Bittker and Eustice

FEDERAL INCOME TAXATION
OF CORPORATIONS AND
SHAREHOLDERS

Fourth Edition

―――――――

1985 Cumulative Supplement
to Abridged Student Edition

For Student Use Only

Bittker and Eustice

FEDERAL INCOME TAXATION OF CORPORATIONS AND SHAREHOLDERS

Fourth Edition

1985 Cumulative Supplement
to Abridged Student Edition

by
JAMES S. EUSTICE
Professor of Law, New York University

For Student Use Only

WARREN, GORHAM & LAMONT
Boston ● New York

HOW TO USE
THIS SUPPLEMENT

This cumulative supplement brings the fourth edition of Bittker and Eustice's *Federal Income Taxation of Corporations and Shareholders,* Abridged Student Edition, up-to-date. Each entry in the supplement is keyed to a chapter, paragraph, and, where appropriate, a specific page of the student edition. An italicized instruction line located under the reference to the student edition tells you exactly where the new material belongs in relation to the original text and/or footnotes of the student edition. When using the student edition, you can quickly find whether or not there have been post-publication developments by finding the corresponding place in the supplement. The sequences of both the student edition and the supplement are identical. To further aid locating material in the supplement, the top of each page carries a reference to the paragraph number of the student edition to which it is related. The supplement also contains a series of cumulative tables of citations to Internal Revenue Code sections, regulations, and case decisions, and a cumulative index to both the student edition and the supplement.

As in the abridged student edition, the original pagination, index, and tables have been retained from the professional edition rather than revised, despite the dangling cross-references that necessarily result, to permit use of the original printing plates in order to achieve economies necessary to produce a student supplement.

CHAPTERS UPDATED IN THIS SUPPLEMENT

Special Alert

With the ink scarcely dry on the TEFRA Subchapter C amendments, the Senate Finance Committee is in the process of revising the corporate income tax system on a scale not seen since the 1954 Code. These tentative proposals are heavily influenced by the American Law Institute Subchapter C Project,[1] the principal thrust of which is to require corporate level recognition of gain on distributions and transfers of appreciated property if the transferee claims a stepped-up basis for that property. In effect, the two tier tax system of present law would be extended to dispositions of appreciated property, as well as current operating income.

Also slated for total revision are the net operating loss carryover limitations of §382 which, in effect, would prohibit any shift of tax loss history benefits to new owners. Moreover, the present reorganization definitions in §368 would be replaced by an elective nonrecognition system keyed to corporate asset basis treatment (viz., the price for nonrecognition would be preservation of historic asset bases). Shareholder treatment in an acquisitive transaction no longer would be linked to treatment at the corporate level, depending instead upon whether a particular shareholder received stock or other property in the transaction.

If the proposals are enacted, the collapsible corporation rules of §341 would be repealed, and much (if not most) of the material in Chapters 11, 12, 14, and 16 would become substantially obsolete.

These proposals are contained in a preliminary report of the Staff of the Senate Finance Committee, entitled "The Reform and Simplification of the Income Taxation of Corporations," submitted on September 22, 1983.[2] Statutory language reflecting the proposals is not yet publicly available, but the general outlines of their

---

[1] See Beghe, The American Law Institute Subchapter C Study: Acquisitions and Distributions, 33 Tax Law. 743 (1980); Land, Unallocated Premium in Corporate Acquisitions Under the American Law Institute Subchapter C Proposals, 34 Tax Law. 341 (1981); Wolfman, "Continuity of Interest" and the American Law Institute Study, 33 Taxes 840 (1979).

[2] 98th Cong., 1st Sess., Comm. Print S. 98-85, issued by CCH as Extra Edition No. 45, Oct. 6, 1983.

content will be noted at the appropriate points in this Supplement. The proposals fall into six principal categories: (1) acquisitions and liquidations; (2) special limitations on net operating losses and other tax attributes; (3) ordinary distributions; (4) basis of stock in controlled subsidiaries; (5) entity classification; and (6) foreign rules. Each of these categories contains various specific recommendations, many of which are interrelated and contingent upon adoption of other recommendations.[3]

---

[3] A summary of these proposals is reprinted in Tax Notes, Vol. 21, No. 1, at p. 65, October 3, 1983.

Chapter 1

INTRODUCTORY

¶ 1.01. THE CORPORATE INCOME TAX

Page 1-3:

Correct tenth line of first full paragraph.

Change "$25,000" to "$50,000."

Page 1-4:

Add new note 6.1 to sentence ending on first line of text.

[6.1] The Economic Recovery Tax Act (ERTA) of 1981, P.L. No. 97-34, 95 Stat. 172, lowered the rates on the first two brackets to 16 percent and 19 percent for 1982, and to 15 and 18 percent for 1983 and thereafter.

The Senate Finance Committee has proposed to phase out the graduated-rate benefits of §11(b) for large corporations with taxable income in excess of $1,000,000 by imposing a 51 percent rate on taxable income between $1,000,000 and $1,400,000; S.2062, §108 (effective for taxable years beginning in 1984). The current version of this provision is §44 of the Deficit Reduction Act of 1984, H.R. 2163; and passed as §66(a) of the Tax Reform Act of 1984, P.L. No. 98-369 (effective for years beginning after 1984).

Add to end of note 8.

[8] The ERTA of 1981, supra note 6.1 (this Supplement), amended §6621 to require annual adjustments of interest rates keyed to 100 percent of the prime rate during September; TEFRA 1982 further modified the §6621 rules by adjusting the rates twice a year (in September and May, effective for January and July); moreover new §6622 now provides for compounding.

¶ 1.02.   UNDISTRIBUTED CORPORATE INCOME

Page 1-5:

Add new note 9.1 to sentence ending on line 9.

[9.1] The ERTA of 1981, P.L. No. 97-34, 95 Stat. 172, reduced the top marginal rate for individuals to 50 percent for 1982 and thereafter; the brackets are widened and rates are further reduced for 1983 and 1984; and the brackets are to be indexed for inflation, commencing in 1985 and annually thereafter, thereby further moderating the disparity between individual and corporate rates.

Page 1-6:

Add new note 9.2 to heading "Individual Liability" in Table 1-1.

[9.2] When fully effective (by 1984), the individual rate reductions effected by the ERTA of 1981, supra note 9.1 (this Supplement), will significantly reduce the text figures, substantially more so in the upper brackets. Thus, at the $500,000 taxable income level, individual tax liability on a joint return will be $231,350 instead of $316,725, while at $1,000,000 of taxable income, the tax will drop from $666,725 to $480,350.

Add to note 10.

[10] Code section reference in line 5 should be §1348, not §348. The ERTA of 1981, supra note 9.1 (this Supplement), repealed §1348, as of 1982, in view of the general reduction in the top individual tax rate to 50 percent commencing in 1982.

Page 1-7:

Add to text at end of first paragraph.

Section 1023 ultimately was repealed by the Crude Oil Windfall Profit Tax Act of 1980, P.L. No. 96-223, 94 Stat. 229.

¶ 1.03.   DISTRIBUTED CORPORATE INCOME

Page 1-10:

Add new note 13.1 to heading "Table 1-2."

[13.1] The figures in Table 1-2 will be significantly modified as a result of the individual rate changes effected by the ERTA of 1981, P.L. No. 97-34, 95 Stat. 172, and this is especially so at the higher income levels. Thus, in the case of $500,000 of taxable income, an individual proprietor's net after taxes will increase from $183,275, under 1979 rates, to $268,650, at 1984 rates; while at $1,000,000 of taxable income, the after-tax net will rise from $333,276 to $510,650. The sole share-holder's net after taxes on $500,000 of income will rise from $120,051 to $163,225; while the after-tax net on $1,000,000 will increase from $201,051 to $298,225.

Add to note 14, first paragraph.

14 Under the ERTA of 1981, supra note 13.1 (this Supplement), the top rate on individual capital gain was reduced to 20 percent (for sales after June 9, 1981), while the top rate on ordinary unearned income was reduced to 50 percent (for 1982).

Page 1-11:

Add to note 14, third paragraph.

14 The alternative minimum tax of §55 was reduced to a top rate of 20 percent by the ERTA of 1981, supra note 13.1 (this Supplement), (by eliminating the 25 percent bracket).

Add new note 14.1 to heading "Table 1-3."

14.1 The figures in Table 1-3 will change dramatically as a result of the individual rate reductions for ordinary income and capital gain effected by the ERTA of 1981, supra note 13.1 (this Supplement). Thus, the sole shareholder net after capital gain taxes at the $5,000,000 annual income level will increase from $1,913,401, at 1979 rates, to $2,332,600, at 1984 rates (actually, the top capital gain rate of 20 percent applies to sales after June 9, 1981); at the $10,000,000 annual income level, the after-tax net rises from $3,668,401 to $4,492,500 under the new statutory rate system effective in 1984.

A significant effect of the 1981 Act rate cuts is that the after-tax net is greater for individual proprietors at all six income levels in Table 1-3.

¶ 1.05. THE CORPORATION AS AN ENTITY

Page 1-14:

Replace citation for DiPardo *at the end of note 15 with the following.*

15 78-1 USTC ¶ 9224.

Page 1-18:

Add to note 20, second paragraph.

20 See also Silvano Achiro, 77 TC 881 (1981), and David F. Keller, 77 TC 1014 (1981), aff'd, 723 F.2d 58 (10th Cir. 1983) (personal-service corporations upheld as viable entities, and respected for

tax purposes; also, withstood IRS reallocation attacks under §§482, 61, and 269). Accord with *Keller* is John L. Fatland, ¶ 84,489 P-H Memo TC (pre-§269A case). But compare Frederick H. Foglesong Co., 77 TC 1102 (1981) (§482 applied to allocate 98 percent of service corporation's income to dominant shareholder as true "earner" of that income). But on appeal, *Foglesong* was reversed, 691 F.2d 848 (7th Cir. 1982) (no §482 where shareholder worked exclusively for his own personal-service corporation). In both *Achiro* and *Keller,* IRS lost on §482 because terms of service agreements held to be arm's length; this conclusion then constituted a defense to §61 assignment of income attack. *Keller* was followed in Bernard Pacella, 78 TC 604 (1982). But see §269A, added by §250 of the Tax Equity and Fiscal Responsibility Act (TEFRA) of 1982, P.L. No. 97-248, 96 Stat. 324, which gives the IRS power to reallocate income and deductions in *Keller*-type situations (infra ¶¶ 15.06 and 16.21 (this Supplement)).

See generally Wood, The *Keller, Foglesong,* and *Pacella* Cases: 482 Allocations, Assignments of Income, and New §269A, 10 J. Corp. Tax. 65 (1983); Manning, The Service Corporation—Who Is Taxable On Its Income: Reconciling Assignment of Income Principles, Section 482, and Section 351, 37 U. Miami L. Rev. 653 (1983).

More recently, see Hospital Corp. of Am., 81 TC 520 (1983) (foreign corporate entity respected; had business purpose and business activity, even though one of reasons for creation was tax avoidance); LeBeau & Dostart, Offshore Tax Planning May Be Favorably Affected by Recent *Hospital Corp.* Decision, 60 J. Tax. 294 (1984).

Page 1-19:

Add to note 24, first paragraph.

[24] Frederick H. Foglesong Co. v. CIR, 621 F.2d 865 (7th Cir. 1980) (Tax Court decision reversed on assignment of income theory; "no need to crack walnuts with a sledgehammer"; IRS should use more precise theories, such as §482, §531, and constructive receipt; *Rubin* approach adopted.). See McFadden, Section 482 and the Professional Corporation: The *Foglesong* Case, 8 J. Corp. Tax. 35 (1981); and Feuer, Section 482, Assignment of Income Principles and Personal Service Corporations, 59 Taxes 564 (1981). But compare Charles Johnson, 78 TC 882 (1982) (shareholder taxed as true earner of corporate income under §61 and *Earl* principles since he had control of earning process).

On remand, 77 TC 1102 (1981), *Foglesong* reached the same result, this time under §482, à la *Rubin* (dominant shareholder held the true earner of corporation's income, and hence taxable on that income via §482 allocation). But *Foglesong* again was reversed, 691 F.2d 848 (7th Cir. 1982) (no §482 where shareholder worked exclusively for his personal-service corporation).

Add to note 24, second paragraph.

[24] Silvano Achiro, supra note 20 (this Supplement) (service corporation, which performed management services for affiliated sister corporations, withstood IRS attempt to reallocate 100 percent of its income to affiliated corporations under §§482, 61, and 269); Daniel F. Keller, supra note 20 (this Supplement) (if service corporation withstands §482 attack, as it did here, no §61 assignment of income because standards are the same on this issue); Bernard Pacella, 78 TC 604 (1982) (same); John L. Fatland, ¶ 84,489 P-H Memo TC (same). See also Wm. H. Bell, ¶ 82,660 P-H Memo TC (same as *Davis*; corporation "real," and earned its income; but some reallocation under §482 to reflect arm's-length prices); Hospital Corp. of Am., 81 TC 520 (1983) (foreign subsidiary not a sham; enough of a viable business entity to withstand attack under §61 and sham entity doctrines; tax avoidance present, but cannot disregard entity solely on this ground). But compare Louis G. Horn, ¶ 82,741 P-H Memo TC (where "support corporation" of PC ignored as sham and income taxed to PC as true earner; no business purpose except tax avoidance, and support corporation didn't carry on any business activity; *Bell* and *Davis* distinguished). See LeBeau & Dostart, supra note 20 (this Supplement).

The moral of *Achiro, Keller, Foglesong,* and *Pacella* is that arm's-length economic terms in service corporation arrangements will provide a defense to IRS adjustments under §§482 and 61. But new §269A, added by §250 of TEFRA, supra note 20 (this Supplement), provides §482-type powers to IRS to reallocate income in *Keller* situations (see infra ¶¶ 15.06 and 16.21 (this Supplement)).

See generally Gombinski & Kaplan, Demise of the Tax Motivated Personal Service Corporation, 1 J. Copyright, Entertainment & Sports L. 73 (1982); Wood, supra note 20 (this Supplement); and Manning, supra note 20 (this Supplement).

Add to note 25.

[25] See Isenberg, Musings on Form and Substance in Taxation, 49 U. Chi. L. Rev. 859 (1982).

Page 1-20:

Add to note 27.

[27] See Louis G. Horn, supra note 24 (this Supplement) (corporation ignored as sham; no business purpose and no business activity).

Page 1-21:

Add to note 30.

[30] See also Charles Johnson, 78 TC 882 (1982); compare Hospital Corp. of Am., supra note 24 (this Supplement).

Add to note 32.

[32] But see Silvano Achiro, 77 TC 881 (1981) (no §482 allocation of service corporation's income to affiliated sister corporations because service agreements on arm's-length terms); Daniel F. Keller, supra note 20 (this Supplement) (same); Bernard Pacella, 78 TC 604 (1982) (same); John L. Fatland, ¶ 84,489 P-H Memo TC (same); compare new §269A of TEFRA, supra note 20 (this Supplement), giving the IRS §482-type allocation powers in *Keller* situations; and Frederick H. Foglesong Co., 77 TC 1102 (1981) (§482 allocation of service corporation's income to dominant shareholder earner of that income sustained), rev'd, 691 F.2d 848 (7th Cir. 1982) (no §482 where shareholder worked exclusively for his personal-service corporation).

Compare Hospital Corp. of Am., supra note 24 (this Supplement) (§482 applied to reallocate 75 percent of foreign subsidiary's income to U.S. parent to compensate parent for use of its intangibles, which was the major factor in generating subsidiary's income).

See generally Wood, supra note 20 (this Supplement); Manning, id; LeBeau & Dostart, id; Gombinski & Kaplan, supra note 24 (this Supplement); McFadden, *id;* and Feuer, *id.*

¶ 1.06.   SPECIAL CLASSES OF CORPORATIONS

Page 1-22:

Add to note 35.

[35] Halpern, Real Estate Investment Trusts and the Tax Reform Act of 1976, 31 Tax Law. 329 (1978).

¶ 1.07.   THE CORPORATION VS. THE PARTNERSHIP

Page 1-26:

Correct first line of example (1).

Add "ordinarily" after "partner" and before "does."

Page 1-27:

Delete last sentence of paragraph 6 and substitute.

A partner cannot be an "employee" of his firm for purposes of these more lucrative benefits, even though he may receive a "salary" under §707(c).

Add to note 45.

[45] See also Armstrong v. Phinney, 394 F.2d 661 (5th Cir. 1968) (partner an "employee" for §119 exclusion).

A partner can, however, be an employee for purposes of self-employed retirement plans (although the benefits of these plans are less lucrative than those available for corporate retirement plans). But 1982 legislation, TEFRA of 1982, P.L. No. 97-248, 96 Stat. 324, substantially conforms the tax treatment of corporate and self-employed retirement plans by 1984.

¶ 1.08. CURRENT PROPOSALS: INTEGRATION OF CORPORATE AND INDIVIDUAL TAXES

Page 1-29:

Add new note 45.1 to end of third line of text.

45.1 The Treasury Report on Tax Simplification and Reform, released November 27, 1984, adopts this approach (would allow a corporate-level deduction for one half of dividends paid from previously taxed earnings).

Add to note 46.

46 Warren, The Relation and Integration of Individual and Corporate Income Taxes, 94 Harv. L. Rev. 719 (1981) (analysis of integration proposals and of ALI Draft Report on Subchapter C).

It could be argued that the new ACRS and safe-harbor leasing rules enacted by ERTA of 1981, P.L. No. 97-34, 95 Stat. 172, have substantially achieved at least one type of integration system (viz., elimination of the corporate tax on new investment); for closely held corporations, Subchapter S and the newly proposed §385 regulations achieve a comparable effect. The Subchapter S Revision Act of 1982, P.L. No. 97-354, 96 Stat. 1669, substantially broadened the scope and utility of Subchapter S corporations, infra Chapter 6 (this Supplement), thereby moving even closer to the effective elimination of corporate-level taxes for closely held enterprises.

Chapter 2

DEFINITION OF A CORPORATION

¶ 2.01. INTRODUCTORY

Page 2-2:

Add to note 5.

⁵ As to Rev. Rul. 77-214, see New York State Bar Ass'n Tax Section, Report on Foreign Entity Characterization for Federal Income Tax Purposes, 35 Tax. L. Rev. 167 (1980). See also MCA, Inc. v. US, 1980-2 USTC 9617 (C.D. Cal. 1980) (extending theory of Rev. Rul. 77-214 to find corporate status for putative foreign partnership on ground that relationship of partners created lack of "separate interests" and hence corporate characteristics predominated). But *MCA* was reversed, 685 F.2d 1099 (9th Cir. 1982) (the independent interest theory adopted by lower court was rejected; also, U.S. regulations' rules on status applied here, not some special expansive construction because foreign entity involved).

See Mentz, Foreign Entity Characterization: To Be or Not to Be, 39 NYU Inst. Fed. Tax. Ch. 32 (1981); Hamilton, *MCA Inc.*—Classification Of Foreign Entities As Associations Or Partnerships, 59 Taxes 303 (1981).

¶ 2.02. "ASSOCIATIONS" IN GENERAL

Page 2-7:

Add to note 11.

¹¹ But see Prop. Regs. §§301.7701-2(a)(2), 301.7701-2(a)(3), 301.7701-2(g), Ex. (1) (Nov. 14, 1980) (organization a corporation per se if no member has personal liability). The effective date of these proposals was postponed until taxable years beginning after 1982 by IR 82-118, Oct. 15, 1982, and they were withdrawn in late 1982.

Add new note 13.1 at end of paragraph numbered (3).

¹³·¹ But see Prop. Regs. §§301.7701-2(a)(2), 301.7701-2(a)(3), 301.7701-2(g), Ex. (1) (Nov. 14, 1980) (lack of personal liability a super-factor; corporation per se if no personal liability); Rosen, Effect of Proposed Amendments to Section 7701 Regulations Leveraged Leases, 9 J. Corp. Tax. 57 (1982). The effective date of these proposed regulations was postponed until years beginning after 1982, IR 82-118, Oct. 15, 1982.

But these proposals were withdrawn in IR 82-145, Dec. 16, 1982, which stated that a new study of entity classification was in progress with special focus on the significance of the limited liability characteristic (possible approaches here include a minimum capital requirement, either as a ruling guideline or a substantive rule, and reconsideration of the *Larson* acquiescence). In addition, Rev. Proc. 83-15, 1983-1 CB 674 (no ruling on classification status of limited liability companies until resolution of study) was superseded by Rev. Proc. 83-22, 1983-1 CB 680, now found in Rev. Proc. 84-22, 1984-1 CB 449.

¶ 2.03.   TRUSTS AS "ASSOCIATIONS"

Page 2-8:

Add to note 15.

¹⁵ See also Gelinas, Mineral Royalty Trust Transactions: The Use of the Grantor Trust to Avoid Corporate Income Tax, 37 Tax L. Rev. 222 (1982).

Page 2-9:

Add to note 18, second paragraph.

¹⁸ See also John B. Hynes, 74 TC 1266 (1980) (one-man grantor "business" trust held an association; had associates, limited liability, unlimited life, and centralized management).

But see Elm St. Realty Trust, 76 TC 803 (1981) (Acq.) (trust not an association, even though powers granted trustee gave it *potential* to operate a business; no "associates" because beneficiaries did not create trust or have power to participate in management or exercise significant control; also, interests not freely transferable); Howard v. US, 1984-1 USTC ¶ 9494 (Cl. Ct. 1984) (business trust taxable as an association; had corporate characteristics, associates, and carried on business).

Page 2-10:

Add new sentence to text after sentence ending with note 19.

Also, recently proposed regulations deny investment trust status if the trust has multiple classes of ownership; instead, such an organization will be either a partnership or an association.[19.1]

[19.1] Prop. Regs. §301.7701-4(c) (May 2, 1984).

Add to note 20.

[20] See Rev. Proc. 79-1, 1979-1 CB 481, for ruling guidelines on classification of organizations as "liquidating trusts." Rev. Rul. 80-150, 1980-1 CB 316 (trust established under state law for purpose of liquidating assets that could not be readily sold within §337 time frame held valid "liquidating trust"; primary purpose of trust was liquidation and distribution of assets, not business). Rev. Proc. 79-1 was revised and liberalized by Rev. Proc. 80-54, 1980-2 CB 848; and Rev. Proc. 80-54 was again revised and liberalized by Rev. Proc. 82-58, 1982-2 CB 847.

See generally Westin, Tax Planning With Shareholders' Liquidating Trusts, 5 J. Corp. Tax. 328 (1979); Del Negro, Using Trusts in Twelve Month Liquidations in the Light of Rev. Proc. 79-1 Restrictions, 51 J. Tax. 138 (1979); Westin, Shareholder's Liquidating Trusts After Revenue Procedure 80-54, 9 J. Corp. Tax. 63 (1982).

¶ 2.04. PARTNERSHIPS AS "ASSOCIATIONS"
Page 2-11:
Add to note 24.

[24] But see Prop. Regs. §§301.7701-2(a)(2), 301.7701-2(a)(3), 301.7701-2(g), Ex. (1) (Nov. 14, 1980) (cannot be partnership if no member has personal liability). The effective date of these proposals was delayed until years beginning after 1982, IR 82-118, Oct. 15, 1982.

But these proposals were withdrawn by IR 82-145, Dec. 16, 1982, pending a new study of entity classification with special focus on significance of limited liability characteristic. See supra ¶ 2.02, note 13.1 (this Supplement). See also Rev. Proc. 84-22, 1984-1 CB 449 (no ruling on status).

Page 2-12:
Add to note 25.

[25] See also Prop. Regs. §301.7701-2(a)(5) (Oct. 24, 1980) (references to ULPA include Revised ULPA of 1976), adopted by T.D. 7889, Apr. 25, 1983.

Compare Rev. Rul. 77-214, 1977-1 CB 408, cited supra ¶ 2.01, note 5; and see MCA, Inc. v. US, 1980-2 USTC 9617 (C.D. Cal. 1980), rev'd, 685 F.2d 1099 (9th Cir. 1982), discussed supra ¶ 2.01, note 5 (this Supplement) (partners' lack of separate interests, due to related control features, caused finding of corporate status even though organization flunked corporate tests on face of documents; organized as foreign partnerships, but theory of Rev. Rul. 77-214 extended to deny partnership status where relationship of partners caused lack of separate interests). But *MCA* was reversed, 685 F.2d 1099 (9th Cir. 1982); the appellate court rejected the independent interest theory adopted by the court and applied the U.S. regulation rules in finding partnership status (rather than some "special" expansive construction because of foreign entity involvement).

See generally Mentz, Foreign Entity Characterization: To Be or Not to Be, 39 NYU Inst. Fed. Tax. Ch. 32 (1981); Hamilton, *MCA Inc.*—Classification of Foreign Entities as Associations or Partnerships, 59 Taxes 303 (1981).

Add to note 27.

[27] Prop. Regs. §301.7701-2(c)(4) (Oct. 24, 1980), amended to state that if limiteds have right to remove general partner, all facts and circumstances must be considered in determining whether organization has centralized management (except that a substantially restricted right of removal will not cause finding of centralized management per se), adopted by T.D. 7889, Apr. 25, 1983.

Page 2-13:

Add to note 30, first paragraph.

[30] See Prop. Regs. §§301.7701-2(a)(2), 301.7701-2(a)(3), 301.7701-2(g), Ex. (1) (Nov. 14, 1980) ("limited liability" companies cannot be partnerships because no member has personal liability; must have personal liability of some member to avoid corporate status). See Rosen, Effect of Proposed Amendments to Section 7701 Regulations Leveraged Leases, 9 J. Corp. Tax. 57 (1982).

But the effective date of these proposals was delayed until years after 1982, IR 82-118, Oct. 15, 1982. These proposals were withdrawn on December 16, 1982, pending a further study of entity classification, with special focus on the significance of limited liability characteristic; see supra, ¶ 2.02, note 13.1 (this Supplement). See also Rev. Proc. 84-22, 1984-1 CB 449 (no ruling on status).

Page 2-14:

Add to note 31, first paragraph.

[31] Rev. Proc. 84-67, 1984-39 IRB 19 (no ruling on limited partnership status unless agreement provides that general partner has at least one percent interest in all partnership items, and, on liquidation, general partners will contribute deficit balances in their capital accounts or excess of 1.01 percent of limiteds' capital contributions over generals' capital contributions).

Add to note 31, second paragraph.

³¹ Peel, Definition of a Partnership: New Suggestions on an Old Issue, 1979 Wis. L. Rev. 989 (1979); and Weidner, The Existence of State and Tax Partnerships—A Primer, 11 Fla. St. U.L. Rev. 1 (1983).

Add to note 33.

³³ See Rev. Rul. 79-106, 1979-1 CB 448 (IRS agrees to follow *Larson* as association status classification; four-factor approach of regulations accepted; factors that will not be considered independently of major factors listed; generally backed away from expansive sweep of proposed regulations and litigating position in *Larson*). But Service is reconsidering here; see IR 82-145, Dec. 1982, discussed supra ¶ 2.02, note 13.1 (this Supplement).

See Katz, Service Agrees to Follow the Tests of Partnership Recognition as Stated in *Larson,* 51 J. Tax. 12 (1979).

Page 2-17:

Add to note 35.

³⁵ But see Rev. Rul. 79-106, supra note 33 (this Supplement).

¶ 2.06. PROFESSIONAL ASSOCIATIONS AND PROFESSIONAL CORPORATIONS

Page 2-21:

Add to note 49, after Davis *case.*

⁴⁹ and Wm. H. Bell, ¶ 82,660 P-H Memo TC (same as *Davis,* although partial reallocation under §482). But see Louis G. Horn, ¶ 82,741 P-H Memo TC ("support" corporation ignored as sham because no business purpose and no business activity, and its income taxed to dominant PC corporation as true earner; *Davis* and *Bell* distinguished).

Add to end of note 49, runover paragraph.

⁴⁹ See also Silvano Achiro, 77 TC 881 (1981) (no reallocation of service corporation's income to affiliated sister corporations under §§482, 61, or 269; term is arm's length); Daniel F. Keller, 77 TC 1014 (1981), aff'd, 723 F.2d 58 (10th Cir. 1983) (one-man professional corporation partner of medical partnership survived reallocation attack under §§482, 269, and 61; term is arm's length because PC's shareholder received compensation that was comparable to what he would have received individually); see Bernard Pacella, 78 TC 604 (1982) (same). Compare Frederick H. Foglesong Co., 77 TC 1102 (1981) (bulk of service corporation's income allocated to dominant shareholder under §482 as true earner of that income). See generally

supra ¶ 1.05, note 24 (this Supplement). But *Foglesong* was reversed, 691 F.2d 848 (7th Cir. 1982) (no §482 where shareholder worked exclusively for his personal-service corporation).

New §269A, added by §250 of the Tax Equity and Fiscal Responsibility Act (TEFRA) of 1982, P.L. No. 97-248, 96 Stat. 324, provides §482-type powers to the IRS in *Keller* case patterns (infra new ¶¶ 15.06 and 16.21 (this Supplement)). See infra paragraph numbered 3, ¶ 2.06 (this Supplement).

Page 2-22:

Add to note 51.

[51] See also Earnest Booth, M.D., P.C., ¶ 82,423 P-H Memo TC (medical PC liable for §531 tax on accumulation; no business reason to accumulate).

Add new note 51.1 to sentence ending on line 14.

[51.1] See, e.g., A. La Mastro, 72 TC 377 (1979); Bianchi v. CIR, 553 F.2d 93 (2d Cir. 1977); compare E. Catalano, ¶ 79,183 P-H Memo TC (1979).

See also Isaacson, Rosenbaum, Spiegleman & Friedman, P.C. v. US, 1979-2 USTC ¶ 9463 (Ct. Cl. 1979) (reasonable compensation issue a question of federal tax law, not state law); Rosenbaum, The Court of Claims' Handling of a Legal PC's Reasonable Compensation: Problems Remain, 55 J. Tax. 138 (1981). See also supra note 49 (this Supplement).

Page 2-23:

Add to note 53.

[53] H.R. 6410, The Pension Equity Tax Act of 1982, introduced by Congressman Rangel, proposed to do just that by cutting down on the benefits of §401 qualified plans, expanding the benefits of self-employed plans, and subjecting the plans of personal-service corporations to treatment under the self-employed plan rules. Essential parts of this legislation were incorporated in the Senate Finance Committee Revenue Raiser Tax Package in July 1982, which passed the Senate.

These provisions passed as §§235-250 of TEFRA of 1982, supra note 49 (this Supplement).

Add new paragraph 3 to end of section.

3. TEFRA amendments affecting professional corporations. The 1982 Act [53.1] amendments dealt harshly with personal-service corporations. Thus, new §269A, added by §250 of the Act, gives

---

[53.1] P.L. No. 97-248, 96 Stat 324.

the Service §482-type allocation powers where a personal-service corporation performs substantially all of its services for, or on behalf of, another corporation, partnership or entity, and the principal purpose of forming, or availing of, such corporation is securing any tax benefit for its employee-owner that would not otherwise be available. (The Committee Report specifically refers to cases such as *Keller* as the prototype abuse.)

A "personal-service corporation" is defined by §269A(b)(1) as a corporation the principal activity of which is the performance of personal services and such services are substantially performed by "employee-owners"; an employee owner is one who is any more than a 10 percent shareholder (with expanded §318 attribution). For purposes of the application of §269A, all related persons (under §§267, 707(b), and 1563(a)) are aggregated and treated as "one entity." The effect of new §269A is to specifically give the Service the allocation weapons that the courts refused to allow in cases like *Keller*. See Prop. Regs. §1.269A (Mar. 30, 1983).

Section 269A is effective for years beginning in 1983 (but Senator Dole, in a floor statement during the consideration of TEFRA, indicated that §269A was not intended to apply to plans already in place for the year 1983; see Prop. Regs. §1.269A(d)). Thus, new §269A seems destined merely to close the gate for new *Keller*-type PC partner corporations in 1983; those already in the trough will be allowed to feed for another year, until the TEFRA parity rules become effective in 1984, infra. See generally Prop. Regs. §1.269A (Mar. 30, 1983).

On a more basic level, however, the new pension provisions of TEFRA (Act §§235–250) took a giant step towards parity in the tax treatment for corporate and noncorporate retirement plans. The thrust of these amendments cut back on the more generous benefits of corporate plans, while concurrently expanding the benefits of noncorporate plans to a more or less comparable level (by 1984).

In keeping with this comparability theme, new Act §247 (uncodified) provides a special transition rule that permits personal-service corporations to liquidate under §333 without triggering corporate-level recognition on their untaxed receivables.[53.2] Thus,

---

[53.2] See new ¶ 11.25 (this Supplement). See generally Gombinski & Kaplan, Demise of the Tax Motivated Personal Service Corporation, 1 J. Copyright, Entertainment & Sports L. 73 (1982); Wood, The *Keller, Foglesong,* and *Pacella* Cases: §482 Allocations, Assignments

the heyday of the professional corporation—or at least the tax-motivated version of this creature—seems to be finally drawing to a close, since there will no longer be any significant tax advantages for setting up (or even keeping) such organizations.

---

of Income, and New §269A, 10 J. Corp. Tax. 65 (1983); and Manning, The Service Corporation—Who Is Taxable On Its Income: Reconciling Assignment of Income Principles, Section 482, and Section 351, 37 U. Miami L. Rev. 653 (1983).

¶ 2.07. ONE-MAN ASSOCIATIONS

Page 2-23:

Add to note 57.

[57] See also John B. Hynes, 74 TC 1266 (1980), which so holds. But compare Elm St. Realty Trust, 76 TC 803 (1981). For the effect of "unitary" or "related" partner status on classification of putative foreign partnerships as a corporation, see Rev. Rul. 77-214, 1977-1 C.B. 408, cited supra ¶ 2.01, note 5; MCA, Inc. v. US, 1980-2 USTC 9617 (C.D. Cal. 1980), rev'd, 685 F.2d 1099 (9th Cir. 1982), discussed supra ¶ 2.01, note 5 (this Supplement).

¶ 2.09. CORPORATIONS IN THE PROCESS OF WINDING UP

Page 2-25:

Add to note 63.

[63] But see Garris Invest. Corp., ¶ 82,038 P-H Memo TC (1982) (corporation with cancelled charter not taxable entity even though continued as nominal owner of legal title).

Correct note 64.

[64] The *Lowndes* and *Owens* cases should be deleted, since those decisions did not technically involve entity existence termination issues (*Lowndes* disregarded the corporation, while *Owens* held that a purported sale of stock by the corporation's sole shareholder was in fact a liquidating distribution of its assets).

Page 2-26:

Add to note 71.

[71] See Westin, Tax Planning With Shareholders' Liquidating Trusts, 5 J. Corp. Tax. 328 (1979); Rev. Proc. 79-1, 1979-1 CB 481 (guidelines for ruling on liquidating trust status); supra ¶ 2.03, note 20 (this

Supplement). Rev. Proc. 79-1 was revised and liberalized by Rev. Proc. 80-54, 1980-2 CB 848; see Westin, Shareholder's Liquidating Trusts After Revenue Procedure 80-54, 9 J. Corp. Tax. 63 (1982). Rev. Proc. 80-54 was further revised and liberalized by Rev. Proc. 82-58, 1982-2 CB 847.

¶ 2.10. DISREGARD OF THE CORPORATE ENTITY: NOMINEE AND DUMMY CORPORATIONS

Page 2-29:

Add to note 80.

[80] See also Ogiony v. CIR, 617 F.2d 14 (2d Cir. 1980) (corporation not a "dummy"; entity respected); and Jones v. CIR, 640 F.2d 745 (5th Cir. 1981) (corporation not an agent for shareholder; true owner of property and earner of income); Ltr. Rul. 8105048 (Nov. 4, 1980), 1981 CCH Fed. Tax Rep. Vol. 10, ¶ 6956 (same); Garris Invest. Corp., ¶ 82,038 P-H Memo TC (1982) (same).

But see Roccaforte v. CIR, 77 TC 263 (1981) (corporation mere title holding agent for shareholders to avoid state usury laws; partnership was true economic owner of property for tax purposes; corporate entity respected, but corporation functioned as mere agent for the partnership-owner; taxpayer successfully satisfied the six-factor test for corporate-agency treatment enunciated by *National Carbide*). Six dissenters thought that case should be controlled by its former opinion in *Strong*. On appeal, *Roccaforte* was reversed, 708 F.2d 988 (5th Cir. 1983) (no corporate agency where relations with principal dependent on fact that corporate agent is owned by the principal; ownership dependency defeats agency relationship as a matter of law). The Tax Court adhered to *Roccaforte* in a reviewed decision, Florenz R. Ourisman, 82 TC 171 (1984) (corporation mere nominee agent, even though owned by its principal). Moncrief v. US, 730 F.2d 276 (5th Cir. 1984) (corporate agency found when agent only owned by a 25 percent partner; *Roccaforte* distinguished, and *Raphan* followed).

See also Vaughn v. US, 1983-2 USTC ¶ 9558 (Cl. Ct. 1983), aff'd, 740 F.2d 941 (Fed. Cir. 1984) (corporate agency rejected when owned by same controlling interests; also failed on burden of proof to establish other criteria) (follows *Roccaforte* where common control of principal and agent by same interests); compare Raphan v. US, 1983-2 USTC ¶ 9613 (Cl. Ct. 1983) (corporate agent found where no common control; owner of agent only 50 percent partner in principal; agent mere title-holding nominee).

Add to note 81.

[81] See generally Miller, The Nominee Conundrum: The Live Dummy Is Dead, But the Dead Dummy Should Live, 34 Tax L. Rev. 213 (1979).

Chapter 3

ORGANIZATION OF A CORPORATION – SECTION 351 AND RELATED PROBLEMS

¶ 3.01.   INTRODUCTORY

Page 3-3:

Add to note 2.

[2] Rev. Proc. 73-10 was revised and updated by Rev. Proc. 81-57, 1981-2 CB 674, which was updated by Rev. Proc. 83-59, 1983-2 CB 575.

Page 3-6:

Add to note 11.

[11] See also Rev. Rul. 79-70, 1979-1 CB 144 (purchase of securities for cash from new corporation does not make lender a "transferor" for §351 control definition either).

¶ 3.02.   POTENTIAL ABUSES OF §351: INDIRECT EXCHANGES

Page 3-8:

Add to note 14.

[14] For new variations of the swap-fund technique, see Rev. Proc. 82-56, 1982-2 CB 846 (no §351 ruling on transfer of widely held real estate interests or widely held oil and gas property interests if (1) the transfer results from promoter solicitation, or (2) the transferee's stock is readily marketable), superseded by Rev. Proc. 83-22, 1983-1 CB 680, and Rev. Proc. 84-22, 1984-1 CB 449. See Winston, The IRS' No-Ruling Policy on Exchange Offers, 61 Taxes 375 (1983).

Page 3-9:

Add to note 16.

[16] See also Rev. Rul. 80-221, 1980-2 CB 107 (issue of new preferred for cash in §351 exchange, followed thirteen months later by "planned" redemption in kind; held, corporate level sale of asset for cash per theory of Rev. Rul. 70-140). See infra ¶ 9.64, note 207.1 (this Supplement).

¶ 3.03.   TRANSFER OF "PROPERTY"

Page 3-12:

Add to note 26.

[26] See also Rev. Rul. 79-194, 1979-1 CB 145 (disregard "nominal" property transfers).

Page 3-13:

Add to note 33.

[33] Stafford v. US, 611 F.2d 990 (5th Cir. 1980) (error for court to grant summary judgment on property vs. services question); for later proceedings, see 727 F.2d 1043 (11th Cir. 1984).

Page 3-14:

Add to note 34, first paragraph.

[34] Rev. Rul. 79-288, 1979-2 CB 139 (corporate "name" and goodwill associated with that name held property; but "name" not property where not protectable under applicable law and no goodwill associated with that name); Stafford v. US, supra note 33 (this Supplement) (collection of cases on property vs. services question; letter of intent and loan commitment held "property"). See also Hospital Corp. of Am., 81 TC 520 (1983) (diversion of corporate opportunity to negotiate and perform contract with foreign client not a transfer of property under §§351 and 367).

Add to text at end of section.

Amendments to §351, by §5(e)(1) of H.R. 5043, the Bankruptcy Tax Act of 1980, expanded the category of "nonproperty" items to include: (a) debt of the transferee not evidenced by a "security" (which presumably allows the creditor holder to claim an immediate bad-debt loss therefor under §166); and (b) interest on the transferee's debt accrued during the transferor's holding period. The nonproperty status of services, nonsecurity debts and accrued interest are set out in new Subsection 351(d) (and the last sentence of §351(a), relating to stock issued for services, was deleted). This provision is effective generally for transfers after 1980.

New §351(d)(2) thus reverses the holding of Rev. Rul. 77-81, 1977-1 CB 97, that creditors' exchanges of non-security debt claims for stock constituting control of the debtor did not constitute a "purchase" for purposes of §382(a), infra ¶ 16.22. Hence, vulnerability to §382(a) treatment has been significantly expanded by the new Act.[34.1]

[34.1] For prior law (holding that an exchange of debt for stock of the debtor corporation qualified as a property transfer under §351), see Private Ltr. Rul. 8245010, 1982 P-H Fed. Tax Serv. ¶ 55,414.

¶ 3.04. "EXCHANGE" FOR "STOCK OR SECURITIES"; PROBLEMS OF CLASSIFICATION

Page 3-17:

Add to note 43, first paragraph.

[43] Bradshaw v. US, 683 F.2d 365 (Ct. Cl. 1982) (installment sale notes, ranging in maturity from two and one-half to six and one-half years, held not to constitute "securities").

Add to note 43, second paragraph, following Rev. Proc. 72-9 citation.

[43] Rev. Proc. 72-9 has been superseded by Rev. Proc. 84-22, 1984-1 CB 449.

Page 3-18:

Add to note 46, first paragraph.

[46] Contra to *Wham* is Rev. Rul. 80-228, 1980-2 CB 115 (intracompany account is taxable boot on assumption in §351 transfer); see also Ltr. Rul. 8026012, [1980] 9 P-H Fed. Taxes ¶ 55,201. See also Rev. Rul. 80-240, 1980-2 CB 116.

Add to note 46, end of runover paragraph.

[46] *Wham* was affirmed, 600 F.2d 1052 (4th Cir. 1979) (no economic change of substance effected by the exchange here, hence no boot).

¶ 3.05. "STOCK OR SECURITIES": THE CONTINUITY OF INTEREST DOCTRINE

Page 3-20:

Add to note 54.

[54] See also Rev. Rul. 80-284, 1980-2 CB 117; Rev. Rul. 80-285, 1980-2 CB 119 (discussed infra ¶ 3.19, this Supplement); and Rev. Proc. 81-10, §3.01(20), 1981-1 CB 647 (no ruling under §351 unless continuity of interest test satisfied), superseded by Rev. Proc. 84-22, 1984-1 CB 449.

In Rev. Rul. 73-472 and Rev. Rul. 73-473, supra ¶ 3.01, note 11, the Service held that property for debt exchanges were taxable sales, but that §351 applied if the transferor had the requisite 80 percent stock control.

Add to text at end of section.

The market discount rules of §1276, added by the Tax Reform Act of 1984,[54.1] can result in the creation of a market discount under §1278(a)(2)(A) whenever the basis of such obligation is less than its face immediately after its acquisition by the taxpayer.[54.2] Thus, securities issued in a §351(a) exchange (after July 18, 1984) can create market discount to the transferor-holder through the operation of the substituted-basis rules of §358(a). For example, if A transfers land having a basis of $20 to newly organized X corporation for X stock worth $50 and a $50 debt security, A would take a $10 basis in the security; this $40 spread would be market discount under §1278(a)(2), resulting in ordinary income characterization in the hands of A.

[54.1] The Tax Reform Act of 1984, P.L. No. 98-369, §41(a), 98 Stat. 678.

[54.2] None of the exceptions in §1278(a)(1)(B) applies here. See infra new ¶ 4.23 (this Supplement); Eustice, The Tax Reform Act of 1984, ¶ 2.02[4] (Warren, Gorham & Lamont, Inc. 1984). The statute should be amended to exempt acquisitions in substituted-basis transactions to avoid this result (i.e., market discount should only arise when the debt is acquired by "purchase"). But see Joint Committee Staff "General Explanation," at pp. 95–96 (Dec. 31, 1984).

¶ 3.06. "SOLELY" IN EXCHANGE: THE RECEIPT OF "BOOT"

Page 3-21:

Add to note 55, second paragraph.

[55] See P.L. No. 96-471, The Installment Sales Revision Act of 1980,

which adds new §453(f)(6) and allows § 453 reporting for installment boot in §1031 and §356 nonrecognition exchanges (the formula of revised §453 disregards nonrecognition property in computing contract price, gross profit ratios, and payments, unlike Rev. Rul. 65-155, which counted such property). While this amendment does not specifically cover §351(b) exchanges, it seems likely that similar rules should apply here as well. But see the "related party" rules of §§453(e) and 453(g). See generally Temp. Regs. §15A.453-1(b)(3)(i). Regulations under §453(f)(6) as applied to §351 exchanges were proposed in Prop. Regs. §1.453-1(f)(3)(ii), May 3, 1984. See New York State Bar Ass'n Tax Section, A Report on Proposed Regulations Under Section 453(f)(6)—Installment Obligations Received in Certain Nonrecognition Exchanges, 24 Tax Notes 297 (July 16, 1984); Friedman, An Analysis of Nonrecognition Exchanges and Installment Rules Under the Recent Proposed Regulations, 61 J. Tax. 158 (1984).

See generally Dentino & Walker, Impact of the Installment Sales Revision Act of 1980 on Evidences of Indebtedness in a Section 351 Transaction, 9 J. Corp. Tax 330 (1983); Jacobs, Something Simple: A Tax-Free Incorporation, 37 Tax L. Rev. 133 (1983); and Bogdanski, Closely Held Corporations, 11 J. Corp. Tax 268 (1984). For basis aspects under the regulations, see infra notes 113 and 119 (this Supplement).

Add to note 56.

[56] But the Tax Reform Act of 1984 amended §267(b)(3) to cover related corporate groups, so that §267(f) now can apply as well to the incorporation of, or transfer of property to, a controlled subsidiary (presumably §351 would take precedence here). See ¶ 5.05 (this Supplement).

Page 3-22:

Add new note 56.1 in fourth line of paragraph (1).

[56.1] The Installment Sales Revision Act of 1980 (P.L. No. 96-471) amended §§1239(b)(2) and 1239(b)(3) by substituting the word "taxpayer" for "individual" (this amendment extends the reach of §1239 to sales between parent and subsidiary corporations and between brother-sister subsidiary corporations).

Add to note 57.

[57] See also Robishaw v. US, 1979-1 USTC ¶ 9307 (Ct. Cl. Tr. Div. 1979) (time for measuring §1239 control is before the sale in question, rather than after; followed theory of Rev. Rul. 75-514), aff'd per curiam, 616 F.2d 507 (Ct. Cl. 1980). See Prop. Regs. §1.1239-1(c)(3) (Jan. 6, 1983) (test relationship before or immediately after sale or exchange of depreciable property).

Page 3-23:

Add to note 58.

[58] But Rev. Rul. 76-514 was revoked by Rev. Rul. 83-65, 1983-1 CB 10; IRS agreed to follow Loewen v. CIR, 76 TC 90 (1981), that no ITC trigger on lease of building to corporate transferee after incorporation of business.

¶ 3.07. ASSUMPTION OF LIABILITIES

Page 3-26:

Add to note 67.

[67] But see Rev. Rul. 78-422, 1978-2 CB 129 (§304 prevails over §351 and §357(a) if overlap). But new §304(b)(3)(B), added by §226(a) of TEFRA of 1982, P.L. No. 97-248, 96 Stat. 324, exempts assumed, etc. purchase-money debt from §304 treatment, contrary to Rev. Rul. 78-422. (The Committee Reports also state that §357(b) is not applicable here either.)

Compare Rev. Rul. 80-240, 1980-2 CB 116 (§§304 and 357 not applicable where transferor mere "agent" for new corporate transferee to effect the borrowing and acquisition of stock of target company; form used merely to satisfy nontax rules; transaction not a debt "assumption" on facts); for ruling guidelines on transactions of the type described in Rev. Rul. 80-240, see Rev. Proc. 80-34, 1980-2 CB 768, which was superseded by Rev. Proc. 84-22, 1984-1 CB 449. But these guidelines (and the consequent no-ruling status) were deleted by Rev. Proc. 84-52, 1984-26 IRB 18.

Page 3-27:

Add to note 69, second paragraph.

[69] Compare Wham Constr. Co. v. US, 600 F.2d 1052 (4th Cir. 1979); contra to *Wham* is Rev. Rul. 80-228, 1980-2 CB 115; see also Rev. Rul. 80-240, 1980-2 CB 116 (transitory borrowing by "agent" and subsequent novation not true assumption transaction).

Page 3-29:

Add to note 72.

[72] See generally Greiner, Behling & Moffett, Assumption of Liabilities and the Improper Purpose—A Reexamination of Section 357(b), 32 Tax Law. 111 (1978).

Add to note 73.

[73] See also Rev. Rul. 79-258, 1979-2 CB 143 (§357(b) not applicable where parent incurred new debt, used proceeds to pay off old

debt which creditor would not allow to be assumed, and subsidiary then assumed new debt).

According to H.R. Rep. No. 97-760, 542 (the Conference Committee Report to TEFRA, supra note 67 (this Supplement)), new §304(b)(3)(B) (which exempts purchase-money debt which is assumed in a §351 exchange from the rules of new §304) is also immune from §357(b). See infra ¶ 9.32 (this Supplement).

Add to note 74, second paragraph.

74 Diedrich v. CIR, 457 US 191 (1982) (donor taxable on transfer of property with obligation to pay donor's gift tax liability).

Page 3-30:

Correct fourth complete sentence of text.

Delete last six words and put period in place of comma.

Add to note 75, first paragraph.

75 See also Regs. §§1.1001-2(a), 1.1001-2(b) (Dec. 11, 1980); for recent applications of *Crane* principle to tax transferor on excess of debt over basis (regardless of property value), see Millar v. CIR, 577 F.2d 212 (3d Cir. 1978); Est. of Levine v. CIR, 634 F.2d 12 (2d Cir. 1980); Evangelista v. CIR, 629 F.2d 1218 (7th Cir. 1980); Jerold Delman Est., 73 TC 15 (1979); for comparable basis treatment, see Paul Brountas, 73 TC 491 (1979); but see Regs. §1.1001-2(a)(3) (1980). On appeal, *Brountas* was reversed, 692 F.2d 152 (1st Cir. 1982).

But in an important recent decision by the Fifth Circuit, *Tufts* was reversed, 651 F.2d 1058 (5th Cir. 1981), and the court held that the transferor of property subject to nonrecourse debt could not realize more than the fair market value of the transferred property, even though such amount was less than the debt (in effect, the court revitalized footnote 37 of the *Crane* case, despite contrary decisions by the Second, Third and Seventh Circuits). Certiorari was granted in *Tufts* on May 3, 1982, and the Supreme Court reversed, 461 US 300 (1983) (amount realized includes face of nonrecourse debt if debt included in basis; footnote 37 of *Crane* rejected, and principles of Reg. §1.1001-2 accepted). In a related development, the Supreme Court held the donor to be taxable in a "net gift" transaction where property was transferred upon the donee's agreement to pay the donor's gift tax liability, Diedrich v. CIR, 457 US 191 (1982). See Andrews, On Beyond *Tufts*, 61 Taxes 949 (1983).

But see new §7701(g), added by §75(c) of the Tax Reform Act of 1984, P.L. No. 98-369, 98 Stat. 678 (in computing amount realized on property transferred subject to nonrecourse debt, property value is deemed to equal the amount of the debt). This provision inadvertently seems to have codified the 1979 proposed regulations' rule, which paved the way for the Tax Court's decision in *Brountas*; see Eustice, The Tax Reform Act of 1984, ¶ 5.05[5][a].

Add to note 75, second paragraph.

[75] See also Bernstein, Avoiding Zero Basis Problems in Capital Contributions of Debt Obligations, 50 J. Tax. 302 (1979).

But see Jackson v. CIR, 708 F.2d 1402 (9th Cir. 1983) (no §357(c) where transferor remained personally liable on debt and corporation did not assume debt on transferred property). See Comment by Bogdanski, Closely Held Corporations, 10 J. Corp. Tax. 357 (1984).

Page 3-31:

Add to note 76, first paragraph.

[76] Rev. Rul. 80-199, 1980-2 CB 122 (IRS will follow *Focht* for pre-§357(c)(3) transfers but will not follow *Thatcher* and *Bongiovanni*). Compare Wm. P. Orr, 78 TC 1059 (1982) (§357(c) gain on assumption of customer deposit liabilities which, for this purpose, were treated like cash loans to transferor; *Focht* distinguished).

Add to note 76, third paragraph.

[76] See generally Truskowski, Section 358(d) and the Cash Basis Taxpayer, 56 Taxes 555 (1978); and Banoff, Incorporation of Partnerships With Negative Capital Accounts: Can Gain Be Avoided? 60 Taxes 411 (1982).

Page 3-33:

Add to note 82.

[82] See also Rev. Rul. 78-330, 1978-2 CB 147 (parent shareholder's cancellation of subsidiary's debt prior to merger into sister subsidiary in order to avoid §357(c) gain did not violate §357(b), citing *Simpson*).

¶ 3.08. "CONTROL": THE 80 PERCENT RULE

Page 3-33:

Add to note 84.

[84] Rev. Rul. 78-130, 1978-1 CB 114 (control must be direct; not by §318 attribution).

Page 3-35:

Add to text at end of section.

In determining the existence of the requisite 80 percent control under §368(c), the attribution principles do not apply.[88.1] Thus, control must be obtained and held directly by the transferors in order to constitute a valid §351 exchange.

[88.1] Rev. Rul. 56-613, 1956-2 CB 212; Brams v. CIR, 734 F.2d 290 (6th Cir. 1984).

¶ 3.09. TWO OR MORE TRANSFERORS
Page 3-35:
Add to note 89.

[89] See also Rev. Rul. 79-194, 1979-1 CB 145 (nominal property transfer does not qualify for transferor status); Rev. Rul. 79-70, 1979-1 CB 144 (property for debt securities only not qualified for transferor status); Rev. Rul. 84-44, 1984-1 CB 105 (must transfer property to corporation issuing the stock to be included in control group; transfer to its subsidiary not sufficient).

¶ 3.10. CONTROL "IMMEDIATELY AFTER THE EXCHANGE"
Page 3-37:
Correct citation error in third line of note 96.

[96] Change "Rev. Rul. 77-123" to "Rev. Rul. 76-123."

Add to note 96, after Rev. Rul. 77-449 citation.

[96] Fisher, Does Rev. Rul. 77-449 Signal a Change in IRS Application of the Step-Transaction Doctrine? 51 J. Tax. 96 (1979); Rev. Rul. 83-34, 1983-1 CB 79 (double drop-downs to 80 percent subsidiaries covered by Rev. Rul. 77-449 principle too); Rev. Rul. 83-156, 1983-2 CB 66 (drop down to subsidiary and subsidiary contribution to joint venture partnership tax-free successive §351 and §721 transfer).

Page 3-38:
Add to note 99.

[99] See also Rev. Rul. 79-70, 1979-1 CB 144 (loss of control through binding agreement to sell 40 percent to third party investor killed §351; buyer not a property transferor where it purchased securities for cash from new corporation).
Compare Rev. Rul. 79-194, 1979-1 CB 145 (one property transferor's resale to another property transferor did not affect §351 qualification; however, if buyer only a de minimis property transferor, will

be disregarded and resale per binding obligation breaks §351 if seller drops below 80 percent).

Page 3-40:

Add to note 103, second paragraph.

[103] See generally Tillinghast & Paully, The Effect of the Collateral Issuance of Stock or Securities on the Control Requirement of Section 351, 37 Tax L. Rev. 251 (1982).

Page 3-41:

Add to note 104.

[104] See also Rev. Rul. 79-194, supra note 99 (this Supplement).

Page 3-43:

Add to note 109.

[109] See Rev. Rul. 82-150, 1982-2 CB 110 (call option may be the economic equivalent of present ownership if exercise a foregone conclusion).

¶ 3.11.　THE TRANSFEROR'S BASIS

Page 3-44:

Add to note 111.

[111] But see §§1276–1278, added by the Tax Reform Act of 1984; if the bonds have "market discount," ordinary income will result to the holder if the bonds are issued after July 18, 1984. See supra note 54.2 (this Supplement).

Page 3-45:

Add to note 113.

[113] But boot gain reported under §453 (supra note 55, this Supplement) has an immediate §358 basis effect under Prop. Regs. §1.453-1 (f)(3)(ii); compare the transferor's basis results under §362(a), infra note 119 (this Supplement).

Page 3-46:

Add to note 115.

[115] For basis results under §358 where gain is reported under the installment sale rules of §453, see supra note 113 (this Supplement).

Page 3-47:

Add to note 116.

[116] See generally Truskowski, Section 358(d) and the Cash Basis Taxpayer, 56 Taxes 555 (1978).

¶ 3.12.   THE TRANSFEREE CORPORATION'S BASIS

Page 3-49:

Add to note 119.

[119] But if the transferor reports boot gain under §453, the corporate transferee's basis step-up is delayed until reporting of the transferor's gain by Prop. Regs. §1.453-1(f)(3)(ii).

Add to note 120.

[120] Service will not apply *Holdcroft* rule if distortion of income does not arise from corporate deduction. Point to Remember No. 2, 32 Tax Law. 182 (1978); Rothman, Transfers to Controlled Corporations: Related Problems, BNA Portf. No. 348, at A-20 (1978), discussing Ltr. Rul. 7830010; Rev. Rul. 80-198, 1980-2 CB 113 (IRS agrees to allow corporate deduction for assumed "expense" liabilities similar to cited letter ruling); Rev. Rul. 83-155, 1983-2 CB 38 (corporate assumption of guaranteed payment to retired partner deductible under Rev. Rul. 80-198).

¶ 3.13.   CORPORATE GAIN OR LOSS ON ISSUE OR SALE OF STOCK: §1032

Page 3-51:

Add to note 126.

[126] The House version of the Bankruptcy Tax Act of 1980 (H.R. 5043) proposed to subject equity-for-debt exchanges to the debt discharge rules of new §108 if the value of the stock was less than the face of the discharged debt. (This provision would not apply, however, if the canceled debt was a security.) The Senate dropped this provision, retaining a limited exception in §108(e)(8)(B) for cases where a de minimis amount of stock was issued or where an unsecured creditor received a disproportionately lower percentage of stock (less than 50 percent) than other participating unsecured creditors. In addition, a special ordinary income recapture rule was added in §108(e)(7) for a creditor who subsequently disposed of stock received in satisfaction of his debt (where the satisfaction transaction produced an ordinary loss deduction for the creditor). The Senate version ultimately passed in 1980. See generally infra ¶ 14.58 (this Supplement).

For analysis of equity-for-debt swap transactions, see Heng &

Parker, Tax-Free Debt Repurchase Using Stock-for-Debt Exchanges, 60 Taxes 527 (1982); Walter, Tax Aspects of Recent Innovative Financings—Strategies for Existing Discount Debt and for New Securities, 60 Taxes 995 (1982); and Addendum, 61 Taxes 184 (1983). See also Note, Debt-Equity Swaps, 37 Tax L. Rev. 677 (1984); and Chirelstein & Lopata, Recent Developments in the Step-Transaction Doctrine, 60 Taxes 970 (1982). But see S. 2688 (introduced in July 1982), which would treat such transactions as if stock had been issued for cash, and cash used to buy in the debt (hence triggering §108 gain). This provision did not pass, however, in the 1982 legislation.

But H.R. 4170, the Tax Reform Act of 1984, proposed (in §59) to add new §108(e)(10), providing for the generation of debt discharge gain where a solvent debtor discharges its debts with stock worth less than the amount of the debt. There was no comparable provision in the Senate Finance Committee bill, but the final Conference version accepted the House proposal and enacted §108(e)(10) in §59 of the Tax Reform Act of 1984. See Eustice, The Tax Reform Act of 1984, ¶ 3.03[5][a].

Page 3-52:

Add to note 130.

[130] See also National Can Corp. v. US, 520 F. Supp. 567 (N.D. Ill. 1981) (parent has no basis for subsidiary's bonds converted into parent stock); contra, ITT & Cos., 77 TC 60 (1981) (parent has basis in bonds equal to value of parent's stock), aff'd per curiam, 704 F.2d 252 (2d Cir. 1983). *National Can* was affirmed, 687 F.2d 1107 (7th Cir. 1982) (parent denied §165 loss deduction or §171 bond premium deduction on conversion of subsidiary's bonds into parent's stock; *ITT* case distinguished on grounds that latter decision involved tax consequences of subsequent retirement of bonds after their acquisition by parent).

Page 3-53:

Add to text at end of runover paragraph.

But recent legislation [132.1] amended §1032 to provide nonrecognition treatment on the lapse or repurchase of any option to buy or sell stock of the corporation (including treasury stock).

[132.1] The Tax Reform Act of 1984, H.R. 4170, §57; The Deficit Reduction Act of 1984, H.R. 2163, §42; The Tax Reform Act of 1984, P.L. No. 98-369, §57, 98 Stat. 678. For general background, see Pesiri, Untangling the Warrant Web, 23 Tax Notes 525 (Apr. 30, 1984); Eustice, The Tax Reform Act of 1984, ¶ 3.03[6].

Page 3-54:

Add to note 134.

[134] See also Duncan Indus., Inc., 73 TC 266 (1979) (stock issue discount held deductible as loan origination fee and amortizable over term of debt). PLR 8248010 (Tech. Adv.), 1982 P-H Fed. Taxes ¶ 55,459 (preferred stock issued to cancel warrants subject to §1032 where holder given right to accept either common or preferred stock pursuant to modification of warrants).

But recent legislation extended §1032 nonrecognition for stock issued to cancel warrants (supra note 132.1 (this Supplement)).

¶ 3.14. CONTRIBUTIONS TO CAPITAL

Page 3-56:

Add to note 141.

[141] Cf. City Gas Co. of Fla., 74 TC 386 (1980) (refundable security deposits by utility's customers held not income to corporate payee; mere security device to insure payment of bills by customers). But decision reversed and remanded, 689 F.2d 943 (11th Cir. 1982) (test is primary purpose of payment—security deposit or prepaid income).

Add to note 143.

[143] But §2(a) of H.R. 5043, the Bankruptcy Tax Act of 1980, proposed to amend §108 and §118 to provide, in §108(f)(1), that debt cancelled in a capital contribution would be deemed to have been satisfied for cash equal to the basis of the debt. See infra ¶ 14.58 (this Supplement).

The Senate Finance Committee favorably reported H.R. 5043 on November 19, 1980. While the stock-for-debt rules proposed by the House bill were dropped in the Senate version, the capital contribution portion of the House bill was retained as §108(e)(6). This version of the bill passed in December 1980; for 1984 legislation, adding new ¶ 108(e)(10), see supra note 126 (this Supplement).

Page 3-57:

Add to note 144, second paragraph.

[144] *Putoma* affirmed, 600 F.2d 734 (5th Cir. 1979) (§118 overrides inclusionary tax benefit rule; cancellation also held exempt "gift" under §102). But *Putoma* result overruled by Bankruptcy Tax Act of 1980, §108(e)(6).

Compare Dwyer v. US, 622 F.2d 460 (9th Cir. 1980) (shareholder had interest income when he cancelled corporation's debt and accrued interest on complete liquidation of corporation, even though corporation had been denied interest deduction under §267).

Page 3-59:

Correct fifth line of second paragraph in note 149.

[149] Add "stock" after "its" and before "issue," and delete word "issue."

Add to note 149, end of second paragraph.

[149] But see Nolan, Deferred Compensation and Employee Options Under the New Section 83 Regulations, 57 Taxes 790, 793-795 (1979). Rev. Rul. 80-76, 1980-1 CB 15 (majority shareholder of parent transferred parent's stock to key employee of subsidiary; held, no gain or loss to shareholder-transferor—instead, add basis of transferred stock to basis of remaining stock; subsidiary gets deduction equal to value of stock; and subsidiary has no gain or loss). But see Henry C. Tilford, 75 TC 134 (1980) (shareholder sale of stock to corporation's key employee held deductible loss per *Downer;* regulations invalid, and committee report statement on which regulations were based not the "law" re shareholder sales in compensatory transaction). On appeal, *Tilford* was reversed, 705 F.2d 828 (6th Cir. 1983) (held, regulations valid). In Leroy Frantz, 83 TC 162 (1984), the Tax Court overruled its prior decisions in *Tilford* and *Smith* and agreed to follow the Circuit Court view that a shareholder's non-pro rata surrender of stock resulted in a nontaxable capital contribution.

Page 3-60:

Add to note 151, end of runover paragraph.

[151] *Smith* was reversed sub nom. Schleppy v. CIR, 601 F.2d 196 (5th Cir. 1979) (no loss deduction allowed; add basis of contributed stock to basis of stock still held by contributing shareholder).

Accord with *Downer* is Henry C. Tilford, 75 TC 134 (1980) (also, regulations treating compensatory stock sale to employer as capital contribution by selling shareholder held invalid), rev'd, 705 F.2d 828 (6th Cir. 1983).

But in Leroy Frantz, supra note 149 (this Supplement), the Tax Court abandoned its previous decisions and concluded that such transactions were tax-free capital contributions by the surrendering shareholder.

Add to note 151, second paragraph.

[151] See generally Bolding, Non-Pro Rata Stock Surrenders: Capital Contribution, Capital Loss or Ordinary Loss, 32 Tax Law. 275 (1979); Wray, Transfer of Property by Shareholders to Corporate Employees Under Section 83, 52 J. Tax. 152 (1980).

¶ 3.15.   TRANSFER UNDER §351 VS. "SALE"

Page 3-61:

Add new note 153.1 to first full sentence of text.

153.1 For a successful example of this technique, see Bradshaw v. US, 683 F.2d 365 (Ct. Cl. 1982) (sale of undeveloped land to newly organized corporation held true sale and taxable as capital gain to transferors).

Add to note 154, end of first paragraph.

154 See generally Hirotashi Yamamoto, 73 TC 946 (1980), aff'd by unpublished order (9th Cir., Dec. 7, 1981) (§1239 of *prior* law not applicable to shareholder property sales to 100 percent subsidiary of taxpayer's 100 percent owned parent corporation; transaction not a §351 exchange either since taxpayer received no stock of subsidiary in exchange for the property transfer).

Add to note 155, following Rev. Proc. 72-9 citation.

155 Rev. Proc. 72-9 is currently found in Rev. Proc. 84-22, 1984-1 CB 449. For possible application of the new market discount rules of §1276, see supra note 54.2 (this Supplement).

Page 3-62:

Correct second line from bottom in note 158.

158 Word "gained" should read "gain."

Add to note 158.

158 Compare Bradshaw v. US, supra note 153.1 (this Supplement) (separate sale respected; short-term installment notes true debt, and not securities).

Page 3-63:

Add to note 161, second paragraph.

161 Bradshaw v. US, supra note 153.1 (this Supplement) (sale treatment upheld; notes not equity, and not securities).

Page 3-64:

Add to note 162.

162 See generally Bradshaw v. US, supra note 153.1 (this Supplement).

¶ 3.16. TRANSFER UNDER §351 VS. DIVIDEND

Page 3-65:

Add to note 167.

[167] But new §304(b)(3)(A), added by §226(a) of TEFRA of 1982, P.L. No. 97-248, 96 Stat. 324, overrules *Haserot* and provides for §304 primacy over §351 in an overlap situation (except for the assumption of purchase-money debt, in which case new §304(b)(3)(B) provides for §357(a) primacy over §304). See infra ¶ 9.32 (this Supplement). Compare Stanley H. Brans, ¶ 83-025 P-H Memo TC, aff'd, 734 F.2d 290 (6th Cir. 1984).

Add to note 168.

[168] See Rev. Rul. 80-239, 1980-2 CB 103 (transfer of all the stock of X Corporation to new Y Corporation for Y stock and cash borrowed by Y from a bank and repaid with funds distributed to Y from X—held, taxable dividend to transferor from X under step transaction doctrine; §351(b)(1)(A) boot rules not applicable; Y a mere conduit for distribution of cash by X). See Blanchard, The Service's Recent Attack: Taxation of Section 351 Exchanges Between Shareholders and Newly Organized Holding Companies, 35 Tax Law. 163 (1981) (analyzing Rev. Rul. 80-239). See new §304(b)(3)(C), added by TEFRA of 1982, supra note 167 (this Supplement), for special rules dealing with the creation of bank holding companies. See also new §304(b)(3)(B) (§357 overrides §304 as to assumed purchase-money debt in a §351 exchange), added by §226(a) of TEFRA of 1982.

¶ 3.17. "MIDSTREAM" TRANSFERS OF POTENTIAL INCOME UNDER §351

Page 3-66:

Add to note 170.

[170] Manning, The Service Corporation—Who Is Taxable On Its Income: Reconciling Assignment of Income Principles, Section 482, and Section 351, 37 U. Miami L. Rev. 653 (1984).

Page 3-67:

Add to note 173.

[173] Rev. Rul. 80-198, 1980-2 CB 113 (*Brown*-type assignment of income taxable to assignor-transferor per *Earl-Eubank*).

Add to note 174.

[174] Accord with *Biggs* is Rev. Rul. 80-198, supra note 173 (this Supplement).

Add to note 175, second paragraph.

[175] Accord with *Hempt* is Rev. Rul. 80-198, supra note 173 (this Supplement).
Shore was affirmed, 631 F.2d 624 (9th Cir. 1980).

Page 3-68:

Add to note 177.

[177] For applicability of §482 if income distorted as result of transfer, see Rev. Rul. 80-198, supra note 173 (this Supplement). Richard H. Foster, 80 TC 34 (1983) (§482 can apply in §351 context and did here).

Add to note 178, first paragraph.

[178] Rev. Rul. 80-198, supra note 173 (this Supplement) (application of §482 if transfer distorts income stream).
But compare Stewart v. CIR, 714 F.2d 977 (9th Cir. 1983) (although §482 did not apply because of lack of two businesses, transferor taxed on profits from transferee's resale under *Court Holding Co.* doctrine and substance vs. form principle; essentially the same result here as a §482 reallocation).

Add to note 178, end of second paragraph.

[178] Adess, The Role of Section 482 in Nonrecognition Transactions —The Outer Edges, 57 Taxes 946 (1979); and Note, Section 482 and the Nonrecognition Provisions: Resolving the Conflict, 77 Nw. U.L. Rev. 670 (1982).

Page 3-69:

Add to note 182.

[182] See also Rev. Rul. 79-127, 1979-1 CB 189 (LIFO election by transferee triggered recapture of transferor's inventory write-downs).
Stewart v. CIR, supra note 178 (this Supplement) (shareholder transferor taxed on profits from transferee's resale under *Court Holding Co.* and *Hallowell* substance vs. form principle).
But compare Stewart v. US, 1983-2 USTC 9580 (D. Ariz. 1982), aff'd, 739 F.2d 411 (9th Cir. 1984) (shareholder installment sale to corporation and corporate *pledge* of property as security for loan; later foreclosure sale by creditor did not result in taxable gain to shareholder).

¶ 3.18. COLLATERAL PROBLEMS OF INCORPORATING A GOING BUSINESS

Page 3-71:

Add to note 195.

[195] But Rev. Rul. 70-239 was revoked by Rev. Rul. 84-111, 1984-30 IRB 6.

Page 3-72:

Add to note 196.

[196] Banoff, Incorporation of Partnerships With Negative Capital Accounts: Can Gain Be Avoided? 60 Taxes 411 (1982).

See PLR 8333004, 1983 P-H Fed. Taxes, Vol. 11, ¶ 55,262 (theory of Rev. Rul. 70-239 applied to deny §1244 stock status).

But Rev. Rul. 70-239 was revoked by Rev. Rul. 84-111, 1984-30 IRB 6 (tax consequences to parties depend on form of transfer and will differ depending on whether transaction involves a partnership-level asset transfer, partner-level asset transfer after liquidation of partnership, or partner interest transfer followed by corporate liquidation of partnership).

¶ 3.19. RELATION OF §351 TO REORGANIZATION PROVISIONS

Page 3-74:

Add to note 199.

[199] Rev. Rul. 79-289, 1979-2 CB 145 (so holds).

Add to note 201.

[201] See also Rev. Rul. 79-274, 1979-2 CB 131 (overlap of B reorganization and §351; voting preferred received pro rata by transferors held §306 stock if transferee has earnings and profits in its first taxable year). See generally Corry, Preferred Stock Issued in Tax-Free Exchanges: Does Section 306 Apply? 35 Tax L. Rev. 113 (1979).

But see new §306(c)(3), added by §226(b) of TEFRA of 1982, P.L. No. 97-248, 96 Stat. 324, providing for "section 306 stock" classification if cash would have resulted in dividend treatment under the newly revised §304 rules, infra ¶ 9.32 (this Supplement).

Page 3-75:

Add to note 203.

[203] See also Rev. Rul. 78-130, 1978-1 CB 114 (illustration of §351, Type D reorganization and Type C reorganization overlap).

Rev. Rul. 68-357 and Rev. Rul. 76-123 were distinguished in Rev. Rul. 84-44, 1984-1 CB 105 (stock not aggregated where one corporation merged into subsidiary for stock of parent and another corporation transferred assets to the parent for less than control; second transferor was only transferor of property to corporation issuing stock and hence §351 control not obtained).

Add new paragraph (5) to text at end of section.

(5) Inspired by some of the broader implications of Rev. Rul. 76-123 (supra ¶ 3.02, note 21), use of §351 as an alternative acquisition method to the tax-free reorganization provisions of §368 has been suggested in view of the considerably more relaxed limitations of the former. Thus, if an acquisition transaction can be tailored to fit the §351 mold, greater flexibility is obtained than would be available under the traditional §368(a) rules. For example, by creating a preliminary holding company, owned jointly by the acquiring corporation and those shareholders of the target company who want nonrecognition treatment, the remaining shareholders of the target can be bought out for cash, debt securities, nonvoting stock (or a combination thereof), presumably without rendering the initial incorporation transaction taxable under §351 (in an extreme case, the acquiring corporation could even obtain a cost basis for the acquired corporation's stock or assets if proper planning is adopted).[203.1]

But the transaction described above was rejected on continuity of interest grounds in two recent rulings,[203.2]

[203.1] For analysis of the various possibilities inherent in this technique, see Greenberg, The Use of Holding Companies to Obtain Tax Advantages, 57 Taxes 847, 855 (1979); Freeman, Holding Companies: Section 351 as a Lever to Avoid Restrictions Inherent in Section 368, Section 306, and Sections 304 and 302, 6 J. Corp. Tax. 332 (1980).

[203.2] Rev. Rul. 80-284, 1980-2 CB 117 (stock acquisition route); Rev. Rul. 80-285, 1980-2 CB 119 (asset acquisition route). Both rulings held that the acquisition essentially constituted a taxable "purchase" of stock and assets respectively in view of the large amounts of cash involved, over 80 percent). See also Rev. Proc. 81-10, §3.01(20), 1981-1 CB 647 (no-ruling area), superseded by Rev. Proc. 82-22, 1982-1 CB 649 (same), and Rev. Proc. 84-22, 1984-1 CB 449 (same). For analysis of these rulings, see Rosenberg, Use of Section 351 by

even though the "technical" requirements of §351 were satisfied. The rulings curiously omitted any reference to Rev. Rul. 76-123, however, and likewise refrained from noting the Service's concession that continuity of interest principles do not apply in recapitalization reorganizations (infra ¶¶ 14.11 and 14.17). One can sympathize with the Service's discomfort over the use of §351 as an end-around the more restrictive reorganization definition provisions of §368(a); a more appropriate forum for this debate, however, would appear to be Congress, rather than the rulings division and the courts.

On reconsideration, however, the Service revoked the 1980 rulings in Rev. Rul. 84-71,[203.3] holding that if §351 fits, it applies, even though the §351 transaction is part of a "larger acquisition" transaction that would not qualify under §368.

Minority Stockholder in Acquisitions Challenged by New Rulings, 54 J. Tax. 76 (1981); Silverman, Comment: The Nonrecognition Sieve, 36 Tax L. Rev. 557 (1981); Bowen, The Reach of Section 351, 59 Taxes 926 (1981); and Samuels, The Limited Role of Section 351 in Corporate Acquisitions, 60 Taxes 955 (1982).

But Rev. Rul. 80-284 and Rev. Rul. 80-285 were revoked by Rev. Rul. 84-71, 1984-1 CB 106; moreover, Rev. Proc. 84-43, 1984-1 CB 552 deleted §3.01(25) from the no-ruling list in Rev. Proc. 84-22.

[203.3] Supra note 203.1 (this Supplement); see Friedrich, Recent Developments, 11 J. Corp. Tax. 290 (1984).

Chapter 4

THE CORPORATION'S
CAPITAL STRUCTURE

PART A. CAPITAL STRUCTURE

¶ 4.01. INTRODUCTORY

Page 4-2:

Add new note 2.1 to end of first sentence of first paragraph.

[2.1] But see new § 163(f)(1), added by the Tax Equity and Fiscal Responsibility Act (TEFRA) of 1982, P.L. No. 97-248, 96 Stat. 324 (no interest deduction on unregistered public debt obligations; publicly traded debt with maturity of more than one year must now be in registered form to qualify for interest deduction).

Page 4-5:

Add to note 10.

[10] Regulations under §385 were finally proposed, however, on March 20, 1980, and became final on December 29, 1980 (though with a delayed effective date, May 1, 1981, which date was further postponed until January 1, 1982, and then delayed once again until July 1, 1982). New regulations were proposed on December 30, 1981. The effective date of the §385 regulations was again delayed, until at least April 1983, leaving their status in ever-increasing uncertainty. On July 6, 1983, the regulations were withdrawn, probably never to be seen again (at least not in the foreseeable future). See T.D. 7920, Nov. 2, 1983.

¶ 4.02. STOCK VS. DEBT: MAJOR
LITIGATION AREAS AND STAKES

Page 4-6:

Add to note 111 (first paragraph).

[111] For a recent article on the debt-equity area generally, see Taylor,

Debt-Equity and Other Tax Distinctions: How Far Can We Go? 62 Taxes 848 (1984).

Add to note 111 (second paragraph).

[111] The 1985 P-H Tax Service paragraph is the same citation.

Correct first line of note 14.

[14] Citation to *Zilkha* should be "52 TC," not "55 TC."

Add to note 14.

[14] See Prop. Regs. §1.385-12 and Final Regs. §1.385-10 for possible classification of preferred stock as debt. The new proposed regulations on December 30, 1981 drop these provisions, however.

All versions of the regulations were withdrawn on July 6, 1983; see T.D. 7920, Nov. 2, 1983.

Add to note 15.

[15] Rev. Proc. 76-19 has been superseded by what is now Rev. Proc. 84-22, 1984-1 CB 449.

Texas Farm Bureau v. US, 725 F.2d 307 (5th Cir. 1984) (held equity as a matter of law; reversible error for jury to find debt).

Page 4-7:

Add to note 16.

[16] See Prop. and Final Regs. §1.385-4 (determined status at time of creation; but purported debt can turn into stock at later time on "second look"; however, once classified as stock, interest cannot be reclassified as debt). Final Regs. §1.385-4 and new Prop. Regs. §1.385-4 (same).

Add new note 16.1 to end of second full paragraph.

[16.1] If purported debt is reclassified as stock, Prop. and Final Regs. §1.385-4 treated such interests as preferred stock (new proposed regulations same).

Page 4-8:

Add new text to end of section.

With the withdrawal of the §385 regulations on July 6, 1983, and the likelihood (at this writing) that the Treasury will abandon its attempt to draft regulations under §385, matters seem poised for a return to the decisional morass that has prevailed in this area for five decades.

¶ 4.03. STOCK VS. DEBT: FORMAL CHARACTERISTICS: HYBRID SECURITIES

Page 4-8:

Add to note 19.

[19] Jones v. US, 569 F.2d 618 (5th Cir. 1981) (subordination not fatal on facts because imposed by state laws and regulations).

Page 4-9:

Add to note 21.

[21] But compare Rev. Rul. 83-98, 1983-2 CB 40 (adjustable rate convertible notes held equity on facts; Rev. Rul. 68-54 and Rev. Rul. 73-122 distinguished). See also Paulsen v. CIR, 716 F.2d 563 (9th Cir. 1983) (infra ¶ 14.11; hybrid equity aspects of reorganization, continuity-of-interest doctrine).

Add reference to note 22 at end of first full paragraph of text.

Page 4-10:

Add to note 24.

[24] For treatment of hybrid instruments issued by public corporations, see Prop. Regs. §1.385-5, where the approach was a mechanical analysis of objective factors reminiscent of the association regulations; for treatment of hybrids issued by closely held corporations, see Prop. Regs. §1.385-6(b) (generally treated as stock). For permissible alternative to hybrids see Prop. Regs. §1.385-10 (locked interests).

Final Regs. §1.385-5 continues the proposed regulations' factor analysis approach, finding debt status if the value of the instrument's equity features (contingent payment of principal or interest, and convertibility) do not exceed 50 percent of total value. Thus, if the value of the instrument's equity features is not predominant, debt classification will result. The second Prop. Regs. §1.385-5(d) (Dec. 30, 1981) revises and clarifies the valuation rules for determining the value of the "straight debt portion" of the instruments (assumptions give highest potential value to equity features). However, Prop. Regs. §1.385-5(c)(5)(v) states that stock redemption debt not contingent where local law limits payments to earned surplus; and Prop. Regs. §1.385-5(c)(5)(iv) states that nonrecourse debt is not per se contingent (but if issued for property, debt must not exceed value of property).

But Final Regs. §1.385-6(c) finds equity status per se for proportionately held hybrids; but see new Prop. Regs. §1.385-8(d)(2) "exception," where at least 20 percent of instruments held by independent creditors (not per se equity here; instead, test under general hybrid rules of §1.385-5 and "second look" rules of §1.385-6).

Final Regs. §1.385-8 adopted the proposed regulations "locked interest" provisions without change; new Prop. Regs. §1.385-8 (same). But the §385 regulations were withdrawn on July 6, 1983. See T.D. 7920, Nov. 2, 1983.

Add new text to end of section.

Withdrawal of the §385 regulations on July 6, 1983, and publication of the ARCN ruling (Rev. Rul. 83-98, supra note 21 (this Supplement)) stemmed from the Treasury's disenchantment with the mechanical rules of the hybrid instrument provisions; apparently it was felt that regulatory bright lines encouraged tax-motivated bright ideas, and that a retreat to vagueness was necessary to restrain overly aggressive exploitation of the regulation's definitional safe harbors. As of late 1983, it seems clear that the Treasury will avoid any but the most cursory regulation guidelines in the hybrid instrument area (for that matter, issuance of *any* regulations under §385 seems highly unlikely in the near future). Thus, "all the facts and circumstances" will be the sole operative test as to whether a particular instrument constitutes debt or equity paper. Those who relied on the various regulation versions in structuring hybrid instruments appear to have been unduly optimistic as to the weight that could be placed on these proposals (which, of course, never became legally effective). See T.D. 7920, Nov. 2, 1983.

¶ 4.04. STOCK VS. DEBT: CLASSIFICATION OF NONHYBRID SECURITIES

Page 4-10:

Add to note 28.

[28] Lane v. US, 724 F.2d 1311 (11th Cir. 1984) (advances and guarantees were equity; no intent to repay); compare Bauer v. CIR, 748 F.2d 1365 (9th Cir. 1984) (advances were debt); Texas Farm Bureau v. US, 725 F.2d 307 (5th Cir. 1984) (advances equity as a matter of law).

Page 4-11:

Add to note 29.

[29] See Prop. Regs. §1.385-6 for effect of proportionality on classification of purported debt instruments at the time of the instruments'

issuance; Prop. Regs. §1.385-7 focused on the effects of proportionality at the time of potential enforcement (or lack of it) of the purported obligations.

Under the Final Regs. §1.385-6, proportionality is the key issue (or super factor) for classification as debt or equity, i.e., straight debt held disproportionately will be treated as debt per se. If the debt is held proportionately, initially it will be treated as equity if: (a) it is a "hybrid," §1.385-6(c); (b) it is issued for property and the interest rate is unreasonable, §§1.385-6(d) and 1.385-6(e); or (c) the debtor is excessively "thin," §§1.385-6(f) and 1.385-6(g). Pro rata held debt that escapes initial equity classification can be reclassified as equity under "second look" rules if: (a) there is a substantial change in terms (in which case the revised instrument is treated as a new issue and retested), §1.385-6(j); (b) interest payments are not enforced with due diligence when due, §1.385-6(k); and (c) demand (or matured) obligations are not enforced with due diligence, §1.385-6(l).

Under new Prop. Regs. §1.385-6, proportionality has become a "mega-factor." Proportionality is defined objectively under new Prop. Regs. §1.385-6(a) (debt will be pro rata if more than 50 percent overlap with stock holdings, tested with "special" §318 attribution rules). However, debt held by a 25 percent shareholder will be deemed to be pro rata if the debtor corporation is excessively thin (viz., ratio exceeds 10:1), due to the high risk nature of such a loan and the creditor's substantial equity position. On the other hand, Prop. Regs. §1.385-6 (a)(2)(iv) provides a special exception for stock redemptions qualifying under §302(a), if the interest rate meets §483(c) (currently 9 percent). Under the new proposals, the treatment of pro rata held hybrids is in Prop. Regs. §1.385-6(d), the debt for property rules are in Prop. Regs. §§1.385-6(e) and 1.385-6(f), the excessive debt rules are in Prop. Regs. §§1.385-6(g), 1.385-6(h) and 1.385-6(j), and the "second look" rules are in Prop. Regs. §§1.385-6(k), 1.385-6(l) and 1.385-6(m). The excessive or inadequate issue price rules of Final Regs. §1.385-3(a) were moved to the proportionality provisions in Prop. Regs. §1.385-6(c) (moreover, such provisions apply only after initial debt status is found). But the proportionality rules do not apply to debt held by independent creditors (defined in Prop. Regs. §1.385-6 (b)), or to cases where the corporation's stock and debt instruments are widely held and readily marketable.

On July 6, 1983, however, the §385 regulations were withdrawn; see T.D. 7920, Nov. 2, 1983.

Add to note 30.

[30] Texas Farm Bureau v. US, 725 F.2d 307 (5th Cir. 1984) (advances to affiliated corporation held equity as a matter of law, even though not strictly pro rata); Bauer v. CIR, supra note 28 (this Supplement) (advances not pro rata and were held to be debt).

Add to note 31, second paragraph.

[31] Electronic Modules Corp. v. US, 695 F.2d 1367 (Fed. Cir. 1982) (parent's advances to subsidiary for working capital held true debt because reasonable expectation of repayment); compare Texas Farm Bureau v. US, supra note 30 (this Supplement) (held equity as a matter of law).

Add to note 31, third paragraph.

[31] Inductotherm Indus., ¶ 84,281 P-H Memo TC (parent's advances to subsidiary held "equity" capital contributions, which rendered subsidiary solvent and hence permitted §332 liquidation and §381 carryover of tax history).

Page 4-12:

Add to note 36.

[36] But see Bauer v. CIR, supra note 28 (this Supplement) (used asset basis to compute ratio; also included non-shareholder debt; but corporation still not thin). Prop. Regs. §1.385-3(c) generally computed debt-equity ratios by use of asset basis rather than values; moreover, such computations exclude trade payables, and generally compute the debt-equity ratio as of the end of the corporation's year. Final Regs. §1.385-6(g) adopted a similar approach; new Prop. Regs. §1.385-6(h) (same).

The new proposed regulations permit use of the stretched out depreciation rates of §312(k) to determine asset bases, however (thus preventing an undue consumption of shareholder basis equity through the artificially high recovery rates permitted by the ACRS rules).

But the §385 regulations were withdrawn on July 6, 1983; T.D. 7920, Nov. 2, 1983.

Page 4-13:

Add to note 37, first paragraph.

[37] Bradshaw v. US, 683 F.2d 365 (Ct. Cl. 1982) (not equity capital contribution even though thin — 50 to 1 — because reasonable assurance of ability to repay when due, price fair, and prospects bright; corporation had adequate resources to pay off debts, and did); Bauer v. CIR, supra note 28 (this Supplement) (range of 2:1 and 8:1 not thin; evidence that corporation could have obtained outside loans and could have easily paid off advances).

Add to end of note 37.

[37] Proposed Regs. §§1.385-6, 1.385-7, and 1.385-9 generally utilized a debt-equity ratio of 1:1 as a safe haven; for the treatment of

excessive debt-equity ratios generally, see Prop. Regs. §1.385-8 (ratio in excess of 10:1 resulted in classification as equity, but for this purpose, compute ratio by using either asset bases or values).

The final regulations dropped per se equity classification for excessively thin corporations; under the final regulations, excessive debt structure is only significant if the debt is held proportionately to stock.

Final Regs. §1.385-6(e) continued the proposed regulations' one-to-one safe-harbor limit for determining a reasonable interest rate, while Regs. §1.385-6(f) established a dual safe-harbor zone for pro rata held debt (viz., the "inside" debt-equity ratio must not exceed 3:1, *and* the outside ratio must not exceed 10:1). In computing these ratios, asset bases, rather than values, are utilized. But new Prop. Regs. §1.385-6(g), while retaining the 3:1 and 10:1 safe-harbor zones for determining thinness (using asset bases), allows the use of §312(k) depreciation rates in §1.385-6(h) to determine these ratios.

But new Prop. Regs. §1.385-6(f)(2) raised the reasonable interest rate/safe-harbor rate to 3:1. Moreover, two new safe-harbor rates were added to the reasonable interest rate list, viz., the §482 test rates (11 to 13 percent), and two points over prime.

But the regulations were withdrawn on July 6, 1983; T.D. 7920, Nov. 2, 1983.

Page 4-14:

Add new note 39.1 to end of second line of text.

[39.1] See generally Prop. Regs. §§1.385-3(a), 1.385-6(c), and 1.385-6(d), where debt is issued for property transferred by shareholders.

For similar provisions under the Final Regs., see §§1.385-3(a) and 1.385-6(d) and 1.385-6(e); new Prop. Regs. §§1.385-6(c), 1.385-6(e), and 1.385-6(f). The new Prop. Regs. §1.385-6(f)(2) safe harbor for determining reasonable interest rates now provides that rates between the §6621 rate (currently 20 percent), the §482 rates (11 to 13 percent), prime (plus 2 points), or comparable government debt will suffice if the debt is recourse and the debt-to-equity ratio does not exceed 3:1.

But the regulations were withdrawn on July 6, 1983; T.D. 7920, Nov. 2, 1983.

Add to note 44.

[44] Electronic Modules Corp. v. US, supra note 31 (this Supplement) (reasonable expectation of repayment of advances by parent to subsidiary; thus, advances held true debt); Adelson v. US, 737 F.2d 1569 (Fed. Cir. 1984) (non-shareholder's advances to client companies held bona fide debt; taxpayer basically not a shareholder and parties intended to create debt, not equity, interests). On remand, 1984-2 USTC

¶ 9787 (Cl. Ct. 1984), held dominant motive business and losses allowed as business bad debt. Lane v. US, supra note 28 (this Supplement); Bauer v. CIR, supra note 28 (this Supplement).

Page 4-15:

Add to note 45.

⁴⁵ But regulations proposed under §385 on March 20, 1980 generally shift from the subjective intent approach of present law to the use of objective criteria in classifying debt and equity intersts.

The final regulations generally continue this objective factor approach as the touchstone for their classification analysis, although proportionality has assumed "super factor" status under these latter provisions, and the new proposed regulations go even further in this direction.

Withdrawal of the regulations on July 6, 1983 leaves the definitional question of debt or equity status in the case law morass until such time as further proposals are promulgated, which proposals, as of late 1983, seem an unlikely prospect in the foreseeable future.

¶ 4.05. STOCK VS. DEBT: TREASURY AUTHORITY TO ISSUE REGULATIONS

Page 4-16:

Add to text at end of section.

Reports of the demise of §385 were premature as regulations at last were proposed under this provision on March 20, 1980 (a mere eleven years after enactment).[49.1] The proposals were prospective only, being limited to interests in corporations created after 1980. The general approach of the proposed regulations was the promulgation of various objective "safe harbors" within which interests in the corporation were certain to be classified as debt; moreover, the all-or-nothing approach of present law was abandoned. Furthermore, the proposed regulations were "selective" in their coverage, dealing only with the major problem areas as perceived by the Treasury; hence, existing case law continued to apply to those areas not dealt with in the proposals. Also, classification

---

[49.1] See generally Pike, Proposed Debt-Equity Regulations: Potent New Standards for Characterizing Purported Debt, 7 J. Corp. Tax. 195 (1980); Gershman, Debt-Equity Proposals Provide Guidance But Pose Problems for Small Corporations, 53 J. Tax. 194 (1980); Beghe, Redrawing the Lines Between Corporate Debt and Equity Interests: The Proposed Regulations Under Section 385, 58 Taxes 931 (1980).

as "debt" was not further refined into the two principal categories of indebtedness, "securities" and "non-securities"; accordingly, existing case law was still relevant on this issue as well.

The §385 regulations were promulgated in final form by T.D. 7747, on December 29, 1980,[49.2] although with an initially delayed effective date, until May 1, 1981, which date, however, was further extended until January 1, 1982, and then extended again until July 1, 1982.[49.3] The final version of the §385 regulations was more limited in scope than the proposed regulations, though the proposals' general themes of selective application, objective safe harbors, and prospective effect were reaffirmed in the final regulations. The two principal changes to the proposed regulations that were made by the final regulations were: (1) the rule providing for per se equity classification where the debtor's capital structure was excessively thin (Prop. Regs. §1.385-8) was dropped; and (2) the final regulations concentrated their main classification analysis on whether or not the purported debt obligations were held proportionately to stockholdings (in effect, pro rata stock and debt holdings have assumed "super factor" status under the final regulations). The new proposed regulations issued on December 30, 1981 further extended this approach. Again, proportionality is the key to application of the regulations, and has now assumed "mega-factor" status.

[49.2] For analyses of the Final Regs., see Beghe, An Interim Report on the Debt-Equity Regulations Under Code Section 385, 59 Taxes 203 (1981); Bush, The Debt Equity Regulations: Do Stock Redemptions and Other Areas Require Special Attention? 39 N.Y.U. Inst. on Fed. Tax. Ch. 1 (1981); Bloom & Bush, Final Regulations Under Section 385 Contain Complex Rules and Safe Harbors, 54 J. Tax. 274 (1981); Bloom & Bush, Pinpointing the Problem Areas That Still Exist Under the Final Section 385 Regulations, 54 J. Tax. 322 (1981); Natbony, Cleaning the Augean Stables: The Debt-Equity Regulations, 8 J. Corp. Tax. 3 (1981); Levin and Bowen, the Section 385 Regulations Regarding Debt Versus Equity: Is the Cure Worse than the Malady? 35 Tax Law. 1 (1981); and Stone, Distinguishing Corporate Debt From Stock Under Section 385, 36 Tax L. Rev. 341 (1981).

[49.3] In announcement IR 82-80, the §385 regulations were again postponed (by T.D. 7822) until ninety days after final revisions to the regulations are published in the Federal Register, but in no event before January 1, 1983. On July 1, 1982, the Treasury agreed to further delay the effective date until at least April 1983, in return for withdrawal of proposed legislation to block the regulations. As matters now stand, the fate of the regulations is becoming ever more tenuous.

The new proposals create more "bright-line" objective tests, and expand the breadth of the various safe-harbor rules.[49.4]

However, on July 6, 1983, the regulations were withdrawn. See T.D. 7920, Nov. 2, 1983. At this writing, it seems most likely that the entire project will be scrapped, and that the Treasury will recommend repeal of §385 (thus returning the definitional problem to the place from whence it came—the courts). For analyses of the various phases of the §385 regulations, see the 1983 No. 3 Supplement.

[49.4] For analysis of these proposals, see Bloom & Bush, New Re-proposed Regs. on Section 385 Compared to the Prior Regs., 56 J. Tax. 153 (1982). See also Manning, Hyper Lexis and the Law of Conservation of Ambiguity: Thoughts on Section 385, 36 Tax Law. 9 (1982); Kaplan & Yoder, New Variations On An Old Enigma: Debt-Equity Regulations, 1981 U. Ill. L. Rev. 567 (1981).

¶ 4.06.   EQUITY-FLAVORED SECURITIES: CONVERTIBLES, OPTIONS, ETC.

Page 4-16:

Add to note 50.

[50] The Lee article in 44 St. John's L. Rev. 1081 (1980) was a special edition of that publication, which was also numbered Vol. 44.

Page 4-18:

Add to text at end of third line.

Legislation enacted in 1982 changed the straight-line ratable accrual system for issue discount reporting to an "economic interest" computation formula based on compound interest and present value principles, the general effect of which is to bunch the interest amounts in later years.[53.1]

[53.1] See §§1232A and 163(e), added by TEFRA of 1982. Recent legislation (the Tax Reform Act of 1984, H.R. 4170, §41, and the Deficit Reduction Act of 1984 proposed to H.R. 2163, §25(a)) replace present §§1232 and 1232A with new §§1271–1275 and expand the scope of the original-issue discount rules to transactions not covered by present law. See infra new ¶ 4.23 (this Supplement). This legislation passed as the Tax Reform Act of 1984, P.L. No. 98-369, §41(a), 98 Stat. 678.

Page 4-19:

Add to note 59.

[59] For application of 1969 rules, see Seaboard Coffee Serv., Inc., 71 TC 465 (1978) (no original-issue discount on issue of untraded bonds for untraded stock); Microdot, Inc. v. US, 728 F.2d 593 (2d Cir. 1984) (no original-issue discount in recapitalization-reorganization exchange); Golden Nugget, Inc., 83 TC 28 (1984) (same).

Add to text after first full paragraph.

The Technical Corrections Act of 1982 removed the reorganization exception from the definition of issue price in §1232(b)(2) (thereby revitalizing the relevance of the pre-1969 case law), so that it is now possible to generate issue discount in reorganization exchanges (to the extent that the face of the new bonds exceeds the greater of the old bonds' value or their adjusted issue price).[59.1] Moreover, recent legislation[59.2] extended the issue discount rules to a much wider range of debt for property transactions (abolishing the major exceptions of current law).

[59.1] See §1232(b)(4); Gulf Mobile & Ohio R.R. v. US, 579 F.2d 892 (5th Cir. 1978).

[59.2] See the Tax Reform Act of 1984, H.R. 4170, §41(a); the Deficit Reduction Act of 1984, H.R. 2163, §25(a); and the Tax Reform Act of 1984, P.L. No. 98-369, §41(a), 98 Stat. 678 (adding §§1271–1275); infra new ¶ 4.23 (this Supplement).

Page 4-20:

Add to note 60.

[60] See recent legislation, which materially expanded the scope of the debt-for-property original-issue discount rules. The Tax Reform Act of 1984, H.R. 4170, §41; the Deficit Reduction Act of 1984, H.R. 2163, §25(a); and the Tax Reform Act of 1984, P.L. No. 98-369, §41(a), 98 Stat. 678 (adding new §§1271–1275); infra new ¶ 4.23 (this Supplement).

Page 4-21:

Add to note 62.

[62] Regulations were proposed August 29, 1980 raising the test rate of §483 to 9 percent and the imputed rate to 10 percent. These regulations became final on July 1, 1981 in T.D. 7781.

Recent legislation materially expanded the scope of the original-issue discount accrual rules (and concomitantly contracted the role of the §483 characterization rules), but computation of the §483 imputed interest element was conformed to the economic interest principles applicable to original-issue discount. See infra new ¶ 4.23 (this Supplement).

Add to note 63.

[63] See Ltr. Rul. 8052018, 1981 P-H Fed. Tax Serv. ¶ 54,976 (parent has no §171 amortizable bond premium on excess value of its stock over face of subsidiary's debt on conversion of debt into parent stock; premium attributable to conversion feature). See also National Can Corp. v. US, 520 F. Supp. 567 (N.D. Ill. 1981) (no §171 deduction to parent on conversion of subsidiary debt into parent stock; also no §162 or §165 deduction for excess of stock value over face of debt because of §1032), aff'd, 687 F.2d 1107 (7th Cir. 1982). But cf. ITT & Cos., 77 TC 60 (1981), aff'd per curiam, 704 F.2d 252 (2d Cir. 1982) (parent gets basis in subsidiary's debt equal to value of parent's stock at date of conversion). Contra is National Can Corp. v. US, supra (parent has no basis for subsidiary's debt). See also Husky Oil Co., 83 TC 717 (1984) (no interest deduction after debt converted into stock of parent, even though debt still outstanding; *ITT* case not cited).

Page 4-23:

Add to note 67, second paragraph.

[67] Tandy Corp. v. US, 1979-1 USTC ¶ 9160 (D. Tex. 1979) (followed *Bethlehem Steel* and *Columbia Gas*), aff'd, 626 F.2d 1186 (5th Cir. 1980); accord with *Tandy* is Husky Oil Co., supra not 63 (this Supplement) (even though debt was converted into stock of *parent*).

Query the effect of the recently enacted amendments to §354 by the Bankruptcy Tax Act of 1980 making accrued interest taxable in various nonrecognition exchanges (infra ¶ 14.20 (this Supplement), and ¶ 14.34).

Add to note 69.

[69] But see Duncan Indus., Inc., 73 TC 266 (1979) (stock issue discount held amortizable as loan organization fee over term of related debt transaction; §1032 not applicable on facts).

Page 4-24:

Add to note 71, fourth paragraph.

[71] Pesiri, Untangling the Warrant Web, 23 Tax Notes 525 (Apr. 30, 1984).

Correct paragraph 7 of text.

First line of second paragraph should be "option*or*," not "option*er*."

Add to note 72.

[72] As a result of amendments to §1234(b) by the Tax Reform Act of 1976, the grantor's gain on lapse of the option is a short-term capital gain. PLR 8248010 (Tech. Adv.), 1982 P-H Fed. Taxes ¶ 55,459 (corporate buy-back of warrants for cash allowable §165 loss deduction; but §1032 nonrecognition on exchange of its preferred stock to cancel warrants). See also Robert E. Whiting, ¶ 84,182 P-H Memo TC (reductions in amounts due on shareholders' stock subscription and in par value of stock were equivalent to tax-free stock dividend).

Page 4-25:

Add to note 73.

[73] Rev. Rul. 80-134, 1980-1 CB 187 (unilateral extension of expiration date by issuing corporation had effect of grant of new warrants; hence, issuer had ordinary income from lapse of old warrants).

But §1032 was extended to cover the lapse of options (and amounts paid to cancel options) to purchase or sell the corporation's stock; the Tax Reform Act of 1984, H.R. 4170, P.L. No. 98-369.

Add to text at end of runover paragraph.

But recent legislation extended §1032 nonrecognition treatment to cover the lapse of (or payments to cancel) outstanding options to purchase the corporation's stock.[74.1]

―――――――――

[74.1] See the Tax Reform Act of 1984, H.R. 4170, §57 (and a comparable provision in the Senate Finance Committee Bill, the Deficit Reduction Act of 1984, H.R. 2163, §42), which passed as §57 of the Tax Reform Act of 1984, P.L. No. 98-369, 98 Stat. 678. See Pesiri, supra note 71 (this Supplement); Eustice, The Tax Reform Act of 1984, ¶ 3.03[6].

Page 4-26:

Add to note 79, first paragraph.

[79] See Simmonds Precision Prods., Inc. 75 TC 103 (1980) (property acquired for options; valuation of options for basis purposes deferred until date of exercise; compensatory option principles of Regs. §1.421-6 applied; options here did not have readily ascertainable fair market value). Cf. ITT & Cos., supra note 63 (this Supplement) (parent's basis for bonds of subsidiary equal to value of parent stock issued on conversion of bonds); contra, National Can Corp. v. US, 687 F.2d 1107 (7th Cir. 1982).

Page 4-27:

Add new note 80.1 to end of first full paragraph of text.

[80.1] Extension of §1032 to lapsed options would appear to favor the §362(c) adjustment approach in view of the capital characterization of such transactions. See the Tax Reform Act of 1984, H.R. 4170, §57; the Deficit Reduction Act of 1984, H.R. 2163, §42; and the Tax Reform Act of 1984, P.L. No. 98-369, §57, 98 Stat. 678. See Pesiri, supra note 71 (this Supplement).

¶ 4.07.　STOCK VS. DEBT:　CAPITAL ASSET STATUS

Page 4-28:

Add to note 81.

[81] The dealer segregation rules of §1236 were materially tightened by the Economic Recovery Tax Act (ERTA) of 1981, P.L. No. 97-34, 95 Stat. 172 (identification period reduced from 30 days to one day). The Tax Reform Act of 1984, §107(b), tightened the §1236 identification rules even further by authorizing regulations to shorten the time when identification must be made. See Eustice, The Tax Reform Act of 1984, ¶ 5.05[6][a] (Warren, Gorham & Lamont, Inc. 1984).

Add new note 82.1 to end of paragraph numbered (3).

[82.1] For new revisions of the original-issue discount rules, see infra new ¶ 4.23 (this Supplement).

This same legislation also adds new §1276, which characterizes accrued "market discount" as interest income to the holder on the sale or disposition of the obligation, infra new ¶ 4.23 (this Supplement). See also ¶ 3.05 (this Supplement).

Page 4-29:

Add to note 85, second paragraph.

[85] Campbell Taggart, Inc. v. US, 744 F.2d 442 (5th Cir. 1984) (*Corn Products* applied to holding company loss on sale of subsidiary when transaction was solely to protect its reputation as an acquirer of corporations; no investment motive; pure business motive case).

Add to note 85, third paragraph.

[85] Arkansas Best Corp., 83 TC 640 (1984) (partial capital loss, under *Windle,* and partial ordinary loss, under *Corn Products,* for holding company's forced sale of subsidiary stock; mixed motive case and a substantial investment motive for initial part of transaction, although later portion of transaction solely business motivated).

Page 4-30:

Add new paragraph numbered (9) to end of section.

(9) Accrued market discount now is characterized as interest to the holder on the sale or disposition of the obligation by recently enacted legislation.[86.1]

[86.1] The Tax Reform Act of 1984, H.R. 4170, §41; the Deficit Reduction Act of 1984, H.R. 2163, §25(a); the Tax Reform Act of 1984, P.L. No. 98-369, §41(a), 98 Stat. 678, adding new §1276; infra new ¶ 4.23 (this Supplement), and ¶ 3.05 (this Supplement).

¶ 4.08. STOCK VS. DEBT: REPAYMENT OF "LOAN," REDEMPTION OF "STOCK," OR DIVIDEND?

Page 4-31:

Add to note 89, first paragraph.

[89] Rev. Rul. 80-143, 1980-1 CB 19 (gain attributable to unearned issue discount held capital gain; *Leavin* and *Bolnick* followed).

Add to text at end of first complete paragraph.

The issue discount rules of §1232 were changed again in 1982 [90.1] by repealing the straight-line level accrual rules of §1232 and instead requiring that discount be accrued under a constant interest rate system reflecting economic accrual compound interest concepts (the general result of which is to bunch interest in the later years of the obligation).

Recent legislation [90.2] once again revised the issue discount rules, this time extending them to a far wider range of transactions than was the case under prior law.[90.3] Moreover, even "market" discount has been characterized as interest under this legislation.[90.4]

[90.1] See §§1232A and 162(e), added by TEFRA of 1982.

[90.2] The Tax Reform Act of 1984, H.R. 4170, §41, the Deficit Reduction Act of 1984, H.R. 2163, §25(a), and the Tax Reform Act of 1984, P.L. No. 98-369, §41(a), 98 Stat. 678, adding new §§1271–1275.

[90.3] See infra new ¶ 4.23 (this Supplement).

[90.4] New §1276, added by §41 of the Tax Reform Act of 1984, P.L. No. 98-369, 98 Stat. 678; such discount would not accrue ratably, however, unless the holder so elected. See infra new ¶ 4.23 (this Supplement).

Add to text after sentence ending with note 91.

But new §1232(d), added by TEFRA of 1982, denies §1232 capital gain treatment for retirement of "registration required debt," defined by §163(f)(2) as long-term (more than one year) publicly traded obligations of corporate issuers. This provision was moved to §1287 in the Tax Reform Act of 1984 (without change).

¶ 4.09.   STOCK VS. DEBT: CHARACTER OF INVESTOR'S LOSS ON SALE OR WORTHLESSNESS

Page 4-34:

Add to note 95.

[95] But new §165(j), added by TEFRA of 1982, P.L. No. 97-248, 96 Stat. 324, denies a worthlessness deduction for unregistered debt if such obligation was required to be in registered form by §163(f)(2).

Page 4-35:

Add to note 96.

[96] But see new §165(j), denying §165 worthlessness deductions for unregistered debt if the debt was required to be in registered form by §163(f)(2).

Page 4-36:

Add to note 101.

[101] Compare Lorch v. CIR, 605 F.2d 657 (2d Cir. 1979) (*Stahl* distinguished on facts).

Michtom was reversed by the full Court of Claims, 45 AFTR2d 1664 (Ct. Cl. 1980) (capital loss, per *Lorch*). Case citation is Michtom not Michton. Accord, Meisels v. US, 732 F.2d 132 (Fed. Cir. 1984).

Page 4-37:

Add to note 102, first paragraph.

[102] See also Henry J. Benak, 77 TC 1213 (1981) (worthless note issued on redemption of §1244 stock held non-business bad debt short-term capital loss per *Whipple-Generes*).

Add to note 102, second paragraph.

[102] But see Alfred H. Tolzman, ¶ 81,689 P-H Memo TC (no dominant business motive per *Generes,* even though no direct stock owner-

ship interest in debtor (taxpayer a 25 percent partner in partnership that owned 50 percent of debtor)).

Add to note 104, first paragraph.

[104] Compare Alfred M. Tolzman, supra note 102 (this Supplement) (business-employee motive for guaranty not dominant) with Est. of Allen, ¶ 82,303 P-H Memo TC (president-shareholder's motive for guaranty of corporate debt was to protect salary and job).

Page 4-38:

Add to note 105.

[105] But see Bowers v. CIR, 678 F.2d 509 (4th Cir. 1982) (sole shareholder's loan to client of his corporation may be business bad debt because motive for loan was to maintain high income as corporate employee, even though taxpayer not in business of lending and loan not to protect continued employment).

In a subsequent decision, Bowers v. CIR, 716 F.2d 1047 (4th Cir. 1983) (business bad-debt treatment allowed on theory that dominant motive for loan to client was to maintain taxpayer's income level as employee of his corporation).

Add to note 107.

[107] Adelson v. US 737 F.2d 1569 (Fed. Cir. 1984) (lower court decision remanded for further evidence on dominant motive for taxpayer's advances to client companies, viz., whether advances were to further his consulting business or were to obtain equity interests on clients); on remand, 1984-2 USTC ¶ 9787 (Cl. Ct. 1984) (held business bad debt; dominant motive for advance business).

Page 4-39:

Add to note 107, end of runover paragraph.

[107] *Lorch* was affirmed, 605 F.2d 657 (2d Cir. 1979). See also Henry J. Benak, supra note 102 (this Supplement) (substantial investment motive); Alfred H. Tolzman, supra note 102 (this Supplement) (business motive not dominant).

Add to note 108.

[108] See generally Inductotherm Indus., ¶ 84,281 P-H Memo TC (advances to subsidiary were equity, which made subsidiary solvent and thus resulted in tax-free §332 liquidation rather than bad-debt loss).

Add to note 109.

[109] See Natbony, Twice Burned or Twice Blessed—Double Deduc-

tions in the Affiliated Corporation Context, 6 J. Corp. Tax. 3 (1979). See also Campbell Taggart, Inc. v. US, 744 F.2d 442 (5th Cir. 1984) (holding company allowed *Corn Products* ordinary loss on sale of stock acquired solely to protect its business reputation as an acquirer of business); Arkansas Best Corp., 84 TC 640 (1984) (holding company's forced sale of subsidiary resulted in partial capital loss, investment motive, and partial ordinary loss, business motive).

Correct third line of text in paragraph numbered 4(3).

Change "90 percent or more" to "more than 90 percent."

¶ 4.10. OUTSIDE LOANS GUARANTEED BY SHAREHOLDERS

Page 4-40:

Add to note 111, first paragraph.

[111] Alfred H. Tolzman, ¶ 81,689 P-H Memo TC (guarantor's payment of interest on guaranteed debt, which accrued *after* his liability became primary and fixed held deductible under §163); Henry J. Benak, 77 TC 1213 (1981) (guaranty payment non-business bad debt).

Page 4-41:

Add to note 112.

[112] But contra is Vaughn v. US, 719 F.2d 196 (6th Cir. 1983) (guarantor partial payment for release of guaranty liability still capital loss even though no subrogation).

Add to note 113.

[113] Tennessee Sec. Inc. v. CIR, 674 F.2d 570 (6th Cir. 1982) (guaranty loss capital per *Whipple* and *Generes* because business motive not dominant). See also Vaughn v. US, supra note 112 (this Supplement) (guarantor partial payment for release of guaranty liability held a capital loss).

Page 4-42:

Add to note 114.

[114] With *Stahl,* compare Lorch v. CIR, 605 F.2d 657 (2d Cir. 1979). See also Meisels v. US, 732 F.2d 132 (Fed. Cir. 1984).

Fred H. Lenway & Co. was affirmed by unpublished order (9th Cir., May 19, 1980).

Add to note 115.

¹¹⁵ For proposed regulations under §385 dealing with shareholder-guaranteed loans, see Prop. Regs. §1.385-11, and Final Regs. §1.385-9, which adopt the approach of *Ellisberg* and *Plantation Patterns* in appropriate situations (where there is a lack of reasonable expectation that the corporation can repay the debt and the lender in substance is looking to the shareholder-guarantors for ultimate collection). But these provisions were dropped by the new 1981 proposed regulations.

Page 4-43:

Add to note 117, first paragraph.

¹¹⁷ See Rev. Rul. 79-4, 1979-1 CB 150 (shareholder-guarantor treated as true borrower per *Plantation Patterns*). J.C. Hunter, ¶ 82,381 P-H Memo TC (guaranty payment held indirect capital contribution; treat as if borrowing by shareholder-guarantor and capital contribution of funds to corporation); Lane v. US, 724 F.2d 1311 (11th Cir. 1984) (guaranty losses held equity capital contributions).

Add to note 117, following Falkoff *citation.*

¹¹⁷ *Falkoff* was reversed, however, 604 F.2d 1045 (7th Cir. 1979) (transaction was respected and treated as true corporate-level borrowing); compare Jos. Creel, 72 TC 1173 (1979) (shareholder held true borrower and corporate payment of debt deemed a constructive dividend to shareholder).

¶ 4.11. LOSS ON "SECTION 1244 STOCK"

Page 4-45:

Add new note 120.1 at end of sixth line of text.

¹²⁰·¹ Regulations were proposed to reflect these 1978 amendments in September 1979. These regulations became final on June 1, 1981 in T.D. 7779. See Barrack & Dodge, Section 1244: Is the Intent of Congress Finally Achieved? 6 J. Corp. Tax. 4 (1980).

Add to note 121.

¹²¹ Prop. Regs. §1.1244(a)-1(b)(2) continues the distributee-partner trap noted above. The new proposals also deal with a stock issuance through underwriters (if underwriter acts as selling agent, purchase of stock therefrom qualifies, but if underwriter purchases and resells, buyer will not qualify). The final regulations adopted these proposals without material change.

Page 4-46:

Add to note 124.

[124] See Prop. Regs. §§1.1244(c)-2(b)(2), 1.1244(c)-2(b)(3), and 1.1244(c)-2(b)(4) for "designation" and allocation rules where ceiling is exceeded. See Regs. §§1.1244(c)-2(b)(2), 1.1244(c)-2(b)(3), and 1.1244(c)-2(b)(4) for the final version of these proposals (which were adopted without material change).

Page 4-47:

Correct fourth line of text.

Word "quality" should read "qualify."

Add to note 126.

[126] See Regs. §1.1244(c)-1(g)(2) (§1244 limited to "largely operating company"), approved in H.L. Davenport, 70 TC 992 (1978). See Prop. Regs. §1.1244(c)-1(g)(2) (same). Final Regs. §1.1244(c)-1(e)(2) (same).

Page 4-48:

Add to note 127.

[127] But §492 of H.R. 4170, the Tax Reform Act of 1984, proposed to allow §1244 treatment for preferred stock as well. This provision passed in §481 of the Tax Reform Act of 1984, P.L. No. 98-369, 98 Stat. 678.

Page 4-49:

Add new section.

¶ 4.12.　CANCELLATION OF INDEBTEDNESS ASPECTS TO CORPORATE DEBTOR

1. In general. The corporation that retires its "equity" instruments at less than their stated par value has never been deemed to realize "income" as a result of such a transaction; rather, §118 treats any profit from the cancellation as a tax-free capital contribution, supra ¶ 3.14. By contrast, a corporate debtor that retires its debt obligations at a discount may derive taxable income therefrom under §61(a)(2), unless it made a timely election to exclude such gains under the provisions of §108 (and reduce asset bases under the concomitant rules of §1017), or unless the transaction was not deemed to result in taxable "income" by virtue of one of the numerous "exceptions" to the cancellation of indebtedness rules (such as capital contributions and insolvency) approved by the courts and the regulations in this area.[131.1]

While the tangled tax treatment of debt cancellation income is beyond the scope of this work, several comments are appropriate to the matters considered in this chapter. The capital contribution exception to debt cancellation income has been considered supra ¶ 3.14; satisfaction of debts through issuance of the debtor's stock is dealt with supra ¶ 3.13; debt cancellation problems of liquidating corporations are considered infra ¶ 11.69; and, finally, debt restructurings and debtor corporation reorganizations pursuant to insolvency proceedings are considered infra ¶¶ 14.17, 14.20, and 14.58. In general, the debtor corporation does not derive taxable income from the bargain cancellation of its debts if (a) the cancellation is a contribution to its capital under §118; (b) the debtor issues its own stock in exchange for the debt under §1032; (c) the debts are assumed by an acquiring corporation under §357 (discussed infra ¶ 14.55); or (d) the debtor is insolvent before and after the cancellation transaction. In other circumstances, gain from the cancellation of a corporation's debts will be taxable, unless the debtor qualifies to exclude such income under §108 and reduce the basis of its assets in the manner prescribed by §1017.

2. Changes effected by the Bankruptcy Tax Act of 1980. On March 12, 1980, the Ways and Means Committee reported H.R. 5043, the Bankruptcy Tax Act of 1980, which passed the House on March 24, 1980. The original version of this legislation would have repealed the election rules of §108 and §1017 (to exclude debt cancellation income and reduce basis) for solvent debtors; moreover, debt cancellation gains realized in the course of insolvency proceedings were required to reduce various tax attributes of the debtor (loss carryover deductions, etc.) before

---

[131.1] See generally Regs. §§1.61-12(a), 1.61-12(b); Eustice, Cancellation of Indebtedness and the Federal Income Tax: A Problem of Creeping Confusion, 14 Tax L. Rev. 225 (1959); Bittker & Thompson, Income From the Discharge of Indebtedness: The Progeny of *United States v. Kirby Lumber Co.*, 66 Calif. L. Rev. 1159 (1978).

See generally Carolina, Clinchfield & O. Ry., 82 TC 888 (1984) (definition of "cancellation" of old debt as opposed to "substitution" of new debt); OKC Corp., 82 TC 638 (1984) (debt discharge gain was ordinary income from lost profits claim settlement, not §108 item).

reduction in asset bases could be made. The revised version of the Act, however, retained the §108 and §1017 election for solvent debtors (but only with respect to depreciable property); moreover, the debtor (solvent or insolvent) would be entitled to elect to apply the debt discharge gain first to reduce depreciable property bases before reducing other tax attributes. H.R. 5043 was favorably reported by the Senate Finance Committee on November 19, 1980 and ultimately passed in the closing hours of the lame-duck session in December of 1980. These provisions are considered in greater detail infra ¶ 14.58 (this Supplement).

The Tax Reform Act of 1984 eliminated the application of §1032 in cases where debt is cancelled for less than its face amount through the issuance of stock by a *solvent* debtor; in such case new §108(e)(10) provides for the generation of debt cancellation gain to the extent the value of the stock is less than the face value of the cancelled debt.[131.2]

[131.2] The Tax Reform Act of 1984, P.L. No. 98-369, §59, 98 Stat. 678, adding new §108(e)(10). See Note, Debt-Equity Swaps, 37 Tax L. Rev. 677 (1984); see Eustice, The Tax Reform Act of 1984, ¶ 3.03 [5][a].

PART B.　DEBT-FINANCED ACQUISITIONS

¶ 4.20.　IN GENERAL

Page 4-50:

Correct note 132.

[132] Citation in third line should be "A.B.A.J.," not "A.B.A.T."

¶ 4.22.　OTHER ASPECTS OF CORPORATE DEBT SECURITIES: §§453, 1232, AND 249

Page 4-54:

Add to text after first complete paragraph.

The Installment Sales Revision Act of 1980 drastically overhauled the rules of §453, providing, inter alia, for repeal of the 30 percent initial payment limitation and the two-payment rule, recognizing that §453 can apply to contingent payment sales, and dealing with some of the more flagrant abuses spawned by the *Rushing* case and its progeny.[138.1]

[138.1] For analysis of this important legislation, see Ginsburg, Future Payment Sales After the 1980 Revision Act, 39 N.Y.U. Inst. on Fed. Tax. Ch. 43 (1981).

Page 4-55:

Add to note 141.

[141] For legislation changing the timing rules for OID income and deduction (to reflect "true" economic interest, which tends to bunch the interest amounts in later years), see new §§1232A and 163(e), enacted September 3, 1982, §231 of TEFRA of 1982, P.L. No. 97-248, 96 Stat. 324, effective for bonds issued after May 3, 1982. The purpose of this amendment was to inhibit zero-coupon bond transactions where level OID rate computations of current law give artificially higher interest deductions in early years. The OID rules were revised extensively once again by the Tax Reform Act of 1984, infra new ¶ 4.23 (this Supplement), to cover a wide range of transactions.

Page 4-56:

Add to note 143.

[143] Regulations were proposed July 5, 1979 (Prop. Regs. §1.1232-3A(b)(2)) to eliminate the exclusion for short-term debt from the OID rules; but these proposals were withdrawn on September 19, 1979 (IR News Release (Sept. 14, 1979), [1979] 10 CCH Stand. Fed. Tax Rep. ¶ 6839).

But both the Tax Reform Act of 1984, H.R. 4170, and the Deficit Reduction Act of 1984, H.R. 2163, proposed to extend the OID accrual rules to certain short-term obligations held by accrual-basis taxpayers, banks, and dealers (new §§1281–1283); see §41(a) of the Tax Reform Act of 1984, P.L. No. 98-369, 98 Stat. 678, for the final version of this legislation (adding new §§1281–1283).

See infra new ¶ 4.23 (this Supplement).

Add to end of note 144.

[144] But the Technical Corrections Act of 1982 removed the reorganization exception from the §1232(b)(2) definition of issue price, so it is now possible to generate OID in reorganization exchanges (new §1232(b)(4) measure of OID is excess of face of new debt over greater of value or issue price of old debt). See Microdot Inc. v. US, 728 F.2d 593 (2d Cir. 1984) (for 1969 law; no OID in a reorganization); Golden Nugget, Inc., 83 TC 28 (1984) (same).

The Tax Reform Act of 1984 moved §1232(b)(4) to new §1275 (a)(5) and expanded its coverage to untraded debt, infra ¶ 14.17 (this Supplement).

Page 4-57:

Add to text at end of paragraph numbered (2).

Congress amended the issue discount rules in 1982 [148.1] to require economic accrual of discount at a constant interest rate (in lieu of the 1969 Act imposition of straight-line accrual), the general effect of which is to bunch discount interest reporting in the later years of the obligation. Recent legislation [148.2] further revised the debt issue discount rules by extending these provisions to a considerably broader range of transactions, and by characterizing "market discount" as interest at the holder level.[148.3]

[148.1] TEFRA of 1982, supra note 141 (this Supplement), adding §§1232A and 163(e).

[148.2] Tax Reform Act of 1984, H.R. 4170, §41, the Deficit Reduction Act of 1984, H.R. 2163, §25(a), and the Tax Reform Act of 1984, P.L. No. 98-369, §41(a), 98 Stat. 678, adding new §§1271–1275, infra new ¶ 4.23 (this Supplement).

[148.3] Id. (adding new §1276).

Page 4-58:

Add to note 150.

[150] See also Seaboard Coffee Serv., Inc., 71 TC 465 (1978) (call premium not accruable from issue date to earliest call date because obligation contingent; no fixed obligation to call).

Regs. cite should be Regs. §1.163-4(c).

Add new heading.

¶ 4.23.　DEBT DISCOUNT:　NEW LEGISLATION RELATING TO ORIGINAL-ISSUE DISCOUNT, UNSTATED INTEREST, MARKET DISCOUNT, AND BELOW-MARKET-RATE LOANS

1. General background. The time value of money occupied center stage in both the House and Senate versions of the 1984 legislation, due in large part to the belated recognition by Congress that the original-issue discount (OID) and imputed interest rules in §§1232 and 483 of prior law were significantly unreflective of true market interest factors.

The OID concept first entered the law in 1954 as an income characterization rule in §1232(a)(2). This section provided that OID on corporate evidences of debt would be treated as "ordinary gain" to the holder on the sale or retirement of the obligation (to the extent such discount accrued during the period the bond was held by the taxpayer). No attempt was made to match the timing of the holder's income to the corporate debtor's interest deduction for such discount, however. Moreover, §1232(a)(2) only applied to long-term corporate debt obligations that were capital assets in the hands of the holder, and the cases were in conflict as to whether debt issued for "property" was covered by this provision (supra ¶¶ 4.06, 4.08, 4.22).

In 1964, the "unstated interest" rules of §483 (relating to deferred payment sales of property) were enacted, but this provision, like §1232(a)(2), was only an income *characterization* rule rather than a timing rule. If interest stated in the deferred payment sale contract failed to meet a minimum safe-harbor threshold rate (based on a simple interest rate), the statute imputed interest at a higher rate, compounded semi-annually, which amount was spread ratably over the term of the payment period, depending on the seller's and buyer's methods of accounting.

In 1969, §1232 was amended to provide for the ratable accrual of OID over the term of the obligation in an attempt to match the holder's interest income inclusion to the corporate issuer's interest deduction (supra ¶ 4.22). Accrual of both discount interest income and the correlative discount interest deduction was on a straight-line basis, however, and did not provide for the compounding of interest. But TEFRA of 1982, in new §1232A and §163(e), finally adopted an economic accrual system for OID income and deductions which reflected compound interest concepts.

On the other hand, §483 was not changed by TEFRA, so that the relatively low simple interest safe-harbor rules continued to apply to deferred payment debt obligations issued for property. While the §483 rates have been adjusted on several occasions, they have not kept pace with market rates. Moreover, §483 utilized a *single* interest rate factor (both for the safe-harbor test rate and the imputed interest rate computations), regardless of the maturity of the obligations, thereby failing to reflect the fact that lenders typically demand different returns depending on the term of the loan. Similarly, the regulations under §482 (infra ¶ 15.06) imputed an arm's-length interest rate on loans and deferred payment sales between commonly controlled taxpayers when inadequate interest was charged, but the regulations likewise employ a single, simple interest safe-harbor rate to test the adequacy of stated interest, and assume a higher single, simple interest rate if this test is not satisfied.

While the OID rules of §1232 and §1232A were placed on an economic accrual system in 1982 by TEFRA, these provisions did not apply to the following situations: noncorporate debt; open account debt not evidenced by a written instrument; short-term debt; tax-exempt obligations; debt issued for property where neither the debt nor the property was publicly traded (and, until changed by the Technical Corrections Act of 1982, even when one or both sides involved traded securities, the OID rules did not apply to debt issued pursuant to a "reorganization," infra ¶ 14.17); debt issued for the use of property; debt issued for services; and debt that was not a capital asset in the hands of the holder (§483 did not impute interest to the *seller*-holder here either). Thus, where a particular debt obligation was not covered by the OID rules of §1232, the potential for mismatching of income and deductions attributable to OID and the noneconomic accrual of interest on such obligations continued to exist.

Moreover, from the standpoint of the holder of an obligation, "market discount" frequently can be viewed as a substitute for stated interest (e.g., where the value of the bond declines after its issuance because of an increase in prevailing interest rates). Prior law treated market discount as capital gain, despite the fact that the investor's yield may be indistinguishable, as a practical matter, from OID both being in substance a surrogate for adequately stated market interest (although some price declines may be attributable, in whole or in part, to risk factors as well as to changes in prevailing interest rates).

Finally, Congress concluded that the treatment of below-market-interest-rate loans under prevailing case law (infra ¶ 15.08) did not properly characterize such transactions to reflect their true economic consequences—that is, courts generally have held that no income was imputed to either the borrower or the lender (absent §482 adjustments, infra ¶ 15.06), despite the clear economic benefits to the borrower that resulted from the bargain interest rate.

To deal with the just described problems, the following statutory changes were made:

(1) The OID rules of §§1232 and 1232A were replaced by new §§1271 –1275, which extended the economic accrual system to a significantly broader range of transactions (and substantially subsumed, thereby, the rules of prior §483);

(2) To the limited extent §483 continues to apply, its interest rates (as well as those in the §482 regulations) were conformed to true market compound interest computation concepts;

(3) Market discount that accrued in the hands of the holder of the obligation were recharacterized as interest income to the holder on the sale or retirement of the debt (except for purposes of the foreign tax rules, infra Chapter 17) under new §§1276–1278; and

(4) Below-market-interest-rate loan transactions were recharacterized (by new §7872) to impute a designated market interest rate (and thereby subjected to the OID rules) and to provide for various collateral tax consequences to the parties as well (e.g., gift, compensation, dividend) to the extent of the bargain interest element.

These new provisions relating to debt obligations are among the more complex and far-reaching features of the 1984 legislation.[152]

2. Original issue discount and unstated interest (§§1271–1275 and §483). The key to the expanded OID periodic inclusion and deduction rules is §1274, which defines issue price in the case of various debt-for-property transactions and substantially displaces §483. Under this provision, debt issued for "property" (defined broadly to include all tangible and intangible assets of any sort, except money) can give rise to OID where neither the debt nor the property is traded, where the debt is not a capital asset in the hands of the holder, where the debt is issued for the *use* of property or for services,[153] but *not* where the debt is not evidenced by a written instrument (e.g., open-account debt).[154] Short-term (i.e., ma-

---

[152] See generally Eustice, The Tax Reform Act of 1984, ¶ 2.02. Sheffield, Debt Issued for Traded and Non-traded Property, 62 Taxes 1022 (1984).

[153] This provision is found in new §467; see Eustice, The Tax Reform Act of 1984, ¶ 2.03[4].

[154] Both the House and Senate versions of the bill covered open-

turity of one year or less) debt, however, is still excluded from this provision, as are tax-exempt obligations and U.S. savings bonds.

Exceptions to the expanded OID rules of §1274 are found in §1274(c)(4), which include the following debt-for-property transactions: (1) sales of farms by individuals or small businesses for $1,000,000 or less; (2) sales of principal residences; (3) sales for $250,000 or less; (4) annuities;[154.1] (5) contingent price sales which qualify for capital treatment under §1235; and (6) certain land transfers between related persons subject to §483(f). Section 483 (as amended) initially applied to the first three of these exceptions, however (although the next two are also exceptions to §483 as well),[155] but subsequent amendments modified the coverage of §483 as to the first two exceptions.[156]

If debt is issued for cash, the rules of prior law continue to apply; and if either the debt or the property for which it is issued consists of traded securities, the market value of the traded leg will determine issue price. Where neither side is traded, however, issue price (and the consequent generation of OID) will be determined first by testing to see whether an imputed safe-harbor discount rate on that deferred payment is met (set at 110 percent of a specially determined rate called the "applicable federal rate"), and then, if such safe-harbor rate is not satisfied, imputing interest on the deferred payments at 120 percent of the designated applicable federal rate.[156.1] The applicable federal rate is to be determined twice a year, and will vary with the maturity of the instrument (i.e., "short-term"

---

account debt, but the final Conference version of the legislation, in §1275(a)(1), required a written debt instrument.

[154.1] The exception for annuities is found in §1275(a)(1)(B).

[155] See Eustice, The Tax Reform Act of 1984, ¶ 2.02[2].

[156] By Congressional Resolution of June 29, 1984, the Conference bill was amended and new §483(e) was added, exempting sales of principal residences (to the extent of $250,000) and sales of farms (without limit); but note that §1274 will apply if the farm is sold for more than $1 million. See Eustice, The Tax Reform Act of 1984, ¶ 2.02[2][b]. For current proposals (which were passed in revised form) to revise the OID and §483 rules applicable to deferred-payment sales of property, see Eustice, The Tax Reform Act of 1984, Appendix C; and for discussion of these amendments, see text at end of this paragraph of this section.

[156.1] Rev. Rul. 84-163, 1984-47 IRB 25 (setting out the applicable federal rates).

rates are three years or less, "mid-term" rates are between three and nine years, and long-term rates are over nine years). Thus, if the stated redemption price exceeds either (1) the present value of all payments due under the obligation (using a discount rate equal to 110 percent of the applicable federal rate, compounded semi-annually), or (2) the stated *principal* amount (i.e., there is a balloon interest payment at retirement), OID interest will be imputed on the transaction using a compound present value discount rate equal to 120 percent of the applicable federal rate. However, the discounted principal amount so determined cannot exceed the fair market value of the property acquired for such debt if the transaction is a potentially abusive situation (e.g., a tax shelter).[157]

Section 483, although considerably contracted due to the expansion of the OID rules to cover most debt-for-property transactions, nevertheless will continue to apply to transactions not subject to the new OID rules (e.g., those situations that are exceptions to new §1274).[158] However, the imputed interest rates (both the safe-harbor test rate and the general imputed interest rate) are conformed to those applicable to the OID rules. Thus, new §483 uses compound safe-harbor and imputed interest rates, which vary according to the maturity of the obligation and are computed on an economic accrual basis (although *timing* of income and deductions continue to be governed by the parties' accounting methods). Moreover, the §482 regulations will be revised to provide safe-harbor and imputed interest rates consistent with those applicable under amended §483.

In the closing hours of the 98th Congress, the deferred payment sale rules of §§1274 and 483 were revisited, revised in several respects, and partially delayed in others in a chaotic legislative compromise that was eventually worked out between groups pushing for the total repeal of these provisions on the one hand, and those

---

[157] Section 1274(b)(3). But cf. §7701(g); Eustice, The Tax Reform Act of 1984, ¶ 5.05[5][a].

The new matching rules of §267 (infra ¶ 5.05, this Supplement), do not apply to OID, but do apply to §483; see T.D. 7991 (Nov. 30, 1984), issuing proposed and temporary regulations under new §267; Regs. §1.267(a)-2T(b), questions 2 and 3.

[158] But see supra note 156 (this Supplement); §483(e) also exempts sales of principal residences (to the extent of $250,000) and sales of farms (without limit).

struggling to retain the essential structure of the rules that had so arduously just been enacted on the other. This legislation [158.1] modified the transition rules of §44(b) of the Tax Reform Act of 1984 by providing for new minimum interest test rates and new interest imputation rates in the case of sales of real estate and used personal property before July 1, 1985, for $2,000,000 or less; the test rate in such cases will be 9 percent compounded semi-annually, and the imputation rate will be 10 percent, compounded semi-annually. Deferred payment sales in excess of $2,000,000 will be subject to a "blended" rate, based on a weighted average between the 9 percent and 10 percent rates and 110 percent and 120 percent of the applicable T-bill rates. In the case of property used in the active business of farming, both the buyer and seller must report the applicable interest under the cash basis of accounting.

Assumptions of pre-existing debt are generally made subject to the new §1274 and §483 regime, but assumed debt issued before October 15, 1984 is grandfathered (if the sale does [not] [158.2] exceed $100,000,000), while four intricately crafted exceptions are provided for assumptions of loans with respect to certain specified types of property: (1) residences (e.g., either principal residences or vacation homes, if such property was not depreciable within the prior two-year period and also was not "dealer" property at any time in the hands of the seller); (2) farms (real and personal property used as a farm by the seller for three years, and also to be used in an *active* farming business by the buyer); (3) active trades or businesses (qualifying as an active business, or line of business, within the meaning of §355); and (4) real property used in an active business (other than holding for rental). The exceptions for sales of farms and business are limited to sales by "qualified persons," defined as an individual, estate, testamentary trust, corporation (or partnership) with no more than thirty-five shareholders (or partners) who dispose of their entire interest in the business (or line of business) and who are 10 percent owners of the farm or business

---

[158.1] H.R. 5361, §2 (P.L. No. 98-612), enacted Oct. 31, 1984. For the background of this legislation, see BNA DTR No. 199, p. G-3 (Oct. 15, 1984); BNA DTR No. 206, p. G-1 (Oct. 24, 1984); Tax Notes (Oct. 22, 1984), pp. 285, 291, and 293; and Tax Notes (Oct. 29, 1984), pp. 389 and 396.

[158.2] For explanation of the "typo," which omitted the word "not," see Tax Notes (Oct. 29, 1984), pp. 389 and 396.

(with attribution). Finally, transactions with sale prices in excess of $100,000,000 [158.3] are not exempt assumptions.

3. Market discount (§§1276–1278). New §1276 generally requires that gain on the disposition of a market discount bond must be recognized by the holder (but not the debtor-issuer) as interest income, to the extent of accrued market discount (i.e., the excess of stated redemption price over the holder's basis,[159] allocated in equal linear daily installments during the period held by the taxpayer). In effect, rules similar to the §1232 OID provisions applicable between 1954 and 1969 will apply to these obligations (i.e., market discount builds up on a straight-line basis, by reference to the taxpayer's holding period, but is only taxable on the disposition of the obligation).

While "disposition" is generally a gain-triggering event (i.e., a gift triggers gain up to the value of the obligation), §1276(d)(1) provides for exceptions for cases similar to those that govern dispositions of recapture property under §1245(b) (including, for this purpose, reorganization exchanges). Market discount bonds exchanged in a reorganization, however, will result in a carryover of the market discount taint into the property received in exchange for such obligations (infra ¶ 14.17, this Supplement) under §1276(c)(2). Installment obligations to which §453B applies are not treated as market discount bonds (in view of the special triggering regime applicable to such obligations).

4. Below-market-interest-rate loans (§7872). Congress concluded generally that a loan at below-market interest rates (or on an interest-free basis) is the economic equivalent of a loan bearing interest at market rates, coupled with a correlative payment by the lender to the borrower of an amount to fund the payment of interest by the borrower. If an interest-free loan is made by a corporation to its shareholders, present law treats the transaction as the tax

---

[158.3] Supra note 158.2.

[159] See Eustice, The Tax Reform Act of 1984, ¶ 2.02[4]. By keying the definition of market discount to the spread between basis and face (at the time the debt is acquired by the taxpayer), §1278(a)(2)(A) fails to exempt transactions where market discount is artificially created because the debt is issued in a substituted-basis transaction (e.g., §368(a)(1)(E) recapitalization exchange of old debt for new debt or a §351 exchange). See ¶ 3.05, note 54.2 (this Supplement).

equivalent of a deduction by the corporate-lender for distribution of a dividend in the amount of the value of the economic benefits conferred by the bargain interest rate, since no interest is imputed to either the lender or the borrower on such a loan. Had the corporation instead charged full market interest for the loan, and then distributed such interest as a dividend, the corporate-lender would derive taxable income without an offsetting deduction, while the shareholder-borrower would have taxable dividend income offset by an interest deduction. By forgoing interest on the loan, the lender can avoid any taxable income, which is the economic equivalent of a deduction.

To prevent this distortion (and others as well), both the House and Senate versions of the 1984 legislation recharacterized below-market-interest-rate loans as arm's-length transactions to reflect their true economic consequences, and the final version of the 1984 Act accepted this proposal as new §7872.[160] Thus, an arm's-length market interest is imputed on the loan transaction (using the rates designated in the new OID rules of §1274(d), supra), and the resulting interest amount is deemed to have been paid by the lender to the borrower as a dividend (or as compensation, a gift, or some other taxable event, as the case may be). In the case of gift loans and demand loans, imputed interest (and the correlative taxable dividend, compensation, or gift) accrues *ratably* on a daily basis during the period the loan continues to be outstanding;[161] low-interest term loans, however, create OID, which is taxable under the economic accrual principles of §1272, while the spread between face and issue price is immediately taxable as a dividend, compensation, or gift, as the case may be.

For example, if X Corporation makes a $100 demand loan to its sole shareholder A without interest, interest income will be imputed to X (and A will have a correlative interest deduction, subject to §§265, 267 and 163(d)) based on the designated market rates (i.e., the federal short-term rate) during the term the loan is outstanding. Moreover, A will receive an equivalent amount of

---

[160] See Eustice, The Tax Reform Act of 1984, ¶ 2.02[3].

[161] Section 7872(a)(2). Term gift loans were treated as demand loans by the final Conference version of the new law, in view of the close family relationships involved; while the interest element on a term gift loan accrues ratably, the taxable gift is computed under the term loan rules by virtue of §7872(d)(2).

dividend income equal to the imputed interest factor (thus, resulting in a wash for A if the interest is deductible).

If the loan is a ten-year term loan, and is determined to give rise to $40 of OID (under the discounted present value rules of new §1274(d), using the federal long-term rate), the OID interest income and deduction will accrue periodically under the economic accrual principles of §1272, but the $40 spread will result in an immediate dividend distribution from X to A in the year of the loan.[162]

The new imputed interest rules for below-market-interest-rate loans can be viewed as a backstop to the more generally applicable amendments to the OID rules of §§1271–1275 and the unstated interest rules of §483 (supra, paragraph 2), as well as to the rules concerning arm's-length dealing between related taxpayers found in §482 (infra, ¶ 15.06); thus, they are part of an overall statutory regime in which the failure to charge adequate market-based interest will be grounds for recharacterization of the transaction to reflect the true economic interest element attributable to the time value of money.[163]

---

[162] Thus, the Service's argument in Herman Greenspun, 72 TC 931 (1979) (that the spread between face and present value represents an immediately taxable benefit to the borrower) has been codified by the new §7872(b)(1) term loan rules.

[163] See generally Eustice, The Tax Reform Act of 1984, Chapter 2.

Chapter 5

THE CORPORATION
INCOME TAX

¶ 5.01. INTRODUCTORY: CORPORATE TAX RATES

Page 5-2:

Add new note 1.1 at end of runover paragraph.

[1.1] The Economic Recovery Tax Act (ERTA) of 1981, P.L. No. 97-34, 95 Stat. 172, lowers the rate on the bottom two brackets in two stages: for 1982, the first bracket rate drops from 17 percent to 16 percent, and the second bracket rate from 20 percent to 19 percent; for 1983 and thereafter, the rates are 15 percent and 18 percent respectively. Thus, by 1983, the average rate on the first $100,000 of taxable income is 25.75 percent.

Add new note 1.2 to sentence ending on line 6 of second full paragraph.

[1.2] Under the ERTA of 1981, supra note 1.1 (this Supplement), (when fully effective in 1983), the first four brackets are 15, 18, 30, and 40 percent respectively.

Add new note 1.3 to sentence ending on line 8 of second full paragraph.

[1.3] The top marginal rate for individuals was reduced to 50 percent, starting in 1982, by the ERTA of 1981, supra note 1.1 (this Supplement).

Add to text at end of second full paragraph.

Recent legislation [1.4] phases out the graduated rate benefits for

---

[1.4] See the Deficit Reduction Act of 1984, H.R. 2163, §44 (Senate Finance Committee bill); there was no comparable provision in the House version of this legislation, but the final legislation in §66 of the Tax Reform Act of 1984, P.L. No. 98-369, 98 Stat. 678, accepted the Senate proposal.

large corporations by subjecting taxable income between $1,000,000 and $1,405,000 to a 51 percent rate (thereby eliminating the tax benefit of graduated rates on the first $100,000 of taxable income). Thus, new §11(b) imposes an additional 5 percent tax on taxable income over $1,000,000 (with a maximum of $20,250).

Correct next-to-last line on page.

The rate differential is 18 points, not 14.

Page 5-3:

Add new note 1.5 to end of runover paragraph.

[1.5] The ERTA of 1981, supra note 1.1 (this Supplement), lowered the top marginal rate on ordinary income for noncorporate taxpayers to 50 percent (for 1982); the top capital gain rate (for sales after June 9, 1981) was also lowered to 20 percent; thus the rate spread between ordinary income and capital gain was narrowed to 30 percentage points. No change in the corporate capital gain rate occurred.

Add to note 2.

[2] In February 1982, the Treasury proposed to limit existing §56 to individuals, Subchapter S corporations, and personal holding companies, and to enact a new alternative minimum tax for all other corporations, infra ¶ 5.01, paragraph (5) (this Supplement), but this proposal did not pass.

Add new note 2.1 at end of paragraph 4(a).

[2.1] But see new §57(a)(12), added by the ERTA of 1981, supra note 1.1 (this Supplement) (new tax preference item to reflect more rapid write-off for leased property under the accelerated cost recovery system).

Page 5-4:

Correct fifth line from top of page.

The fraction is 18/46, not 18/16.

Add new paragraph 5 to end of ¶ 5.01.

5. *New alternative minimum tax on corporations.* On February 26, 1982, the Treasury proposed to replace the existing "add-on" minimum tax rules of §56 with a new alternative minimum tax on the expanded "minimum taxable income" of regular corporations (viz., corporations other than Subchapter S corporations and personal holding companies, which latter entities would con-

tinue to be subject to existing §56), effective in 1983. The minimum tax base for this new provision would be regularly computed taxable income plus a list of fourteen tax preference items arising from various special deductions (nine of which were new), less a $50,000 exemption. The tax would be 15 percent of this expanded taxable income base (if higher than the regularly computed §11 tax), and no credits (other than the foreign tax credit) would be allowed; however, the excess of minimum tax paid over regular tax liability would be carried over as a credit available against future regular tax liability for fifteen years (such credit to be applied only after all other credits are exhausted).

Instead of the above proposals, the Senate Finance Committee decided to retain the existing add-on minimum tax rules, but adopted an alternative approach to scale down various corporate tax preference items: Under the Finance Committee Bill, the amount of various corporate preference items would be reduced by 15 percent (e.g., percentage depletion for coal and iron ore, excess bad-debt reserves, interest on debt to carry tax-exempt securities, deferred DISC income, §1250 recapture potential on structures, rapid amortization of pollution-control facilities and mineral exploration and development costs). This version passed the Senate in July 1982, and became law as §204(a) of the Tax Equity and Fiscal Responsibility Act (TEFRA) of 1982,[2.2] which added new §291 to the Code.

The 1982 amendments of TEFRA that relate to the treatment of various items of tax preference significantly revised both the structure and scope of the minimum tax rules of §§55–58. In addition, the new legislation enacted a 15 percent reduction in selected corporate preference items in new §291. As to the minimum tax changes, the new legislation now limits the "add-on" minimum tax provisions of §56 exclusively to corporate taxpayers, while the alternative minimum tax rules of §55 would continue to apply only to tax preference items of noncorporate taxpayers.[2.3] Those items

---

[2.2] P.L. No. 97-248, 96 Stat. 324.

[2.3] New §55, however, is a vastly expanded version of the 1978 version of this provision, which applied to only two preference items, long-term capital gains and "excess itemized deductions." Under new §55(b), alternative minimum taxable income now includes all of the twelve tax preference items enumerated in §57(a) that are generated by noncorporate taxpayers; in addition, since the starting point for determi-

of tax preference in §57(a) to which the add-on corporate minimum tax applies are as follows:

(1) Section 57(a)(2) (excess accelerated depreciation on real property)

(2) Section 57(a)(4) (excess amortization of certified pollution-control facilities)

(3) Section 57(a)(7) (excess of bad-debt reserve additions over actual loan losses of banks and financial institutions)

(4) Section 57(a)(8) (excess of percentage depletion deductions over adjusted basis)

(5) Section 57(a)(9)(B) (long-term capital gains)

(6) Section 57(a)(12)(B) (excess Accelerated Cost Recovery System (ACRS) deductions on fifteen-year real property over fifteen-year straight-line depreciation thereon)

The 15 percent preference reduction rules of new §291 apply to the following corporate tax preferences:

(1) In the case of depreciable real estate (§1250 property), the excess of a recapture amount determined under §1245 over the amount of recapture determined under §1250

(2) Percentage depletion of iron ore and coal in excess of basis

(3) Financial institution preference items (i.e., the excess of additions to bad-debt reserves over actual loan losses) and interest paid or incurred to carry tax-exempt securities

(4) Deferred DISC income

---

nation of the §55(a) tax base is "adjusted gross income," non-§62 itemized deductions are generally not allowed (although new §55(e) does permit deductions for casualty losses, charitable contributions, medical expenses, interest on residence-related debt, and investment interest, up to the amount of investment income, in computing the taxable base). The rate under §55(a) is 20 percent of "expanded taxable income" in excess of $40,000 (on a joint return) if such tax is higher than the regular $1 tax.

In short, new §55 may well be the precursor of a broad-based flat-tax system for noncorporate taxpayers. See Graetz, The 1982 Minimum Tax Amendments as a First Step in the Transition to a "Flat-Rate" Tax, 56 S. Calif. L. Rev. 527 (1983).

(5) Accelerated amortization of pollution-control facilities
(6) Intangible drilling costs of an integrated oil company, and mineral exploration and development costs

With respect to the above corporate preference items, new §291 simply reduces such preference by 15 percent. For example, in the case of depreciable real estate, if application of the §1245 recapture rules would produce recapture income in excess of the amount of recapture determined under §1250, 15 percent of such excess would be converted to ordinary gain under §291(a)(1). Similarly, §291 (a)(2) reduces the excess percentage depletion deduction for coal and iron ore by 15 percent, while §291(a)(3) reduces the two items of financial institution preference by 15 percent.[2.4]

In order to prevent a statutory overkill through the combination of the 15 percent add-on minimum tax of §56 and the 15 percent tax preference scale-down rules of §291, new §57(b) provides that only 71.6 percent of the items that are subject to §291 reduction treatment will be deemed to be tax preference items for the corporate minimum tax.

The combination of new §291 and the minimum tax rules of §§56 and 57 illustrate with renewed force that those tax benefits that Congress giveth, can eventually (or, in some cases, quickly) be taken away. The general feeling that pervaded the 1982 legislative backdrop of TEFRA was that the 1981 tax reduction (the Economic Recovery Tax Act) had been overly generous, and hence corrective measures were in order to redress the balance. These provisions, like many others, were simply reflective of this view.[2.5]

[2.4] New §291(a)(4) includes 57.5 percent of DISC income as the §995 deemed dividend (instead of the former 50 percent amount); and §291(a)(5) reduces amortizable basis for computing the pollution-control facility amortization deduction by 15 percent. Finally, §291(b)(1) generally reduces intangible drilling cost (IDC) deductions and mineral exploration and development costs by 15 percent, and requires that such amounts instead be capitalized and written off over a prescribed period (thirty-six months for capitalized IDCs, and four years for capitalized mineral exploration and development costs).

[2.5] For example, cutting back (and eventual expiration by 1984) of the safe-harbor leasing benefits of §168(f)(8), TEFRA §208; and reduction of future-year accelerated deductions in the ACRS system, TEFRA §206.

The Tax Reform Act of 1984 increased the preference scale-down percentage of §291 to 20 percent (and reduced the §57(b) preference inclusion percentage to 59 5/6 percent) in §68(a) of the Act, P.L. No. 98-369, 98 Stat. 678.

¶ 5.02. THE CORPORATION'S GROSS INCOME

Page 5-5:

Add new note 4.1 to end of paragraph numbered (1).

[4.1] The Bankruptcy Tax Act of 1980 narrowed the exclusion of §108 for bargain debt cancellations effected by solvent corporations, infra new ¶ 14.58 (this Supplement).

Moreover, the Tax Reform Act of 1984, P.L. No. 98-369, §59, 98 Stat. 678, eliminated §1032 protection for debt cancellations by solvent corporations with stock having a value less than the face of the cancelled debt (new §108(e)(10)).

¶ 5.03. DEDUCTIONS

Page 5-6:

Add to note 7.

[7] See Hillsboro Nat'l Bank v. CIR, 460 US 370 (1983) (no tax benefit income to corporation on recovery by shareholders of taxes previously deducted by corporation due to §164(e)).

Add to note 8.

[8] Campbell Taggart, Inc. v. US, 744 F.2d 442 (5th Cir. 1984) (pure holding company engaged in business and could use *Corn Products* doctrine to get ordinary loss on sale of subsidiary); Arkansas Best Corp., 83 TC 640 (1984) (holding company in business, but lost on *Corn Products* issue for forced divestiture of subsidiary because substantial investment motive).

Page 5-7:

Add new note 9.1 at end of first sentence of paragraph 6.

[9.1] Regulations under §465 were proposed on June 4, 1979.

Add new note 9.2 at end of third sentence of paragraph 6.

[9.2] The ERTA of 1981, P.L. No. 97-34, 95 Stat. 172, extended the "at risk" limitations to investment credit property as well in new §§46 (c)(8) and 46(c)(9). Moreover, new §47(c) will trigger recapture of ITC where the property ceases to be at risk.

Section 432(a) of the Tax Reform Act of 1984, P.L. No. 98-369, 98 Stat. 678, added new §465(c)(7), which exempts certain active businesses conducted by closely held Subchapter C corporations from the loss limitation at-risk rules of §465.

Page 5-8:

Add new note 11.1 to end of paragraph 9.

[11.1] The ERTA of 1981, supra note 9.2 (this Supplement), raised the corporate ceiling for charitable contributions to 10 percent.

Page 5-9:

Add new paragraph 16 to text at end of section.

16. *Safe-harbor leasing rules.* The new safe-harbor leasing rules of §168(f)(8), enacted by the ERTA of 1981, supra note 9.2 (this Supplement), are limited to corporate lessors (other than Subchapter S corporations and PHCs).[15.1]

[15.1] These provisions, in effect, permitted the lessor to "purchase" certain tax benefits, arising from depreciation (or ACRS) deductions and investment tax credits, that could not currently be used by the seller-lessee. For temporary regulations under these provisions, see T.D. 7791 (Oct. 20, 1981), promulgating Regs. §§5c.168(f)(8)-1 through 5c.168(f)(8)-11. For analysis, see Melnick, Equipment Leasing Under ERTA, TMM 81-21, Oct. 19, 1981; and Bostick & Davis, Structuring Safe-Harbor Leasing Transactions Under the New Temporary Regulations, 56 J. Tax. 130 (1982).

Legislation approved by the Senate Finance Committee in July 1982 materially cut back on the tax benefits of safe-harbor leasing transactions (and phase out these provisions by 1984); and this proposal became law on September 3, 1982 as part of TEFRA of 1982.

¶ 5.04. SPECIAL DEDUCTION PROBLEMS ARISING FROM CORPORATE-SHAREHOLDER RELATIONSHIP

Page 5-11:

Add to note 19.

[19] Wm. Wagner, 78 TC 910 (1982) (litigation expenses in defense of suit re installment sale of taxpayer's stock held capital per *Hilton*; origin of claim was sale transaction).

See Schenk, Arrowsmith And Its Progeny: Tax Characterization by Reference to Past Events, 33 Rutgers L. Rev. 317 (1981).

Add to note 20, second paragraph.

[20] Dolese v. US, 605 F.2d 1146 (10th Cir. 1979) (fight for control in divorce litigation; some expenses paid by corporation nondeductible personal expenses, but some were held deductible for preservation of corporate assets; proxy fight analogy applied).

Page 5-12:

Add to note 21.

[21] Dolese v. US, supra note 20 (this Supplement) (expense deductible to extent related to preservation of corporation's business; not deductible to extent expense personal to divorce proceeding between husband and wife shareholders).

Add to note 23.

[23] See Ellis Banking Corp. v. US, 688 F.2d 1376 (11th Cir. 1982) (fees for investigation of potential target corporation, held part of the cost of acquisition of the stock).

Add to note 24, second paragraph.

[24] But cf. §195 (enacted in 1980), providing an election to amortize start-up costs, business investigation costs, and preopening costs of a new business over five years à la §248 (this section apparently does not apply to acquisition costs, however; but see §195(d), business begins when "acquired").

Page 5-15:

Add to note 32.

[32] But see Ltr. Rul. 8023025 (Feb. 28, 1980), [1980] 10 CCH Stand. Fed. Tax Rep. ¶ 6971 E (repurchase of warrants issued to lenders as part of loan agreement in order to relieve itself of an obligation under the loan agreement resulted in an ordinary loss rather than a capital expense; *Jim Walter Corp.* and *Harder Servs., Inc.* distinguished); Markam & Brown, Inc. v. US, 648 F.2d 1043 (5th Cir. 1981) (redemption of stock pursuant to buy-sell agreement held nondeductible capital expenditure; redemption not necessary to save the corporation; *Five Star* distinguished; removal of animosity not enough to support deductibility). But see PLR 8248010, 1982 P-H Fed. Taxes ¶ 55,459 (corporation allowed §165 loss deduction on buy-back of warrants for cash; but §1032 applied on exchange of preferred stock for warrants). But §57 of the Tax Reform Act of 1984, P.L. No. 98-369, 98 Stat. 678, extended §1032 to cover the lapse of options and payments to cancel options to buy or sell the corporation's stock.

Add to note 33.

[83] But see Regs. §1.162-1(a) (1975), which appears to eliminate the "frustration of public policy doctrine" except to the extent explicitly covered by other provisions of §162.

Add to note 34.

[84] But see J.C. Bradford, 70 TC 584 (1978) (damages paid for fraudulent use of inside information held nondeductible capital expenditure). Rev. Rul. 80-119, 1980-1 CB 40 (legal expenses and out-of-court settlement payments by shareholder-director re *claim* for violation of §10(b) of Securities Exchange Act of 1934 held nondeductible capital expenditure attributable to taxpayer's acquisition of his stock).

Page 5-17:

Add to note 41.

[41] McCrory Corp. v. US, 651 F.2d 828 (2d Cir. 1981) (capitalized merger costs attributable to the issue of acquiring corporation's stock not deductible on subsequent disposition of acquired properties; such costs are never deductible).

Page 5-18:

Add to note 43.

[43] Duncan Indus., Inc., 73 TC 266 (1979) (stock issue discount held deductible on facts as amortizable loan origination fee because stock issue tied into loan transaction).

Add to note 44, following Doernbecher *citation.*

[44] Rev. Rul. 79-2, 1979-1 CB 98 (shareholder expenses of abandoned public stock offering deductible as ordinary loss when plan abandoned).

Add to note 46.

[46] But see §195 (elective five-year write-off for start-up, investigation, and pre-opening costs of new business).

¶ 5.05. NONDEDUCTIBLE ITEMS
Page 5-19:

Add new text to end of paragraph 1.

The Tax Reform Act of 1984 [47.1] extended the related-party category of §267(b)(3) to cover "controlled corporate groups,"

[47.1] P.L. No. 98-369, §174(b), 98 Stat. 678; see Eustice, The Tax

defined in new §267(f)(1) by reference to the definition in §1563(a) (infra ¶ 15.03), but substituting a more-than-50 percent test in lieu of the 80 percent test. Intragroup losses covered by §267(f)(1) are not disallowed, however; rather, they are deferred by new §267(f)(2) under principles similar to the deferred intercompany transaction rules applicable to consolidated returns (infra ¶ 15.23).

Reform Act of 1984, ¶¶ 2.03[5], 3.04[2][b] (Warren, Gorham & Lamont, Inc. 1984). Proposed and Temporary Regulations under new §267 were issued November 30, 1984, in T.D. 7991.

Add new text to end of paragraph 2.

Section 174 of the Tax Reform Act of 1984, P.L. No. 98-369, 98 Stat. 678, replaced the present disallowance rule of §267(a)(2) with a new matching provision whereby the accrual-basis payor's deduction is delayed (but not denied) until such time as the related payee includes such amount in gross income. This provision replaced a more limited matching rule in §267(f), which applied only to S corporations and their related (2 percent) shareholders. New §267 covers a wider range of "related" taxpayers as well, most notable in this respect is the broadening of §267(b)(3) to cover "controlled corporate groups," defined in new §267(f) by reference to the definition in §1563(a) (infra ¶ 15.03), but substituting a more-than-50 percent test in lieu of the 80 percent test.[48.1]

[48.1] See Eustice, supra note 47.1 (this Supplement); for Proposed and Temporary Regulations, see T.D. 7991 (Nov. 30, 1984).

Page 5-21:

Add new paragraph 9 to text at end of section, and note 50.1.

9. *"Golden parachute" payments—§280G.* The Tax Reform Act of 1984 [50.1] enacted §280G, which denies a deduction for payments of "excessive" compensation to corporate officers that were triggered by changes in corporate control (any payment that violates securities laws or regulations is a per se "parachute payment").

[50.1] Section 67(a) of the Act, P.L. 98-369; a companion special excise tax is imposed on the recipients of such payments in §4999. See generally Eustice, The Tax Reform Act of 1984, ¶ 3.05[3]; Moore and Tilton, Golden Parachute Restrictions Require Planning on Existing, Proposed Arrangements, 61 J. Tax. 324 (1984).

Only excessive payments above a designated base period amount are subject to the disallowance rule, however, and in this respect new §280G represents a partial statutory codification of "unreasonable compensation" principles.

¶ 5.06. DIVIDENDS-RECEIVED DEDUCTION AND RELATED PROBLEMS

Page 5-22:

Add to note 51.

[51] See generally Schaffer, The Income Tax on Intercorporate Dividends, 33 Tax Law. 161 (1979).

Page 5-24:

Correct fourth line of paragraph 6 of text.

Citation should be "§882," not "§881."

Add to note 54.

[54] *TSN* was reversed, 624 F.2d 1328 (5th Cir. 1980) (held true dividend to seller despite subsequent capital contribution by buyer).

See also Rev. Rul. 82-11, 1982-1 CB 51 (sale of stock after record date, but before ex-dividend date; held, corporate purchaser not entitled to §243 deduction, has no income on collection of dividend, and basis for shares is portion of purchase price not attributable to accrued dividend right, so no capital loss on resale of stock; corporate seller got §243 deduction because in effect it sold dividend right per *Lake* and *Hort* dividend substitution principles).

Accord with Rev. Rul. 82-11 is Silco, Inc. v. US, 591 F. Supp. 480 (N.D. Tex. 1984) (owner on record date the taxable person). For similar results under amendments by the Tax Reform Act of 1984, see infra new paragraph 9 of this section (this Supplement).

Page 5-25:

Add to note 57, first paragraph.

[57] For application of Rev. Rul. 77-226 principles, see GCM 39290, 23 Tax Notes 238 (Oct. 15, 1984).

Page 5-27:

Add to note 62.

[62] Rev. Rul. 80-238, 1980-2 CB 96 (writing a call on stock held by corporate shareholder does not shorten holding period for §246(c) purposes).

Add new paragraph 9 to text at end of section.

9. New restrictions on dividends-received deduction. To counter various abuses that had developed in connection with the intercorporate dividends-received deduction, proposals submitted by the Staff of the Senate Finance Committee on September 22, 1983 would further restrict the deduction in the following manner:

(1) The holding period on stock eligible for the deduction would be lengthened to one year (conforming to the long-term capital gain period);

(2) Leveraged stock investments would be neutralized by extending §265(2) to deny 85 percent of the interest deduction on debt incurred to purchase or carry any stock eligible for the dividends-received deduction; and

(3) Payments by short sellers "in lieu of dividends" would be added to the basis of the stock sold short, rather than allowed as an ordinary deduction (Rev. Rul. 62-42, 1962-1 CB 133, would be overruled).

Legislation in both the House (H.R. 4170, the Tax Reform Act of 1984) and the Senate (H.R. 2163, the Deficit Reduction Act of 1984) picked up on those suggestions and proposed to tighten the dividends-received deduction rules in several significant respects as follows:

(1) The House bill (§51 of H.R. 4170) proposed to reduce the deduction for dividends on "debt financed portfolio stock" (new §245A) to the extent of the leveraged basis percentage (i.e., if half of stock basis is attributable to debt financing, the deduction would be reduced to 42.5 percent). Such reduction, however, would not exceed the amount of any interest deduction allocable to such dividend.

(2) The Senate Finance Committee approach to leveraged stock investments initially was to deny the allocable interest deduction under §265(2) to the extent such interest is attributable to the 85 percent exempt portion of the dividend; but the final version of the bill (§31 of H.R. 2163; adding new §246A) adopted the same approach as the House bill.

(3) Both the House (§53(a) of H.R. 4170, adding new

§1059) and the Senate (§35(a) of H.R. 2163, adding §1059) proposed to require a corporate shareholder to reduce underlying stock basis to the extent of the non-taxed portion of any "extraordinary dividend" (defined as a dividend distribution equal to at least 5 percent of pre-ferred stock basis or 10 percent of common stock basis) on such stock that has been held for one year or less. The amount of property dividends for this purpose would be fair market value.

For example, an extraordinary dividend of property with a basis of $40 and a value of $100 would result in a stock basis reduction of $94 (i.e., $100, the *amount* of the dividend for this purpose, less the taxable portion thereof, which is $40 basis less $34 of §243 deduction).

(4) Moreover, both the House (§53(b) of H.R. 4170) and the Senate (§35(b) of H.R. 2163) proposed to amend the holding period rule of §246(c) to exclude any period dur-ing which the taxpayer has substantially diminished the risk of loss from holding the stock.

(5) Finally, both the House (§56(a) of H.R. 4170) and the Senate (§41(a) of H.R. 2163) proposed to require pay-ments in lieu of dividends on stock sold short to be added to stock basis unless the short sale is held open for at least 16 days (or more than one year in the case of extraordi-nary dividends), in new §263(h).

The final Conference version of the Tax Reform Act of 1984 [62.1] adopted all of the above proposals (and went even further

---

[62.1] Tax Reform Act of 1984, P.L. No. 98-369, 98 Stat. 678, §51 (new §246A limitation on leveraged portfolio stock acquisitions), §53(a) (new §1059 basis reduction for extraordinary dividends), §53(b) (new §246(c) holding-period rules), and §56(a) (new capi-talization rule of §263(h) for payments in lieu of short-sale dividends). See also new §7701(f), added by §53(c) of the 1984 Act, authorizing regulations to prevent the use of related parties to avoid provisions that deal with the linking of borrowing to investment or diminishing risks.

See generally Eustice, The Tax Reform Act of 1984, ¶¶ 3.03[3] (dividend-received deduction limitations), 3.04[3][c] (new §7701(f) regulations), 5.05[6][c] (short-sale expenses).

See also Silco, Inc. v. US, supra note 54 (this Supplement), for de-cision under pre-1984 law, which reached results comparable to the new legislation.

in the case of the §246(c) holding period, extending it from 15 to 45 days).

¶ 5.07. ORGANIZATION, REORGANIZATION, AND LIQUIDATION EXPENDITURES

Page 5-27:

Add to note 63, second paragraph.

[63] NYS Bar Ass'n, Tax Section, Report on the Ancillary Tax Effects of Different Forms of Reorganizations, 34 Tax L. Rev. 477 (1979).

Page 5-31:

Add to note 79, second paragraph.

[79] See McCrory Corp. v. US, 651 F.2d 828 (2d Cir. 1981).

Page 5-32:

Add new note 81.1 to end of runover paragraph.

[81.1] See generally McCrory Corp. v. US, supra note 79 (this Supplement) (court adopted bifurcated approach to capitalized merger costs; merger costs attributable to acquisition of target's assets were deductible on subsequent disposition of those assets by acquiring corporation; but expense attributable to issuance of the stock utilized to effect the acquisition never deductible).

See also §195 (election to amortize start-up costs of new business over five years); supra ¶ 5.04, note 24 (this Supplement).

Page 5-34:

Add new note 83.1 to end of first full paragraph.

[83.1] But see McCrory Corp. v. US, 496 F. Supp. 1286 (S.D.N.Y. 1980) (acquiring corporation's expenses of tax-free statutory merger acquisition *not* added to basis of acquired assets; costs must be capitalized as separate asset of surviving corporation and are deductible only when it liquidates). But on appeal, *McCrory* was reversed and remanded, supra note 79 (this Supplement) (costs attributable to asset acquisition via merger added to asset basis and deductible on later disposition of acquired assets; costs attributable to stock issued by acquiring corporation never deductible).

But cf. §195 (election to amortize start-up, investigation, and pre-opening costs of new business over five years); supra ¶ 5.04, note 24 (this Supplement).

Page 5-36:

Add to note 92.

[92] See also El Paso Co. v. US, 694 F.2d 703 (Fed. Cir. 1982) (expenses of forced divestiture proceedings incurred by parent corporation attributable to successful plan and abandoned plans are generally deductible §162 expenses; transaction in substance a partial liquidation because of contraction effects; no continuing benefit for taxpayer or its subsidiaries).

Add to note 93.

[93] See El Paso Co. v. US, supra note 92 (this Supplement) (divestiture proceeding expenses deductible; but no deduction for organization of subsidiary divestiture vehicle, start-up costs of new subsidiary's business, and costs of obtaining ruling on tax consequences of reorganization transaction).

Add to note 96.

[96] See also El Paso Co. v. US, supra note 92 (this Supplement) (divestiture proceeding expenses incurred by parent corporation deductible; but costs of reorganization, start-up of new subsidiary, and obtaining tax ruling nondeductible capital expenses).

Page 5-37:

Add to note 98.

[98] See generally Gerli & Co., 73 TC 1019 (1980) (attorney's fees for obtaining §367 ruling on liquidation of foreign subsidiary under §332 held capital expenditure), rev'd on other grounds, 668 F.2d 691 (2d Cir. 1982).

Add new paragraph 4 to end of section.

4. *Special problems in corporate asset acquisitions with assumed liabilities—current expense vs. capital cost treatment.* As noted previously (supra ¶ 5.04, paragraph 1), property "acquisition costs" are not currently deductible by the acquiring party, but instead must be capitalized as part of the cost basis of the acquired stock or properties. Liabilities of the acquired party that are taken over by the buyer likewise are subject to this general rule of capitalization (and this includes "expense-type" obligations that would otherwise ordinarily be deductible).[99] Like all seemingly

---

[99] See, e.g., GCM 39274, 24 Tax Notes 944 (Sept. 3, 1984), and cases cited; see generally, Landis, Liabilities and Purchase Price, 27 Tax L. 67 (1973).

well settled principles of taxation, however, numerous problems and ambiguities can arise here, depending upon the type of liability assumed, its maturation (viz., the extent to which it is a past, present, or future obligation), the form of the acquisition (viz., stock or assets, taxable or tax-free), and the details of the parties' business bargain.[100]

Thus, assumed *future* liabilities generally are not deemed to be part of the purchase price and can be deducted only when actually incurred by the acquiring party (although the line between present and future liabilities is not always a bright one). Assumed "expense" liabilities in the context of a §351 incorporation are given special treatment by §357(c) (since 1978),[101] and liabilities assumed in a tax-free reorganization likewise operate under a special statutory regime.[102] These problems are dealt with throughout this work in the context where they arise and are referred to here merely as a guide for the reader in a search for their treatment.[103]

---

[100] Landis, supra note 99.

[101] Supra ¶ 3.07, paragraph 3; see also ¶ 3.12, note 120.

[102] Infra ¶ 14.55 and ¶ 16.13, paragraph 4.

[103] In addition to the references in notes 101 and 102, see infra ¶ 11.45, paragraph 2, ¶ 11.65, note 202, ¶ 11.68, and new ¶ 11.72 (this Supplement). See also supra ¶ 4.06 and ¶ 4.23 (this Supplement).

Chapter 6

CORPORATE ELECTIONS
UNDER SUBCHAPTER S

¶ 6.01.   INTRODUCTORY

Page 6-2:

Add to note 1.

[1] For extensive treatment of the Subchapter S rules, see Eustice & Kuntz, Federal Income Taxation of Subchapter S Corporations, (Warren, Gorham & Lamont, 1982).

Add to note 3.

[3] The shareholders' limit was raised to twenty-five by the Economic Recovery Tax Act (ERTA) of 1981, P.L. No. 97-34, 95 Stat. 172, and it was raised again to thirty-five by the Subchapter S Revision Act of 1982, P.L. No. 97-354, 96 Stat. 1669, which became law on October 21, 1982 and is effective for years beginning in 1983. See Eustice & Kuntz, supra note 1 (this Supplement).

Page 6-4:

Add to note 4.

[4] New §1371(a)(1), added by the Subchapter S Revision Act of 1982, supra note 3 (this Supplement), states that "except as otherwise provided in this subchapter, and except to the extent inconsistent with this subchapter, subchapter C shall apply to an S corporation and its shareholders." Thus, the statute now explicitly recognizes a role for Subchapter C, but one that gives way to Subchapter S if the former rules are inconsistent with the basic pass-through system adopted by the new legislation.

Page 6-5:

Add new text at end of section.

On April 1, 1982, legislation was introduced jointly in the House and Senate (H.R. 6055 and S. 2350) entitled the Subchapter

S Revision Bill of 1982. The principal thrust of this legislation was to conform the treatment of Subchapter S corporations more closely to the partnership model by making them pass-through conduits to their shareholders for items of income, deduction, and credits; moreover, the proposals materially liberalized eligibility requirements and changed the procedures for terminating Subchapter S status. These proposals, the Subchapter S Revision Act of 1982, supra note 3 (this Supplement), became law on October 21, 1982 and are effective for years beginning after 1982.[6.1]

[6.1] See Eustice, Subchapter S Corporations and Partnerships: A Search for the Pass-Through Paradigm, 39 Tax L. Rev. 345 (1984).

¶ 6.02. ELIGIBILITY TO ELECT UNDER SUBCHAPTER S

Page 6-5:

Add to note 7.

[7] The Subchapter S Revision Act of 1982, P.L. No. 97-354, 96 Stat. 1669, in new §1361(b)(2) adds to the list of ineligible corporations (besides the exclusion under present law for affiliated group membership) the following: financial institutions, DISCs or former DISCs, possessions (§936) corporations, and insurance companies.

Add to note 9, second paragraph.

[9] See Prop. Regs. §1.1371-1(d)(4), April 17, 1980, reflecting the 1976 and 1978 amendments.

Page 6-6:

Add new note 10.1 at end of first full paragraph.

[10.1] See Prop. Regs. §§1.1371-1(d)(1) and 1.1371-1(d)(2), April 17, 1980, reflecting these amendments.

Add to text at end of first full paragraph.

The ERTA of 1981 [10.2] expanded the shareholder group once again to twenty-five shareholders, effective for years beginning after 1981. The Subchapter S Revision Act of 1982 [10.3] again raised the maximum shareholder limit to thirty-five shareholders, effective for years beginning in 1983, new §1361(b)(1)(A).

[10.2] P.L. No. 97-34, 95 Stat. 172.

[10.3] Supra note 7 (this Supplement).

Add to note 11, following CHM Co. *case citation.*

[11] In re Weisser, 44 AFTR2d 5854 (M.D. Fla. 1979) (accord with *CHM Co.*; Rev. Rul. 74-9 distinguished because shareholder not bankrupt). *Mason* was affirmed per curiam, 646 F.2d 1309 (9th Cir. 1980). See also §5(d) of H.R. 5043, the Bankruptcy Tax Act of 1980, which amended §1371 to permit a bankrupt shareholder's estate to be a qualified shareholder (effective for any bankruptcy case begun after October 1, 1979, which ultimately passed in December of 1980). New §1361 (c)(3) continues this rule.

Page 6-7:

Add to note 12, first paragraph.

[12] American Nurseryman Publishing Co., 75 TC 271 (1980) (accord, even though state court later declared transfer to grantor trust void ab initio as mistake).

Add to note 12, second paragraph.

[12] See Prop. Regs. §1.1371-1(d)(3)(i), April 17, 1980.

Add to note 13.

[13] See Prop. Regs. §1.1371-1(d)(3)(ii), April 17, 1980.

Add to text at end of paragraph 2.

The ERTA of 1981 [13.1] revised and broadened the qualified trust-shareholder categories of §1371(e) by adding trusts which are deemed to be completely owned by a person other than the grantor under §678 to the list of qualified shareholders. Also, a new category of qualified trust shareholder, the "qualified Subchapter S trust," is added by §1371(g), if the individual beneficiary specially elects to be treated as the owner of the trust under §678. Such a trust is one which (a) distributes all its income currently to one individual U.S. beneficiary, and (b) has terms which narrowly focus the benefits of its income and corpus on a single U.S. beneficiary in the manner described in §1371(g)(3)(C) (viz., there can only be one income beneficiary at a time, corpus can only be distributed to the current income beneficiary, such income interest can only last for life, and the trust must distribute all its assets to

---

[13.1] Supra note 10.2 (this Supplement).

the person who is the income beneficiary at the time of its termination. These provisions are effective for 1982.

The Subchapter S Revision Act of 1982 [13.2] did not make any significant changes as to the type of permissible shareholders other than to place the definitional structure of former §1371 in new §1361. Thus, new §1361(b)(1)(B) continues the basic rule that shareholders must be individuals, estates, and qualified trusts; new §1361(c)(2) continues the qualified trust shareholder rules of former §1371(e); and new §1361(d) continues the special qualified Subchapter S trust rules of former §1371(g) (though in slightly broader form).

[13.2] Supra note 7 (this Supplement).

Page 6-8:

Add to text after note 16.

Legislation passed in 1982 now allows differences in voting rights of common stock without causing violation of the one-class-of-stock rule. This provision of the Subchapter S Revision Act of 1982,[16.1] new §1361(c)(4), is effective for years beginning in 1983.

[16.1] Supra note 7 (this Supplement).

Page 6-9:

Add to note 19.

[19] Proposed Regulations under §385 (all versions), supra ¶ 4.05 (this Supplement), were silent on this issue. The §385 regulations were withdrawn on July 6, 1983. But T.D. 7920 §5 (Nov. 2, 1983) reinstated the language of previously withdrawn Regs. §1.1371-1(g), notwithstanding the uniformly hostile judicial reaction to those regulations. However, in view of the 1982 amendments in §1361(c)(5) (infra, this Supplement), courts may be more reluctant to strike down the reincarnated regulations in the future.

The 1982 proposals provide that a corporation's election will not be terminated if it has outstanding straight-debt instruments (i.e., nonhybrid debt) held by persons who are eligible to hold Subchapter S stock. Straight-debt, for this purpose, is unconditional and nonconvertible debt bearing a fixed interest rate. Obligations that do not meet this safe-harbor test will be tested for second-class-of-stock status under "general" classification principles. These proposals passed, as new §1361(c)(5), supra note 7 (this Supplement).

Add to text at end of paragraph 3.

The Subchapter S Revision Act of 1982 [19.1] continues the basic requirement of prior law that the corporation can have only one class of stock, new §1361(b)(1)(D). While the stated reason for the one-class-of-stock limitation has usually been to preserve simplicity in the allocation of corporate income and losses, the thrust of the 1982 legislation is to conform the tax treatment of Subchapter S corporations to the partnership rules, and "special allocations" are expressly permitted in the latter area by §704(b). In view of the partnership parity policy that underlies the new Subchapter S legislation, failure to permit special allocations through differing equity interests (viz., different classes of stocks) unfortunately perpetuates one of the principal discontinuities of prior law in the tax treatment of Subchapter S corporations and partnerships.

New §1361(c)(4) does permit variance in voting rights among the common stockholders, and new §1361(c)(5) provides a safe-harbor exemption for certain types of "straight debt" (held by eligible shareholders) in applying the one-class-of-stock limitation. Safe-harbor "straight debt" is defined by new §1361(c)(5)(B) as a written unconditional promise to pay on demand or on a specified date a sum certain in money if the interest rate (and payment dates) are not contingent, and the obligation is not convertible (directly or indirectly) into stock. Hybrid "bent debt" (viz., convertible or contingent debt), however, will continue to expose the corporation to loss of Subchapter S status if such obligations are classified as a second class of stock. Presumably, "warrants" should not cause problems under this provision in view of the IRS' long-held views that these instruments do not constitute stock or securities. The straight debt safe-harbor is limited solely to one-class-of-stock determinations, however, so that these obligations could be treated as equity for other purposes. New §1361(c)(5)(C) authorizes regulations to provide for the treatment of straight debt obligations under Subchapter S and for the coordination of such treatment with other Code provisions.[19.2]

[19.1] Supra note 7 (this Supplement).

[19.2] See supra ¶ 4.05 (this Supplement) for description of the §385 regulations saga, which bodes poorly for regulations under the Subchapter S provisions.

Add new note 19.3 to end of paragraph 4.

[19.3] Cf. § 875(1) (nonresident alien or foreign corporation considered to be engaged in U.S. business if a partner in a partnership is so engaged); Ward v. US, 661 F.2d 226 (Ct. Cl. 1981) (nonresident alien spouse owner per community property law of foreign country and thus no valid election). New §1361(b)(1)(C) continues to prohibit nonresident alien shareholders.

Page 6-10:
Add to note 20.

[20] Rev. Rul. 72-201 was revoked by Rev. Rul. 80-169, 1980-1 CB 188 (no termination for short year return period). In Rev. Rul. 72-320, the Subchapter S corporation was the corporation that transitorily acquired the stock of the spun-off subsidiary.

See also Rev. Rul. 73-496, 1973-2 CB 312 (transitory acquisition of stock of subsidiary, followed by prompt §334(b)(2) liquidation not fatal).

Add new note 20.1 to end of first complete sentence of text.

[20.1] The 1982 legislation, in new §1361(b)(2), lists five types of "ineligible" corporations for electing "S corporation" status: (1) members of an affiliated group (whether or not they may be consolidated); (2) financial institutions; (3) insurance companies; (4) §936 possessions corporations; and (5) DISCs or former DISCs. However, existing corporations with foreign subsidiaries or DISC subsidiaries could retain their status so long as their election does not terminate and a majority of their stock is not transferred.

The "affiliated group" limitation in new §1361(b)(1)(A) is more rigorous than prior law, however, since the affiliated group definition of §1504 is applied without the exceptions of §1504(b) (e.g., foreign corporations, possessions corporations, etc.). Section 6(c)(1) of the Subchapter S Revision Act grandfathers foreign subsidiaries and DISC subsidiaries so long as there is not a more than 50 percent change of stock ownership within the meaning of new §1378(c)(2) (Act §6(c)(4) of the effective date rules).

Add to note 22.

[22] See also Rev. Rul. 69-591, 1969-1 CB 191 (de facto existence of new subsidiary even though no formal issue of shares; okay to file consolidated return); McClelland Farm Equip. Co. v. US, 601 F.2d 365 (8th Cir. 1979) (premature filing of election held effective).

Page 6-11:
Add to text at end of section.

The 1982 legislation modified the election mechanics somewhat by providing that elections on or before the fifteenth day of the third month of the taxable year (in lieu of seventy-five days) will be effective for the entire year only if the corporation meets all qualifying requirements for the entire year and any persons who held stock up to the time the election is made may consent to it; if these requirements are not met, or the election is made after the two-and-one-half-month period, it is effective for the following year. These provisions are found in new §§1362(a), 1362(b), and 1362(c). See T.D. 7872 (Jan. 26, 1983) for Temporary Regulations dealing with elections, consents, revocations, and taxable years under the new law. Temp. Regs. §18.1361-1 deals with qualified Subchapter S trusts, §18.1362-1 deals with the corporate election, and §18.1362-2, the shareholder consents.

¶ 6.03. TERMINATION OF THE ELECTION

Page 6-11:

Add to note 26.

[26] The 1982 legislation significantly changes the termination rules as to method, effect, and timing. Moreover, the new law gives the IRS power to waive "inadvertent" terminations if the defects are cured within a reasonable time after their discovery. These provisions are found in new §§1362(d), 1362(e), and 1362(f). For Temporary Regulations on revocations under the new law, see Temp. Regs. §§18.1362-3 and 18.1362-4, T.D. 7872 (Jan. 26, 1983).

Page 6-12:

Add to note 28.

[28] T.J. Henry Assocs., Inc., 80 TC 846 (1982) (Acq.) (intentional termination by transfer of one share to nonconsenting new shareholder held effective); under the new Subchapter S legislation, however, such maneuvers are unnecessary since revocation is the proper route, but termination is prospective only).

Page 6-13:

Add new note 28.1 at end of sixth line of text.

[28.1] See Prop. Regs. §§1.1372-3(b) and 1.1372-4(b)(1), April 17, 1980.

Add to text at end of paragraph numbered 1.

The 1982 legislation requires a majority vote to terminate the S corporation's election; thus, a new shareholder who acquires 50 percent or less of the corporation's stock could not cause termination of its election even by an express refusal to consent. In fact, an affirmative refusal to consent by a new shareholder no longer would have any effect under these proposals. (If majority control were obtained, the termination mechanism would be by revocation.) These provisions are found in new §1362(d)(1).

Add to text at end of second paragraph of paragraph numbered 2.

The 1982 legislation, however, allows voluntary terminations by revocation with a majority vote of the shareholders. If the revocation is made by the fifteenth day of the third month, it will be effective for the entire year; if made subsequently, it is effective for the following year. But the revocation can specify that it is effective on the date filed, or a later prospective date, and this specification will control. These provisions are found at new §1362(d)(1).

If a short taxable year results from a revocation during the corporation's taxable year, the special termination year rules of new §1362(e) come into play, which are described in new paragraph 6 of this section (this Supplement).

For Temporary Regulations on these provisions, see Temp. Regs. §§18.1362-3 and 18.1362-4, T.D. 7872 (Jan. 26, 1983).

Add to note 30.

[30] Rev. Rul. 72-201 was revoked by Rev. Rul. 80-169, 1980-1 CB 188 (no termination for short-year return period).

Page 6-14:

Add new note 30.1 to end of runover of paragraph numbered 3.

[30.1] See also Rev. Rul. 72-320, 1972-1 CB 270; and Rev. Rul. 73-496, 1973-2 CB 312 (no loss of Subchapter S status by purchase of subsidiary's stock, followed by prompt liquidation under §332-§334 (b)(2); same where creation of subsidiary will not terminate Subchapter S election); see also supra ¶ 6.02, note 20.

The 1982 legislation provides that a disqualifying event terminates the S corporation's election as of the date of the disqualifying event, and will result in two short taxable years (one as an S corporation, and one as a regular corporation). These provisions are found at new §§1362(d)(2) and 1362(e).

Add to text at end of runover of paragraph numbered 3.

The Subchapter S Revision Act of 1982 [30.2] rules in new §1362 (d)(2) for involuntary terminations usually result in the application of the short taxable year rules of new §1362(e). [30.3]

Accidental terminations can now be forgiven under new §1362(f) if the Service determines that the termination was "inadvertent," the disqualifying event is corrected within a reasonable period after discovery, and both the corporation and the shareholders agree to be treated as if the election had been in effect for the terminated period. The Committee Report [30.4] admonished the Service to be "reasonable" in applying this amnesty provision where no tax avoidance would result from continued Subchapter S treatment. Two examples of "inadvertent" terminations cited in the Report are (1) violation of the passive income test where a corporation in good faith, though erroneously, determined that it had no accumulated earnings, and (2) where the one-class-of-stock rule was inadvertently breached. The termination waiver of §1362(f) can be retroactive for all years, or merely retroactive to the period in which the corporation again became eligible for Subchapter S treatment.

[30.2] P.L. No. 97-354, 96 Stat. 1669.

[30.3] See infra paragraph 6 of this section (this Supplement).

[30.4] S. Rep. No. 97-640 at 12.

Add to end of first full text paragraph, paragraph numbered 4.

Regulations §1.1372-4(b)(5)(iv) redesignated as §1.1372-4 (b)(5)(iii) by Prop. Regs., April 17, 1980.

Add to text at end of paragraph numbered 4.

The 1982 legislation drops the foreign income restrictions as a terminating event. Thus, excessive amounts of foreign-source income will no longer cause termination of Subchapter S corporation status. Moreover, under new §1373(a), an S corporation is to be treated as a partnership, and its shareholders as partners, in applying the foreign tax credit rules of §901, the Subpart F rules of §951, and the boycott rules of §999.

Add to note 31.

[31] Rev. Rul. 79-294, 1979-2 CB 305 (computation of gross receipts from commodity futures transactions; gross receipts equal net

gain from closing transaction—no gross receipts if take delivery or if sustain a loss); John D. Thompson, 73 TC 878 (1980) (discount income derived from collections of purchased tax refund claims not passive investment income; profits not equivalent to "interest" because no "lending" transaction); Bradshaw v. US, 683 F.2d 365 (Ct. Cl. 1982) (collections on installment notes from sale of land not passive investment income; not "sale" of notes, despite constructive sale treatment under §1232; moreover, corporation, as assignee of notes in §351 exchange, stepped into shoes of original installment seller).

Page 6-15:

Add to note 32.

[82] Accord with *Howell* is Bradshaw v. US, supra note 31 (this Supplement) (mere passiveness of corporate activity not fatal).

Add to seventh line of first full paragraph of text.

Regs. §1.1372-4(b)(5)(iv) redesignated as §1.1372-4(b)(5)(iii) by regulations proposed April 17, 1980.

Add to note 34.

[84] Rev. Rul. 79-294, supra note 31 (this Supplement) (commodity futures transactions result in gross receipts only if net gain on closing transaction).

Page 6-17:

Add to note 38, runover paragraph, following Winn citation.

[88] *Winn* was affirmed, 595 F.2d 1060 (5th Cir. 1979). See also John J. McIlhinney, ¶ 79,473 P-H Memo TC (rents passive income); and Crouch v. US, 692 F.2d 97 (10th Cir. 1982) (rents passive income; no exception for "active rents," and rents not business income on facts because services not significant).

Add to note 38, end of runover paragraph.

[88] See Rev. Rul. 81-197, 1981-2 CB 166 (distinction between "rents" and "service fees" in the case of airplane charters; rents where mere passive lease; service fee where lessor performs significant services).

Add to text at end of paragraph numbered 5.

New §1362(d)(3)(A) abolishes the passive investment income limitation for corporations that have no accumulated profits from post-1981 nonelection years. (For new corporations, it will not be

possible to have accumulated earnings under new §1371(c)(1).)
But if the S corporation has accumulated earnings from Subchapter
C years (which existing corporations that have not elected ordinarily
would have), the passive investment income limitations continue to
apply, and if they are exceeded, the election terminates (though
only prospectively).

Under new §1362(d)(3), however, the excess passive investment income rules will cause termination of Subchapter S status
only if such income exceeds 25 percent (raised from 20 percent) of
gross receipts for three consecutive years; such termination is effective for the *following* year. During the three-year waiting period,
however, new §1375 imposes a tax on the passive income in excess
of 25 percent (at the top 46 percent rate). The definition of passive
investment income in new §1362(d)(3)(D) is modified to exclude
interest on deferred payment sales of inventory, and to include in
gross receipts only the net gain from the sale of nonsecurity capital
assets (e.g., commodities). It seems clear, however, that the new
passive investment income rules should be considerably less onerous
to comply with than prior law.

6. *Effect of Termination.* Under new §1362(e), if an S corporation's status terminates for less than its entire taxable year,
then there will be two short-taxable-year periods, one in which the
corporation is treated as an S corporation and one in which it is
taxed as a regular corporation. The income for the regular corporation year is taxed on an annualized basis, and all items of income,
deduction and credit are allocable between the two periods on a
daily basis (unless *all* shareholders elect to apply normal accounting
rules to both periods).

Thus, new §1362(e)(1)(A) provides that the S short year ends
on the day before the effective date of termination of S corporation
status (although new §1362(e)(6)(B) extends the due date of its
final S short-year return to the due date of the C short-year return,
including extensions); the C short-year period commences with the
date of termination under §1362(e)(1)(B). The income allocation rules are found in §1362(e)(2) (the daily allocation rule),
and §1362(e)(3) (election to allocate income under normal accounting rules). The annualization requirement for the C short-
year period is provided by new §1362(e)(5). Finally, new §1362
(e)(6)(A) provides that the short years created by §1362(e) only
count as one year in determining corporate carryovers and carry-

backs. See Temp. Regs. §§18.1362-3, 18.1362-4, and 18.1377-1, issued in T.D. 7872 (Jan. 26, 1983).

7. *Coordination with §338.* If control of an S corporation's stock is purchased by another corporation, which then elects §338 (infra ¶ 11.47 (this Supplement)), S corporation status terminates as of the day before the terminating event, viz., the date when its stock is acquired. Thus, the deemed asset sale required by §338 occurs in the acquired corporation's C short-year period, and any recapture income triggered by the §338 election is reportable in the C short-year return. If the acquired corporation is included in the acquiring corporation's consolidated return, only income attributable to the period beginning on the day after the acquisition date goes into the consolidated return since §338(a) provides that the deemed sale occurs on the acquisition date and the deemed repurchase occurs on the day after the acquisition date. In effect, the acquired corporation has a one day separate return short year as an unconsolidated C corporation.[38.1]

[38.1] See infra ¶¶ 11.47 and 15.24 (this Supplement). Section 201(g) of the Technical Corrections Act of 1983 (H.R. 3805), provided in new §1362(e)(6)(C) that the daily allocation rules of §1362 (e)(2) will not apply to any items resulting from the application of §338 (e.g., recapture income and the like). This provision moved to §621(g) of H.R. 4170, the Tax Reform Act of 1984, and passed as §721(g) of the Tax Reform Act of 1984, P.L. No. 98-369, 98 Stat. 678.

¶ 6.04.   ELECTION AFTER TERMINATION

Page 6-17:

Add after second sentence of text.

(The reelection waiting period of former §1372(f) is continued in new §1362(g) without change; however, the Committee Report [39.1] states that the five-year waiting period will not apply for old-law terminations).

[39.1] S. Rep. No. 97-640 at 11.

¶ 6.05. TAXATION OF CORPORATE INCOME TO SHAREHOLDER

Page 6-19:

Add after first full paragraph.

The Subchapter S Revision Act of 1982 [44.1] abandoned the year-end deemed dividend system of former §1373(b) and adopted a conduit pass-through approach based on the partnership model, in new §1366. Moreover, corporate items of income, loss, deduction, and credit flow through to shareholders on a per-share, per-day allocation basis by virtue of new §1377(a)(1).[44.2]

[44.1] P.L. No. 97-354, 96 Stat. 1669.

[44.2] See infra new paragraph 3 of this section (this Supplement).

Page 6-20:

Add to note 44, third paragraph.

[44] Briskin, Use of Subchapter S Corporations to Shift Income Among Family Members, 59 Taxes 557 (1981).

The 1982 legislation dropped the year-end taxability rule for shareholder income pass-through treatment, and instead switched to a ratable allocation on a per-share/per-day basis like that used under the present law for loss pass-through reporting (infra ¶6.07). A shareholder who dies during the year will include his allocable share of the corporation's income in his final return.

Add to note 45, first paragraph.

[45] Repeal of §1348 by ERTA of 1981, P.L. No. 97-34, 95 Stat. 172, makes characterization as dividend, rather than personal service, income less significant, since the top §1 rate is now 50 percent for both categories of income. As to prior law, see William H. Crook, 80 TC 27 (1983) (deemed dividend from S Corporation constituted investment income for purposes of §163(d) limitation).

The 1982 amendments to Subchapter S abandon the constructive dividend system and pass-through corporate income on a conduit basis in the same way as partnerships. See new §1366, infra paragraph 3 of this section (this Supplement).

Add to note 47, runover paragraph.

[47] Note that safe-harbor leasing benefits of §168(f)(8) added by ERTA of 1981, P.L. No. 97-34, 95 Stat. 172, were not available to Subchapter S corporate lessors (viz., they could *sell* and lease back, but they could not buy and lease back).

Page 6-21:

Add to note 49, second paragraph.

⁴⁹ Regulations under §1377(d) were adopted January 12, 1979, as Regs. §1.1377-4.

Page 6-23:

Add to first sentence of text after note 53.

The retirement income credit of §37 was repealed by the Tax Reform Act of 1976 and replaced by a new credit for the elderly.

Page 6-24:

Add to note 54, after Davis.

⁵⁴ But compare Louis G. Horn, ¶ 82,741 P-H Memo TC (Subchapter S "support" Corporation ignored as sham and its income was taxed to dominant PC as true earner of the income; no business purpose and no business activity).

Add new note 54.1 at end of first full paragraph of text.

⁵⁴·¹ See generally Richard L. Johnson, 77 TC 837 (1981) (allocation rules of §1375(c) can only be invoked by IRS, not shareholders; similar in this respect to §482). On appeal, *Johnson* was affirmed, 720 F.2d 963 (7th Cir. 1983) (court suggested that Treasury should clarify its regulations on this point, however, like those in §482).

The 1982 amendments also allow IRS adjustments to reflect adequate compensation for capital as well as services, new §1366(e).

Add to note 55, second paragraph.

⁵⁵ See generally Shop Talk, Interplay of Investment Credit Recapture and Subchapter S, 53 J. Tax. 127 (1980), discussing ITC recapture problems where ITC property of a Subchapter S corporation is acquired in a tax-free reorganization.

Under the 1982 amendments, ITC (like other items) will pass through to shareholders on a per-share, per-day allocation basis. Moreover, election of Subchapter S will not trigger ITC recapture under §47, and any recapture tax liability will remain at the corporate level. See new §§1366(a), 1377(a)(1), and 1371(d).

Section 201(e) of the Technical Corrections Act of 1983 (H.R. 3805) would provide for adjustment to earnings and profits of an S corporation for any ITC recapture tax generated by §47 (new §1371 (d)(3)). Presumably *accumulated* earnings would be reduced to reflect such additional tax liability. This provision moved to §621(e) of H.R. 4170, the Tax Reform Act of 1984, and passed as §721(e) of the Tax Reform Act of 1984, P.L. No. 98-369, 98 Stat. 678.

Page 6-25:

Add to text at end of section.

3. *Subchapter S Revision Act of 1982.* The 1982 legislation [56.1] shifts completely to a conduit system, based for all practical purposes on the partnership analogue. Thus, each shareholder is allocated his pro rata share (on a daily basis) of each item of corporate income, deduction, loss, and credit that may have special tax effect to him, and his pro rata share of residual corporate income or loss. The character of such items likewise passes through in the same manner as the partnership conduit system. Thus, the elaborate constructive dividend rules previously described will no longer apply (and present law concepts of earnings and profits, undistributed taxable income (UTI), and previously taxed income (PTI) are eliminated under the new system for years after 1982).

New §1366 establishes the conduit pass-through system for items of corporate income, loss, deduction, or credit, based on the partnership analogue; new §1377(a)(1), in addition, conforms the allocation system for income and losses, providing for a per-share, per-day allocation of all corporate items to the shareholders. Moreover, the new pass-through system is unrelated to distributions, accumulations, or earnings and profits (which, by virtue of new §1371(c)(1), can no longer be generated by an S corporation). Finally, new §1367 provides that shareholders adjust their stock basis annually to reflect the amount of passed-through income and losses in a manner similar to the partner basis adjustment rules of §705.

Under new §1363(a), the S corporation is not subject to tax, except for the one-shot capital gain tax rules of new §1374 (formerly §1378),[56.2] and the special tax on excess passive investment income provided by new §1375.[56.3] New §1363(b) provides generally that the taxable income of an S corporation shall be computed in the same manner as an individual, except that no deduction is allowed for personal exemptions and the various individual "itemized deductions," but the deduction for organization expenses of §248 is allowed. Moreover, new §1371(a)(2) treats an S corporate shareholder of a C corporation as an individual for

---

[56.1] Supra note 44.1 (this Supplement).

[56.2] Infra ¶ 6.06.

[56.3] Infra ¶ 6.06A (this Supplement).

purposes of the Subchapter C rules (viz., no §243 deduction, and property dividends are taxable at value). Finally, new §1363 (c)(1) provides that elections are generally made at the corporate level, except for those specified in §1363(c)(2) (§§108, 163(d), 617, and 901), which are made at the shareholder level.[56.4]

New §1378 provides that the taxable year of an S corporation will be required to be a calendar year, unless it can establish a business purpose (to the satisfaction of IRS) to adopt a fiscal year.[56.5] Existing Subchapter S corporations can retain their fiscal years, however, until there has been a change of more than 50 percent of its stock ownership. (In applying the stock ownership rules, transfers of stock to family members or by reason of death will not count.) Moreover, new §267(f) in effect places Subchapter S corporations on the cash method of accounting for purposes of deducting business expenses and interest owed to a related cash-basis taxpayer (including a shareholder who owns 2 percent or more, with attribution, of its stock). The deduction delay rule of new §267(f)(1) preempts the deduction disallowance rule of §267 (a)(2) (though *not* the loss denial rule of §267(a)(1)). Recent legislation (§174 of the Tax Reform Act of 1984) extended the matching rule of §267(f) to all §267(a)(2) accruals between related parties (and replaced the disallowance rule of §267(a)(2) with a deduction delay rule keyed to payee includability), supra ¶ 5.05 (this Supplement).

In keeping with the partnership theme, distributions (whether of cash or property) ordinarily will have no direct tax consequences to the shareholders other than to reduce their stock basis (new §1368), since an S corporation typically will not have any current or accumulated earnings and profits (new §1377(c)(1)). How-

---

[56.4] For Temporary Regulations on elections, consents, and refusals, see Temp. Regs. §18.1379-2, added by T.D. 7872 (Jan. 26, 1983).

[56.5] Section 305(d)(1) of the Technical Corrections Act of 1982 modified the effective date rules of new §1378 to make the new taxable year rules effective on date of enactment, October 1, 1982. See also Temp. Regs. §18.1378-1, added by T.D. 7872 (Jan. 26, 1983). See generally Rev. Proc. 83-25, 1983-1 CB 689, for automatic approval of an S corporation's adoption of a fiscal year in cases comparable to the partnership fiscal year rules (i.e., where the corporation's year is the same as over half of its shareholders' year; where income deferral to over half of its shareholders is not more than three months; and when the year is the corporation's "natural business year").

ever, the distributing corporation will be required to recognize gain on the distribution of appreciated property (whether as a dividend-in-kind, in redemption of stock, or in a partial liquidation), as if such property had been sold for its value, new §1363(d).[56.6] If the S corporation has accumulated earnings and profits (either from pre-election years or pre-enactment years), distributions can give rise to dividend income under new §1368(c) if they exceed the S corporation's "accumulated adjustment account" (defined by new §1368(e) as its undistributed net income, which resembles the PTI account rule of present law, infra ¶ 6.08).[56.7]

Undistributed income will increase stock basis, while losses and tax-free distributions will reduce stock basis under new §1367, as is the case under present law. Distributions in excess of stock basis are treated as a sale of the stock under §301(c)(3) under new §1368. Losses reduce stock basis (down to zero), then are applied to debt basis, but unlike present law, losses in excess of stock and debt basis will carry over to future years under new §1366(d)(3) (infra ¶ 6.07). Moreover, unlike present law, debt basis will be restored in the event of subsequent earnings by the S corporation (and such restoration of basis is made prior to restoration of stock basis), see new §1367(b)(2)(B).

In sum, the pass-through, conduit, distribution, and basis rules of the new Subchapter S system are essentially the same as those applicable to partnerships. Moreover, the role of the earnings and profits concept will be virtually eliminated for S corporations under the new rules since an S corporation cannot have current earnings and profits and can only have accumulated earnings if it was a profitable pre-electing corporation. (Existing Subchapter S corporations can have an accumulated earnings account, but this is

---

[56.6] As initially drafted, §1363(d) literally covered *any* distribution of appreciated property (although the committee report exempted distributions in complete liquidation). Section 201(a) of the Technical Corrections Act of 1983 would reduce the scope of the provision, however, by adding new §1363(e), which exempts distributions in complete liquidations and distributions pursuant to a tax-free reorganization. This provision moved to §621(a) of H.R. 4170, the Tax Reform Act of 1984, and passed as §721(a) of the Tax Reform Act of 1984, P.L. No. 98-369, 98 Stat. 678. See also §7701(g), added by the 1984 Act (property transferred subject to nonrecourse debt presumed to have value equal to debt).

[56.7] But §305(d)(2) of the Technical Corrections Act of 1982

ordinarily the exception rather than the general rule.) Thus, the operations under the new system will be considerably simpler for taxpayers and their advisers, which is the principal reason for this legislation.

---

added new §1368(e)(3), allowing an election (by *all* shareholders) to treat distributions as coming first from accumulated earnings and profits.

¶ 6.06.   PASS-THROUGH OF LONG-TERM CAPITAL GAIN

Page 6-25:

Correct second line of text.

Change "it" to "if."

Page 6-26:

Add to note 58.

[58] See also George Buono, 74 TC 187 (1980) (corporate-level sale resulted in pass-through capital gain even though some of shareholders arguably were dealers; corporation's subdivision activity not enough per se to make it a dealer; also, taxpayer satisfied test of Regs. §1.1375-1(d) because gain would have been capital at their level as well; hence, court did not have to decide questionable validity of regulation).

The 1982 rules of new §1366(c) specifically impose a conduit system on S corporations so that the character of each item of corporate income and deduction is determined at the corporate level and that characterization passes through to the shareholders, à la the partnership rules.

Page 6-27:

Add new note 59.1 to end of first full paragraph of text.

[59.1] See Warrensburg Board & Paper Corp., 77 TC 1107 (1981) (§1378 applies to involuntary capital gain transactions, as well as to "planned" sales); Paramount Land Co. v. US, 727 F.2d 322 (4th Cir. 1984).

Page 6-28:

Add new note 61.1 to end of example (1) in text.

[61.1] The ERTA of 1981, P.L. No. 97-34, 95 Stat. 172, reduced the top capital gain rate for noncorporate taxpayers to 20 percent for sales after June 9, 1981 (including sales made by Subchapter S corporations).

Page 6-29:

Correct second and third lines of text.

Change "238,600" to "238,400" in second line, and change "586,400" to "586,600" in third line.

Add to text at end of section.

The 1982 legislation retains the general capital gain pass-through system of present law (including the one-shot election corporate-level tax thereon, now found in §1374), but extends conduit treatment universally to all the corporation's items of income and deduction. Thus, not only will a corporation's capital gains pass through as such to its shareholders, so also will its items of capital loss, short-term capital gain or loss, and §1231 gains and losses.

¶ 6.06A.   CORPORATE TAX ON EXCESS PASSIVE INVESTMENT INCOME—NEW §1375

The passive investment income rules were extensively revised by the 1982 legislation.[63.1] Newly organized corporations, or existing corporations with no accumulated earnings from nonelection years, will no longer be disqualified by reason of excessive receipts of passive income. However, for a corporation with accumulated earnings from years in which it was a regular Subchapter C corporation, a tax will be imposed by new §1375 (at the top §11 rate of 46 percent) on the corporation's passive income in excess of 25 percent of gross receipts. (If such income exceeds 25 percent of gross receipts for three consecutive years, its election terminates, though only prospectively.)

The tax base for purposes of the special 46 percent tax of §1375(a) is "excess net passive income," which is defined by §1375(b) as that portion of the net passive income (i.e., gross passive income less directly connected deductions) that bears the same ratio as gross passive income in excess of 25 percent of gross receipts bears to gross passive income for the year. For example, if the corporation has net passive income of $100, gross passive income of $200, and gross receipts of $400, 50 percent of the net income is taxable (i.e., gross passive income exceeds 25 percent of

---

[63.1] See supra ¶ 6.03, paragraph 5 (this Supplement).

gross receipts by $100, which excess is 50 percent of gross passive income).

Taxable passive income cannot exceed the corporation's taxable income, however, so that if the entire passive income consisted of tax-exempt income, no tax should be payable under §1375 (although the section literally could apply here if the corporation had other §63 taxable income for the year, a result, however, that does not seem to have been contemplated by Congress).

¶ 6.07. PASS-THROUGH OF CORPORATE NET OPERATING LOSS

Page 6-30:

Add to note 67, end of third paragraph.

[67] Accord with *Abdalla* is Sam W. Klein, 75 TC 298 (1980) (NOL taken into account before reductions in basis for liquidating distributions). On appeal, the Tax Court holding in *Abdalla* was affirmed, 647 F.2d 487 (5th Cir. 1981) (Tax Court upheld only because Service did not cross appeal; court would have denied entire NOL here because corporation's year ended after shareholder's year, and stock basis eliminated by §§165, 166 worthlessness loss at end of shareholder's year). The 1982 legislation specifically adopts the *Abdalla* principle that loss pass-throughs and basis adjustments are taken into account before the worthlessness deduction rules of §165(g) apply, see new §1367(b)(3).

Section 201(d) of the Technical Corrections Act of 1983 extends the priority rule of §1367(b)(3) to cover debt losses under §§165(g) and 166(d) (in addition to §165(g) stock worthlessness losses). This provision moved to §621(d) of H.R. 4170, and passed as §721(d) of the Tax Reform Act of 1984, P.L. No. 98-369, 98 Stat. 678.

Add to note 67, fourth paragraph.

[67] Rev. Rul. 80-236, 1980-2 CB 240 (no step-up in stock basis for purported cash contributions to capital which in fact were never made). Rev. Rul. 81-187, 1981-2 CB 167 (no basis step-up by giving unsecured demand note that remained upaid at end of year; must have actual economic outlay to get basis and mere promise to pay is not payment).

Page 6-31:

Add to text after first full paragraph.

The new 1982 amendments retain the general basis limitation for loss pass-through deductibility, new §1366(d)(1), but, in a significant departure from prior law, allow an unlimited carryover for "excess losses" to later years, new §1366(d)(2). This provision comports with the partnership model and allows the shareholder to make use of suspended losses in subsequent years if basis is restored by later profits or additional investment. Moreover, new §1366(d)(3) goes even further by allowing a carryover for deferred losses to a period following the termination of the corporation's Subchapter S status, viz., to its "post-termination transition period," which is defined by new §1377(b) as the longer of one year after termination, the due date for the final S-year return (including extensions), or 120 days after a determination that the corporation's election has terminated. (Such a "determination" is a final court decision, a closing agreement, or an agreement between the IRS and the corporation.) If a shareholder can increase his *stock* basis during this period, the deferred loss will be allowed to that shareholder.

Add to note 70.

[70] The 1982 amendments change existing law and require debt basis restoration (before stock basis) in the event of subsequent profits, new §1367(b)(2)(B).

Page 6-32:

Add to note 71.

[71] For *Abdalla* decision on appeal, see Abdalla v. CIR, supra note 67 (this Supplement) (discussion of relationship between shareholder level deductions under §§165 and 166 and NOL pass-through under §1374 where stock becomes worthless during taxable year).

The 1982 amendments codify the *Abdalla* principle (that loss pass-through deductions and basis adjustments precede the §165 worthlessness deduction), new §1367(b)(3). This provision states that new §§1366 and 1367 shall be applied before the application of §165(g) to any taxable year of the shareholder or the corporation in which the stock becomes worthless. (No mention was made, however, of worthless debt losses under §165 or §166, although a similar ordering rule would seem to be applicable to these losses as well. But §721(d) of the Tax Reform Act of 1984 extended this rule to debt losses under §§165 and 166 as well.)

Add new note 71.1 to end of first full paragraph.

[71.1] Under the 1982 amendments, however, capital losses (long- and short-term) will pass through as such to the shareholders under the general conduit system of new §1366 adopted by these provisions.

Add to note 72, first paragraph.

[72] See generally Dreicer v. US, 665 F.2d 1292 (D.C. Cir. 1981) (§183 does not require reasonable expectation of profit; only need actual profit objective, even though prospect of achieving it seems dim).

¶ 6.08.   DISTRIBUTIONS OF PREVIOUSLY TAXED INCOME

Page 6-33:

Add to note 73.

[73] See Fred G. Bonner, ¶ 79,435 P-H Memo TC (illustration of §316(a)(2) nimble dividend rule—not a PTI distribution because post-distribution current earnings turned distribution into real dividend).

Page 6-34:

Add to note 77.

[77] See generally Rev. Rul. 79-52, 1979-1 CB 283 (merger of brother-sister Subchapter S corporations having same shareholders; right to make previously taxed income (PTI) distributions carries over to surviving corporation).

Page 6-36:

Add to note 82, first paragraph.

[82] Compare Rev. Rul. 80-154, 1980-1 CB 68 (cash dividend linked to reinvestment as payment for additional stock treated as non-taxable stock dividend under §305(a)).

Page 6-37:

Add to note 84.

[84] E.B. Grain Co., 81 TC 70 (1983) (§7503 extends seventy-five day rule when last day falls on nonbusiness day); contra, Rev. Rul. 83-116, 1983-32 IRB 21. See Rev. Rul. 79-52, 1979-1 CB 283 (surviving corporation in merger of brother-sister Subchapter S corporations can make PTI distribution within seventy-five days of close of merged corporation's taxable year).

Add to text at end of section.

The 1982 amendments generally abandon the PTI system of former law in favor of a more simplified approach based on the partnership model.[84.1] As a general rule, all distributions (whether of money or property) will be treated as §§ 301(c)(2) and 301 (c)(3) distributions, viz., return of capital transactions under new §1368(b). If an S corporation has *accumulated* earnings and profits (it can never have *current* earnings under the new rules, see §1371(c)(1)), then distributions will continue to be treated as capital transactions to the extent of the corporation's "accumulated adjustment account," as defined in §1368(e) (viz., its undistributed net taxable income). This latter concept resembles the PTI account of present law and consists generally of the shareholder's ratable share of undistributed net taxable income (calculated in a manner similar to the shareholder's basis adjustment computations). Distributions in excess of this account will be taxable as dividends, to the extent of any accumulated earnings, and distributions in excess of accumulated earnings switch back into capital transaction treatment, new §1368(c).[84.2] The PTI-type account is transferable during S corporation years, and even survives termination of S corporation status (generally for at least one year), so that tax-free cash (only) distributions can be made after termination during this grace period, see new §§1371(e) and 1377(b).

For newly created S corporations (viz., those organized after 1982), new §1368 will provide for stock basis recovery treatment for all distributions by S corporations, since they cannot generate current earnings by virtue of new §1371(c)(1). Moreover, new §1368(d) provides an ordering rule in the case of distributions, which applies the pass-through and stock basis adjustment provisions of §§1366 and 1367 before consideration of the distribution rules. Thus, if a corporation has losses during the same year as it makes a distribution, the loss pass-through rules are applied before the distribution rules, so that the full loss (to the extent of stock basis) could be availed of before the distribution is applied against that stock basis.

[84.1] Distributions of appreciated property result in a deemed corporate-level sale, however, under §1363(d); new §1363(e) (in §721(a) of the Tax Reform Act of 1984) narrowed the present scope of §1363(d) by exempting distributions in complete liquidation and distributions pursuant to a reorganization that are tax-free at the shareholder level.

[84.2] New §1368(e)(3), added by §305(d)(2) of the Technical Corrections Act of 1982, allows an election, by *all* shareholders, to treat distributions as first coming from accumulated earnings and profits.

The ability to make tax-free distributions even survives termination of S corporation status, so that *cash* (though not property) can be distributed on a nontaxable basis (to the extent of the corporation's accumulated adjustments account) during the post-termination transition period of §1377(b) (which is at least one year, and can be even longer).

The PTI rules of former law do have continuing application, however, by virtue of new §1379(c), which provides that post-1982 distributions from pre-1983 undistributed taxable income can continue to qualify for nondividend treatment under former §§1375(d) and 1375(f). (These rules presumably apply *after* the distribution has exhausted its tax-free sources under new §1368, and should also apply to property distributions as well as cash).[84.3]

[84.3] See generally Ellett & Tull, Previously Taxed Income and the New S Corporation, 61 Taxes 569 (1983).

¶ 6.09.   RELATION OF OTHER CORPORATE PROVISIONS TO SUBCHAPTER S

Page 6-37:

Add to note 85.

[85] The 1982 amendments specifically provide that Subchapter C applies to Subchapter S corporations and their shareholders except where otherwise provided, or except where such treatment would be inconsistent with the S corporation rules. The amendments also state that an S corporation shareholder of a C corporation is to be treated like an individual shareholder. See new §1371(a).

Add new note 85.1 to end of third sentence.

[85.1] Under the 1982 amendments, operations in S corporation years will not generate *current* earnings and profits (and hence cannot augment any existing accumulated earnings of the S corporation), new §1371(c)(1). Accumulated earnings of an S corporation can be reduced in S corporation years only by dividends from accumulated earnings (viz., distributions in excess of the corporation's accumulated adjustment account, a PTI-type account), new §1371(c)(3). Thus, earnings and profits will play a very minor role under the new system.

Add new note 85.2 to end of fourth sentence.

[85.2] Under the 1982 amendments, distributions of appreciated property (whether as a dividend, redemption, or partial liquidation distribution) will be taxable to the distributing corporation as if such property had been sold at its value, new §1363(d). This provision does not apply to complete liquidation distributions, however. Moreover, proposed §1363(e) (in §201(a) of the Technical Corrections Act of 1983) would also exempt distributions pursuant to a reorganization that is tax-free at the shareholder level. This provision passed as §721 of the Tax Reform Act of 1984.

Page 6-38:
Add to note 88.

⁸⁸ But the Installment Sales Revision Act of 1980 extended §453 benefits to §337 liquidation sales in new §453(h).

¶ 6.10.   ADVANTAGES OF SUBCHAPTER S ELECTION
Page 6-41:
Add new note 93 at end of last complete sentence of text.

⁹³ But the unreasonable compensation issue is not totally avoided by use of a Subchapter S corporation since the maximum tax stakes of §1348 are still present if the compensation is held to be excessive and treated as a dividend to the shareholder employee; see Gary N. Cromer, ¶ 80,263 P-H Memo TC.

But the top marginal rate on *all* income will be 50 percent (in 1982) as a result of the ERTA of 1981, P.L. No. 97-34, 95 Stat. 172, which should eliminate this problem.

Page 6-42:
Add new ¶ 6.11.

¶ 6.11.   LEGISLATIVE CHANGES TO SUBCHAPTER S

In June 1979, significant changes in the Subchapter S provisions were submitted in tentative draft form by the Staff of the Joint Committee, the general thrust of which would simplify the operation of Subchapter S and conform these provisions more closely to the partnership rules. These tentative draft proposals were expanded and reissued on April 30, 1980 as Staff Recommendations for Simplification of the Rules Relating to Subchapter S Corporations, found in Volume 10 of 1980 CCH Fed. Tax. Rep. at ¶ 6165.⁹⁴

⁹⁴ See Kadens, Proposed Subchapter S Amendments—A Boon to Private Investment Corporations, 58 Taxes 379 (1980); Chang, Recommendations for Restructure of Tax Rules Relating to Subchapter

The principal features of the draft proposal were:

(1) The passive investment income and foreign-source income limitations would be eliminated.

(2) The one-class-of-stock requirement would be modified to permit differences in voting rights of common stock and to allow use of certain limited-interest debt obligations, which in substance constitute equity capital.

(3) The rules on election terminations would be changed to deny a new shareholder the power to terminate the election, and to allow revocations by shareholders owning only 80 percent of the stock. Moreover, if an election is terminated, the termination generally will be effective as of the date of the event that caused the termination.

(4) The character of the corporation's various items of income, deductions, and credits would pass through to shareholders in the same manner as for partnerships (and such items would be allocated on a daily basis).

(5) Shareholders would be entitled to carry over unusable losses until such time as stock basis is increased, thus conforming the treatment of Subchapter S shareholders to that of partners in a partnership.

(6) The distribution rules of §1375 would be changed in several important respects, viz., property distributions (at fair market value) would be allowed, and all distributions, regardless of when made, would be applied against stock basis (with the excess taxable as capital gain, unless §341 applied). If the corporation has pre-election accumulated earnings, distributions nevertheless would be tax-free to the extent of PTI (and PTI accounts could be transferred to new shareholders as well). Moreover, the new distribution rules would continue to apply for at least one year after the election is terminated.

On the other hand, gain would be recognized to the distributing corporation upon any nonliquidating distributions of inventory and "investment" type property, while gains on the sale, redemption, or other disposition

S: A Comparative Summary, 34 Tax L. Rev. 403 (1981); Chase & Masjen, What Is Happening to Subchapter S Corporations, 39 NYU Inst. on Fed. Tax. Ch. 2 (1981).

of debt obligations would be recaptured as ordinary income to the extent losses had been passed through and used to reduce basis of the obligations.

(7) The treatment for pension plans and fringe benefits of Subchapter S shareholder-employees would be conformed to the rules applicable to partner-employees.

(8) Finally, a Subchapter S corporation's taxable year would generally be conformed to that of its shareholders (similarly to the partnership rules).

The likelihood that some, if not all, of these proposals would be enacted seemed higher than usual in view of their relatively noncontroversial nature. The trend toward conformity of the Subchapter S rules with those applicable to partnerships had been obvious for the last decade. Moreover, simplification of the Subchapter S provisions was a task whose time was long overdue.

On April 1, 1982, legislation was introduced jointly in the House (H.R. 6055) and the Senate (S. 2350) entitled the Subchapter S Revision Act of 1982. To a large extent, these proposals followed the 1980 Staff Recommendations described above, and were to be effective for years beginning in 1983. They were accepted by the House Ways and Means Subcommittee on Select Revenue Measures in July 1982, and became law on October 21, 1982 as the Subchapter S Revision Act of 1982.[95]

The principal changes in the final legislation from the 1980 Staff version are:

(1) A limited retention of the excess passive income limitation for corporations having accumulated earnings at the close of the year (for three consecutive years).

(2) A special corporate-level tax of 46 percent on excess passive investment income.

(3) Revocations need only majority vote, rather than 80 percent.

(4) S corporations would recognize gain on a nonliquidating distribution of any appreciated property, and the ordinary income recapture rule on debt obligations was dropped.

---

[95] P.L. No. 97-354, 96 Stat. 1669.

(5) The number of permissible shareholders was raised to thirty-five, and various corporations were made ineligible for Subchapter S treatment.

(6) Debt basis will be restored by subsequent corporate earnings, and such restoration is made before stock basis is increased.

(7) The concept of earnings and profits is virtually eliminated for Subchapter S corporations.

These provisions are reflected in the annotations at the appropriate points of this chapter. Enactment of the new 1982 legislation materially alters the tax structure and stakes for Subchapter S corporations and should substantially increase the importance and utility of these provisions.[96]

---

[96] For analyses of these provisions, see Coven & Hess, The Subchapter S Revision Act of 1982; An Analysis and Appraisal, 50 Tenn. L. Rev. 569 (1983); Kanter, To Elect or Not to Elect Subchapter S— That Is a Question, 60 Taxes 882 (1982); Shaw & August, An Analysis of the Subchapter S Revision Act: Eligibility, Election, Termination, 58 J. Tax. 2 (1983); Shaw & August, Subchapter S Revision Act Makes Significant Changes in Taxing S Corporation Operations, 58 J. Tax. 84 (1983); Huffaker & Doering, Opportunities and Problems With Sub S Holdings of Estates and Trusts, 58 J. Tax. 130 (1983); Lang, Subchapter S Revision Act of 1982: Dealing With Transition Rules, 60 Taxes 928 (1982); Shaw & August, Subchapter S Revision Act: Distributions, Taxable Years, and Other Changes, 58 J. Tax. 300 (1983); Ginsburg, Subchapter S and Accumulated Earnings and Profits: A Different View, Tax Notes, Nov. 22, 1982; Katz, Subchapter S: A Step Toward Sanity, 10 J. Corp. Tax. 118 (1983); Newman & Lang, The Subchapter S Revision Act of 1982, 37 Tax Law. 93 (1983); Eustice, Subchapter S Corporations and Partnerships: A Search for the Pass-Through Paradigm, 39 Tax L. Rev. 345 (1984).

Chapter 7

DIVIDENDS AND
OTHER NONLIQUIDATING
DISTRIBUTIONS

PART A. DISTRIBUTIONS IN CASH

¶ 7.01. INTRODUCTORY

Page 7-4:

Add to note 6.

⁶ But the Staff of the Senate Finance Committee, in a preliminary report submitted on September 22, 1983, proposed to repeal the earnings and profits limitation (or, if this approach was felt to be too far-reaching, alternative restrictions on the earnings and profits computation rules were recommended, e.g., to deal with §312(a)(2), §312(e), timing mismatches, and the measure of earnings and profits primarily by taxable income concepts).

Recent legislation adopted the latter approach, choosing to refine the earnings and profits concept more closely to "economic" earnings. The Tax Reform Act of 1984, P.L. No. 98-369, §61(a), 98 Stat. 678; infra ¶ 7.03 (this Supplement).

¶ 7.02. "DIVIDEND": A TERM OF ART

Page 7-5:

Add to note 7, second paragraph.

⁷ See Ltr. Rul. 8022010, 1980 P-H Fed. Taxes ¶ 55,134 (distribution by corporation of dividend to partnership in which distributing corporation was a partner did not result in gross income to corporate-partner where partnership distributed its pro rata share of the dividend receipt; corporation merely reacquired an allocable portion of its own cash).

Page 7-7:

Add to note 10.

[10] See also Falkoff v. US, 604 F.2d 1045 (7th Cir. 1979).

Page 7-8:

Add new note 10.1 at end of runover sentence.

[10.1] But see Rufus K. Cox, 78 TC 1021 (1982), holding that §301(c)(3) "gain" did not constitute a "sale" so as to allow installment reporting of that gain under the pre-1980 version of §453 (which required a casual "sale" of property; query the 1980 version, which merely speaks of a "disposition").

Add to note 11, second paragraph.

[11] See Zukerman, Note, Aggregation of Bases Under Sections 301(c)(2) and (3), 33 Tax. Law. 937 (1980).

Page 7-10:

Add to note 15, following Anderson citation.

[15] The full citation to the *Anderson* per curiam affirmance is 583 F.2d 953 (7th Cir. 1978).

Page 7-11:

Add to note 17, first paragraph.

[17] Contra to *Steel Improvement* is Rev. Rul. 69-447, 1969-2 CB 153.

Add to note 17, second paragraph.

[17] Rev. Rul. 74-164 (part (b)) does not specifically hold that the ending deficit is $60,000, although this conclusion seems the only sensible result in that situation.

¶ 7.03. EARNINGS AND PROFITS

Page 7-12:

Add to note 18, first paragraph.

[18] But the Staff of the Senate Finance Committee, in a preliminary report submitted on September 22, 1983, proposed to repeal (or substantially restrict) the earnings and profits rules of present law.

Instead, §61(a) of the Tax Reform Act of 1984 adds new §312(n), which restricts the computation of earnings and profits "to more accurately reflect economic gain or loss"; infra annotations to this section and ¶ 7.04 (this Supplement).

Add to note 18, second paragraph, following Rev. Proc. 72-9 citation.

[18] Rev. Proc. 72-9 has been superseded by Rev. Proc. 84-22, 1984-1 CB 449.

Page 7-18:

Add to note 35, following Meyer.

[35] But §5(f) of H.R. 5043, the Bankruptcy Tax Act of 1980, proposed new §312(1), excluding debt cancellation income from earnings only to the extent such cancelled debt gain applied to reduce basis under §1017; the Senate Finance Committee amended §5(f) to provide further that any deficit in earnings would be reduced by the capital account of shareholders whose interests are eliminated in a bankruptcy proceeding. This version of the bill ultimately passed in December 1980.

Page 7-20:

Add to note 42.

[42] See also Rev. Rul. 79-20, 1979-1 CB 137 (each corporate member of a partnership must make the §312(k) adjustment).

Add new note 42.1 to end of last line of text.

[42.1] In order to take account of the new accelerated cost recovery system established by the Economic Recovery Tax Act (ERTA) of 1981, P.L. No. 97-34, 95 Stat. 172, §312(k)(3) provides for a special stretched-out straight-line amortization schedule for the five categories of recovery property covered by the new Act; thus, three-year recovery property must be depreciated for earnings and profits purposes over a five-year period, five-year property over twelve years, ten-year property over twenty-five years, fifteen-year real property over thirty-five years, and fifteen-year public utility property over thirty-five years. These provisions are effective for property placed in service in 1981.

The Deficit Reduction Act of 1984, H.R. 2163, in §47(b) proposed to raise the §312(k)(3) term for real estate to 40 years, and this proposal passed in §61(b) of the Tax Reform Act of 1984, P.L. No. 98-369, 98 Stat. 678.

Page 7-23:

Add to note 53, following Gross *citation.*

[53] 236 F.2d 612 (2d Cir. 1954). For a recent illustration of the successful use of the mortgaging-out technique to pay tax-free dividends, see Falkoff v. US, 604 F.2d 1045 (7th Cir. 1979).

The Staff of the Senate Finance Committee, in a preliminary report submitted on September 22, 1983, proposed either to repeal outright the earnings and profits limitation, or at least restrict it to prevent results like the *Falkoff* decision. But legislation, discussed infra (this Supplement), contains no such provision.

Add to text at end of section.

Legislation approved by the Senate Finance Committee,[53.1] and ultimately passed in 1984, modified the computation of earnings and profits to more accurately reflect "economic" again or loss. Thus, the corporation's taxable income now must be adjusted for earnings and profits purposes to require:

(a) Capitalization of otherwise deductible construction period interest, taxes, and carrying charges in the basis of the related property;

(b) Capitalization of intangible drilling expenses, with a five-year write-off;

(c) Capitalization of the deductions allowed by §§173, 177, and 248 (i.e., circulation expenses, trademark and trade name expenditures, and organization expenditures);

(d) Increase of earnings by the amount of gain not recognized under §311 on the distribution of appreciated property, a rare event after 1984 (infra ¶ 7.21);

(e) Increase or decrease of earnings by changes in the last in, first out inventory recapture account;

(f) Full current reporting of installment sale gains;

(g) Reporting of long-term contracts on the percentage of completion basis; and

(h) Reduction of earnings by redemption distributions only to the extent of the redeemed stock's "ratable share" of such earnings (infra ¶ 9.65).

The new earnings and profits rules of §312(n) do not apply, however, in computing the *amount* of the taxable dividend income to a 20 percent corporate shareholder (and its adjusted basis in the stock of the distributing corporation) by virtue of §301(f)(1),

---

[53.1] The Deficit Reduction Act of 1984, H.R. 2163, §47(a), adding new §312(n) to the Code, which passed as §61(a) of the Tax Reform Act of 1984.

which provision was added in Conference.[53.2] This rule does not affect the computation of either the distributing corporation's or the distributee-shareholder's earnings and profits; rather, it only affects the amount of taxable dividend income to the corporate shareholder.[53.3]

[53.2] Tax Reform Act of 1984, P.L. No. 98-369, §61(d), 98 Stat. 678. See generally Eustice, The Tax Reform Act of 1984, ¶ 3.02[2][b].

[53.3] For explanation of the purpose of this special rule, see H.R. Rep. No. 98-861, 98th Cong., 2d Sess., p. 842 (1984).

¶ 7.04. TAX ACCOUNTING PRINCIPLES IN COMPUTING EARNINGS AND PROFITS AND DIVIDEND INCOME

Page 7-24:

Add to note 54, second paragraph.

[54] See also Rev. Rul. 79-68, 1979-1 CB 133 (no earnings adjustment for advance receipts of an accrual basis corporation that are properly deferrable); Rev. Rul. 79-69, 1979-1 CB 134 (cash-basis corporation charges earnings for estimated taxes paid regardless of ultimate tax liability—adjust in later year to reflect true tax).

Add to text after sentence ending with note 54.

Recent legislation approved by the Senate Finance Committee,[54.1] and ultimately passed in 1984, modified several of the above accounting rules in the computation of earnings and profits in order to more accurately reflect economic gain or loss. Thus, new §312(n) now requires:

(a) Capitalization of construction period carrying charges, §312(n)(1);

(b) Capitalization (and write-off over five years) of intangible drilling costs, §312(n)(2);

(c) Capitalization of the deductions allowed by §§173, 177, and 248, §312(n)(3);

[54.1] The Deficit Reduction Act of 1984, H.R. 2163, §47(a), adding new §312(n), which passed as §61(a) of the Tax Reform Act of 1984. See supra ¶ 7.03 (this Supplement).

    (d) Adjustments reflecting changes in the last in, first out inventory accounts, §312(n)(5);

    (e) No use of §453, §312(n)(6); and

    (f) Mandatory percentage of completion accounting for long-term contracts, §312(n)(7).

Page 7-26:

Add to note 59, end of first paragraph.

[59] Bush Bros. & Co., 73 TC 424 (1979), aff'd, 668 F.2d 252 (6th Cir. 1982) (no constructive receipt on facts; shareholders did not have unqualified rights to distribution on earlier asserted date).

¶ 7.05. CONSTRUCTIVE DISTRIBUTIONS

Page 7-30:

Add to note 71.

[71] But see White Tool & Mach. Co., ¶ 80,443 P-H Memo TC, aff'd, 677 F.2d 528 (6th Cir. 1982) (no constructive dividend to shareholders of brother-sister corporations where excessive rental payments reallocated under §482; no direct economic benefit to shareholders from payments, and §482 adequately corrected any tax distortion).

But see Stinnett's Pontiac Serv., Inc. v. CIR, 730 F.2d 634 (11th Cir. 1984) (advances between brother-sister corporations held to be equity and resulted in constructive dividend fall-out to controlling shareholder per *Sammons*).

Add to note 72.

[72] Accord with *Sammons* is Stinnett's Pontiac Serv., Inc. v. CIR, supra note 71 (this Supplement).

Add to note 73.

[73] See also Stinnett's Pontiac Serv., Inc. v. CIR, supra note 71 (this Supplement).

Page 7-31:

Add to note 74.

[74] Gilbert L. Gilbert, 74 TC 60 (1980) (transfer of funds by brother corporation to sister corporation not true "loan"; funds were used by sister to redeem part of its stock so that controlling shareholder ended up as 100 percent owner after redemption; held constructive dividend to controlling shareholder).

See also Regs. §1.385-7(e), Ex. (5) (brother-sister loans that are reclassified as equity under §385 principles are deemed a constructive dividend from "lender" to shareholder and a capital contribution by shareholder to "borrower"); new Prop. Regs. §1.385-7(e), Ex. (5) (same). See also PLR 8207010, Vol. 9, 1982 P-H Fed. Tax Serv. ¶ 54,827 (lateral advances not certifiable as loans result in triangular constructive dividend fall-out to parent). But the §385 regulations were withdrawn on July 6, 1983; T.D. 7920, Nov. 2, 1983.

Page 7-32:

Add to note 75, end of runover paragraph.

[75] See Alterman Foods, Inc. v. US, 1979-1 USTC ¶ 9175 (Ct. Cl. Tr. Div. 1979) (parent's withdrawals from 100 percent subsidiary were dividends; not true debt), aff'd per curiam, 611 F.2d 866 (Ct. Cl. 1980).

Add to note 76, second paragraph.

[76] But see PLR 8114004, 1981 P-H Fed. Taxes ¶ 55,200 (no dividend on cancellation because original withdrawals were not true loans; dividend occurred on earlier receipt of funds).

Page 7-33:

Add to note 79, first paragraph.

[79] See also Jos. Creel, 72 TC 1173 (1979); compare Falkoff v. US, 604 F.2d 1045 (7th Cir. 1979).

Add to note 79, second paragraph.

[79] See also Dolese v. US, 605 F.2d 1146 (10th Cir. 1979) (payment of costs of shareholder divorce litigation partly personal, and hence a dividend, and partly for corporate business purpose); Tennessee Sec., Inc. v. CIR, 674 F.2d 570 (6th Cir. 1982) (corporation's payment of shareholders' personal guaranty liability held constructive dividend to shareholder-guarantors).

Page 7-34:

Add to note 82, second paragraph.

[82] Rev. Rul. 79-9 is analyzed by Davis & McGill, Corporate Charitable Contributions and the Constructive Dividend Problem, 8 J. Corp. Tax. 323 (1982).

Page 7-35:

Add to end of note 84.

[84] Howard Johnson, 74 TC 1316 (1980) (corporate payment of premium on split-dollar life insurance policies held by trust for benefit

of taxpayer-shareholder's family held constructive dividend to tax-payer).

Add to note 86, second paragraph.

[86] See Bank of America v. US, 1979-1 USTC ¶ 9170 (N.D. Cal. 1978) (bargain sale dividend to corporate shareholder did not permit IRS to impute full sale price to distributing corporation under §482). On remand, Baumer v. US, 518 F. Supp. 813 (N.D. Ga. 1981) (option dividend held taxable at grant because value ascertainable, but tax-payer won because that year not before the court). On appeal, *Baumer* was reversed on the valuation point, 685 F.2d 1318 (11th Cir. 1982) (option had no ascertainable value at grant, so value at date of exercise). See also Ruddick Corp. v. US, 643 F.2d 747 (Ct. Cl. 1981); compare Richard H. Foster, 80 TC 34 (1983); infra note 140 (this Supplement).

Page 7-36:

Add to note 88, end of second paragraph.

[88] See generally Jassy, Dividend Treatment of Distributions of Options to Acquire Assets of the Distributing Corporation, 34 Tax L. Rev. 607 (1979); Gann, Taxation of Stock Rights and Other Options: Another Look at the Persistence of *Palmer v. Commissioner,* 1979 Duke L.J. 911. See also Baumer v. US, 685 F.2d 1318 (11th Cir. 1982) (option had no ascertainable value at grant, so value at date of exer-cise).

Page 7-37:

Add to note 91, second paragraph.

[91] But see Gerald R. Redding, 71 TC 597 (1979) (distribution of controlled subsidiary via a transferable short-term rights offering held valid §355 transaction; *Palmer* lives if §355 applies). On appeal, *Redding* was reversed, 630 F.2d 1169 (7th Cir. 1980), holding that *Palmer* was overruled by the 1954 Code (if a spread existed at the date of the distribution, theory of Rev. Rul. 70-521 followed).

Page 7-38:

Add to note 93, end of first full paragraph.

[93] See Loftin & Woodward, Inc. v. US, 577 F.2d 1206 (5th Cir. 1978) (use of value as measure of constructive distribution the general and preferred rule; only use cost where no evidence of value and where use of value would be inappropriate). See also Ireland v. US, 621 F.2d 731 (5th Cir. 1980) (measure amount of dividend to shareholder from personal use of company plane by value of private charter fare, not cost of operating plane or value of commercial fare).

Add to note 94, end of first sentence.

⁹⁴ See Rev. Rul. 79-50, 1979-1 CB 138 (if insured is principal shareholder, amount of benefit is constructive dividend). See also Herman Greenspun, 72 TC 931 (1979), aff'd, 670 F.2d 123 (9th Cir. 1982), Max Zager, 72 TC 1009 (1979), and Jos. Creel, 72 TC 1173 (1979), *aff'd per cur.,* 649 F.2d 1133 (5th Cir. 1981), for recent applications of *J. Simpson Dean* principle. For additional *Dean* cases finding no income to the borrower from an interest-free loan, see Jack Baker, 75 TC 166 (1980), aff'd, 677 F.2d 11 (2d Cir. 1982); Suttle v. CIR, 625 F.2d 1127 (4th Cir. 1980). But contra to *Dean* is Hardee v. US, 1982-2 USTC 9459 (Ct. Cl. Tr. Div. 1982). But *Hardee* was reversed, 708 F.2d 661 (Fed. Cir. 1983) (*Dean* followed; exemption a rule of law changeable only by Congress; moreover, use of borrowed funds held irrelevant to finding of no income).

Add to note 94, end of last sentence.

⁹⁴ Contra to *Crown* is Dickman v. US, 104 S. Ct. 1086 (1984) (taxable gift on interest-free demand loan equal to value of use of funds during term of use). For recent legislation, see infra note 94.1 (this Supplement).

Add to text after sentence ending with note 94.

Recent legislation⁹⁴·¹ overruled *Dean* and now imputes an interest element (and a concomitant dividend, compensation, or gift element, as the case may be) in below-market-interest-rate loan transactions. In the corporate-shareholder context, an interest-free (or below-market rate) loan by a corporation to its shareholders will result in the following tax consequences: imputed interest income to the lender and a correlative deduction to the borrower (based on statutorily prescribed rates); and taxable dividend income to the borrower equal to the spread between the principal amount of a term loan and the present value of such amount (compounded semiannually using designated market rates), or the

---

⁹⁴·¹ See supra new ¶ 4.23 (this Supplement). The Tax Reform Act of 1984, H.R. 4170, §162, adding new §7872; the Deficit Reduction Act of 1984, H.R. 2163, §176, adding new §§7872 (gift loans) and 7873 (other low-interest-rate loans); the Tax Reform Act of 1984, P.L. No. 98-369, 98 Stat. 678, §172 (adding new §7872 to cover both types of low-rate loans). See Eustice, The Tax Reform Act of 1984, ¶ 2.02[3].

amount of the annually imputed interest in the case of demand loans.[94.2]

[94.2] For example: A ten-year term loan without interest by X Corporation to its shareholder A would result in original-issue discount treatment to X and A (accruable ratably over the ten-year term by X and A, supra new ¶ 4.23 (this Supplement), but A's current dividend would be the full amount of such discount. A demand loan, by contrast, would result in annual dividend income to A equal to his imputed interest deduction.

Page 7-39:

Add to note 95, following Goldstein *citation.*

[95] But see E.W. Stuchell, ¶ 78,236 P-H Memo TC (1978) (arm's-length purchase price for long-term contract between corporation and shareholders not constructive distribution; not necessary to determine values each year where initial terms fair).

Add to note 97.

[97] Tulia Feedlot, Inc. v. US, 1983-2 USTC 9516 (Cl. Ct. 1983) (deductibility of fees for later years upheld where amount of fees was reasonable, fees were ordinary and necessary in the taxpayer's business, and were not proportional to stock holdings).

Page 7-40:

Add to note 97, end of runover paragraph.

[97] See also Olton Feed Yard, Inc. v. US, 592 F.2d 272 (5th Cir. 1979) (guaranty fee paid to shareholder-guarantor of corporate debt held constructive dividend; fee not necessary, even though reasonable).

Add to note 98.

[98] But see Elliots, Inc. v. CIR, 716 F.2d 1241 (9th Cir. 1983) (*McCandless* automatic dividend rule rejected; test for deductibility of shareholder compensation is reasonableness, and payee's sole shareholder statutes not determinative; also, fact that no dividends paid not fatal; reasonableness focus is from view of an independent investor, i.e., would he compensate this employee in this amount, somewhat on the order of the §482 arm's-length test).

¶ 7.06. DIVIDENDS-RECEIVED EXCLUSION AND CREDIT FOR INDIVIDUALS

Page 7-43:

Add to text at end of section.

Under an amendment to §305 by the ERTA of 1981, P.L. No. 97-34, 95 Stat. 172, new §305(e) allows a $750 annual exclusion ($1,500 on a joint return) for distributions pursuant to dividend reinvestment plans of certain public utilities. The exclusion applies for distributions after 1981 and terminates for distributions after 1985. See infra ¶ 7.62, note 205 (this Supplement). Proposed legislation would have terminated this provision at the end of 1982, however, but this provision was dropped in Conference. But the Senate in §185 of the Deficit Reduction Act of 1984, H.R. 2163, proposed to repeal §305(e) for distributions after 1984; however, no comparable provision existed in the House version of the 1984 tax bill, H.R. 4170, the Tax Reform Act of 1984, and the Conference version of the final Act did not accept the Senate proposal.

¶ 7.07. ASSIGNMENT OF DIVIDEND INCOME AND RELATED PROBLEMS

Page 7-43:

Correct second line of note 105.

[105] Citation should be "17 Tax L. Rev.," not "Reg."

Page 7-44:

Add to note 107 (first paragraph).

[107] See Silco, Inc. v. US, 591 F. Supp. 480 (N.D. Tex. 1984) (owner on record date the taxable person on the dividend).

Add to note 108 (first paragraph).

[108] But see Blake v. CIR, 697 F.2d 473 (2d Cir. 1982) (gift of stock to charity, followed by expected sale and use of proceeds to buy donor's yacht at inflated price—held, donor taxable on stock sale proceeds and §170 contribution of yacht; court distinguished *Grove* and backed off from *Palmer* and Rev. Rul. 78-197).

Add to note 109.

[109] Accord with *Jones* is Dayton Hydraulic Co. v. US, 592 F.2d 937 (6th Cir. 1979) (liquidation too far advanced to shift tax burden; assets had been sold by corporation).

Correct last line of text.

Code citation should be "§691," not "§161."

Page 7-45:

Add to note 113.

[113] See generally Boozman, Note, Income and Gift Tax Treatment of a Waiver of Rights to Future Undeclared Dividends by a Corporate Shareholder, 32 Vand. L. Rev. 889 (1979).

Page 7-46:

Add to note 116.

[116] See also Rev. Rul. 82-11, 1982-1 CB 51 (sale after record date but before payment and ex-dividend dates; held part of selling price allocable to accrued dividend rights and taxed as dividend substitute (with §243 deduction)). Accord, Silco, Inc. v. US, supra note 107 (this Supplement).

Page 7-47:

Add to note 118.

[118] See also Rev. Rul. 82-11, supra note 116 (this Supplement) and Silco, Inc. v. US, supra note 107 (this Supplement).

Add to note 119.

[119] Rev. Rul. 82-11, supra note 116 (this Supplement) holds that seller of dividend rights gets the §243 deduction while buyer has tax-free capital recovery of dividend distribution); accord, Silco, Inc. v. US, supra note 107 (this Supplement).

Compare §1232B, added by the Tax Equity and Fiscal Responsibility Act (TEFRA) of 1982, P.L. No. 97-248, 96 Stat. 324, subjecting "stripped bonds" (i.e., bonds with separation of ownership between the bond and future interest coupons) to the original-issue discount rules of §1232A (economic accrual); now found in §1286 after the Tax Reform Act of 1984 restructuring of the OID rules (no change occurred in the stripped bond rules, however).

Page 7-48:

Add to note 121, first paragraph.

[121] *Waterman* is a Fifth Circuit decision.

Page 7-49:

Add to note 122, first paragraph.

[122] *TSN Liquidating* was reversed on appeal, 624 F.2d 1328 (5th Cir. 1980) (threshold dividend taxable as such to seller despite subsequent reinvestment by buyer; mere infusion of assets into purchased corporation after its acquisition not enough per se to invoke *Waterman* principle).

But see Blake v. CIR, supra note 108 (this Supplement) (court applied step doctrine approach of *Basic, Inc.* case to tax donor on proceeds of donated stock used to buy other property from donor at inflated price; transactions linked by parties' "understandings").

Add to text at end of section.

For recent legislation restricting the §243 deduction in the case of leveraged "portfolio" stock investments and requiring a reduction in a corporate shareholder's stock basis for the untaxed portion of extraordinary dividends on stock held one year or less, see supra ¶ 5.06 (this Supplement).[122.1]

[122.1] The leveraged investment limitation does not apply to cases where the corporate shareholder has, or obtains, 50 percent control, or to cases where the dividend qualifies for the 100 percent dividends-received deduction (i.e., a parent-subsidiary relationship).

The basis reduction rule does not apply where the corporate recipient of the extraordinary dividend holds the underlying stock for more than one year.

PART B.   DISTRIBUTIONS IN KIND

¶ 7.20.   INTRODUCTORY

Page 7-50:

Add to text at end of section.

As discussed in ¶ 7.21, however, corporate-level nonrecognition treatment on the distribution of appreciated property has been steadily eroding since the 1954 Code (commencing in 1962 with the passage of §1245); and recent legislative enactments would virtually eliminate corporate-level tax-free treatment for such distributions.[124.1]

[124.1] The Tax Reform Act of 1984, H.R. 4170, §54(a); the Deficit Reduction Act of 1984, H.R. 2163, §36(a); the Tax Reform Act of 1984, P.L. No. 98-369, §54(a), 98 Stat. 678.

¶ 7.21. CORPORATE INCOME OR LOSS ON DISTRIBUTION OF PROPERTY

Page 7-54:

Add to note 137.

[137] See also Hillsboro Nat'l Bank, 73 TC 61 (1979) (corporation deducted tax paid on behalf of its shareholders; tax recovered by shareholders and corporation held taxable under tax benefit doctrine), aff'd, 641 F.2d 529 (7th Cir. 1981); reversed, 460 US 370 (1983). The majority opinion (five Justices), formulated the test for tax benefit includability as whether the later event was "fundamentally inconsistent" with allowance of the prior deduction; that is, if the event had occurred in the same year, no deduction would be allowed. The majority held that §164(e) prevented includability here; two concurring Justices would only apply the inclusion rule to an actual recovery, and none occurred here. One dissent thought that inclusion was required under the majority's fundamental inconsistency test, and the other dissenter argued that the proper adjustment mechanism was denial of the prior deduction (where the statute had not yet run when the adjustment event occurred).

Page 7-55:

Add to note 139, end of second paragraph.

[139] Bush Bros. & Co., 73 TC 424 (1979) (corporation taxed because tax avoidance, no business purpose, expected shareholder sale, and corporate influence; multiple distributions over period of years; four dissents thought *Hines* controlled).

See Loengard and Cobb, Who Sold the Bush Brothers' Beans?: The Commissioner's Power to Ignore the Transfer of an Asset Prior to Sale, 35 Tax L. Rev. 509 (1980).

Bush Bros. & Co. was affirmed, 668 F.2d 252 (6th Cir. 1982) (on basis of concurring opinion that corporation actively participated in shareholder-level resale transaction).

Add to note 140, end of second paragraph.

[140] Compare Bush Bros. & Co., supra note 139 (this Supplement).

Add to note 140, third paragraph.

[140] But see Bank of America v. US, 1979-1 USTC ¶ 9170 (N.D. Cal. 1978) (IRS attempt to use §482 to impute full selling price for bargain sale dividend distribution to corporate parent rejected; §311(a) protected distributing corporation here because no distortion of income). See also Ruddick Corp. v. US, 643 F.2d 747 (Ct. Cl. 1981) (no invocation of §482 on dividend in kind unless transactional taint—i.e., tax avoidance or no business purpose; distortion caused by §§301 and 311 rules have been approved by Congress and IRS cannot use §482 income distortion attack to override §311 et al. rules). But see Richard H. Foster, 80 TC 34 (1983). On remand in Ruddick Corp., 1983-2 USTC 9480 (Ct. Cl. 1983), §482 was applied because tax avoidance taint was found due to (a) lack of business purpose for dividend, and (b) pre-existing plan for resale of distributed property by parent-shareholder.

See also Roger Dolese, 82 TC 830 (1984) (disproportionate distribution by partnership rearranged under §482 principles; but *Court Holding Co.* doctrine did not apply).

See generally Adess, The Role of Section 482 in Nonrecognition Transactions—The Outer Edges, 57 Taxes 946 (1979); and Note, Section 482 and the Nonrecognition Provisions: Resolving the Conflict, 77 Nw. U.L. Rev. 670 (1982).

Page 7-56:

Add to note 144.

[144] See also Bush Bros. & Co., supra note 139 (this Supplement); Adess, supra note 140 (this Supplement); Bank of America v. US, supra note 140 (this Supplement); and Ruddick Corp. v. US, supra note 140 (this Supplement). *Ruddick Corp.* was distinguished in General Elec. Co. v. US, 1983-2 USTC 9532 (Ct. Cl. 1983), where loss property was distributed in a §332 liquidation of the parent's §931 subsidiary (a tax-exempt entity) and resold to another affiliate (this distortion was not sanctioned by Congress; rather Congress had shown a clear policy not to allow losses of a §931 corporation to be offset against profits of related entities).

See also Roger Dolese, supra note 140 (this Supplement).

Page 7-58:

Replace first full paragraph in text with the following.

There are now (culminating with the 1984 Tax Reform Act) so many exceptions to the statement in §311(a) that the corporation shall not recognize gain or loss on the distribution of property with respect to its stock that the former "general rule" has presently become the rare exception to corporate recognition on non-liquidating distributions of appreciated property to its shareholders.[147.1]

[147.1] See Javaras, Corporate Distributions of Property: Recent Judicial and Legislative Changes, 62 Taxes 587 (1984).

Add to note 148.

[148] But see §7701(g), added by the Tax Reform Act of 1984, which may require the distributing corporation to recognize additional gain up to the face of the nonrecourse debt since that provision mandates that property transferred subject to such debt is deemed to have a value equal to the debt. See Eustice, The Tax Reform Act of 1984, ¶ 5.05[5][a].

Add new paragraph to text after paragraph ending with note 148.

If more than one property is distributed, the Service has recently ruled that §311(c) computations are made asset by asset (rather than on an aggregate property basis); [148.1] also, specific liens are assigned to the property securing that debt, while general liabilities are assigned in proportion to relative values of the distributed properties.

[148.1] Rev. Rul. 80-283, 1980-2 CB 108.

Correct last line of text.

Reference to §453(d) should be changed to §453B(a) as redesignated (without change in substance) by the Installment Sales Revision Act of 1980.

Page 7-59:

Add to note 150.

[150] Recent legislation specifically provides in new §386 that corporate distributions of a partnership interest will be treated as a distribution of the corporation's proportionate share of the partnership's recognition property (defined as any property which would trigger corporate-level gain if distributed directly by the corporate-partner). See the Tax Reform Act of 1984, H.R. 4170, §75(a); the Deficit Reduction Act of 1984, H.R. 2163, §59(a); the Tax Reform Act of 1984, P.L. No. 98-369, §75(a), 98 Stat. 678 (adding new §386).

For a decision applying a look-through approach under prior law as well, see Holiday Village Shopping Center v. US, 1984-2 USTC ¶ 9549 (Cl. Ct. 1984).

See generally Eustice, The Tax Reform Act of 1984, ¶ 3.02[1][c].

Add text to end of paragraph 6.

New legislation, the Corporate Takeover Tax Act of 1982, which was incorporated in TEFRA of 1982, significantly broadened the scope of §311(d) by tightening the principal exceptions to its application. See ¶¶ 9.64 and 9.64A (this Supplement).

Add new paragraphs 8 through 12 to text.

8. *Distributions by foreign corporations of U.S. real property.* Under §897(d)(1) of the Foreign Investment Real Property Tax Act of 1980, distributions of an interest in U.S. real property by a foreign corporation are taxable at the corporate level, notwithstanding §311(a).

9. *Corporate Takeover Tax Act of 1982.* Proposed legislation would have applied a new toll charge provision requiring corporate recognition of gain on the distribution of appreciated property in any case where a corporate distributee obtains a stepped-up basis for the distributed property. But this special proposal was not adopted; instead, the exceptions to §311(d)(2) were materially tightened by TEFRA of 1982. See ¶¶ 9.64 and 9.64A (this Supplement).

10. *Distributions by Subchapter S corporations.* The Subchapter S Revision Act of 1982,[151.1] in new §1363(d), requires recognition of gain on any nonliquidating distribution of appreciated property by a Subchapter S corporation. Since shareholders of a Subchapter S corporation will obtain a stepped-up basis for distributed property without ordinary dividend consequences under the new revisions to Subchapter S, it was felt that a toll charge should be imposed on such transactions. (This recognized gain will flow through to shareholders under the conduit pass-through rules of these proposals, less any corporate level tax imposed by new §1374.) But the Tax Reform Act of 1984[151.2] narrowed the scope of §1363(d) by adding §1363(e), which exempts distributions in complete liquidation and distributions pursuant to a reorganization that are nontaxable to the distributee (and hence do not obtain a basis step-up).

[151.1] P.L. No. 97-354, 96 Stat. 1669.
[151.2] P.L. No. 98-369, §721(a), 98 Stat. 678, adding new §1363(e).

11. Senate Finance Committee Staff Proposals. A preliminary report of the Staff of the Senate Finance Committee, submitted on September 22, 1983, proposed to repeal §311(a) for all distributions of appreciated property which result in a stepped-up basis to the distributees.

12. Recent legislation. The Tax Reform Act of 1984 [151.3] essentially abolished §311 nonrecognition treatment for corporate distributions of appreciated property (whether as an ordinary dividend-in-kind or in redemption of its stock) by treating such distribution as a deemed sale at value to the distributees. The principal inspiration for this legislation was several widely publicized royalty trust distribution transactions, but the legislation goes well beyond these situations. Note also that the deemed corporate-level sale could be subject to §1239 recharacterization if the shareholders are sufficiently related.

While corporate-level taxability for distributions in kind will become the general rule, rather than the exception, under this legislation (i.e., *General Utilities* will shrink to *G.U.*), several exceptions nevertheless still remain:

(a) Losses will not be recognized;

(b) Distributions not subject to Subpart A (i.e., §§301–307) are exempt (e.g., complete liquidations and distributions pursuant to a tax-free reorganization or division);

(c) Carryover basis distributions to an 80-percent corporate shareholder are exempt (but *only* through 1984);

(d) Partial liquidation distributions on qualified stock under §302(b)(4) and §311(e)(1) (infra ¶ 9.64 (this Supplement) are exempt; and

(e) "Qualified dividends," defined by new §311(e)(3) as dividends to noncorporate shareholders of property used in the active conduct of business (other than inventory and receivables), are exempt.

[151.3] The Tax Reform Act of 1984, H.R. 4170, §54(a); the Deficit Reduction Act of 1984, H.R. 2163 §36(a); the Tax Reform Act of 1984, P.L. No. 98-369, §54(a), 98 Stat. 678.

See generally Eustice, The Tax Reform Act of 1984, ¶ 3.02[1]; ABA Tax Section Special Task Force Report, Income Taxation of Corporations Making Distributions With Respect to Their Stock, 37 Tax L. Rev. 625 (1984).

¶ 7.22.   TAXABILITY OF DISTRIBUTION TO INDIVIDUAL DISTRIBUTEES

Page 7-60:

Add to note 152, first paragraph.

[152] For valuation of "stapled stock" dividend, see Rev. Rul. 80-213, 1980-2 CB 101. See generally Corry, Stapled Stock—Time For a New Look, 36 Tax L. Rev. 167 (1981). Cordner v. US, 671 F.2d 367 (9th Cir. 1982) (dividend-in-kind of rare coins taxable at market, not face, value). For new restrictions on stapled stock, see §269B, added by §136 of the Tax Reform Act of 1984, P.L. No. 98-369, 98 Stat. 678.

Page 7-61:
Correct seventh line of text.
Change "divided" to "dividend."

Page 7-62:
Correct twelfth line of text.
Change "either" to "earlier."

Page 7-63:
Add to note 159.

[159] But see §897(f), added by the Foreign Investment Real Property Tax Act of 1980, which provides that distributions by domestic corporations of U.S. real property to foreign shareholders take a carryover basis (increased by gain recognized to the distributing corporation and taxes paid thereon by the distributees).

Correct note 160.

[160] Reference to §453(d) should be changed to §453 B as a result of the Installment Sales Revision Act of 1980 (substance of this provision unchanged, however).

¶ 7.23.   TAXABILITY OF DISTRIBUTION TO CORPORATE DISTRIBUTEES

Page 7-65:

Add to text at end of first runover paragraph.

Recent legislation [162.1] however, limits A's tacked holding period for the distributed property to its holding period for the X

[162.1] The Tax Reform Act of 1984, H.R. 4170, §54(b); the Deficit

stock, by virtue of new §301(e). Moreover, this same legislation [162.2] requires A to reduce its basis in the X stock by the untaxed portion of the distribution if such distribution constitutes an "extraordinary dividend" (i.e., equals 10 percent of A's X stock basis) and the X stock is disposed of by A within one year. In computing the amount of this reduction, the *value* of the distributed property is treated as the amount of the distribution. Thus, A would have to reduce its X stock basis by 85,000 if the §243 deduction was 85 percent, and by $100,000 if the deduction was 100 percent (or if the dividend was "eliminated" in a consolidated return, infra ¶ 15.23). Finally, the 1984 Act materially tightened §311 to the extent that, after 1984, *all* distributions of appreciated property to corporate shareholders (even controlling parent corporations) will be taxable to the distributing corporation (supra ¶ 7.21, paragraph 12, this Supplement). Consequently, corporate shareholders will be treated virtually the same as individual shareholders in the case of property dividends.

Reduction Act of 1984, H.R. 2163, §35(e); the Tax Reform Act of 1984, P.L. No. 98-369, §54(b), 98 Stat. 678. After 1984, however, all distributions of appreciated property to corporate shareholders will be taxable to the distributing corporation under §311(d)(1), so this rule should have no effect after that date.

[162.2] The Tax Reform Act of 1984, H.R. 4170, §53(a); the Deficit Reduction Act of 1984, H.R. 2163, §35(a); the Tax Reform Act of 1984, P.L. No. 98-369, §53(a), 98 Stat. 678; adding new §1059; supra ¶ 5.06 (this Supplement).

Page 7-66:

Add new text at end of section.

But, as a result of the 1984 Tax Reform Act amendments to §311 (supra ¶ 7.21, paragraph 12, this Supplement), distributions of appreciated property to *all* corporate shareholders will trigger taxable gain to the distributing corporation after 1984; hence, the amount of the distribution will, in effect, be the value of the distributed property, and in this respect, the tax consequences for corporate distributees of appreciated property will be the same as that applicable to individual shareholders (save for the §243 deduction).

¶ 7.24.   DISTRIBUTIONS IN KIND: EFFECT ON EARNINGS AND PROFITS

Page 7-67:

Add to note 164.

[164] Recent legislation requires earnings to be *increased* by the untaxed portion of the potential gain inherent in the distributed property, the Tax Reform Act of 1984, §61(a), adding new §312(n)(4). This provision apparently would not apply, however, to a carryover basis distribution to an 80 percent corporate shareholder during 1984 *only* (after 1984, all distributions to any corporate shareholder trigger taxable gain to the distributing corporation).

Add new note 164.1 to end of first runover paragraph.

[164.1] But under recent legislation (supra note 164, this Supplement) X's earnings would be increased by the $5,000 of untaxed gain on the distributed property (presumably creating current earnings which, in turn, could thereby increase the taxable dividend amount to A). By virtue of the Tax Reform Act of 1984 amendments to §311(d), however, most dividends in kind will be taxable to the distributing corporation. See supra ¶ 7.21 (this Supplement).

Page 7-68:

Add to note 167.

[167] See Rev. Rul. 79-149, 1979-1 CB 132 (livestock raised and purchased for breeding purposes not §312(b) inventory).

There is a question as to whether new §312(n)(4) (supra note 164, this Supplement) would require an additional increase to earnings to reflect the *untaxed* portion of the appreciation on the distributed inventory.

Page 7-69:

Add new note 167.1 at end of third line of text.

[167.1] Compare Rev. Rul. 74-164, 1974-1 CB 74, discussed supra ¶ 7.02, note 17. The ruling is silent on the size of the ending deficit, however, although the result noted in the text seems to be the most sensible interpretation of the statute in this situation.

Add new example (3) to text.

(3) If X instead had accumulated earnings of $10,000 at the start of the year, A's dividend income would be $50,000, since the distribution would be fully covered by earnings ($10,000 of accumulated, and $40,000 of current gen-

erated by §312(b)(1)(A)); X's earnings would be reduced to zero as a result of the §312(b)(1)(B) adjustment.

Add to note 168.

[168] There is a question as to whether new §312(n)(4) (supra note 164, this Supplement) would require a double increase in the distributing corporation's earnings.

Page 7-70:

Correct note 170, first paragraph.

[170] Reference to §453(d) should be changed to §453 B as a result of redesignation by Installment Sales Revision Act of 1980.

Page 7-71:

Add new paragraph to text after example.

Recent legislation [172.1] requires an increase in earnings and profits in the rare case where gain is not taxed to the distributing corporation on the distribution under §311 (except for carryover basis distributions to 80 percent corporate shareholders during 1984). Such increase presumably creates current earnings and profits; moreover, such an increase is apparently permanent in view of the lack of any correlative decrease provision comparable to §312(b)(1)(B), although this result may not have been intended.[172.2]

[172.1] Supra note 164 (this Supplement).
[172.2] See Joint Committee Staff "General Explanation," p. 179.

PART C.   DISTRIBUTIONS OF CORPORATION'S OWN OBLIGATIONS

¶ 7.40.   DISTRIBUTIONS OF CORPORATION'S OWN OBLIGATIONS

Page 7-73:

Add to note 175, second paragraph.

[175] PLR 8316019 (Tech. Adv.), 1983 P-H Fed. Taxes, ¶ 54,983 (if notes true debt, dividend taxable at time of distribution based on value of notes and interest is deductible; if not true debt, dividend occurs when notes paid and interest part of dividend).

Add to note 715, third paragraph.

[175] Rufus K. Cox, 78 TC 1021 (1982) (no installment-sale reporting for §301(c)(3) gain; notes taxable currently at their fair market value).

Add to note 176.

[176] See also Baumer v. US, 580 F.2d 863 (5th Cir. 1978) ("open" dividend treatment on facts because of valuation contingencies). But see remand, Baumer v. US, 518 F. Supp. 813 (N.D. Ga. 1981) (grant of bargain option having ascertainable value at the time of taxable dividend), rev'd, 685 F.2d 1318 (11th Cir. 1982) (value at exercise date).

Page 7-74:

Add to note 177.

[177] See Senate Finance Committee Staff preliminary report, submitted September 22, 1983, proposing either to repeal the earnings and profits limitation, or at least restrict the §312(a)(2) charge to earnings on a distribution of securities.

Both the House and Senate versions of recent legislation (the Tax Reform Act of 1984, H.R. 4170, §60, and the Deficit Reduction Act of 1984, H.R. 2163, §47(c)) proposed to amend §312(a)(2) to lower the charge to earnings for debt dividend distributions to the present value of such obligations; moreover, the distributed debt would specifically be subject to the new original-issue discount system, supra new ¶ 4.23 (this Supplement). These proposals passed as §61(c) of the Tax Reform Act of 1984, P.L. No. 98-369, 98 Stat. 678, amending §312(a)(2), and adding §§312(o) and 1275(a)(5) (effective for distributions after Mar. 15, 1984). See Eustice, The Tax Reform Act of 1984, ¶ 3.02[2][c].

PART D.   DISTRIBUTIONS OF STOCK AND STOCK RIGHTS

¶ 7.61.   STOCK DISTRIBUTION RULES, 1954–1969
Page 7-80:

Add to note 198.

[198] Rev. Rul. 82-158, 1982-2 CB 77 (stock issued in an acquisitive reorganization not a §305(b) or §305(c) transaction; not a distribution with respect to the distributing corporation's stock); Robert E. Whiting, ¶ 84,182 P-H Memo TC (reduction of shareholders' stock subscription obligations and correlative reduction of stock par value held equivalent to a §305 tax-free stock dividend and did not give rise to shareholder-level debt cancellation gain).

Page 7-81:

Correct citation in first line of paragraph 2 of text.
Section 302(b)(1) should read §305(b)(1).

Correct citation in third line of paragraph 3 of text.
Section 302(b)(2) should read §305(b)(2).

Page 7-82:

Correct citation in first and fifth lines of text in runover paragraph.
Section 305(b)(*1*) should read §305(b)(2).

¶ 7.62. STOCK DISTRIBUTION RULES, 1969 AND LATER YEARS

Page 7-84:

Add to note 204, end of first paragraph.

[204] Stone, Back to Fundamentals: Another Version of the Stock Dividend Saga, 79 Colum. L. Rev. 898 (1979).

Page 7-85:

Add to note 205.

[205] See also Rev. Rul. 79-42, 1979-1 CB 130 (similar plan to Rev. Rul. 76-53; Rev. Rul. 77-149 distinguished); Rev. Rul. 83-68, 1983-1 CB 75 (principle of Rev. Rul. 76-258 followed even though not all shareholders had right to redeem distributed stock; since one shareholder had redemption right, all shareholders fully taxed on stock dividend).
Compare Rev. Rul. 80-154, 1980-1 CB 68 (cash dividend used to pay for additional stock held tax-free §305(a) stock dividend; not a §305(b)(1) cash option because election was to capitalize earnings, not to take cash *or* stock; while declaration of cash dividend raises a presumption of taxability, presumption can be rebutted if resolution ties up the cash so that shareholders never receive it, never exercise control over it, and cash is used to pay for additional stock). Rev. Rul. 82-158, 1982-2 CB 77 (stock issued in an acquisitive reorganization not a §305(b) or §305(c) distribution with respect to stock).

Add to text at end of runover paragraph.

New §305(e), added by the ERTA of 1981,[205.1] carves out a limited and temporary exception to §305(b) treatment for certain

---

[205.1] P.L. No. 97-34, 95 Stat. 172.

dividend reinvestment plans of public utilities (applicable to distributions after 1981 and before 1985). Under this provision, individual shareholders can elect to exclude up to $750 from income if they receive qualified stock (generally newly issued common stock specially designated by the corporation for such plans) from a qualified public utility. Stock excluded from income under this provision has a zero basis, but it must be held for more than one year to receive capital gain treatment. Moreover, sales of other common stock of the distributing corporation within the one-year period will be deemed to be sales of the excluded stock. Finally, the distributing corporation cannot reduce earnings and profits by the distribution of such stock, whether or not a shareholder elects to exclude it from income.

Pending legislation proposed to accelerate the termination of this provision to December 31, 1982, but failed to pass. But §185 of the Deficit Reduction Act of 1984, H.R. 2163, again proposed to repeal §305(e) for distributions after 1984; however, there was no comparable provision in the House version of this legislation (H.R. 4170), and once again this proposal failed to pass.

Add new note 206.1 to end of first sentence in paragraph 4.

[206.1] See Rev. Rul. 84-141, 1984-39 IRB 6 (constructive receipt of taxable §305(b)(4) stock dividend on preferred where holder of preferred had right to elect to receive common stock equal to cash dividends that had been passed for two consecutive quarters).

Page 7-86:

Add to note 207.

[207] But Rev. Rul. 83-42, 1983-1 CB 76 (actual distribution on convertible preferred to compensate for dilution caused by stock dividend on common taxable under §305(b)(4); antidilution exception limited to deemed distributions resulting from conversion ratio adjustments).

Add to note 208, second paragraph.

[208] Minasian and Welz, Guidelines for Determining When Discount Preferred Stock Will Create Taxable Income, 53 J. Tax. 2 (1980).

Add to note 209, second paragraph.

[209] Principle of Rev. Rul. 75-468 followed and extended in Rev Rule. 81-190, 1981-2 CB 84 (unanticipated value fluctuations occurring

after it was too late to change the terms of the tender offer as a business matter caused premium to exceed 10 percent safe harbor; but such premium did not result in taxability under §305(b) because not bargained for, not intended, not foreseeable, and not possible to renegotiate terms once values changed). For digest of private rulings that no taxable call premium exists if the preferred is immediately callable, see Shoptalk, 61 J. Tax. 444 (1984).

Page 7-87:

Add to note 210.

[210] But see Rev. Rul. 83-119, 1983-2 CB 57 (but if excess redemption premium on preferred, taxability on spread results under §§305(b) (4) and 305(c); control shift recapitalization via exchange of preferred (redeemable at death) for common, but redemption price of preferred exceeded its value, thereby creating redemption premium taxable over the life expectancy of the preferred shareholder, or at death if earlier). For general valuation principles in "estate freeze" recapitalizations, see Rev. Rul. 83-120, 1983-2 CB 170.

Add to note 211.

[211] See generally Walter, "Preferred Stock" and "Common Stock": The Meaning of the Terms and the Importance of the Distinction for Tax Purposes, 5 J. Corp. Tax. 211 (1978).

Page 7-88:

Add to note 214.

[214] See generally Regs. §1.305-3(b)(3) (last sentence).

Page 7-89:

Add to note 220.

[220] Rev. Rul. 82-158, supra note 205 (this Supplement) (stock issued in an acquisitive reorganization not a §305(b) or §305(c) distribution with respect to stock).

Page 7-90:

Add to note 222.

[222] See generally Regs. §1.305-3(b)(3) (last sentence).

Page 7-92:

Add to note 227.

[227] Rev. Rul. 83-119, supra note 210 (this Supplement) (in a control shift recapitalization, which also purported to freeze the equity value

of the retiring shareholder, the redemption price of the preferred was found to exceed its value, thereby creating a taxable §305(b)(4) dividend over life expectancy of holder, or when stock redeemed at his death). For general valuation principles in equity freeze recapitalizations, see Rev. Rul. 83-120, supra note 210 (this Supplement).

Page 7-94:

Add to note 232.

²³² For valuation factors in equity freeze transactions, see Rev. Rul. 83-120, supra note 210 (this Supplement).

¶ 7.63. STOCK RIGHTS

Page 7-98:

Add to note 244.

²⁴⁴ But see Gerald R. Redding, 71 TC 597 (1979) (distribution of controlled subsidiary via rights offering qualified as tax-free §355 distribution). But *Redding* was reversed on appeal, 630 F.2d 1169 (7th Cir. 1980) (distribution of rights the taxable event per Rev. Rul. 70-521 principles; *Palmer* overruled by 1954 Code amendments); (accord, Baumer v. US, 518 F. Supp. 813 (N.D. Ga. 1981), rev'd other grounds, 685 F.2d 1318 (11th Cir. 1982). See also Rev. Rul. 80-292, 1980-2 CB 104 (subsidiary's distribution of rights to purchase its stock directly to shareholders of parent; rights nontransferable; held, tax-free §305(a) stock dividend from subsidiary to parent, and taxable §301 dividend by parent to its shareholders per Rev. Rul. 70-521 principles).

See generally Jassy, Dividend Treatment of Distributions of Options to Acquire Assets of the Distributing Corporation, 34 Tax L. Rev. 607 (1979); Gann, Taxation of Stock Rights and Other Options: Another Look at the Persistence of *Palmer v. Commissioner,* 1979 Duke L.J. 911.

Add to text at end of section.

New §311, as revised and materially tightened by the Tax Reform Act of 1984,²⁴⁵ will considerably complicate the tax results of Rev. Rul. 70-521, since that ruling assumed that §311(a) applied to the rights distribution; under revised §311(d)(1), however, the distribution would consist of zero basis "property" (i.e., the rights), trigger gain on the spread between value and exercise price,²⁴⁶ and thereby result in taxable dividend treatment (and

---

²⁴⁵ Supra ¶ 7.21, paragraph 12 (this Supplement).
²⁴⁶ The option premium "suspension" rules of Rev. Rul. 58-234, 1958-1 CB 279, may allow the distributing corporation to suspend

basis) for corporate distributees as well.[247] The earnings and profits effects (both to the distributing corporation and to corporate distributees) likewise will change, although precisely how is by no means clear.[248] Perhaps *Palmer* deserves another look in light of these imponderables.

---

taxability on that gain until the rights are exercised or lapse; supra ¶ 4.06, paragraph 7.

[247] Since gain is recognized to the distributing corporation, there would accordingly be a distributable amount equal to that gain; query whether the distributee's dividend (and basis) would be "suspended" until the distributing corporation's gain matures under the option premium suspense rules, supra note 246.

[248] The distributing corporation's earnings would go up by the taxable gain amount (but *when* is unclear, supra note 246), and would be reduced, presumably by a comparable amount; similarly, a corporate distributee's earnings would be increased by a like amount (the timing of such increase is not clear, however, supra note 246).

Chapter 8

ACCUMULATED EARNINGS
AND UNDISTRIBUTED INCOME

PART A. THE ACCUMULATED EARNINGS TAX

¶ 8.01. INTRODUCTORY

Page 8-2:

Add to note 1.

[1] But the Economic Recovery Tax Act (ERTA) of 1981, P.L. No. 97-34, 95 Stat. 172, reduced the top individual rate to 50 percent, commencing in 1982, and accordingly repeals §1348 since this provision is no longer needed.

Hence, in view of the close proximity between the top individual rate (50 percent) and the top corporate rate (46 percent) corporate accumulations primarily to avoid shareholder taxes should be the exception, rather than the general rule; accordingly, the significance of §531 may be significantly downgraded for 1982 and following.

Add to text at end of first paragraph.

But §1023 was repealed by the Crude Oil Windfall Profit Tax Act of 1980, P.L. No. 96-223, 94 Stat. 229.

Page 8-4:

Add to note 5, first paragraph.

[5] See generally Cunningham, More Than You Ever Wanted to Know About the Accumulated Earnings Tax, 6 J. Corp. Tax. 187 (1979).

Page 8-5:

Add new note 6.1 to end of second full sentence of text.

[6.1] The rate differentials between §§1 and 11 were virtually eliminated (for 1982 and thereafter) by the ERTA of 1981, supra note 1 (this Supplement) (top §1 rate is 50 percent; top §11 rate is 46 percent).

Add new note 6.2 to end of fourth full sentence of text.

[6.2] When the ERTA of 1981, supra note 1 (this Supplement), rates became effective (in 1982) intentional absorption of the §531 penalty will almost never be justified economically).

Add new note 7.1 to end of last full sentence of text in section.

[7.1] The tax stakes of the §531 gamble have been materially shifted since the rate changes enacted by ERTA of 1981, supra note 1 (this Supplement); with the top individual rate only 50 percent (for 1982), intentionally incurring the §531 penalty tax will cause genuine economic pain.

¶ 8.02. THE FORBIDDEN PURPOSE: §532
Page 8-6:
Add to note 8.

[8] But these proposals were withdrawn in May 1979 when regulations dealing with computation of the §531 tax in context of consolidated returns were reproposed. Infra ¶ 15.23, paragraph 8 (this Supplement).

Add to note 9.

[9] Amendments to Regs. §1.532-1(a)(1) were proposed on Dec. 19, 1980 to apply the §531 tax to a U.S. corporation formed or availed of to avoid the §881 tax imposed on its foreign corporate shareholders. Moreover, the §531 tax can be imposed not only on the U.S.-source income of a foreign corporation, but also on the foreign-source income of that corporation if it is effectively connected to a U.S. trade or business, Prop. Regs. §1.532-1(c). But these proposals were withdrawn, June 3, 1983. But for recent legislation, see infra new ¶ 17.25 (this Supplement).

Add to note 10.

[10] But see Wilcox Mfg. Co., ¶ 79,092 P-H Memo TC (subsidiary liable for tax where accumulation unreasonable on facts).

Page 8-7:
Add to text after note 13.

But recent legislation [13.1] specifically provides that application

---

[13.1] The Tax Reform Act of 1984, H.R. 4170, §58(a), adding new §532(e); the Deficit Reduction Act of 1984, H.R. 2163, §43(a)

of the §531 tax is to be determined without regard to the number of shareholders of the corporation.

(same); the Tax Reform Act of 1984, P.L. No. 98-369, §58(a), 98 Stat. 678 (same), effective for years beginning after date of enactment (July 18, 1984).

Page 8-9:

Add to note 16.

[16] Since the ERTA of 1981, P.L. No. 97-34, 95 Stat. 172 (with the top individual rate of 50 percent for 1982 and following), it can be argued that the §531 tax should not ordinarily be asserted by IRS, since not much in the way of individual shareholder tax can be avoided (or even deferred) by corporate accumulations (especially if one considers potential capital gains taxes payable at the shareholder level if they sell their stock following the accumulation). But the §531 tax has *not* been repealed (either explicitly or implicitly), regardless of the force of the above economic argument.

Page 8-11:

Add to note 25.

[25] Thompson Eng'g Co., 80 TC 672 (1983) (shareholder loans evidence of unreasonable purpose; also, no dividends and sole shareholder in high bracket).

Page 8-13:

Add to note 29.

[29] See also Est. of Fred W. Lucas, 71 TC 838 (1979) (§531 tax could only be imposed on accumulations in excess of guidelines); accord, Doug-Long, Inc., 72 TC 158 (1979).

**¶ 8.03. "REASONABLE NEEDS OF THE BUSINESS":
IN GENERAL**

Page 8-19:

Add to note 47.

[47] See also Doug-Long, Inc., 72 TC 158 (1979) (estimated tax payments count as current expense); Grob, Inc. v. US, 565 F. Supp. 391 (E.D. Wis. 1983) (general application of *Bardahl*; allowed use of peak operating cycle, inflation factor, and estimated tax needs; also product liability self insurance reserve).

Page 8-20:

Add to note 49.

[49] Thompson Eng'g Co., 80 TC 672 (1983) (*Bardahl* not applicable because taxpayer didn't have routine operating cycle).

Add to note 51, following Alma Piston *citation.*

[51] *Alma Piston* was affirmed, 579 F.2d 1000 (6th Cir. 1978). See also Doug-Long, Inc., supra note 47 (this Supplement) (peak needs); Grob, Inc. v. US, supra note 47 (this Supplement) (same; also allowed use of inflation factor and estimated tax needs).

Page 8-21:

Add to note 52.

[52] Grob, Inc. v. US, supra note 47 (this Supplement) (product liability exposure needs). Section 537(b)(4) (added in 1979), now allows reserves for product liability losses.

¶ 8.04. "REASONABLE NEEDS OF THE BUSINESS": ANTICIPATED NEEDS

Page 8-23:

Add to note 60.

[60] Chaney & Hope, Inc., 80 TC 263 (1983) (future needs definite; accumulation for purpose of meeting expected needs of pending merger, partner acceptable once merger became definite).

Page 8-24:

Add to text at end of section.

Section 537(b) lists several special rules which will justify the accumulation: §537(b)(1), §303 redemption needs (infra ¶ 8.07); §537(b)(2), excess business holding redemption needs (infra ¶ 8.07); and §537(b)(4), reasonable product liability loss reserves.

¶ 8.06. "REASONABLE NEEDS OF THE BUSINESS": WHAT IS "THE" BUSINESS?

Page 8-28:

Add to note 81, first paragraph.

[81] Chaney & Hope, Inc., 80 TC 263 (1983) (accumulation for needs of sister-corporation affiliate not reasonable).

¶ 8.07. "REASONABLE NEEDS OF THE BUSINESS": STOCK REDEMPTIONS

Page 8-30:

Add to note 84, first paragraph.

[84] Lamark Shipping Agency, Inc., ¶ 81,284 P-H Memo TC (1981) (redemption of 95 percent shareholder; no corporate business purpose; shareholder tax avoidance purpose, capital gain bail-out).

¶ 8.08. PRESUMPTIONS AND BURDEN OF PROOF PROBLEMS

Page 8-33:

Add to note 93.

[93] James H. Rutter Mfg. Co., 81 TC 937 (1983) (IRS opportunity for discovery has no effect on scope of facts that must be included in a §534(c) statement to shift burden of proof).

Page 8-34:

Add to note 96, runover paragraph.

[96] See also H.C. Cockrell Co., 71 TC 1036 (1979) (only activity net-leased warehouse and two vacation homes leased to sole shareholder—held a mere holding company; fact that notice of deficiency did not specify grounds for §531 tax did not prevent IRS from invoking holding company issue).

¶ 8.09. COMPUTATION OF ACCUMULATED EARNINGS TAX

Page 8-35:

Add new note 96.1 to end of first paragraph in section.

[96.1] For 1982 and following, the new top individual rate of 50 percent, established by ERTA of 1981, P.L. No. 97-34, 95 Stat. 172, generally reverses the stakes of this gamble; if the §531 tax is incurred, the economic costs will usually exceed the additional shareholder taxes that would be due from payment of dividends.

Moreover, the new "safe-harbor" leasing rules of §168(f)(8) should go a long way to eliminate the need for this gamble, since a purchase and lease of property under these provisions can effectively eliminate the §531 tax base (as well as taxable income). Note, however, the purchased ITCs in a safe-harbor lease deal will not shelter the §531 tax since investment tax credits are not allowed against the §531 tax, §46(a)(4). But safe-harbor leasing was phased out by TEFRA in 1982.

Page 8-36:

Add to note 97.

[97] Lamark Shipping Agency, Inc. ¶ 81,284 P-H Memo TC (1981) (*GPD* issue not decided because taxpayer did not argue it).

Add to note 98.

[98] Accord with Rev. Rul. 72-306 is Doug-Long, Inc., 73 TC 71 (1979) (protest of deficiency is a contest and Regs. §1.535-2(a)(1) valid); and Mariani Frozen Foods, Inc., 81 TC 448 (1983).

Add new note 98.1 to end of second sentence of paragraph 1.

[98.1] New legislation restricts the allowance of capital losses in computing accumulated taxable income under §535(b), especially for "mere holding companies," which are denied any deduction for net capital losses. See the Tax Reform Act of 1984, H.R. 4170, §58(b), adding new §§545(b)(2), 545(b)(5), 545(b)(7), 545(b)(8); the Deficit Reduction Act of 1984, H.R. 2163, §43(b) (same); the Tax Reform Act of 1984, P.L. No. 98-369, §58(b), 98 Stat. 678.

Page 8-37:

Add to note 99.

[99] See also Rev. Rul. 78-430, 1978-2 CB 181 (accumulated taxable income base may be increased by §482 reallocation).

Correct note 100, second line of first paragraph.

[100] Substitute "qualify" for "quality."

Add to note 100, end of second paragraph.

[100] As to triple tax exposure, see also Est. of Fred W. Lucas, 71 TC 838 (1979). See generally, Doernberg, The Accumulated Earnings Tax: The Relationship Between Earnings and Profits and Accumulated Taxable Income in a Redemption Transaction, 34 U. Fla. L. Rev. 715 (1982).

Correct note 100, third paragraph.

[100] Citation to *Fulman v. US* should be 434 US 528 (1978).

Page 8-38:

Add to note 102.

[102] For analysis of these, and other, possible uses of the consent dividend procedures of §565, see Buchholtz, Consent Dividends May

Allow a Step-Up in Basis or Increase the Foreign Tax Credit, 56 J. Tax. 148 (1982). See also PLR 8224117, Vol. 9, 1982 P-H Fed. Tax Serv. ¶ 55,158 (IRS considering limitations on expansive use of §565 consent dividend technique). But §565 now a "no-ruling" area, Rev. Proc. 82-55, 1982-2 CB 845, now found in Rev. Proc. 84-22, 1984-1 CB 449.

Page 8-39:

Add to text at end of section.

The ERTA of 1981 [103.1] raised the minimum accumulated earnings tax credit to $250,000 (effective for years beginning after 1981). The new credit does not apply, however, for certain personal-service corporations, viz., those whose principal business consists of the performance of services in the fields of law, accounting, health, engineering, architecture, actuarial science, performing arts, or consulting.

[103.1] Supra note 96.1 (this Supplement). See generally Rev. Rul. 84-101, 1984-28 IRB 5.

PART B.   PERSONAL HOLDING COMPANIES

¶ 8.20.   INTRODUCTORY

Page 8-40:

Add to note 104.

[104] Compare Daniel F. Keller, 77 TC 1014 (1981), aff'd, 732 F.2d 1014 (10th Cir. 1983) (no §482 because arm's-length terms, and this was defense to §61 as well) with Chas. Johnson, 78 TC 882 (1982) (shareholder taxed as true earner of income under §61 because had control of earning process). See also Louis G. Horn, ¶ 82,741 P-H Memo TC.

Page 8-41:

Add to end of text in paragraph 2.

The §541 rate was lowered to 50 percent by the ERTA of 1981 [105.1] (effective for years beginning in 1982).

[105.1] P.L. No. 97-34, 95 Stat. 172.

Add to note 106, second paragraph.

[106] Fletcher v. US, 674 F.2d 1308 (9th Cir. 1982) (distribution before corporation designated as a PHC not qualified for §547 deficiency dividend). See generally Bauman, Jr., Deficiency Dividends and Other Solutions For Avoiding Personal Holding Company Tax, 59 J. Tax. 202 (1983).

Page 8-42:

Add to note 107.

[107] Also, the safe-harbor leasing benefits of §168(f)(8), established by the ERTA of 1981, supra note 105.1 (this Supplement), are not available to PHC lessors, and, in any event, were repealed by TEFRA in 1982 (effective for 1984).

Page 8-43:

Add to note 110.

[110] When the new rates for individuals established by the ERTA of 1981, supra note 105.1 (this Supplement), become fully effective, however, it is difficult to imagine any case where incurring the §541 tax would be preferable to distributing dividends to its shareholders.

Correct second line of text in first complete paragraph.

Insert word "tax" after "company."

Add to note 111.

[111] Mariani Frozen Foods, Inc., 81 TC 448 (1983) (no state-of-mind defense for FPHC tax either, infra ¶ 17.21).

¶ 8.21. PERSONAL HOLDING COMPANY INCOME: THE 60 PERCENT INCOME TEST

Page 8-44:

Add to note 114.

[114] See also Rev. Rul. 79-60, 1979-1 CB 211 (consolidated return aspects of §542(b)); Rev. Rul. 74-432, 1974-2 CB 175; and Rev. Rul. 76-320, 1976-2 CB 181 (insurance company subsidiary before and after 1974 statutory change).

Page 8-45:

Amend last clause of sentence in note 116, second paragraph.

[116] ". . . since loss of deductions under §465 can push the PHC into the 84 percent bracket . . ." (reduced to 73 percent, for 1982, as a result of the new 50 percent rate in §541).

¶ 8.22. PERSONAL HOLDING COMPANY INCOME: §543(a)

Page 8-46:

Add new note 119.1 to end of first sentence of paragraph 1.

[119.1] Mariani Frozen Foods, Inc., 81 TC 448 (1983) (§551 constructive dividends as §543 PHC income).

Page 8-47:

Add to note 120, second paragraph.

[120] See also The Krueger Co., 79 TC 65 (1982) (interest imputed under §482 constituted PHC interest income).

Add to note 121, first paragraph.

[121] See Lake Gerar Dev. Co., 71 TC 887 (1979) (interest on purchase-money mortgage is personal holding company interest). See also Investors Ins. Agency, Inc. v. CIR, 677 F.2d 1328 (9th Cir. 1982) (payment held to be interest, even though no underlying debt; label controlled; since parties "intended" payment to be interest and treated it as such, they were bound by their labels).

Add to note 122.

[122] Dothan Coca-Cola Bottling Co., Inc. v. US, 745 F.2d 400 (11th Cir. 1984) (receipts were "rent" for lease of tangible assets, not royalties for use of franchise).

Page 8-49:

Add to note 126, first paragraph.

[126] Feldman, Active vs. Passive Rental Income: A Questionable Result Under the Proposed Regulations for Personal Holding Companies, 6 J. Corp. Tax. 316 (1980).

But the "active" rents exception in the proposed regulations was rejected by the Tax Court in Walt Eller et al., 77 TC 934 (1981) (no statutory distinction in §543 between active and passive rents; test is a mechanical definition; hence, rents are rents for PHC income definition purposes); See Cook & Allen, *Eller* Considered: Are Substantial Services Irrelevant In Determining Personal Holding Company Rents? 10 J. Corp. Tax. 139 (1983).

But the 1968 proposed regulations were withdrawn on November 29, 1983 for reason of excessive "age."

Add to note 126, second paragraph.

[126] See Johnson Inv. & Rental Co., 70 TC 895 (1978) (rent vs. royalty classification; key is fixed amount vs. contingent on use).

Page 8-52:

Insert in second line of text in second full paragraph after "enacted."
(which provision is now found in §§543(a)(6)(B) and 543(a)(6)(C))

Page 8-53:

Add to note 133, second paragraph.

[133] Contra, Allied Indus. Cartage Co., 72 TC 515 (1979), aff'd per curiam, 647 F.2d 713 (6th Cir. 1981), and Silverman & Sons Realty Trust, ¶ 79,404 P-H Memo TC, aff'd, 620 F.2d 314 (1st Cir. 1980) (lease between brother-sister corporations not PHC income; use not imputed to individual shareholders merely by virtue of their ownership of the lessee; statute requires actual use); Rev. Rul. 84-137, 1984-38 IRB 15 (agrees, and revokes Rev. Rul. 65-259).

See Rudolph, Shareholder Rent as PHC Income—A Misguided Missile Now Partially Disarmed, 8 J. Corp. Tax. 118 (1981).

Page 8-54:

Add to note 135, third paragraph.

[135] *Foglesong* was reversed and remanded on other grounds, 621 F.2d 865 (7th Cir. 1980) (assignment of income theory not applicable to impute corporate income to dominant shareholder). Thos. B. Byrnes, Inc., 73 TC 416 (1979) (shareholder not named or described individually in agreement even though he did the actual work). On remand of *Foglesong,* corporation's income allocated to shareholder under §482, 77 TC 1102 (1981), but reversed again, 691 F.2d 848 (7th Cir. 1982) (no §482 where work solely for own corporation).

¶ 8.24. DEFINITION OF "PERSONAL HOLDING COMPANY": EXEMPTIONS

Page 8-57:

Add new paragraph (6) at end of section.

(6) Section 5(a) of H.R. 5043, the Bankruptcy Tax Act of 1980, added another exception in §542(c)(9) for corporations involved in an insolvency reorganization proceeding; this provision was enacted in December of 1980.

¶ 8.25. COMPUTATION OF PERSONAL HOLDING COMPANY TAX

Page 8-57:

Add to text at end of first sentence.

The §541 rate was reduced to 50 percent (for 1982) by the ERTA of 1981.[141.1]

[141.1] P.L. No. 97-34, 95 Stat. 172.

Page 8-58:

Add to note 142.

[142] Regarding deduction of federal income taxes, see also Rev. Rul. 79-59, 1979-1 CB 209 (loss carryovers and carrybacks generally denied, except for loss of preceding year which is allowed in computing personal holding company tax even though also allowed as carryback in computing §11 tax); Kluger Assocs., Inc. v. CIR, 617 F.2d 323 (2d Cir. 1980) (contested taxes not accruable); LX Cattle Co. v. US, 629 F.2d 1096 (5th Cir. 1980) (same); Mariani Frozen Foods, Inc., 81 TC 448 (1983) (same).

Chapter 9

STOCK REDEMPTIONS AND PARTIAL LIQUIDATIONS

PART B.   STOCK REDEMPTIONS UNDER §302

¶ 9.20.   INTRODUCTORY
Page 9-11:

Add to note 17.

[17] Rev. Proc. 73-35 was superseded by Rev. Proc. 81-62, 1981-2 CB 684.

¶ 9.21.   CONSTRUCTIVE OWNERSHIP OF STOCK: §318.
Page 9-12:

Add to note 19.

[19] See also Complete Fin. Corp., 80 TC 1062 (1983) (example of different types of attribution, including chain attribution).

Add to note 21.

[21] See also, Coven, The Affinity Provisions of the IRC: A Case Study in Nonsimplification, 45 Tenn. L. Rev. 557 (1978); and Loeb, What Constitutes Ownership of Stock, 21 N.Y.U. Inst. on Fed. Tax. 417 (1963).

Page 9-14:

Add to note 24.

[24] But see Estate of Weiskopf, 77 TC 135 (1981) (trusts not beneficiaries of estate at time of redemption from estate because beneficiary status effectively terminated under local law through distribution—only a remote possibility that distributees would be liable).

Page 9-15:

Add to note 29, first paragraph.

[29] But Patterson Trust v. US, 729 F.2d 1089 (6th Cir. 1984), is contra to Rev. Rul. 68-601 (optioned stock treated as outstanding for denominator in computing dividend equivalent effect; followed "plain language" of statute).

¶ 9.22. SUBSTANTIALLY DISPROPORTIONATE REDEMPTIONS: §302(b)(2)

Page 9-19:

Add to note 34.

[34] Rev. Rul. 81-41, 1981-1 CB 121 (redemption of voting preferred can qualify under §302(b)(2) if redeemed shareholder owns no common; second 80 percent test only applies if shareholder owns some common stock).

Page 9-21:

Add to note 38.

[38] For illustration of a series redemption case, see PLR 8316019 (Tech. Adv.), 1983 P-H Fed. Taxes ¶ 54,983 (plan existed because redeemed shareholder knew of other shareholder's intention to resign and redeem his shares, allowing taxpayer to regain control): but see Glacier State Elec. Supply Co., 80 TC 1047 (1983) (not a series case where second potential redemption required by corporate buy-sell plan).

Add to note 39, second paragraph.

[39] Rev. Proc. 72-9 and Rev. Proc. 77-45 were superseded by Rev. Proc. 79-14, 1979-1 CB 496, which was superseded by Rev. Proc. 80-22, 1980-1 CB 654, and is now found in Rev. Proc. 84-22, 1984-1 CB 449.

Add to note 40.

[40] See also Prop. Regs. §1.385-6 (must have "reasonable" interest rate if debt held proportionately, with §318(a)(1) family attribution); see Pike, Proposed Debt-Equity Regulations: Potent New Standards for Characterizing Purported Debt, 7 J. Corp. Tax. 195, 208 (1980). See Final Regs. §§1.385-6(d) and 1.385-6(e), adopted Dec. 29, 1980 (but not effective until 1982), adopting this requirement. But see Prop. Regs. §1.385-5(c)(5)(v), and §1.385-6(a)(2)(iv) (§483 test rate, 9 percent, adequate). Thus, if redemption satisfies §302(a), notes issued for redeemed stock will initially qualify as debt if the stated interest rate meets the §483(c) test rate of 9 percent; moreover, the note will not be contingent even though payment is limited under local law to earned surplus.

See also new Prop. Regs. §1.385-6(f)(2) safe-harbor interest rate for recourse debt of a corporation whose debt-equity ratio does not exceed 3:1 (acceptable rates are §6621 rate (20 percent), §482 rates (11 to 13 percent, prime plus 2 points, or comparable T-bill rates).

But the §385 regulations were withdrawn on July 6, 1983, T.D. 7920, Nov. 2, 1983.

For recent legislation that significantly expanded the scope of the original-issue discount rules (and the imputed interest rules) in the case of below-market-interest-rate credit sales, see supra new ¶ 4.23 (this Supplement).

Page 9-22:

Add to note 42, following Rickey *citation.*

[42] *Rickey* was affirmed, 592 F.2d 1251 (5th Cir. 1979).

¶ 9.23. TERMINATION OF SHAREHOLDER'S ENTIRE INTEREST: §302(b)(3)

Page 9-23:

Add to note 45, first paragraph.

[45] Gardner & Randall, Distributions in Redemption of Stock: Changing Definitions for a Termination of Interest, 8 J. Corp. Tax 240 (1981) (general discussion of current developments, except for *Rickey* waiver issue).

Add to note 46.

[46] See also Prop. and Final Regs. §1.385-6 (must have reasonable interest rate if debt held proportionately, with §318(a)(1) family attribution); Pike, Proposed Debt-Equity Regulations: Potent New Standards for Characterizing Purported Debt, 7 J. Corp. Tax. 195 (1980); new Prop. Regs. §1.385-6(a)(2)(iv) (§483 rate reasonable here). Under these new proposals, notes issued in a qualified §302(a) redemption are not contingent even though local law limits payment to earned surplus, and such notes will initially qualify as debt (subject to the "second look" rules) if they bear the 9 percent §483(c) test rate. See also Prop. Regs. §1.385-6(f)(2) general safe-harbor interest rate, described supra ¶ 9.22, note 40 (this Supplement). But the §385 regulations were withdrawn on July 6, 1983, T.D. 7920, Nov. 2, 1983.

For application of §483 and §1232 (now §§1274 et seq.), see supra new ¶ 4.23 (this Supplement).

Page 9-24:

Add to note 46, end of carryover paragraph.

[46] Service changed acquiescence to nonacquiescence in *Est. of Milton S. Lennard.* Wm. M. Lynch, 83 TC 597 (1984) (note sub-

ordinated to bank loan and secured by pledge of remaining shareholder's stock held true debt, not retained equity interest).

Add to note 48.

[48] Nazum, Waiver of the Family Ownership Rules Under Section 302(c)(2)(A): Retention or Reacquisition of a Prohibited Interest, 11 J. Corp. Tax. 19 (1984); Wm. N. Lynch, supra note 46 (this Supplement) (creditor status found).

Add to note 49.

[49] Rev. Rul. 83-116, 1983-2 CB 264 (ten-year period not extended by §7503 Saturday, Sunday rule); contra, E.B. Grain Co., 81 TC 70 (1983).

Add to text on last line before note 50.

. . . and to retain records.[50]

Page 9-25:

Correct Haft *citation in note 50, second paragraph.*

[50] Citation should be Robin Haft Trust v. CIR.

Add to note 50, second paragraph, following Rickey *citation.*

[50] *Rickey* was affirmed, 592 F.2d 1251 (5th Cir. 1979).

Correct last line in note 50, second paragraph.

[50] The regulations citation should be Regs. §1.302-4(a)(2).

Add to note 53.

[53] But Rev. Rul. 68-388 distinguished in Rev. Rul. 79-67, 1979-1 CB 128 (distribution of stock by estate to beneficiary followed by redemption from beneficiary respected—purpose was to allow shift of control to unredeemed shareholder; distinguishing feature was distribution in kind, rather than sale, of stock to beneficiary).

But Rickey v. US, 592 F.2d 1251 (5th Cir. 1979), held that an estate could cut off §318(a)(3) estate-beneficiary attribution by filing the waiver; "flexible" reading of attribution rules adopted.

Contra to *Rickey* is David Metzger Trust, 76 TC 42 (1981) (trust cannot cut off attribution from beneficiary by filing waiver; *Rickey* distinguished, though on tenuous grounds, despite appealability to 5th Circuit); but accord with *Rickey* is Cruvant v. US, — F. Supp. — (D.C. La. 1982) (trust can waive §318 effect).

Metzger Trust was aff'd, 693 F.2d 459 (5th Cir. 1982) (no waiver *by* trust entity; *Rickey* not extended from estate waiver to trust waiver;

opinion noted limited changes in the Tax Equity and Fiscal Responsibility Act (TEFRA) re entity waiver rules, infra note 55 (this Supplement)).

Page 9-26:

Add to note 55.

[55] The *Crawford* rule was extended to trusts in Rodgers P. Johnson Trust 71 TC 941 (1979) (trust waiver effective to cut off *chain family* attribution; Rev. Rul. 59-233 rejected). But see David Metzger Trust, 76 TC 42 (1981) (trust cannot cut off attribution from beneficiary by filing waiver), aff'd, 693 F.2d 459 (5th Cir. 1982).

Rickey v. US, supra note 53 (this Supplement), goes even further; here, the estate was allowed to cut off §318(a)(3) estate-beneficiary attribution by filing the waiver; "flexible" interpretation of attribution rules adopted (in effect, court wrote §302(c)(2) waiver rules into *all* of attribution provisions, at least where the facts were equitable for that view). See Andrews, Comment: Estate Waiver of the Estate-Beneficiary Attribution Rule in Nonliquidating Redemptions Under Section 302 and Related Matters: The *Rickey* Case in the Fifth Circuit, 35 Tax L. Rev. 147 (1979); Comment, Stock Redemptions and the Estate Attribution Rules, 128 U. Pa. L. Rev. 650 (1980). Contra to *Rickey* is David Metzger Trust, supra. But Cruvant v. US, supra note 53 (this Supplement) followed *Rickey* in allowing a trust to waive §318 with respect to *its* redemption (waiver timely too, because filed as soon as authority existed permitting it).

Legislation was approved as §228 of 96 Stat. 324, TEFRA of 1982, P.L. No. 97-248, which added new §302(c)(2)(C) to deal with the entity waiver problem raised by *Crawford* and *Rickey*. New §302(c)(2)(C) generally approves the *Crawford* result (viz., entities can waive remote chain *family* attribution), but disapproves of *Rickey* (viz., entities cannot waive entity-beneficiary attribution). This provision is effective for distributions after August 31, 1982. See text infra (this Supplement).

Add new text to end of first complete sentence.

The decisions allowing attribution waiver did not, however, impose any of the special restrictions in §302(c)(2) upon the beneficiary whose constructive ownership was being waived; thus, they did not preclude the beneficiary from acquiring an interest in the corporation, require a notification agreement from the beneficiary, nor reopen the statute of limitations in the event of an acquisition by that beneficiary.[55.1]

[55.1] H. Rep. No. 760, 97th Cong., 2d Sess., at 545 (1982).

The Conference Committee Report to the TEFRA legislation (without any specific provision in either the House or Senate Bill) provided a new special rule in §302(c)(2)(C) permitting the waiver of §318(a)(1) family attribution (only) [55.2] if those through whom ownership is attributed to the entity join in the waiver (and accept all of the conditions of §§302(c)(2)(A) and 302(c)(2)(B)). Thus, the new rules of §302(c)(2)(C) permit an estate,[55.3] trust,[55.4] partnership, or corporation to waive any stock ownership that would be attributed to such entity through a combination of the family attribution rules of §318(a)(1) and the beneficiary-to-entity attribution rules of §318(a)(3). Such related beneficiary must, however, join in the entity's waiver and subject himself to the waiver limitations and conditions of §§302(a)(2)(A) and 302(a)(2)(B).[55.5]

To illustrate: (a) Trust T owns 50 percent of X's only class of stock, individual A owns 50 percent, and A is the father of B, who is a beneficiary of Trust T. X redeems all of T's X stock. Under §318, T still owns 100 percent of X after the redemption, viz., all of A's stock, which is attributed first to B under the family rules of §318(a)(1), and then up to T under trust attribution rules of §§318(a)(5)(A) and 318(a)(3)(B)

[55.2] The Conference Report specifically disapproved of the *Rickey* (Rickey v. US, 427 F. Supp. 484 (W.C. La. 1977)) decision; see H. Rep. No. 760, supra note 55.1 (this Supplement) (though without any inference as to the correctness of that decision). See new §302(c)(2)(C)(ii)(II). See generally Owen, Waiver of Family Attribution By Entities May Still Present Problems Despite TEFRA, 58 J. Tax. 202 (1983).

[55.3] Thus codifying *Crawford,* though with the restrictions on the constructive-owner beneficiary provided in §§302(c)(2)(A) and 302(c)(2)(B).

[55.4] Codifying David Metzger Trust, supra note 55 (this Supplement) (no entity beneficiary waiver).

[55.5] While new §302(c)(2)(C)(i)(II) makes the related beneficiary jointly and severally liable to any deficiency (including interest and penalties) resulting from prohibited acquisition, the Conference Report (H. Rep. No. 760, supra note 55.1) states that it is intended that such additional taxes first should be assessed against the redeeming entity (unless it no longer exists or has insufficient funds to pay), and that the beneficiary whose acquisition caused the deficiency should be proceeded against before any other beneficiary.

(i).[55.6] Under new §302(c)(2)(C), however, T (if joined by B) [55.7] can waive the attribution of A's stock to B and thus prevent any post-redemption ownership by T in X.[55.8]

(b) If B also owned some of X's stock directly, new §302(c) (2)(C) would not allow waiver of attribution from B to T. (Thus, T's interest would not be completely terminated under §302(b)(3), or would §302(b)(2) help here, since a §318 waiver is not available for substantially disproportionate redemptions.) [55.9]

(c) In Example (a), if B actually acquired a stock interest in X within ten years of the redemption,[55.10] the waiver would be purged and T's redemption would, in view of its 100 percent deemed ownership in X, most likely result in dividend treatment to T. The resulting deficiency would first be asserted against T, but if insufficient funds are available in T, B would be liable for the tax (including interest and penalties).[55.11]

[55.6] Unless B's interest in T is both contingent and "remote" (actuarially worth 5 percent or less).

[55.7] Though not A; see §302(c)(2)(C)(ii)(II).

[55.8] Accordingly, T's redemption will qualify under §302(b)(3) as a complete termination of T's interest in X. The ten-year preredemption limitation rules of §302(c)(2)(B) are unaffected by these amendments.

[55.9] If all of B's direct ownership in X was redeemed in tandem with T's redemption, Rev. Rul. 72-472, 1972-2 CB 202, discussed supra note 54, indicates that new §302(c)(2)(C) could now become available to T. (In the ruling, B's redemption qualified for waiver protection under §302(c)(2), and, since after B's redemption he owns no stock in X, other than by attribution from his father, A, the provisions of new §302 (c)(2)(C) could presumably save T from this two-step attribution result.)

[55.10] Constructive acquisitions do not count for this purpose; Rev. Rul. 71-562, 1971-2 CB 173.

[55.11] Supra note 55.5 (this Supplement).

Page 9-27:

Add to note 56.

[56] Rev. Rul. 79-334, 1979-2 CB 127 (Rev. Rul. 72-380 followed where redeemed shareholder accepted appointment by will as trustee of a trust that held corporation's voting stock); Jack O. Chertkof, 72 TC 1113 (1979) (*Lennard* distinguished where redeemed shareholder got management contract six months after redemption, which agree-

ment gave him broad powers over corporation's only business asset enabling him to control all major corporate policy decisions). *Chertkof* was affirmed, 649 F.2d 224 (4th Cir. 1981). See generally Rose, The Prohibited Interest of Section 302(c)(2)(A), 36 Tax L. Rev. 131 (1981). See also Rev. Rul. 81-233, 1981-2 CB 83 (being appointed custodian of donated stock under Uniform Gifts to Minors Act held a tainted interest under Rev. Rul. 71-426).

Dunn was affirmed, 615 F.2d 578 (2d Cir. 1980) (held true debt and shareholder mere creditor despite payment deferral clause in redemption note).

See also LaVerne v. Seda, 82 TC 484 (1984) (retention of interest as employee fatal to waiver, and hence equivalent to dividend because 100 percent owner via §318; employee interest *substantial* here; concurring opinion opts for per se tainting rule). Compare Wm. N. Lynch, supra note 46 (this Supplement) (independent contractor relationship not fatal; occasional consulting, even for compensation allowed; not an employee here). But see Rev. Rul. 84-135, 1984-37 IRB 5 (pension rights not a tainted interest).

Add to note 57.

[57] *Dunn* was affirmed, 615 F.2d 578 (2d Cir. 1980). Cross-reference at end of note should be to note 39, not 30. Wm. N. Lynch, supra note 46 (this Supplement) (notes true debt even though subordinated to bank loan and secured by pledge of remaining shareholder's stock).

Page 9-28:

Add new note 59.1 to third line of paragraph (a) after the words "related person."

[59.1] Rev. Rul. 82-129, 1982-2 CB 76 (tax-free partition of jointly owned community property stock not an "acquisition" for this purpose).

Add to note 61, first paragraph.

[61] Rev. Rul. 57-387 was modified by Rev. Rul. 77-293.

Page 9-29:

Add to note 61, runover paragraph.

[61] See also Rev. Rul. 79-67, 1979-1 CB 128 (purpose for transfer from estate to beneficiary was to set stage for §302(c)(2) waiver and thereby allow control shift through redemption; not tax avoidance); Wm. N. Lynch, supra note 46 (this Supplement) (gift to son was solely for purposes of control shift; no tax avoidance and hence waiver of attribution effective).

See generally Kuntz, Stock Redemptions Following Stock Transfers, An Expanding Safe Harbor, 58 Taxes 29 (1980).

¶ 9.24. REDEMPTION NOT ESSENTIALLY EQUIVALENT TO DIVIDENDS: §302(b)(1)

Page 9-32:

Add to note 70, first paragraph.

[70] But see Rev. Rul. 81-289, 1981-2 CB 82 (pro rata redemption a dividend, even though public company; must be meaningful reduction in interest).

Add to note 71, following Benjamin *citation.*

[71] *Benjamin* was affirmed, 592 F.2d 1259 (5th Cir. 1979).

Add to end of note 71.

[71] See also Rev. Rul. 81-289, 1981-2 CB 82 (if pro rata, redemption a dividend, even though public company); PLR 8316019 (Tech. Adv.), 1983 P-H Fed. Taxes ¶ 54,983 (principles of Rev. Rul. 78-401 and Rev. Rul. 75-502 applied—no §302(b)(1) where retain more than 50 percent control); contra to Rev. Rul. 78-401 is Patterson Trust v. US, 729 F.2d 1089 (6th Cir. 1984) (reduction from 80 percent to 63 percent meaningful).

Page 9-33:

Add to note 73.

[73] Rev. Rul. 80-26, 1980-1 CB 66 (IRS will not follow *Haft* family hostility exception; also acquiescence in *Squier* changed to nonacquiescence, although prospectively only). Contra to *Haft,* under §267 attribution rules, is David Miller, 75 TC 182 (1980). Also contra to *Haft* on §318 attribution exception for family hostility is David Metzger Trust, 76 TC 42 (1981) (bad blood exception of *Haft* not followed unless reduction in interest occurs *with* §318 attribution; here, trust 100 percent owner before and after, so dividend equivalent redemption even though redemption motivated by intra-beneficiary hostility; also §267 applied to deny interest deductions), aff'd, 693 F.2d 459 (5th Cir. 1982). But see Patterson Trust v. US supra note 71 (this Supplement) (reduction from 97 to 93 percent (with attribution) meaningful in view of factional hostility).

Add to note 75, first paragraph.

[75] Rev. Rul. 81-289, 1981-2 CB 82 (pro rata redemption a dividend, even though public company). See Friedrich, IRS Views *Davis* as Requiring Reduction in Interest in All Cases, 9 J. Corp. Tax. 184 (1982).

Add to note 75, second paragraph.

75 See generally Zinn & Silverman, Redemptions of Stock Under Section 302(b)(1), 32 Tax Law. 91 (1978); Postlewaite & Finneran, Section 302(b)(1): The Expanding Minnow, 64 Va. L. Rev. 561 (1978); Blumstein, When Is a Redemption "Not Essentially Equivalent to a Dividend"? 7 J. Corp. Tax. 99 (1980).

Page 9-34:

Add to note 77.

77 Mary G. Roebling, 77 TC 30 (1981) (redemption of preferred stock qualified for §302(b)(1) under *Himmel* analysis even though taxpayer continued to own common stock; significant enough reduction in vote, earnings, and assets shares to meet *Davis* line).

But see Mary Johnston, 77 TC 679 (1981) (series of redemptions resulted in separate dividend equivalent transactions; no firm and fixed plan because parties did not stand by their purported agreement; hence, each redemption tested separately, and not meaningful in its own right); compare Glacier State Elec. Supply Co., 80 TC 1047 (1983) (meaningful reduction under *Davis*; not a series case because of presence of buy-sell plan).

Add to note 78.

78 But in Ltr. Rul. 7933006 (Oct. 13, 1979), the Service discussed *Himmel* and expressly rejected its approach, holding that only vote (not dividend rights or liquidation preferences) counts for meaningful reduction of interest test under *Davis*.

See also Rev. Rul. 81-289, supra note 75 (this Supplement).

Page 9-35:

Add to note 79.

79 See also Patterson Trust v. US, supra note 71 (this Supplement) (reduction from 80 to 63 percent meaningful per se; alternatively, reduction from 97 to 93 percent meaningful in view of special facts showing internecine hostilities); Mary G. Roebling, 77 TC 30 (1981) (redemption of preferred stock pursuant to plan to redeem all preferred stock in a series of redemptions qualified under §302(b)(1); significant enough reduction in vote, earnings, and assets shares to meet *Davis* and *Himmel* tests); and Rev. Rul. 81-289, supra note 75 (this Supplement) (pro rata redemption by public corporation still a dividend because no meaningful reduction in interest).

¶ 9.25. REDEMPTIONS IN CONJUNCTION WITH "BOOTSTRAP" ACQUISITIONS OF STOCK: BUY-SELL PLANS, ETC.

Page 9-36:

Add to note 82, second paragraph.

[82] *Benjamin* was affirmed, 592 F.2d 1259 (5th Cir. 1979) (plan must be definite and fixed); compare Bleily & Collishaw, Inc., 72 TC 751 (1969) (single plan even though no binding agreement; "gentleman's agreement" enough). *Rickey* was affirmed, 592 F.2d 1251 (5th Cir. 1979). See also Jack Paparo, 71 TC 692 (1979) (second step not part of plan because too speculative and contingent).

Add to note 84.

[84] Jake E. Roth, ¶ 83,651 P-H Memo TC (although formally structured as a dividend, distribution treated as part of redemption proceeds which completely terminated taxpayer's interest in two corporations— including payments from a related corporation that were also part of the integrated complete redemption transaction).

Page 9-37:

Add to note 85, second paragraph.

[85] *TSN Liquidating* was reversed, 618 F.2d 1328 (5th Cir. 1980) (threshold dividend taxable as such to selling corporate shareholder despite subsequent capital contribution by buyer; buyer's reinvestment not fatal per se under *Waterman*).

Add to note 85 (third paragraph).

[85] Principles of Rev. Rul. 77-226 applied in GCM 39290, Jan. 4, 1984, 23 Tax Notes 238 (Oct. 15, 1984).

Add to note 86.

[86] But the Installment Sales Revision Act of 1980, by eliminating the 30 percent initial payment limitation, also did away with problems presented by the *Farha* decision; see also Clarence J. Monson, 79 TC 827 (1982) (held *Zenz* for §302(b)(3), but not part of §453 sales payment; *Farha* distinguished, but not very convincingly).

Page 9-38:

Add to note 87, third paragraph.

[87] More currently, see Adams v. CIR, 594 F.2d 657 (8th Cir. 1979) (purchase, then redemption of part, then reissue as stock dividend; held, redemption dividend equivalent because owned 100 percent before and after; taxpayer held to wrong choice of form).

Page 9-41:

Add to end of note 96.

[96] See also Rev. Rul. 80-240, 1980-2 CB 116 (agency theory applied to shareholder's accommodation borrowing for benefit of corporation; shareholder mere transitory debtor on facts); State Pipe & Nipple Corp., ¶ 83-339 P-H TC Memo (1983) (taxpayer escaped *Wall* treatment on showing that documents reflected mutual mistake; corporation obligated to redeem and taxpayer merely acting as agent); but see Glacier State Elec. Supply Co., 80 TC 1047 (1983) (redeeming shareholder real owner—not mere agent or conduit).

Correct cross-reference to Citizens Bank *in note 97.*

[97] Cross reference should be note 92, not 82.

Correct last line of second paragraph of text.

Add "and conditional" after "executory."

Page 9-42:

Add to note 103, first paragraph.

[103] See Rev. Rul. 78-422, 1978-2 CB 129 (purchase-money liability assumption by related sister corporation not protected by §357(a); §304 applied). But see new §304(b)(3)(B) (added by §226(a) of TEFRA of 1982, P.L. No. 97-248, 96 Stat. 324) which overrules the principle of Rev. Rul. 78-422 that §304 prevails over §357; new §304(b)(3)(B) provides that purchase-money debt for the acquisition of stock can be assigned in a §351 exchange without §304 consequences; thus, the new law gives the purchaser of stock a second chance to escape *Wall* treatment by assigning his purchase-money obligations to a new (or existing) corporation in a §351 transaction. But §102(h)(3)(B) of H.R. 3805, the Technical Corrections Act of 1983 (introduced August 4, 1983), proposed to limit the exception of §304(b)(3)(B) to stock acquired from "unrelated" sellers. This provision was moved to §612(b)(3) of H.R. 4170, the Tax Reform Act of 1984, which passed as §712(*l*)(3) of the Tax Reform Act of 1984, adding new §304 (b)(3)(B)(iii).

Page 9-43:

Add to note 105.

[105] See also Rev. Rul. 78-422, 1978-2 CB 129 (assumption of stock purchase obligation by sister corporation not protected by §357(a); §304 applied); contra, new §304(b)(3)(B); supra note 103 (this Supplement).

Page 9-44:

Correct citation in eleventh line of text of paragraph 4.

Section 302(b)(2) should read §305(b)(2)

Add to note 108.

[108] This amnesty presumably also includes the bargain element attributable to the artificially low redemption price term in *Holsey*. See Regs. §1.305-3(b)(3), last sentence, and §305(c).

PART C.   REDEMPTIONS BY AFFILIATED CORPORATIONS: §304

¶ 9.31.   REDEMPTIONS BY AFFILIATED CORPORATIONS UNDER §304

Page 9-48:

Correct line nine of text.

Change "agaist" to "against."

Add to note 119, first paragraph.

[119] Tiger, Redemptions Through Use of Related Corporations: New and Old Problems Under Section 304, 39 Tax L. Rev. 77 (1984).

Page 9-49:

Correct third from last line of text.

Citation should be "§302(b)(3)," not "§303(b)(3)."

Page 9-50:

Add to note 123.

[123] See Jack Paparo, 71 TC 692 (1975) (brother-sister redemption not meaningful per *Davis;* hence, dividend per §§302(d) and 301).
   Falkoff was reversed on other grounds, 604 F.2d 1045 (7th Cir. 1979) (no earnings and profits at time of distribution so no dividend per §301(c)(2)).

Correct line seven of text.

Change "predicted" to "predicated."

Page 9-51:

Add to text at end of paragraph 1.

Section 226(a) of TEFRA [128.1] amended the brother-sister rules of §304(a)(1) in two important respects: First, in determining the amount of dividend income resulting from a §304(a)(1) transaction, new §304(b)(2)(A) provides for a hypothetical (though not a "real") dividend transfer laterally from the issuing corporation to the acquiring corporation (thus adopting a rule comparable to the parent-subsidiary dividend measurement rule of §304(b)(2)(B)); and second, new §304(b)(3) resolves the jurisdictional dispute in a §304–§351 overlap transaction in favor of §304.[128.2]

[128.1] P.L. No. 97-248, 96 Stat. 324.

[128.2] See infra ¶ 9.33 (this Supplement); and for amendments made by the Tax Reform Act of 1984, id.

Correct fifth line of text under paragraph 2.

Should read "dividend under §301," not "§302."

Add to note 130, second paragraph.

[130] Rev. Rul. 80-189, 1980-2 CB 106, revoked Rev. Rul. 69-261 and agreed to follow cases holding no constructive dividend to parent on subsidiary redemption).

Add to note 130, third paragraph.

[130] But Rev. Rul. 80-189, supra, agrees with *Broadview* that subsidiary gets "cost" basis for purchased parent stock.

Page 9-52:

Add to note 132.

[132] See Stewart & Randall, A Proposed Solution to the Statutory Overlap of Sections 304(a)(1) and 304(a)(2), 9 J. Corp. Tax. 125 (1982).

¶ 9.32. COLLATERAL PROBLEMS INVOLVING "CROSS-OWNERSHIP" AND §304

Page 9-53:

Add to note 135, second paragraph.

[135] Rev. Rul. 78-422, 1978-2 CB 129, also held that §304 prevails

over §357(a) (moreover, assumption taxable at once because "novation" of transferor-shareholder's debt). Compare Rev. Rul. 80-240, 1980-2 CB 116 (no §304 where shareholder mere transitory borrowing agent for acquiring corporation and was not true "owner" of acquired stock; merely a conduit for passage of stock to acquiring corporation); Rev. Proc. 81-10, §4.01(5), 1981-1 CB 647 (ruling guidelines). Rev. Proc. 81-61, 1981-2 CB 683 (Service will not rule whether §§304, 351(a), or 351(b) apply to transfers to existing affiliates; but short-term debt, securities, and liability assumptions are property for §317, though stock of affiliate is not). But Rev. Proc. 83-42, 1983-1 CB 778 (IRS will rule on §§304-351 overlaps after TEFRA amendments). See also Rev. Proc. 84-52, 1984-1 CB 551. See Stanley H. Brans, ¶ 83,025 P-H Memo TC (no §351 via §318; just §304 dividend), aff'd, 734 F.2d 290 (6th Cir. 1984).

New §304(b)(3)(A) adopts the §304 primacy rule of Rev. Rul. 73-2; but new §304(b)(3)(B) rejects the primacy of §304 over §357 espoused by Rev. Rul. 78-422 (purchase-money debt for acquisition of stock assignable in §351 exchange without §304(a)(1) consequences). See infra ¶ 9.33 (this Supplement).

Page 9-54:

Add to note 136.

[136] Compare Rev. Rul. 80-239, 1980-2 CB 103 (transfer of stock to new corporation for stock and cash held dividend on facts since transferee corporation mere conduit for passage of cash from transferred corporation), described supra ¶ 3.16, note 168 (this Supplement); Blanchard, The Service's Recent Attack: Taxation of Section 351 Exchanges Between Shareholders and Newly Organized Holding Companies, 35 Tax Law. 163 (1981) (analyzing Rev. Rul. 80-239). See also Rufus K. Cox, 78 TC 1021 (1982) (installment sale to new sister corporation resulted in §301(c)(3) capital gain, but not reportable on installment method because transaction not a "sale" for §453— query 1980 version of §453 that only requires a disposition, rather than a sale).

For the legislative solution to the use of new affiliates as an end around the bail-out defenses of §304, see new §304(b)(2)(A) (earnings created in the acquiring company by shifting an appropriate amount from the acquired company, on the order of the parent-subsidiary redemption rules). This legislation passed as §226(a) of TEFRA of 1982, P.L. No. 97-248, 96 Stat. 324, new §304(b)(2)(A). See infra ¶ 9.33 (this Supplement).

Page 9-54:

Add to note 138, runover paragraph, following 10-42 Corp. citation on page 9-55.

[138] IRS has acquiesced in *10-42 Corp.* case.

Sections 1239(b)(2) and 1239(b)(3) were amended by the Install-ment Sales Revision Act of 1980 (P.L. 96-471) to substitute the word "taxpayer" for "individual," thereby considerably broadening the scope of those provisions (e.g., sections will now cover intercorporate sales of depreciable property).

Add new heading.

¶ 9.33. HOLDING COMPANY BAIL-OUTS AND TEFRA AMENDMENTS TO §304

1. Problems. The relationship of §304 to §351 (and §357) spawned more than its share of controversy and confusion ever since the *Haserot* [138.1] decision nearly twenty years ago, which concluded that §351 controlled over §304 if the two provisions conflicted. For example, if A transferred all his stock of wholly owned X Corp. to his wholly owned Y Corp. for additional Y stock and cash, the ex-change of X stock for Y stock is literally governed by §351; the cash "boot," however, could either be taxed solely by §351(b) (as capital gain), or solely by §304(a)(1) (which would result in divi-dend treatment), depending upon which of these two provisions was deemed to apply.[138.2] Although the Service refused to follow *Haserot,* and at least one Circuit agreed,[138.3] the situation was suffi-ciently uncertain to merit some sort of legislative correction lest the anti-bailout defenses of §304 be drastically eroded.

If the acquiring corporation was a newly organized holding company (and hence without current or accumulated earnings and

[138.1] Henry McK. Haserot, 41 TC 562 (1964), rev'd and remanded, Haserot v. CIR, 355 F.2d 200 (6th Cir. 1965), Henry McK. Haserot, 46 TC 864 (1966), aff'd sub nom. CIR v. Stickney, 399 F.2d 828 (6th Cir. 1968). But see Stanley H. Brans, ¶ 83,025 P-H Memo TC, aff'd 734 F.2d 290 (6th Cir. 1984).

[138.2] Variations on this pattern included (a) The issuance of Y Corp. "securities" (in which case the exchange would be totally tax-free under §351(a)); or, alternatively, (b) a borrowing on the security of his X stock, and then transferring that stock to Y for additional Y stock and Y's assumption of the debt (relying on the rules of §357 to avoid boot treatment for the liability).

[138.3] Rev. Rul. 73-2, 1973-1 CB 171 (§304 controls over §351); Rev. Rul. 78-422, 1978-2 CB 129 (§304 controls over §357); see also Coates Jr. v. CIR, 480 F.2d 468 (9th Cir. 1973), cert. denied, 414 US 1045 (1973) (rejecting *Haserot* §351 priority view). See also Rev. Rul. 80-239, 1980-2 CB 108.

profits), even the application of §304(a)(1) to such a transaction would not result in dividend consequences to the transferor, since the acquiring corporation was treated as the distributing corporation in such a case and it had no earnings and profits (hence the distribution fell under §301(c)(2) and resulted in capital gain under §301(c)(3) if it exceeded stock basis).[138.4]

On the other hand, the formation of bank holding companies resulted in one published ruling, limited guidelines for the issuance of private letter rulings, and a general refusal to rule on the overlap of §§304 and 351 (since the area was under extensive study).[138.5] If the assumed liability was incurred by the transferor as a "mere intermediary agent for a newly created transferee," the Service ruled (in Rev. Rul. 80-240) that neither §304 nor §351 applied to the transaction, since there was no liability assumption or property distribution by the transferee.

Thus, the application of §304 to §351 exchanges (whether of newly created holding companies or to existing controlled corporations) was highly uncertain; moreover, the extent to which §357 applied (or did not apply) in the context of these transactions was equally unclear.

2. Changes to §304 by Act §226. New §304(b)(3)(A) specifically provides for the primacy of §304 over §351 (and §368) by stating that "subsection (a) (and not part III) shall apply to any property received in a distribution described in subsection (a)." [138.6] However, §304(b)(3)(B) provides an exception to §304 treatment for liabilities assumed (or taken subject to) by the acquiring corporation in the §351 exchange if such liabilities were

---

[138.4] Section 304(a)(1), §304(b)(2)(A) of old law; see, e.g., Fehrs Fin. Co. v. CIR, 487 F.2d 184 (8th Cir. 1973); Rufus K. Cox, 78 TC 1021 (1982) (no §453 reporting for §301(c)(3) capital gain via §§304(a)(1)–304(b)(2)(A)).

[138.5] Rev. Rul. 80-240, 1980-2 CB 116; Rev. Proc. 81-10, §4.01(5), 1981-1 CB 647; Rev. Proc. 81-61, 1981-2 CB 683; Rev. Proc. 82-22, §§4.01(5) and 5.04, 1982-1 CB 469; Rev. Proc. 83-22, 1983-1 CB 680, §5.08. But in Rev. Proc. 83-42, 1983-1 CB 778, the IRS resumed issuance of rulings on §§304–351 overlaps. See also Rev. Proc. 84-52, 1984-1 CB 551.

[138.6] Thus overruling *Haserot,* supra note 138.1 (this Supplement), and adopting the principle of Rev. Rul. 73-2 and *Coates Jr.,* supra note 138.3 (this Supplement).

incurred by the transferor to acquire the transferred stock.[138.7] The Conference Committee Report notes that §304 should not apply to the assumption of acquisition debt incurred to acquire the stock and then assumed by a controlled corporation acquiring such stock in a §351 exchange, since this form of transaction is merely an alternative to a direct debt-financed acquisition of such stock by the acquiring company.[138.8] Though stock acquisition debt assumed in a §351 exchange is protected from §304 treatment by the new legislation, other liabilities assumed or taken subject to in the exchange will constitute distributions of property under §304.[138.9] Thus, subsequent borrowing on the security of the transferred stock cannot be assumed by the acquiring corporation in a §351 without §304 consequences. (So to this extent, at least, the holding of Rev. Rul. 78-422 [138.10] that §304 will override §357 has been codified.)

Another significant change effected by the 1982 legislation was its revision of the earnings and profits source rules applicable to brother-sister redemptions under §304(a)(1). New §304(b) (2)(A) now provides a deemed distribution rule similar to that governing parent-subsidiary redemptions under §§304(a)(2) and 304(b)(2)(B), viz., the issuing corporation whose stock is acquired first is deemed to have distributed the property to the acquiring corporation, which is then considered to have distributed it to the transferor-shareholder.[138.11] But amendments of the Tax Re-

---

[138.7] For this purpose, extension, renewal, or refinancing of such a liability will similarly qualify for exclusion from §304 treatment, §304(b)(3)(B)(ii).

The nonapplication of §304 to assumed acquisition debt thus reverses the contrary holding in Rev. Rul. 78-422, supra note 138.3 (this Supplement).

[138.8] H. Rep. No. 760, 97th Cong., 2d Sess., at 542 (1982). The Report also states that §357(b) will not apply here either. But see §102(h)(3)(B) of H.R. 3805, the Technical Corrections Act of 1983 (introduced August 4, 1983) (this rule will not apply if stock is acquired from a person related to buyer under §318); this provision passed in §712(*l*)(3) of the Tax Reform Act of 1984, P.L. No. 98-369, 98 Stat. 678 (adding new §302(b)(3)(B)(iii)).

[138.9] H. Rep. No. 760, supra note 138.8 (this Supplement), at 543.

[138.10] Supra note 138.3 (this Supplement).

[138.11] This provision thus overrules (or makes unnecessary) the cases cited supra note 138.4 (this Supplement), and Rev. Rul. 80-239, supra note 138.3 (this Supplement). But see §102(h)(1) of H.R. 3805, the

form Act of 1984 (1984 Act) revised this ordering rule for dividends, treating the distribution as if it first came from the acquiring corporation (to the extent of its earnings), and then from the issuing corporation. Thus, in the case of a newly organized transferee corporation (or an existing transferee without earnings), dividend consequences can result to the extent that the acquired corporation has available earnings to cover the distribution, and, if both corporations have earnings, dividend treatment will result to the extent of their combined earnings.

> *To illustrate:* Assume that A owns all of X (which has earnings of $100) and transfers the X stock to newly organized Y Corp. for stock of Y worth $100 and $100 of notes. Under prior law, the $100 of notes would be treated as a non-dividend distribution under §§301(c)(2) and 301(c)(3) (assuming that §304, rather than §351(b) or §351(a), applied). Under amended §304(b)(3)(A), §304 clearly applies to the notes (although §351 would still govern the receipt of Y stock), and dividend treatment for the value of the notes would result to A under new §304(b)(2)(A) by virtue of the deemed distribution of the notes from X to Y.[138.12]

Technical Corrections Act of 1983, limiting the amount of the deemed dividend to the combined earnings and profits of the issuing and acquiring corporations. This provision passed in §712(*l*)(1) of the Tax Reform Act of 1984, which amended §304(b)(2) to measure the amount (and source) of dividends in both brother-sister and parent-subsidiary redemption transactions under the same rules; namely, first as a dividend from the acquiring corporation to the extent of its earnings and then as a dividend from the issuing corporation.

[138.12] H. Rep. No. 760, supra note 138.8 (this Supplement), at 543, specifically states that this "deemed distribution" to Y is not a "real dividend" to Y, thus reaching the same result as occurs under the parent-subsidiary redemption rule, which was agreed to by Rev. Rul. 80-189, 1980-2 CB 106.

X's earnings formerly were reduced by the *face* of the notes under §312(a)(2), even though the amount of Y's deemed distribution (and of A's actual distribution) was measured by the *value* of the notes, but the Tax Reform Act of 1984 changed this result. See supra ¶ 7.40 (this Supplement). But see supra note 138.11 (this Supplement) (deemed dividend distribution limited to combined earnings of issuing and acquiring corporations). See also amendments to §312(a)(2), supra ¶ 7.40 (this Supplement).

Alternatively, if Y were an existing corporation with an *accumulated* deficit of $100, the results to A nevertheless were the same before the 1984 Act amendments, since the hypothetical distribution from X to Y presumably created *current* earnings to Y, which then were taxable to A under §316(a)(2).[138.13] If Y's deficit was from current operations, however, Y presumably was able to offset its current operating deficit against its hypothetical dividend income in computing the amount of A's §316(a)(2) dividend.[138.14] Under the 1984 Act amendments, however, A's dividend would be unaffected by Y's deficit (whether current or accumulated), since the amount of the dividend is measured first by the earnings of Y, to the extent thereof, and then of X, to the extent thereof, without any hypothetical intercorporate distributions.

Alternatively, suppose that neither X nor Y has earnings, but that Y distributes appreciated property (basis of 10, value of $100) to A instead of notes. The property was deemed first to have been distributed by X to Y (X presumably was entitled to §311(a) protection on this deemed distribution, and Y was in receipt of a deemed dividend of $10, the property's basis, but no deemed income because X has no earnings), and then as a distribution by Y to A, which triggered $90 of §311(d)(1) gain to Y (and current earnings) and a $90 dividend to A (less any taxes payable by Y as a result of its §311(d)(1) gain).[138.15] Under the Tax Reform Act of 1984, Y would have

---

[138.13] See supra ¶ 7.02 (this Supplement).

[138.14] If neither X nor Y have earnings, could Y nevertheless be deemed to have received §301(c)(3) gain as a result of its hypothetical distribution from X, and hence have some available earnings for purposes of §316(a)(2)? If so, what basis would Y use in computing its constructive §301(c)(3) gain? Presumably, Y would use a carryover basis from A for the X stock as a result of the deemed capital contribution of that stock under §304(a)(1). See Fehrs Fin. Corp. v. CIR, supra note 138.4 (this Supplement). But see supra note 138.11 (this Supplement).

[138.15] See Regs. §§1.311-2(a)(1) and 1.311-2(a)(2) (§311(d) applies to §304 distributions). X was entitled to §311(a) protection on its deemed dividend-in-kind to Y before amendments to §311(d) by the Tax Reform Act of 1984; Y, however, was subject to §311(d)(1) (unless one of the exceptions applied, which seemed unlikely here), infra ¶ 9.64A (this Supplement). After the 1984 Act amendments,

taxable gain under §311(d)(1) on the distribution, creating $90 of current earnings (less taxes) and resulting in a comparable dividend to A; no further dividend income would result to A, since X has no available earnings.

New §304(c)(2) also makes clear that §304(a)(1) applies to the creation of a new controlled corporation (rather than being limited to transactions involving the stock of existing brother-sister corporations), even though some of the transferors receive only stock in the transferee corporation. Thus, if A and B own all of X Corp., and transfer their X stock to newly organized Y Corp. in exchange for Y stock and short-term notes, §304(a)(1) will apply to the notes, while §351(a) will apply to the Y stock received by A and B. If A instead received all the Y stock, while B received solely the Y notes, §304(a)(1) applies to the B-Y exchange (although B should obtain §302(a) sale treatment here, assuming that he has no §318 relationship to A or Y).

The bifurcation rule of the 1982 law version of §304(b)(3) (A), coupled with the expanded control group definition of §304 (c)(2), offered some interesting planning possibilities. Thus, suppose that A owned all of X Corp. and B owned all of Y Corp. (A and B being unrelated.) If A sold all of his X stock to Y for cash and stock of Y, §304 did not apply to the transaction (unless A received 50 percent of Y's stock in the exchange, or was related to B or Y via §318). Accordingly, A's exchange with Y would result in a fully taxable capital gain or loss to A (and a cost basis purchase of X stock by Y). If, however, A transferred his X stock to newly organized Z Corp. for cash (or notes of Z) and Z stock, while B concurrently transferred his Y stock to Z solely for Z stock, §304(a)(1) applied to A's receipt of the nonstock consideration, while §351(a) (or §368(a)(1)(B)) [138.16] would apply to A and

---

however, all distributions to corporate shareholders will result in §311(d)(1) gain to the distributing corporation, but the 1984 Act amendments to §304(b)(2) dropped the hypothetical intercorporate dividend rule of the 1982 law, supra note 138.11 (this Supplement).

[138.16] Z would acquire control of both X and Y, and the cash segment of the A-Z exchange is excised from §368 by §304(b)(3)(A). Application of §304 to A in this example assumes that A obtains at least 50 percent of Z's stock. But see §102(h)(2) of H.R. 3805, the Technical Corrections Act of 1983 (introduced August 4, 1983), which removes the possible application of §368 to the stock received by A.

B's receipt of Z stock. Depending upon A's proportionate interest in X after the exchange, capital gain or dividend income would result to A upon his receipt of the boot.[138.17] Presumably, these same results would occur if X and Y were publicly held, as long as a significant number of X and Y shareholders participated in order to meet the 50 percent control line of §304(c). (The net result of this analysis seemed to open the way for the payment of cash in the functional equivalent of a Type B reorganization, but amendments by the Tax Reform Act of 1984 to §304(b)(3)(A) cured this potential anomaly.[138.18])

In a similar vein, the 1982 law earnings and profits source rule of §304(b)(2)(A) offered some planning possibilities that were probably not intended by the 1982 amendments. For example, if A owned 100 percent of X and 50 percent of Y (while B owned the other 50 percent), A's sale of his Y stock to X will be a §304(a)(1), §302(d), §301 dividend [138.19] to A (measured by the earnings of *both* X and Y). But Y's earnings account was reduced as a result of its hypothetical dividend to X under former §304(b)(2)(A) (before its amendment in 1984), leaving the possibility that later distributions to B would not be subject to dividend treatment

---

This provision passed as §712(*l*)(2) of the Tax Reform Act of 1984, which amended §304(b)(3)(A) to preempt *only* §351, not §368.

[138.17] If A owned (constructively) less than 50 percent of X, §302(b)(2) would apply; (in fact, if A owned less than 50 percent of Z, §304 apparently doesn't even apply here); if A owned exactly 50 percent of X, §302(b)(1) would apply, Rev. Rul. 75-502, 1975-2 CB 111; if A owned more than 50 percent, but less than 80 percent, presumably a dividend would result to A, Rev. Rul. 78-401, 1978-2 CB 127; if A is deemed to own 80 percent of X through his ownership of Z, dividend treatment for the boot seems assured.

[138.18] See supra ¶ 3.19 and infra ¶ 14.13 (this Supplement). Compare Rev. Rul. 80-284, 1980-2 CB 117; and Rev. Rul. 80-285, 1980-2 CB 119. But see Rev. Rul. 84-71, 1984-1 CB 106, revoking these rulings. However, the Tax Reform Act of 1984, in §712(1)(2) (supra note 138.16), eliminated this possibility by confining the primacy of §304 solely to §351.

[138.19] Since A's ownership of Y has remained at 50 percent (through his 100 percent ownership of X). If A is a corporate shareholder, dividend consequences are essentially abated by the §243 deduction. But see §712(*l*)(1) of the Tax Reform Act of 1984 (deemed distribution would now flow first from X, the acquiring corporation, to A, and then from Y to A, thus preventing the result described in the text example). See supra note 138.11.

under §316. This stripping of Y's earnings account by the deemed dividend rule of §304(b)(2)(A) seemed possible, however, only where the §304(a)(1) transaction resulted in dividend treatment to the selling shareholder. Thus, if B sold his Y stock to X, §304 (a)(1) applied, but B got sale treatment under §302(b), and hence Y's earnings account was not reduced by §304(b)(2)(A).

New §§304(b)(3)(C) and 304(b)(3)(D) provide special limited rules for the treatment of distributions of securities to certain minority shareholders incident to the formation of bank holding companies.[138.20]

The 1984 Act also amended the constructive ownership rules of §304(c)(3) to restrict the flow of attributive ownership under §318 in de minimis situations. Thus, new §304(c)(3)(B) attributes out of corporations only to 5 percent shareholders, and attributes into corporations only stock owned by 5 percent-or-more shareholders, and then only to the extent of their ownership (stock owned by 50 percent-or-more shareholders, however, is attributed in under §318 in full).

The new amendments to §304 apply generally to transfers occurring after August 31, 1982, in taxable years ending after such date (although the bank holding company provisions have a special August 16 rule for applications on file with the Federal Reserve Board before such date that are completed before 1983).[138.21]

[138.20] See supra note 138.5 (this Supplement).

[138.21] See Bloom, The Stark Reality of the New Liquidation and Redemption Rules, 10 J. Corp. Tax. 3 (1983); Ginsburg, Taxing Corporate Acquisitions, 38 Tax L. Rev. 171 (1983); Steines, Taxation of Corporate Distributions—Before and After TEFRA, 68 Iowa L. Rev. 937 (1983); Faber, How the New Tax Law Changes the Rule Affecting the Bailout of Corporate Earnings, 49 J. Tax. 281 (1983); deKosmian, Partial Liquidations, Section 311(d) Redemptions and Section 304 Under TEFRA, 61 Taxes 918 (1983); Tiger, Redemption Through Use of Related Corporations: New and Old Problems Under Section 304, 39 Tax L. Rev. 77 (1984).

For treatment of the 1984 Act amendments to §304, see Eustice. The Tax Reform Act of 1984, ¶ 3.04[3].

PART D.　REDEMPTIONS TO PAY DEATH
TAXES: §303

¶ 9.40.　REDEMPTIONS UNDER §303

Page 9-55:

Add to note 139, second paragraph.

[139] See ABA Tax Section Report, Overall Impact of the Tax Reform
Act of 1976 on §303, 32 Tax Law. 243 (1979); Blum and Trier, Plan-
ning for Maximum Benefits of Section 303 Redemptions With Estate
Tax Deferral, 53 J. Tax. 236 (1980); Kahn, Closely Held Stocks —
Deferral and Financing of Estate Tax Costs Through Sections 303 and
6166, 35 Tax Law. 639 (1982).

Regulations under §303 reflecting the amendments effected by the
Tax Reform Act of 1976 and ERTA 1981 were proposed on August
22, 1984.

Add to note 140, first paragraph.

[140] But § 1023 was repealed by the Crude Oil Windfall Profit Tax
Act of 1980.

Page 9-56:

Add new note 140.1 to second sentence of paragraph (1).

[140.1] Rev. Rul. 84-76, 1984-22 IRB 6 (stock redeemed must be
owned by decedent at death to qualify for §303 if such stock was not
includable in his gross estate, even though it counts for percentage test
of §303(b).

Correct fifth line of note 141.

Citation should be "§306(b)(5)" not "§303(b)(5)." See generally Rev. Rul. 82-72, 1982-1 CB 57 (§303 redemption of §306
stock); Prop. Regs. §1.303-1(f).

Add to note 142.

[142] The Economic Recovery Tax Act (ERTA) of 1981, P.L. No.
97-34, 95 Stat. 172, eased the aggregation rules of §303(b)(2)(B) by
lowering the inclusion threshold from 75 percent to 20 percent. See
Prop. Regs. §1.303-1(a)(2).

Page 9-57:

Add to text at end of line 4.

The ERTA of 1981 [142.1] reduced the 50 percent line to 35 percent
(for decedents dying after 1981).

―――――――――

[142.1] Supra note 142 (this Supplement). See Prop. Regs. §1.303-
1(a).

Add to note 143, second paragraph.

¹⁴³ The ERTA of 1981, supra note 142 (this Supplement), consolidated §§6166 and 6166A into one section and repealed §6166A. See Kahn, supra note 139 (this Supplement); Anderson, Letter Rulings Indicate Approval of Serial Redemptions Along With Deferral Under 303, 59 J. Tax. 370 (1973).
See Prop. Regs. §1.303-1(c) for distribution timing rules.

Page 9-58:

Add to note 145, first paragraph.

¹⁴⁵ The ERTA of 1981, supra note 142 (this Supplement), further eased the rules for §6166 deferred tax payment treatment by lowering the 65 percent qualification line to 35 percent. See Prop. Regs. §1.303-1(d).

Add to note 145, second paragraph.

¹⁴⁵ See Anderson, supra note 143 (this Supplement).

Add to note 147, first paragraph.

¹⁴⁷ But §1023 was repealed by the Crude Oil Windfall Profit Tax Act of 1980.
See generally Prop. Regs. §1.303-1(e).

PART E. PARTIAL LIQUIDATIONS UNDER §346

¶ 9.50. INTRODUCTORY

Page 9-59:

Add to text at end of section.

Proposed legislation, initially approved by the Senate Finance Committee and the House Ways and Means Subcommittee on Select Revenue Measures (entitled the Corporate Takeover Tax Act of 1982), would have repealed the partial liquidation provisions of §346, effective September 1, 1982, and substituted new §346, titled "definition and special rule." Under this provision, existing §346 (a)(1) (series of redemptions in complete liquidation, infra ¶ 9.51) would have been retained as §346(a) and defined as a complete liquidation. The contraction provisions of §346(a)(2) (infra ¶ 9.52) would have been repealed, but the "two-business" provisions of §346(b) (infra ¶ 9.53) would have been shifted to new

§302(e) and limited to noncorporate shareholder-distributees. Proposed §346(b) provided a broad grant of regulatory authority to deal with transactions that may have the effect of a partial liquidation. The proposed legislation would have deleted all references to partial liquidations and confined §§331(a) and 336(a) exclusively to complete liquidation transactions. These provisions passed the Senate in July 1982. But the Conference Committee version (August 1982) retained partial liquidation treatment (in new §302(e)) for individual shareholders.

Thus, new §346(a) continues the former §346(a)(1) "series" rule, but defines it as a complete liquidation; new §346(b) contains the regulatory delegation rule (which could prove to be a strong foundation for broad anti-reincorporation regulations, see infra ¶ 14.54); all partial liquidations are shifted to §302 (§§331, 334(a), and 336 are now limited to complete liquidation transactions); partial liquidation sale treatment is limited by new §302 (b)(4) to noncorporate shareholders; and the definition of partial liquidation in old §346 was shifted to new §302(e) without significant change. (New §302(e)(1) contains the "contraction" definition, while new §302(e)(2) contains the "two-business" rules of former §346(b).) See infra new ¶ 9.54 (this Supplement).

Page 9-60:

Add to note 149, first paragraph.

[149] Golden, Thinking Small? Problems and Opportunities Presented by Partial Liquidations, 58 Taxes 887 (1980); Ward, The TEFRA Amendments to Subchapter C: Corporate Distributions and Acquisitions, 2 J. Corp. L. 277 (1983); Ginsburg, Taxing Corporate Acquisitions, 38 Tax L. Rev. 171 (1983); deKosmian, Partial Liquidations, Section 311(d) Redemptions and Section 304 Under TEFRA, 61 Taxes 918 (1983).

Add to note 149, second paragraph.

[149] Rev. Proc. 73-36 superseded and updated by Rev. Proc. 81-42, 1981-2 CB 604.

¶ 9.51. ONE OF A SERIES OF DISTRIBUTIONS IN COMPLETE LIQUIDATION: §346(a)(1)

Page 9-60:

Add to text at end of first paragraph.

Legislation enacted in 1982 (supra ¶ 9.50, this Supplement) officially classified these serial liquidation transactions as complete liquidations. This provision passed (as new §346(a)) in August of 1982 and became law on September 3, 1982.[149.1]

[149.1] See generally Joseph Olmsted, ¶ 87,381 P-H Memo TC (complete liquidation found, even though long delay in liquidation process, because of an intent to liquidate, a continuing purpose to liquidate, and corporate activities oriented toward liquidation).

Page 9-62:

Correct eleventh line of second paragraph.

Holding period reference should be "one year," not "six months."

¶ 9.52.   CORPORATE CONTRACTIONS: §346(a)(2)

Page 9-63:

Add to text at end of first runover paragraph.

Legislation proposed in 1982 (supra ¶ 9.50, this Supplement) would have repealed the partial liquidation provisions of §346 (a)(2). But the final Conference Committee version only repeals partial liquidation treatment for corporate shareholders, and this version passed as new §§302(b)(4) and 302(e)(1), effective for distributions after August 31, 1982. See infra ¶ 9.54 (this Supplement).

Page 9-66:

Add to note 168, first paragraph.

[168] Nord Krauskopf, ¶ 84,386 P-H Memo TC (no contraction; no significant reduction in business capital or activities).

Add to note 168, second paragraph, following Rev. Rul. 76–279 citation.

[168] Rev. Rul. 79-275, 1979-2 CB 137 (not a contraction where distribute unrelated assets; must distribute contracted business assets or proceeds of their sale);

Add to note 168, second paragraph, following Rev. Rul. 75-223 citation.

[168] Rev. Rul. 75-223 distinguished by Rev. Rul. 79-184, 1979-1 CB 143 (parent's sale of *stock* of subsidiary and distribution of proceeds

not §346(a)(2) partial liquidation because no basis for attributing business of subsidiary to parent via §381; mere sale of investment asset by parent and distribution of dividend).

Add to end of note 168.

[168] See generally Rose, Representations Required by IRS for Rulings on a Partial Liquidation of a Subsidiary's Business Go Further Than Necessary, 9 J. Corp. Tax. 151 (1982). Rev. Proc. 82-40, 1982-2 CB 761 (no contraction ruling unless distribution results in at least a 20 percent reduction in gross revenues, net assets, and employees).

Partial liquidations via the corporate-level contraction route typically are pro-rata, although they need not be, Rev. Rul. 82-187, 1982-2 CB 80.

Add new sentence to end of first full paragraph.

However, the principal advantage of the partial liquidation contraction rules of former §346 (now found in new §302(e)(1)) over §302 is the pro-rata character of such distributions,[169.1] since a pro-rata transaction cannot ordinarily meet the requirements of §302(b). New §302(e)(1) now specifically tests for a contraction effect at the corporate level.

[169.1] While partial liquidations usually are pro-rata, they need not be, Rev. Rul. 82-187, 1982-2 CB 80.

Page 9-67:

Add to note 172.

[172] Rev. Rul. 79-257, 1979-2 CB 136 (not necessary to redeem stock where distributing company wholly owned by one shareholder); Rev. Rul. 81-3, 1981-1 CB 125 (same if pro-rata distribution). But see Rev. Proc. 82-31, 1982-1 CB 486 (no ruling on §346 status where lack of redemption if more than one class of stock or there are other outstanding rights, e.g., warrants, options, convertible debt, etc., affecting the corporation's stock).

¶ 9.53. TERMINATION OF ONE OUT OF TWO OR MORE BUSINESSES: §346(b)

Page 9-68:

Add to note 176.

[176] Legislation enacted in 1982 (infra ¶ 9.54, this Supplement) shifted the provisions of §346(b) to new §302(e) and limited their application to noncorporate shareholder-distributees. New §§302(b)(4) and 302(e)(2), effective for distributions after August 31, 1982.

Page 9-69:

Add to note 178.

[178] Rev. Rul. 79-275, 1979-2 CB 137 (interpretation of "attributable"); Kenton Meadows Co., ¶ 84,379 P-H Memo TC (corporation did not distribute full proceeds of terminated business, hence no §346(b) transaction).

Page 9-71:

Add to note 181.

[181] Kenton Meadows Co., supra note 178 (this Supplement) (single integrated business, not two separate businesses; §355 cases allowing split of single business not applicable under §346(b) rules); Nord Krauskopf, supra note 168 (this Supplement) (terminated business not a separate business; merely an incident to taxpayer's main business activity).

Page 9-72:

Add new note 182(a) to last sentence of section.

[182a] For an illustration of the dangers of proceeding without a ruling here, see Kenton Meadows Co., supra note 178 (this Supplement) (flunked §346 and thus a dividend to shareholders; moreover, corporation also taxable on appreciated assets under §311(d)(1)).

Add new heading.

¶ 9.54. PARTIAL LIQUIDATIONS AFTER TEFRA AMENDMENTS

1. In general. Partial liquidation distributions qualifying under §346 offered numerous significant tax benefits to both the distributing corporation and its distributee shareholders (especially in the context of the consolidated return regulations) viz., (a) the distributee shareholders received capital gain or loss treatment with respect to the distribution under §331(a)(2) (assuming that §341 did not apply); [182.1] (b) the distributed property obtained a stepped-

---

[182.1] Corporate distributees in a consolidated return generally received nonrecognition treatment on partial liquidation distributions in kind under Regs. §1.1502-14(b)(1); if distributed cash exceeded the distributee's stock basis, gain could be recognized under Regs. §1.1502-14(b)(2)(i); while loss could be recognized under Regs. §1.1502-

up (or down) fair market value basis to the distributee under §334(a); [182.2] (c) gain or loss was not recognized to the distributing corporation under §336 (except for various recapture items, LIFO inventory distributions, and distributions of installment obligations); [182.3] and (d) the distributing corporation, since it was not completely liquidated, preserved its general tax history (e.g., net operating loss carryovers, earnings deficits, investment tax credit (ITC) carryovers, etc.) [182.4] and tax basis with respect to any undistributed assets.

These tax benefits formed the inspiration for the structure of several recent highly publicized acquisitions. For example, P Corp. could buy all (or 80 percent control) of the stock of target T Corp., include T in its consolidated return,[182.5] have T make selected partial liquidation distributions to P (with no current recapture to

---

14(b)(2)(ii) if the distribution consisted solely of cash, but any gain or loss so recognized was deferred under Regs. §1.1502-14(b)(2)(iii), subject to recapture under Regs. §1.1502-14(b)(3) (when the distributee ceased to be a member of the group, or one of the excess loss account (ELA) triggers of Regs. §1.1502-19(b)(2) occurred). See infra ¶ 15.23. See Ginsburg, Taxing Corporate Acquisitions, 38 Tax L. Rev. 171 (1983).

[182.2] Basis results in a consolidated return were determined under Regs. §1.1502-31(b)(2)(ii) by reference to the distributee corporation's basis in the stock exchanged (or deemed exchanged) in the partial liquidation (the basis result here was analogous to that which occurred under the §334(b)(2) rules).

[182.3] See generally infra ¶¶ 11.61–11.66. By contrast, asset sales are taxable at the corporate level, since §337 does not apply to partial liquidation transactions.

In the consolidated return content, however, matters were much more favorable: (a) no ITC recapture occurred by virtue of Regs. §1.1502-3(f)(2)(i); (b) any gain recognized to the distributing corporation was treated as a deferred intercompany transaction under Regs. §1.1502-14(c)(1); and (c) any ultimately recognized gain could be sheltered in the consolidated return by losses or tax credit carryovers from other members of the group (see infra ¶¶ 15.23 and 15.24).

[182.4] See infra Ch. 16. Partial liquidations could, however, trigger §382(a) if coupled with the requisite change of stock ownership. Infra ¶ 16.22.

[182.5] Rev. Rul. 80-169, 1980-1 CB 188 (include in consolidated return on day after acquisition date); for the possibility of short-term (one-day) membership, see Private Ltr. 8118011, 1981 P-H Fed. Tax Serv. ¶ 55,261.

T),[182.6] and obtain a stepped-up basis for T's distributed assets without recognition of gain or loss to P. Moreover, P could cause T to distribute virtually all of its assets (though not so much as to constitute a complete liquidation) and obtain the above-noted tax benefits of a partial liquidation, while effecting the economic equivalent of a complete liquidation of T. Alternatively, had P merely purchased the wanted assets directly from T, gain or loss would have been recognized in full to T, and P would simply obtain a cost basis for those assets under §1012 (without inheriting any of T's tax history).

2. Changes effected by TEFRA §222. The final 1982 legislation significantly modified the treatment of partial liquidations, although less drastically than some of the earlier versions.[182.7] Essentially, the treatment of partial liquidations for individual shareholders was retained intact, although the applicable provisions of old §346 were shifted to new §§302(b)(4) and 302(e). The serial liquidation type of partial liquidation in old §346(a)(1) was retained as new §346(a), but this transaction was redefined for what it was, a complete liquidation. All references to "partial liquidations" in old §§331(a) and 336(a) were deleted.[182.8]

[182.6] And no ITC recapture at all, Regs. §1.1502-3(f)(2)(i). Later, recapture income triggered in P's consolidated return could also be sheltered by the group's losses, or loss carryovers.

[182.7] The original version of the Stark Bill, H.R. 6295, abolished virtually all of the partial liquidation rules (except for §346(b)-type transactions); similarly, the original Senate Finance Committee version of H.R. 4961 repealed all the partial liquidation rules except for §346 (b)-type transactions involving individual shareholder distributees. The Bill that passed the Senate, however, retained all the partial liquidation rules for individual shareholders (i.e., contraction distributions and §346(b)-type distributions), although that version of the Bill had no statutory definition of partial liquidation. See generally Ward, The TEFRA Amendments to Subchapter C: Corporate Distributions and Acquisitions, 2 J. Corp. L. 277 (1983); Ginsburg, supra note 182.1 (this Supplement); Bloom, The Stark Reality of the New Liquidation and Redemption Rules, 10 J. Corp. Tax. 3 (1983); Steines, Taxation of Corporate Distributions—Before and After TEFRA, 68 Iowa L. Rev. 937 (1983); and deKosmian, Partial Liquidations, Section 311(d) Redemptions and Section 304 Under TEFRA, 61 Taxes 918 (1983).

[182.8] Similar language deletions were made to §§306(b)(2), 312(e), 331(b), 334(a), and 336(b).
Moreover, the flush sentence in §346(a) (including a §302(a) stock

Under new §302(e)(1), the contraction definition of old §346(a)(2) is retained, although only for individual stockholders, while new §§302(e)(2) and 302(e)(3) contains virtually the same language as old §346(b), although again only for individual stockholders. Corporate shareholders thus are excluded from qualifying for partial liquidation treatment, with the result that dividend treatment ordinarily will occur to such shareholders.[182.9] The Conference Report specifically notes that an actual stock redemption is not required for partial liquidation treatment to apply and intends that such treatment be continued for §302(e) partial liquidations.[182.10] The Report also adds that §302(e) partial liquidations can be pro rata, and that distributions in partial liquidation that terminate a shareholder's interest will qualify for §302(a) sale treatment regardless of §302(c)(2).[182.11]

The tax consequences to the distributing corporation with respect to partial liquidation distributions will now be governed by §311, rather than §336. If the distribution is a dividend, as it will ordinarily be if a corporate shareholder is involved, §311(a) (and §§311(b) and 311(c)) will apply to it;[182.12] if the distribution qualifies as a §302(e) partial liquidation, however, §311(d) must be faced, and significant changes in that provision were effected by the 1982 legislation and again in 1984 by the Tax Reform Act of 1984 (which are considered infra ¶ 9.64A (this Supplement)).

---

redemption as a partial liquidation for purposes of the §562(b) dividends-paid deduction) was finally moved to its proper home in §562(b)(1) (after a twenty-eight-year wait). The genesis for the initial location of this sentence was the product of a more restrained and genteel legislative process, during which Congress exhibited considerably more restraint as to what could be done in the House-Senate Conference—an ironical twist indeed when one considers the freewheeling spectacle of recent legislative exercises.

[182.9] But such dividends will not create PHC dividend income to a corporate shareholder by virtue of new §543(a)(1)(C).

[182.10] H. Rep. No. 760, 97th Cong., 2d Sess., at 530, citing *Fowler Hosiery* and Rev. Rul. 81-3.

[182.11] Id. Presumably this means that §318 attribution rules will not apply to such distributions (although this sentence could also mean that the waiver benefits of §302(c)(3) are not available to escape attribution; however, the former view seems closer to what the Conferees appeared to have in mind). See also Rev. Rul. 82-187, 1982-2 CB 80.

[182.12] See supra ¶ 7.21 (this Supplement).

In determining whether stock is held by a noncorporate share-holder for purposes of §302(e), new §302(e)(5) provides that stock held by partnerships, estates and trusts shall be treated as if it were directly held proportionately by their partners and bene-ficiaries.[182.13]

New §346(b) contains a broad delegation of authority to draft regulations insuring that "the purposes of [this section] (which repeal the special tax treatment for partial liquidations) may not be circumvented through the use of sections 355, 351, 337, or any other provision of law or regulations (including the consolidated return regulations)." [182.14]

The new partial liquidation rules are generally effective for distributions after August 31, 1982, although an incredibly com-plex array of special grandfather rules is contained in Act §222 (f)(2) (which will no doubt be readily ascertainable by the special interests that succeeded in obtaining them).

3. *To Illustrate.* The new partial liquidation rules can be illus-trated by the following examples in which T Corp. operates an active five-year-old business directly, and also has two operating subsid-iaries, X and Y, both of which have also been owned for over five years by T.

Example 1: T sells its operating business and distributes the sale proceeds ratably to its three equal shareholders (P Corp., individual A, and partnership B, all of whose partners are in-dividuals).[182.15] If §302(e)(1) applies, which it presumably

---

[182.13] If some partners or beneficiaries are corporations, and some are individuals, special allocations will be necessary to insure that the entity-level capital gain or loss and dividend income is assigned to the proper member who is entitled to it; these computations, needless to say, can become quite complex.

[182.14] An example of the type of transaction envisioned here is con-tained in S. Rep. No. 494, Vol. 1, July 12, 1982, at 188.

The real "juice" in this provision, however, could well give the Treasury renewed vigor to deal with the liquidation-reincorporation problem by more extensive and detailed regulation rules. See infra ¶ 14.54.

[182.15] If a trust, estate, or partnership has corporate beneficiaries or partners, §302(e)(5) treats the stock owned by such entities as if it were owned proportionately by their beneficiaries or partners.

would here,[182.16] A and B obtain §302(a) treatment by virtue of §302(b)(4), while P Corp. would have a dividend under §301.[182.17]

Example 2: X sells all of its assets, distributes the sales proceeds to T in complete liquidation under §332, and T distributes these proceeds ratably to its shareholders, P Corp., A and B. Again, §302(e)(1) apparently would apply,[182.18] and the tax consequences to P, A, and B would be the same as Example (1).

Example 3: Alternatively, T sells the X stock and distributes the proceeds ratably to P, A, and B. The Service has ruled that such a transaction is not a valid contraction,[182.19] so P, A, and B all would receive dividend treatment here.

Example 4: T distributes the X and Y stock ratably to P, A, and B; subsequently, T distributes all of its remaining active business assets in kind to P, A, and B and dissolves. Arguably, the distribution of X and Y stock is tax-free under §355,[182.20] while the subsequent asset distribution would constitute a complete liquidation of T; however, new §346(b) would apply to characterize this transaction as a partial liquidation,[182.21] resulting in the same tax consequences to P, A, and B as Example (2).

[182.16] The transaction is a valid "contraction"; see supra ¶ 9.52; Rev. Rul. 75-223, 1975-1 CB 109; and Rev. Rul. 79-184, 1979-1 CB 143. See also Rev. Rul. 74-544, 1974-2 CB 108.

[182.17] Subject to the 85 percent §243 deduction, but not resulting in personal holding company income to P by virtue of new §543(a)(1)(C). For new restrictions on the dividends received deduction effected by the Tax Reform Act of 1984 (dealing with "leveraged" purchases of portfolio stock and "extraordinary dividends"), see supra ¶ 5.06 (this Supplement).

Similarly, if B had a corporate partner, a proportionate share of the distribution to B would be a dividend equal to such partner's interest in B. Query, is the corporate partner's proportionate interest determined by reference to its interest in profits, in capital, or both?

[182.18] See Rev. Rul. 75-223 and Rev. Rul. 79-184, supra note 182.16 (this Supplement). The same result under §302(e) should apply if X liquidated into T and T made the sale.

[182.19] Rev. Rul. 79-184, supra note 182.16 (this Supplement).

[182.20] See Rev. Rul. 75-223, supra note 182.16 (this Supplement); and Rev. Rul. 77-191, 1977-1 CB 94.

[182.21] See supra note 182.14 (this Supplement). See also Rev. Rul.

Example 5: Alternatively, T is wholly owned by P, and P, T, X, and Y file consolidated returns. The transactions in *Examples 1–4* would all give rise to dividend treatment to P, which amount, however, is eliminated under the consolidated return regulations.[182.22] Thus, partial liquidation treatment is no longer possible in the consolidated return context.[182.23]

76-429, 1976-2 CB 97; Rev. Rul. 77-191, supra note 182.20 (this Supplement); and TASCO [Tel. Ans. Serv. Corp.], 63 TC 423 (1974).

[182.22] Regs. §1.1502-14(a). P's basis for any assets distributed in kind is a carryover basis from T, increased by any recognized gain to T on the distribution, even though such gain is deferred under Regs. §1.1502-14(c)(1); Regs. §§1.1502-31(a) and 1.1502-31(b)(1).

[182.23] See infra ¶ 15.23, and supra notes 182.1–182.3 (this Supplement). For taxability of the distributing corporation in the case of distributions to corporate shareholders after amendments to §311(d) by the Tax Reform Act of 1984, see supra ¶ 7.21 and infra ¶ 9.64(A) (this Supplement).

PART F. COLLATERAL PROBLEMS ARISING FROM PARTIAL LIQUIDATIONS AND STOCK REDEMPTIONS

¶ 9.64. RECOGNITION OF CORPORATE GAIN OR LOSS ON DISTRIBUTION IN REDEMPTION

Page 9-79:

Add to note 201.

[201] But see Master Eagle Assocs., Inc. v. US, 508 F. Supp. 124 (S.D. N.Y. 1981) (shareholder sale following redemption in kind not imputed to corporation under *Court Holding Co.* principles); see supra ¶ 7.21, note 139 annotations (this Supplement).

Add to note 202.

[202] Rev. Rul. 80-221, 1980-2 CB 107, so holds (sale of "putable" preferred stock for cash by issuing corporation, followed thirteen months later by redemption in kind with wanted assets, held taxable corporate level sale of asset; §311(a) not applicable).

The Service's former acquiescence in *Standard Linen* was changed to nonacquiescence in January 1983, 1983-3 IRB 5. See also Rev. Rul. 83-38, 1983-1 CB 76 (holds corporate-level sale where purchase of stock mere transitory step to exchange of purchased stock for wanted assets; distribution was not with respect to shareholder status, which was merely incidental to sale transaction). See infra note 207.1 (this Supplement) and ¶ 9.64A (this Supplement).

Page 9-80:

Add to note 205, end of runover paragraph.

[205] Rev. Rul. 79-275, 1979-2 CB 137 (§311(d)(1) applies even though dividend equivalent redemption); Kenton Meadows Co., supra note 178 (this Supplement) (same).

Add to note 206.

[206] Legislation proposed in 1982 would have repealed the partial liquidation provisions of §346 so that §336 would govern only complete liquidation distributions; see supra ¶ 9.50 (this Supplement). This legislation passed in August of 1982; consequently, partial liquidation distributions are governed at the corporate level by new §311(d) (see infra new paragraph 3 in this section (this Supplement)).

Add to note 207.

[207] See Rev. Rul. 79-314, 1979-2 CB 132 (reciprocal exchanges by more than 10 percent shareholders of their respective interests in each other protected by §311(d)(2)(A)); Rev. Rul. 80-101, 1980-1 CB 70 (same for reciprocal exchanges in complete liquidation of one of the corporate parties).

Add new note 207.1 at end of next to last sentence.

[207.1] See, e.g., Rev. Rul. 79-273, 1979-2 CB 125 (§311(d)(2)(B) protected distribution). For description of recent attempts to use §311 (d)(2)(B) to purchase a subsidiary by acquiring the parent's stock and then swapping that stock for the subsidiary, see Shop Talk, 55 J. Tax. 127 (1981), 53 J. Tax. 328 (1980), and 53 J. Tax. 264 (1980). But see Rev. Rul. 83-38 and Rev. Rul. 80-221, supra note 202 (this Supplement). See also Rollin & Sherck, Fragmenting a Business Enterprise to Improve the Tax Position of Corporations and Stockholders, 59 Taxes 870 (1981); Axelrod, Esmark's Tax-Free Disposition of a Subsidiary: Too Good To Be True? 9 J. Corp. Tax. 232 (1982); Henderson, Federal Tax Techniques for Asset Redeployment Transactions, 37 Tax L. Rev. 325 (1982).

Amendments to §311(d)(2) by §223 of TEFRA of 1982, P.L. No. 97-248, 96 Stat. 324, effectively put an end to the transactions described above; see infra new paragraph 3 in this section (this Supplement). See also Rev. Rul. 83-38, supra note 202 (this Supplement) (pre-TEFRA law). See also infra ¶ 9.64A (this Supplement).

Page 9-81:

Add new note 209.1 at end of second full paragraph of text.

[209.1] See 55 J. Tax. 330 (1981), discussing recent private ruling sanctioning use of §311(d)(2)(A) to effect a charitable bail-out plan; viz., gift of 10 percent of stock of personal holding company to charity (§170 deduction for value, and no gain to donor), followed by redemption in kind with portfolio securities (no gain to corporation per §311 (d)(2)(A) exception).

Add new paragraphs 3–5 to text at end of section.

3. 1982 amendments. Legislation initially proposed in 1982 would have materially expanded the scope of §311(d) by completely repealing the exceptions in §§311(d)(2)(A), 311(d) (2)(B), 311(d)(2)(C), and 311(d)(2)(G), effective September 1, 1982. The inspiration for this legislation stemmed from several takeover transactions structured to fall within the exemptions to §311(d).[209.2] It was felt that property exchanged for the distributing corporation's stock was economically equivalent to a direct sale of the property and hence these two transactions should be treated symmetrically. Elimination of the principal exceptions in §311(d)(2), coupled with repeal of the partial liquidation rules, would result generally in the recognition of gain to a continuing corporation when it distributes appreciated property in redemption of its stock.

Three exceptions to §311(d)(1) were proposed to be retained in §311(d)(2), however: those for §303 redemptions, certain distributions by private foundations, and distributions by regulated investment companies.

The Conference Committee version (August 1982), however, was more limited in scope; the existing exceptions in §§311(d)(2) (A) and 311(d)(2)(B) generally continued for *individual* shareholders (although in considerably tightened form), while §311 (d)(1) would apply to corporate distributee-shareholders.

The final version of new §311(d), which passed in August of 1982 as §223 of TEFRA of 1982,[209.3] followed the general con-

---

[209.2] Supra note 207.1 (this Supplement).

[209.3] *Id.* See Ward, the TEFRA Amendments to Subchapter C: Corporate Distributions and Acquisitions, 2 J. Corp. L. 277 (1983); Ginsburg, Taxing Corporate Acquisitions, 38 Tax L. Rev. 171 (1983); and deKosmian, Partial Liquidations, Section 311(d) Redemptions and

tours of the Conference version. Thus, new §311(d)(2)(A) provides for nonrecognition on distributions in kind to corporate shareholders if the dividend basis rule applies to the transaction; new §311(d)(2)(B) exempts partial liquidation distributions from corporate-level gain recognition if the distribution is made with respect to "qualified stock," defined by new §311(e)(1) as an individual shareholder who has owned at least 10 percent of the distributing corporation's stock (*with* expanded §318 attribution rules) for at least five years; and new §311(d)(2)(C) exempts qualified distributions of a subsidiary's stock to noncorporate shareholders if the distribution satisfies new §311(e)(2); viz., it is made with respect to "qualified stock" (i.e., to a 10 percent, five-year, noncorporate shareholder), the subsidiary is essentially an operating subsidiary whose business has been conducted for at least five years and was not acquired in a taxable transaction within such period, and more than 50 percent of the subsidiary's stock is distributed.

For analysis of these amendments, see new ¶ 9.64A (this Supplement).

4. 1983 proposals. A preliminary report by the Staff of the Senate Finance Committee for the reform of Subchapter C, submitted on September 22, 1983, proposed the complete repeal of §311 for all distributions of appreciated property (whether as dividends or in redemption of stock) if the distribution results in a stepped-up basis to the distributee. These proposals, if enacted, would repeal §§311(d)(2) and 311(e) as part of the overall repeal of the *General Utilities* doctrine. Hearings were held on October 24, 1983, but at this writing the core provisions of these proposals have not been formally introduced.

5. 1984 legislation. Recent legislation (§54(a) of the Tax Reform Act of 1984, which passed the House on April 11, 1984, §36(a) of the Deficit Reduction Act of 1984, which passed the Senate on April 13, 1984, and §54(a) of the Tax Reform Act of 1984, P.L. No. 98-369, 98 Stat. 678, which became law on July 19, 1984) further contracted the scope of §311, though it did not completely repeal that provision as was suggested by the Finance Committee Staff proposals. See supra ¶ 7.21 and infra ¶ 9.64A (this Supplement).

Add new heading.

¶ 9.64A.   DISTRIBUTIONS OF APPRECIATED PROPERTY IN REDEMPTION OF STOCK—NEW §311(d) RULES AFTER TEFRA AMENDMENTS

1. In general. A direct purchase of part of the assets of one corporation ordinarily results in a fully taxable gain or loss to the selling company; similarly, nonliquidating distributions of appreciated property in redemption of part of the distributing corporation's stock were also taxable to the distributing corporation under §311 (d)(1),[209.4] unless such distribution qualified for one of the various exceptions in former §311(d)(2) (the most generally applicable of which were §311(d)(2)(A), complete termination redemptions of a 10 percent shareholder who had held the redeemed stock for one year, and §311(d)(2)(B), a distribution of stock or obligations of a 50 percent-owned operating subsidiary).[209.5] Several recent widely publicized acquisitions were tailored to fit the exception of §311(d)(2)(B), viz., the purchase of an appropriate amount of the parent's stock, and then an exchange of the purchased parent's stock for stock of its wanted subsidiary,[209.6] with the result that the distributing parent corporation would, if this plan succeeded, avoid paying tax on the appreciation inherent in the distributed subsidiary's stock. Had the sale instead been structured as a direct sale of the subsidiary's stock, however, such gain would have been taxable in full to the seller-corporation.

The original version of the 1982 legislation (the Stark Bill) simply repealed most of the significant exceptions to §311(d) (2);[209.7] so too did the original version of the Senate Finance Committee Bill, H.R. 4961. But the Bill, as finally passed by the Senate

---

[209.4] But cf. §7701(g), also added by the Tax Reform Act of 1984 (property transferred subject to nonrecourse debt deemed to have value equal to debt); Eustice, The Tax Reform Act of 1984, ¶ 5.05[5][a].

[209.5] See generally supra ¶ 9.64 (this Supplement).

[209.6] For description of various transactions structured to fit one of these exceptions of §311(d)(2), see Shop Talk, 55 J. Tax. 127 (1981), 53 J. Tax. 328 (1980), and 53 J. Tax. 264 (1980). But see Rev. Rul. 83-38, 1983-10 IRB 10, and Rev. Rul. 80-221, 1980-2 CB 107; see generally Axelrod, Esmark's Tax-Free Disposition of a Subsidiary: Too Good to Be True? 9 J. Corp. Tax. 232 (1982).

[209.7] I.e., §§311(d)(2)(A), 311(d)(2)(B), 311(d)(2)(C), and 311(d)(2)(G); H.R. 6925 (original) and H.R. 6725 (revised).

and generally accepted by the Conference Committee, was more limited in scope, being tailored to conform more closely to the partial liquidation amendments of Act §222.[209.8] The final legislation retained the basic structure of §311(d)(2), but significantly contracted the exceptions of former §311(d)(2)(A) (now §§311 (d)(2)(B) and 311(e)(1)), and former §311(d)(2)(B) (now §§311(d)(2)(C) and 311(e)). Neither of these latter exceptions will apply to distributions to corporate shareholders; such distributions, however, will not be taxable to the distributing corporation under new §311(d)(2)(A) if the property's basis in the hands of the distributee is determined under the dividend rules of §301 (d)(2) (as would typically be the case under the new law in view of the repeal of partial liquidation treatment for pro rata property distributions to corporate shareholders).[209.9]

However, the 1982 amendments retained the basic nonrecogtion principle of *General Utilities,* as codified in §311(a), although the new legislation represents a further, and continuing, erosion of that doctrine. The principal theme of amended §311(d) is the imposition of a corporate-level tax on distributions of property that result in both a stepped-up basis and sale or exchange treatment at the distributee-shareholder level. This approach can also be viewed as an extension of §1239-type limitations to situations involving exchanges of corporate property for the distributing corporation's stock (although the tax penalty imposed here is corporate-level recognition rather than characterizations as ordinary gain).

However, proposals by the Staff of the Senate Finance Committee for the reform of Subchapter C were submitted on September 22, 1983, which would, if enacted, finally repeal the *General Utilities* doctrine and require corporate level recognition of gain on all distributions of appreciated property that result in a stepped-up basis to the distributee. Moreover, recent amendments by the Tax Reform Act of 1984 essentially repealed the *General Utilities* doctrine (for all stepped-up basis distributions, whether by way of an ordinary dividend or in redemption of the distributing corporation's

---

[209.8] Supra ¶ 9.54 (this Supplement).

[209.9] *Id.* But see amendments effected by the Tax Reform Act of 1984 to §311(d) (infra new paragraph 4 of this section), under which *all* distributions to corporate shareholders now are taxable by §311 (d)(1) (namely, there are no exceptions applicable for corporate shareholders).

stock and for all distributions of appreciated property to corporate shareholders), but retained most of the exceptions of §311(d)(2), except for the carryover basis distribution to corporate shareholders in former §311(d)(2)(A) (supra ¶ 7.21 (this Supplement) and infra new paragraph 4 of this section).

2. *Section 311(d)(2) as revised by TEFRA §223.* New §311 (d)(2) provides that §311(d)(1) will not apply to a distribution of property in redemption of stock if (a) the distribution is to a corporate shareholder, and the basis of the distributed property is determined under §301(d)(2) (viz., the dividend-in-kind rules), §311(d)(2)(A); [209.10] (b) the distribution is a qualified partial liquidation under new §302(b)(4)[209.11] and is made with respect to "qualified stock," as defined in new §311(e)(1) (generally stock held by a noncorporate shareholder continuously for five years and constituting at least 10 percent in value of the distributing corporation), §§311(d)(2)(B), and 311(e)(1); or (c) the distribution consists of stock or obligations of a "controlled corporation" and meets the requirements of new §§311(e)(2),[209.12] 311(d)(2)(C), and 311(e)(2).

The key to the new §311(d)(2) exceptions for partial liquidation distributions and subsidiary stock distributions is the definition of "qualified stock" in §311(e)(1), which provides that such stock is stock that is held by a noncorporate shareholder who at all times during the lesser of the five-year period preceding the distribution, or the period during which the distributing corporation (or its predecessor) was in existence, held at least 10 percent in value of

---

[209.10] This exception presumably applies even though there is an actual redemption of stock; compare Regs. §1.311-2(a)(1) (as to prior law, §311(d)(1) applied even though the redemption was treated as a dividend under §301). If §302(a) applies, however, this exception is inapplicable and gain would result to the distributing corporation. Moreover, §1239 could apply to such gain if the requisite relationship existed between the two corporations; see Rev. Rul. 75-514, 1975-2 CB 116. For abolition of this exception by the Tax Reform Act of 1984, see infra new paragraph 4 of this section.

[209.11] Supra ¶ 9.54 (this Supplement).

[209.12] The distribution is made with respect to qualified stock, as defined in §311(e)(1) (i.e., to 10 percent, five-year, noncorporate shareholders), and consists generally of at least 50 percent of the value of the controlled corporation's stock (which corporation must be predominantly an operating business, which it has conducted for five years).

the distributing corporation's stock. If a partial liquidation distribution occurs with respect to such "qualified stock," the redeeming shareholder's interest need not be completely terminated thereby (as was the case under the prior §311(d)(2)(A) exception). Moreover, in determining the 10 percent minimum ownership requirement, new §311(e)(1)(B) provides for §318 attribution (except that the "family" definition of §267(c)(4) is adopted, including spouses of such individuals).[209.13]

If the distribution of appreciated property does not qualify for partial liquidation treatment under §§302(b)(4) and 302(e) (viz., the pre-1982 law rules of §346, which now apply only to distributions to noncorporate shareholders),[209.14] or if the property distribution is not with respect to qualified stock, the distributing corporation will be taxable in full under §311(d)(1) on any potential gain attributable to such property as if it had been sold for its value. Similarly, if a redeeming corporate distributee obtains §302(a) sale treatment with respect to such distribution (because the redemption was substantially disproportionate under §302(b)(2), completely terminated its interest under §302(b)(3), or was not substantially equivalent to a dividend under §302(b)(2)),[209.15] the distributing corporation will be taxable under §311(d)(1), since the special exception for corporate shareholders in §311(d)(2)(A) applies only to dividend equivalent distributions.

Distributions of controlled subsidiary stock (and obligations) have an especially arduous road to travel before they can qualify for the newly tightened exception of §311(d)(2)(C). Not only must the distribution be in exchange for qualified stock (to a 10 percent, five-year, noncorporate shareholder) but the following requirements of new §311(e)(2) must be met:

(1) Substantially all the assets of the subsidiary must consist of one or more qualified businesses.[209.16]

[209.13] Section 267(c)(4) defines family to include brothers, sisters (whole or half), spouse, ancestors, and lineal descendants. Thus, the attributive network for the stock concentration test is a broad one indeed, and corporations contemplating a property distribution in redemption of their stock will have to run a genealogical scan of their stockholders' lists to be certain of qualification under this provision. Compare Regs. §1.311-2(b) as to prior law (no §318).

[209.14] Supra ¶ 9.54 (this Supplement).

[209.15] See supra ¶¶ 9.22, 9.23, and 9.24 (this Supplement).

[209.16] A "qualified business" is defined by new §311(e)(2)(B)(i)

(2) No substantial part of its nonbusiness assets [209.17] were acquired from the distributing corporation by a contribution
to capital or a §351 exchange within the five-year period
preceding the distribution.

(3) More than 50 percent of the value of the subsidiary's stock
is distributed with respect to qualified stock.

In short, the subsidiary must essentially be an operating company;
its active business must have been conducted for five years (and not
purchased in a taxable transaction within such five-year period);
stock representing more than 50 percent of the subsidiary must be
distributed; and the distributees must be substantial (10 percent),
long-term (five-year), noncorporate shareholders. If all of these
conditions are satisfied, then the distributing corporation will not
recognize gain on the distribution of that stock in exchange for its
own stock; but if only one of these conditions is violated, the distribution will result in taxable gain under §311(d)(1).

The effective date rules for new §311(d)(2) are generally for
distributions after August 31, 1982, but the usual special-interest
grandfather rules apply here as well, and can be found in TEFRA
§223(b).

3. To Illustrate. These amendments can be illustrated by the
following examples, in which T is the distributing corporation
(which directly operates two five-year-old businesses), X is a wholly
owned operating subsidiary of T, and Y is a 50 percent-owned
operating subsidiary of T. T has the following equal shareholders:
Corp. P, individual A, and partnership B (all of whose equal partners are individuals).

Example 1: T distributes the assets of one of its two businesses
(or the proceeds from the sale of those assets) ratably to its
three shareholders, P, A, and B. The distribution constitutes a
partial liquidation as to noncorporate shareholders A and B
under §§302(b)(4) and 302(e)(2) (old law §346(b)); assuming that their stock is "qualified stock" under §311(e)
(1),[209.18] no gain would be recognized to T on the distribution

---

as an active business conducted for five years that was not acquired, by
any person, within such five-year period in a taxable transaction.

[209.17] "Nonbusiness assets" are defined by §311(e)(2)(B)(ii) as
any asset not used in the active conduct of a trade or business.

[209.18] A would so qualify if he had held the T stock for five years;

under §311(d)(2)(B). As to corporate shareholder P, the distribution, being pro rata, would be a dividend and, accordingly, T would be protected from recognition of gain under §311(d)(2)(A).[209.19]

Example 2: If partnership B only owned 5 percent of T directly (while P owned 50 percent of T and A owned 45 percent), the distribution to B would be taxable to T under §311(d)(1), since none of the exceptions would apply.[209.20]

---

as to B, presumably the 10 percent minimum ownership line is satisfied here, since, under §318, B would be deemed to own any stock of its partners (but note that B already owns more than 10 percent directly in its own right). Compare §302(e)(5) (noncorporate entity-owned stock tested for corporate shareholder status by looking through a partnership, estate, or trust and treating its stock as owned proportionately by the entity's partner or beneficiaries). The Tax Reform Act of 1984 adopted a similar look-through rule in §311(e)(1)(C), infra this note.

If one of B's partners was a corporation, the distribution to B would not qualify as a partial liquidation (to the *extent* of that partner's proportionate interest) by virtue of §302(e)(5); but would T be protected here by §311(d)(2)(A), even though T would also be taxable under §311(d)(1), since the distribution did not qualify under §302(b)(4) and hence §311(d)(2)(B) could not apply to the extent of the corporate partner's interest? It would seem that no exception covers T here since the distribution was not in fact made to a corporate shareholder. But §712(j) of the Tax Reform Act of 1984, P.L. No. 98-369, 98 Stat. 678, added new §311(e)(1)(C), which tests for qualified stock status at the beneficiary level and treats the distribution to various pass-through entities as if made directly to the beneficiaries in proportion to their interests in the entity. For a similar look-through rule in testing for partial liquidation status, see §302(e)(5).

[209.19] P would take the property at a basis equal to the lower of T's basis (plus any recognized recapture gain) or the property's value under §301(d)(2), and would get the 85 percent dividend-received deduction of §243. But after the Tax Reform Act of 1984, this exception was abolished, and thus T will be taxable on this distribution to P (infra new paragraph 4 of this section).

[209.20] The treatment of A and B would still be a partial liquidation sale under §§302(b)(4) and 302(e), however, while the distribution to P would be a dividend. Moreover, T would be protected by §311(d)(2)(A) with respect to the P distribution (but not after 1984), while §311(d)(2)(B) would apply to the A distribution.

If A were one of three equal partners in partnership B (so that B owned 50 percent by virtue of its own 5 percent and the §318 attribution of A's stock to B), §311(d)(2)(B) would then apply to the B

Example 3: If T distributed the property to P in exchange for all of P's stock in T, §302(b)(3) (rather than §302(b) (4))[209.21] applies and P gets §302(a) treatment (assuming no §318 attribution problems exist); but T is taxable under §311 (d)(1), since no exception exists in §311(d)(2).[209.22]

Example 4: If instead, T distributed the property to A in redemption of all of A's stock in T, A is entitled to §302(b)(4) partial liquidation treatment (as well as §302(b)(3)); [209.23] now, however, T would be protected by §311(d)(2)(B) (if A held qualified stock under the §311(e)(1) rules).

Example 5: If T distributes all of the X stock (its 100 percent-owned subsidiary) to P in exchange for all of P's T stock, §355(a) should give nonrecognition treatment to P, and thus §311(d)(1) would not be applicable to the distribution, since the exchange of X stock for T stock is not a distribution to which subpart A applies).[209.24] If, however, the split-off exchange by T to P of its X stock did not qualify as a §355 transaction, T would not be protected by any of the exceptions of §311(d)(2) (unless the distribution resulted in a dividend to P, which would be unlikely here, and, after 1984, even this exception no longer applies).

Example 6: If T distributes all of the X stock to A in a §355 tax-free split-off, the results would be the same as Example (5); but if the distribution did not qualify for §355, T could qualify for §311(d)(2)(C)[209.25] if the stock of T held by A is "quali-

---

distribution, since B now would hold "qualified stock" by virtue of §311(e)(1)(B). But under new §311(e)(1)(C), added by the Tax Reform Act of 1984, each partner of B will have to satisfy the 10 percent stock ownership test in his own right.

[209.21] The partial liquidation rules of §302(b)(4) do not apply to corporate distributees.

[209.22] Section 311(d)(2)(A) does not apply, since P did not take a §301(d)(2) basis for the distributed property.

[209.23] According to H. Rep. No. 760, 97th Cong., 2d Sess., at 530 (1982), A need not be concerned with §§318 and 302(c)(2) in such a case.

[209.24] See Regs. §1.311-2(a)(2).

[209.25] Section 311(d)(2)(B) would not apply since a distribution of stock is not a partial liquidation under §302(e); see Rev. Rul. 79-184, 1979-1 CB 143.

fied stock" under §311(e)(1) and if the requirements of §311 (e)(2) are met.[209.26]

Example 7: If T distributes the Y stock (its 50 percent-owned subsidiary) ratably to P, A, and B, the distribution would be a dividend to the distributee shareholders and T would be protected by §311(a); if P, A, and B all exchanged T stock for the Y stock, dividend treatment would still result to P, A, and B since the transaction is pro rata; T would be protected by §311(d)(2)(A) on the distribution to P, but no exception would apply to the A and B distributions and the regulations require recognition under §311(d)(1) even though the exchange resulted in §301 dividend treatment to these distributees.[209.27]

4. Tax Reform Act of 1984 amendments. The recent 1984 legislation [209.28] materially contracted §311 even further by turning §311(d) into a general recognition section for *all* distributions of appreciated property subject to Part A (i.e., §§301–307). Thus, under revised §311(d)(1), all distributions of appreciated property will be treated as a deemed sale at value [209.29] to the distributee (see §1239). However, most of the exceptions of §311(d)(2) were retained (although the carryover basis dividend to corporate share-

[209.26] Namely, X is a five-year-old operating subsidiary and there was no substantial contribution of nonoperating assets by T to X during the five-year period prior to the distribution.

Note that T could not qualify for §311(d)(2)(C) if it distributed the Y stock to A (Y being T's 50 percent-owned subsidiary) by virtue of §311(e)(2)(A)(iv) (which requires the distribution of *more* than 50 percent in value of the subsidiary's stock).

[209.27] Regs. §1.311-2(a)(1). But under changes effected by the Tax Reform Act of 1984, infra, T would be taxable on the entire distribution of Y stock, even if it is a "pure" dividend distribution.

[209.28] The Tax Reform Act of 1984, H.R. 4170, §54(a) (which passed the House on April 11, 1984), the Deficit Reduction Act of 1984, H.R. 2163, §36(a) (which passed the Senate on April 13, 1984), and the Tax Reform Act of 1984, P.L. No. 98-369, §54(a), 98 Stat. 678 (which became law on July 18, 1984). See supra ¶ 7.21 this Supplement); Eustice, The Tax Reform Act of 1984, ¶ 3.02[1] (Warren, Gorham & Lamont, Inc. 1984).

[209.29] But see new §7701(g) (property transferred subject to nonrecourse debt deemed to have value at least equal to debt); Eustice, The Tax Reform Act of 1984, ¶ 5.05[5][a].

holders exception of §311(d)(2)(A) was limited to shareholders that control—that is, 80 percent within the meaning of §368(c)—the distributing corporation, and this exception only exists as a transition rule through 1984). An additional exception was added for "qualifying dividends," defined by new §311(e)(3) as dividends on qualified stock of "active business" assets, other than inventory and receivables. The other exceptions of §§311(d)(2)(B) and 311(d)(2)(C), supra, continued intact (although they are moved back one notch to §§311(d)(2)(A) and 311(d)(2)(B)), resulting in the ironic twist that partial liquidation qualification now is treated more favorably at the corporate level than ordinary dividends in kind (the prototype *General Utilities* case). In fact, the 1984 amendments went beyond what even the Senate Finance Committee staff proposed in the case of distributions to corporate shareholders.

¶ 9.65.   EFFECT OF REDEMPTION ON CORPORATION'S EARNINGS AND PROFITS

Page 9-82:

Add to note 210, second paragraph.

[210] *Uris* was affirmed, 605 F.2d 1258 (2d Cir. 1979).

Add new note 210.1 to text at fourth line from bottom of page after paragraph 4.

[210.1] See Rev. Rul. 82-72, 1982-1 CB 57 (capital account allocated between common and preferred at time of preferred stock dividend in proportion to relative values of common and preferred).

Page 9-83:

Add to note 212, end of second paragraph.

Rev. Rul. 79-376, 1979-2 CB 133 (IRS gives up and agrees to follow *Jarvis;* Rev. Rul. 70-531 revoked; acquiescence in *Jarvis* and *Anderson*). See Note, Rev. Rul. 79-376: Effect of Section 312(e) Redemption Distribution on Earnings and Profits, 34 Tax L. 817 (1981). See also Rev. Rul. 82-72, supra note 210.1 (this Supplement) (application of §312(e) to §303 redemption of §306 stock).

But the Senate Finance Committee Staff Report for the reform of Subchapter C, submitted September 22, 1983, proposes either to repeal the earnings and profits limitation for dividends, or at least to restrict the earnings charge under §312(e) to overrule *Jarvis* et al. The Senate

Finance Committee tax bill, the Deficit Reduction Act of 1984, H.R. 2163, §47(a), proposed to add new §312(n)(8), repealing *Jarvis* and adopting the "ratable share" limitation of Rev. Rul. 70-531, and this provision passed in §61(a) of the Tax Reform Act of 1984, P.L. No. 98-369, 98 Stat. 678.

Page 9-85:

Add to text at end of section.

The Tax Reform Act of 1984,[218] however, repealed *Jarvis* and adopted the ratable share limitation of Rev. Rul. 70-531.

---

[218] The Tax Reform Act of 1984, P.L. No. 98-369, §61(a), 98 Stat. 678, adding new §312(n)(8).

Chapter 10

PREFERRED STOCK BAIL-OUTS

¶ 10.03. THE DEFINITION OF "SECTION 306 STOCK"

Page 10-6:

Add to note 9, runover paragraph.

⁹ See also Rev. Rul. 79-163, 1979-1 CB 131 (stock not common stock if it *either* is limited as to dividends *or* limited as to liquidation rights, viz., must be "uncapped" as to both earnings and assets to be common stock, even though it is only stock with vote).

But see Rev. Rul. 81-91, 1981-1 CB 123 (not "section 306 stock" because shared in future earnings and growth, even though preferred as to annual dividends and on liquidation).

Add to note 9, third paragraph.

See also Walter, "Preferred Stock" and "Common Stock": The Meaning of the Terms and the Importance of the Distinction for Tax Purposes, 5 J. Corp. Tax. 211 (1978).

Add to last sentence of first paragraph of note 10.

¹⁰ The 1978 regulation thus incorporates the "nimble dividend" concept of §316(a)(2); see also Regs. §1.306-1(b)(2), Ex. (1).

Add to note 11.

¹¹ For recent legislation to extend the taint of §306 to preferred stock issued by a newly organized holding company in a §351 transaction, see DER No. 133, July 12, 1982, p. J.-13, and DER No. 136, July 15, 1982, p. J-10 (amendments to the Corporate Takeover Tax Act of 1982, H.R. 6725), which passed as §226(b) of the Tax Equity and Fiscal Responsibility Act (TEFRA) of 1982, P.L. No. 97-248, 96 Stat. 324, adding new §306(c)(3). See infra new paragraph 4 of this section (this Supplement).

Page 10-7:

Add to note 13.

[13] See §227(a) of TEFRA of 1982, supra note 11 (this Supplement), adding new §306(c)(4) (apply §318 in testing for dividend equivalence, though without regard to the 50 percent limitation).

Correct note 14, first paragraph, last sentence.

[14] Citation should be "§306(b)(5)," not "§303(b)(5)."

Add to note 14, second paragraph.

[14] But §1023 was repealed by the Crude Oil Windfall Profit Tax Act of 1980, so that the date-of-death basis rules of §1014 once again will result in a purging of §306 taint at death.

Page 10-8:

Add paragraph 4 to text at end of section.

4. *Stock received in a §351 exchange—TEFRA amendments to §306(c).* A potential device to set the stage for the future bail-out of corporate earnings at capital gain rates involved the issuance of preferred stock in connection with the formation of a new corporation under §351; if the new corporation had no earnings for its first year, the preferred stock would not constitute §306 stock by virtue of §306(c)(2).[16.1] Moreover, such a transaction did not fall within the type of transactions covered by §306(c)(1). Thus, the formation of a holding company issuing both common and preferred stock afforded similar bail-out opportunities to the issuance of a preferred stock dividend, but stock issued in such an exchange did not give rise to tainted "section 306 stock."

New §306(c)(3), however, provides a special rule for preferred stock [16.2] issued in a §351 exchange. Under this provision, such stock will be tainted as "section 306 stock" if the distribution of cash in lieu of such stock would have been taxable as a dividend (to *any* extent) under rules similar to the rules of §304(b)(2); [16.3] viz., if the hypothetical cash distribution would have caused §304

[16.1] See Rev. Rul. 77-108, 1977-1 CB 86; Rev. Rul. 79-274, 1979-2 CB 131; Corry, Preferred Stock Issued in Tax-Free Exchanges: Does Section 306 Apply? 35 Tax L. Rev. 113 (1979).

[16.2] Technically, preferred stock is stock that is not "common stock"; see supra ¶ 10.03, note 9.

[16.3] Supra ¶ 9.33 (this Supplement).

(rather than §351 or §368) to apply to such receipt (and dividend consequences would have resulted therefrom), the stock would be tainted in full as "section 306 stock." Moreover, by virtue of a new §306(c)(4), §318 attribution rules apply in testing for dividend effect (without the 50 percent limitation).

> *To illustrate:* If A and B own X Corp. equally, and transfer their X stock to new Y Corp., taking back Y common and preferred ratably, the preferred will be tainted as "section 306 stock" if X has *any* accumulated (or current) [16.4] earnings and profits because a cash distribution by Y would have resulted in dividend treatment to A and B under §§304(a)(1) and 304 (b)(2)(A). If, however, A took back Y common, while B took the Y preferred, the preferred would not be tainted in B's hands, since a cash distribution would have qualified for §302(a) sale treatment (assuming A and B were not related under §318).[16.5]

These provisions are effective for transfers occurring after August 31, 1982 in taxable years ending after such date.[16.6] Note, however, that §306(c)(3) only comes into play if §351 applies to the transaction; hence, if the exchange fails to qualify under §351 (because the transferors do not control the transferee),[16.7] the preferred would not be tainted by this provision (even though the exchange qualified for tax-free treatment as a Type B reorganization).[16.8] However, the more egregious escapes from §306 via the holding company creation route seem to have been effectively halted by the 1982 amendments.

[16.4] See Regs. §§1.306-3(a) and 1.306-3(d). Thus, post-exchange earnings in the same taxable year of X could cause a retroactive taint of the preferred; see supra ¶ 10.03, note 10 (this Supplement).

[16.5] The same result would occur if B's proportionate interest in X shifted substantially enough to meet §302(b)(2).

[16.6] A special effective date rule applies to bank holding company formations, TEFRA §226(c)(2).

[16.7] Note that §318 does *not* apply to determine §351 or §368 "control."

[16.8] Because control was acquired solely for voting stock, whether common, or preferred (or both). But see Rev. Rul. 79-274, supra note 16.1. Such stock may, however, be tainted by §306(c)(1)(B).

¶ 10.04.　DISPOSITIONS OF "SECTION 306 STOCK"

Page 10-12:

Add to note 25.

[25] Query whether a dividend in kind of §306 stock (resulting in a basis "purge" to the distributee under §301(d)(1), would be protected by §311(a); for similar opportunities under §§336 and 337, see infra ¶ 10.05, note 30.

Add new note 26.1 at end of second paragraph.

[26.1] But §1023 was repealed by the Crude Oil Windfall Profit Tax Act of 1980, thus rendering §306(a)(3) superfluous.

¶ 10.05.　EXCEPTIONS TO §306(a)

Page 10-13:

Add to note 29.

[29] But legislation proposed in 1982 entitled The Corporate Takeover Tax Act of 1982 (and approved by the Senate and House Tax Committees in July 1982) repealed the partial liquidation rules, effective September 1, 1982. Thus, §331 would apply only to complete liquidations, as would the exception in §306(b)(2).

The final version of this legislation, however, retained the partial liquidation rules for noncorporate shareholders, now found in new §§302(b)(4) and 302(e); thus, the exception of §306(b)(2) will apply if the transaction qualifies as a partial liquidation under new §302(b)(4).

Page 10-14:

Correct sixth and seventh lines of text.

Delete material in parenthetical, "unless it is all "common" stock."

Add to note 34.

[34] Rev. Rul. 80-33, 1980-1 CB 69 (although valid business purpose for preferred stock issue, stock held "section 306 stock" because bond dividend could have accomplished same business objective; hence tax avoidance and no amnesty).

¶ 10.06. USES OF "SECTION 306 STOCK"

Page 10-15:

Add to note 36.

[36] But the repeal of §1023 in 1980 reinstates the "purging" of §306 taint on death as a result of the new basis obtained under §1014.

Chapter 11

COMPLETE LIQUIDATIONS
AND RELATED PROBLEMS

PART A. THE GENERAL RULE OF §331(a)(1)

¶ 11.02. MEANING OF "COMPLETE LIQUIDATION"
Page 11-6:

Add to note 6.

   [6] See generally Joseph Olmsted, ¶ 84,381 P-H Memo TC (complete liquidation found despite stretched-out liquidation process).

Page 11-7:

Add to note 9, first paragraph.

   [9] Joseph Olmsted, supra note 6 (this Supplement) (serial liquidation over long period found to be a liquidation on facts).

Add new note 10.1 to first sentence after note 10.

   [10.1] See generally Joseph Olmsted, supra note 6 (this Supplement), which found liquidation status on the facts despite a long delay in the liquidation process.

¶ 11.03. LIQUIDATING DISTRIBUTIONS AND
SHAREHOLDER GAIN OR LOSS
Page 11-7:

Add new note 10.2 to end of first sentence of text.

   [10.2] But see Braddock Land Co., 75 TC 324 (1980) (distribution re creditor status not subject to §331 treatment; shareholder-creditors' cancellation of their claims for accrued salaries in course of corporation's complete liquidation disregarded as sham and taxed to distributees as ordinary income). See also Dwyer v. US, 622 F.2d 460 (9th Cir.

1980) (shareholder taxed on accrued interest when he cancelled debt on complete liquidation, even though deduction had been denied under §267).

Dwyer seems essentially contra to *Putoma*, supra ¶ 3.14, note 144 (this Supplement). See generally Brod, Liquidations Involving Shareholder-Creditors—Tax Traps for the Unwary, 7 J. Corp. Tax. 352 (1981).

Page 11-8:

Add to note 14, first paragraph, following Jones *citation.*

[14] Accord with *Jones* is Dayton Hydraulic Co. v. US, 592 F.2d 937 (6th Cir. 1979) (liquidation too ripe to shift shareholder tax burden thereon).

Page 11-9:

Add new note 14.1 at end of first sentence of text.

[14.1] For possibility of constructive receipt at shareholder level when funds readily available at will of shareholder, see Rev. Rul. 80-177, 1980-2 CB 109.

Add to note 15, first paragraph.

[15] Concord Control, Inc. v. CIR, 615 F.2d 1153 (6th Cir. 1980) (existence of going concern value not inconsistent with finding of absence of goodwill; but case remanded for further explanation of computation of going concern value). See Henszey, Going Concern Value After *Concord Control,* 61 Taxes 699 (1983).

Page 11-10:

Add to note 17.

[17] See Schenk, Arrowsmith And Its Progeny: Tax Characterization by Reference to Past Events, 33 Rutgers L. Rev. 317 (1981).

Page 11-12:

Add to end of note 21, second paragraph.

[21] See also Regs. §1.483-1(e)(1) (section applies even though obligation valued and transaction treated as closed for determining gain or loss). For legislation modifying §483 and essentially replacing this provision with expanded coverage under the original-issue discount rules, see supra new ¶ 4.23 (this Supplement).

Page 11-14:

Add new comment to text at end of paragraph 2.

Enactment of the Installment Sales Revision Act of 1980 (P.L. No. 96-471) may narrow the "open liquidation" window of *Burnet v. Logan,* especially in view of new §453(j)(2), which confers authority on the Service to provide for taxable basis recovery methods in situations where the selling price is not readily ascertainable.[26.1] On the other hand, new §453(h) now allows shareholders to report corporate-level installment sales pursuant to a §337 liquidation as installment sales of their stock (infra ¶ 11.65), thus obviating resort to the open liquidation doctrine in order to obtain deferred-gain reporting treatment. Moreover, it could be argued that §453(j)(2), and any regulations issued thereunder, can only apply to corporate assets that qualify for §453(a), or §453(h), treatment; consequently, the open liquidation rules may be unaffected by the distribution of corporate assets that do not themselves contribute qualified §453 obligations.

[26.1] Section 2 J of the Senate Finance Committee Report to this legislation echoes the Service's views in Rev. Rul. 58-402 that cost recovery treatment under *Logan* will be "limited to those rare and unusual cases . . . where the fair market value of a purchaser's obligation cannot reasonably be ascertained." See Goldberg, Open Transaction Treatment for Deferred Payment Sales After the Installment Sales Act of 1980, 34 Tax Law. 605 (1981). See infra note 191.1 (this Supplement).

Add to note 27.

[27] But cf. §7701(g), enacted by the Tax Reform Act of 1984 (property transferred subject to nonrecourse debt deemed to have value at least equal to amount of debt); Eustice, The Tax Reform Act of 1984, ¶ 5.05[5][a].

Page 11-15:

Add to note 28, second paragraph.

[28] See also Rev. Rul. 78-25, 1978-1 CB 270 (*Arrowsmith* capital loss for paying shareholder; but §1341 applies too). See Schenk, supra note 17 (this Supplement).

¶ 11.04. BASIS OF PROPERTY RECEIVED IN COMPLETE LIQUIDATION

Page 11-16:

Add to note 33, second paragraph, following Crane *citation.*

[33] See M.Q. Peterson, ¶ 71,021 P-H Memo TC (if liabilities exceed value, basis is value of property, not face of debt). See also Tufts v. CIR, 651 F.2d 1058 (5th Cir. 1981), rev'd, — US — (S. Ct. 1983). But see §7701(g), supra note 27 (this Supplement).

Page 11-17:

Add to text after second word of twelfth line.

"property received in the"

¶ 11.05. LIQUIDATION FOLLOWED BY REINCORPORATION

Page 11-19:

Add to text at end of first runover paragraph.

Legislation introduced in 1982, the Corporate Takeover Tax Act of 1982 proposed to repeal the partial liquidation provisions of §346 and substitute new §346(b), granting broad regulatory authority to deal with various transactions that have the economic effect of a partial liquidation (supra ¶ 9.50, this Supplement). These regulations could provide the Treasury with a potent weapon in the liquidation-reincorporating area. This latter aspect of the proposed legislation passed, as §222(d) of the Tax Equity and Fiscal Responsibility Act (TEFRA) of 1982.[37.1] Moreover, the Tax Reform Act of 1984[37.2] revised the definition of a nondivisive D reorganization in new §368(c)(2) to coordinate this provision with the control line applicable to §304. This amendment will further strengthen the Service's hand in combating the liquidation-reincorporation device.[37.3]

[37.1] P.L. No. 97-248, 96 Stat. 324. See ¶ 9.54 (this Supplement).

[37.2] Tax Reform Act of 1984, P.L. No. 98-369, §64(a), 98 Stat. 678, adding new §368(c)(2).

[37.3] See infra ¶ 14.54 (this Supplement); Eustice, The Tax Reform Act of 1984, ¶ 3.04[4] (Warren, Gorham & Lamont, Inc. 1984).

Page 11-20:

Add to note 39, second paragraph.

[39] Capital Sales, Inc., 71 TC 416 (1978) (no "transfer" of assets where liquidating brother corporation's franchise cancelled by unrelated franchise holder and reissued to continuing sister corporation); rev'd sub nom. Simon v. CIR, 644 F.2d 339 (5th Cir. 1981).

Page 11-21:

Add to note 43.

[43] See also Viereck v. US, 1983-2 USTC ¶ 9664 (Cl. Ct. 1983).

Add to note 44.

[44] See also Viereck v. US, supra note 43 (this Supplement).

PART B.   NONRECOGNITION OF SHAREHOLDER GAIN IN ELECTIVE ONE-MONTH LIQUIDATIONS UNDER §333

¶ 11.21.   NONRECOGNITION OF GAIN UNDER §333

Page 11-24:

Add to note 52.

[52] For possible application of §312(b) principles to create earnings and profits in a §333 liquidation, see Rev. Rul. 79-149, 1979-1 CB 132.

Page 11-25:

Add to note 55, first paragraph.

[55] But Rev. Rul. 69-486 was distinguished by Rev. Rul. 83-61, 1983-1 CB 78 (distribution of cash to some shareholders and property to others will not be rearranged where local law does not give shareholders right to a ratable share of each asset—trust ruling won't be extended to area of corporate liquidations).

¶ 11.23.   THE ELECTION AND OTHER CONDITIONS OF §333

Page 11-27:

Add to note 59.

[59] See also Rev. Rul. 79-82, 1979-1 CB 141 (if corporation is owned by a partnership, the partnership is the qualified electing shareholder, but each partner reports respective gains under §333(e) or §333(f) as the case may be).

Page 11-28:

Correct last line of paragraph (d) of text.

Line should read "vote on the adoption of the plan" not "vote on the adoption plan."

Page 11-29:

Add to note 62, second paragraph.

[62] But see DiAndrea, Inc., ¶ 83,788 P-H Memo TC (choice of seller

a mistake of fact and shareholder could revoke improvident §333 election under *Meyer*; thus corporation got §337 protection; *Aaron Cohen* distinguished because mistake of fact point not raised).

Page 11-30:

Add new heading.

¶ 11.25. SPECIAL LIQUIDATION RULE FOR PERSONAL-SERVICE CORPORATIONS

In view of the parity provisions of TEFRA of 1982,[66.1] which moved substantially towards equalization of the tax treatment for corporate and noncorporate retirement benefit plans, Act §247 (uncodified) provides a special transition rule allowing personal-service corporations to liquidate under §333 (for 1983 and 1984 only) without triggering corporate-level recognition of their untaxed receivables. (Other recapture tax items will be triggered by such liquidations, however.) Although the distribution of corporate receivables is not taxable to the distributing corporation (and initial nonrecognition treatment at the shareholder level applies to the receipt of such assets), the *character* of the income passes through to shareholders and thus will be taxable as ordinary income on collection or other disposition of those receivables.

[66.1] P.L. No. 97-248, 96 Stat. 324.

PART C. NONRECOGNITION OF PARENT CORPORATION'S GAIN OR LOSS ON LIQUIDATING A SUBSIDIARY: §332

¶ 11.40. INTRODUCTORY

Page 11-30:

Add to note 67 at end of runover paragraph.

[67] Rev. Proc. 73-17 updated and superseded by Rev. Proc. 81-68, 1981-2 CB 723.

¶ 11.41. CONDITIONS OF §332

Page 11-34:

Add to note 77, first paragraph.

[77] See Inductotherm Indus., ¶ 84,281 P-H Memo TC (subsidiary

held to be solvent on finding that parent's advances were "equity" capital contributions; hence, §332 applied on liquidation, and §381 tax history carried over to parent).

Page 11-37:

Add to note 81, end of runover paragraph.

81 See Crescent Oil, Inc., ¶ 79,026 P-H Memo TC (no §332 because parent did not own requisite 80 percent at time plan adopted).

Add to note 82.

82 Compare Rev. Rul. 84-2, 1984-1 IRB 6 (reincorporation of nominal assets solely to protect corporate name did not vitiate §332).

Page 11-38:

Add to note 85, first paragraph.

85 Compare Rev. Rul. 84-2, supra note 82 (this Supplement).

¶ 11.42.   EFFECT OF SUBSIDIARY INDEBTEDNESS TO ITS PARENT

Page 11-39:

Add to note 90, first paragraph.

90 See Brod, Liquidations Involving Shareholder-Creditors—Tax Traps for the Unwary, 7 J. Corp. Tax. 352 (1981); supra ¶ 11.03, note 10.1 (this Supplement).

Page 11-40:

Add to note 90, at end of second full paragraph.

90 Compare Rev. Rul. 78-330, 1978-2 CB 147 (parent cancellation of brother-subsidiary debt prior to merger into sister subsidiary in order to avoid §357(c) gain held not violation of §357(b)).

¶ 11.44.   BASIS OF PROPERTY RECEIVED BY PARENT CORPORATION: §334(b)

Page 11-42:

Add new note 96.1 to end of first sentence of text.

96.1 In the case of high basis assets, however, §334(b)(1) is desirable since the potential loss on such property shifts upstream to the distributee-parent. For possible application of §482 to reallocate that loss from the parent to the subsidiary, see General Elec. Co. v. US, 1983-2 USTC ¶ 9532 (Cl. Ct. 1983).

Add to note 98 (after Griswold).

[98] but see Security Indus. Ins. Co. v. US, 702 F.2d 1234 (5th Cir. 1983) (stock purchase, liquidation, reincorporation transfer held §334 (b)(2) stepped-up basis liquidation; no mention in opinion of *Griswold*).

Page 11-43:

Add to end of note 99.

[99] See McGaffey, Tax Aspects of Liquidating a Subsidiary Recently Acquired by Purchase, 56 Taxes 858 (1978).

Add new note 100.1 at end of clause in fourth line of text.

[100.1] Rev. Rul. 80-358, 1980-2 CB 110 (twelve-month period starts with date parent first deemed to own subsidiary's stock via §318).

Page 11-44:

Add to note 102, second paragraph.

[102] The General Explanation of TEFRA, prepared by the Joint Committee Staff (Dec. 31, 1982) at 734, states that the 80 percent qualified purchase requirement of §338(d)(3) "may be satisfied through the combination of stock purchases and redemptions."

Add to note 103.

[103] *Chrome Plate* was affirmed, 614 F.2d 990 (5th Cir. 1980) (not a valid purchase because stock acquired in §351 transaction). See also PLR 8021001, 1980 P-H Fed. Taxes ¶ 55,115 (acquisition of additional stock by intervening capital contribution did not violate purchase requirement where parent had previously acquired requisite 80 percent by qualified purchase; Rev. Rul. 57-296 distinguished; but Service continued to reject *Madison Square Garden* rule, supra note 102, until changes effected by TEFRA in 1982. See new §338(d)(3), id.

Correct note 104.

Citation should read "Baker Commodities, Inc. v. CIR."

Page 11-45:

Add to note 105, second paragraph.

[105] Rev. Rul. 80-358, 1980-2 CB 110 (delay in liquidation of first tier subsidiary for more than twelve months after purchase of its stock killed §334(b)(2) treatment for liquidation of second tier subsidiary).

Page 11-46:

Correct sixth line of example text.

liabilities of *X* . . . assumed by *P*

Page 11-47:

Add to note 111, following R.M. Smith *citation.*

[111] *R.M. Smith, Inc.* was affirmed on the goodwill valuation issue, 591 F.2d 248 (3d Cir. 1979).

See generally Yost, Delayed Section 334(b)(2) Liquidation: The *Smith* Case—A Pyrrhic Victory for the IRS, 5 J. Corp. Tax. 263 (1978).

Page 11-48:

Add to note 112, second paragraph.

[112] *Chrome Plate* was affirmed, 614 F.2d 990 (5th Cir. 1980) (*Kimbell-Diamond* rule totally preempted by 1954 Code). See generally, Dubroff & Daileader, *Kimbell-Diamond* Revisited: A Critique of Judicial Analysis of the Exclusivity of Section 334(b)(2), 43 Albany L. Rev. 739 (1979); Dolan, *Kimbell-Diamond, Chrome Plate* and Taxpayer Intent in the Liquidation of Subsidiaries: Should Congress Reexamine Section 334(b)(2)? 8 J. Corp. Tax. 281 (1982). For another blunder example, see New York Fruit Auction Corp., 79 TC 564 (1982) (parent purchased stock and merged downstream into new subsidiary; held no basis step-up for subsidiary's assets).

Legislation was proposed in 1982 to repeal §334(b)(2) and replace it with an elective basis step-up mechanism, §338, described infra ¶ 11.47 (this Supplement). The Senate Finance Committee Report to this Bill, H.R. 4961, S. Rep. No. 97-494, at p. 192 (July 12, 1982), specifically notes that §338 is intended to preempt *Kimbell-Diamond*. This legislation was enacted as §224 of TEFRA of 1982, P.L. No. 97-248, 96 Stat. 324.

Add to note 112, third paragraph.

[112] See also Security Indus. Ins. Co. v. US, 702 F.2d 1234 (5th Cir. 1983) (stock purchase, liquidation, and transfer of operating assets to another subsidiary, held §334(b)(2) liquidation despite reincorporation transfer of assets).

Add new paragraph 3 to text at end of section.

3. *1982 legislation.* The Corporate Takeover Tax Act of 1982 (approved by the Senate Finance Committee, §229 of H.R. 4961, and by the House Ways and Means Subcommittee on Select Revenue Measures, H.R. 6725) proposed to repeal §334(b)(2), effec-

tive September 1, 1982. In its stead, a new elective basis step-up provision, §338, would be added under which the purchasing corporation would have seventy-five days after a qualified stock purchase (which is generally similar to that in existing §§334(b)(2) and 334(b)(3)) to elect to treat the stock acquisition transaction as a deemed asset purchase under §337 (infra ¶ 11.64). No formal liquidation of the purchased subsidiary would be required in order to obtain this cost-basis treatment for its assets. As a further result of the §338 election, the purchased corporation's tax history would be purged. This legislation passed and became law on September 3, 1982 as §224 of TEFRA of 1982.[112.1]

Under this new system, all actual §332 liquidations will result in a carryover of basis (and of the tax history) from the liquidated subsidiary. Thus, the purchasing corporation has a choice; either liquidate the subsidiary and inherit its basis and tax history, or make the §338 election and treat the acquisition as a purchase of assets. (A third choice is not to make the election, leaving the purchased subsidiary with its own asset basis and tax history.) The principal intent of these amendments is to harmonize the tax results of an asset purchase and a stock purchase acquisition transaction. These provisions are described infra new ¶ 11.47 (this Supplement).

[112.1] See supra note 112 (this Supplement).

¶ 11.45. SPECIAL PROBLEMS OF §334(b)(2) LIQUIDATIONS

Page 11-54:

Add to note 127, second paragraph, following R.M. Smith *citation.*

[127] *R.M. Smith, Inc.* was affirmed on the goodwill valuation issue, 591 F.2d 248 (3d Cir. 1979). *Concord Control, Inc.* was remanded for further explanation of "going concern value" computation method, 615 F.2d 1153 (6th Cir. 1980). See Henszey, Going Concern Value After *Concord Control,* 61 Taxes 699 (1983).

Add to note 128, first paragraph.

[128] See Harold C. Lang, ¶ 82,149 P-H Memo TC (wrong order of steps; reorganization and no basis step-up). For another wrong-way illustration, see New York Fruit Auction Corp., 79 TC 564 (1982) (downstream merger of parent into newly purchased subsidiary; no basis step-up for subsidiary's assets).

But see Security Indus. Ins. Co. v. US, 702 F.2d 1234 (5th Cir. 1983) (stock purchase, liquidation, retransfer of assets to another subsidiary; held §334(b)(2) liquidation which purged acquired corporation's tax history).

Add to note 128, second paragraph.

[128] With *Yoc Heating,* compare Harold C. Lang, supra, and New York Fruit Auction Corp., supra; but see Security Indus. Ins. Co. v. US, supra (follows *Yoc Heating*; also stock purchase and liquidation held §334(b)(2) liquidation, despite retransfer of operating assets to another subsidiary).

Page 11-55:

Add to note 129, second paragraph.

[129] Pugh, Combining Acquired and Acquiring Corporations and Their Subsidiaries: Some Anomalies of Form and Substance, 35 Tax L. Rev. 359 (1980).

Add new heading.

¶ 11.47.   CERTAIN STOCK PURCHASES TREATED AS ASSET PURCHASES: §338

1. In general. Nearly thirty years of experience with the intricacies of §334(b)(2) exposed various deficiencies in the operation of these provisions, ranging from excessive complexity and discontinuities of the interim adjustment rules, to the potential for creative manipulation inherent in the stretched-out period during which the purchased subsidiary could be kept alive before it was finally terminated.[129.1] It was asserted that the asset purchase theory of §334

[129.1] See generally Ginsburg, Taxing Corporate Acquisitions, 38 Tax L. Rev. 170 (1982); Bonovitz, Taxable Dispositions of a Corporate Business Before and After TEFRA, 60 Taxes 812 (1982); Brogan, Corporate Stock and Asset Acquisitions After TEFRA, 68 A.B.A.J. 1373 (1982); Battle, Section 338—Stock Purchases Treated as Asset Purchases for Tax Purposes, 60 Taxes 980 (1982); Ward, The TEFRA Amendments to Subchapter C: Corporate Distributions and Acquisitions, 2 J. Corp. L. 277 (1983); Bloom, The Stark Reality of the New Liquidation and Redemption Rules, 10 J. Corp. Tax. 3 (1983); Silverman & Serling, An Analysis of the TEFRA Changes Affecting Corporate Distributions and Acquisitions, 59 J. Tax. 274 (1983); Yancy, Section 338: The Result of the Legal Evolution of the Tax Treatment of Two-Step Asset Acquisitions, 61 Texas L. Rev. 1109 (1983); Heinkel, IRC Section 338—An Analysis and Proposals for Reform, 59 Notre Dame L. Rev. 158 (1983); New York State Bar Association Tax Sec-

(b)(2) was inconsistent with allowing continuation of the purchased subsidiary's life for as long as five years after its acquisition. During this period, inclusion in the buyer's consolidated return allowed the acquired company's tax attributes to be used by the consolidated group (subject to various limitations, infra ¶ 15.24). Moreover, recapture income generated on the eventual liquidation could be sheltered by any losses of other members of the group, a result not available where assets are directly purchased. Finally, selectivity in tax results (stepped-up basis for some assets, and survival of tax history for others) could be arranged through a variety of either pre-acquisition or post-acquisition planning techniques.

For these reasons, The Corporate Takeover Tax Act of 1982 (H.R. 6725, the House version, and a comparable Senate bill, H.R. 4961) proposed to replace §334(b)(2) (including any nonstatutory equivalent) with a new elective provision, §338, under which the acquiring corporation could elect (within a considerably shortened time span of seventy-five days) to treat the stock purchase as a deemed §337 asset purchase. Pursuant to this election, the acquired corporation (denominated as "target" in the legislation) will be treated as having sold all of its assets to an unrelated corporation under §337, become reborn as a "new" corporation, and then immediately repurchased its assets, all without having to go through the ritual of a formal liquidation. Thus, if an election is made under §338, all taxable acquisitions, whether of stock or assets, will be governed by a uniform statutory system, viz., §337. If the purchasing group files consolidated returns, the new subsidiary will enter the group with a clean slate, its tax attributes having been purged outside of the consolidation as a result of the §338 elective deemed asset sale. If the election is not made, the purchased subsidiary retains its tax history and asset bases; a later liquidation under §332 will result in a §381 carryover of its tax history and a §332(b)(1) carryover of asset basis to the parent.

These proposals are effective for acquisitions after August 31, 1982; they passed the Senate in July, were approved by the Con-

---

tion, Report of the Committee on Corporations on Section 338, 37 Tax Law. 155 (1983); Henderson, Planning Possibilities Under Section 338, 36 So. Cal. Tax Inst. Ch. 9 (1984).

For various technical amendments to §338 effected by the Tax Reform Act of 1984, P.L. No. 98-369, §712(k), 98 Stat. 678, see Eustice, The Tax Reform Act of 1984, ¶ 3.03[1].

ference Committee in August of 1982, and became law on September 3, 1982 as §224 of TEFRA of 1982.[129.2] The Tax Reform Act of 1984 made numerous technical modifications to §338, which are reflected in the following material.

Under this new system, all actual §332 liquidations will result in a carryover of basis (and of the tax history) from the liquidated subsidiary. Thus, the purchasing corporation has a choice; either liquidate the newly purchased subsidiary and inherit its basis and tax history, or make the §338 election and treat the acquisition as a purchase of assets. (A third choice is not to make the election, leaving the purchased subsidiary intact with its own asset basis and tax history.) The principal intent of these amendments is to harmonize the tax results of an asset purchase and a stock purchase acquisition transaction. Thus, conformity of the tax treatment for stock purchases to that applicable to asset purchases is the principal theme of new §338, and, when its provisions are elected, both sides of the acquisition will be treated as if the transaction had been structured as a purchase of assets.

2. *Principal features of §338.* Students of §334(b)(2) will find much that is familiar in new §338, especially the definition of "purchase" and the time frame during which a qualified stock purchase must be made. But §338 is definitely a new provision, and contains within it many new and, at times, potentially complex rules (especially the anti-selectivity rules in §§338(e) and 338(f)). The principal features of §338 are the following:

(a) Qualified acquisition. A "qualified stock purchase" is defined by §§338(d)(3) and 338(h)(3) in essentially the same way as existing §§334(b)(2) and 334(b)(3), viz., the purchase of 80 percent control within the twelve-month acquisition period ("purchase" being essentially a cost-basis acquisition from unrelated parties).[129.3] Unlike §334(b)(2), however, the option attribution rules of §318(a)(4) do not apply, §338(h)(3)(A)(iii). Similar to the chain acquisition rules of §334(b)(3), purchases of stock of one corporation are also deemed to be purchases of stock owned by that corporation to the extent that (and beginning on the date that)

[129.2] P.L. No. 97-248, 96 Stat. 324.

[129.3] New §338(h)(3)(A) essentially tracks the "purchase" definition of old §334(b)(3). Similarly, §§338(h)(1) and 338(h)(2) define the acquisition time frame in the same manner as old §334(b)(2).

the buyer would be considered as owning such stock under §318(a) by virtue of new §338(h)(3)(B).[129.4] The qualified purchase can be made in whole or in part by any corporate member of an "affiliated group," §338(h)(7),[129.5] but only corporations can be quali-

---

[129.4] See S. Rep. No. 494, 97th Cong., 2d Sess., at 194 (1982) for illustration of the chain rules of §338(h)(3)(B). (This example did not appear in the Conference Report, but should still be applicable in view of the substantially identical statutory language, but the example was included in the Joint Committee Staff General Explanation of this legislation at 136.)

Under this example, T owned 50 percent of S and P purchased T's stock in five equal 20 percent amounts on January 1, April 1, July 1, October 1, and December 31, of 1983. P is not deemed to own any S stock until the third purchase on July 1 (at which time it constructively owns 30 percent, viz., 60 percent of T's 50 percent. At the end of the remaining purchases, P is deemed to have purchased 50 percent of S and has until June 30, 1984 to complete a qualified acquisition with respect to the remaining S stock.

Section 712(k)(5) of the Tax Reform Act of 1984 clarified and conformed the chain subsidiary purchase rules more closely to the former §334(b)(3) rules: viz., (a) the term "purchase" now includes a "deemed purchase" under §338(a)(2), new §338(h)(3)(B) (i.e., the purchasing corporation's election as to the target triggers a deemed purchase of any stock in subsidiaries owned by the target, and so on down the chain of second- and third-tier subsidiaries); (b) the related seller exception of §338(h)(3)(A)(iii) will not apply to an acquisition of stock from a related corporation (including, by virtue of new §338 (h)(3)(B), a "deemed purchase" under §338(a)(2)) if at least 50 percent of the related corporation's stock was acquired by purchase, new §338(h)(3)(C)(i); (c) the carryover basis exception of §338(h)(3) (A)(i) will not apply if stock of the distributing corporation was acquired by purchase and the acquiring corporation elected §338 with respect to such stock, new §338(h)(3)(C)(ii); and (d) §338(h)(3) (A)(ii) was amended to require that the stock must be acquired in a transaction in which gain was recognized in full to the seller, and cannot be acquired in a substituted-basis transaction either.

[129.5] For this purpose, an affiliated group has the same meaning as §1504, but without any of the exceptions in §1504(b) (e.g., foreign corporations, possessions corporations, tax-exempt corporations, etc.), §338(h)(5). See infra ¶ 15.21. Thus, any member that fails the 80 percent stock tests of §1504(a) will not be an "affiliate" under §338.

Section 712(k)(6)(A) of the Tax Reform Act of 1984, P.L. No. 98-369, 98 Stat. 678, redesignated §338(h)(7) as §338(h)(8), and provided that purchases by members of an acquiring affiliated group shall be treated as made by one corporation, namely, various member purchases will be aggregated.

fied buyers of the target's stock (hence, noncorporate purchasers will have to organize a new corporation to effect the acquisition if §338 benefits are desired).[129.6]

Thus, the type of acquisition governed by new §338 is essentially the same type of transaction that was covered by old §334(b)(2), viz., an acquisition of control (80 percent) within a one-year period from unrelated sellers in a cost-basis acquisition transaction.

(b) The election. The election must be made by the purchasing corporation within seventy-five days of the acquisition date (i.e., that date within the twelve-month acquisition period on which 80 percent control is acquired), and, once made, is irrevocable.[129.7] If all or part of the target's stock is transferred to other members of the purchasing corporation's affiliated group, presumably the initial purchasing corporation continues to be the member entitled to make the election.[129.8] If split acquisitions are made by a purchasing affiliated group (e.g., half of target's stock is purchased by parent, P, and half by its subsidiary, S), identification of the proper electing member is less clear, although it would seem that the controlling parent is the most likely candidate here.[129.9]

(c) Effect of the election. Section 338(a) treats all of the assets of the target corporation as having been sold on the acquisi-

---

[129.6] Thus, stock acquisitions by partnerships, trusts, estates, and individuals cannot qualify for §338 treatment.

[129.7] Section 338(g). The term acquisition date is defined by §338(h)(2) as the first date upon which there is a qualified stock purchase, and §338(d)(3) defines such a purchase as the acquisition of control, by purchase within a twelve-month period.

Section 712(k)(4) of the Tax Reform Act of 1984 added six months to the time for making the election (i.e., by the fifteenth day of the ninth month after the acquisition date month). See Temp. Regs. §5f.338-1, added by T.D. 7942, Feb. 7, 1984. See also new Temp. Regs. §§1.338-1T and 1.338-2T, added by T.D. 7975, Sept. 4, 1984.

[129.8] See H. Rep. No. 760, 97th Cong., 2d Sess., at 538 n.2 (1982), specifically noting that §338(h)(7) (treating acquisitions by affiliates of the purchasing corporation as an acquisition by the purchasing corporation) will prevent intra-group transfers of purchased stock from disqualifying a §338 election, citing Chrome Plate v. US, 614 F.2d 990 (5th Cir. 1980).

[129.9] Neither the Senate Report nor the Conference Report give any clue on this point, however. See supra note 129.5 (this Supplement) (member purchases will be aggregated and treated as if made by one corporation).

tion date (at their fair market value) in a single transaction governed by §337, and then subsequently repurchased by a "new" corporation on the day after the acquisition date.[129.10] It should be noted that §337 will apply to such a sale *without* regard to any of the exceptions in §337(c) (for §§341, 332, and 333). The deemed sale price rules are found in §338(b), which provides that the price at which the assets are deemed to have been sold and repurchased is an amount equal to the purchasing corporation's "grossed-up" basis in the target's stock on the acquisition date, plus adjustments (under regulations) for liabilities of the target corporation and "other relevant items" (it seems likely that these adjustments will strongly resemble the current regulations under §334 (b)(2) in view of the similar statutory language).[129.11]

[129.10] Thus, any recapture income required to be recognized as a result of the deemed §337 sale will occur outside of the purchasing group's consolidated return. See H. Rep. No. 760, supra note 129.8 (this Supplement) at 537 and 539. Under new §338(h)(11), added by §712(k)(6)(B) of the Tax Reform Act of 1984, valuation can be made under formulas provided by regulations.

If the purchased corporation was itself a member of another consolidated group, presumably its recapture tax liability remains with the seller-group. Arguably, however, the purchased corporation may have its own one-day separate return, in which it is responsible for its own recapture tax liability generated by the §338 sale. The Conference Report is unclear on this point, merely stating that it is the intent not to include such amounts in the acquiring group's consolidated return, but instead to include them "in the return of the 'old' corporation." H. Rep. No. 760, supra note 129.8 (this Supplement) at 539.

But see new §§338(h)(8) and 338(h)(9), added by the Technical Corrections Act of 1982, to deal with this problem. Under §338(h)(8) (redesignated as §338(h)(9) by the Tax Reform Act of 1984), the target corporation is not treated as a member of an affiliated group with respect to the deemed sale of its assets (i.e., it bears the recapture tax liability, and thus the buyer will inherit that liability); but §338(h)(9) (redesignated as §338(h)(10)) provides an alternative election to treat the transaction as a nonqualified asset sale by the target corporation (i.e., the seller group has full recognition of gain or loss on the target's assets, but the stock sale is tax free).

The economic burden for such liabilities will have to be dealt with in the purchase agreement (at least if the acquisition is a negotiated transaction). See Temp. Regs. §5f.338-2, added by T.D. 7942, Feb. 7, 1984.

[129.11] However, the "earnings and profits" adjustment in the §334 (b)(2) regulations will not be necessary under §338; for prior law, see R.M. Smith, Inc., 69 TC 317 (1977); Silverman, Leave It to *Smith* (or,

The "grossed-up basis" is defined by §338(b)(2) as an amount equal to the basis of the purchasing corporation's basis in the stock on the acquisition date (i.e., when 80 percent control was acquired), grossed-up to equate 100 percent stock ownership by the acquiring corporation; but §338(c)(1) limits the acquired corporation's §337 nonrecognition to the highest stock ownership percentage held by the acquiring corporation during the one-year period after the acquisition date.[129.12] Thus, if the acquiring corporation buys less than 100 percent of the acquired corporation's stock, the deemed asset sale nevertheless will be considered to be at full asset values, but §337 nonrecognition will be limited to the acquiring corporation's actual ownership percentage.

The deemed sale and purchase price rules of §§338(a) and 338(b) were modified by §712(k)(1) of the Tax Reform Act of 1984. The target company now is deemed to have sold all of its assets at their fair market value, §338(a)(1), and, under new §338(b)(1), repurchased those assets at their "adjusted fair market value"; adjusted fair market value is defined by §338(b)(2) as the excess of asset values over the net unrealized appreciation in the target corporation's stock already held by the acquiring corporation on the acquisition date (thus, no basis step-up will be allowed for potential gain in the target company's stock already held by the acquiring corporation unless the acquiring company elects to be taxed on that gain).

The constructive liquidation mandated by §338(a) is not, however, a true liquidation, so that minority shareholders will not be subject to imputed recognition on their target stock.[129.13]

"Refinements" on Section 334(b)(2)), 33 Tax L. Rev. 545 (1978); and Yost, Delayed Section 334(b)(2) Liquidation: the *Smith* Case— A Pyrrhic Victory for the IRS, 5 J. Corp. Tax. 263 (1978).

See §712(k)(1) of the Tax Reform Act of 1984, which provides for certain technical amendments to the deemed purchase basis rules of §338(b).

[129.12] Full §337 nonrecognition will apply here, however, if the acquired corporation is actually liquidated within such one-year period. Note also that the liquidating corporation's assets will carry over at the stepped-up §338 figure under new §334(b). But §712(k)(2) of the Tax Reform Act of 1984 denies §337 nonrecognition if the target liquidates under §333, thus conforming §338 with the comparable chain liquidation rules of §337(c)(3).

[129.13] H. Rep. No. 760, supra note 129.8 (this Supplement) at 537; S. Rep. No. 494, supra note 129.4 (this Supplement) at 193. For contrary results in the context of a taxable merger squeeze-out via §334

Additional purchases of target stock after the acquisition date (i.e., the control date) will be treated as qualified acquisitions if made on or before the close of the twelve-month acquisition period; moreover, additional stock purchases within the one-year period after the requisite control acquisition date can be counted in determining the acquired corporation's §337 nonrecognition percentage by virtue of §338(c)(1). (But §712(k)(6)(A) of the Tax Reform Act of 1984 added new §338(h)(7), which limits such additional stock purchases to those that qualify as a "purchase" or a §302(a) redemption by the target corporation.) However, post-acquisition adjustments to the target company's stock basis (e.g., capital contributions, or stock basis increases under the consolidated return regulation investment basis adjustment rules) will *not* be taken into account since they represent basis adjustments to stock of the deemed "new" corporation. On the other hand, post-acquisition adjustments in the *purchase price* of the target's stock should be taken into account as a "relevant item" under §338(b)(1)(B) (redesignated as §338(b)(2) in 1984), and so should any adjustments in the target's recapture tax liabilities as a result of these purchase price adjustments.[129.14] The Committee Reports [129.15] specifically note, however, that any recapture *income* of the target corporation is *not* to be included in the consolidated return of the purchasing group (and this includes post-acquisition recapture income generated by post-acquisition purchase price adjustments).

A special rule in §338(c)(2) was added by the Conference Committee to deal with situations where part of the acquired corporation's stock was purchased and part was redeemed.[129.16] If in

---

(b)(2), see May B. Kass, 60 TC 218 (1973). But the Tax Reform Act of 1984, in §717(k)(6)(B), adding new §338(h)(14), provides that §341 will apply to minority shareholder sales of target stock within one year of the acquisition date without regard to §338.

[129.14] Since the purpose of §338 is to give comparability of tax treatment to direct asset purchases, this is the result that would occur in the case of such an acquisition.

[129.15] S. Rep. No. 494, supra note 129.4 (this Supplement) at 193; H. Rep. No. 760, supra note 129.8 (this Supplement) at 537.

[129.16] The so-called *Zenz* combined stock purchase, stock redemption transaction. See supra ¶ 9.25. Query whether the purchaser can "back into" the requisite 80 percent control via this route? See Madison Square Garden Corp. v. CIR, 500 F.2d 611 (2d Cir. 1974). The Joint Com-

connection with a qualified stock purchase to which §338 election is made, the acquired corporation makes a distribution in complete redemption of a shareholder's stock under §302(b)(3), §336 (rather than §311(d)) will apply at the corporate level to such distribution.[129.17]

The Tax Reform Act of 1984, in §712(k)(6)(B), added new §338(h)(12), which deals with the case where the target corporation had already adopted a plan of complete liquidation during the twelve-month period preceding the acquisition date. In that case, if the plan is not rescinded before the acquisition date and §338 is elected, then §337 applies under principles similar to the rules of §338(c)(1) and the target will be deemed to have distributed all its assets at the close of the acquisition date.

(d) Anti-selectivity all-or-nothing rules. A major theme of new §338 is consistency of treatment where the purchasing corporation acquires two or more members of the same affiliated group, or combines a direct asset purchase from target (or its affiliate) with a qualified stock purchase. In order to obtain the basis step-up benefits of a §338 election, the purchasing corporation is required by §§338(e) and 338(f) either to step up the basis of all of target's assets and those of any of its affiliates, or none of them. This all-or-nothing "group-wide" consistency rule applies whether assets of the target, or one of its affiliates, have been purchased, or the controlling stock of target has been purchased and a §338 election has been made.[129.18]

Thus, §338(e) imposes a deemed §338 election in any case where there is a direct acquisition (by purchase) of any asset (other than in the ordinary course of business) of the target (or of one of its affiliates) within the "consistency period," defined by §338(h)(4) as "one year before the start of the twelve-month acquisition

---

mittee Staff General Explanation, at 134, specifically states that the 80 percent requirement can be met in this manner.

[129.17] In the absence of such a rule, the distributing corporation probably would have been taxed under new §311(d), in view of the significant contraction in the scope of the exceptions to that provision. See supra new ¶ 9.64A (this Supplement).

[129.18] See also §338(i), authorizing extraordinarily broad regulations to effectuate the consistency treatment rules, viz., to prevent circumvention of these rules "through the use of *any* provision of law or regulations (including the consolidated return regulations)."

period and one year after the end of such period" (and the consistency zone can be expanded if there is found to be a "plan" to avoid its parameters), §338(h)(4)(B).[129.19] However, §338(e) does not apply to carryover basis asset acquisitions (i.e., tax-free reorganizations), nor to certain other asset acquisitions as may be provided by regulations.[129.20]

Section 338(f) likewise requires consistent treatment for all qualified stock acquisitions of members of the same affiliated group during the consistency period; viz., any election as to the first stock purchase binds subsequent stock purchases within the consistency period. For example, if P buys one of target's subsidiaries and elects §338, any later qualified purchases (either of target's stock or of one of its subsidiaries) within a one-year period will be bound by the first election. Nonelection of §338 on the first purchase similarly will preclude any election for subsequent acquisitions during the one-year consistency period. Target affiliates, for this purpose, are defined by §338(h)(6) as a member of the target corporation's affiliated group (which is defined in §338(h)(5) by reference to the consolidated return definition in §1504(a)) at any time during the consistency period, which ends on the acquisition date.[129.21]

Note, however, that the consistency rules do not apply to the following: purchases by noncorporate buyers; corporations that are not affiliated by virtue of *corporate* shareholder relationships; corporate groups that do not meet the stock ownership tests of §1504; carryover basis asset acquisitions (e.g., tax-free reorganizations and

---

[129.19] Moreover, §338(e)(3) provides an anti-avoidance rule that empowers the Service to treat stock acquisitions pursuant to a plan as if they were qualified stock purchases. The anti-avoidance rules in §§338 (e)(3), 338(h)(4)(B), and 338(i) seem destined to materially revive analysis of the subjective "motives" of the acquiring corporation as an important consideration in the application of §338, a result that undercuts the stated purpose of replacing the *Kimbell-Diamond* intent test with an exclusive, objective statutory rule. See infra text at note 129.33 (this Supplement).

[129.20] See §338(e)(2)(D) (property located outside of the United States), and §338(e)(2)(E) (blanket delegation to except asset acquisition by regulation). The former provision was dropped in 1984, leaving only the regulation delegation rule.

[129.21] Certain foreign corporations are exempted from the "target affiliate group" by §338(h)(6)(B), except as provided by regulations (and subject to such conditions as those regulations may prescribe).

§351 transactions); and asset acquisitions that do not constitute a "purchase" (e.g., leases, or licenses).

3. *To illustrate.* The application of the new §338 rules can be illustrated by the following examples, in which T is the target corporation; X and Y are wholly owned subsidiaries of T; and P is the acquiring corporation and it has one wholly owned subsidiary, S (and both groups file consolidated returns).

Example 1: P (or S) purchased all of T's stock for cash and made the §338 election. P was deemed to have purchased X and Y's stock as well as T's stock; accordingly, the T group's taxable year closed, each member was deemed to have sold its assets under §337 with no gain or loss (except for recapture) at a price equal to its allocable share of P's purchase price (plus any adjustment for recapture tax liability), and then repurchased these assets at the same price and entered P's consolidated group with a clean slate (each member having purged its tax history, and stepped up, or down, its asset bases prior to includability in P's consolidated return).

But under the Tax Reform Act of 1984 amendment in §338(h)(3)(B), the X and Y stock now is deemed to have been sold and repurchased by T (and will be controlled by P's election, or nonelection of §338 as to T under the §338(f) consistency rules). Also, new §338(h)(15) allows a combined deemed sale return by the T, X, and Y group.

Example 2: The same results would occur if, within the two-year consistency zone of §338(h)(4), P acquires assets from T, X, or Y, or if P buys X and Y stock in a series of stock purchases, regardless of the order. However, these provisions would not apply if T, X, and Y did not constitute an affiliated group under §1504.[129.22]

Example 3: If P acquired one or more of T's affiliates in a basis carryover reorganization, the consistency rule of §338(e) does not apply by virtue of §338(e)(2)(B).

[129.22] Because, for example, X and Y both had outstanding issues of *participating* preferred stock owned by persons other than T. See infra ¶ 15.21. But changes in the consolidated return eligibility rules of §1504 were effected by the Tax Reform Act of 1984.

Example 4: If P only purchased 80 percent of T's stock, the deemed §338(b) sale price would be grossed-up to 100 percent, but T, X, and Y would only obtain §337 nonrecognition for 80 percent of their gain by virtue of §338(c)(1), unless P acquired the rest of T's stock within one year, or completely liquidated T, X, and Y within such period.[129.23]

But X and Y would get full §337 protection after the Tax Reform Act of 1984 amendments in §338(h)(3)(B) because T will be deemed to have sold and repurchased *all* of its X and Y stock.

Example 5: If P purchased 80 percent of T's stock, and T distributed property in complete redemption of the rest of its stock, T would be protected by §336 because of the special rule in §338(c)(2).

Example 6: If P already owned 20 percent of T's stock, and bought the remaining 80 percent in a qualified purchase, the gross-up pricing rules of §338(b) formerly resulted in a 100 percent basis step up to T, X, and Y, and presumably they were able to count P's preexisting ownership for applying §337 nonrecognition under §338(c)(1).

But under the new gross-up basis rules of §338(b) after the Tax Reform Act of 1984 amendments, basis would not be grossed-up to the extent of P's potential gain in old-and-cold T stock unless P elects to recognize its gain on that stock.[129.24]

[129.23] On the liquidation of T (and X and Y), P would inherit T's (and X and Y's) stepped-up asset basis that resulted from the §338 election by virtue of §334(b)(1). But the Tax Reform Act of 1984, in §712(k)(6)(A), adds new §338(h)(7), which requires that additional stock acquisitions must be by purchase or a §302(a) redemption by target.

[129.24] While §338(c)(1) speaks of cases where P owns less than 100 percent of T's stock, by implication, it would seem that if P owned all of that stock as a result of both prior minority ownership and a qualified 80 percent control purchase, §337 would apply in full to the deemed sale. But see §712(k)(1)(B) of the Tax Reform Act of 1984, which revised the deemed basis rules of §338(b) now will deny a basis step-up for any unrealized appreciation attributable to the previously held target stock unless P elects to be taxed on the gain atributable to its old-and-cold T stock.

Example 7: P buys 20 percent of T's stock in January, and 20 percent each in March, May, July, and September. A qualified purchase results (for T, X, and Y stock), the acquisition date occurs with the July purchase (when 80 percent control was acquired), and the acquisition period ends twelve months after the January purchase. The fact that P had options to acquire any of T's stock is disregarded.

The deemed sale price for the T group's assets is grossed up to 100 percent of the value of T's stock and the deemed asset sales occur as of the July control acquisition date.[129.25] Thus, any recapture income to the T group as a result of its deemed asset sales (including the grossed-up sale price portion reflected by the September sale portion) is reportable in T's final return preceding the July acquisition date, and T (and its affiliates) enter P's consolidated return immediately after such date (with a clean slate) as if their assets had been purchased by the P group.

The deemed sale price also includes any recapture tax liability generated in the T group as a result of these deemed asset sales. A statutory circle exists, however, since the deemed sale price includes recapture tax liability while recapture tax liability depends on the deemed sale price. If consistency with §337 asset sales is the goal, recapture tax liability should be computed based on the actual (grossed-up) stock sale price, and then adjusted upward for the resulting recapture tax liability.

Example 8: If T owned only 80 percent of X and Y, P had to acquire 100 percent of T's stock in a qualified purchase to enable it to step up the basis of X and Y's assets (although not of their stock), since P was only deemed to have purchased its §318 attributive percentage of any stock owned by T (even

---

[129.25] By virtue of §338(c)(1), T, X, and Y would get 100 percent §337 protection since P acquired the rest of T's stock within one year of the July acquisition date. But see new §388(h)(7), supra note 129.23 (this Supplement) (such additional stock acquisitions must be by purchase or by a §302(a) redemption).

T's deemed acquisition of X and Y now occurs on the July acquisition date under the Tax Reform Act of 1984 amendments to §338 (h)(3)(B).

though T, X, and Y could be included in P's consolidated return).[129.26]

But after the Tax Reform Act of 1984 amendments to §338(h)(3)(B), a qualified purchase of X and Y would result by virtue of T's deemed repurchase of the X and Y stock.

Example 9: If P makes additional investments in T (or X and Y) after acquiring control, such amounts will not be reflected in asset basis because they occur with respect to the stock of "new" corporations T, X, and Y.[129.27]

Example 10: If T owned 80 percent of X and X owned 80 percent of Y, and P buys 80 percent of T stock and elects §338, the deemed purchase rules of new §338(h)(3)(B) will result in a qualified purchase of the T stock by P, of the X stock by T, and of the Y stock by X (prior to the Tax Reform Act of 1984 amendments, only the T stock acquisition by P would have qualified).

4. Collateral implications of §338 and general comments. The policy of new §338 to conform the tax treatment of stock purchase acquisitions to that applicable to direct asset acquisitions seems to have been effectively accomplished by the 1982 amendment. Thus, if assets are sold in a §337 transaction, recapture income stays with the selling corporation, its tax history disappears upon the eventual (with twelve months) liquidation mandated by §337, and the acquiring corporation obtains a §1012 cost basis for the purchased properties. Similarly, if stock control is purchased and a timely §338 election is made, asset basis will be stepped up inside of the acquired corporation, its tax history will be purged, and any recapture tax

---

[129.26] See S. Rep. No. 494, supra note 129.4 (this Supplement) at 195; and H. Rep. No. 760, supra note 129.8 (this Supplement) at 537.

[129.27] Similarly, any stock basis adjustments required by the consolidated return regulation investment basis rules would not be considered here either.

Moreover, additional recapture income generated in the acquiring corporation's consolidated return as a result of post-acquisition adjustments to the purchase price of the acquired corporation's stock is to be accounted for "separately" according to the Committee Reports; see S. Rep. No. 494, supra note 129.4 (this Supplement) at 194, and H. Rep. No. 760, supra note 129.8 (this Supplement) at 537. Presumably "separate return limitation year"-type computations will be made with respect to such amounts. See infra ¶ 15.24.

liability resulting from the deemed §337 sale remains in the acquired corporation (and recapture income is not includable in the acquiring corporation's consolidated return). Moreover, the statutory time frames applicable to asset purchases and stock purchases are essentially comparable under the new legislation: The selling corporation has one year to liquidate if the §337 route is adopted, while the acquiring corporation has one year to effect a "qualified stock" purchase and seventy-five additional days (now about eight and one-half months) to elect §338 if the stock acquisition route is followed.[129.28]

If the §338 election is not made, asset basis (and tax history) of the acquired corporation will be preserved; on a subsequent liquidation under §332, basis and tax history will carry over to the distributee parent under §§334(b) and 381(a)(1). Thus, a corporation that purchases stock control of another corporation has the following choices: (a) make the §338 election, under which the assets of the acquired corporation will obtain a new cost basis and its tax history will be purged;[129.29] (b) waive the §338 election and leave the acquired corporation's basis and tax history intact; or (c) liquidate the acquired corporation under §332 and carry over its asset bases and tax history under §§334(b) and 381(a)(1).

While one of the principal purposes of new §338 is to inhibit loss corporations (or loss affiliated groups) from acquiring the stock of profitable corporations and sheltering its income in the acquiring group's consolidated return, the converse pattern (profit corporation acquiring a loss corporation) seems considerably easier to accomplish under the new law. Thus, if profit corporation P buys

---

[129.28] Moreover, use of partial liquidation techniques to obtain selective basis step-ups has likewise been eliminated by the new legislation, supra ¶ 9.54 (this Supplement), since distributions to corporate shareholders in what were formally partial liquidation transactions now will result in dividend treatment, and carryover asset basis consequences to the corporate distributee (although any recapture gain triggered by the distribution still will be deferred under the consolidated return regulations). But see changes to §311(d) effected by the Tax Reform Act of 1984, supra ¶¶ 7.21 and 9.64A (this Supplement), which will treat all such distributions as taxable sales by the distributing corporation (after 1984).

[129.29] Recapture gain must be reported outside of the acquiring group's consolidated return, and the acquired corporation enters the consolidated group with a "clean slate."

loss company T's stock and liquidates T under §332, the tax basis and loss history of T will carry over to P under §§334(b) and 381 (a)(1), subject to §382(a) (which can be avoided if T's business is continued) [129.30] and §269 (which can be avoided if there is a reasonable business purpose for the acquisition). [129.31] Under prior law, a §334(b)(2) liquidation was not a §381 transaction, and thus the liquidated subsidiary's tax history was purged by the distribution transaction. Under the new §§332–334(b) rules, however, all §332 liquidations are basis carryover transactions, with the result that tax history will survive, subject only to the tax-motivated acquisition defenses of §269. But the Tax Reform Act of 1984 added new §269(b) to extend §269 to tax-motivated nonelections of §338.

New §338, by eliminating the formal requirement for an actual liquidation of the purchased corporation, should also considerably simplify the structuring problems that arose under prior law where preservation of the purchased corporation's legal existence was a vital commercial component of the acquisition (e.g., because of favorable leases, nonassignable franchises, and regulatory restrictions). Now, by simply electing §338, a complete liquidation of the acquired corporation is deemed to have occurred, coupled with a constructive "reincorporation" of the acquired corporation, thus avoiding the risk under prior law that an actual liquidation-reincorporation transaction would result in the denial of §334(b)(2) treatment.[129.32] Conversely, if carryover treatment is desired, stock purchases followed by a §332 liquidation will yield the sought-after basis (and tax history) preservation result, since the new legislation abolishes the deemed asset purchase principle of the *Kimbell-Diamond* case.[129.33]

[129.30] See infra ¶ 16.22.

[129.31] See infra ¶ 16.21. But §712(k)(8) of the Tax Reform Act of 1984 amended §269 and specifically provided (in newly designated §269(b)) that if the principal purpose for *liquidating* the target corporation (pursuant to a plan adopted within two years of the acquisition date) is tax avoidance, then §269(a) can deny the target's carryovers.

[129.32] See, e.g., Harold C. Lang, ¶ 82,149 P-H Memo TC (1982); Pugh, Combining Acquired and Acquiring Corporations and their Subsidiaries: Some Anomalies of Form and Substance, 35 Tax L. Rev. 359 (1980).

[129.33] S. Rep. No. 494, supra note 129.4 (this Supplement) at 192 (1982); H. Rep. No. 760, supra note 129.8 (this Supplement) at 536.

If "selective" tax treatment is desired, life under the new statutory regime is made considerably more difficult—though not impossible—by new §338. Thus, new §338(i) grants awesome regulatory authority to the Service for combatting various tax-motivated maneuverings, which, when coupled with §§338(e)(3) and 338(h)(4)(B), should at least serve to restrain the overly optimistic tax-planning schemes that may be attempted in circumventing the consistency rules. On the other hand, the relative ease with which §1504 "affiliation" can be broken [129.34] leaves a ready escape from the consistency rules of §§338(e) and 338(f), since corporate affiliation status is the key to the application of these provisions. Moreover, selective asset acquisitions can be made by lease or license (or in a carryover basis acquisition) without triggering the application of §338(e). Moreover, if the affiliated target corporations are not owned by a common parent *corporation* stockholder, selective acquisitions of stock and assets can be effected without fear of §§338(e) or 338(f).

In any event, it is clear that the acquisition ground rules have undergone a major substantive change; no doubt the tax-planning "game" will continue, however, but the game will be played on a new playing field and under a new official rulebook.

5. September 1983 Reform Proposals. After scarcely a year under the new TEFRA regime, and inspired, perhaps, by the rapid passage of §338 in 1982, the Staff of the Senate Finance Committee issued a preliminary report on the reform and simplification of Subchapter C in September of 1983, which proposed to extend the elective basis step-up (or elective basis carryover) approach of §338 to *all* qualified corporate acquisitions, whether of stock or assets, and whether the consideration consists of stock or cash. Qualified stock acquisitions are defined as 80 percent control acquisitions within a twelve-month period (like §338), and qualified asset acquisitions are those constituting the acquisition of "substantially all" the acquired corporation's assets.

In effect, the new proposed system would provide for specific taxpayer electivity of carryover- or cost-basis treatment, which would replace the transactional electivity of present law. Qualified

---

[129.34] E.g., by having affiliated subsidiaries issue participating preferred stock to outsiders. But see amendments to §1504(a) by the Tax Reform Act of 1984, infra ¶ 15.21 (this Supplement).

asset acquisitions are presumed to be carryover-basis, unless cost treatment is elected; stock acquisitions carry the same presumption, i.e., carryover-basis unless a cost-basis is elected. But acquisitions from "related parties" (with §318) are not eligible for the cost-basis election. If carryover-basis treatment is elected, then no gain or loss is recognized to the acquired corporation; if cost-basis treatment is election, then gain or loss would be fully recognized to the transferor corporation (viz., §§336 and 337 would be repealed). However, a special nonrecognition election (and correlative carryover-basis rule) is provided for goodwill purchase premium, even in cost-basis acquisitions.

Shareholder tax treatment would be determined independently of corporate level recognition or nonrecognition; viz., regardless of whether the acquired and acquiring corporations elected carryover or cost-basis treatment, shareholders who receive stock in a qualified acquisition would be entitled to nonrecognition treatment to that extent. Qualified stock would consist of stock of the acquiring corporation and/or its parents in the direct chain of ownership. If cash or other nonqualifying consideration is received, recognized gain or loss (or dividend) treatment can result, depending on the mixtures of consideration (i.e., all cash, full capital gain or loss; part stock and cash could result in a dividend if the distribution is essentially pro rata).

The choice between cost- and carryover-basis treatment would be made on a corporation-by-corporation basis (i.e., selectivity by entities is allowed, but not by assets). Thus some, but not all, of the anti-selectivity provisions of §§338(e) and 338(f) would be repealed.

Specific legislation reflecting these proposals has not yet, at this writing, been forthcoming, although considerable sentiment for their enactment seems to be building in the tax community. These proposals, however, did not find their way into the Tax Reform Act of 1984 legislation; whether this represents merely a lost opportunity or a fatal flaw in timing remains to be seen.[129.35]

[129.35] For further analysis of the Tax Reform Act of 1984 changes in the Subchapter C area, see Eustice, The Tax Reform Act of 1984.

PART D.   THE LIQUIDATING CORPORATION'S INCOME AND LOSS

¶ 11.61.   EFFECT OF THE DISTRIBUTION ITSELF: §336

Page 11-56:

Add to note 130.

[130] Recent legislative amendments of §346, supra ¶ 9.50 (this Supplement), confine §336 exclusively to complete liquidations. This amendment passed as §222(b) of TEFRA of 1982, P.L. No. 248, 96 Stat. 324.

Correct text in sixth line.

Change reference of §453(d) to §453 B (provision redesignated, without change, by Installment Sales Revision Act of 1980).

Page 11-57:

Add to note 132.

[132] But new §336(b) (added by P.L. No. 96-223, 1980, and effective for plans adopted after 1981) provides a recapture rule for distributions of LIFO inventory similar to §311(b); viz., ordinary income will result to the liquidating corporation to the extent of the excess of FIFO value over LIFO value of the distributed inventory.

See also §897(d)(1) of the Foreign Investment Real Property Tax Act of 1980 (distribution of U.S. real property by a foreign corporation taxable to distributing corporation notwithstanding §336).

Add to note 133, first paragraph.

[133] See Eugene J. Ramm, 72 TC 671 (1979) (ITC recapture in §333 liquidation distribution to 50 percent shareholder); but see Long v. US, 1979-2 USTC ¶ 9612 (W.D. Tenn. 1979) (no §47 recapture on liquidation distribution by Subchapter S corporation where shareholder continued business of liquidating corporation; §47(b) "change of form"; Regulations rejected). But *Long* was rev'd, 652 F.2d 675 (6th Cir. 1981) (Regs. valid; not a mere change of form because basis step-up on liquidation).

For application of §482 to reallocate potential loss on distributed assets in a §332 liquidation to the liquidating subsidiary (which could not use such loss because it was the tax equivalent of a foreign corporation), see General Elec. Co. v. US, 1983-2 USTC ¶ 9532 (Cl. Ct. 1983).

Recently enacted legislation imposed a look-through rule on the distribution of partnership interests (the distributing corporation now will be taxed under the recapture rules as if it had distributed its ratable share of the recapture property directly); the Tax Reform Act of 1984,

P.L. No. 98-369, §75(a), 98 Stat. 678, adding new §386. See Eustice, The Tax Reform Act of 1984, ¶ 3.02[1][c].

For a decision anticipating this legislation, see Holiday Village Shopping Center v. US, 1984-2 USTC ¶ 9549 (Cl. Ct. 1984).

Add to text at end of section.

Proposals by the Staff of the Senate Finance Committee on the reform and simplification of Subchapter C have recommended the repeal of §336 (and §337), or, failing that, at least the substantial restriction of these corporate-level nonrecognition rules where distributed property obtains a new basis in the hands of the transferee. See infra new ¶ 11.61A (this Supplement).[133.1]

[133.1] See ABA Tax Section Special Task Force Report, Income Taxation of Corporations Making Distributions With Respect to Their Stock, 37 Tax L. 625 (1984).

Add new section heading.

¶ 11.61A.   PROPOSED REPEAL OF §336

On September 22, 1983, the Staff of the Senate Finance Committee submitted its preliminary report on the reform and simplification of Subchapter C. A centerpiece of this study was the Staff recommendation for repeal of §336 (and §337 as well), thus requiring full corporate-level recognition of gain or loss on liquidating distributions of corporate assets (if the liquidation does not give rise to a carryover-basis under §334(b), supra ¶ 11.44). Thus, complete liquidation distributions-in-kind of appreciated (or depreciated) corporate assets would be treated as a deemed sale at fair market value by the liquidating corporation to its shareholders, under this proposal.

The Staff report listed a number of optional relief possibilities as alternatives to the outright repeal of §336: (1) shareholder credit for their pro rata shares of the corporate tax; (2) exemption of certain historic assets from the corporate-level tax; (3) elective deferral of taxes until the shareholders dispose of the distributed assets; (4) the corporate capital gain rate could be reduced; (5) the shareholder capital gain rate on the liquidation could be reduced; or (6) the corporate capital gain tax on the liquidation could be phased in over a period of years (a twelve-year schedule was suggested).

No specific legislative provisions reflecting these proposals have been presented at this writing, however, and this proposal did not become part of the Tax Reform Act of 1984 legislation.[133.2]

[133.2] See ABA Tax Section Special Task Force Report, supra note 133.1 (this Supplement).

¶ 11.62. INCOME OF THE LIQUIDATING CORPORATION: "TIMELY" LIQUIDATIONS AND RELATED PROBLEMS

Page 11-58:

Add to note 136, first paragraph.

[136] Byrne, The Tax Benefit Rule as Applied to Corporate Liquidations and Contributions to Capital: Recent Developments, 56 Notre Dame Law. 215 (1980).

Page 11-60:

Add to note 140, first paragraph.

[140] See also General Elec. Co. v. US, 1983-2 USTC ¶ 9532 (Cl. Ct. 1983) (§482 applied to reallocate loss to subsidiary on sale by parent after §332 liquidation of §931 subsidiary).

Page 11-63:

Add to note 147, second paragraph.

[147] But see Bliss Dairy, Inc. v. US, 645 F.2d 19 (9th Cir. 1981) (Ninth Circuit continued to follow *South Lake Farms;* no tax benefit recapture on distribution in kind of previously expensed property because no recovery by distributing corporation), but rev'd, 460 US 370 (1983); *Tennessee-Carolina* followed in Bonaire Dev. Co., 76 TC 789 (1981), aff'd other grounds, 679 F.2d 159 (9th Cir. 1982) (item not deductible). Accord with *South Lake Farms* is Ballou Constr. Co. v. US, 526 F. Supp. 403 (D. Kan. 1981), rev'r, 706 F.2d 301 (10th Cir. 1983).

Add to note 147, fourth paragraph.

[147] See also Byrne, supra note 136 (this Supplement); and Note, Tax Treatment of Previously Expensed Assets in Corporate Liquidations, 80 Mich. L. Rev. 1636 (1982).

Add to text after last sentence of runover paragraph.

But the Supreme Court, in Bliss Dairy, Inc. v. US,[149.1] applied the tax benefit doctrine to tax a liquidating corporation on the distri-

---

[149.1] Supra note 147 (this Supplement). See Blum, The Role of

bution of previously expensed assets to its shareholders in a §333 liquidation, notwithstanding the putative protection of §336. Under the majority view (decided 6 to 3), no actual recovery is necessary in order to trigger tax benefit recapture income for a liquidating corporation; rather, the test for application of the inclusionary aspect of the doctrine is whether the subsequent event (in this case distribution in kind in complete liquidation of unconsumed assets that had previously been deducted) was "fundamentally inconsistent" with the prior allowance of a deduction (viz., if the subsequent events had occurred in the same taxable year, no deduction would have been allowed). Two dissenters would have affirmed, requiring an actual recovery for application of the doctrine, while the third dissenter would have corrected the transactional discontinuity by denying the earlier deduction (if the statute of limitations was still open at the time of the later event).

Thus, the majority opinion overrules *South Lake Farms* and accepts the conclusion of *Tennessee-Carolina* that tax benefit principles can override §336. The case was remanded to determine the proper amount of includability, which the Court held was the cost of the deducted property on hand at the time of liquidation.

Add new paragraph 5 to text at end of section.

5. *Relation of §482 to distribution of property in complete liquidation.* The Service recently has been asserting §482 as an alternative to assignment of income arguments in the case of corporate distributions of property under §311 (supra ¶ 7.21) and incorporation transfers (supra ¶ 3.17). In a case of first impression, the Claims Court in *General Electric Co. v. US* [149.2] upheld the application of §482 to reallocate to a subsidiary a loss sustained by its parent on the parent's resale of property distributed in a complete liquidation under §§332 and 334(b)(1). On the facts of this case, the potential loss was not usable by the subsidiary (because it was the tax equivalent of a foreign corporation), so the parent obtained the property in a complete liquidation (with a

---

The Supreme Court in Federal Tax Controversies—*Hillsboro National Bank* and *Bliss Dairy, Inc.,* 61 Taxes 363 (1983); Cartano, The Tax Benefit Rule in Corporate Liquidations, 10 J. Corp. Tax. 216 (1983).

[149.2] 1983-2 USTC ¶ 9532 (Cl. Ct. 1983).

carryover basis) and claimed the loss on its resale to another subsidiary. The court held that income was distorted as a result of this transaction, and that such distortion was not congressionally sanctioned; accordingly, §482 applied to reassign the loss to the related entity which generated it. The theory of this decision seems equally applicable to distributions of appreciated property when the parent can make more effective use of the potential gain in the distributed property, and it may well even apply when the distribution results in a stepped-up basis under §334(a).

¶ 11.63.   THE COURT HOLDING CO. DOCTRINE AND ITS LIMITATIONS

Page 11-66:

Change second line of note 153 to read:

[153] liquidation under §333, on which gain would not be recognized. See supra note 150.

Page 11-69:

Add to note 158, second paragraph.

[158] Jos. R. Bolker, 81 TC 782 (1983) (shareholder §1031 exchange after §333 liquidation not imputed to corporation under *Court Holding*; shareholder made the exchange; corporation didn't negotiate or participate in transaction); DiAndrea, Inc., ¶ 83,788 P-H Memo TC (taxpayer error as to *Cumberland—Court Holding Co.* choice of seller question a mistake of "fact"; so could revoke improvident §333 election and get §337).

¶ 11.64.   §337: THE "ANTI-COURT HOLDING CO." PROVISION

Page 11-70:

Add to note 160, second paragraph.

[160] Rev. Proc. 75-32 was superseded and updated by Rev. Proc. 81-52, 1981-2 CB 625.

Page 11-75:

Add to note 174, first paragraph.

[174] See also Rev. Rul. 79-3, 1979-1 CB 143 (end of twelve-month period computation; if plan adopted other than on first day of month,

it ends at midnight of day before corresponding day in month one year later; if adopted on first day of month, ends at midnight on last day of eleventh month). The one year rule of §337(a) is not extendable by §7503 (Saturday, Sunday, or holiday rule), Rev. Rul. 83-116, 1983-2 CB 264; contra, E.B. Grain Co., 81 TC 70 (1983).

Add to note 174, fourth paragraph.

[174] John L. Bear, ¶ 79,304 P-H Memo TC (sale of property serially over two-year period; no §337), aff'd, 650 F.2d 1167 (10th Cir. 1981).

Add to note 176, first paragraph.

[176] Rev. Rul. 80-150, 1980-1 CB 316 (illustration of valid liquidating trust); see annotations to ¶ 2.03, note 20 (this Supplement).

Page 11-77:

Add new text to end of section.

Section 5(c) of H.R. 5043, the Bankruptcy Tax Act of 1980, proposed to liberalize the applicability of §337 to insolvent corporations by providing, in new §337(g)(1), that §337 treatment will apply to a corporation that (a) adopts a plan of complete liquidation after commencement of an insolvency proceeding; (b) distributes all its assets prior to the termination of that proceeding; (c) distributes nothing to its shareholders. In effect, the creditors will be treated as the proprietary owners of the liquidating corporation in such a case, which comports with the realities of the situation. The major advantage of new §337(g) is found in the flexible distribution-term period of §337(g)(1)(B) (viz., after adoption of the plan of liquidation and prior to termination of the insolvency proceeding). However, new §337(g)(2) denies nonrecognition treatment for property acquired after adoption of the plan of liquidation. These provisions are effective for any bankruptcy case begun after October 1, 1979.

H.R. 5043 was favorably reported by the Senate Finance Committee on November 19, 1980, with two liberalizing amendments, viz., the stretched-out liquidation rule of §337(g) would apply even though distributions are made to shareholders, and assets can be retained to pay administrative claims beyond the close of the bankruptcy proceedings. This revised version of the bill passed in December of 1980.

4. Deemed §337 sales under new §338. Under legislation enacted in 1982 (supra ¶ 11.47, this Supplement), certain qualified stock acquisitions will be treated as deemed §337 sales by the acquired corporation if the purchasing company makes a timely election under §338. This provision, which is effective September 1, 1982, treats the target company as if it had sold all of its assets in a single §337 transaction, become a "new" corporation, and then immediately repurchased its properties. This deemed liquidation does not require either an actual liquidation or sale by the acquired company; all adjustments are made on an as-if basis. These proposals passed the Senate in July, were approved by the Conference Committee in August of 1982, and became law on September 3, 1982.

5. *Proposed repeal of §337.* On September 22, 1983, the Staff of the Senate Finance Committee submitted its preliminary report on the reform of Subchapter C. A centerpiece of this report was the Staff's recommendation that §337 (and §336) be repealed, and that gain or loss be recognized at the corporate level in all cases where the transferee elects cost-basis treatment for assets acquired from the transferor corporation in a "qualified acquisition." A qualified asset acquisition is an acquisition of substantially all of the transferor's assets; and a qualified stock acquisition is the acquisition of 80 percent control within a twelve-month period.

The new corporate acquisition proposals are considered in greater detail in new ¶ 11.67A of this Supplement, and in new ¶ 14.21 of this Supplement.

¶ 11.65.   §337: NONQUALIFYING ASSETS AND DISPOSITIONS

Page 11-77:

Add to first line of text in section.

(including deemed §337 sales under §338 elections, supra ¶ 11.47, this Supplement).

Page 11-78:

Add to note 183, first paragraph.

[183] Bear v. CIR, 650 F.2d 1167 (10th Cir. 1981) (not bulk sale, thus no §337).

Add to note 184, second paragraph.

[184] But new §337(f) (added by P.L. No. 96-223, 1980) applies a recapture rule on the sale of LIFO inventory for amounts attributable to the excess of FIFO or LIFO values, which rule applies to sales under plans adopted after 1981.

See also §897(d)(2) of the Foreign Investment Real Property Tax Act of 1980, which taxes sales of U.S. real property by foreign corporations notwithstanding §337.

Page 11-79:

Correct seventh line of text.

Change §453(d) to §453B(a) (redesignated by Installment Sales Revision Act of 1980), and change §453(d)(1) to §453B(a)(1).

Correct tenth line of text.

Change §453(d)(4)(B) to §453 B(d)(4)(B).

Correct last line of paragraph (a) of text.

Change §453(d)(4)(B) to §453 B(d)(4)(B).

Correct fourth line of paragraph (b) of text.

Change §453(d)(4)(A) to §453 B(d)(4)(A).

Add to note 189.

[189] Liberty Nat'l Bank & Trust Co., ¶ 79,074 P-H Memo TC (accord with *Family Record Plan* re "installment obligations"; loss allowed). *Liberty* was affirmed, 650 F.2d 1174 (10th Cir. 1981) (sale of receivables at a loss allowed even though no reporting under §453).

Page 11-80:

Add to note 191, first paragraph, following West-Shore Fuel *citation.*

[191] *West-Shore Fuel* was affirmed, 598 F.2d 1236 (2d Cir. 1979) (merger is a sale of assets at corporate level, not a sale of stock).

Add to note 191, second paragraph, following Pityo *citation.*

[191] Correct citation of *Weaver* case to read "accord, James H. Weaver, 71 TC 443 (1978)." See also Wm. J. Goodman, 74 TC 684 (1980) (valid installment sale even though seller trustee of buyer-trust; not fatal per se). Under new §453(e) of the Installment Sales Revision Act of 1980, related party sales will be denied §453 treatment if the buyer resells within two years.

Add to text after note 191.

But the Installment Sales Revision Act of 1980 (P.L. No. 96-471) now provides, in new §453(h), that shareholders of a corporation liquidating under §337 can utilize §453 in reporting their liquidating gain attributable to the corporation's installment sale of its property.[191.1] Regulations under §453(h) were proposed on January 13, 1984 as Prop. Regs. §1.453-2. The principal features of these regulations are the following:

(a) Shareholders report collections on corporate-level obligations as if they were collected on an installment sale of their stock;

(b) All liquidation distributions are treated as stock sale proceeds;

(c) Assumptions of corporate debt increase stock basis;

(d) Qualified installment obligations include all deferred payment rights from sales of corporate assets within the §337(a) or §337(g) time frames (the nature of such assets does not affect qualified installment obligation status —for example, loss assets, recapture property);

(e) The rules apply to §337(c)(3) chain liquidations;

(f) The rules are not applicable to §337(c)(1) nonqualified §337 liquidations (e.g., §341(b), unless §341(e)(4) applies, §333, or §332);

(g) If distributions span more than one taxable year, shareholders must file amended returns for the earlier year to reflect true gain; and

(h) Shareholders' installment sale treatment is treated as such for all purposes (e.g., §§483, former 1232, and new 1274).

[191.1] Receipt of the corporation's installment obligation is not deemed to be a "payment" to the distributee shareholders; instead, the shareholders report collections on the corporation's notes as if such collections were derived from the sale of their stock. Such treatment also applies to installment sales of inventory in bulk by the liquidating corporation. See Bogdanski, The 453(h) Regulations: Hard Choices, 11 J. Corp. Tax 177 (1984).

Page 11-82:

Add new note 197.1 at end of third line of text.

[197.1] For mechanics of this election (which must be made with a timely filed original return), see Prop. Regs. §§1.337-6(a)(2), 1.337-6(c).

Page 11-83:

Add to note 199.

[199] See also Byrne, The Tax Benefit Rule as Applied to Corporate Liquidations and Contributions to Capital: Recent Developments, 56 Notre Dame Law. 215 (1980).

Add to note 201, first paragraph, following Storz citation.

[201] For allocation of price on remand in *Storz*, see ¶ 79,140 P-H Memo TC.

Page 11-84:

Add to note 202, second paragraph.

[202] Accord with *James Pierce Corp.* is Commercial Sec. Bank, 77 TC 145 (1981) (selling corporation deemed to have paid assumed expenses because it accepted reduced cash selling price to reflect these assumed liabilities).

Page 11-85:

Add to note 207, first full paragraph, following Storz citation.

[207] For *Storz* on remand, see ¶ 79,140 P-H Memo TC. Peterson v. US, 723 F.2d 43 (8th Cir. 1983) (sale of matched futures contracts with locked-in profit not protected by §337; mere sale of "ripe" ordinary income item).

Add to note 208.

[208] But see Peterson v. US, supra note 207 (this Supplement) (sale of futures contracts with locked-in ordinary profits denied §337).

Add to note 209, first paragraph.

[209] Bliss Dairy, Inc. v. US, 460 US 370 (S. Ct. 1983) (Court adopted §§336–337 parity principle by applying §337 tax benefit recapture cases to decide §336 question). See supra note 147 and note 149.1 (this Supplement). But see Peterson v. US, supra note 207 (this Supplement) (followed *Storz* and denied §337 on sale of property with ripe ordinary income profit potential).

Page 11-86:

Add to note 211.

[211] But *South Lake Farms* was overruled by *Bliss Dairy*, supra note 209 (this Supplement).

Add to note 212.

[212] Bliss Dairy, Inc. v. US, supra note 209 (this Supplement), adopts the parity principle for construing exceptions to nonrecognition under §§336 and 337. But see Peterson v. US, supra note 207 (this Supplement) (followed *Storz*).

Add to note 213.

[213] Recent legislation enacted §386, a special "look-through" rule for determining recapture gain on the sale of a partnership interest (treated as if a direct sale by partner). The Tax Reform Act of 1984, §75(a), P.L. No. 98-369, 98 Stat. 678. See supra note 133 (this Supplement).

¶ 11.66.   § 337: NONQUALIFYING LIQUIDATIONS

Page 11-89:

Add to note 226.

[226] Compare Jos. R. Bolker, 81 TC 782 (1983) (§336 applied even though shareholder exchanged distributed property in a §1301 transaction after acquiring it in a §333 liquidation; corporation didn't participate in the exchange; thus, nonrecognition treatment for each step in the chain of transactions). DiAndria, Inc., ¶ 83,788 P-H Memo TC (taxpayer allowed to revoke an improvident §333 election because of mistake of fact as to applicability of *Court Holding Co.* rule and thereby obtain §337 protection).

Add to note 227.

[227] But legislation enacted on September 3, 1982 repealed §334(b) (2) and this limited exception in §337(c)(2)(B) as part of its new elective basis step-up provisions in §338, supra ¶ 11.47 (this Supplement). Under new §338, the parent and all of its affiliates in a purchased group obtain §337 sale-repurchase treatment; §337(c)(2) thus would not apply to a §338 transaction because no actual liquidation under §332 occurs.

Page 11-90:

Add to note 228, second paragraph.

[228] The 1982 legislation enacting §338 (supra ¶ 11.47, this Supplement) does not affect the chain liquidation rules of §337(c)(3).

Similarly, deemed §337 sales under §338 by a chain of purchased corporations are not affected by §337(c)(2) since no actual §332 liquidation occurs.

Regulations were proposed under §337(c)(3) on Jan. 10, 1984 as Prop. Regs. §1.337-6 (five examples in Prop. Regs. §1.337-6(c) illustrate the operation of these provisions; membership in the chain which must liquidate is determined on the basis of stock owned on the date the first liquidation is made to such corporation).

Page 11-91:

Add to note 229.

[229] For legislative limitations of the partial liquidation provisions of §346, see supra ¶ 9.50 (this Supplement). New §§302(b)(4) and 302(e) apply only to noncorporate shareholders.

¶ 11.67.   §337 AND REINCORPORATIONS OR OTHER REORGANIZATIONS

Page 11-92:

Add to note 230, first paragraph, following Rev. Proc. 72-9 citation.

[230] Rev. Proc. 72-9 has been superseded ultimately by Rev. Proc. 84-22, 1984-1 CB 449.

But see PLR 8027017, [1980] 9 P-H Fed. Taxes ¶ 55,246 (asset sale for cash, followed by transfer of cash to regulated investment company for stock, followed by liquidation; held, §337 protected sale because transfer to regulated investment company not a tax-free reorganization under continuity of business enterprise principles, infra ¶ 14.51).

Add new text after sentence ending with note 231.

But the Tax Reform Act of 1984 [231.1] modified the control definition for nondivisive Type D reorganizations in new §368(c)(2) to conform to the control line applicable under §304(c); thus, it will be considerably easier to find a Type D reorganization for reincorporation transactions under the new law.[231.2]

[231.1] P.L. No. 98-369, §64(a), 98 Stat. 678.
[231.2] See Eustice, The Tax Reform Act of 1984, ¶ 3.04[4].

Add to note 232.

[232] See generally Comment by Austin, The Applicability of Section 337 to Sales to Third Parties in a "C" Reorganization: The *FEC*

Liquidating and *General Housewares* Decisions, 66 Calif. L. Rev. 623 (1978); Ordower, Separating Statutory Frameworks: Incompatibility of the Complete Liquidation and Reorganization Provisions of the Internal Revenue Code, 25 St. Louis U.L.J. 9 (1981).

General Housewares was affirmed, 615 F.2d 1056 (5th Cir. 1980) (§337 can apply in tandem with Type C reorganization; provisions not mutually exclusive; corporation sold some of stock acquired for its assets and used proceeds to pay debts).

Add new heading.

¶ 11.67A.   CURRENT PROPOSALS: CORPORATE ACQUISITIONS AND COST-BASIS ELECTION

1. In general. The Staff of the Senate Finance Committee, in a preliminary report on the reform and simplification of Subchapter C submitted on September 22, 1983, proposed a fundamental restructuring of the rules governing corporate acquisitions and liquidations. The report recommends that §§336 and 337 be repealed, and that corporate transferors recognize gain or loss on any transfer of assets that results in a cost-basis for the property to the transferee. The treatment of corporate acquisitions would be placed on a specific electivity system, viz., cost-basis or carryover-basis treatment would be expressly elected by the parties, rather than, as under present law, being elected transactionally.

2. Principal features of the cost-basis acquisition proposals. The key to the new proposed corporate acquisition regime is basis; if cost-basis is elected, then gain or loss is recognized at the corporate level, while if basis is preserved through a carryover-basis election, no gain or loss will result to the corporate transferor. Thus, a cost-basis election acquisition will trigger full corporate-level recognition of both gain and loss (with, however, an exception for "unallocated acquisition premium," viz., excess consideration paid for goodwill and the like, for which the parties could separately elect carryover-basis and nonrecognition treatment).

(a) Qualified acquisition. These proposals would apply to two basic types of acquisitions, qualified asset acquisitions and qualified stock acquisitions. The former are those constituting an acquisition of "substantially all" of the acquired corporation's assets; the latter are acquisitions of stock control (80 percent) within a twelve-month period. Stock acquisitions from related sellers (under §318)

would not count in determining whether qualified control was acquired, and asset acquisitions from related corporations (under more than 50 percent common control) could not obtain cost-basis treatment (viz., carryover-basis treatment would be mandatory in this case). However, elective cost-basis or carryover-basis treatment would *not* be affected by the type of consideration paid (i.e., cash, stock, or debt).

(b) The election. Asset acquisitions would be presumed to be carryover basis transactions, unless cost basis is affirmatively elected; stock acquisitions similarly would be presumed to be a carryover-basis election unless cost-basis is affirmatively elected. Asset acquisition elections would be made jointly by the two corporate parties (unless the acquisition is by merger, in which case the surviving corporation would elect); stock acquisition elections would be made by the acquiring corporation. Once made, an election would be irrevocable, and the election timetable follows the current rule for §338 (that is, within fifteen days of the ninth month following the month in which the acquisition occurs).

(c) Selectivity. The election between cost- and carryover-basis treatment would be on a corporation-by-corporation basis (not an asset-by-asset basis). Thus, selectivity as to entities would be permitted (unlike §338 of present law), but asset selectivity would be prohibited. As to the latter, a two-year consistency period (which could increase to three years in the case of stock acquisitions) would be provided to prevent avoidance of the asset selectivity prohibition. The election as to the acquired corporation would govern any assets held by such corporation within one year of the acquisition and ultimately acquired during the consistency period.

(d) Corporate treatment. Election of cost-basis treatment for the acquisition would result in full recognition of gain or loss at the corporate level, regardless of the type of consideration paid by the acquiring corporation. A special exception is provided for acquisition premium (e.g., goodwill), for which the parties can separately elect nonrecognition and carryover-basis treatment. The election covers all assets of the acquired corporation, but separate elections can be made for separate entities owned by the acquired corporation. The rules of §338, supra ¶ 11.47 (this Supplement), would be conformed to reflect the above proposals, viz., full corporate-

level recognition and basis adjustment of all assets to fair market value.

Thus, qualified stock acquisitions in a cost-basis election transaction will trigger corporate-level recognition of gain or loss and inside asset-basis adjustments (to fair market value) for the acquired corporation, regardless of how the transferor's shareholders are taxed (i.e., they could receive tax-free treatment to the extent they receive qualified consideration, viz., stock of the acquiring corporation, independently of corporate-level recognition or nonrecognition).

3. Examples. Assume that T, the acquired corporation, has directly owned assets and also wholly owns two subsidiaries, X and Y; P is the acquiring corporation and has one wholly owned subsidiary, S.

Example 1: P or S acquires all the assets of T, including the stock of X and Y, for cash and a cost-basis election is made as to T only; T recognizes gain or loss on all of its assets (including the X and Y stock) and P obtains a fair market value basis for T's directly owned assets (but not on the X and Y stock). If cost-basis treatment was elected only as to the X and Y subsidiaries of T, X and Y both would recognize gain or loss, and P would obtain a fair market value basis for the X and Y stock (and X and Y would obtain a fair market value basis for their respective assets).

Example 2: P or S acquires all of the stock of T for cash and elects cost-basis treatment for T, X, and Y; T, X and Y recognize gain or loss on all of their assets (but T will not recognize gain or loss on the X and Y stock), and the basis of the T, X, and Y assets (including the X and Y stock), is adjusted to their fair market values.

Example 3: In the above examples, both asset and stock acquisitions are presumed to be carryover-basis acquisitions. To obtain cost-basis treatment, an affirmative election would be required.

The results would not change in Example 1 and 2 even if P acquired T's assets or stock for P stock.

Example 4: If both T and P were 51 percent owned subsidiaries of H, cost-basis treatment could not be elected, viz., carryover-basis treatment would be mandatory for both stock and asset acquisitions from such "related" persons.

Example 5: If T had dropped assets into X or Y within one year of the acquisition in Example 1, those assets would be governed by the election applicable to T in Examples 1 and 2.

4. General comments. The proposed acquisition rules described above would replace the present liquidation and cost-basis rules of §§336, 337, 334, and 338; electivity and flexibility are their dominant themes. However, valuation of assets will be required in every cost-basis stock acquisition, and valuation questions will also arise in asset acquisitions where a "premium" price is alleged to have been paid for goodwill. The proposed system also is strongly flavored by §338 principles (except that corporate-level gain or loss (although only at one level in the case of corporate chains) now would be recognized in view of the recommended repeal of §337). Another major theme of these proposals is consistency of treatment to corporate sellers and buyers; the tax "price" for cost-basis treatment will be corporate-level recognition of gain or loss, regardless of the tax treatment at the shareholder level. But such treatment is expressly elective by the parties, and hence should be negotiated as part of the overall acquisition terms.

¶ 11.68. THE LIQUIDATING CORPORATION'S DEDUCTIONS

Page 11-94:

Correct sixth line of text.

Change "in" to "of."

Page 11-95:

Correct first line in second paragraph of note 238.

[238] Should be "corporation."

Page 11-96:

Add to note 246.

[246] See also Gerli & Co., 73 TC 1019 (1980) (attorney's fees incurred by parent in obtaining §367 ruling for liquidation of foreign subsidiary, held capital expenditure).

¶ 11.69. THE LIQUIDATING CORPORATION'S INDEBTEDNESS

Page 11-98:

Add to note 252.

[252] For discussion of amendments to the debt cancellation rules by H.R. 5043, the Bankruptcy Tax Act of 1980, see infra ¶ 14.58 (this Supplement).

¶ 11.71. BOOTSTRAP ACQUISITIONS AND THE LIQUIDATING CORPORATION

Page 11-101:

Add to note 258, second paragraph.

[258] For yet another chapter in the *Berenson* saga, see Berenson v. CIR, 612 F.2d 695 (2d Cir. 1980) (reversed and remanded with order for Tax Court to try again on its valuation findings).

Add new section to end of chapter.

¶ 11.72. ACQUIRING CORPORATION PROBLEMS— BASIS AND PURCHASE PRICE ALLOCATION

In an asset purchase transaction, the principal tax questions faced by the acquiring corporation center around the appropriate tax basis for the acquired assets, which amount, in view of the taxable character of the acquisition, will be "cost" under §1012.[261] Unlike a stock purchase, however, the parties are generally free to allocate the purchase price among the various categories of acquired assets,[262] and such allocation, being at arm's length, ordinarily will be respected by the Service.[263] In the absence of a specific alloca-

---

[261] See generally Rogers, Purchase Price Allocations in Taxable Acquisitions: New Frontiers—New Hazards, 62 Taxes 813 (1984).

[262] As noted previously (supra note 124), allocation of purchase price to asset bases under §334(b)(2) is governed by the regulations, rather than by the purchase contract terms, and the same rule presumably will apply under §338 (the replacement for §334(b)(2) in 1982).

[263] The parties themselves are generally bound by their specific allocations, absent unusual facts that show that the allocation lacked economic substance or independent significance (or, in the view of some courts, an even stricter standard holds the parties to their agreement

tion by the parties, the price must be allocated to the various assets (including goodwill and going concern value) in proportion to their respective fair market values.[264]

Buyers generally prefer to acquire assets, rather than stock, for two principal reasons: first, the transaction can be more precisely structured to fit the buyer's needs (viz., unwanted assets and liabilities can be excluded from the acquisition); and second, the incidence of various recapture tax liabilities falls on the seller rather than the buyer (although this fact is typically reflected in an increased price to take account of the seller's potential tax liability resulting from the sale). When stock control is acquired, by contrast, the buyer assumes ownership of the entire corporate package, including its liabilities (known and unknown). The tax problems of the buyer in a stock acquisition have been considered previously in this chapter;[265] herein, the focus will be on the buyer's tax consequences in a taxable acquisition of assets, viz., one where the transaction does not constitute a tax-free reorganization (which matters are considered infra Chapter 14).

In all cash acquisitions, the buyer's major concern is allocation of the price among the various categories of assets (the buyer's allocation priorities are first to ordinary income-type property, then to depreciable or amortizable assets, and lastly to non-depreciable property, such as land and goodwill). Since the seller's allocation priorities are usually adverse to the buyer's, an allocation by agreement generally will be respected in view of the conflicting tax stakes involved in the negotiations,[266] and both parties to the agreement

---

unless the contract is unenforceable due to fraud, mistake, undue influence, or duress—CIR v. Danielson, 378 F.2d 771 (3d Cir. 1967)).

The IRS usually will accept specific allocations where the interests of the parties are adverse, viz., where the tax consequences to the seller and the buyer are mutually hostile; if the seller is fully protected from gain recognition by §337 (or by the presence of loss carryovers), and is thus indifferent to how the price is allocated among various assets, the Service may challenge the allocation as being unreasonable—see, e.g., Black Industries, Inc., ¶ 79,061 P-H Memo TC.

See generally Rogers, supra note 261, at pp. 813–815.

[264] Williams v. McGowan, 152 F.2d 570 (2d Cir. 1945); similar allocation principles apply under former §334(b)(2) (supra ¶ 11.45) and, since 1982, under § 338, its replacement (supra ¶ 11.47).

[265] Supra ¶¶ 11.44, 11.45, and 11.47.

[266] The seller prefers an allocation to nonrecapturable capital gain assets, such as land and goodwill, while the buyer generally prefers

(and the IRS as well) typically will be bound by its terms.[267] Absence of a specific allocation agreement, on the other hand, invites inconsistent treatment on both sides of the transaction, which in turn will bring the IRS into the picture (in order to avoid whipsaw exposure where the parties take favorable positions with respect to their particular interests).

If the purchase price instead consists of debt obligations of the buyer, the new OID rules of §1274 and the amended imputed interest rules of §483 [268] may turn part of the buyer's principal payments into currently deductible interest if the minimum interest test rates established by these provisions are violated. On the other hand, if the price also includes stock of the buyer (in whole or in part) and the transaction does not qualify as a tax-free reorganization, the value of the buyer's stock generally constitutes its "cost" for the property, at least if the stock is traded; [269] and if stock purchase warrants also are used as part of the consideration, includability in the buyer's cost basis presumably depends upon whether the warrants have a readily ascertainable value.[270]

Liabilities of the seller that are assumed (or taken subject to) by the buyer are included in cost basis at face (less any OID or imputed interest inherent in the obligations),[271] and this treatment also applies to expense obligations of the seller that are assumed and paid by the buyer. On the other hand, future liabilities that are assumed by the buyer generally do not enter into basis (nor are they currently deductible) until the liability is actually incurred by the buyer,[272] and the same is generally true with respect to contingent liabilities that are assumed in the transaction.

If a buyer's purchase price is partially contingent upon certain

---

allocation to ordinary assets and recapture potential assets; but if the adverse interests do not exist (because the seller is insulated from potential gain recognition), the parties' allocation will have to withstand a challenge of reasonableness in order to be respected by the Service; supra note 263 (this Supplement).

[267] Assuming adverse tax interests on both sides of the transaction, supra notes 266 and 263 (this Supplement).

[268] Supra ¶ 4.23 (this Supplement).

[269] See supra ¶ 3.13, note 130; infra ¶ 14.33, note 289.

[270] Supra ¶ 4.06, note 79; Simmonds Precision Products, Inc., 75 TC 103 (1980).

[271] Supra ¶ 5.07, new paragraph 4 (this Supplement).

[272] *Id.*

specified events (e.g., achievement of designated levels of profitability), a portion of such payments will be subject to either the OID rules of §1234 or the imputed interest rules of §483.[273] The treatment of the remainder of such payments depends upon the underlying asset to which they relate (i.e., if made for franchises, trademarks, or trade names, §1253(d)(1) governs the buyer's treatment, permitting a deduction under §162(a) when paid;[274] other payments are excluded from basis until the contingency is fixed, and at that time the buyer obtains additional basis credit in the assets acquired).[275]

---

[273] See also infra ¶ 14.56 for the effect of contingent price terms on tax-free reorganization transactions.

[274] Rogers, supra note 261 (this Supplement), at p. 829.

[275] *Id.* See also Holden Fuel Oil Co., ¶ 72,045 P-H Memo TC; Yates Inds., Inc., 58 TC 91 (1972); Liquid Paper Corp. v. US, 1983-1 USTC 9305 (Cl. Ct. 1983), applying doctrine of Associated Patentees, Inc., 4 TC 979 (1945) (Acq.), to various contingent price payments.

Chapter 12

COLLAPSIBLE CORPORATIONS

¶ 12.01. INTRODUCTORY

Page 12-2:

Add to note 2.

    [2] The Economic Recovery Tax Act (ERTA) of 1981, P.L. No. 97-34, 95 Stat. 172, further liberalized the treatment of capital gain for noncorporate taxpayers by lowering the top rate on sales after June 9, 1981, to 20 percent (including the alternative minimum tax rate, which eliminated the 25 percent bracket). Moreover, individual rates on ordinary income were lowered to a top rate of 50 percent (for 1982), so that the rate differential under the new law schedules will be 30 points (starting in 1982; for 1981, however, the spread can reach 50 points).

Page 12-3:

Add to text at end of section.

    Proposals by the Staff of the Senate Finance Committee for the reform and simplification of Subchapter C, submitted on September 22, 1983, would repeal the collapsible corporation rules of §341 for *domestic* corporations because such corporations would be required to recognize gain on any cost-basis transfer of their assets under the new system. However, because foreign corporations generally do not recognize gain on the sale or distribution of their assets in complete liquidation, the collapsible rules would be retained for such entities.

¶ 12.03. THE FRAMEWORK OF §341

Page 12-5:

Add to note 9, first paragraph.

    [9] Proposed legislation, H.R. 4961, The Corporate Takeover Tax

Act of 1982, would have repealed the "contraction" provisions of §346(a)(2), and limited §346(b) partial liquidation treatment to individual shareholders only. Hence, distributions formerly covered by §346(a)(2) (and §346(b) to the extent that there were corporate distributees) would result in dividend treatment; see supra ¶ 9.50 (this Supplement).

The final version of this legislation, however, retained the partial liquidation rules for both contractions and "two-business" situations but limited sale treatment thereunder to noncorporate shareholders, new §§302(b)(4) and 302(e). Thus, §341(a)(2) continues to apply to such transactions. See supra new ¶ 9.54 (this Supplement).

Section 341 will not apply to the "special transitional liquidation" under §333 permitted by the Tax Equity and Fiscal Responsibility Act (TEFRA) of 1982, P.L. No. 97-248, 96 Stat. 324, §247 for personal-service corporations, supra ¶ 11.25 (this Supplement).

Moreover, deemed §337 sales under new §338 are not subject to the limitations of §341. But see §712(k)(6)(B), the Tax Reform Act of 1984, adding new §338(h)(14) (§341 will apply to minority shareholders' stock sales within one year after the acquisition). This provision became law on July 18, 1984. P.L. No. 98-369, 98 Stat. 678.

Page 12-6:

Add to note 10, second paragraph.

[10] See Falkoff v. US, 604 F.2d 1045 (7th Cir. 1979) (successful use of mortgage bail-out to avoid dividend treatment because no earnings in year of distribution; hence tax-free under §301(c)(2)).

Page 12-7:

Add to note 14.

[14] But as a result of rate changes enacted by the ERTA of 1981, P.L. No. 97-34, 95 Stat. 172 (which lowered the top noncorporate rate to 50 percent and the top noncorporate capital gain rate to 20 percent), this calculus has been materially altered. Thus, §341 treatment cannot exceed a top bracket rate of 50 percent, while the combined effective rate for corporate level ordinary gain and shareholder level capital gain is 56.8 percent (while the combined capital gain tax at both levels is 42.2 percent).

Add to note 15.

[15] Rev. Proc. 82-60, 1982-2 CB 788, modifies Rev. Proc. 82-22, §4.01-8 ("ordinarily" no ruling on §341(b) status), by providing that a favorable ruling will issue if the corporation has been in existence twenty years, not more than 10 percent of its stock has changed hands, and it has conducted substantially the same business for that period. These rules are currently found in Rev. Proc. 84-22, 1984-1 CB 449.

¶ 12.04.   THE DEFINITION OF "COLLAPSIBLE CORPORATION"

Page 12-8:

Add to note 17.

[17] More currently, see King v. US, 641 F.2d 253 (5th Cir. 1981) (corporation availed of for collapsible purpose); Natbony, The Onion or the Pearl? Peelings From Collapsibility and Dealership, 11 J. Corp. Tax. 91 (1984).

Page 12-9:

Add to note 18.

[18] More currently, see King v. US, supra note 17 (this Supplement) (principally modifies construction, etc.); Natbony, supra note 17 (this Supplement).

Add to note 19.

[19] For an expansive definition of construction, see King v. US, supra note 17 (this Supplement) (construction by utility continued until entire system complete; in effect, continuous construction here); Mirsky & Willens, New Developments Augur a Changed View in Applying the Collapsible Corporation Rules, 57 J. Tax. 2 (1982); Natbony, supra note 17 (this Supplement).

Page 12-10:

Add to note 20.

[20] Calvin A. Thomas, ¶ 81,387 P-H Memo TC (1981) (preliminary activities not construction per *Cohen*).

Add to note 21, first paragraph.

[21] King v. US, supra note 17 (this Supplement) (development of intangible utility franchise is §341 production of property; also, construction continued until entire system completed). See Natbony, supra note 17 (this Supplement).

Page 12-12:

Add to note 25, second paragraph.

[25] King v. US, supra note 17 (this Supplement) (one-shot sale of option to acquire tract of land held dealer sale of "section 341 asset"). But see Calvin A. Thomas, supra note 20 (this Supplement) (property not held for sale; *Van Heusden* distinguished). See also Combs v. US, 655 F.2d 90 (6th Cir. 1981) (co-op conversion resulted in §341 treatment for sale of stock because shareholders intended to profit from

sale of individual apartments; viz., dealer intent here, even though shareholders not otherwise real estate dealers). See Natbony, supra note 17 (ths Supplement).

Add to note 27.

[27] It should be noted, however, that untaxed receivables generated by the corporation from services or sales would also constitute "produced property" under the more generalized definition of §341(b)(1); see supra note 21.

Page 12-15:

Correct sixth line of first full paragraph.

Change "Moeover" to "Moreover."

Page 12-16:

Add to note 33.

[33] King v. US, supra note 17 (this Supplement) (construction continued beyond formation of view to sell; also, view to sell existed at time of purchase of "section 341 asset"); Natbony, supra note 17 (this Supplement).

Page 12-17:

Correct note 34.

[34] Regulations citation in second line should be §1.341-4(c)(3).

Page 12-18:

Add to text after sentence ending with note 39.

But recent legislative amendments by the Tax Reform Act of 1984 specified the substantial realization percentage as two thirds. These amendments passed both the House and Senate in April 1984 and became law on July 18, 1984.[39.1] They were enacted as a general effort to tighten the definitional net of §341 by rejecting *Kelley* and instead adopting the approach of *Abbott* that property remains collapsible until less than a substantial portion of the taxable income to be realized from the property remains unrealized. To further

[39.1] The Tax Reform Act of 1984, H.R. 4170, §164, amending §341 (b)(1)(A) and §341(d)(2) (passed House on April 11, 1984); the Deficit Reduction Act of 1984, H.R. 2163, §51 (same) (passed Senate on April 13, 1984); the Tax Reform Act of 1984, §84(a) (same), P.L. No. 98-369, 98 Stat. 678.

buttress the substantial realization rule of §341(b)(1)(A), the 70-30 rule of §341(d)(2) (infra ¶ 12.06) also were tightened by requiring aggregation of like kind §1221(1) properties.[39.2]

[39.2] For proposed regulations under these amendments, see Prop. Regs. §§1.341-2(a)(1)(iii), 1.341-2(a)(2), 1.341-2(a)(4), 1.341-4(a), 1.341-4(c), and 1.341-5(d) (Aug. 31, 1984).

¶ 12.06. THE STATUTORY LIMITATIONS OF §341(d)

Page 12-22:

Add to note 46, first paragraph.

[46] But 1984 legislative amendments overrule Rev. Rul. 72-48 and require realization of two thirds of the potential income; see supra ¶ 12.04, note 39.2 (this Supplement).

Add to note 47.

[47] The Tax Reform Act of 1984, P.L. No. 98-369, §84(b), 98 Stat. 678, revised §341(d)(2) to permit aggregation, under regulations, of all §1221(1) properties for purposes of the §341(d)(2) computation.

Page 12-23:

Add to note 50.

[50] King v. US, 641 F.2d 253 (5th Cir. 1981) (shareholder's gain *all* attributable to collapsible property; shareholder appreciation traceable to construction of collapsible property).

Add to text after note 50.

Recent legislation now authorizes aggregation of all §1221(1) properties for purposes of making the §341(d)(2) 70-30 computation,[50.1] so that collapsible treatment will continue until there has been substantial realization (viz., two-thirds), in the *aggregate*, of the potential income from the corporation's collapsible §1221(1) properties.

[50.1] Supra note 47 (this Supplement). See Prop. Regs. §1.341-4(c).

Page 12-24:

Add to note 51.

[51] See also Rev. Rul. 79-235, 1979-2 CB 135 (also can tack holding period of property exchanged in tax-free §1031 transaction).

Add to note 52.

[52] See Rev. Rul. 79-226, 1979-2 CB 134 (in applying three-year rule, can exclude separate properties upon which gain has been fully realized by the corporation; and hence with respect to which corporation would not be collapsible).

¶ 12.07. THE AMNESTY OF §341(e)
Page 12-28:

Add to second paragraph of note 58.

[58] See generally George V. Buono, 74 TC 187 (1980) (corporate-level capital gain even though some of shareholders arguably dealers; corporation's subdivision activity not enough to turn it from investor into dealer); Calvin A. Thomas, ¶ 81,387 P-H Memo TC (1981).

But see King v. US, 641 F.2d 253 (5th Cir. 1981) (more than 20 percent shareholder dealer in similar property, so corporation's assets were "section 341(e) assets").

¶ 12.08. AVOIDANCE OF §341 BY A §341(f) CONSENT
Page 12-35:

Add to note 71, second paragraph.

[71] Regulations became final in T.D. 7655 (Nov. 28, 1979). The final regulations, in Regs. §1.341-7(a)(2)(ii), provide a "small shareholder" exception (viz., a person who qualifies for the protection of §341(d)(1)) from the notice requirements of §341(f) and such a shareholder's stock will not taint corporate assets as "subsection (f) assets."

Page 12-36:

Add to note 72.

[72] Final regulations adopted November 28, 1979, same.

Add to note 73.

[73] Final regulations adopted November 28, 1979, same.

Page 12-37:

Add new note 75.1 to end of first complete paragraph.

[75.1] But see Regs. §1.341-7(a)(2)(i) (sale only means sale for long-term capital gain; thus not applicable if loss, short-term or ordinary). For a recent decision involving §341(f) consents, see King v. US, 641 F.2d 253 (5th Cir. 1981).

Page 12-37:

Add to notes 74, 75, and 76.

[74] Final regulations, same. But see current legislation, discussed infra new text at note 76.1 (this Supplement), denying §341(f)(3) exemption from gain trigger where the transferee is a foreign corporation.
[75] Final regulations, same. See King v. US, supra note 75.1 (this Supplement).
[76] Final regulations, same.

Add to text at end of paragraph 1.

But recent legislation [76.1] sharply restricted the use of §341(f) by foreign corporations by authorizing regulations denying effect to a §341(f) consent by a foreign corporation, and by providing that the §341(f)(3) exceptions for various nonrecognition asset transfers (supra note 74) would not apply where the transferee is a foreign corporation.

[76.1] The Tax Reform Act of 1984, H.R. 4170, §138, adding new §341(f)(8); the Deficit Reduction Act of 1984, H.R. 2163, §126 (same); the Tax Reform Act of 1984, §135 (same). These proposals passed the House and Senate in April 1984 and became law on July 18, 1984.

Page 12-38:

Add to note 77, first paragraph.

[77] But the ERTA of 1981, P.L. No. 97-34, 95 Stat. 172, further amends these computations by (a) lowering the top noncorporate tax rate to 50 percent (for 1982); (b) widening, and indexing (in 1985) the §1 brackets; and (c) lowering the top noncorporate capital gain rate to 20 percent. Hence, reducing the price to reflect a potential corporate tax of 46 percent may not be worthwhile to a shareholder whose maximum tax exposure (even if §341 applies) is 50 percent as opposed to 20 percent.

¶ 12.09. PEACEFUL COEXISTENCE WITH §341
Page 12-39:

Add new note 77.1 to end of paragraph (1).

[77.1] But see the new computations engendered by the ERTA of 1981, P.L. No. 97-34, 95 Stat. 172, where collapsible treatment to a selling shareholder cannot exceed a 50 percent rate, while incurring double level taxes (even at capital gain rates) can result in a combined effective rate of 42.2 percent (or 56.8 percent if the corporate gain is ordinary).

Add to note 78.

[78] But see recent legislation, discussed supra new text at note 39.1 (this Supplement), overruling *Kelley* and requiring realization of two thirds of the potential collapsible income.

Add to note 79.

[79] But see recent legislation, discussed supra new text at note 39.1 (this Supplement), overruling *Kelley* and requiring realization of two thirds of the potential collapsible income.

Add to note 80.

[80] George V. Buono, 74 TC 187 (1980) (capital gain to shareholders of selling Subchapter S corporation even though some of shareholders arguably were dealers; corporation's activities in obtaining subdivision approval not enough to turn it from investor into dealer; gain would have been capital in hands of shareholders too, so test of Regs. §1.1371-1(d) satisfied). See also Calvin A. Thomas, ¶ 81,387 P-H Memo TC (1981).

Add new note 80.1 to end of paragraph numbered (4).

[80.1] But see current legislation (supra ¶ 12.06 note 47 and new text at note 50.1 (this Supplement)) providing for aggregation of §1221(1) properties in making the 70-30 computation under §341(d)(2).

Page 12-40:

Add new note 82 at end of text, paragraph (8).

[82] But §1023 was repealed by the Crude Oil Windfall Profit Tax Act of 1980, thus reopening the date-of-death basis purging technique under §1014, which once again is fully applicable.

Chapter 13

CORPORATE DIVISIONS

¶ 13.02. DIVISIVE REORGANIZATIONS BEFORE 1954
Page 13-6:

Correct fourth line from bottom of text.

Should be "statute," not "statue."

¶ 13.03. THE 1954 LEGISLATION: §355 IN OUTLINE
Page 13-10:

Add to note 15.

[15] In Gerald R. Redding, 71 TC 597 (1979), distribution of a controlled subsidiary via short-term rights offering was held to constitute a valid tax-free §355 transaction. But *Redding* was reversed on this point, 630 F.2d 1169 (7th Cir. 1980) (not a good §355 because distribution via rights offering not a distribution with respect to the parent's stock. See O'Dell & Boyd, Using Stock Rights in a Corporate Spin Off: The *Redding* Case, 8 J. Corp. Tax. 140 (1981); Note, Redding v. Commissioner: Step Transaction Doctrine Applied to Distribution of Stock Warrants in a Section 355 Spin-Off, 35 Tax L. Rev. 257 (1981).

But see Rev. Rul. 83-142, 1983-2 CB 68 (purported sale of second tier subsidiary stock to parent, followed by immediate dividend of cash back to parent disregarded as a circular cash "wash" and transaction qualified for §355; form of transaction dictated by local law requirement).

Page 13-14:

Add to note 20, second paragraph.

[20] Rev. Proc. 75-35 was superseded and updated by Rev. Proc. 81-41, 1981-2 CB 588.

¶ 13.04. THE ACTIVE BUSINESS REQUIREMENT IN GENERAL: §355(b)

Page 13-15:

Add to note 23.

[23] But see Rev. Rul. 82-219, 1982-2 CB 82 (can still be in active business even though no income during one of the five years because of insolvency of taxpayer's sole customer).

Page 13-16:

Add to note 26.

[26] See Helfand & Lafving, Filling the Serbonian Bog With Quicksand—Proposed Section 355 Regulations Further Obscure Corporate Separations, 5 J. Corp. Tax. 345 (1979) (Part I); 6 J. Corp. Tax. 53 (1979) (Part II); 6 J. Corp. Tax. 133 (1979) (Part III).

Page 13-19:

Correct sixth line of text.

Add "infra" before ¶ 15.06 citation.

Page 13-20:

Correct sixth line of text.

Change "if" to "it."

Page 13-23:

Add to note 41, second paragraph.

[41] But Rev. Rul. 58-54 declared obsolete by Rev. Rul. 76-566, 1976-2 CB 450.

Page 13-26:

Correct note 51.

[51] Regulations citation should be §1.955-5(a)(1).

Page 13-27:

Add to note 54.

[54] Rev. Rul. 79-394, 1979-2 CB 141 (subsidiary held engaged in active business on facts even though it had no paid employees of its own; corporation used employees of sister subsidiary under reimbursement arrangement; after distribution, it hired these employees directly to perform the services); amplified by Rev. Rul. 80-181, 1980-2 CB 121 (not necessary that services be reimbursed; §482 would accomplish same result in any event).

¶ 13.05. THE FIVE-YEAR RULE: PREDISTRIBUTION BUSINESS HISTORY

Page 13-31:

Add to note 68.

[68] See Rev. Rul. 74-5, 1974-1 CB 82 (indirect acquisition case—e.g., P buys stock of T and T distributes stock of S to T; valid §355 distribution by T to P, but no good if P then distributes the S stock to its shareholders because §355(b)(2)(D) rule violated).

Page 13-32:

Add to note 69, second paragraph.

[69] See GCM 39264, 24 Tax Notes 661 (August 13, 1984), discussed at 61 J. Tax 294 (1984), applying Rev. Rul. 57-144 rule (such an acquisition is irreversible too; cannot be purged; thus, parent must wait five years to distribute).

Page 13-35:

Add to note 79, first paragraph.

[79] But Rev. Rul. 58-68 was revoked by Rev. Rul. 83-114, 1983-2 CB 66 (threshold capital contribution not a device per se; depends on facts and valid business purpose here).

¶ 13.06. THE "DEVICE" RESTRICTION: §355(a)(1)(B)

Page 13-37:

Add to note 83.

[83] Rev. Rul. 58-68 was revoked by Rev. Rul. 83-114, 1983-2 CB 66 (planned post-distribution merger not a device; also, threshold capital contribution not a device per se; depends on facts and valid business purpose here).

Page 13-38:

Add to note 86, first paragraph.

[86] See also Rev. Rul. 83-23, 1983-1 CB 82 (transfer of stock compelled by foreign law requirement requiring higher level of local ownership not a device).

Page 13-40:

Add to note 91, first paragraph.

[91] Rev. Rul. 58-68 was revoked by Rev. Rul. 83-114, 1983-2 CB 66 (planned post-distribution merger not a device).

¶ 13.07. DISTRIBUTION OF ALL STOCK AND SECURITIES IN CONTROLLED CORPORATIONS

Page 13-44:

Add to note 99, first paragraph.

[99] See also Gerald R. Redding, 71 TC 597 (1979) (distribution of controlled subsidiary via rights offering held a valid §355 transaction; rights merely a procedural device to effect the distribution and to permit distributing corporation to raise capital concurrently therewith; control effectively distributed in "single" step). On appeal *Redding* was reversed, 630 F.2d 1169 (7th Cir. 1980) (distribution of "control" must be to shareholders of parent, and such requirement not satisfied in instant case because exercising rights holders not all stockholders of parent).

¶ 13.08. NON-PRO RATA DISTRIBUTIONS

Page 13-48:

Add to note 106, first paragraph.

[106] But see Rev. Rul. 79-314, 1979-2 CB 132 (reciprocal redemption exchanges by two corporations that owned more than 10 percent of each other's stock held protected from gain recognition by §311(d)(2)(A) exception). See also Rev. Rul. 80-101, 1980-1 CB 70 (principle of Rev. Rul. 79-314 applied in case where one of exchanging corporations completely liquidated; X owned 70 percent of Y and Y owned 25 percent of X; on complete liquidation of Y, held §§311(a)(2) and 311(d)(2)(A) applied to protect both X and Y).

But the Corporate Takeover Tax Act of 1982 (S. 2687, incorporated as §227 of H.R. 4961, and H.R. 6725, approved by the Ways and Means Committee) proposed to repeal most of the exceptions of §311(d)(2) for corporate shareholder-distributees (effective September 1, 1982), including the one relied on in the above rulings.

The final version of this legislation, which became law on September 3, 1982 (supra ¶ 9.64 of this Supplement), eliminated §311(d)(2) protection for distributions to corporate shareholders (unless the distribution was a carryover basis dividend and even that exception was eliminated in 1984). The 1982 legislation, §223 of the Tax Equity and Fiscal Responsibility Act (TEFRA) of 1982, P.L. No. 97-248, 96 Stat. 324, 1982, overrules the holdings of the above rulings, however. See supra new ¶ 9.64A (this Supplement).

¶ 13.09. JUDICIAL LIMITATIONS ON TAX-FREE CORPORATE DIVISIONS

Page 13-51:

Add to note 114, third paragraph.

[114] Rev. Rul. 83-23, 1983-1 CB 82 (spin-off to satisfy foreign decree requiring 60 percent direct ownership of local business by nationals had business purpose; no device either because transfer of 20 percent interest compelled by foreign law); Rev. Rul. 82-130, 1982-2 CB 83 (spin-off of real estate subsidiary by parent in high-technology business to facilitate parent's public offering of its stock a valid purpose); Rev. Rul. 82-131, 1982-2 CB 83 (spin-off of unregulated subsidiary by regulated parent to justify parent's rate increase for its regulated business a valid purpose); Rev. Rul. 83-114, 1983-2 CB 66 (followed Rev. Rul. 76-527; business purpose for spin-off was to attract investment capital to distributed subsidiary which was required to be divested by antitrust decree).

See also PLR 84-21-062, 61 J. Tax. 186 (1984) (a valid business purpose for spin-off to increase value of parent stock as defensive tactic to prevent hostile takeover attempt).

¶ 13.10. "BOOT" UNDER §355

Page 13-54:

Add to end of note 120.

[120] Section 4(e)(2) of H.R. 5043, the Bankruptcy Tax Act of 1980, amended §355(a)(3) to make a distribution that is attributable to accrued interest on the distributing corporation's securities taxable to the extent such interest accrued during the creditor's holding period. The effective date of this legislation is proceedings commencing after 1980, unless taxpayers elect October 1, 1979, and it passed in December of 1980.

Note also the new market discount rules of §§1276 and 1278(a) (2)(A), added by the Tax Reform Act of 1984, defining market discount as the spread between *basis* and face of obligations issued after July 18, 1984 and taxing such discount as ordinary income on disposition of the security. See supra new ¶ 4.23 (this Supplement).

Page 13-55:

Add to note 123, first paragraph.

[123] See also Rev. Rul. 78-442, 1978-2 CB 143 (existence of §357(c) gain from preliminary incorporation transfer prior to spin-off did not create §355(a)(3) "boot" re stock of spun-off subsidiary; same theory as Rev. Rul. 69-461, 1969-2 CB 52, supra ¶ 13.05, note 66).

¶ 13.11.   BASIS, HOLDING PERIOD, EARNINGS AND PROFITS, ETC.

Page 13-57:

Add new text to end of paragraph 1.

Before amendment by the Tax Reform Act of 1984,[130.1] a spin-off literally could qualify as a "purchase" of the distributed subsidiary's stock by a distributee that acquired at least 80 percent of that stock in the distribution (since §338(h)(3)(A)(i) only provided that carryover basis acquisitions failed the "purchase" definition, assuming that the distributee did not own 50 percent of the distributing corporation). But new §338(h)(3)(A)(ii) now forecloses this possibility by denying purchase status for substituted stock basis acquisitions as well.

The substituted basis rules of §358 also can operate to create "market discount" under the new Tax Reform Act of 1984 amendments,[130.2] since market discount arises in an acquisition of debt issued after July 18, 1984, where the holder's basis is less than the face of the obligation (i.e., if, as part of a §355 distribution, the distributee exchanges securities of the parent for securities of the distributed subsidiary, market discount will result if the basis of the exchanged securities is less than the face of the securities received).

[130.1] P.L. No. 98-369, §712(k)(5)(D), 98 Stat. 678; see Eustice, The Tax Reform Act of 1984, ¶ 3.03[1][b] (Warren, Gorham & Lamont, Inc. 1984).

[130.2] See supra new ¶ 4.23 (this Supplement); Eustice, The Tax Reform Act of 1984, ¶ 2.02[4].

Page 13-59:

Add to note 133, first paragraph.

[133] While new legislation (supra annotation to note 106, this Supplement) sharply expands the reach of §311(d) by repealing most of the exceptions in §311(d)(2), continued nonrecognition under §311 for tax-free §355 distributions will not be affected by these amendments. But see new §1363(d), added by the Subchapter S Revision Act of 1982, P.L. No. 97-354, 96 Stat. 1669, which literally could cause recognition to the distributing corporation in a §355 transaction. But §721(a) of the Tax Reform Act of 1984 contracted the scope of §1363(d) by providing in new §1363(e) that gain will not be triggered on the distribution of property permitted to be received tax-free under §355.

Add to note 133, second paragraph.

[133] Note that §351(e)(2), added by the Bankruptcy Tax Act of 1980, would also prevent the tax-free incorporation of assets under §351 if the transferor in a Title 11 case was acting under a plan to satisfy its debts with the transferee's stock or securities. While such a split-off to creditors might meet the new "divisive G" reorganization test of §368(a)(1)(G) (and be tax-free to creditor security holders under §355(a)(1)), the distributing corporation would have the same taxable exposure referred to in Rev. Rul. 70-271 when it "satisfied" its debts with stock of the controlled subsidiary (unless possibly §108 could apply to the gain resulting from this type of debt satisfaction).

¶ 13.12.   CORPORATE DIVISIONS AND SECTION 306
Page 13-61:

Add to note 140.

[140] Legislation approved by the House Ways and Means Committee, supra annotation to note 106 (this Supplement), would apply §318 attribution principles in testing such dividend equivalence, and hence §306 stock status. This legislation passed in TEFRA of 1982, P.L. No. 97-248, 96 Stat. 324.

¶ 13.13.   THE MONOPOLY OF §355
Page 13-63:

Correct first line of paragraph 2.

Change "asssets" to "assets."

Page 13-64:

Add to note 144.

[144] But see Gerald R. Redding, 71 TC 597 (1979) (distribution via rights offering tax-free under §355), rev'd, 630 F.2d 1169 (7th Cir. 1980) (taxable distribution of rights; amount of dividend is value of rights per Rev. Rul. 70-521 principles).

¶ 13.14.   NONQUALIFYING CORPORATE DIVISIONS
Page 13-64:

Add to text after note 146.

On the distribution of the controlled corporation's stock §311(a) generally protected the distributing corporation from recognition of gain; but recent legislation [146.1] significantly restricted the scope of §311 nonrecognition for ordinary distributions of appreciated property, so that failure of the spin-off distribution to qualify under §355 will result in taxable gain to the distributing corporation under these amendments, unless the distribution qualifies for one of the exceptions of §311(d)(2) (which ordinarily would not apply to a failed spin-off).[146.2]

[146.1] The Tax Reform Act of 1984, §54(a), amending §311(d), P.L. No. 98-369, 98 Stat. 678, supra ¶¶ 7.21, 9.64A (this Supplement).

[146.2] A conceivable candidate would be former §311(d)(2)(A) (carryover basis dividend to 80 percent controlling parent corporation), supra ¶¶ 7.21 and 9.64A (this Supplement), but that exception only exists on a transitional basis through 1984. Another possibility is §311(d)(2)(B) (formerly §311(d)(2)(C)), but this exception is an extremely narrow one.

Page 13-65:

Add to text at end of first paragraph.

On the distribution of the controlled corporations' stock in complete liquidation, §336 presumably applies to protect the distributing corporation from recognition of gain or loss (unless the distribution is deemed under §346(b), to have the effect of a partial liquidation, in which event §311(d) rather than §336 would govern).[148.1]

[148.1] See infra note 151, supra ¶ 9.64A (this Supplement). If §311(d) applies by virtue of §346(b), recent legislation enacted in 1984 now subjects the distributing corporation to recognition of gain on the distributed stock, supra note 146.1 (this Supplement), unless §311(d)(2)(B) (formerly §311(d)(2)(C)) applies, which is unlikely in most cases.

Page 13-66:

Add to note 151.

[151] New legislation enacted in 1982 (supra annotation to note 106, this Supplement) restricted the partial liquidation provisions of §346 (see generally discussion supra new ¶ 9.54, this Supplement). In place of existing §346, a new provision in §346(b) gives broad regulatory authority to the Service to deal with transactions having the economic effect of a partial liquidation, which provision could offer a potent new weapon in the reincorporation area. Partial liquidations are limited by new §§302(b)(4) and 302(e) to noncorporate shareholders. For corporate-level recognition, see new ¶ 9.64A (this Supplement).

See also the recent legislative amendments in 1984 that further restricted the application of the §311 nonrecognition rules, supra note 146.1 (this Supplement).

Page 13-67:

Correct fifth line of text in paragraph 3.

Change "profts" to "profits."

Add to note 155.

[155] But §311(d) was materially tightened in 1982, supra new ¶ 9.64A (this Supplement); and recent amendments in 1984 further tightened §311(d), supra note 146.1 (this Supplement).

Page 13-68:

Add to note 157, third paragraph.

[157] Rev. Rul. 75-223 was distinguished and expanded by Rev. Rul. 79-184, 1979-1 CB 143 (parent's sale of subsidiary's stock and distribution of proceeds taxable dividend rather than §346(a)(2) partial liquidation).

New legislation, TEFRA of 1982, P.L. No. 97-248, 96 Stat. 324, limits the contraction provisions of former §346(a)(2) and business termination distributions of §346(b) to individual shareholder-distributees. Serial distributions in §346(a)(1) are defined as complete liquidations. See supra ¶ 9.50 (this Supplement). These provisions passed the Senate in July, were approved by the Conference Committee in August of 1982, and became law on September 3, 1982 as new §§302(b)(4) and 302(e). See new ¶ 9.54 (this Supplement). This legislation also materially tightened the exceptions of §311(d)(2); see supra new ¶ 9.64A (this Supplement).

Recent legislation enacted in 1984, supra note 146.1 (this Supplement), further expanded the potential for corporate-level recognition on nonliquidating distributions of appreciated property, supra ¶¶ 7.21 and 9.64A (this Supplement). Under these amendments, most nonqualifying §355 transactions now result in recognition of gain at the distributing corporate level. The only available exception under the 1984 legislation for a failed split-off would be §311(d)(2)(B), formerly §311(d)(2)(C), which was continued without change.

¶ 13.15.   SECTION 367

Page 13-68:

Amend text to read as follows.

Divisive transactions involving foreign corporations and having an expatriating effect must obtain clearance under §367 (although no longer in advance of the distribution) to qualify for nonrecognition treatment under §355. Other types of divisive transactions involving foreign corporations no longer need Service approval (although certain "toll charges" may be imposed thereon).

Chapter 14

CORPORATE
REORGANIZATIONS

PART A. GENERAL CONSIDERATIONS

¶ 14.01. INTRODUCTORY

Page 14-3:

Add to note 2, first paragraph.

  ² See, e.g., Rev. Rul. 79-155, 1979-1 CB 153 (modifications in terms of debt assumed in merger substantial enough to create an "exchange"). See also Rev. Rul. 81-204, 1981-2 CB 157 (exchange of mortgage "pools" involving identical mass asset "pots" not a taxable §1001 exchange; properties did not differ materially in kind or extent).

Page 14-4:

Add new note 2.1 at end of second full paragraph.

  ²·¹ But §1023 was repealed by the Crude Oil Windfall Profit Tax Act of 1980.

Page 14-8:

Add to note 7, first paragraph, following Rev. Proc. 72-9 citation.

  ⁷ Rev. Proc. 72-9 was superseded by Rev. Proc. 82-22, 1982-1 CB 469, and is currently found in Rev. Proc. 84-22, 1984-1 CB 449.

Add to text at end of section.

The Staff of the Senate Finance Committee submitted a preliminary report on the reform and simplification of Subchapter C on September 22, 1983, which proposed the replacement of the Type A, B, and C acquisitive reorganization rules of present law, with a single elective nonrecognition-carryover-basis system at the corporate level. Shareholders, in turn, would be permitted to receive stock tax-free in a qualified acquisition without regard to the treatment of the transaction at the corporate level or the terms of the exchange with other shareholders. Under this proposal, the limitations of present law now applicable to acquisitive reorganizations, i.e., continuity of interest, continuity of business enterprise, corporate-shareholder parallel treatment, the business purpose requirement and the qualified consideration rules, would be repealed.

¶ 14.02. THE STATUTORY PATTERN
Page 14-10:

Add to text at end of section.

Proposals were submitted by the Staff of the Senate Finance Committee on September 22, 1983, to repeal the acquisitive reorganization rules of present §§368(a)(1)(A), 368(a)(1)(B), and 368(a)(1)(C), and replace these provisions with a single elective nonrecognition-carryover-basis system at the corporate level. These proposals are considered infra ¶ 14.21 (this Supplement) and at other relevant points in this chapter.

¶ 14.03. JUDICIAL LIMITATIONS: IN GENERAL
Page 14-12:

Add to text at end of section.

But proposals submitted by the Staff of the Senate Finance Committee on September 22, 1983, would drastically revise and simplify the acquisitive reorganization rules of present law and, in the process, repeal the judicially imposed business purpose, continuity of business enterprise, and continuity of proprietary interest limitations.

¶ 14.05. OTHER GENERAL CONSIDERATIONS
Page 14-14:

Add to note 10, third paragraph.

[10] See also Fiflis, Accounting for Mergers, Acquisitions and Investments in a Nutshell: The Interrelationships of, and Criteria for, Pur-

chase or Pooling, the Equity Method, and Parent-Company-Only and Consolidated Statements, 37 Bus. L. Rev. 89 (1981).

Page 14-15:
Add to note 11, second paragraph.

[11] The Bankruptcy Tax Act of 1980, H.R. 5043, repealed the provisions of existing law dealing with insolvency reorganizations in §§371 and 372 and replaced them with a new statutory structure dealing more broadly with the entire area of insolvency proceedings. These provisions are considered in new ¶ 14.20 and ¶ 14.58 of this Supplement.

PART B. "REORGANIZATION" DEFINED

¶ 14.10. INTRODUCTORY
Page 14-17:
Add to text at end of section.

Proposals by the Staff of the Senate Finance Committee, submitted on September 22, 1983, would drastically overhaul and simplify the acquisitive reorganization rules of the Type A, B, and C reorganizations and replace them with a single elective nonrecognition-carryover-basis system applicable to all qualified acquisitions of stock or assets, regardless of the type of consideration paid. These proposals are considered infra ¶ 14.21 (this Supplement) (if enacted, the material in ¶¶ 14.12–14.15 would be repealed, and the discussions therein would be of historical interest only).

¶ 14.11. CONTINUITY OF PROPRIETARY INTEREST AND PLAN OF REORGANIZATION

Page 14-18:
Add new note 12.1 at end of paragraph 1.

[12.1] See generally Hutton, Musings on Continuity of Interest—Recent Developments, 56 Taxes 904 (1979). For discussion of recent reform proposals by the ALI Subchapter C Project, see Wolfman, Continuity of Interest and the American Law Institute Study, 57 Taxes 840 (1979).

See also McGaffey & Hunt, Continuity of Shareholder Interest in Acquisitive Reorganizations, 59 Taxes 659 (1981) (focusing on "cash-option" merger transactions).

Page 14-21:

Correct first line of text.

Delete second "that."

Add to note 24.

[24] Superior Coach of Fla., Inc., 80 TC 895 (1983) (historic shareholders cashed out—no continuity of interest; stock of target purchased by shareholder of acquiring corporation who then merged target into acquiring corporation); Security Indus. Ins. Co. v. US, 702 F.2d 1234 (5th Cir. 1983) (same; cash purchase of target stock by holding company, immediate liquidation of target; reincorporation of operating assets in another subsidiary).

Add to note 25.

[25] Rev. Rul. 80-105, 1980-1 CB 78 conversion of federal non-stock mutual S&L to state stock S&L held valid Type F reorganization).

Page 14-22:

Add to note 26 at end of runover paragraph.

[26] Capital Savings & Loan Ass'n v. US, 607 F.2d 970 (Ct. Cl. 1979) (merger of state capital stock savings & loan into non-stock mutual savings & loan held a valid A reorganization; Rev. Rul. 69-6 rejected; interests received in merger not boot even though withdrawable at will; sufficient proprietary characteristics to satisfy continuity of interest test); Rocky Mt. Fed. Savings & Loan Ass'n v. US, 473 F. Supp. 779 (D. Wyo. 1979) (same); Herold T. Paulsen, 78 TC 291 (1982) (same), rev'd 716 F.2d 563 (9th Cir. 1983) (no continuity; contra to above cited decisions), cert. granted, Feb. 21, 1984.

Add to note 28, first paragraph.

[28] But cf. Rev. Rul. 77-449, 1977-2 CB 110 (successive drop-downs to second-tier grandchild subsidiary valid §351 exchanges; each drop-down a separate §351, even though single plan to transfer assets to second-tier subsidiary); Rev. Rul. 83-34, 1983-1 CB 79 (same even where only 80 percent ownership of subsidiaries). See also Rev. Rul. 84-30, 1984-1 CB 114 (continuity not violated where target corporation passed acquiring corporation stock upstream to its grandparent).

Add to note 28, second paragraph.

[28] Murray, How to Avoid Loss of Continuity of Interest Through Stock Remoteness in a Reorganization, 59 J. Tax. 8 (1983); Murray, IRS Revocation of "Stock Remoteness" Posture May Have Positive

Effect on Reorganizations, 60 J. Tax. 352 (1984) (discussion of Rev. Rul. 84-30).

Page 14-23:

Add to note 31.

[31] See also Rev. Rul. 80-284, 1980-2 CB 117, and Rev. Rul. 80-285, 1980-2 CB 119, holding no §351 where only 14 percent and 19 percent continuity respectively by target company's shareholders; transaction essentially a stock or asset "purchase" under continuity of interest principles even though transaction literally satisfied language of §351. No mention was made by the Service of Rev. Rul. 76-123, which seems essentially inconsistent with the 1980 pronouncements; nor, for that matter, did the Service note its recent concession that continuity of interest principles do not apply to recapitalizations, another curious omission. But these rulings were revoked in Rev. Rul. 84-71, 1984-1 CB 106.

Superior Coach of Fla., Inc., 80 TC 895 (1983), and Security Indus. Ins. Co. v. US, 702 F.2d 1234 (5th Cir. 1983) (continuity killed by cash purchase of target stock; historic shareholders terminated and continuity of interest failed; no reorganization).

Page 14-25:

Add new note 36.1 at end of first paragraph of text.

[36.1] But see McDonald's of Zion, Inc., 76 TC 972 (1981) (no post-merger holding period for acquiring company's stock so long as sale discretionary with target company shareholders; even though pre-merger intent to sell out, not fatal to reorganization; sale an independent transaction because reorganization and sale not mutually interdependent).

But on appeal *McDonald's* was reversed, 688 F.2d 520 (7th Cir. 1982) (continuity broken under step transaction principles where intended sale by target shareholders of acquiring corporation's stock; court imposed consistency of treatment on IRS here; since IRS required post-acquisition continuity rule for favorable ruling, it could not deny that requirement where the tax stakes favored the buyer corporation, as here).

For analysis of Tax Court decision in *McDonald's,* see Prusiecki, Continuity of Interest in Tax-Free Mergers: New Opportunities After *McDonald's of Zion,* 55 J. Tax. 378 (1981).

Page 14-27:

Add to note 44.

[44] See also Pierson v. US, 472 F. Supp. 957 (D. Del. 1979) (can pay 20 percent cash in a Type B), rev'd, 621 F.2d 1227 ¶ 9322 (3d Cir. 1980). Page citation to *Reeves* is 71 TC 727. *Reeves* also rev'd sub nom. Chapman v. CIR, 618 F.2d 856 (1st Cir. 1980).

Page 14-28:

Add to note 45, third paragraph.

[45] Accord with Rev. Rul. 77-315 are Microdot, Inc. v. US, 728 F.2d 593 (2d Cir. 1984) (no continuity of interest requirement in recapitalization), and Golden Nugget, Inc., 83 TC 28 (1984).

Page 14-29:

Correct paragraph (c) of text.

Delete first word in paragraph (c) ("finally").

Page 14-30:

Add to note 51.

[51] Faber, The Use and Misuse of the Plan of Reorganization Concept, 38 Tax L. Rev. 515 (1983).

Add to note 52.

[52] See also Regs. §1.368-1(d)(1)(iii) (date of B reorganization acquisition is date that exchange of all stock under the plan or reorganization is complete).

Page 14-31:

Add to note 53.

[53] See Simon v. CIR, 644 F.2d 339 (5th Cir. 1981) (steps as a whole were a reorganization).

Add to note 54.

[54] See also ITT & Cos., 77 TC 60 (1981) (subsequent conversion of subsidiary bonds into parent stock following prior tax-free acquisition of subsidiary by parent not part of original plan of reorganization).

Add new paragraph 11.

11. *Current proposals.* The Staff of the Senate Finance Committee submitted a preliminary report on the reform and simplification of Subchapter C on September 22, 1983, a centerpiece of which was a proposal to replace the present acquisitive reorganization provisions of §§368(a)(1)(A), 368(a)(1)(B), and 368(a)(1)(C) with an elective nonrecognition-carryover-basis system at the corporate level. The type of consideration paid would be irrelevant under these proposals and, as a consequence, the con-

tinuity-of-interest limitation would be repealed. These proposals are considered infra ¶ 14.21 (this Supplement).

If enacted, most of the material in ¶¶ 14.12–14.15 would be repealed.

¶ 14.12. STATUTORY MERGERS AND CONSOLIDATIONS (TYPE A)

Page 14-33:

Add to note 57.

[57] See also West-Shore Fuel, Inc. v. US, 598 F.2d 1236 (2d Cir. 1979) (shareholders not entitled to use §453 in all debt mergers; transaction a corporate-level asset sale, not a shareholder level stock sale). But see §453(h), added by the Installment Sales Revision Act of 1980, which allows shareholder use of §453 in such cases.

Page 14-35:

Add new note 63.1 to first sentence of second full paragraph.

[63.1] Superior Coach of Fla., Inc., 80 TC 895 (1983), and Security Indus. Ins. Co. v. US, 702 F.2d 1234 (5th Cir. 1983), so held.

Add to note 64, second paragraph.

[64] Pugh, Combining Acquired and Acquiring Corporations and Their Subsidiaries: Some Anomalies of Form and Substance, 35 Tax L. Rev. 359 (1980).

¶ 14.13. ACQUISITIONS OF STOCK FOR VOTING STOCK (TYPE B)

Page 14-39:

Add to note 73, second paragraph.

[73] Accord with the *Reeves* result is Pierson v. US, 472 F. Supp. 957 (D. Del. 1979) (acquiring corporation can pay up to 20 percent cash in a Type B without violating solely requirement if acquire at least 80 percent for voting stock, even though cash and stock paid in same transaction). But *Pierson* was reversed on appeal, sub nom. Heverly v. CIR, 621 F.2d 1227 (3d Cir. 1980); and *Reeves* itself was rev'd sub nom. Chapman v. CIR, 618 F.2d 856 (1st Cir. 1980).

Add new paragraph to text after note 74.

Judicial acceptance of *Southwest Consolidated*'s dictum that "solely means solely" was interrupted by a narrowly divided Tax

Court decision in *C.E. Graham Reeves* [74.1] where a plurality of six judges held that cash paid in a Type B reorganization does not per se violate the statute if the requisite 80 percent control is acquired in one transaction solely for voting stock. The exchange in *Reeves* was held to satisfy this test, regardless of *prior* cash purchases by the acquiring corporation of 8 percent of the target company's shares (which purchases the court held to be "irrelevant" for this purpose). The plurality opinion's test for §368(a)(1)(B) is a narrow one, however, since the transaction in which the 80 percent stock control is acquired must be one in which only voting stock is paid as consideration. Two concurring judges would go even further and allow payment of up to 20 percent cash in the same transaction as the stock for stock control acquisition transaction (a view which was subsequently adopted by a Delaware district court decision in the same case [74.2]). Five judges dissented in *Reeves,* however, stating that the weight of precedent required a decision for the government on the "solely" question and that the majority's view created too much uncertainty in an area which had long been considered to be well settled. [74.3]

[74.1] 71 TC 727 (1979).

[74.2] Pierson v. US, supra note 73 (this Supplement).

[74.3] In Pierson v. US, id., the court found this prior precedent to be either readily distinguishable, or at best unpersuasive; instead, after analyzing the prior legislative history (which it found to be inconclusive) and the congressional policies of the reorganization provisions, payment of some cash in a Type B reorganization was held to be permissible under the existing statutory scheme. The government's inability to articulate any policy reason, save the literal language of §368(a)(1) (B), for taxing the transaction in the *Reeves* and *Pierson* decisions, seemed to strongly influence the majority judges in *Reeves* and the judge in *Pierson.*

One of the principal effects of the *Reeves* and *Pierson* decisions, if ultimately sustained, will be to ease the definitional pressures on the Type B provisions in the situations discussed infra in paragraphs 1–7. But in the first two appeals from these decisions, Heverly v. CIR, 621 F.2d 1227 (3d Cir. 1980); Pierson v. US, 621 F.2d 1227 (3d Cir. 1980); Chapman v. CIR, 618 F.2d 856 (1st Cir. 1980), the lower court position was reversed, largely on the grounds of Judge Wilbur's dissent in *Reeves* that stare decisis was too well established on this question to tolerate any new judicial departures.

The Hartford litigation was settled in May, 1981, upon payment by ITT of $18.5 million; the shareholders will obtain tax-free exchange treatment, if they treat basis consistently, and will not be deemed to have received additional income as a result of ITT's payment. In short, the "litigation" was settled, but the "law" is not.

See generally Silverman & Trow, Cash Consideration in a "B" Reorganization: Where Are *Reeves* and *Pierson* Taking Us? 51 J. Tax. 2 (1979); Romano, Comment, The "Solely for Voting Stock" Requirement of B Reorganizations; Reeves v. Comm'r, 79 Colum. L. Rev. 774 (1979); Wolfman, Federal Income Taxation of Business Enterprise, 1979 Supp. at 485; Steines, Policy Considerations in the Taxation of B Reorganizations, 31 Hastings L.J. 993 (1980); Note, The "Solely for Voting Stock" Requirement in a (B) Reorganization After *Reeves v. Commissioner* and *Pierson v. United States*, 66 Va. L. Rev. 133 (1980); Fissel, Case Comment, *Reeves v. Commissioner*, 71 TC 727 (1979), 48 U. Cin. L. Rev. 1058 (1979); Barrack and McKinley, The Tax Court's *Reeves* Decision: A Relaxation of the B Reorganization Requirements? 57 Taxes 421 (1979); Thompson, Qualifying as a "B" Reorganization: The ITT-Hartford Cases: Alternatives to Use of a "B," 39 NYU Inst. on Fed. Tax. Ch. 7 (1981); and McMahon, Defining the "Acquisition" in B Reorganizations Through the Step Transaction Doctrine, 67 Iowa L. Rev. 31 (1981).

Page 14-40:

Add to note 76, first paragraph.

[76] See generally McMahon, supra note 74.3 (this Supplement), on defining "the acquisition" for purposes of the Type B definition; and Henry, The Impact of *Reeves v. Comm'r* on the Creeping Control "B" Reorganization: The Need for Legislative Reexamination of Section 368(a)(1)(B), 10 J. Corp. Tax. 195 (1983).

Correct last line of text.

Change "persumably" to "presumably."

Page 14-42:

Add to note 79.

[79] Rev. Rul. 79-274, 1979-2 CB 131 (overlap of B reorganization and §351; voting preferred received pro rata can be section 306 stock if transferee has earnings for its first year). For analysis of Rev. Rul. 79-274, see Corry, Preferred Stock Issued in Tax-Free Exchanges: Does Section 306 Apply? 35 Tax L. Rev. 113 (1979). But see new §§304(b)(3) and 306(c)(3), added by the Tax Equity and Fiscal Responsibility Act (TEFRA) of 1982, P.L. No. 97-248, 96 Stat. 324, supra ¶ 9.33 (this Supplement).

Add to note 80, second paragraph.

[80] Accord with *Reeves* on the "solely" question is Pierson v. US, supra note 73 (this Supplement). But *Reeves* and *Pierson* were reversed

on appeal by the First and Third Circuits, supra note 73 (this Supplement). See generally McMahon, supra note 74.3 (this Supplement).

Add to note 81.

[81] See Rev. Rul. 79-100, 1979-1 CB 152 (shareholder-level stock purchases not boot; directors' qualifying shares in bank purchased by new directors per grant of nonassignable option).

Page 14-43:

Add to note 85.

[85] See also Rev. Rul. 79-4, 1979-1 CB 150 (acquiring corporation's payment of shareholder-guarantor's debt held boot; shareholder treated as true debtor, not mere guarantor of target corporation's debt).

Page 14-44:

Add to note 87.

[87] See Rev. Rul. 79-4, 1979-1 CB 150 (shareholder-guarantor held true debtor under debt-equity analysis principles so that acquiring corporation's discharge of such debt ruled boot to shareholder).

Compare Rev. Rul. 79-89, 1979-1 CB 152 (acquiring corporation's contribution of cash to acquired corporation to enable it to pay off debt guaranteed by one of the two shareholders not boot; contribution not a condition of exchange, and stock-for-stock exchange values equal).

Page 14-47:

Add to note 97.

[97] But *Bercy Indus.* was reversed, 640 F.2d 1058 (9th Cir. 1981) (triangular forward merger into shell subsidiary of acquiring corporation sufficient to allow post-merger carrybacks despite §381(b)(3); transaction not a type F and no opinion as to whether it was a Type B, although court seemed to view it as the functional equivalent of a Type B). See new §368(a)(1)(F), as amended by TEFRA of 1982, supra note 79 (this Supplement) (Type F limited to single operating company).

Add to note 98.

[98] See also Rev. Rul. 79-274, supra note 79 (this Supplement) (overlap of §351 and B reorganization; voting preferred issued pro rata as section 306 stock). For analysis of Rev. Rul. 79-274, see Corry, supra note 79 (this Supplement). See new §§304(b)(3) and 306(c)(3), added by TEFRA of 1982, supra note 79 (this Supplement).

¶ 14.14. ACQUISITIONS OF PROPERTY FOR VOTING STOCK (TYPE C)

Page 14-50:

Add to note 107.

[107] But recent legislation enacted in 1984 requires the complete liquidation of the transferor pursuant to the plan of reorganization, new §368(a)(2)(G), added by §63 of the Tax Reform Act of 1984, P.L. No. 98-369, 98 Stat. 678 (effective on date of enactment, July 18, 1984). The complete liquidation requirement is waivable by regulations, but the parties will be treated as if the acquired corporation had in fact been liquidated in such a case.

Page 14-51:

Correct fourth line from top of page.

Delete the word "not."

Add to text at end of first runover paragraph.

But recent legislation enacted in 1984 [109.1] now requires complete liquidation of the transferor corporation pursuant to the plan of reorganization, unless regulations waive this requirement; in such a case, however, a complete liquidation will be deemed to have occurred.

[109.1] Supra note 107 (this Supplement), adding new §368(a)(2)(G). See H. Rep. No. 98-861, 98th Cong., 2d Sess., pp. 844–846. See also Eustice, The Tax Reform Act of 1984, ¶ 3.03[3] (Warren, Gorham & Lamont, Inc. 1984).

Page 14-52:

Add to note 114.

[114] See also Rev. Rul. 78-47, 1978-1 CB 114 (substantially all test applied re "business assets" in downstream transfer); Smothers v. US, 642 F.2d 894 (5th Cir. 1981) (necessary operating assets the benchmark for substantially all test).

Page 14-58:

Add to note 130, first paragraph.

[130] Rev. Rul. 81-247, 1981-2 CB 87 (post-acquisition drop-downs under §368(a)(2)(C) do not violate continuity of business enterprise regulations).

Page 14-59:

Add to note 131.

[131] Rev. Rul. 78-130, 1978-1 CB 114 (not a Type D because no direct control of transferee, but transaction qualified alternatively as a triangular Type C); Rev. Rul. 84-30, 1984-1 CB 114 (valid type C even though target passed acquiring corporation's stock upstream to its grandparent; continuity of interest not violated).

Add new paragraph 5 to end of section.

5. *Problems and opportunities when the transferor did not liquidate.* In some cases, the transferor corporation which has exchanged its operating assets for stock in a Type C reorganization may prefer not to liquidate pursuant to the reorganization (which it did not have to do, supra note 107). Since its tax history was stripped-out by §381(a)(2),[135.1] passing over automatically to the acquiring corporation (infra Ch. 16), the transferor could continue in existence as a holding company with a "clean slate" of earnings and profits. Alternatively, it could distribute out the acquiring corporation's stock tax-free to its shareholders under §354 (infra ¶ 14.34) and retain other untransferred assets (assuming they were not significant enough to violate the substantially all requirement), thereby avoiding the possible boot dividend consequences that would result to the shareholders if those assets were distributed in the reorganization.[135.2] Finally, if the corporation's asset bases were high enough to tolerate the receipt of boot (within the §368 (a)(2)(B) zone) without significant corporate-level gain, it could likewise avoid shareholder boot dividend risks by retaining such property (with only a nominal recognition of gain, if any).

Because of these, and other, abuse possibilities stemming from the fact that the transferor is not required to liquidate in a Type C reorganization, proposals by the Staff of the Senate Finance Committee (submitted on September 22, 1983) would amend the law in this respect and require the transferor to completely liquidate within twelve months of the acquisition in order to obtain nonrecognition treatment on the transaction (infra ¶ 14.32, this Supplement). Recent legislation enacted in 1984[135.3] now requires

---

[135.1] See Rev. Rul. 73-552, 1973-2 CB 116, discussed supra note 107; Rev. Rul. 76-188, 1976-1 CB 99, discussed supra note 131.

[135.2] Rev. Rul. 73-552, supra note 135.1 (this Supplement).

[135.3] The Tax Reform Act of 1984, §63, adding new §368(a)(2)

complete liquidation by the transferor pursuant to the plan of reorganization, unless waived by regulations. If the liquidation requirement is waived, however, the waiver will be conditioned on the parties being treated as if a complete liquidation had in fact occurred.

(G); supra note 107 (this Supplement). See Eustice, supra note 109.1 (this Supplement).

¶ 14.15. MERGER WITH CONTROLLED SUBSIDIARY (HYBRID TYPE A)

Page 14-60:

Add to note 137, second paragraph.

[137] Testa, The "A," "B," "C" Matrix of Triangular Reorganizations, 38 NYU Inst. on Fed. Tax. Ch. 1 (1980). Regulations under §368 (a)(2)(E) were proposed on December 29, 1980.

Page 14-61:

Correct third line of text.

Delete the first word, "of."

Add to note 139.

[139] Rev. Rul. 79-273, 1979-2 CB 125 (same as Rev. Rul. 73-427, viz., cash reverse merger treated as taxable stock purchase and *Zenz* redemption where target distributed stock of unwanted subsidiary).
See Blanchard, The Effect of the Step-Transaction Doctrine on Reverse Subsidiary Mergers: An Analysis, 55 J. Tax. 72 (1981) (discussion of nonqualified §368(a)(2)(E) deals).

Add to text before start of paragraph 2.

Amendments to the reorganization rules by the Bankruptcy Tax Act of 1980, H.R. 5043, generally extend the tax-free triangular rules of §§368(a)(2)(D) and 368(a)(2)(E) to bankruptcy reorganizations under new §368(a)(1)(G) (infra ¶ 14.20, this Supplement). In addition, these provisions sanction asset dropdowns in bankruptcy reorganizations, and also amend §368(b) to include the parent of an acquiring subsidiary as a "party" to the reorganization. See generally infra ¶ 14.20 (this Supplement). These provisions were reported by the full Ways and Means Committee on March 12, 1980, passed the House on March 24, 1980, were reported by the Senate Finance Committee on November 19, 1980, and ultimately passed in December 1980.

Page 14-62:

Add to note 140, first paragraph.

[140] Rev. Rul. 81-247, 1981-2 CB 87 (drop-down does not violate continuity of business enterprise regulations).

Add to note 140, second paragraph.

[140] Cook & Coalson, The "Substantially All of the Properties" Requirement in Triangular Reorganizations—A Current Review, 35 Tax Law. 303 (1982).

Add to note 141.

[141] Regulations under §368(a)(2)(E) were proposed on Dec. 29, 1980, as Prop. Regs. §1.368-2(j). Their principal features are: (a) there must be a bulk acquisition of control in the transaction, Prop. Regs. §§1.368-2(j)(3)(i), 1.368-2(j)(3)(ii); (b) the substantially-all test applies to both the target company and the merging subsidiary, but, for this purpose, property transferred to the disappearing subsidiary which is used to pay boot to the target company, dissenters, creditors, or reorganization expenses is disregarded, Prop. Regs. §1.368-2(j)(3)(iii); (c) the parent can drop the target's stock into a controlled subsidiary under §368(a)(2)(C) (*but,* the target cannot drop more than 10 percent of *its* net assets into a controlled subsidiary), Prop. Regs. §1.368-2 (j)(4); and (d) the parent can assume liabilities of the target, Prop. Regs. §1.368-2(j)(5). See generally, Comment, Report on Reverse Triangular Mergers and Basis-Nonrecognition Rules in Triangular Reorganizations, New York State Bar Association, Tax Section, 36 Tax L. Rev. 395 (1981). See also Cook & Coalson, supra note 140 (this Supplement).

Add new note 141.1 to end of first full sentence of text.

[141.1] But Prop. Regs. §1.368-2(j)(7), Ex. (4), holds that parent must acquire complete control of target *in* the acquisition, i.e., threshold redemption by target of its preferred stock (less than 10 percent of total stock outstanding too) violated §368(a)(2)(E) control acquisition requirement (note, however, that similar transaction apparently does not spoil a Type B, since acquiring corporation only has to *end up* in control of target).

Rev. Rul. 84-104, 1984-29 IRB 7 (no §368(a)(2)(E) for "consolidations," but consolidation under National Bank Act considered a "merger" because one of parties survived, so valid reverse merger).

Add to note 142.

[142] But see Rev. Proc. 82-50, 1982-2 CB 839 (no ruling on whether §368(a)(1)(B) or §351 applies via Rev. Rul. 67-448 if transaction structured as a §368(a)(2)(E) reverse merger, but fails to qualify as such because it violates substantially all, or control requirements).

Page 14-63:

Add to note 143, first full paragraph.

[143] See also Rev. Rul. 78-397, 1978-2 CB 150 (circular cash flow, to meet state law minimum-capital requirement, disregarded as transitory step).

Add to note 144.

[144] Prop. Regs. §1.368-2(j)(3)(ii) (must acquire 80 percent control in the merger).

Add to note 145.

[145] Prop. Regs. §1.368-2(j)(5) (parent can assume target's liabilities in a reverse merger).

Page 14-64:

Add new note 146.1 to text at end of paragraph (e).

[146.1] Rev. Rul. 79-155, 1979-1 CB 153 (convertible debt jointly assumed by parent and subsidiary; debt convertible into stock of parent and into stock of subsidiary if parent disposed of subsidiary; held, not stock of subsidiary yet, until conversion).

Page 14-65:

Add to note 147.

[147] But Prop. Regs. §1.358-6(c) (Dec. 29, 1980) allows use of target's net asset basis as the basis for its stock in the target (as if the parent had acquired the target's net assets and retransferred them back to the target).

Add new note 148.1 to end of second paragraph of subparagraph (g).

[148.1] But regulations under §368(a)(2)(E) were proposed on Dec. 29, 1980, Prop. Regs. §1.368-2(j) (summarized supra note 141, this Supplement). Concurrently, regulations dealing with subsidiary-level nonrecognition and parent's basis for its subsidiary's stock in triangular acquisitions also were proposed on Dec. 29, 1980, Prop. Regs. §§1.1032-2, 1.358-6 (which are considered infra ¶ 14.33, this Supplement).

¶ 14.16. TRANSFER OF ASSETS TO CONTROLLED CORPORATIONS (TYPE D)

Page 14-71:

Add to note 163 (second paragraph).

[163] See also Rev. Rul. 78-130, 1978-1 CB 144 (overlap of §351, Type C, and Type D reorganizations; assets of first-tier subsidiary transferred to new second-tier subsidiary of sister first-tier subsidiary for stock of latter not a Type D because no direct control, but valid triangular Type C; assets of second-tier subsidiary transferred to new second-tier subsidiary for stock of transferor's parent a Type D because control test met here). See also Rev. Rul. 84-30, 1984-1 CB 114 (lateral asset transfer by second-tier "nephew" subsidiary to first-tier "aunt" subsidiary held valid Type C reorganization; presumably not a Type D because of lack of direct control of transferor).

Correct last line of section.

Add "as a Type" after "and" and before "F."

Add new paragraph 4 to text at end of section.

4. *Current legislation.* The Staff of the Senate Finance Committee, in its preliminary report on the reform and simplification of Subchapter C, submitted on September 22, 1983, recommended two significant changes in the nondivisive Type D reorganization definition: (1) the control threshold would be lowered from 80 percent to 50 percent; and (2) §318(a) principles would apply in determining such control. Under these proposals, the scope of the Type D reorganization would expand materially, and thereby prove considerably more effective in combatting the liquidation-reincorporation device, infra ¶ 14.54, which is the purpose of this proposal. This proposal was adopted by the 1984 tax legislation in slightly altered form.[164.1]

[164.1] The Tax Reform Act of 1984, §64(a), added a special §368 (c)(2) "control" definition for nondivisive type D reorganizations keyed to the control definition in §304(c) and effective on the date of enactment (July 18, 1984). See Eustice, The Tax Reform Act of 1984, ¶ 3.04[4].

¶ 14.17. RECAPITALIZATIONS (TYPE E)

Page 14-72:

Add to note 165, first paragraph.

[165] See Rev. Proc. 78-33, 1978-2 CB 532 (guidelines and information to be included in ruling requests); updated by Rev. Proc. 81-60, 1981-2 CB 680. Rev. Rul. 82-34, 1982-1 CB 59 (no business continuity requirement). But see Rev. Proc. 82-30, 1982-1 CB 485 (no ruling on whether transaction constitutes Type E, or §1036, except where recapitalization part of a larger transaction and not possible to determine tax consequences of larger transaction without determination of recapitalization status). See generally Microdot, Inc. v. US 728 F.2d 593 (2d Cir. 1984); Golden Nugget, Inc., 83 TC 28 (1984).

Page 14-73:

Add to note 170.

[170] Rev. Rul. 83-119, 1983-2 CB 57 (estate freeze recapitalization; value of new preferred less than value of old common and thus created §305(b)(4) taxable dividend); for valuation factors in determining values of common and preferred, see Rev. Rul. 83-120, 1983-2 CB 170. Friedman, New Ruling Requires Creative Planning in Structuring Recapitalizations, 60 J. Tax. 146.

Page 14-74:

Add to note 172, end of first full paragraph.

[172] Rev. Rul. 69-135 was distinguished in Rev. Rul. 79-155, 1979-1 CB 153 (issuer of stock on conversion also an obligor on debt, even though not the only one, since both parent and subsidiary jointly assumed convertible debt in merger agreement and right to convert into parent stock granted in amended security pursuant to the initial reorganization transaction).

Add to note 172, third paragraph.

[172] Lipton, Debt-Equity Swaps for Parent-Subsidiary: A Current Analysis of a Useful Technique, 59 J. Tax. 406 (1983) (focus on Rev. Rul. 69-265).

Add to note 175, first paragraph.

[175] James H. Johnson, 78 TC 564 (1982) (exchange of old common for new class of common a recapitalization).

Add to note 175, second paragraph.

[175] Rev. Rul. 72-57 was modified by Rev. Rul. 78-351, 1978-2 CB 148.

Page 14-75:

Add to note 181.

[181] But see Rev. Rul. 83-119, 1983-2 CB 57 (can have §305(b)(4), §305(c) dividend here if excess redemption premium on new preferred, and was on facts).

Add to note 182.

[182] Rev. Rul. 83-119, supra note 181 (this Supplement) (excess redemption premium on new preferred issued for old common in "estate freeze" transaction resulted in §305(b)(4) dividend where value of preferred less than its redemption price; dividend taxable over life of holder since not redeemable till death).

Page 14-76:

Add to note 183.

[183] See Rev. Rul. 83-119, supra note 181 (this Supplement), for example.

Add to note 184.

[184] See also Rev. Rul. 83-119, supra note 181 (this Supplement).

Add to note 186, first paragraph.

[186] See generally Lorch v. CIR, 605 F.2d 657 (2d Cir. 1979) (bond for stock exchange as recapitalization).

Add to note 186, second paragraph.

[186] See Ltr. Rul. 8052018, 1981 P-H Fed. Tax Serv. ¶ 54,976 (parent has no §171 amortizable bond premium for excess of value of its stock over face of subsidiary's debt on conversion of that debt into parent's stock; excess value "attributable" to conversion feature). Accord with Letter Ruling is National Can Corp. v. US, 520 F. Supp. 567 (N.D. Ill. 1981) (no §162 deduction either because of §1032), aff'd, 687 F.2d 1107 (7th Cir. 1982).

But see ITT & Cos., 77 TC 60 (1981), aff'd per curiam, 704 F.2d 252 (2d Cir. 1983) (parent gets basis in subsidiary's bonds equal to value of parent's stock at date of conversion). Contra is National Can Corp. v. US, supra (parent has zero basis for bonds). See Lipton, supra note 172 (this Supplement).

Page 14-77:

Add to note 187, end of first paragraph.

[187] But §4(e)(1) of H.R. 5043, the Bankruptcy Tax Act of 1980, overrules the *Carman* case principle and amends §354(a)(2) to

make property attributable to accrued interest (including accrued original-issue discount) on the exchanged debt securities taxable to the exchanging creditor. See infra ¶ 14.20 (this Supplement) and infra ¶ 14.34.

Add new note 187.1 to end of fourth line of text.

[187.1] But new §351(d)(2), added by the Bankruptcy Tax Act of 1980, excludes "non-security" debts from the definition of property under §351.

Add new text after sentence ending with note 187.1.

Recent legislation enacted in 1984 significantly expanded the scope of the original-issue discount (OID) rules (and concurrently downgraded the coverage of §483).[187.2] Moreover, this legislation also characterized accrued "market discount" as interest in the hands of the holder under an approach similar to the rules of §1232 before its amendment by the Tax Reform Act of 1969 (i.e., ordinary income would be taxed on disposition, rather than currently as accrued, to the extent such discount accrued ratably during the taxpayer's holding period for the bond).[187.3] Thus, if bonds with accrued market discount (i.e., having an adjusted basis less than face) are exchanged for stock or securities in a recapitalization, such discount taint would carry over into new stock or securities and be taxed as interest income to the exchanging creditor *when* such property is disposed of by sale, retirement, or other "disposition."[187.4]

[187.2] The Tax Reform Act of 1984, H.R. 4170, §41(a), adding §§1271–1278 (passed the House on April 11, 1984); the Deficit Reduction Act of 1984, H.R. 2163, §25(a) (same) (passed the Senate on April 13, 1984); the Tax Reform Act of 1984, P.L. No. 98-369, §41(a), 98 Stat. 678 (enacted July 18, 1984); supra new ¶ 4.23 (this Supplement). See Eustice, The Tax Reform Act of 1984, ¶ 3.03[5].

[187.3] Under new §1276(b)(1), market discount accrues ratably on a *straight-line* basis (unlike OID, which, after the TEFRA of 1982, was changed to an economic accrual method in §1232A). From 1969 to 1982, OID also accrued (and was currently taxed) ratably on a straight-line basis. Unlike issue discount, however, market discount would only be taxed on "disposition" (i.e., sale, retirement, or gift, but not in a tax-free nonrecognition exchange transaction).

[187.4] Sections 1276(a)(1), 1276(a)(3), 1276(c)(2)(B), 1276 (d)(1)(B).

Add to note 188, last paragraph.

[188] While §483 could apply to an exchange of old stock for new bonds (and conceivably even to an exchange of old bonds for new bonds), it ordinarily would not apply to an exchange of old bonds for new stock (unless the issue of such stock was deferred for the statutory period), infra ¶ 14.56. For taxability of any accrued market discount on the exchanged bonds, see supra notes 187.3 and 187.4 (this Supplement).

Page 14-78:

Add new note 188.1 at end of second line of text.

[188.1] H.R. 5043, the Bankruptcy Tax Act of 1980, initially proposed to amend §§108 and 1032 in new §108(f)(1), which provided that stock issued to satisfy debt generally would not be subject to §1032, and the transaction would be treated as if the debt were satisfied for cash equal to the value of the stock. This provision would not apply to registered "security" debt in a §354 transaction, however, except to the extent there was accrued interest on the debt. See infra ¶¶ 14.20 and 14.58 (this Supplement).

But this provision was revised on February 28, 1980 to permit the debtor to elect to apply the amount of its debt discharge gain either first to reduce depreciable property basis or, alternatively, to reduce other tax attributes; see revised §§108(b)(5) and 108(d)(7). The revised version of the Bankruptcy Tax Act of 1980 was reported by the House Ways and Means Committee on March 12, 1980 and passed the House on March 24, 1980. These provisions were effective for bankruptcy proceedings commencing on or after October 1, 1979 and for other transactions occurring after 1980.

In reporting H.R. 5043 on November 19, 1980, however, the Senate Finance Committee dropped the equity-for-debt provisions of §108(f)(1) and retained the rules of present law, viz., no tax consequences result to the debtor from the satisfaction of its debts with stock (unless only a de minimis amount of stock is issued). The Finance Committee also modified the House version of the bill by providing that if a package of stock and other property is issued to cancel debts, the other property is deemed to have satisfied an equivalent amount of debt, and the stock will be deemed to have satisfied the balance. Finally, the Finance Committee version provides in new §108(e)(7) for an ordinary income recapture rule to the creditor who subsequently sells the stock (to tne extent of the creditor's prior ordinary loss or bad debt deduction). This version of the bill ultimately passed in December of 1980.

But Senator Danforth introduced legislation in June 1982, S. 2688, which would make equity-for-debt exchanges taxable to the debtor corporation where the value of the newly issued stock is less than the face of the canceled debt. For description of the types of transactions that inspired this proposal, see Heng & Parker, Tax-Free Debt Repurchases Using Stock-for-Debt Exchanges, 60 Taxes 527 (1982). This legislation did not pass, however. See also Walter, Tax Aspects of Recent Innovative Financings—Strategies for Existing Discount Debt and for New Securities, 60 Taxes 995 (1982) (analyzing equity-for-debt swaps); Lipton, note 172 supra (this Supplement); Note, Debt-Equity Swaps, 37 Tax L. Rev. 677 (1984).

But §59(a) of the Tax Reform Act of 1984, P.L. No. 98-369, 98 Stat. 678, now provides for the creation of debt cancellation gain in cases where the exchange is effected by a solvent corporation, new §108(e)(10). This provision was contained only in the House bill, but was accepted by the conference in the final legislation. See Eustice, The Tax Reform Act of 1984, ¶ 3.03[5][a].

Page 14-79:

Add to note 191.

[191] Since 1980, use of §453 seems possible here as well in view of the abolition of the two-payment rule and the 30 percent initial payment limitation; see §483(f)(6) (bonds must not be tradeable under §§453 (f)(4) and 453(f)(5) limitations, however).

Add to note 193.

[193] TEFRA of 1982 changed the straight-line ratable accrual method of the 1969 legislation to an economic accrual method based on a yield-to-maturity compound present value interest formula.

Add to text after note 194.

Recent legislation enacted in 1984 [194.1] materially revised and expanded the OID rules once again (supra new ¶ 4.23, this Supplement), extending the scope of these provisions to a significantly wider range of transactions (including reorganization exchanges, whether or not involving traded securities). Under these amendments, issue discount can arise whether or not the bonds are traded. If the bonds are traded, then the issue price will be determined by the value of the traded property; if not traded, the new bonds' issue price would be their discounted present value, using a prescribed statutory rate keyed to federal securities (and using compound interest principles).

Moreover, accrued market discount (i.e., the excess of face of

---

[194.1] The Tax Reform Act of 1984, §41(a), replacing §§1232 and 1232A with new §§1271–1275; supra new ¶ 4.23 (this Supplement). See Eustice, The Tax Reform Act of 1984, ¶¶ 2.02[2], 3.03[5][b].

the bond over the holder's adjusted basis for the bonds) generally will be characterized as interest and taxed as such to the holder on the disposition of the bond, except that such discount will carry over into new bonds received in exchange therefore in a tax-free transaction.[194.2]

[194.2] The Tax Reform Act of 1984, §41(a), adding new §§1276-1278. Bond-for-bond recapitalization exchanges would not trigger current tax on accrued market discount income (at least if the face of the new bonds does not exceed the face of the old), by virtue of §§1276 (d)(1)(B) and 1276(c)(2)(A); rather, the discount taint would carryover into the new bonds. See Eustice, The Tax Reform Act of 1984, ¶¶ 2.02[4], 3.03[5][a], 3.03[5][b].

Add to note 195.

[195] See generally Walter, supra note 188.1 (this Supplement). Accord with Rev. Rul. 77-415 is Microdot, Inc. v. US, 728 F.2d 593 (2d Cir. 1984); and Golden Nugget, Inc., 83 TC 28 (1984).

But see new §1232(b)(4), added by §306(a)(9)(C)(ii) of the Technical Corrections Act of 1982. Under this legislation, reorganization exchanges of traded debt for debt after December 13, 1982 can create OID if the face of the new obligations exceeds the fair market value of the old bonds. Such OID is limited, however, to the "adjusted issue price" of the old bonds (if greater than value), which term is defined as original issue price plus previously includable OID thereon. See Walter, Recent Innovative Financing Techniques—An Addendum, 61 Taxes 184 (1983). This provision is now found at new §1275(a)(4) of the 1984 Act amendments to the OID rules, supra note 194.1 (this Supplement), but also covers reorganization exchanges of untraded debt as well as traded debt.

Add new note 195.1 to sentence after note 195.

[195.1] Husky Oil Co., 83 TC 717 (1984) (no deduction for unamortized issue costs of old debt where exchanged for new debt; instead, such costs are spread over life of new debt).

Add to text after sentence ending with note 196.

But legislation adopted in 1982[196.1] eliminated the reorganization exception of §1232(b)(2), so that recapitalization exchanges of traded debt can give rise to OID, limited, however, to the spread between the face of the new bonds and the greater of the old bonds'

[196.1] New §§1232(b)(2), 1232(b)(4), added by §306(a)(9)(C)(ii) of the Technical Corrections Act of 1982.

value or adjusted issue prices (initial issue price plus accrued OID).[196.2] Recently enacted legislative changes in 1984 further broadened the possibility for OID by covering exchanges of non-traded debt as well.[196.3]

[196.2] This rule would continue as §1275(a)(4) of the 1984 Act revisions to the OID rules, supra note 194.1 (this Supplement). For the new treatment of market discount on recapitalization exchanges (which will give rise to taxable interest to the holder, though *not* an interest deduction to thet corporate debtor), see supra note 194.2 (this Supplement).

[196.3] Supra note 194.1 (this Supplement), adding new §§1274 and 1275(a)(4). The amount of OID on exchanges of untraded debt would be determined by the discounted present value of the new bonds, using a prescribed satutory rate keyed to various federal securities, and compounded semiannually.

Page 14-80:

Add new note 196.4 at end of first complete sentence.

[196.4] But could not have OID in reorganization exchange since 1969 amendments to §1232(b)(2); see Rev. Rul. 77-415, 1977-2 CB 311, discussed supra note 195. But see new §1232(b)(4), added by §306 (a)(9)(C)(ii) of the Technical Corrections Act of 1982 (can have OID in bond-for-bond recapitalization if face of new exceeds greater of value of old or "adjusted issue price" of old, viz., original issue price plus accred OID); and new §1275(a)(4), added by the Tax Reform Act of 1984 (can have OID on exchanges of untraded debt). See Walter, supra note 195 (this Supplement).

Add to note 197.

If basis of the old debt exceeds face of the new debt, exchanging creditor arguably may get §171 bond purchase premium deduction over life of the new debt in view of §171(b)(1)(A) and §171(b)(1)(B) definition of bond premium as excess of *basis* of the debt over face.

But see supra note 186 (this Supplement).

Add new sentence to text after end of paragraph.

But, as a result of legislation in late 1982,[197.1] issue discount can be created in recapitalization exchanges of traded debt if the face of the new bonds exceeds the greater of the old bonds' value or "adjusted issue price" (i.e., original issue price plus accrued

---

[197.1] New §§1232(b)(2) and 1232(b)(4), added by §306(a)(9) (C)(ii) of the Technical Corrections Act of 1982.

OID). Recent legislative amendments to the OID rules enacted in 1984 [197.2] continued this provision and expanded the possible creation of OID to recapitalization exchanges of untraded debt as well [197.3] (in this latter case, the issue price of the new bonds will be determined by their discounted present value, using a statutorily prescribed rate based on comparable federal debt instruments of short-, medium-, or long-term maturity, as the case may be, and compounded semiannually). [197.4] Market discount taint on the old debt will carry over into the new obligations and be taxable as interest to the holder on disposition of the new securities. [197.5]

[197.2] The Tax Reform Act of 1984, §41(a), adding §§1271-1275; supra new ¶ 4.23 (this Supplement).

[197.3] New § 1275(a)(4), supra note 197.2 (this Supplement).

[197.4] New §1274(d), supra note 197.2 (this Supplement).

[197.5] Supra notes 187.4, 194.2 (this Supplement).

Page 14-84:

Add to note 205, first paragraph.

[205] But §1023 was repealed by the Crude Oil Windfall Profit Tax Act of 1980.

Page 14-85:

Add to note 209.

[209] Moreover, the redeeming taxpayer could use §453 installment sale rules here as well, if the bonds are not traded per §§453(f)(4) and 453(f)(5). Moreover, §483 could apply here as well. Recently enacted legislation, supra note 197.2 (this Supplement), will apply the OID rules of new §1274 in lieu of §483. Accord with Rev. Rul. 77-415 is Microdot, Inc. v. US, 728 F.2d 593 (2d Cir. 1984; and Golden Nugget, Inc.; 83 TC 28 (1984).

Add to note 210, first paragraph.

[210] See also §453 (as amended in 1980) for possible installment sale treatment if bonds not traded (no longer any two-payment rule).

Add to note 210, second paragraph.

[210] But recently enacted legislation in 1984 (supra note 197.2 (this Supplement)) will create OID on debt dividends to the extent the face of the debt exceeds its discounted present value, new §1275(a)(5), added by §61(c) of the Tax Reform Act of 1984. Moreover, this amendment modified the charge to earnings and profits under §312

(a)(2) for debt dividends (limiting such charges to the *value* of the distributed debt), supra ¶ 7.40 (this Supplement).

Add to text after sentence ending with note 210.

Recently enacted legislation extended the OID rules to debt dividends and to other exchanges of stock (whether traded or not) for debt (whether traded or not), regardless of the status of the exchange as a recapitalization reorganization.[210.1]

[210.1] New §1273(b)(3) (traded), and new §§1274 and 1275 (a)(4) (untraded), supra note 197.2 (this Supplement); supra new ¶ 4.23 (this Supplement).

Page 14-86:

Add to note 216.

[216] Accord with Rev. Rul. 77-415 is Microdot, Inc. v. US 728, F.2d 593 (2d Cir. 1984); and Golden Nugget, Inc., 83 TC 28 (1984).

¶ 14.18.   CHANGES IN IDENTITY, FORM, OR PLACE OF ORGANIZATION (TYPE F)

Page 14-87:

Add to note 218.

[218] See generally Metzer, An Effective Use of Plain English—The Evolution and Impact of Section 368(a)(1)(F), 32 Tax Law. 703 (1979); Solomon, The Judicially Expanded "F" Reorganization and Its Uncertain Operating Rules, 7 J. Corp. Tax. 24 (1980).

Add to note 219.

[219] Rev. Rul. 80-105, 1980-1 CB 78 (conversion of federal non-stock mutual S&L into state stock S&L held Type F).

Page 14-88:

Add to note 223, first paragraph.

[223] See also Security Indus. Ins. Co. v. US, 702 F.2d 1234 (5th Cir. 1983) (purchase of subsidiary stock, liquidation, and reincorporation of operating assets in another subsidiary not a Type F; no continuity of interest; continuity broken by cash purchase).

Add to note 226, first paragraph.

[226] Next to last line of first paragraph, insert word "in" after "exclusive."

See also Rev. Rul. 79-289, 1979-2 CB 145 (overlap of D and F reorganization; held, §357(c) not applicable to Type F).

Add to note 227.

[227] But *Bercy* was reversed on the loss carryback issue, 640 F.2d 1058 (9th Cir. 1981) (post-merger carryback allowed after forward triangular merger into new shell subsidiary even though transaction not a Type F or Type B; no tracing problems here, so §381(b)(3) limitation not applicable; transaction functional equivalent of a Type B stock acquisition, even though court did not decide whether transaction constituted a Type B).

Page 14-89:

Add to note 231 (second paragraph).

[231] But *Bercy* was reversed, supra note 227 (this Supplement). See also Mariani Frozen Foods, Inc., 81 TC 448 (1983) (merger of holding company subsidiary into its parent not a Type F where subsidiary's asset promptly resold by parent after merger; no business continuity).

Page 14-90:

Add to note 232, second paragraph.

[232] See also Security Indus. Ins. Co. v. US, supra note 223 (this Supplement) (no Type F; continuity broken by cash purchase of stock).

Add to note 233.

[233] See also Rev. Rul. 78-441, 1978-2 CB 152 (de minimis rule applies to Rev. Rul. 75-561 Type Fs).

Add to note 234, first paragraph.

[234] See Rev. Rul. 79-71, 1979-1 CB 151 (post-fusion business continuity test of Rev. Rul. 75-561 satisfied where service corporation and corporation engaged in business of leasing facilities to service corporation were merged into a new corporation and leasing activities discontinued; previous integration of premerger activities, coupled with use of facilities by new corporation after merger, enough to satisfy business continuity). But see Mariani Frozen Foods, Inc., supra note 231 (this Supplement); see also National Tea Co., 83 TC 8 (1984) (postreorganization loss not attributable to prefusion business and thus could not be carried back to transferor-subsidiary's prior year; loss-tracing rule of Rev. Rul. 75-561 a proper limitation and was not satisfied here).

Add new paragraph numbered 4 to text at end of section.

4. Type F reorganizations involving multiple operating companies—TEFRA §225. After nearly fourteen years of judicial expansions of the Type F reorganization definition in §368(a)(1)(F) to include fusions of active affiliated corporations if there was (a) identity of relative shareholder proprietary interest, and (b) uninterrupted business continuity,[234.1] Congress overturned these decisions (including the limited concessions in Rev. Rul. 75-561) and adopted the Service's original views first expressed in Rev. Rul. 69-185 by adding "three little words" to §368(a)(1)(F), "of one corporation." In keeping with the freewheeling Conference Committee legislative approach, no such provision existed in either the House or Senate Bills; undeterred by this technicality, the Conference amended the Type F definition effective for transactions occurring after August 31, 1982.[234.2]

The Conference Report notes, however, that the new limitation "does not preclude the use of more than one entity to consummate the transaction provided only one *operating* company is involved."[234.3] It may well be that fusion of an operating subsidiary

[234.1] See, e.g., Stauffer's Est. v. CIR, 903 F.2d 611 (9th Cir. 1968); Associated Mach. v. CIR, 403 F.2d 622 (9th Cir. 1968); Home Constr. Corp. v. US, 439 F.2d 1165 (5th Cir. 1971); Performance Sys., Inc. v. US, 382 F. Supp. 525 (M.D. Tenn. 1973); MovieLab, Inc. v. US, 494 F.2d 693 (Ct. Cl. 1974); Eastern Color Printing Co., 63 TC 27 (1974) (Tax Court's original view that Type F not available to fusion of multiple operating companies modified to permit upstream merger of operating subsidiary into its parent holding company).

See also Aetna Cas. & Sur. Co. v. US, 568 F.2d 811 (2d Cir. 1976) (merger of 61 percent-owned subsidiary into newly owned 100 percent subsidiary held Type F, at least for §381(b)(3) purposes); Bercy Indus., Inc. v. CIR, 640 F.2d 1058 (9th Cir. 1981) (triangular forward merger of unrelated operating company into newly organized shell subsidiary; held, post-fusion carrybacks allowable because losses "traceable").

After initially rejecting Type F treatment for fusions of multiple operating corporations, Rev. Rul. 69-185, 1969-1 CB 108, the Service relented in Rev. Rul. 75-561, 1975-2 CB 129, permitting Type Fs of multiple operating corporations if (a) there is identity of relative shareholder ownership, (b) the same (or an integrated business), and (c) uninterrupted business continuity (also, loss carrybacks must be traceable to the same business).

See also infra ¶¶ 14.53, 14.54, and 16.12.

[234.2] Prior law will continue to apply, however, to plans adopted before such date and consummated by the close of 1982, TEFRA §225(b)(2).

[234.3] H. Rep. No. 760, 97th Cong., 2d Sess., at 541 (1982). (The example given is the reincorporation of an operating company in a different state.)

with its passive holding company parent (as in the *Eastern Color* case) [234.4] can still be a Type F under the new restrictive definition; on the other hand, fusions of multiple operating subsidiaries, or combinations of an operating parent and its operating subsidiary, will no longer be Type Fs.[234.5] Curiously, the new legislation may have failed to reach the decision in *Bercy Industries*,[234.6] in which the court did not hold that the transaction was a true Type F reorganization.[234.7]

[234.4] Supra note 234.1.

[234.5] E.g., transactions like those involved in *Home Construction, Performance Systems*, and *MovieLab*, supra note 234.1

[234.6] Supra note 234.1.

[234.7] *Bercy*, supra note 234.1, involved a forward triangular merger into a newly created shell subsidiary. Moreover, reverse triangular mergers under §368(a)(2)(E) and Type B reorganizations still do not invoke the carryback limitations of §381(b)(3). See Barbosa, An Analysis of "F" Reorganizations Involving a Single Operating Corporation After TEFRA, 11 J. Corp. Tax. 3 (1984).

¶ 14.19. TRANSACTIONS INVOLVING INVESTMENT COMPANIES

Page 14-91:

Add to note 236, first paragraph.

[236] See also Freeman, Leveraged Buy-Outs: Cash Company and Investment Company Reorganizations, 6 J. Corp. Tax. 239 (1979). Regulations under §368(a)(2)(F) were proposed on December 30, 1980.

Add to end of note 236.

Regulations were proposed on December 28, 1979 in Prop. Regs. §1.368-1(d) to restrict cash company mergers under continuity of business enterprise principles; concurrently, Rev. Rul. 79-434, 1979-2 CB 155, Rev. Rul. 79-433, 1979-2 CB 155, and Rev. Proc. 79-68, 1979-2 CB 600, were promulgated to deal with various aspects of the proposed continuity of business enterprise regulations. See infra ¶ 14.51 (this Supplement). These proposals became final on December 29, 1980. See infra ¶ 14.51 (this Supplement).

Add new headings.

¶ 14.20.   INSOLVENCY REORGANIZATIONS (TYPE G)

1. General. In order to reform and modernize the tax rules applicable to insolvency reorganizations, reflecting the recently enacted bankruptcy legislation of 1978, the House Ways and Means Select Subcommittee introduced H.R. 5043, the Bankruptcy Tax Act of 1979, on November 1, 1979. This bill represented the joint efforts of the tax and bankruptcy bars, working together with Congress, to draft legislation that would bring some order to the chaotic state of present law as it applied to insolvency proceedings. These proposals, in slightly revised form, were reported by the full Ways and Means Committee as the Bankruptcy Tax Act of 1980 on March 12, 1980, passed the House on March 24, 1980, were reported by the Senate Finance Committee on November 19, 1980, and ultimately passed in December of 1980.

In general, Section 4 of H.R. 5043 replaced existing §§371 and 372 with a new set of specific reorganization provisions tailored to the special exigencies of insolvency reorganizations. A new category of reorganization (Type G) was adopted in §368 (a)(1)(G), which provision strongly resembled the language and operation of the Type D reorganization (supra ¶ 14.16). Moreover, triangular reorganizations involving insolvent corporations were greatly facilitated under the new Act. The new Type G reorganization can be acquisitive or divisive in character. Finally, the continuity of interest limitations of present law were significantly eased for insolvency reorganizations, a feature of the new legislation that was one of its most notable characteristics. These provisions were effective generally for insolvency proceedings commencing on or after October 1, 1979, although the ultimately enacted Finance Committee version pushed this effective date forward to 1981 (unless taxpayers elect the earlier date).

The Economic Recovery Tax Act (ERTA) of 1981 [236.1] amended §368(a)(3)(D) as to reorganizations involving economically distressed financial institutions, extending the new Type "G" reorganization provisions to such transactions free of the continuity of interest requirement if (a) substantially all the transferor's assets are acquired, (b) substantially all its liabilities are

---

[236.1] P.L. No. 97-34, 95 Stat. 172. See Rev. Proc. 82-13, 1982-1 CB 447.

assumed, and (c) the appropriate bank regulatory agency certifies that certain conditions exist, or will exist in the near future in the absence of action by such agency. These provisions apply to transfers after 1980.

2. Technical analysis. A Type G reorganization is defined by new §368(a)(1)(G) as "a transfer by a corporation of all or part of its assets to another corporation in a title 11 or similar case; but only if, in pursuance of the plan, stock or securities of the corporation to which the assets are transferred are distributed in a transaction which qualifies under Section 354, 355, or 356." A "title 11 or similar case" is defined by new §368(a)(3) (A) as a case under Title 11 of the U.S. Code (viz., the Bankruptcy Act) or a receivership, foreclosure, or similar proceeding in a federal or state court. New §368(a)(3)(B) defines a qualified transfer of assets as one where the transfer is under the jurisdiction of a court in a bankruptcy proceeding and the transfer is pursuant to a plan of reorganization approved by the court. In the case of overlaps with other types of reorganizations, or with §§332 or 351, §368(a)(3)(C) gives the Type G reorganization provisions exclusive jurisdiction over the transaction. Moreover, new §351 (e)(2) denies §351 treatment for any transfer of property by a debtor corporation pursuant to a bankruptcy reorganization plan to the extent stock or securities received in the plan are used to satisfy a transferor corporation's debts.

Thus, transfers of assets and exchanges of stock and securities pursuant to a court approved insolvency reorganization plan will constitute tax-free reorganizations to the transferor corporation under §§368(a)(1)(G) and 361, and to the exchanging stockholders and security holders under §368(a)(1)(G) and §354 or §355. Moreover, §381(a)(2) was amended to provide that the tax history of the debtor corporation carries over to the transferee if the transaction constitutes a reorganization under §368(a)(1)(G) and §354(b)(1) (i.e., is nondivisive), a result comparable to the present treatment of nondivisive Type D reorganizations. However, §§354(a)(2) and 355(a)(3) were amended to tax exchanging security holders to the extent that consideration received was attributable to interest accrued on their securities during the period they held such obligations. These provisions initially were effective for bankruptcy proceedings commencing on or after October 1, 1979 and to all other transactions occurring after 1980 (but the finally enacted Senate Finance Committee version pushed the effective date forward to 1981, unless taxpayers elect the earlier date).

Finally, "triangular reorganization" treatment (supra ¶ 14.15) was extended to the new Type G reorganizations by the following provisions:

a. New §368(a)(3)(E) allows the "reverse merger" treatment of §368(a)(2)(E) to apply for insolvency reorganizations if stockholders of the debtor corporation receive *no* consideration for their stock, and former creditors of the debtor corporation get voting stock of the acquiring corporation's parent equal to 80 percent of the total value of its debt (viz., *creditors* of the debtor corporation are treated as its stockholders for purposes of the reverse merger rules).

b. The subsidiary merger rules of §368(a)(2)(D) were extended to Type G reorganizations.

c. Drop-downs in nondivisive Type G reorganizations were permitted under an amendment to §368(a)(2)(C).

d. The "party" definition of §368(b) was amended to include parent corporations in Type G asset acquisitions.

Recapitalization exchanges involving the same continuing corporate entity do not constitute Type G reorganizations; these transactions, however, will be affected by the amendments to the cancellation of indebtedness rules, which are considered infra ¶ 14.58 (this Supplement).[236.2]

[236.2] For analysis of these provisions, see Rabinowitz & Rubin, The Bankruptcy Tax Act of 1979—HR 5043: Proposals for New Tax Treatment of Debtors and Creditors, 57 Taxes 911 (1979). For analysis of final legislation, see Eustice, Cancellation of Indebtedness Redux: The Bankruptcy Tax Act of 1980—Corporate Aspects, 36 Tax L. Rev. 1 (1980); Braubach, Insolvency Reorganizations Under the Bankruptcy Tax Act of 1980, 8 J. Corp. Tax. 91 (1981); Scranton, Corporate Transactions Under the Bankruptcy Tax Act of 1980, 35 Tax L. Rev. 49 (1981); Watts, Corporate Acquisitions and Divisions Under the Bankruptcy Tax Act: The New "G" Type Reorganization, 59 Taxes 848 (1981); Bergquist & Groff, Reorganizing the Financially Troubled Corporation After the Bankruptcy Tax Act of 1980, 36 Tax L. Rev. 517 (1981); Plumb, The Bankruptcy Tax Act, 33 So. Calif. Tax Inst. 800 (1981); Asofsky, Reorganizing Insolvent Corporations, 45 N.Y.U. Ins. Fed. Tax. Ch. 5 (1983); and Bacon, Rescue Planning for the Failing or Bankrupt Company, 61 Taxes 931 (1983).

3. *Examples*. In the following examples it is assumed that D Corp. is involved in a "title 11 or similar case" and that its assets are transferred pursuant to a court-approved plan in that proceeding.

a. D transfers all its assets to P Co. for P Co. stock (voting and/or nonvoting), or for a combination of stock and debt securities, which consideration is distributed exclusively to D's debt security holders (D's former shareholders having been wiped out). D recognizes no gain or loss under §§368(a)(1)(G) and 361, and the exchanging security holders recognize no gain or loss under §354(a) (except to the extent accrued interest on their transferred securities is involved). D's tax history carries over to P under § 381 (and §382(b) will be applied by reference to D's creditors as well as its former stockholders).

b. Same as (a) except that P retransfers the D assets to S, a wholly owned subsidiary; same results.

c. Same as (a) except that D merges into S, a controlled subsidiary of P for consideration paid by P; same results.

d. Same as (a) except that S, a controlled subsidiary of P, is merged into D; §368(a)(2)(E) will apply if D's shareholders get nothing and if creditors of D get P voting stock equal to 80 percent of the value of D's debts.

e. D transfers one of its two businesses to P for P stock, which it distributes to its creditors, and transfers its other business (also "substantial" in size) to Q Co. for Q stock, which it likewise distributes to its creditors; even though the transaction is "divisive" in effect, it still qualifies as a Type G reorganization so that D has nonrecognition under §361 (and §351 will not apply), while the distributee creditors get nonrecognition under §355 rather than §354 (query D's nonrecognition rule where it distributes the P and Q stock to its creditors?).

f. To the extent that D's former stockholders participate in the transaction, the above results would be unchanged (except in example (d), the reverse merger situation, in which stockholders of D must not receive any consideration).

g. To the extent creditors of D do not exchange "securities" in the transaction, the entire reorganization may be vulnerable since §368(a)(1)(G) is conditioned on the distribution qualifying under §354 or 356 (and neither provision applies to the *transfer*, as opposed to the *receipt*, of nonsecurity debt). In such a case, D presumably would recognize gain or loss on its asset transfers (unless the transaction met one of the other reorganization definitions), and the creditors of D would similarly have immediate recognition of gain or loss on their respective exchanges.

  i. D, however, may be entitled to §337 treatment in this situation under new §337(g), supra ¶ 11.64 (this Supplement);

  ii. Moreover, §382(a) would not have been triggered to the extent that a creditor received stock in exchange for his claim under the House version of the bill (infra ¶ 16.22, this Supplement), since such an exchange would not be treated as a "purchase." The final version of the bill dropped this provision, however.

4. Collateral aspects. The Bankruptcy Tax Act provisions also contained numerous other changes to the Subchapter C rules, including: (a) amendments to §118, which treat the satisfaction of debt by capital contribution as a cash payment by the debtor (see supra ¶ 3.14, this Supplement); (b) amendments to §337 extending nonrecognition treatment to liquidation sales by insolvent corporations (see supra ¶ 11.64, this Supplement); (c) modifications of §§381, 382(a), and 382(b) to ease the tax history carryover rules for insolvency reorganizations (see infra ¶¶ 16.11, 16.22, and 16.23, this Supplement); and (d) changes in §351 to eliminate nonsecurity debt of the transferee and accrued interest on the transferee's debt from the definition of "property" (see supra ¶ 3.03, this Supplement).

Moreover, a fundamental restructuring of the cancellation of indebtedness rules was effected by the Act, which matters are considered in greater detail, infra ¶ 14.58, this Supplement. For articles on this general area, see supra ¶ 14.05, note 11, and supra note 236.2 (this Supplement).

¶ 14.21. CURRENT PROPOSALS: CORPORATE ACQUISITIONS—CARRYOVER-BASIS ELECTION

1. In general. On September 22, 1983, the Staff of the Senate Finance Committee submitted its preliminary report on the reform and simplification of Subchapter C. A centerpiece of this report was the Staff's proposal to replace the acquisitive reorganization provisions of present §§368(a)(1)(A), 368(a)(1)(B), and 368(a)(1)(C) (and the related triangular acquisition rules of §§368(a)(2)(C), 368(a)(2)(D), and 368(a)(2)(E)) with a single elective nonrecognition-carryover-basis system at the corporate level. The principal limitations of present law now applicable to acquisitive reorganizations—i.e., qualifying consideration (supra ¶¶ 14.11–14.14), continuity of interest (supra ¶ 14.11), continuity of business enterprise (infra ¶ 14.51), parallel treatment at the corporate and shareholder levels (infra ¶¶ 14.32 and 14.34), and the business purpose requirement (infra ¶ 14.51)— would all be repealed.

In effect, the present system of transactional electivity would be replaced with an express election regime keyed to the parties' decision to preserve basis for the acquired corporate assets by electing carryover-basis treatment, in which case the transaction would be entitled to nonrecognition treatment regardless of the type of consideration paid for the acquired properties. If, on the other hand, cost-basis treatment is elected, full recognition of gain or loss by the corporate transferor would be required, again without regard to the form of consideration paid (for the cost-basis election treatment, see supra new ¶ 11.67A of this Supplement). Regardless of what happens at the corporate level, shareholders would be permitted to receive stock tax-free in a qualified acquisition (infra ¶ 14.34, this Supplement).

2. Principal features of carryover-basis proposals. The proposed elective nonrecognition-carryover-basis system has residual elements of §§368, 337, and 338 of present law, principally in the definition of "qualified acquisition," but it is clearly a new regime that is being proposed here, and one that is markedly more simple to apply than present law, and which radically alters some long standing principles which have existed in the reorganization sections since their inception over five decades ago. The principal features of these proposals are the following:

(a) Qualified acquisition. A qualified stock acquisition consists of an acquisition of 80 percent control within twelve months from unrelated parties (as defined in §318, but without the option rule of §318(a)(4)); a qualified asset acquisition consists of a merger or consolidation, or a transaction, or series of transactions in which "substantially all" the assets of one corporation are acquired by the acquiring corporation and/or its affiliates. In applying the substantially all standard, however, pre-transaction asset tailoring would be permitted (viz., the *Elkhorn Coal* doctrine, supra note 115, and infra ¶ 14.52, would not apply here). Acquisitions of stock from related transferors (under §318) would not count for qualified stock acquisition treatment, but asset acquisitions from corporations within a controlled group (i.e., where there was at least 50 percent common ownership) could be qualified asset acquisitions, although carryover-basis treatment would be mandatory in this situation.

The various forms of triangular acquisition under present law (viz., triangular Type C, forward mergers, and reverse mergers) would be treated as stock acquisitions. Moreover, two-step stock and asset acquisitions (infra ¶ 14.53) would be treated as stock acquisitions if stock control was acquired on the first step, regardless of whether assets were acquired as the ultimate step.

(b) The election. Asset acquisitions are presumed to be carryover-basis acquisitions unless the parties specifically elect carryover-basis treatment; in a merger or consolidation, the surviving corporation makes the carryover-basis election, while in other asset acquisitions, both the transferor and transferee corporations must jointly elect carryover-basis treatment. Stock acquisitions likewise are presumed to be carryover-basis transactions unless the acquiring corporation specifically elects cost-basis treatment.

The election would be irrevocable, and the report suggested that it would have to be made within eight and a half months after the acquisition (paralleling the §338 election time frame, supra ¶ 11.47, this Supplement).

(c) Selectivity. The choice between carryover-basis and cost-basis treatment is made on a corporation-by-corporation basis, not

an asset-by-asset basis. In order to prevent avoidance of the prohibition against selective asset basis step-ups, a limited consistency rule (less onerous than those of §338, supra ¶ 11.47, this Supplement) would be imposed with respect to assets held directly by the acquired corporation at any time during the one-year period prior to its acquisition, and acquired at any time within the consistency period (generally a two-year period bracketing the acquisition date). In such a case, the election governing the acquired corporate entity which first held that asset will also apply to that asset.

(d) Corporate-level treatment. If a carryover-basis election is made for the acquisition, no gain or loss is recognized to the corporate transferor (infra ¶ 14.32), asset basis carries over to the transferee (infra ¶ 14.33), and all other tax attributes of the transferor likewise carry over to the transferee under §381 (infra Ch. 16). This result would occur regardless of the type of consideration paid, and without regard to the former judicially imposed continuity of interest, continuity of business enterprise, and business purpose limitations.

Unlike prior law, however, the transferor corporation in a qualified asset acquisition (the prototype of the former Type C reorganization, supra ¶ 14.14) would be required to completely liquidate within twelve months or be taxed on any boot received and any unrealized appreciation on retained assets (which provision is reminiscent of the §337 rule).[236.3] Gain (but *not* loss) so recognized would be treated as long-term capital gain and would be computed by subtracting the aggregate basis of all the assets transferred, from the value of all the consideration received (see infra ¶ 14.32, this Supplement).

[236.3] For shareholder-level treatment under these proposals, see infra ¶ 14.34 (this Supplement). For recently enacted legislation adopting this requirement, see supra ¶ 14.14, note 109.1 (this Supplement) (viz., acquired corporation in a Type C reorganization must completely liquidate by virtue of new §368(a)(2)(G).

PART C.   TREATMENT OF PARTIES TO A REORGANIZATION

¶ 14.31.   STOCK OR SECURITIES VS. BOOT: IN GENERAL

Page 14-95:

Add to note 242.

[242] See also supra ¶ 14.11, note 26; Paulsen v. CIR, 716 F.2d 563 (9th Cir. 1983).

Add to note 244.

[244] But see Paulsen v. CIR, supra note 242 (this Supplement).

Page 14-96:

Add to note 248.

[248] See also Vorbleski v. CIR, 589 F.2d 123 (3d Cir. 1978) (§483 applies to contingent stock issued in Type B reorganization); Jerrold L. Kingsley, 72 TC 1095 (1979).

Page 14-97:

Correct first line of text in second complete paragraph.

Third word should read "difficulties."

Page 14-98:

Add to note 256.

[256] But proposed regulations under §483 (Aug. 29, 1980) raise the test rate to 9 percent and the imputed rate to 10 percent, they became final on July 1, 1981 in T.D. 7781. Recently enacted legislation largely supplanted §483 with expanded coverage by the OID rules (but rates under both the new OID rules and §483 are keyed to market rates and computed under a compound discounted present value formula). See the Tax Reform Act of 1984, §41, adding new §§1271–1275, P.L. No. 98-369, 98 Stat. 678 (enacted July 18, 1984); supra new ¶ 4.23 (this Supplement).

Page 14-99:

Add to note 260.

[260] See also Rev. Rul. 78-408, 1978-2 CB 203 (exchange of warrants for warrants taxable exchange; separate from stock-for-stock Type B reorganization transaction).

See generally Pesiri, Untangling the Warrant Web, 23 Tax Notes 525 (Apr. 30, 1984).

¶ 14.32. TREATMENT OF CORPORATE TRANSFEROR: §§361, 357, AND 358

Page 14-102:

Add to note 268, first paragraph.

[268] But proposals by the Staff of the Senate Finance Committee on September 22, 1983, would overrule *Minnesota Tea* and allow purging distributions of boot to creditors of the transferor, as well as its shareholders.

Correct note 268, second paragraph.

[268] Word in second line should read "transferor," not "transfer."

Page 14-103:

Add to note 274, third paragraph.

[274] See generally Austin, The Applicability of Section 337 to Sales to Third Parties in a "C" Reorganization: The *FEC Liquidating* and *General Housewares* Decisions, 66 Calif. L. Rev. 623 (1978); Ordower, Separating Statutory Frameworks: Incompatibility of the Complete Liquidation and Reorganization Provisions of the Internal Revenue Code, 28 St. Louis U. L.J. 9 (1981).

General Housewares was affirmed, 615 F.2d 1056 (5th Cir. 1980) (§337 can apply in tandem with Type C reorganization; target corporation's sale of part of stock consideration received for its assets and use of proceeds to pay debts protected by §337 even though assets for stock exchange transaction governed by §361; moreover, shareholders obtained §354 nonrecognition even though corporation protected by §337 on stock sale). Compare Ltr. Rul. 8027017, [1980] 9 P-H Fed. Taxes ¶ 55,246 (asset sale for cash, followed by transfer of cash to regulated investment company for stock; followed by liquidation; held, §337 transaction since second step not a tax-free reorganization under continuity of business enterprise principle).

Add text after sentence ending with note 274.

If the transferor corporation is an S corporation, new §1363(d) (enacted by the Subchapter S Revision Act of 1982), arguably could cause recognition of gain on the distribution of the acquiring corporation's stock pursuant to the reorganization. If the transferor liquidates, the Committee Report states that §1363(d) does not apply; the Tax Reform Act of 1984, §721(a), cures this problem (retroactively) by exempting tax-free reorganization distributions from §1363(d) in new §1363(e). Moreover, the new restrictive §311(d) rules enacted by TEFRA and materially tightened once again in 1984 (supra ¶ 9.64A, this Supplement) still do not cover reorganization distributions.

Proposals by the Staff of the Senate Finance Committee, submitted on September 22, 1983, would modify the above discussed rules of §§361(a) and 361(b) as follows:

(a) No gain or loss would be recognized to the corporate transferor in a qualified carryover-basis asset acquisition if all assets were transferred and no boot was received.

(b) If boot was received on the transfer (including for this purpose debt securities), or if appreciated assets were retained, the corporate transferor would be required to distribute all of its assets to its shareholders or creditors pursuant to a plan of complete liquidation within twelve months in order to avoid recognition of gain.

(c) If the transferor fails to so liquidate, *net* gain (viz., the excess of the consideration received over the aggregate basis of the transferred assets) will be recognized to the extent of the boot received and the potential gain in retained assets, and taxed to the corporate transferor as long-term capital gain.

To illustrate:

(a) T transfers all of its assets, with a basis of $20 and a value of $100, for $100 of P stock in a carryover-basis acquisition. No gain is recognized, whether or not T liquidates.

(b) If P pays $50 cash and $50 of stock for all of T's assets, T must completely liquidate, or be taxed on $50 of long-term capital gain.

(c) If T retains $10 of assets (with a basis of $2), and transfers the rest of its assets for $90 of stock), T must also completely liquidate, or be taxed on $8 of capital gain on the retained assets.

Page 14-104:

Add to note 275, first paragraph.

[275] Compare Rev. Rul. 78-330, 1978-2 CB 147 (parent cancellation of subsidiary debt prior to subsidiary merger into affiliated subsidiary in order to avoid §357(c) gain did not constitute §357(b) tax avoidance). See also Rev. Rul. 79-289, 1979-2 CB 145 (§357(c) not applicable to a Type F reorganization even though transaction also a Type D; Rev. Rul. 75-161 and Rev. Rul. 76-188 distinguished).

Add to note 275, second paragraph.

[275] See generally Steiner, Liabilities in Excess of Basis in Corporate Reorganizations—When Should Gain Be Recognized, 6 J. Corp. Tax. 39 (1979).

¶ 14.33. TREATMENT OF CORPORATE TRANSFEREE: §§1032 AND 362

Page 14-107:

Correct note 283.

[283] "condu*c*t" should read "condu*i*t."

Add to note 284.

[284] Prop. Regs. §1.1032-2 (Dec. 29, 1980) provides nonrecognition for the subsidiary on the exchange of its parent's stock in forward subsidiary mergers, triangular Type B, and triangular Type C reorganizations. The general theory of Rev. Rul. 57-278 thus seems to be accepted by the proposed regulations (although apparently without a "conduit" limitation present in the ruling). But the subsidiary can recognize gain or loss if it pays property boot, see Prop. Regs. §1.1032-2(c), Ex. (1). See "Comment" on these proposed regulations, supra ¶ 14.15, note 141 (this Supplement), by New York State Bar Association, Tax Section.

Proposals by the Staff of the Senate Finance Committee on September 22, 1983, would amend §1032 to include parent, grandparent, great-grandparent, etc., stock within the ambit of §1032, without regard to whether the acquisition was taxable or tax-free.

Page 14-108:

Add to note 285, first paragraph, ending on page 14-108.

[285] Prop. Regs. §1.1032-2 is silent on the subsidiary's treatment in a taxable purchase acquisition.

Add to note 285, second paragraph.

[285] Rev. Rul. 80-189, 1980-2 CB 106 (subsidiary gets cost basis for parent's stock in §304(a)(2) acquisition).

Add to note 287.

[287] Arkansas Best Corp., 83 TC 640 (1984) (transferee equitably estopped to deny carryover basis where acquisition occurred fifteen years earlier and was treated as a reorganization by both parties; duty of consistency, or quasi-estoppel, doctrine applied here). See Prop. Regs. §1.453-1(f)(3)(ii) (basis step-up delayed if transferor reports boot gain under §453).

Add to note 289, first paragraph.

[289] But see Arkansas Best Corp., supra note 287 (this Supplement) (transferee estopped to deny carryover basis under duty of consistency doctrine).

Add to note 289, second paragraph.

[289] But OID now can occur in debt for property transactions as a result of amendments made by the Tax Reform Act of 1984, adding new §1274, supra ¶ 4.23 (this Supplement).

Add to note 289, third paragraph.

[289] Simmonds Precision Prods., Inc., 75 TC 103 (1980) (property acquired for options; basis "open" till exercise à la § 1.421-6 compensatory stock option regulations because options did not have readily ascertainable value at grant).

Page 14-109:

Add to note 290.

[290] See Rev. Proc. 81-70, 1981-2 CB 729 (guidelines for estimating basis of stock acquired in a B reorganization where shareholders do not respond to requests for information, and providing for the use of statistical sampling techniques to estimate basis in lieu of surveying each shareholder of acquired corporation).

Add to note 292.

[292] But see Rev. Rul. 80-189, 1980-2 CB 106 (subsidiary has cost basis for parent's stock acquired in §304(a)(2) transaction).

See also Prop Regs. §§1.358-6 and 1.1032-2, proposed on December 29, 1980 (dealing with "zero basis" problems in triangular reorganizations).

See also ITT & Cos., 77 TC 60 (1981), aff'd per curiam, 704 F.2d 252 (2d Cir. 1983) (parents gets cost basis equal to value of its stock on conversion of subsidiary's debt into parent's stock). Contra is National Can Corp. v. US, 520 F. Supp. 567 (N.D. Ill. 1981) (parent has zero basis for subsidiary's debt), aff'd, 687 F.2d 1107 (7th Cir. 1982).

Page 14-111:

Add new note 294.1 to end of paragraph 2.

[294.1] But Prop. Regs. §1.358-6(c)(2) (Dec. 29, 1980) adopts the third method (whether or not a phantom subsidiary is involved). However, a transition rule in Prop. Regs. §1.358-6(c)(5) gives the parent an election to claim the Type B carryover stock basis, if higher, in Rev. Rul. 67-448 type acquisitions.

Add new paragraphs 4 and 5 to text.

4. *Parent's basis for subsidiary stock in triangular reorganizations.* On Dec. 29, 1980, Prop. Regs. §§1.358-6(a) and 1.358-6 (b) were proposed, under which the parent would be allowed to adjust the basis of its subsidiary's stock in the case of triangular Type A, B, and C reorganizations as if the parent had directly acquired the target company's assets or stock in a two-party reorganization and then dropped that property into its subsidiary. Thus, in a triangular asset acquisition (Type A or Type C), the parent can step up the basis in its subsidiary's stock by the net basis (basis less liabilities assumed) of the target company's assets; in a triangular Type B, the parent can step up the basis for its subsidiary's stock by the amount of the shareholders' bases in the target company.

But the proposed regulations, in §§1.358-6(a)(3), 1.358-6 (b)(3), and 1.358-6(c)(3), require a downward adjustment for the value of any consideration not furnished by the parent *in* the reorganization. Read literally, this provision could result in a negative basis to the parent for its subsidiary's stock where the subsidiary effects the acquisition with old and cold parent stock. For example, if the target's asset basis is $700, and the parent's basis for its subsidiary's stock is $100, if the subsidiary gets all of target's assets with old and cold parent stock worth $1,000, the proposed regulations' adjustment mechanics would leave the parent with a minus-$200 basis in its subsidiary's stock (viz., upward adjustment of $700, target's asset basis; downward adjustment of $1,000, value of consideration not furnished by parent). The arguably "correct" answer here is that the parent simply has no basis adjustment for its subsidiary's stock as a result of the acquisition (presumably, the final version of the regulations will reach this result).[294.2]

5. *Current proposals for controlled subsidiary's stock basis.* The Staff of the Senate Finance Committee, in its report on the reform and simplification of Subchapter C, proposed a uniform outside basis rule for a controlled subsidiary's stock in the hands of its parent which would be derived, in *all* cases, by reference to the

---

[294.2] Comment, Report on Reverse Triangular Mergers and Basis-Nonrecognition Rules in Triangular Reorganizations, New York State Bar Association, Tax Section, 36 Tax L. Rev. 395 (1981).

inside net basis of the subsidiary's assets. Adjustments to outside stock basis would be made when and to the extent that changes occurred in inside net asset basis (viz., basis less liabilities). Adjustments would be required to reflect minority interests, e.g., if P only owned 80 percent of S, P's basis for S's stock would only reflect 80 percent of S's net asset basis.

This proposal would replace the rules of present law which give the parent a substituted-stock-basis if the subsidiary is incorporated, a carryover basis if the stock is acquired in a reorganization, and a cost-basis if the stock is purchased. Moreover, the investment basis adjustment rules of the consolidated return regulations would be repealed (infra ¶ 15.23, paragraph 7).

¶ 14.34.   TREATMENT OF STOCKHOLDERS AND SECURITY HOLDERS: §§354, 356, AND 358

Page 14-112:

Add to note 297.

[297] See Rev. Rul. 79-155, 1979-1 CB 153 (terms of security modified to such an extent in reorganization assumption that transaction deemed to constitute an "exchange," but tax-free per §354(a)(1)).

But §4(e)(1) of H.R. 5043, the Bankruptcy Tax Act of 1980 (enacted in December of 1980), amends §354(a)(2) to make property received that is attributable to accrued interest (including accrued OID) taxable to the exchanging creditor (to the extent such interest accrued during his holding period). See supra ¶ 14.20 (this Supplement).

Recently enacted legislation extended the OID rules to all exchanges of property for debt, whether or not traded and whether or not in a reorganization. Moreover, this legislation (in new §1276) also characterizes accrued *market* discount as the equivalent of interest to the holder and taxes such income at the time the bond is disposed of; however, if the bond is exchanged for another bond of equivalent face amount, the discount taint would carryover into the new bond under new §§1276(c)(2) and 1276(d)(1)(B). These provisions were contained in the Tax Reform Act of 1984, §41(a) (which passed on July 18, 1984). See generally supra new ¶ 4.23 (this Supplement).

Page 14-114:

Add to note 300, fourth paragraph.

[300] Accord with Rev. Rul. 77-415 is Microdot, Inc. v. US, 728 F.2d 593 (2d Cir. 1984); and Golden Nugget, Inc., 83 TC 28 (1984). For recently enacted legislation applying the OID rules to the receipt of debt securities having a discounted present value less than their face amount, see supra note 297 (this Supplement).

Add to note 301.

[301] For possibility of reporting "installment obligation" boot under §453, see Rev. Rul. 65-155, supra ¶ 3.06, note 55. For recent legislation approving this technique, see P.L. No. 96-471, The Installment Sales Revision Act of 1980, where new §453(f)(6) provides for §453 treatment in the context of reorganization nonrecognition exchanges (but unlike Rev. Rul. 65-155, §453(f)(6) disregards nonrecognition property in computing the "payments" and total contract price elements of a §453 fraction). See Prop. Regs. §1.453-1(f)(2) (May 3, 1984) for application of §453 to §356(a) boot gain. See generally, NY State Bar Ass'n Tax Section, A Report on Proposed Regulations Under Section 453(f)(6)—Installment Obligations Received in Certain Non-recognition Exchanges, 24 Tax Notes 297 (July 16, 1984); Friedman, An Analysis of Nonrecognition Exchanges and Installment Rules Under the Recent Proposed Regulations, 61 J. Tax. 158 (1984).

Page 14-115:

Add to note 302, second paragraph.

[302] Recently enacted legislation (supra note 297 (this Supplement)) largely supplanted §483 with expanded coverage of the OID rules (new §1273(b)(3) for traded debt exchanges and new §§1274 and 1275(a)(4) for untraded debt exchanges). To the extent the exchange results in the creation of OID on the new debt, this will affect the computation of "principal amounts" under §356(d).

Add to note 302, third paragraph.

[302] But under recently enacted legislation (supra note 297 (this Supplement) any taxable gain attributable to accrued market discount would be taxed as ordinary interest income to the holder under new §§1276(a)(1) and 1276(a)(3).

Page 14-116:

Add new text to end of paragraph 1.

But proposals by the Staff of the Senate Finance Committee (submitted on September 22, 1983) would determine shareholder treatment in a qualified corporate acquisition (supra new ¶ 14.21, this Supplement) independently of corporate-level recognition or nonrecognition, in effect adopting the approach of the *Howard* case. Thus, shareholders would be permitted to receive qualified stock tax-free in an acquisition without regard to the tax treatment of the transaction at the corporate level, or the terms of the exchange with other shareholders. See infra new paragraph 5 of ¶ 14.34 (this Supplement).

Add new note 305.1 to end of third sentence in paragraph 2.

[305.1] But proposals by the Staff of the Senate Finance Committee on September 22, 1983, would abolish the "dividend-within-gain" limitation of present §356(a)(2). See infra new paragraph 5 of ¶ 14.34 (this Supplement).

Page 14-117:
Add to note 307.

[307] Atlas Tool Co. v. CIR, 614 F.2d 860 (3d Cir. 1980) (Tax Court affirmed, boot dividend limited to transferor's earnings account).

Page 14-118:
Add to note 312, second paragraph.

[312] See also Sellers v. US, 1979-1 USTC ¶ 9202 (D.C. Ala. 1977) (boot not dividend equivalent because meaningful reduction, tested by comparison of percentage in target with percentage in acquiring corporation; query, vitality of this test in view of Fifth Circuit opinion in *Shimberg?*). *Sellers* was duly reversed, 615 F.2d 1066 (5th Cir. 1980).

More recently, see James H. Johnson, 78 TC 564 (1982) (receipt of boot in recapitalization to compensate for passed dividends held equivalent to dividend).

But proposals by the Staff of the Senate Finance Committee on September 22, 1983, would adopt the view of the *Wright* case, and reject *Shimberg,* in testing for dividend equivalence under §356(a)(2); infra new paragraph 5 of ¶ 14.34 (this Supplement).

Add to note 312, third paragraph.

[312] Gately & Pratt, Dividend Equivalency—Are The Tests Changing? 7 J. Corp. Tax. 53 (1980). Hurley, Capital Gain Possibilities for Boot in Acquisitive Reorganizations Lessened by *Shimberg* Case, 50 J. Tax. 334 (1979); Peterson, Comment, Determining Dividend Equivalence of "Boot" Received in a Corporate Reorganization—*Shimberg v. United States,* 32 Tax Law. 834 (1979); Golub, "Boot" in Reorganizations—The Dividend Equivalency Test of Section 356(a)(2), 58 Taxes 904 (1980); Fleming, Reforming the Tax Treatment of Reorganization Boot, 10 J. Corp. Tax. 99 (1983); Kayser, The Long and Winding Road: Characterization of Boot Under Section 356(a)(2), 39 Tax L. Rev. 297 (1984).

Add to note 313.

[313] See T.M. Memo 79-12, Pt. to Rem. No. 2, p. 10 (June 4, 1979), re Ltr. Rul. 7912101 (§318 not applicable in §356(a)(2) determination). Proposed legislation accepted by the House Ways and Means Subcommittee on Select Revenue Measures (H.R. 6725) would extend the attribution rules of §318 to §356(a)(2) boot dividend determinations. This proposal passed as §227(b) of TEFRA of 1982, P.L. No. 97-248, 96 Stat. 324 (effective after August 31, 1982).

Rev. Rul. 84-114, 1984-31 IRB (in a recapitalization, test for boot dividend equivalence under §302 principles, including *Zenz* step doctrine; here, boot did not have dividend effect under *Davis* because holder's interest dropped from 28 to 23 percent of vote and also effected a meaningful reduction in dividend and liquidation rights).

Page 14-119:

Add to note 314, first paragraph.

[314] See also Viereck v. US, 1983-2 USTC ¶ 9664 (Cl. Ct. 1983). For current proposals, see preliminary report of the Staff of the Senate Finance Committee, submitted September 22, 1983; these would abolish the dividend-within-gain limitation, and would accept the view of the *Wright* case that dividend equivalence should be tested by reference to a hypothetical redemption of the *acquiring* corporation's stock. See infra new paragraph 5 of ¶ 14.34 (this Supplement).

See also Rev. Rul. 84-114, supra note 313 (this Supplement).

Add to note 314, second paragraph.

[314] Rev. Rul. 81-81, 1981-1 CB 122 (forced cash received in a recapitalization exchange by minority shareholders in lieu of fractional shares of "section 306 stock" not dividend either; Rev. Rul. 66-365 amplified and amnesty of §306(b)(4)(A) applied).

Add to note 315.

[315] But see Sellers v. US, supra note 312 (this Supplement), where dividend equivalence comparison was of percentage interest in target company with interest in acquiring company, a test rejected by the Fifth Circuit in *Shimberg*). *Sellers* was reversed, 615 F.2d 1066 (5th Cir. 1980); see also Viereck v. US, supra note 314 (this Supplement) (boot distribution not a partial liquidation because no contraction of business enterprise; total business continuity so distribution equivalent to a dividend).

Add to note 316.

[316] See also Rev. Rul. 81-81, supra note 314 (this Supplement).

Page 14-121:

Add to note 321.

[321] See Tech. Advice Memo, 1979 P-H Fed. Taxes ¶ 55,756 (where shares specifically identified, can trace; not required to use average cost approach).

Page 14-122:

Add new paragraph 5 to text at end of section.

5. *Current proposals.* The Staff of the Senate Finance Com-

mittee, in its preliminary report on the reform and simplification of Subchapter C submitted on September 22, 1983, proposed to amend the boot rules of §356 in the following manner: (1) shareholder nonrecognition treatment would be determined independently of corporate-level recognition or nonrecognition (in effect accepting the view of the *Howard* case, supra note 303); (2) the dividend-within-gain limitation of present law would be repealed; and (3) boot dividend equivalence would be tested by assuming a hypothetical redemption of the *acquiring* corporation's stock (the *Wright* case approach, supra note 312), rather than of the *acquired* corporation's stock (the *Shimberg* case approach, supra note 312).[325.1]

Thus, shareholders who receive only qualified stock in a qualified corporate acquisition (supra new ¶ 14.21, this Supplement), would be entitled to nonrecognition treatment in full on their exchange, even though other shareholders receive cash, and even though cost-basis and recognition treatment is elected at the corporate level. If a shareholder receives both qualified stock and boot, dividend equivalence is tested by assuming a full issuance of stock followed by a hypothetical redemption of such stock for the boot by the acquiring corporation; if dividend equivalence results, it will be taxed in full as such, regardless of the shareholder's realized gain or loss on the exchange.

[325.1] See Milner, Boot Under the Senate Finance Committee's Reorganization Proposal: A Step in the *Wright* Direction, 62 Taxes 507 (1984).

¶ 14.35. "SECTION 306 STOCK" RECEIVED IN CORPORATE REORGANIZATIONS

Page 14-123:

Add to note 326.

[326] See Rev. Rul. 81-91, 1981-1 CB 123 (stock not "section 306 stock," even though preferred as to dividend and liquidation rights, because participated in earnings and equity growth as well).

Page 14-124:

Add to note 328.

[328] But see Rev. Rul. 79-287, 1979-2 CB 130 (preferred stock received in Type F reorganization in exchange for same number of old

preferred with identical terms not section 306 stock; transaction not substantially the same as receipt of a stock dividend); Rev. Rul. 82-118, 1982-1 CB 56 (same for new preferred received in triangular forward merger where substantially the same as old section 306 stock exchanged therefor). Rev. Rul. 82-191, 1982-2 CB 78 (preferred stock, voting and "limited," issued in recapitalization exchange for all of shareholder's voting common held §306 stock where shareholder purchased all of a new issue of nonvoting common as part of the same plan; thus, transaction as a whole had bail-out potential).

Add to note 329, first paragraph.

[329] Rev. Rul. 81-186, 1981-2 CB 85 (preferred stock received by sole shareholder on recapitalization exchange not §306 stock where taxpayer concurrently gave away all of his common pursuant to a unitary plan; cash dividend would have been §302(b)(3) under *Zenz* principles).

Add to note 329, second paragraph.

[329] See also Rev. Rul. 79-274, 1979-2 CB 131 (receipt of voting preferred pro rata in §351 exchange that also constituted a Type B reorganization; held, preferred section 306 stock if transferee corporation has earnings in its first year; transaction essentially equivalent to a stock dividend even though also qualified as §351 exchange). For analysis of this ruling, see Corry, Preferred Stock Issued in Tax-Free Exchanges: Does Section 306 Apply? 35 Tax L. Rev. 113 (1979).

New §306(c)(3), added by TEFRA §226(b), now specifically covers preferred stock issued in a §351 exchange if cash issued in lieu of such stock would have resulted in a dividend under new §304(b)(2)(A) principles, supra new ¶ 10.03, paragraph 4 (this Supplement).

Page 14-125:

Add to note 334.

[334] Query whether §318 attribution principles apply in determining stock dividend equivalence under §306(c)(1)(B)(ii); see Lowell, Interplay of Section 306 Provisions and Attribution Rules, 47 J. Tax. 206 (1977). Rev. Proc. 82-27, 1982-1 CB 480 (§318 applicability added to no-ruling area; matter under study). Proposed legislation (supra note 313, this Supplement) would specifically make §318 applicable in testing for §306 stock status. This legislation passed as §227(a) of TEFRA of 1982, P.L. No. 97-248, 96 Stat. 324 (effective after August 31, 1982).

Add new text to end of ¶ 14.35.

The TEFRA legislation of 1982 [334.1] modified the section 306 definition rules in two respects: TEFRA §226(b) added §306(c)(3), dealing with preferred stock issued in a §351 exchange (and applies the cash substitution test under principles similar to the rules of new §304(b)(2)); [334.2] and TEFRA §227(a), [334.3] extending §318 to the definitional testing of "Section 306 stock" status (without the 50 percent limitation), viz., as to whether the distribution has a dividend equivalent effect because it is pro rata.

[334.1] P.L. No. 97-248, 96 Stat. 324 (effective after August 31, 1982).

[334.2] Supra note 329 (this Supplement) and new ¶ 10.03, paragraph 4 (this Supplement).

[334.3] Supra note 334 (this Supplement).

PART D.   SPECIAL PROBLEMS IN REORGANIZATIONS

¶ 14.51.   JUDICIAL DOCTRINES AND LIMITATIONS: "BUSINESS PURPOSE," "CONTINUITY OF BUSINESS ENTERPRISE," AND "STEP" TRANSACTIONS

Page 14-127:

Add to note 336.

[336] Compare George R. Laure, 70 TC 1087 (1978) (fusion of dormant loss brother corporation into sister corporation failed to qualify as Type A because of lack of business purpose). But on appeal, *Laure* was reversed, 653 F.2d 253 (6th Cir. 1981) (merger had valid business purpose). Atlas Tool Co. v. CIR, 614 F.2d 860 (3d Cir. 1980) (business purpose satisfied; no requirement of tax avoidance motive to find reorganization on liquidation-reincorporation transaction).

Page 14-128:

Add to note 338.

[338] See also Willens, The Role of Form in Subchapter C, 57 Taxes 717 (1979); Isenberg, Musings on Form and Substance in Taxation, 49 U. Chi. L. Rev. 859 (1982).

Page 14-130:

Add to note 349, first paragraph.

[349] But Rev. Rul. 63-29 was suspended by Rev. Rul. 79-433, 1979-2 CB 155, pending its revision to reflect the new proposed regulations on business continuity, infra. But holding of Rev. Rul. 63-29 was republished by Rev. Rul. 81-25, 1981-1 CB 132 (no business continuity required for *transferee:* Rev. Rul. 79-433 superseded); Rev. Rul. 82-34, 1982-1 CB 59 (no business continuity needed for a recapitalization).

Add to note 349, second paragraph.

[349] See generally Freeman, Leveraged Buy-Outs: Cash Company and Investment Company Reorganizations, 6 J. Corp. Tax. 239 (1979).

Add to note 349, third paragraph.

[349] See also George R. Laure, supra note 336 (this Supplement) (no reorganization on fusion of dormant loss corporation into related sister corporation due to lack of business continuity). But *Laure* was reversed on appeal, supra note 336 (this Supplement) (business enterprise continuity existed, even under new regulations' test because transferee retained significant portion of transferor's historic business assets; 27 percent, by book value, significant).

But see Rose v. US, 640 F.2d 1030 (9th Cir. 1981) (generally similar to *Atlas Tool* in finding reincorporation transaction to be a Type D, but court expressly refused to apply a business continuity requirement for reorganization status here).

Add new paragraphs to text after note 349.

On December 28, 1979, new regulations on continuity of business enterprise were proposed in Prop. Regs. §1.368-1(d), requiring that the transferee corporation either (a) continue the transferor's "historic business" or (b) continue to use a "significant portion" of the transferor's "historic business assets" in a business. The proposals note that the fact that the transferee is in the same line of business as the transferor tends to establish the requisite business continuity, but is not alone sufficient; moreover, if the transferor has more than one business, continuity requires that the transferee need only continue a significant line of the transferor's business. Finally, the transferor's historic business is that which it most recently conducted; however, a business entered into as part of an overall plan to achieve a tax-free reorganization will not qualify. A corporation's historic business assets will include various intangibles, such as goodwill, patents, and the like, whether or not they have a tax basis.

The proposed regulations applied only to *asset* transfers, raising the curious and inexplicable implication that stock-for-stock Type B reorganizations will not be subject to these limitations. The proposals might also have some unintended side effects in the liquidation-reincorporation area, infra ¶ 14.54, where taxpayers are seeking methods to avoid application of the reorganization rules. Moreover, the business continuity proposals could seriously restrict the new Type G insolvency reorganization rules (supra ¶ 14.20) where, as is frequently the case, the reorganizing debtor corporation significantly scales down its "historic" business activities or assets as a consequence of its reorganization in the bankruptcy proceeding.

The proposed regulations set out five examples in §1.368-1(d)(5) illustrating the business continuity doctrine. Example (1) illustrates that the transferee need only continue one of the transferor's lines of business (two of its three equal lines were sold prior to the reorganization, but continuation of one of those businesses was adequate since it was a "significant" line). Example (2) illustrates acceptable asset continuity, while Examples (3), (4), and (5) illustrate situations where the requisite business continuity is lacking. In Example (3), the transferee sold its operating assets and became an investment company three and one-half years prior to the purported reorganization; in Example (4) the transferee acquired the transferor after the latter had sold its operating assets for cash and notes, while in Example (5) the transferee sold off the transferor's assets after the acquisition and discontinued that line of business.[349.1]

[349.1] Concurrently with these proposals, the Service issued Rev. Proc. 79-68, 1979-2 CB 600, suspending issuance of rulings on business continuity pending adoption of the regulations, while Rev. Rul. 79-433, 1979-2 CB 155, suspended Rev. Rul. 63-29, 1963-1 CB 77, pending its revision to reflect the new proposals. Finally, Rev. Rul. 79-434, 1979-2 CB 155, ruled that a corporation that sold its assets and was acquired by an investment company did not satisfy the business continuity requirement (the substance of the transaction was deemed merely to constitute a "purchase of stock" by the transferor). Compare Ltr. Rul. 8027017, [1980] 9 P-H Fed. Taxes ¶ 55,246 (asset sale for cash, followed by transfer of cash to regulated investment company for stock, followed by liquidation; held, §337 applied to first step because second step not a tax-free reorganization under continuity of business enterprise principles; hence, no conflict between §337 and §368).

On Dec. 30, 1980, Regs. §1.368-1(d) was promulgated by T.D. 7745, which provisions essentially adopted intact the 1979 proposed version of these regulations. Several clarifications were made in the final regulations, however. Thus, the continuity of business enterprise principle will be applied to Type B reorganizations, as well as asset acquisitions, see Rev. Rul. 81-92, 1981-1 CB 133. The final regulations also clarified Examples (3) and (5) to limit the various transactions described therein to those that were effected pursuant to the plan or reorganization. Finally, the new regulations state that all the facts and circumstances must be considered in determining whether or not a line of business, or the portion of assets transferred, is "significant." [349.2]

The new regulations are effective for acquisitions occurring thirty days after December 29, 1980. Of special significance is the Treasury's "preamble" to the final regulations (found in Vol. 10, ¶ 6343, 1981 CCH Fed. Tax Serv.), which sets forth its "brief" for the regulations' validity and scope.

[349.2] See also Rev. Rul. 81-247, 1981-2 CB 87 (post-acquisition drop-downs do not violate business continuity); Rev. Rul. 82-34, 1982-1 CB 59 (not apply to a recapitalization).

See generally Fassler, IRS Attacks Tax-Free Reorganizations With Tax-Exempt Bond Funds Following Sale of Assets, 58 Taxes 407 (1980); Beller & Brown, IRS Mounts Double-Barreled Attack on "Cash Reorganizations" With Mutual Funds, 53 J. Tax. 76 (1980); Aidinoff & Lopata, The Continuity of Business Enterprise Requirement and Investment Company Reorganizations, 58 Taxes 914 (1980); Faber, Continuity of Interest and Business Enterprise: Is It Time to Bury Some Sacred Cows? 34 Tax Law. 239 (1981); Bloom, The Resurrection of a Dormant Doctrine: Continuity of Business Enterprise, 7 J. Corp. Tax. 315 (1981); Libin, Continuity of Business Enterprise: The New Regulations, 39 NYU Inst. on Fed. Tax. Ch. 4 (1981); and Westin, Investment Company Reorganization With "Cash Companies" and the Continuity of Business Enterprise Doctrine: One Current View, 16 New Eng. L. Rev. 413 (1981).

Page 14-131:

Add to note 350, end of runover paragraph.

[350] See generally Rev. Rul. 79-250, 1979-2 CB 156 (substance of each of a series of steps will be recognized, and step transaction doctrine not applied, if step has independent economic significance, is not a sham, and was undertaken for a valid business purpose). But compare Rev. Rul. 83-142, 1983-2 CB 68 (disregard transitory interim

steps which would disqualify an otherwise qualified reorganization where steps taken to comply with local law). See also McDonald's of Zion, Inc., 76 TC 972 (1981) (post-fusion stock sales didn't break continuity, even though previously planned and intended; because sales and reorganization not mutually interdependent; end result test of *King Enterprises* rejected). But *McDonald's* was reversed, 688 F.2d 520 (7th Cir. 1982) (continuity broken by planned sales under step transaction principles); see Prusiecki, Continuity of Interest in Tax-Free Mergers: New Opportunities After *McDonald's of Zion,* 55 J. Tax. 378 (1981). See also James H. Johnson, 78 TC 564 (1982) (subsequent sale of stock received in recapitalization not part of recapitalization transaction); ITT & Cos., 77 TC 60 (1981), aff'd per curiam, 704 F.2d 252 (2d Cir. 1983) (conversion transaction not part of prior reorganization transaction in which convertible securities were issued); Chirelstein & Lopata, Recent Developments in the Step-Transaction Doctrine, 60 Taxes 970 (1982).

Further recent step transaction decisions of significance are: Blake v. CIR, 697 F.2d 473 (2d Cir. 1982); Security Indus. Ins. Co. v. US, 702 F.2d 1234 (5th Cir. 1982); and Superior Coach of Fla., 80 TC 895 (1983) (cash purchase of stock, followed by asset fusion transactions linked to destroy continuity of interest).

Add to note 351.

[351] See, e.g., Glacier State Elec. Supply Co., 80 TC 1047 (1983).

Page 14-132:

Add new paragraph 4 to text at end of section.

4. *Current proposals—effect on above doctrines.* Current proposals by the Staff of the Senate Finance Committee, submitted on September 22, 1983, would sharply downgrade in importance (and, in the case of the business purpose and continuity of business enterprise limitations, would repeal these doctrines) in the case of qualified corporate acquisitions (supra new ¶ 14.21, this Supplement). The Staff's proposed new corporate acquisition system would replace considerations of business purpose, continuity of business enterprise, and continuity of proprietary interest, with a specific election system for recognition or nonrecognition treatment at the corporate level. While the step transaction doctrine would continue to have some vitality even under the new elective nonrecognition rules, its role would be a relatively marginal one at most.

¶ 14.52. DISPOSITION OF UNWANTED ASSETS IN CONNECTION WITH A REORGANIZATION

Page 14-132:

Add to note 356.

[356] But recently enacted legislation now requires complete liquidation of the transferor corporation pursuant to the plan of reorganization in order to qualify as a Type C reorganization (unless such liquidation requirement is waived by regulations); the Tax Reform Act of 1984, §63, adding new §368(a)(2)(G) (passed July 18, 1984); there was no comparable provision in the House bill, but the Conference accepted the Senate bill proposal to require liquidation of the acquired corporation in such cases.

Page 14-133:

Add to note 358.

[358] Rev. Rul. 79-273, 1979-2 CB 125 (distribution of stock of unwanted subsidiary in connection with taxable stock purchase via cash reverse merger held a *Zenz* §302(b)(3) complete termination transaction).

Recently enacted legislation lowered the statutory control threshold for nondivisive Type D reorganizations to 50 percent (with §318 attribution) by adopting the control test of §304(c) (i.e., at least 50 percent of vote *or* value, supra ¶ 9.33, this Supplement), thus making it easier to find a reorganization in the above-described transaction; the Tax Reform Act of 1984, §64(a), adding new §368(c)(2) (passed July 18, 1984); there was no comparable provision in the House bill.

Page 14-134:

Add to note 361, first paragraph.

[361] But Rev. Rul. 58-68 was revoked by Rev. Rul. 83-114, 1983-2 CB 66 (not taxable spin-off because of planned merger, or threshold business motivated capital contribution).

Add new note 362.1 to end of first full paragraph of text.

[362.1] But see Rev. Rul. 79-273, 1979-2 CB 125 (former §311(d)(2) protected distributing corporation); for tightening amendments to §311(d)(2) by TEFRA of 1982, see new ¶ 9.64A (this Supplement).

For proposals to repeal §311 entirely, see supra ¶ 7.21, new paragraph 11 (this Supplement) and ¶ 9.64, new paragraph 4 (this Supplement).

Recently enacted legislation in 1984 further tightened (but not completely repeal) §311; see supra ¶ 7.21, new paragraph 12 (this Supplement).

Page 14-135:

Correct second paragraph, fourth line from the bottom.

Change "corporaion" to "corporation."

Page 14-137:

Add to note 369, third paragraph.

[369] NYS Bar Ass'n, Tax Section, Report on the Ancillary Tax Effects of Different Forms of Reorganizations, 34 Tax L. Rev. 477, 527 (1979); Handler, Variations on a Theme: The Disposition of Unwanted Assets, 35 Tax L. Rev. 389 (1980).

Page 14-138:

Add to note 374.

[374] But Rev. Rul. 58-68 was revoked by Rev. Rul. 83-114, 1983-2 CB 66.

Correct fourth line of example (c).

Change "Y" to "Z."

Page 14-140:

Add to note 378.

[378] But Rev. Rul. 58-68 was revoked by Rev. Rul. 83-114, 1983-2 CB 66.

Add new paragraph 3 to text at end of section.

3. *Current proposals.* The Staff of the Senate Finance Committee, in its preliminary report on the reform and simplification of Subchapter C (submitted on September 22, 1983), proposed to completely overhaul the corporate acquisition rules (supra new ¶¶ 11.67A and 14.21, this Supplement). These proposals would specifically permit pre-acquisition tailoring transactions of the type described in this section, without violating the substantially all requirement of those proposals (in effect, the *Elkhorn Coal* doctrine would be repealed under the proposed new acquisition rules).

¶ 14.53.   AFFILIATED CORPORATIONS: SPECIAL ACQUISITION PROBLEMS AND TECHNIQUES

Page 14-141:

Add to note 382, fourth paragraph.

[382] Security Indus. Ins. Co. v. US, 702 F.2d 1234 (5th Cir. 1983)

(cash purchase of stock, liquidation, reincorporation transfer to sister subsidiary not a reorganization; cash purchase killed continuity of interest); Superior Coach of Fla., 80 TC 895 (1983).

Add to end of note 382.

[382] Recent legislation enacted in 1982 (described supra new ¶ 11.47, this Supplement) replaced §334(b)(2) with a new elective provision, §338, under which the parent could elect to have its purchased subsidiary treated as if it had sold its assets in a §337 transaction and then repurchased those assets (without an actual liquidation occuring). This legislation passed as §224 of TEFRA of 1982, P.L. No. 97-248, 96 Stat. 324 (effective generally after August 31, 1982).

Add to note 383.

[383] Under recently enacted legislation in 1982, all actual liquidations under §332 would give rise to §334(b)(1) carryover basis and §381 carryover of tax history treatment. (See annotation to note 382, supra, this Supplement.)

Page 14-142:

Add to note 384, second paragraph.

[384] Pugh, Combining Acquired and Acquiring Corporations and Their Subsidiaries: Some Anomalies of Form and Substance, 35 Tax L. Rev. 359 (1980).

Proposals by the Staff of the Senate Finance Committee (supra new ¶ 14.21 (this Supplement)) would treat the acquisition as a stock acquisition if 80 percent stock control was acquired as the first step in the transaction, regardless of subsequent events.

Page 14-143:

Add to note 391, first paragraph.

[391] See also New York Fruit Auction Corp., 79 TC 564 (1982) (no basis step-up for subsidiary assets on downstream merger of parent into subsidiary after purchase of subsidiary stock; but §338, supra new ¶ 11.47 (this Supplement) would solve this blunder today).

Page 14-144:

Add to note 393.

[393] See also Rev. Rul. 78-397, 1978-2 CB 150 (circular cash flow in §368(a)(2)(D) merger disregarded as transitory step).

Page 14-145:

Add to note 396.

[396] But compare Superior Coach of Fla., Inc., supra note 382 (this

Supplement) (stock purchase by shareholder of acquiring corporation, followed by merger of target into acquiring corporation not a reorganization; continuity killed by stock purchase step).

Page 14-147:

Add to note 401, first paragraph.

[401] But TEFRA amendments to the Type F definition go back to the Rev. Rul. 69-185 rule, and overrule Rev. Rul. 75-561, supra ¶ 14.18 (this Supplement).

Add to text at end of paragraph 3.

But proposals by the Staff of the Senate Finance Committee (supra new ¶ 14.21, this Supplement), would treat all brother-sister fusion acquisitions as mandatory carryover-basis transactions, regardless of the form of the consideration or the structure of the acquisition.

Page 14-149:

Add new note 403.1 at end of paragraph (a) in text.

[403.1] For possible use of §311(a) and §311(d)(2)(A) to effect tax-free exchanges of their respective stock interests, see Rev. Rul. 79-314, 1979-2 CB 132. See also Rev. Rul. 80-101, 1980-1 CB 70 (applying principle of Rev. Rul. 79-314 to situation where one of exchanging corporations was completely liquidated; X owned 70 percent of Y and Y owned 25 percent of X; on complete liquidation of Y, held §§311(a)(2) and 311(d)(2)(A) applied to portion of X stock received back by X on Y's liquidation). But see supra new ¶ 9.64A (this Supplement) for restrictive amendments to §311(d) by TEFRA of 1982, supra note 382 (this Supplement), which overrule these rulings.

Page 14-152:

Add to note 416.

[416] See NYS Bar Ass'n, Tax Section, Report on the Ancillary Tax Effects of Different Forms of Reorganizations, 34 Tax L. Rev. 477, 519 (1979); Murray, How to Avoid Loss of Continuity of Interest Through Stock Remoteness in a Reorganization, 59 J. Tax. 8 (1983).
See also Rev. Rul. 77-449, 1977-2 CB 110 (successive §351 drop-downs per single plan held separate tax-free §351 transactions despite "plan" to pass assets to second-tier subsidiary); Rev. Rul. 83-34, 1983-1 CB 79 (same where first- and second-tier subsidiaries only 80 percent owned); Rev. Rul. 84-30, 1984-1 CB 114 (continuity not violated when stock of acquiring corporation passed upstream to target's grandparent); Murray, IRS Revocation of "Stock Remoteness" Posture May Have Positive Effect on Reorganizations, 60 J. Tax. 352 (1984).

Page 14-154:

Add to note 423.

[423] But see Prop. Regs. §1.358-6 (parent's basis in subsidiary's stock after triangular asset or stock reorganization; generally treat as if a direct acquisition by parent followed by drop-down), and Prop. Regs. §1.1032-2 (extension of §1032 nonrecognition to subsidiary in triangular reorganizations). See supra ¶ 14.33 (this Supplement).

Add new note 424.1 to end of last complete sentence in text.

[424.1] See Rev. Rul. 80-189, 1980-2 CB 106 (subsidiary gets cost basis on purchase of parent's stock from parent's shareholders in §304 (a)(2) transaction).

Compare ITT & Cos., 77 TC 60 (1981), aff'd per curiam, 704 F.2d 252 (2d Cir. 1983) (parent gets cost basis equal to value of its stock upon conversion of subsidiary debt into parent stock) with National Can Corp. v. US, 520 F. Supp. 567 (N.D. Ill. 1981) (parent has no basis for subsidiary's debt on conversion into its stock, aff'd, 687 F.2d 1107 (7th Cir. 1982).

Page 14-155:

Add to note 425.

[425] See also Rev. Rul. 79-273, 1979-2 CB 125 (taxable stock purchase via all cash reverse merger coupled with distribution of stock of unwanted subsidiary treated as §302(b)(3) *Zenz* sale-redemption transaction). See also Prop. Regs. §§1.358-6 and 1.1032-2 (Dec. 29, 1980).

Add to note 426.

[426] But see Prop. Regs. §1.1032-2 (Dec. 29, 1980) (nonrecognition to subsidiary on triangular reorganization acquisition using parent's stock); and Prop. Regs. §1.358-6 (Dec. 29, 1980) (parent's basis for subsidiary's stock after triangular asset or stock reorganization; as if parent acquired assets or stock directly and dropped them into subsidiary). See supra ¶ 14.33 (this Supplement).

Add to text at end of paragraph 5.

Proposals by the Staff of the Senate Finance Committee (supra new ¶ 14.21, this Supplement) would drastically overhaul and simplify the corporate acquisition rules of present law. Under these proposals the following significant changes would be made: (1) all triangular acquisitions would be classified as stock acquisitions under the proposed new system; (2) remote parent stock would constitute qualified consideration so long as the acquiring corporation, or corporations, was in a direct chain with the corporation whose stock was utilized in the acquisition; (3) Section 1032 would be expanded to include nonrecognition on the use of parent (or grandparent, etc.) stock, whether or not the acquisition was tax-free; and (4) a parent's basis for stock in a controlled subsidiary would be determined by reference to the subsidiary's net asset basis (i.e., adjusted basis, less liabilities) in all cases.

¶ 14.54. REINCORPORATIONS: LIQUIDATION VS. REORGANIZATION

Page 14-157:

Add to note 431.

[431] But see new §346(b), added by §222(d) of TEFRA of 1982, P.L. No. 97-248, 96 Stat. 324, granting broad regulatory authority to IRS to deal with various transactions that have the effect of a partial liquidation. See supra ¶¶ 9.50 and 9.54 (this Supplement).

Page 14-159:

Add to note 437, first paragraph.

[437] See also new §346(b), added by TEFRA of 1982, supra note 431 (this Supplement); supra ¶ 9.54 (this Supplement).

Page 14-160:

Add to note 440.

[440] Atlas Tool Co. v. CIR, 614 F.2d 860 (3d Cir. 1980) (no stock exchange necessary where existing 100 percent control).

Add to note 441.

[441] Atlas Tool Co. v. CIR, supra note 440 (this Supplement) (Tax Court finding of D reorganization affirmed); Rose v. US, 640 F.2d 1030 (9th Cir. 1981) (similar to *Atlas Tool* and same results); Viereck v. US, 1983-2 USTC ¶ 9664 (Cl. Ct. 1983) (applied operating-assets test; also transfer of beneficial *use* of assets sufficient to sustain finding of Type D reorganization; constructive acquisition sufficient).

See also Smothers Co. v. US, 1979-1 USTC ¶ 9216 (S.D. Tex. 1979) ("substantially all" test met even though only 15 percent of assets transferred because transferred assets were all of the operating assets), aff'd, 642 F.2d 894 (5th Cir. 1981). Compare Capital Sales, Inc., 71 TC 416 (1978) (no "transfer" where principal asset cancelled and re-issued to affiliate), rev'd, sub nom. Simon v. CIR, 644 F.2d 339 (5th Cir. 1981); Prop. Regs. §1.368-1(d), discussed supra ¶ 14.51 (this Supplement).

Query whether the new business continuity regulations, Regs. §1.368-1(d) (supra ¶ 14.51 (this Supplement)), will have any unintended collateral effects in the liquidation-reincorporation area? See Rose v. US, supra.

Page 14-161:

Add to note 443.

[443] Atlas Tool Co. v. CIR, supra note 440 (this Supplement) (boot dividend limited to transferor's earnings account); Viereck v. US, supra note 441 (this Supplement) (assets distributed and then made available to transferee still part of boot dividend to shareholder-distributee; not transferred so as to reduce amount of boot dividend, even though constructively transferred for purposes of reorganization definition; not partial liquidation either, because no contraction of business enterprise).

Add to note 444.

[444] Accord with *American Mfg. Co.* is Central Soya Co., Inc. v. US, 1980-1 USTC ¶ 9367 (N.D. Ind. 1980).

Page 14-162:

Add to note 445, second paragraph.

[445] Accord with *Griswold* is Harold C. Lang, ¶ 82,149 P-H Memo TC. But compare Security Indus. Ins. Co. v. US, 702 F.2d 1234 (5th Cir. 1983) (seems essentially contra to *Griswold* and *Lang*; stock purchase, liquidation, reincorporation held not a reorganization on continuity grounds).

Legislation enacted in 1982, the Corporate Takeover Tax Act (supra ¶ 11.47, this Supplement), replaced §334(b)(2) with an elective basis step-up mechanism in new §338, thus avoiding the necessity of an initial liquidation. This legislation passed as §224 of TEFRA of 1982, supra note 431 (this Supplement).

Page 14-163:

Add to text after sentence ending with note 451.

Recently enacted legislation in 1984 [451.1] lowered the statutory control threshold for nondivisive Type D reorganizations to 50 percent of vote *or* value in conformity with the control line of §304(c)

[451.1] The Tax Reform Act of 1984, §64(a), adding new §368 (c)(2) (effective on the date of enactment, July 18, 1984). This provision was contained only in the Senate bill, but was accepted in the final conference version of the Act. See Eustice, The Tax Reform Act of 1984, ¶ 3.03[4].

(with §318 attribution rules), thus considerably broadening the scope of this provision and overruling the decisions in *Gallagher*, *Berghash*, and *Breech*.

Page 14-164:

Add to note 453.

[453] Revenue Procedure 72-9 was superseded by Rev. Proc. 79-14, 1979-1 CB 496, which was superseded by Rev. Proc. 80-22, 1980-1 CB 654, and is currently found in Rev. Proc. 84-22, 1984-1 CB 449.

See also new §346(b), added by TEFRA of 1982, supra note 431 (this Supplement).

Add to note 454.

[454] But Rev. Proc. 84-75, 1984-46 IRB 53, amended the no ruling section of Rev. Proc. 84-22 to an "ordinarily no ruling" situation where more than 20 percent common control exists; thus, a liquidation ruling may be obtained even here (apparently, the 1984 Act control amendments inspired this relaxation).

Add to text after sentence ending with note 455.

But the Tax Reform Act of 1984 [455.1] conformed the nondivisive Type D reorganization control definition to the §304(c) control line in new §368(c)(2) (i.e., 50 percent of vote *or* value, with attribution to and from 5 percent shareholders).

[455.1] Supra note 451.1 (this Supplement). See Eustice, The Tax Reform Act of 1984, ¶ 3.04[4].

Page 14-165:

Add to text after sentence ending with note 456.

But the nondivisive Type D control definition was conformed to the control line of §304(c) by the Tax Reform Act of 1984 [456.1] in new §368(c)(2).

[456.1] Supra note 451.1 (this Supplement).

Add to note 458, first paragraph.

[458] See Capital Sales, Inc., supra note 441 (this Supplement) (no "transfer" where principal asset, a franchise, cancelled and reissued to sister corporation; taxpayer had no control over cancellation and reissuance of franchise), rev'd sub nom. Simon v. CIR, supra note 441 (this Supplement).

Add to note 458, second paragraph.

[458] Query what the effect of the new business continuity regulations, Regs. §1.368-1(d), will have on this issue. These provisions may well provide taxpayers with a ready mechanism for avoiding reorganization treatment, at least where the corporation's "historic business" activities and assets are significantly altered. See Note, The Role of the Continuity of Business Enterprise Requirement in Liquidation-Reincorporations, 35 Tax Law. 737 (1982); and Mandelkern, "Continuity of Business Enterprise" and the Liquidation-Reincorporation Battle: Is Treas. Reg. § 1.368-1(d) a Trojan Horse? 34 U. Fla. L. Rev. 822 (1982).

Page 14-166:

Add to note 460.

[460] See also new §346(b), added by TEFRA of 1982, supra note 431 (this Supplement); supra ¶ 9.54 (this Supplement).

Page 14-167:

Add to note 464, second paragraph.

[464] Security Indus. Ins. Co. v. US, supra note 445 (this Supplement) (no Type F where stock purchase for cash; purchase killed continuity of interest).

Page 14-169:

Add to note 468.

[468] But see Security Indus. Ins. Co. v. US, supra note 445 (this Supplement) (no Type F on purchase of stock by holding company, liquidation of purchased subsidiary, and retransfer of its assets to sister subsidiary).

Page 14-170:

Add to text at end of paragraph 4.

Proposals by the Staff of the Senate Finance Committee submitted on September 22, 1983, would materially expand the scope of the Type D reorganization and otherwise combat the liquidation-reincorporation problem by the following amendments: (1) the control line for the nondivisive Type D reorganization would be lowered from 80 percent to 50 percent (with §318 attribution as well); (2) asset acquisitions from related transferors (viz., 50 percent common ownership, with §318), could be denied a cost-basis election (i.e., carryover basis, and carryover of tax history would be mandatory); (3) the boot dividend-within-gain limitation would be repealed; and (4) the earnings and profits limitation for dividend distributions would be repealed.

Recently enacted legislation in 1984 [470.1] adopted only the first of these proposals, lowering the control definition line for nondivisive Type D reorganizations to 50 percent (with §318 attribution, but only to and from 5 percent shareholders), in conformity with the control definition in §304(c).

[470.1] Supra note 451.1 (this Supplement).

Page 14-171:

Add new note 471.1 to end of example (b).

[471.1] But X may be denied §337 treatment under *TASCO* (Telephone Answering Serv. Co., 63 TC 423 (1974), aff'd, 546 F.2d 423 (4th Cir. 1976), cert. denied, 431 US 914 (1977), discussed supra note 460) and §346(b) on the ground that X did not completely liquidate (viz., the transaction, at best, had only a *partial* liquidation effect). This approach would result in full recognition to X (but Y would still get a cost basis for the assets, and A would get capital gain).

Add new note 471.2 to end of example (e).

[471.2] But recently enacted legislation (supra note 451.1 (this Supplement)) now will apply §318 to the Type D control definition (and also will lower the control threshold to 50 percent), so that reorganization and boot dividend treatment will apply to X and A, and Y will take a carryover basis for the acquired assets. Thus, *Berghash* has been overruled.

¶ 14.55. ASSUMPTION OF LIABILITIES: EFFECT ON REORGANIZATION STATUS

Page 14-173:

Add to note 475.

[475] Compare Rev. Rul. 78-330, 1978-2 CB 147 (parent's cancellation of subsidiary's debt to avoid §357(c) gain on merger of subsidiary into another affiliate respected; not §357(b) tax avoidance). Rev. Rul. 79-289, 1979-2 CB 145 (§357(e) not applicable to a Type F reorganization even though transaction also a Type D).

Add new note 475.1 to text at end of second full paragraph.

[475.1] See NYS Bar Ass'n, Tax Section, Report on the Ancillary Tax Effects of Different Forms of Reorganizations, 34 Tax L. Rev. 477, 478 (1979); Levitan, Dealing With Liabilities in a Reorganization, 39 NYU Inst. Fed. Tax. Ch. 8 (1981).

Add to note 476.

[476] See Rev. Rul. 73-301, 1973-2 CB 215 (definition of liability in partnership context under §752; contractual obligation to perform services not a §752 liability).

Page 14-176:

Add to note 488, first paragraph.

[488] See Rev. Rul. 79-155, 1979-1 CB 153 (merger of T into P's controlled subsidiary, S; P and S jointly assumed T's debts and also substantially modified terms thereof; held, §357(a) assumption nonrecognition for T, and §354(a)(1), "exchange" nonrecognition for security holders).

Page 14-177:

Add to note 489.

[489] See also Rev. Rul. 80-240, 1980-2 CB 116 (mere transitory accommodation borrowing in "agency" capacity not true liability assumption transaction; taxpayer not acting for own benefit here; merely assisting in meeting nontax requirements).

¶ 14.56. CONTINGENT CONSIDERATION ACQUISITIONS AND RELATED PROBLEMS

Page 14-181:

Add to note 502.

[502] Rev. Proc. 84-42, 1984-1 CB 521 added an additional guideline for contingent stock and escrowed stock rulings: the issue of contingent stock or release of escrowed stock must not be triggered by events within control of the shareholders, or by an IRS audit, and the trigger mechanism must be objective and readily ascertainable.

Page 14-179:

Add to note 496, second paragraph.

[496] Banoff, Unwinding or Rescinding a Transaction: Good Tax Planning or Tax Fraud, 62 Taxes 942 (1983).

Page 14-182:

Add to note 507, first paragraph.

[507] Jerrold L. Kingsley, 72 TC 1095 (1979), aff'd 662 F.2d 539 (9th Cir. 1981) (and cases cited). The rates under §483 were raised to 9 percent (minimum test line) and 10 percent (imputed) by T.D. 7781 (effective July 1, 1981). But see amendments by the Tax Reform Act of 1984, supra ¶ 4.23 (this Supplement).

Page 14-183:

Add to text at end of paragraph (g).

Recently enacted legislation in 1984 [508.1] largely supplanted §483 with expanded coverage of the OID rules in new §1274; but this provision only applies if the obligation to issue contingent stock is treated as a "debt instrument" under new §1275(a)(1) (which defines such term as "any obligation"). In any event, the imputed interest characterization rule of §483 now will be computed in the same manner as under the OID rules, although the *timing* rules would differ under these two provisions (OID interest is taxed currently on a compound economic accrual basis, while §483 interest is taxable under the normal accounting rules). [508.2]

[508.1] The Tax Reform Act of 1984, §41, adding new §§1274 and 1275 and amending §483; P.L. No. 98-369, 98 Stat. 678 (enacted July 18, 1984). See new ¶ 4.23 (this Supplement).

[508.2] The amount of imputed interest under the two provisions would be the same however, since §483 imputed interest would be under the same formula as §1274 issue discount.

Contingent stock transactions presumably will be handled under the contingent payment rules of §483(g), although new §1275(d) similarly envisions application of the new OID rules to contingent payment obligations. Moreover, the OID rules specifically take priority over §483; §483(d)(1).

Page 14-184:

Add to note 510.

[510] See also Jacobs, Escrows and Their Tax Consequences, 39 NYU Inst. on Fed. Tax. Ch. 5 (1981); Fleming, Rethinking Contingent Price Reorganizations, 9 J. Corp. Tax. 3 (1982).

Add to note 511.

[511] But see Feifer v. US, 500 F. Supp. 102 (N.D. Ga. 1980) (§483 not applicable to release of escrowed stock even though taxpayer's voting rights restricted).

Add to note 512.

[512] See also Rev. Proc. 84-42, supra note 502 (this Supplement), for additional guidelines applicable to contingent stock and escrowed stock rulings.

Add to note 514.

[514] See Rev. Rul. 78-376, 1978-2 CB 149 (in addition to recog-

nition of gain or loss on the forfeiture, basis of remaining shares stepped up by value of shares forfeited).

Page 14-185:

Add to note 516.

[516] See Rev. Rul. 83-73, 1983-1 CB 84.

Page 14-187:

Add to note 525.

[525] See Rev. Rul. 80-58, 1980-1 CB 181, for the Service's treatment of rescissions generally (no gain or loss if return to status quo in same taxable year; otherwise, unwinding transaction a taxable event).

Page 14-190:

Add to note 535.

[535] Rev. Rul. 83-73, 1983-1 CB 84, so holds (purchase price adjustment per indemnity agreement).

Page 14-191:

Add to note 539.

[539] See also Rev. Rul. 72-198, 1972-1 CB 223 (premium ordinary income to grantor on lapse of option to acquire grantor's own stock); Rev. Rul. 80-134, 1980-1 CB 187 (unilateral extension of exercise date by grantor as lapse of old warrant). But § 57(a) of the Tax Reform Act of 1984 extended §1032 protection to the corporate grantor on the cancellation or lapse of options to acquire its stock.

Add new note 539.1 to end of first complete paragraph.

[539.1] If the grantor receives its option premium in kind (i.e., in the optionee's voting stock), and resells that stock before the acquisition takes place, taxability of the sales proceeds presumably could be "suspended" until such time as the option is exercised or lapses.

¶ 14.57. QUASI-REORGANIZATIONS: NONQUALIFYING, OR TAXABLE, "REORGANIZATIONS"

Page 14-192:

Add to note 540, first paragraph, following West-Shore Fuel *citation.*

[540] *West-Shore Fuel* was affirmed, 598 F.2d 1236 (2d Cir. 1979)

(no §453 for shareholders; merger transaction a corporate-level asset sale, not a shareholder-level stock sale).

Add to note 540, second paragraph.

540 See Tufts, The Taxable Merger, 7 J. Corp. Tax. 342 (1981).

Add new heading.

¶ 14.58. INSOLVENCY REORGANIZATIONS— COLLATERAL ASPECTS

Proposals introduced by a House Ways and Means Select Sub-committee on November 1, 1979 (H.R. 5043, §4, the Bankruptcy Tax Act of 1979), reported in revised form by the full Ways and Means Committee on March 12, 1980 (the Bankruptcy Tax Act of 1980), passed by the House on March 24, 1980, reported by the Senate Finance Committee on November 19, 1980, and finally enacted in December 1980, significantly revised the tax treatment of insolvency reorganizations, which matters were considered supra ¶ 14.20, this Supplement. The other principal section of the Act, Section 2, drastically overhauled the debt cancellation rules of prior law in §§108 and 1017 (for descriptions of prior law, see articles supra ¶ 14.05, note 11). While these provisions were not technically part of the tax-free reorganization provisions of Subchapter C, they frequently arise in the context of an insolvency reorganization proceeding, are an integral aspect of that proceeding, and, in many cases, may be even more significant in their tax impact to the respective parties than the Subchapter C rules. It is for this reason that they are considered at this point.

The initial version of Section 2(a) of H.R. 5043 (proposed by the House in November of 1979) substantially revised §108(a) by strictly limiting the exclusion for gains attributable to the discharge of indebtedness to insolvency situations where (a) the discharge occurred in a title 11 proceeding (i.e., the debt was discharged in a Bankruptcy Act proceeding pursuant to a court approved plan), or (b) the debtor taxpayer was insolvent (viz., liabilities exceeded the value of the debtor's assets). In the latter case, the exclusion would be limited by §108(a)(3) to the extent that the debtor was insolvent immediately prior to the discharge. In 1980, however, these proposals were revised by the House to continue the elective exclusion—basis reduction treatment for gains derived by solvent debtors from the discharge of "qualified business indebtedness,"

§§108(a)(1)(C), 108(c), and 108(d)(4) (in which case the basis of *depreciable* property only must be reduced, to the extent thereof, if basis reduction treatment is affirmatively elected by the debtor in the manner prescribed by §108(d)(8)).

The key provision of the initially proposed version of §108, however, was §108(b) which initially reduced various tax attributes of the debtor in a prescribed order (i.e., first, net operating losses of the year of discharge and carryovers *to* such year, then ITC carryovers to or from such year, and then capital losses of such year and carryovers to such year) to the extent the debt cancellation gain was excluded from gross income under §108(a). If any remaining exclusion existed after the above reductions, then basis of the debtor's property was to be reduced under §1017. Such reductions were to be made dollar for dollar (except for credits, where the reduction was 50 cents for each dollar of exclusion). These reductions were to be made after the tax was determined for the year of discharge, current year's losses were reduced before carryovers, and carryovers were reduced on a FIFO basis.

The later revised version of §108, however, provided an election, in new §108(b)(5), for the debtor to reduce the basis of its *depreciable* property before any reduction in tax attributes. The stated purpose of this amendment was to give the debtor "flexibility" in determining whether it wanted to preserve either its net operating loss carryovers, etc., or its depreciation deductions following the debt discharge transaction. To the extent that a debtor elected to reduce its basis for depreciable property (under either §108(b)(5), or §§108(c) and 108(d)(4), revised §1017(d) subjected such reductions to recapture rules similar to §§1245 and 1250, as the case may be, on an early disposition of such property.

The House version of proposed §108(e)(1) provided that the insolvency exceptions of §108(a) were exclusive. However, §§108 (e)(2) and 108(e)(5) provided two additional exceptions, apart from the general exclusion of §108(a): first, reduction of purchase-money debt of a solvent purchaser would be treated as a purchase price adjustment; second, income would not be recognized from the discharge of undeducted expense liabilities. Presumably this latter exception from gross income would not trigger the tax attribute reduction rules of §108(b). Finally, §108(e)(4) provided that debt acquired by "related" persons would be deemed to have been acquired directly by the debtor.

The revised House version of §108 thus treated debt cancellation gains of solvent debtors in substantially the same manner as those of insolvent debtors, affording to both the election either to reduce the basis of depreciable assets (subject to later recapture of such reductions under §§1245 and 1250) or, by not so electing, to cause its various tax attributes (e.g., loss carryovers) to be reduced in the prescribed statutory order of §108(b)(2) (in the case of insolvent debtors) or be currently taxed (in the case of solvent debtors).

Another major substantive change proposed by the House version of the Act was in §108(f), which removed the protection of §§1032 and 118 for corporate debtors that discharged their debts by issuing additional stock or by means of a capital contribution of the debt. Debt cancelled by the issuance of stock was to be treated as if it had been cancelled for cash equal to the value of the stock; debt cancelled in a capital contribution was treated as if it had been paid in cash equal to the creditor's *basis* for the cancelled debt. The first of these rules was inapplicable, however, if the debt was a security within the meaning of §165(g)(2) (so no partial worthlessness deduction could be claimed therefor by the creditor under §166), and the debt constituted a security for purposes of §354 (so that gain or loss would not be recognized to the creditor on the exchange transaction). For purposes of this provision, stock of a parent of the debtor would be treated as stock of the debtor and the "debtor" includes a successor corporation. To the extent gain was deemed to be realized under this provision (whether by a solvent or an insolvent debtor), it was subject to the elective basis reduction or the tax attribute reduction rules of §108(b)(5) or §108(c) noted above.

To illustrate: If D Corp. bought in its "nonsecurity" debt of $100 by issuing stock worth $60, D is deemed to receive $40 of income as a result of the transaction. If the value of the stock was $100, no income would result. If the debt was contributed to D's capital (without the issuance of additional stock by D), income to D would result to the extent the face of the debt exceeded the creditor's basis therefor. If the cancelled debt constituted a security under §165(g)(2), and if the debt for stock exchange qualified for nonrecognition treatment under §354, no debt cancellation income would result from a debt for stock exchange transaction. To the extent income was realized as a result of proposed §108(f), however, it was subject to the treatment prescribed by §§108(a), 108(b), and 108(c).

To the extent income was excluded under §108(a) and a basis reduction is required under §108(b)(2)(D), §108(b)(5), or §108(c), §1017 would take hold (though no longer on an elective basis) and require the basis of the debtor's property to be reduced pursuant to regulations prescribed under this provision (as is the case under present law if §1017 is elected). Basis reduction was limited to the excess of the aggregate basis of properties held by the taxpayer after the discharge over unpaid liabilities (viz., basis cannot be reduced below zero, nor below the amount of the debtor's remaining liabilities). If excluded debt exceeded available property basis, no income would result to the debtor if it was insolvent (although the Service took a contrary position under prior law, see supra ¶ 11.69). The revised version of §108, however, specifically limited the §108(a) exclusion for *elective* basis reductions to depreciable assets to the amount of aggregate asset bases; see §§108 (b)(5)(B), 108(c)(2). Finally, §1017(c)(2) provided that a basis reduction under §1017 did not trigger recapture of investment credits under §47 (thus overruling a contrary position taken by the Service).[541] To the extent that the basis of any property was required to be reduced (either under §108(b)(2)(D), or an election under §108(b)(5) or §108(c) and §108(d)(4)), §1017(d) provided that recapture rules similar to §§1245 and 1250 would apply on the early disposition of such basis-reduced properties.

These provisions were effective for all transactions in any bankruptcy or similar proceeding commencing after October 1, 1979; they would apply to any other transaction occurring after 1980.

In favorably reporting H.R. 5043 on November 19, 1980, the Senate Finance Committee made the following changes in the House version of the bill:

(1) The stock-for-debt rules (though *not* the capital contribution rules) of §108(f)(1) were dropped, thus continuing

---

[541] But see Panhandle Eastern Pipeline Co. v. US, 654 F.2d 35 (Ct. Cl. 1981) (no ITC recapture on §1017 basis reduction); accord, Carolina, Clinchfield & O. Ry., 82 TC 888 (1984); Rev. Rul. 84-134, 1984-37 IRB 4 (revoking earlier rulings to the contrary).

the rule of present law that §1032 precludes any tax consequences to the debtor corporation; [542]

(2) An ordinary income recapture rule was provided in §108 (e)(7) where the stock received by the creditor in satisfaction of debts is later disposed of (the recapture amount is equal to the creditor's ordinary deduction on the satisfaction transaction);

(3) Foreign tax credit carryovers were added to the tax attribute list of §108(b)(2);

(4) Debtors could also elect to reduce basis of "inventory" real estate as if it were depreciable property, under §1017 (b)(3)(E);

(5) Moreover, parent corporations filing consolidated returns could apply the depreciable property basis election to stock of their subsidiaries if the subsidiaries consented to reduce the basis of their depreciable assets under §1017 (b)(3)(D); and

(6) The effective date was pushed forward generally to 1981 unless taxpayers elected the earlier October 1, 1979 date.

On the floor of the Senate, however, the effective date for the tax attribute reductions in §108(b)(2) was delayed for another year (until 1982) under a special transition rule adopted by the full Senate (but this rule applied only to insolvent taxpayers).

This version of the bill ultimately passed on December 13, 1980.[543]

---

[542] But see new note 188.1 at ¶ 14.17 (this Supplement). But recently enacted legislation in 1984 now provides for debt cancellation gain by solvent corporate debtors who cancel debt with stock worth less than the face of the debt; the Tax Reform Act of 1984, §59(a), adding new §108(e)(10). This provision passed the House on April 11, 1984 (but there was no comparable provision in the Senate bill), and was accepted by the Conference in the final legislation (which passed on July 18, 1984).

[543] See Asofsky, Discharge of Indebtedness Income in Bankruptcy After the Bankruptcy Tax Act of 1980, 27 St. L. L. Rev. 583 (1983); and Bacon, Rescue Planning for the Failing or Bankrupt Company, 61 Taxes 931 (1983).

CUMULATIVE TABLE OF PARALLEL CASE REPORT CITATIONS

To enable the user to refer to whichever federal court report system is most accessible, this table lists parallel AFTR and USTC service citations for every federal report citation given in the volume. Cases that are not printed in one of the official federal reports are cited to the AFTR service, and this table lists the parallel USTC citations. Blanks indicate recent developments for which that reporter citation was unavailable at press time.

[Columns should be read across.]

US		AFTR		USTC	
Vol.	Page	Vol.	Page	Vol.	Par.
158	601	3	2602		
220	107	3	2834		
220	187	3	2853		
245	418	3	2959	1	14
247	339	3	2992	1	20
252	189	3	3020	1	32
257	156	3	3123	1	54
265	242	4	3986	1	94
268	536	5	5393	1	137
268	628	5	5398	1	139
269	110	5	5663	1	143
275	175	6	7072	1	263
279	716	7	8875	1	408
281	111	8	10287	2	496
283	404	9	1453	2	736
286	319	11	12	3	938
287	462	11	1112	3	1023
288	406	12	15	3	1064
291	163	13	857	4	1220
292	210	13	1168	4	1277
292	435	13	1180	4	1292
293	282	14	705	35–1	9011
293	295	14	703	35–1	9010
293	465	14	1191	35–1	9043
296	200	16	1126	36–1	9012

US		AFTR		USTC	
Vol.	Page	Vol.	Page	Vol.	Par.
296	344	16	1274	36–1	9020
296	362			36–1	9021
296	365	16	1272	36–1	9023
296	369	16	1270	36–1	9022
296	374	16	1262	36–1	9019
296	378	16	1258	36–1	9015
296	387	16	1264	36–1	9016
298	441	17	1213	36–1	9294
301	385	19	486	37–1	9300
302	63	19	1201	37–2	9532
302	238	19	1226	37–2	9571
302	454	19	1240	38–1	9019
302	573	19	1253	38–1	9040
302	609	19	1258	38–1	9050
303	564	20	1041	38–1	9215
304	282	20	1269	38–2	9312
306	436	22	300	39–1	9410
306	522	22	307	39–1	9432
308	355	23	784	40–1	9123
308	415	23	789	40–1	9150
308	473	23	800	40–1	9160
308	488	23	808	40–1	9161
309	331			40–1	9265
311	112	24	1058	40–2	9787
311	527	24	1087	41–1	9168
313	247	25	1236	41–1	9427
314	701			41–2	9644
315	44	28	215	42–1	9222
315	179	28	567	42–1	9245
315	194	28	573	42–1	9248
316	394	29	196	42–2	9498
316	450	29	193	42–2	9512
318	604	30	1087	43–1	9363
318	693	30	1091	43–1	9379
319	98	30	1096	43–1	9418
319	436	30	1291	43–1	9464
319	590	30	1310	43–1	9486
320	489	31	773	44–1	9108
320	516	31	956	44–1	9127
324	331	33	593	45–1	9215
324	393	33	599	45–1	9234
325	283	33	832	45–1	9311
326	521	34	314	46–1	9133
327	404	34	811	46–1	9188
331	1	35	776	47–1	9217

US		AFTR		USTC	
Vol.	*Page*	*Vol.*	*Page*	*Vol.*	*Par.*
331	210	35	963	47–1	9241
331	737	35	1190	47–1	9288
333	496	36	604	48–1	5922
336	410	37	827	49–1	9204
336	422	37	834	49–1	9223
337	369	37	1363	49–1	9310
338	451	38	978	50–1	9129
339	583	39	327	50–1	5958
343	934	41	590	52–1	66030
344	6	42	649	52–1	9152
345	247	43	367	53–1	9293
350	46	47	1789	55–2	9746
352	82	50	502	57–1	9200
353	382	51	43	57–1	9691

US		AFTR2d		USTC	
Vol.	*Page*	*Vol.*	*Page*	*Vol.*	*Par.*
356	27	1	1158	58–1	9368
356	30	1	1154	58–1	9366
356	260	1	1394	58–1	9428
358	498	3	697	59–1	9262
364	361	6	5851	60–2	9785
366	380	7	1451	61–1	9462
368	337	8	5967	62–1	9104
370	65	9	1625	62–2	9509
373	193	11	1454	63–1	9466
374	65	11	1606	63–2	9531
376	358	13	962	61–4	9330
380	563	15	790	65–1	9375
381	54	15	836	65–1	9387
381	68	15	842	65–1	9386
383	272	17	470	66–1	9280
383	569	17	604	66–1	9317
383	687	17	633	66–1	9319
387	456	19	1891	67–2	12472
391	83	21	1329	68–1	9383
397	301	25	827	70–1	9289
397	572	25	964	70–1	9348
397	580	25	967	70–1	9349
398	1	25	1177	70–1	9405
405	93	29	609	72–1	9259
405	394	29	781	72–1	9292A
412	401	32	5042	73–1	9478

US		AFTR2d		USTC	
Vol.	Page	Vol.	Page	Vol.	Par.
414	982	32	5968	73–2	9730
417	673	34	5200	74–2	9511
422	617	36	5200	75–2	9557
—	—	51	1132	83–1	9328
—	—	53	148, 660	84–1	9240

F.2d		AFTR		USTC	
Vol.	Page	Vol.	Page	Vol.	Par.
24	520	6	7334		
28	803	7	8228	1	333
32	37	7	8668	1	385
33	75	7	8783	5	1569
43	298	9	71	2	573
45	57	9	505		
57	413	10	1558		
60	931	11	854	3	978
60	937	11	857	3	980
67	876	13	415	3	1185
69	809	13	806		
70	655	13	1052	4	1283
71	150	14	259		
71	342	14	270		
74	226	14	828	35–1	9017
74	1015	15	123		
76	106	15	398	35–1	9229
76	442	15	1137	35–1	9166
78	156	16	330	35–2	9442
78	513	16	416	35–2	9484
79	234	16	610	35–2	9547
80	573	17	86	36–1	9030
80	872	17	138	36–1	9048
81	73	17	186	36–1	9068
81	971	17	452	36–1	9077
82	473	17	660	36–1	9195
84	23	17	1245	36–2	9355
84	64	17	1256	36–2	9335
84	415	17	1308	36–2	9324
84	431	17	1313	36–2	9338
84	760	18	207	36–2	9430
85	819	18	520	36–2	9451
87	663	18	791	37–1	9088
88	156	19	96	37–1	9109
88	567	19	158	37–1	9159
88	616	19	174	37–1	9164
90	12	19	769	37–1	9249
90	91	19	810	37–2	9314
93	826	20	599	38–1	9028

F.2d		AFTR		USTC	
Vol.	Page	Vol.	Page	Vol.	Par.
93	883	20	609	38–1	9030
95	404	20	1114	38–1	9171
95	732	20	1301	38–1	9238
96	177	21	103	38–1	9297
99	478	21	1140	38–2	9535
100	415	22	121	38–2	9607
100	418	22	124	38–2	9608
103	283	22	1062	39–1	9481
103	359	22	1071	39–1	9427
103	487	22	1083	39–1	9486
104	177	23	34	39–1	9504
104	865	23	119	39–2	9568
105	311	23	169	39–2	9573
107	390	23	892	39–2	9741
109	479	24	225	40–1	9234
109	933	24	426	40–1	9280
111	961	25	23	40–1	9486
112	508	25	97	40–2	9512
113	103	25	340	40–2	9561
113	718	25	447	40–2	9592
115	337	25	992	40–2	9579
115	481	25	1020	40–2	9767
115	662	25	1044	40–2	9802
116	187	26	1	40–2	9801
116	642	26	189	41–1	9167
116	718	26	197	40–2	9826
116	937	26	223	40–2	9710
120	424	27	452	41–2	9533
120	622	27	491	41–2	9524
120	845	27	529	41–2	9521
122	268	27	837	41–2	9631
122	590	27	887	41–2	9643
122	545	27	892	41–2	9644
123	742	28	404	41–2	9752
125	906	28	1179	42–1	9310
127	514	29	325	42–1	9452
128	885	29	741	42–2	9547
129	684	29	965	42–2	9555
130	791	29	1183	42–2	9648
130	797	29	1189	42–2	9649
130	1011	30	41	42–2	9697
131	50	30	220	42–2	9691
131	426	30	296	42–2	9742
133	308	30	767	43–1	9282
133	990	30	1008	43–1	9293

F.2d		AFTR		USTC	
Vol.	Page	Vol.	Page	Vol.	Par.
135	310	30	1433	43–1	9334
135	882	31	80	43–1	9447
136	22	31	90	43–1	9455
136	812	31	230	43–2	9535
137	128	31	355	43–2	9551
137	306	31	390	43–2	9556
137	424	31	394	43–2	9540
137	537	31	441	43–2	9529
137	600	31	456	43–2	9560
138	27	31	627	43–2	9519
138	104	31	632	43–2	9595
139	280	31	1056	43–2	9682
140	382	32	56	44–1	9170
141	452, 455	32	418	44–1	9226
141	774	32	492	44–1	9254
142	216	32	564	44–1	9262
142	236	32	569	44–2	9419
142	449	32	672		
142	624	32	701	44–1	9235
143	436	32	989	44–2	9371
143	580	32	1026	44–2	9367
143	810	32	1083	44–2	9388
143	1007	32	1111	44–2	9417
144	313	32	1197	44–2	9414
144	466	32	1219	44–2	9407
144	487	32	1237	44–2	9442
145	521	33	74		
145	692	33	115	44–2	9508
145	1001	33	150	44–2	9522
146	177	33	351	44–2	9527
146	970	33	456	45–1	9145
147	376	33	681	45–1	9169
147	602	33	718	45–1	9162
148	452	33	955	45–1	9230
148	599	33	1131	45–1	9233
149	739	33	1468	45–2	9325
149	968	33	1478	45–2	9324
150	334	33	1536	45–2	9353
151	441	34	335	45–2	9418
151	517	34	343	45–2	9403
152	654	34	638	46–1	9124
152	570	34	615	46–1	9120
153	323	34	860	46–1	9193
153	602	34	931	46–1	9170
153	681	34	1025	46–1	9177

F.2d		AFTR		USTC	
Vol.	*Page*	*Vol.*	*Page*	*Vol.*	*Par.*
155	23	34	1292	46–1	9231
156	398	34	1544	46–2	9312
157	321	35	117	46–2	9322
159	324	35	680	47–1	9154
159	921	35	868	47–1	9165
160	84	35	873	47–1	9184
160	150	35	970	47–1	9187
161	817	35	1373	47–1	9265
162	155	35	1427	47–1	9292
162	249	35	1443	47–2	5911
162	628	35	1496	47–1	9294
162	753	35	1557	47–2	9344
163	316, 319	36	48	47–2	9348
164	462	36	423	47–2	9395
165	75	36	645		
166	27	36	741	48–1	9165
167	214	36	929	48–1	9237
167	586	36	959	48–1	9251
168	284	36	1037	48–1	9280
168	957	36	1161	48–2	9329
168	1004	36	1183	48–2	9317
169	186	37	150	48	9346
170	423	37	532	48–2	9399
170	911	37	573	48–2	9415
171	457	37	654	49–1	9109
172	638	37	907	49–1	9176
172	896	37	958	49–1	9205
172	904	37	960	49–1	9168
173	461	37	1137	49–1	9211
174	569	37	1485	49–1	9267
175	422	38	82	49–2	9341
175	641	38	97	49–1	9321
175	772	38	124	49–2	9361
176	190	38	281	49–2	9370
176	570	38	365	49–2	9337
176	646	38	377	49–2	9377
176	573	38	368	49–2	5941
177	513	38	820	49–2	9466, 9471
177	706	38	835	49–2	9443
177	819	38	841	49–2	9470
178	10	38	1014	49–2	9486
178	769	38	1223	50–1	9131
178	987	38	1248	50–1	9123
180	357	39	7	50–1	9232
183	70	39	636	50–2	9410

F.2d		AFTR		USTC	
Vol.	**Page**	**Vol.**	**Page**	**Vol.**	**Par.**
184	157	39	1030	50–1	9441
184	161	39	1034	50–2	9420
185	584	39	1311	51–1	9111
187	557	40	308	51–1	9196
187	718	40	328	51–1	9201
187	1019	40	352	51–1	9237
188	127	40	369	51–1	66010
188	531	40	460	51–1	9265
189	167	40	668	51–1	9319
189	230	40	674	51–1	66013
189	332	40	686	51–1	9340
189	363	40	703	51–1	9312
189	382	40	707	51–1	9307, 9340
189	390	40	712	51–1	9295
190	330	40	1022	51–2	9376
192	392	41	356	51–2	9509
192	718	41	407	51–2	9507
193	178	41	470	52–1	9136
193	594	41	623	52–1	9125
193	827	41	648	52–1	66030
193	996, 1001	41	668	52–1	9171
194	479	41	721	52–1	9199
195	683	41	1116	52–1	9270
195	714	41	1126	52–1	9258
195	724	41	1130	52–1	9248
195	1006	41	1362	52–1	66036
197	620	42	212	52–2	9370
198	235	42	355	52–2	9409
198	357	42	505	52–2	9396
200	165	42	930	52–2	9539
200	308	42	958	53–1	9113
200	592	42	1005	53–1	9138
200	852	42	1039	53–1	66048
202	155	43	286	53–1	9238
202	873	43	450	53–1	9271
203	123	43	643	53–1	9273
203	230	43	652	53–1	9298
203	346	43	678	53–1	9285
205	798	44	151	53–2	9493
206	244	44	266	53–2	9525
206	495	44	291	53–2	9543
207	462	44	494	53–2	9576
208	819	45	37	54–1	9156
209	569	45	175	54–1	66067
209	926	45	266	54–1	9214

F.2d		AFTR		USTC	
Vol.	Page	Vol.	Page	Vol.	Par.
210	607	45	373	54–1	9257
213	523	45	1608	54–1	9409
213	529	45	1614	54–1	9423
213	651, 657	45	1620	54–2	9455
213	914	45	1672	54–2	9445
214	685	45	1805	54–2	9508
214	834	45	1836	54–2	9544
215	673	46	573	54–2	9567
216	41	46	633	54–2	9457, 10954
216	418	46	995	54–2	9626
216	513	46	1017	54–2	9666
216	638	46	1055	54–2	9664
216	748	46	1089	54–2	9648
218	52	46	1418	55–1	9109
218	347	46	1459	55–1	9130
219	51	46	1636	55–1	9188
219	149	46	1659	55–1	9240
219	266	46	1703	55–1	9221
219	682	46	1748	55–1	9191
220	415	47	341	55–1	9298
221	227	47	420	55–1	9339
221	252	47	430	55–1	9335
221	807	47	777	55–1	9390
221	944	47	790	55–1	9381
224	165	47	1368	55–1	9523
224	412	47	1445	55–2	9555
225	467	47	1895	55–2	9624
227	699	48	485	56–1	9101
228	909	48	842	56–1	9181
229	947	48	979	56–1	9249
230	304	49	231	56–1	9268
230	490	49	260	56–1	9306
230	555	49	283	56–1	9314
230	740	49	326	56–1	9315
231	288	49	430	56–1	9326
231	639	49	495	56–1	9419
232	118	49	862	56–1	9428
233	289	49	1208	56–1	9506
233	493	49	1254	56–1	9540
233	739	49	1321	56–2	9629
234	475	49	1457	56–2	9635
235	553	49	1754	56–2	9811
236	159	49	1973	56–2	9808
236	186	41	1986	56–2	9805
236	298	49	2007	56–2	9832

BITTKER AND EUSTICE

F.2d		AFTR		USTC	
Vol.	*Page*	*Vol.*	*Page*	*Vol.*	*Par.*
236	612	50	68	56–2	9861
238	670	50	763	57–1	9201
238	579	50	746	56–2	10085
238	943	50	832	57–1	9232
239	729	50	1210	57–1	9277
239	881	50	1240	57–1	9291
241	197	50	1612	57–1	9376
241	374	52	579	57–1	9455
241	508	50	1683	57–1	9437
242	396	50	1999	57–1	9518
243	125	50	2121	57–1	9590
243	894	51	200	57–1	9576
244	90	51	250	57–1	9678
244	408	51	397	57–1	9632
246	403	51	877	57–2	9735
247	440	52	122	57–2	9920
247	864	52	160	57–2	9921
248	399	52	634	57–2	9929
248	818	52	693	57–2	10015
249	776	52	918	57–2	10050
250	429	52	1082	58–1	9142
250	503	52	1092	58–1	9155
251	682	52	1104	57–2	9823

F.2d		AFTR2d		USTC	
Vol.	*Page*	*Vol.*	*Page*	*Vol.*	*Par.*
251	278	1	542	58–1	9179
251	839	1	840	58–1	9254
252	175	1	916	58–1	9295
252	693	1	986	58–1	9320
252	805	1	1096	58–1	9357
253	121	1	1109	58–1	9352
253	765	1	1214	58–1	9379
253	855	1	1382	58–1	9415
254	105	1	1249	58–1	9383
256	108	1	1883	58–2	9598
256	160	1	1931	58–2	9603
258	537	2	5479	58–2	9753
258	865	2	5660	58–2	9816
259	893	2	5842	58–2	9853
260	949	2	6121	58–2	9940
261	325	2	6202	58–2	9962
261	470	2	6221	58–2	9960

F.2d		AFTR2d		USTC	
Vol.	Page	Vol.	Page	Vol.	Par.
262	150	2	6292	59–1	9130
264	161	3	778	59–1	9279
264	713	3	919	59–1	9315
265	6	3	928	59–1	9318
265	40	3	923	59–1	9316
265	320	3	1150	59–1	9387
266	238	2	6155	58–2	9944
267	26	3	1440	59–1	9455
267	75	3	1497	59–1	9468
267	434	3	1170	59–1	9389
267	829	3	1618	59–2	9516
268	617	4	5035	59–2	9553
269	181	4	5292	59–2	9617
269	463	4	5362	59–2	9626
271	267	4	5759	59–2	9748
271	447	4	5740	59–2	9738
271	748	4	5751	59–1	9256
272	49	4	5856	59–2	9785
273	13	4	5844	59–2	9789
273	543	5	429	60–1	9204
273	928	5	400	60–1	9201
274	713	5	535	60–1	9209
275	120	5	871	60–1	9292
275	424	5	740	60–1	9261
275	598	5	970	60–1	9335
276	417	5	986	60–1	9329
277	526	5	1239	60–1	9419
277	586	5	1223	60–1	9393
277	713	5	1438	60–1	9460
277	879	5	1291	60–1	9414
278	392	5	1277	60–1	9417
278	665	5	1336	60–1	9424
278	946	5	1597	60–2	9505
279	338	5	1572	60–2	9493
279	368	5	1728	60–2	9540
280	38	5	1708	60–2	9521
280	394	6	5178	60–2	9600
281	100	6	5028	60–2	9551
281	507	6	5316	60–2	9647
281	646	6	5531	60–2	9645
281	703	6	5205	60–2	9612
281	823	6	5082	60–2	9565
282	720	6	5603	60–2	9717
283	279	6	5719	60–2	9741
283	395	6	5752	60–2	9768

F.2d		AFTR2d		USTC	
Vol.	*Page*	*Vol.*	*Page*	*Vol.*	*Par.*
283	699	6	5762	60–2	9762
284	322	6	5864	60–2	9795
284	383	6	5951	61–1	9103
284	554	6	5894	60–2	9803
284	723	6	6056	61–1	9153
284	737	6	5910	60–2	9797
285	422	6	6077	61–1	9136
286	200	7	511	61–1	9206
286	285	6	6069	61–1	9138
286	427	7	392	61–1	9172
286	669	7	357	61–1	9148
286	742	7	653	61–1	9230
286	850	6	5967	61–1	9109
287	855	7	1013	61–1	9330
287	860	7	1055	61–1	9332
287	957	7	998	61–1	9304
288	36	7	875	61–1	9312
288	47	7	790	61–1	9281
288	336	7	1035	61–1	9344
288	676	7	909	61–1	9317
288	827	7	1078	61–1	9363
288	904	7	1107	61–1	9359
289	283	7	1220	61–1	9401
289	490	7	1322	61–1	9415
289	531	7	1301	61–1	9428
290	675	7	1395	61–1	9450
290	682	7	1358	61–1	9458
291	669	7	1599	61–2	9506
291	680	8	5010	61–2	9535
291	761	7	1553	61–1	9481
292	469	8	5037	61–2	9549
292	470	8	5119	61–2	9562
292	478	8	5040	61–2	9543
292	524	8	5172	61–2	9583
293	904	8	5232	61–2	9603
294	79	8	5330	61–2	9637
294	82	8	5161	61–2	9582
294	577	8	5552	61–2	9672
294	653	8	5448	61–2	9654
294	795	8	5465	61–2	9655
294	799	8	5557	61–2	9680
296	86	8	5602	61–2	9698
296	925	9	372	62–1	9178
297	915	9	547	62–1	9225
298	35	9	332	62–1	9158

F.2d		AFTR2d		USTC	
Vol.	*Page*	*Vol.*	*Page*	*Vol.*	*Par.*
298	183	9	514	62–1	9212
298	562	9	752	62–1	9304
298	750	9	566	62–1	9224
299	199	9	733	62–1	9271
299	623	9	826	62–1	9283
300	197	9	1015	62–1	9340
300	533	9	954	62–1	9320
300	821	9	1119	62–1	9371
301	192	9	1245	62–1	9362
301	394	9	1252	62–1	9407
301	813	9	1217	62–1	9393
302	786	9	1454	62–1	9465
303	14	9	1382	62–1	9460
303	142	9	1485	62–1	9472
303	580	9	1622	62–2	9503
303	796	9	1393	62–1	9451
303	847	9	1686	62–2	9519
303	922	9	1728	62–2	9537
304	779	10	5057	62–2	9597
305	433	10	5148	62–2	9623
305	681	10	5110	62–2	9598
306	824	10	5414	62–2	9659
307	745	10	5686	62–2	9738
308	39	10	5581	62–2	9723
308	424	10	5641	62–2	9734
308	520	10	5609	62–2	9726
308	575	10	5704	62–2	9745
308	634	10	5721	62–2	9763
309	62	10	5829	62–2	9724
309	202	10	5758	62–2	9768
309	208	10	5794	62–2	9781
310	380	10	5969	63–1	9287
310	947	10	6072	63–1	9123
311	228	11	422	63–1	9171
311	374	11	374	63–1	9162
311	640	10	6136	63–1	9124
311	918	11	423	63–1	9182
311	951	11	433	63–1	9193
312	729	11	511	63–1	9204
312	803	11	656	63–1	9252
313	449	11	777	63–1	9283
313	803	11	767	63–1	9288
314	96	11	953	63–1	9318
314	449	11	901	63–1	9317
314	789	11	1025	63–1	9346

F.2d		AFTR2d		USTC	
Vol.	*Page*	*Vol.*	*Page*	*Vol.*	*Par.*
314	852	11	1028	63–1	9347
315	110	11	1149	63–1	9369
315	784	11	1216	63–1	9388
316	734	11	1499	63–1	9476
317	61	11	1447	63–1	9462
318	651	11	1614	63–2	9520
318	695	11	1663	63–2	9545
318	922	11	1600	63–2	9524
319	647	12	5118	63–2	9587
319	902	12	5093	63–2	9575
320	109	12	5162	63–2	9586
320	356	12	5142	63–2	9603
321	143	12	5362	63–2	9642
321	203	12	5371	63–2	9660
321	253	12	5181	63–2	9589
321	717	12	5622	63–2	9683
321	796	12	5448	63–2	9680
321	840	12	5059	63–2	9682
321	817	12	5487	63–2	9688
322	827	12	5659	63–2	9711
322	872	12	5606	63–2	9707
322	956	12	5300	63–2	9640
323	84	12	5616	63–2	9719
323	316	12	5625	63–2	9726
324	837	12	6054	64–1	9101
324	945	12	5969	63–2	9827
325	28	12	5900	63–2	9806
325	191	12	6005	63–2	9841
325	341	12	6109	64–1	9119
325	551	13	303	64–1	9137
325	820	12	6139	64–1	9116
325	559	13	338	64–1	9155
325	849	12	6103	64–1	9112
325	1022	13	431	64–1	9207
326	67	13	358	64–1	9173
326	600	13	451	64–1	9193
326	860	13	412	64–1	9220
326	878	13	423	64–1	9192
326	988	14	5268	64–1	9214
327	767	13	625	64–1	9240
328	342	13	632	64–1	9249
328	781	13	880	64–1	9306
329	924	13	1077	64–2	9535
330	761	13	1258	64–1	9420
330	1008	13	1283	64–1	9447

F.2d		AFTR2d		USTC	
Vol.	Page	Vol.	Page	Vol.	Par.
331	12	13	1251	64–1	9416
331	321	13	1386	64–1	9474
331	422	13	1367	64–1	9465
333	76	13	1730	64–2	9542
333	382	14	5061	64–2	9580
333	585	14	5001	64–2	9568
333	615	14	5052	64–2	9621
333	653	14	5024	64–2	9578
334	20	14	5154	64–2	9606
334	40	14	5106	64–2	9604
334	44	14	5242	64–2	9625
334	269	14	5086	64–2	9592
334	275	14	5131	64–2	9610
334	936	14	5332	64–2	9674
335	75	14	5260	64–2	9647
335	209	14	5341	64–2	9666
335	473	14	5387	64–2	9689
335	487	14	5378	64–2	9680
335	507	14	5453	64–2	9700
335	518	14	5324	64–2	9675
335	680	14	5504	64–2	9707
335	734	14	5193	64–2	9646
335	738	14	5070	64–2	9593
335	744	14	5206	64–2	9626
336	134	14	5591	64–2	9734
336	339	14	5447	64–2	9705
336	483	14	5649	64–2	9757
336	714	14	5685	64–2	9764
336	809	14	5605	64–2	9743
336	865	14	5597	64–2	9741
337	643	14	5783	64–2	9793
337	1001	14	5667	64–2	9755
338	4	14	5863	64–1	9162
338	691	14	5803	64–2	9803
338	815	14	6009	64–2	9877
338	924	14	6076	65–1	9104
339	503	14	6112	65–1	9123
340	24	15	068	65–1	9147
340	27	15	123	65–1	9180
340	445	15	199	65–1	9183
340	510	15	257	65–1	9201
341	54	15	286	65–1	9205
341	466	15	422	65–1	9257
341	502	15	429	65–1	9259
341	580	15	362	65–1	9240

F.2d		AFTR2d		USTC	
Vol.	Page	Vol.	Page	Vol.	Par.
341	948	15	447	65–1	9262
342	198	15	484	65–1	9280
342	759	15	592	65–1	9300
342	990	15	575	65–1	9291
342	997	15	678	65–1	9331
343	713	15	692	65–1	9332
343	790	15	673	65–1	9330
344	123	15	714	65–1	9347
345	35	15	853	65–1	9388
345	534	15	1107	65–2	9448
345	552	15	979	65–1	9419
345	698	15	1059	65–1	9433
345	761	15	1043	65–1	9439
345	823	15	987	65–1	9420
345	901	15	880	65–1	9395
346	704	15	1172	65–2	9468
348	122	16	5107	65–2	9518
348	278	16	5061	65–2	9525
348	1006	16	5282	65–2	9572
350	225	16	5111	65–2	9537
350	319	16	5591	65–2	9663
350	712	16	5592	65–2	9646
351	568	16	5738	65–2	9686
351	951	16	5853	66–1	9336
352	948	16	6006	65–2	9761
352	991	16	6003	65–2	9763
353	184	16	6030	66–1	9103
354	757	17	13	66–1	9140
354	916	17	97	66–1	9164
354	997	17	11	66–1	9138
355	200	17	71	66–1	9168
355	724	17	183	66–1	9191
355	931	17	358	66–1	9195, 9245
356	514	17	514	66–1	9208
356	668	17	337	66–1	9235
357	483	17	601	66–1	9316
357	647	17	466	66–1	9284
358	294	17	643	66–1	9330
358	333	17	673	66–1	9347
358	342	17	700	66–1	9340
358	867	17	518	66–1	9294
358	892	17	583	66–1	9309
359	191	17	833	66–1	9384
360	113	17	704	66–1	9342
360	260	17	996	66–1	9407

F.2d		AFTR2d		USTC	
Vol.	Page	Vol.	Page	Vol.	Par.
360	382	17	938	66–1	9401
361	93	17	980	66–1	9420
361	257	17	1163	66–1	9446
361	607	17	988	66–1	9436
361	668	17	1171	66–1	9464
361	818	17	1266	66–2	9479
361	939	17	1272	66–2	9483
361	972	17	1184	66–1	9461
362	140	17	1066	66–1	9426
362	212	17	1280	66–2	9497
362	266	17	1213	66–1	9462
362	781	18	5052	66–2	9508
363	262	17	1290	66–2	9498
363	724	18	5413	66–2	9580
363	826	18	5422	66–2	9586
364	101	18	5205	66–2	9555
364	525	18	5337	66–2	9566
364	734	18	5328	66–2	9561
364	746	18	5500	66–2	9610
365	24	18	5018	66–2	9506
365	244	18	5488	66–2	9604
366	874	18	5523	66–2	9618
366	890	18	5517	66–2	9619
367	193	18	5809	66–2	9704
367	276	18	5750	66–2	9708
367	669	18	5732	66–2	9681
367	794	18	5843	66–2	9718
368	125	18	5832	66–2	9716
370	713	18	6082	67–1	9112
370	729	19	393	67–1	9166
367	980	18	5316	66–2	9573
368	125	18	5832	66–2	9716
368	272	18	5937	66–2	9740
368	809	18	5981	66–7	9761
369	119	18	5970	66–2	9751
369	337	18	6094	67–1	9105
369	629	18	6172	67–1	9117
370	729	19	393	67–1	9166
371	189	18	6189	67–1	9131
371	486	19	476	67–1	9188
371	528	19	595	67–1	9183
371	684	19	423	67–1	9169
371	808	19	561	67–1	9231
371	816	19	580	67–1	9207
371	842	19	533	67–1	9189

F.2d		AFTR2d		USTC	
Vol.	Page	Vol.	Page	Vol.	Par.
371	816	19	580	67–1	9207
371	897	19	388	67–1	9179
371	942	19	588	67–1	9200
372	240	19	704	67–1	9236
372	281	19	602	67–1	9203
372	415	19	689	67–1	9243
372	990	19	712	67–1	9248
373	159	19	6205	67–1	9140
373	190	19	693	67–1	9238
373	336	19	745	67–1	9249
373	844	19	838	67–1	9286
374	161	19	880	67–1	9292
375	36	19	1023	67–1	9330
375	351	19	820	67–1	9279
375	662	19	1194	67–1	9363
375	807	19	1195	67–1	9372
375	867	19	1175	67–1	9369
376	314	19	1186	67–1	9375
376	402	19	1281	67–1	9380
376	434	19	1308	67–1	9387
376	623	19	1407	67–1	9389
376	791	19	1425	67–1	9433
377	291	19	1413	67–1	9438
377	403	19	1557	67–1	9471
378	222	19	1623	67–1	9461
378	354	19	1641	67–2	9498
378	686	19	1648	67–2	9501
378	771	19	1356	67–1	9423
379	569	19	1627	67–2	9499
380	1	19	1653	67–2	9497
380	146	19	1731	67–2	9529
380	786	20	5077	67–2	9534
382	298	20	5172	67–2	9571
382	485	20	5268	67–2	9556
382	499	21	5255	67–2	9592
383	883	20	5603	67–2	9671
384	635	20	5611	67–2	9690
384	715	20	5678	67–2	9710
384	1008	20	5730	67–2	9724
385	521	20	5619	67–2	9687
386	510	20	5764	67–2	9743
386	836	20	5838	67–2	9756
386	839	21	395	68–1	9120
387	420	21	376	68–1	9141
387	451	21	5891	68–1	9118

F.2d		AFTR2d		USTC	
Vol.	Page	Vol.	Page	Vol.	Par.
387	475	21	408	68–1	9157
388	184	21	352	68–1	9147
388	223	21	313	68–1	9139
388	886	21	534	68–1	9189
390	205	21	655	68–1	9211
390	877	21	930	68–1	9271
390	965	21	732	68–1	9223
391	584	21	1000	68–1	9292
391	775	21	813	68–1	9245, 12515
391	930	21	957	68–1	9284
392	409	21	1056	68–1	9318
392	458	21	1003	68–1	9297
392	522	21	983	68–1	9279
393	243	21	1133	68–1	9331
393	269	21	1062	68–1	9319
393	983	21	1294	68–1	9367
394	738	21	1189	68–1	9346
395	430	22	5806	68–1	9369
395	861	21	1380	68–1	9406
396	264	21	1438	68–1	9430
398	427	22	5254	68–2	9489
398	694	22	5004	68–2	9438
399	194	22	5161	68–2	9472
399	800	22	5375	68–2	9521
399	828	22	5502	68–2	9551
400	427	22	5481	68–2	9559
400	737	22	5637	68–2	9609
400	483	22	5904	68–2	9653
401	162	22	5621	68–2	9589
401	324	22	5597	68–2	9600
401	333	23	416	68–2	9614
402	272	22	5699	68–2	9624
402	1000	22	5820	68–2	9650
403	502	22	5783	68–2	9643
403	611	22	5771	68–2	9634
403	622	22	5780	68–2	9635
404	411	22	5911		
404	960	22	5947	69–1	9125
405	61	23	408	69–1	9138
405	673	23	320	69–1	9131
405	1300	23	509	69–1	9190
406	76			69–1	9153
406	157	23	425	69–1	9158
406	288	23	401	69–1	9164
406	703	23	544	69–1	9206

F.2d		AFTR2d		USTC	
Vol.	*Page*	*Vol.*	*Page*	*Vol.*	*Par.*
406	1259	23	657	69–1	9226
407	530	23	692	69–1	9236
407	629	23	758	69–1	9246
408	435	23	918	69–1	9275
408	1117	23	1090	69–1	9319
409	904	23	1102	69–1	9321
410	505	23	1289	69–1	9371
410	615	23	1362	69–1	9396
410	888	23	1247	69–1	9372
410	1233	23	1385	69–1	9404
411	231	23	1268	69–1	9375
411	327	23	1474	69–1	9374
411	738	23	1070	69–1	9314
411	818	23	1582	69–1	9398
411	1374	23	1550	69–2	9442
412	800	24	5023	69–2	9495
412	1222	23	1714	69–2	9473
413	97	23	1482	69–1	9428
414	844	24	5426	69–2	9559
414	1283	24	5133	69–2	9478
415	488	21	1512	68–1	9418
415	519	24	5516	69–2	9589
415	531	24	5554	69–2	9626
417	437	24	5797	69–2	9678
417	675	24	5648	69–2	9655
418	381	24	5901	70–1	9101
418	511	24	5866	69–2	9720
419	845	24	5841	69–2	9718
420	332	25	380	70–1	9160
420	702	25	492	70–1	9191
421	910	25	612	70–1	9228
422	2	25	684	70–1	9236
422	402	25	787	70–1	9270
423	49	25	777	70–1	9262
423	494	25	788	70–1	9251
423	1217	25	921	70–1	9307
424	1	25	926	70–1	9328
424	219	25	936	70–1	9327
424	378	25	820	70–1	9279
424	751	25	1016	70–1	9361
424	1330			70–1	9308
425	633	25	626	70–1	9241
425	921	25	314	70–1	9132
426	417	25	1269	70–1	417
426	1293	25	1417	70–1	9445

F.2d		AFTR2d		USTC	
Vol.	Page	Vol.	Page	Vol.	Par.
427	343	25	1280	70–1	9430
427	661	25	1291	70–1	9437
427	1014	25	1398	70–2	9461
427	1202	25	1382	70–1	9458
427	1334	26	5004	70–2	9477
428	49	25	1297	70–1	9439
428	259	25	1434	70–2	9464
429	41	26	5049	70–2	9500
429	426	26	5532	70–2	9595
429	560	26	5361	70–2	9544
429	650	26	5051	70–2	9494
429	1209	26	5154	70–2	9513
430	195	26	5351	70–2	9545
430	1185	26	5185	70–2	9506
431	511	26	5037	70–2	9469
432	741	26	5550	71–2	9620
432	1052	26	5636	70–2	9645
433	309	26	5695	70–2	9657
433	1097	26	5649	70–2	9647
434	1011	26	5837	70–2	9717
434	1357	26	5928	71–1	9110
435	53	26	5877	70–2	9723
435	118	26	5898	71–1	9102
435	1257	27	360	71–1	9148
438	774	27	621	71–1	9214
439	409	27	950	71–1	9273
439	1165	27	837	71–1	9267
441	593	27	1139	71–1	9339
441	999	26	5823	70–2	9714
443	501	27	1402	71–1	9422
444	139	27	1466	71–2	9454
444	1145	27	1520	71–1	9478
444	1385	27	1573	71–1	9483
445	455	28	5102	71–2	9521
445	1306	28	5397	71–2	9575
446	690	27	1488	71–1	9449
447	552	27	1574	71–1	9481
447	612	28	5434	71–2	9588
447	1074	28	5550	71–2	9616
448	141	28	5586	71–2	9631
448	574	28	5644	71–2	9633
449	402	28	5811	71–2	9686
449	759	28	5751	71–2	9678
450	198	29	331	72–1	9159
450	379	28	5676	71–2	9651

F.2d		AFTR2d		USTC	
Vol.	Page	Vol.	Page	Vol.	Par.
450	850	28	5961	71–2	9713
450	961	28	5924	71–2	9518
451	80	28	5992	71–2	9731
451	992	28	6042	71–2	9756
451	1395			72–1	9115
452	137	28	6044	71–2	9755
452	445	28	5881	71–2	9706
452	604	29	321	72–1	9158
452	767	28	6110	72–1	9101
452	1022	28	6173	72–1	9114
453	300	29	305	72–1	9146
453	982	29	360	72–1	9163
453	1100	29	418	72–1	9184
453	1144	29	403	72–1	9182
455	98	29	554	72–1	9242
455	1195	29	633	72–1	9266
456	681	29	779	72–1	9328
457	1150	29	855	72–1	9333
457	1165	29	816	72–1	9317
458	245	29	869	72–1	9341
458	631	29	927	72–1	9351
460	412	29	1138	72–1	9429
460	827	29	1116	72–1	9416
460	1216	29	1194	72–1	9440
460	1130	29	1188	72–1	12843
461	865	29	1446	72–1	9464
462	712	29	1408	72–2	9494
462	751	29	1441	72–2	9510
462	805	30	5275	72–2	9590
462	1281	30	5043	72–2	9485
463	503	30	5144	72–2	9548
464	53	30	5128	72–2	9547
464	394	30	5094	72–2	9537
464	891	30	5208	72–2	9566
466	69	30	5360	72–2	9613
468	370	30	5614	72–2	9689
468	805	30	5421, 5732	72–2	9632, 9744
469	225	30	5699	72–2	9728
469	263	30	5723	72–2	9746
469	340	30	5767	72–2	9751
470	921	31	409	73–1	9133
471	247	31	594	73–1	9162
471	261	31	514	73–1	9161
471	275	31	488	73–1	9136
471	1211	31	614	73–1	9183

F.2d		AFTR2d		USTC	
Vol.	*Page*	*Vol.*	*Page*	*Vol.*	*Par.*
472	449	31	497	73–1	9138
472	590	31	674	73–1	9191
472	867	31	710	73–1	9203
473	274	31	646	73–1	9181
473	1244	31	571	73–1	9176
474	1341			73–1	9327
475	623	31	946	73–1	9292
476	509	31	1056	73–1	9332
476	1312	31	1113	73–1	9347
476	1351	31	1136	73–1	9353
477	599	32	5712	73–2	9640
477	836	31	1170	73–1	9387
477	1029	31	1224	73–1	9404
477	1058	31	1262	73–1	9429
477	1063	31	1215	73–1	9403
478	1049	31	1183	73–1	9380
479	539	31	1325	73–1	9473
479	678	32	5052	73–1	9460
480	66	32	5094	73–2	9484
480	468	32	5251	73–2	9492
480	1304	32	5167	73–2	9501
481	238	32	5209	73–2	9513
481	857	32	5282	73–2	9593
482	600	32	5490	73–2	9583
483	18	32	5404	73–2	9556
483	209	32	5663	73–2	9615
484	462	32	5691	73–2	9630
485	110	32	5850	73–2	9678
486	1	32	5860	73–2	9687
486	632	31	864	73–1	9261
487	184	32	6068	73–2	9767
487	540	32	6147		
487	1246	33	332	74–1	9108
489	161	33	709	74–1	9237
489	197	33	395	74–1	9141
489	957	33	385	74–1	9119
490	218	33	431	74–1	9161
490	241	32	5523	73–2	9591
490	898	33	479	74–1	9168
490	1172	33	570	74–1	9188
494	404	33	960	74–1	9315
494	429	33	839	74–1	9294
494	465	33	1331	74–1	9446
494	693	33	905	74–1	9309
494	1376	33	1111	74–1	9368

F.2d		AFTR2d		USTC	
Vol.	*Page*	*Vol.*	*Page*	*Vol.*	*Par.*
495	653	33	1216	74–1	9396
495	1079	33	1102	74–1	1079
496	532	34	5023	74–1	9467
496	621	33	1226	74–1	9405
497	862	34	5054	74–1	9485
498	225	34	5060	74–1	9474
498	631	34	5634	74–2	9629
500	108	34	5239	74–2	9522
500	611	34	5612	74–2	9618
500	937	34	5667	74–2	9624
500	1041	34	5331	74–2	9527
501	1055	34	5403	74–2	9545
501	1338	34	5582	74–2	9613
503	359	34	5834	74–2	9701
503	1291	34	6007	74–2	9714
503	1406	33	1121	74–1	9369
504	425	34	6030	74–2	9756
505	350	39	5731	74–2	9635
505	873	35	518	75–1	9151
505	1266	35	317	74–2	9827
506	449	34	6153	74–2	9799
506	637	34	6249	74–2	9834
506	972	35	610	75–1	9200
507	262	34	6181	74–2	9806
507	594	35	336	74–2	9845
508	1076	35	348	75–1	9142
508	1251	35	541	75–1	9167
510	43	35	650	75–1	9209
510	230	35	714	75–1	9236
510	259			75–1	9160
510	565	35	1122	75–1	9347
511	107	35	1337	75–1	9405
511	1234	35	811	75–1	9271
512	13	35	990	75–1	9298
513	25	35	1028	75–1	9318
513	391	36	5095	75–1	9477
513	800	36	5078	75–2	9522
514	1199	35	1391	75–1	9423
514	1209	35	1491	75–1	9444
517	75	35	1536	75–1	9478
517	437	35	1478	75–1	9434
519	1233	36	5562	75–2	9645
521	160	36	5607	75–2	9665
522	1281	35	462	75–1	9107
523	1308	36	5942	75–2	9726

F.2d		AFTR2d		USTC	
Vol.	Page	Vol.	Page	Vol.	Par.
524	347	36	6101	75–2	9765
524	729	36	6193	75–2	9778
524	1194	36	6157	75–2	9777
524	1343	36	6251	76–1	9308
525	186	36	6233	75–2	9808
526	135	37	380	76–1	9109
527	621	37	474	76–1	9130
527	945	37	396	76–1	9114
527	1392	37	501	76–1	9128
529	609	37	377	76–1	9191
530	708	37	850	76–1	9243
530	772	37	826	76–1	9225
530	1367	37	696	76–1	9203
531	1343	37	885	76–1	9247
532	1204	37	1119	76–1	9326
533	117	37	1162	76–1	9344
533	152	38	5162	76–1	9467
533	550	37	1223	76–1	9356
533	1114	37	1068	76–1	9324
535	309	38	5476	76–2	9557
535	500	37	1413	76–1	9417
535	1225	37	1433	76–1	9406
539	929	38	5366	76–2	9523
539	1276	38	5417	76–2	9538
539	1312	38	5390	76–2	9540
543	81	38	6051	76–2	9744
544	419	38	6106	76–2	9759
545	1204	39	364	76–2	9809
548	501	39	670	77–1	9163
548	924	39	709	77–1	9160
549	89	39	867	77–1	9218
549	740	39	823	77–1	9161
550	43	39	783	77–1	9203
551	74	39	1333	77–1	9375
551	121	39	1008	77–1	9320
552	478	39	1225	77–1	9324
553	93	39	894	77–1	9270
553	434	40	5087	77–1	9457
553	644	39	1567	77–1	9361
556	889	40	5156	77–2	9479
556	986	40	5026	77–1	9421
556	1019	40	5040	77–1	9423
556	1107	40	5144	77–2	9476
557	1113	40	5444	77–2	9494
558	128	40	5418	77–2	9555

F.2d		AFTR2d		USTC	
Vol.	Page	Vol.	Page	Vol.	Par.
559	1348	40	5807	77–2	9661
561	698	40	5650	77–2	9615
561	753	40	5933	77–2	9685
561	1023	40	5452	77–2	9539
561	1287	40	5716	77–2	9639
566	574	41	310	78–1	16277
568	663	41	745	78–1	9230
568	811	39	400	77–1	9120
568	823	39	1111	77–1	9120
568	1233	41	419	78–1	9144
569	863	41	952	78–1	9301
570	28	41	411	78–1	9140
570	139	41	614	78–1	9216
570	1277	41	1163	78–1	9351
571	1092	41	451	78–1	9147
572	135	41	1264	78–1	9406
572	235	41	1089	78–1	9352
572	1046	41	1366	78–1	9430
573	58	41	989	78–1	9315
577	212	42	5246	78–2	9514
577	283	42	5575	78–2	9607
577	1206	42	5637	78–2	9645
579	1000	42	5320	78–2	9591
582	378	42	5716	78–2	9671
583	313	42	5540	78–2	9621
583	953	42	5876	78–2	9708
583	972	42	5464	78–2	9597
589	123	42	6330	78–2	9839
591	248	43	526	79–1	9179
592	272	43	973	79–1	9299
592	937	43	649	79–1	9213
592	1251	43	1023	79–1	9323
592	1259	43	995	79–1	9319
593	832	43	845	79–1	9268
594	657	43	752	79–1	9234
595	1060	44	5076	79–1	9392
598	1236	43	1092	79–1	9357
598	1375	44	5361	79–2	9499
598	1382	44	5367	79–2	9500
600	1052	44	5260	79–2	9471
601	196	44	5505	79–2	9551
601	365	44	5289	79–2	9472
601	734	44	5576	79–2	9557
602	256	44	5149	79–2	9417
602	338	44	5315	79–2	9491
604	1045	44	5627	79–2	9569

F.2d		AFTR2d		USTC	
Vol.	*Page*	*Vol.*	*Page*	*Vol.*	*Par.*
605	657	44	5180	79–2	9596
605	1146	44	5552	79–2	9540
		46	5349	80–2	9549
618	1328	46	5665	80–2	9640
621	731	46	5387	80–2	9556
622	460	46	5471	80–2	9575
625	1127	46	5413	80–2	9534
—	—	46	5564	80–2	9611
—	—	46	5742	80–2	9637
626	1186	46	5743	80–2	9700
629	1096	46	6050	80–2	9798
629	1218	46	5527	80–2	9607
630	460	46	5471	80–2	9575
640	745	47	1145	81–1	9284
640	1030	47	1070	81–1	9271
640	1058	47	1200	81–1	9303
641	253	47	1330	81–1	9307
641	529	47	874	81–1	9225
642	894	47	1372	81–1	9368
644	339	47	1359	81–1	9411
644	1385	48	5020	81–1	9442
645	19	47	1547	81–1	9429
647	487	48	5281	81–2	9491
648	1043	48	5349	81–2	9518
649	264	48	5194	81–1	9462
650	1167	48	5236	81–2	9489
650	1174	48	5239	81–2	9477
—	—	47	1461	81–1	9425
—	—	48	5319	81–2	9499
—	—	48	5354	81–2	9517
—	—	48	5517	81–2	9537
—	—	48	5537	81–2	9534
—	—	48	5625	81–2	9577
—	—	48	5660	81–2	9574
—	—	48	6034	81–2	9726
661	226	48	5942	81–2	9674
—	—	48	5884	81–2	9683
668	138	49	481	82–1	9129
668	252	49	509	82–1	9118
—	—	49	569	82–1	9167
670	123	49	938	82–1	9218
671	367	49	1353	82–1	9275
674	570	49	1102	82–1	9297
674	1308	49	1401	82–1	9347
677	11	49	1082	82–1	9318
677	72	49	1241	82–1	9301

F.2d		AFTR2d		USTC	
Vol.	*Page*	*Vol.*	*Page*	*Vol.*	*Par.*
677	528	49	1343	82–1	9396
677	1328	50	5104	82–1	9404
678	509	50	514	82–1	9402
679	159	50	5167	82–2	9428
—	—	50	5252	82–2	9459
—	—	50	5238	82–2	9454
685	1099	50	5782	82–2	9552
687	1107	50	5799	82–2	9572
688	520	50	5750	82–2	9581
688	1376	50	5909	82–2	9630
689	943	50	5959	82–2	9643
—	—	50	5767	82–2	9583
—	—	50	5900	82–2	9626
—	—	50	6016	82–2	9650
—	—	50	6046	82–2	9651
690	40	50	5739	82–2	9589
693	459	51	376	82–2	9718
694	703	51	352	82–2	9711
695	1367	51	660	83–1	9113
697	473	51	445	83–1	9121
702	1234	51	1183	83–1	9320
705	828	51	1121	83–1	9310
—	—	51	1015	83–1	9278
—	—	52	22	83–1	9353
—	—	52	5054	83–1	9427
—	—	52	5332	83–2	9452
	None	52	5677	83–2	9480
	None	52	5702	83–2	9516
	None	52	5744	83–2	9532
—	—	52	5770	83–2	9537
706	301	52	5566	83–2	9677
—	—	52	5830	83–2	9558
—	—	52	5866	83–2	9569
714	977	52	5885	83–2	9573
716	563	52	5770	83–2	9537
716	1241	52	5976	83–2	9610
—	—	52	5982	83–2	9613
719	196	52	6153	83–2	9642
—	—	52	6310	83–2	9682
—	—	52	6350	83–2	9664
723	43	53	398	84–1	9103
723	58	53	406	84–1	9046
724	1311	54	6098	84–2	9817
725	307	53	856	84–1	9247
726	1569	53	776	84–1	9214
727	322	53	682	84–1	9190

F.2d		AFTR2d		USTC	
Vol.	*Page*	*Vol.*	*Page*	*Vol.*	*Par.*
727	1043	53	986	84–1	9316
728	593	53	874	84–1	9262
—	—	53	1042	84–1	9315
730	276	53	1479	84–1	7417
730	634	53	1119	84–1	9406
731	1401	53	1210	84–1	9424
732	132	53	1280	84–1	9376
734	290	54	5011	84–1	9495
737	1569	54	5428	84–2	9599
739	411	54	5659	84–2	9701
744	442	54	6135	84–2	9869
745	1400	55	6402	84–2	9910
—	—	55	433	84–2	9996

F. Supp.		AFTR		USTC	
Vol.	*Page*	*Vol.*	*Page*	*Vol.*	*Par.*
45	772	29	1113	42–1	9364
45	962	29	1115	42–2	9616
67	839	35	394	46–2	9354
74	458	36	370	47–2	9364
81	254	37	766	49–1	9101
83	251	37	1273	49–1	9319
101	763	41	567	52–1	9131
103	369	41	961	52–1	9209
103	779	41	1033	52–1	9293
105	292, 307–8	42	115	52–1	9320
126	184	46	1293	54–2	9697
130	586	47	1006	55–1	9409
134	290	48	112	55–2	49153
135	286, 288	48	558	55–2	9753
137	249	48	1150	56–1	9200
137	252	48	1153	55–1	49109
146	444	50	942	57–1	9218
152	66	51	775	57–1	9649

F. Supp.		AFTR2d		USTC	
Vol.	*Page*	*Vol.*	*Page*	*Vol.*	*Par.*
157	244	1	446	58–1	9157
158	627	1	785	58–1	9240
158	887	1	894	58–1	9278
161	807	1	1621	58–1	9511
163	495	1	2035	58–2	9625
163	754	2	5107	58–2	9721
167	756	2	6061	58–2	9937
171	846	3	1110	59–1	9380

F. Supp.		AFTR		USTC	
Vol.	Page	Vol.	Page	Vol.	Par.
171	943	3	1108	59–1	9378
173	793	3	1569	59–2	9493
174	702	4	5127	59–2	9548
175	360	4	5224	59–2	9602
181	752	5	786	60–1	9268
183	901	6	5050	60–2	9530
186	724	6	5588	60–2	9718
187	952	7	423	61–2	9672
188	451	6	5795	60–2	9772
188	461	6	5784	60–2	9773
189	70	7	351	61–1	9120
190	287	7	416	61–1	9168
190	478	7	301	61–1	9144
193	299	7	934	61–1	9249
199	363	9	685	62–1	9257
202	263	9	1305	62–1	9357
203	270	9	1084	62–1	9346
209	286	10	5751	62–2	9758
214	97	11	446	63–1	9175
227	807	13	887	64–1	9235
230	838	13	1747	64–2	9618
232	134	13	1430	64–2	9503
234	681	14	5293	64–2	9584
237	80	14	6104	65–1	9115
238	258	12	5426	63–2	9648
239	401	15	546	65–1	9282
239	794	15	623	65–1	9306
245	369	16	5460	65–2	9551
253	636	17	646	66–1	9333
258	673	18	5793	66–2	9683
259	828	18	5669	66–2	9627
260	100	18	5607	66–2	9599
261	597	18	6191	67–1	9126
263	884	18	5897	66–2	9723
264	969	19	899	67–2	9282
268	52	19	1669	67–2	9596
268	740	19	1545	67–2	9481
269	654	19	1601	67–2	9532
273	460	20	5209	67–2	9554
277	475	20	5616	67–2	9686
280	437	18	5795	66–2	9669
288	770	22	5116	68–2	9509
295	421	23	863	69–1	9215
295	812	23	715	69–1	9225
296	823	23	727	69–1	9227
297	221	23	467	69–1	9182

F. Supp.		AFTR2d		USTC	
Vol.	*Page*	*Vol.*	*Page*	*Vol.*	*Par.*
297	370	23	484	68–2	9625
303	1	24	5474	69–2	9602
304	1080	25	450	70–1	9172
308	1129	25	1257	70–1	9208
320	1328	27	389	71–1	9137
325	1085	27	1166	71–1	9292
327	363	27	896	71–1	9289
333	705	28	5427	71–2	9579
338	602	29	514	72–1	9171
344	1259	30	5037	72–2	9511
345	241			72–2	9760
348	502	30	5551	72–2	9701
349	527	31	902	73–1	9217
350	420	30	5524	72–2	9705
350	726	30	5438	72–2	9624
354	1003	31	640	73–1	9279
362	801	29	1301	72–1	9432
362	897	32	5781	73–2	9677
367	506	33	416	74–1	9149
369	939	33	566	74–1	9189
375	439	34	5034	74–1	9463
382	525	32	5774	73–2	9743
397	719	36	5479	75–2	9609
403	498	36	6287	75–2	9803
407	681	37	864	76–1	9252
412	398	39	1427	76–2	9619
416	689	36	5723	75–2	9749
427	484	39	671	77–1	9275
441	76	41	335	77–2	9740
442	1023	40	6122	78–1	9104
453	956	41	705	78–1	9311
472	957	43	1228	79–2	9432
—	—	47	1393	81–1	9261
—	—	48	5566	81–2	9551
—	—	48	—	81–1	9456
—	—	48	5978	81–2	9638
—	—	50	5058	82–2	9354
—	—	52	5094	83–1	9401
—	—	52	5878	83–2	9573

AFTR2d		USTC	
Vol.	*Page*	*Vol.*	*Par.*
1	863	58–1	9288
1	1278	58–1	9262
5	965	60–1	9298
10	6120	63–1	9119

AFTR2d		USTC	
Vol.	Page	Vol.	Par.
15	536	65–1	9239
17	222	66–1	9206
19	929	67–1	9277
19	1389	67–1	9462
20	5302	67–2	9609
20	5418	67–2	9641
23	559	69–1	9194
25	526	70–1	9188
25	620	70–1	9216
29	965	72–1	9349
29	1466	72–2	9495
30	5396	72–2	9637
31	406	73–1	9123
31	694	73–1	9281
32	5891	73–2	9694
32	5933	72–1	9457
35	511	75–1	9140
36	5186	75–2	9538
36	5591	75–1	9461
36	6367	75–2	9832
37	416	76–1	9126
37	802	76–2	9533
37	1295	76–1	9329
38	5336	76–2	9520
38	5869	76–2	9677
38	6019	76–2	9730
38	6118	76–2	9781
38	6119	76–2	9780
38	6207	76–2	9776
39	849	76–2	9622
40	5357	77–2	9538
40	5429	77–2	9736
40	5688	77–2	9710
40	6047	77–2	9554
41	328	77–2	9741
41	705	78–1	9311
42	5429	77–2	9679
42	5670	78–2	9652
42	5832	78–2	9686
42	6047	78–2	9693
43	617	79–1	9175
43	964	79–1	9160
		79–1	9202
		79–1	9216
43	1017	79–1	9307

AFTR2d		USTC	
Vol.	*Page*	*Vol.*	*Par.*
44	5013	79–1	9170
44	5382	79–2	9463
44	5493	79–2	9547
44	5542	79–2	9560
44	5849	79–2	9648
44	5854		
44	5888	79–2	9612
44	5906	79–2	9633
45	458	80–1	9103
45	542	80–1	9135
45	560	80–1	9156
45	645	80–1	9177
45	653	80–1	9190
45	683	80–1	9187
45	785	80–1	9218
45	817	80–1	9232
45	884	80–1	9265
45	887	80–1	9248
45	1081	80–1	9307
45	1106	80–1	9314
45	1241	80–1	9332
45	1518	80–1	9384
45	1527	80–1	9370
45	1581	80–1	9399
45	1604	80–1	9439
45	1664	80–1	9432
45	5025	80–1	9367
46	5235	80–2	
46	5337	80–2	9617
46	5564	80–2	9611
46	5742	80–2	9637
46	5843	80–2	9729
46	6054		
46	6089	80–2	9799
46	6104	80–2	9759
47	659	81–1	9197
47	846	81–1	9211
47	1066	81–1	9171
47	1372	81–1	9368
47	1359	81–1	9411
47	1393	81–1	9261
47	1461	81–1	9425
47	1547	81–1	9429
48	5020	81–1	9442
48	5194	81–1	9462

AFTR2d		USTC	
Vol.	Page	Vol.	Par.
48	5281	81–2	9491
48	5349	81–2	9518
48	5236	81–2	9489
48	5239	81–2	9477
48	—	81–1	9456
48	5319	81–2	9499
48	5354	81–2	9517
48	5517	81–2	9537
48	5537	81–2	9534
48	5566	81–2	9551
48	5625	81–2	9577
48	5660	81–2	9574
48	5978	81–2	9638
49	491	82–1	9134
50	5054	82–1	9419
51	874	83–1	9229
51	721	83–1	9163
51	778	83–1	9225
51	823	83–1	9168
51	1132	83–1	9328
51	445	83–1	9121
51	1183	83–1	9320
51	1121	83–1	9310
51	1015	83–1	9278
52	22	83–1	9353
52	5054	83–1	9427
52	5332	83–2	9452
52	5566	83–2	9677
52	5677	83–2	9480
52	5770	83–2	9537
52	5830	83–2	9558
52	5866	83–2	9569
52	5878	83–2	9573
52	5885	83–2	9573
52	5976	83–2	9610
52	5982	83–2	9613
52	6153	83–2	9642
52	6310	83–2	9682
52	6350	83–2	9664
52	5702	83–2	9516
52	5744	83–2	9532
52	5770	83–2	9537
52	5094	83–1	9401
54	5370	84–2	9549
54	6580	84–2	9716
54		84–2	9787

CUMULATIVE
TABLE OF CASES

[References are to paragraphs (¶); references to the Supplement are preceded by "S."]

[*References are to paragraphs (¶); references to the Supplement are preceded by "S."*]

[References are to paragraphs (¶); references to the Supplement are preceded by "S."]

[References are to paragraphs (¶); references to the Supplement are preceded by "S."]

Boehm v. CIR 4.09 n.94

Boettger, Lloyd .. 13.04 ns. 36, 46;
        13.05 n.70

Bohart Plumbing &
    Heating Co. 8.25 n.145

Boise Cascade Corp. v. US .. 4.22
    n.143; 11.45 ns. 111, 124, 126

Bolger, David F. 2.10 n.79;
        6.07 n.67; 11.45 n.120

Bolker, Jos. R. S.11.63 n.158;
        S.11.66 n.226

Bolnick, Ted 4.08 n.89;
        S.4.08 n.89

Bondy v. CIR 13.02 n.9

Bone, Thos. E. 6.02 n.22

Bongiovanni v. CIR 3.07 n.76;
    S.3.07 n.76; 3.12 n.120

Bonnaire Dev. Co. .. S.11.62 n.147

Bonner, Fred G. S.6.08 n.73

Bonneville Locks
    Towing Co. 15.02 n.2;
        16.21 n.95

Bonsall v. CIR 13.04 n.54;
        13.09 n.116

Book Production
    Indus., Inc. 11.05 n.39;
    14.31 n.243; 14.54 ns. 462, 463;
        15.21 n.130

Booth, Earnest, M.D. .. S.2.06 n.51

Bordo Prods. Co. v. US .. 4.04 n.28

Borg, Joe E. 6.07 n.67

Borg & Beck Co. 5.07 n.78

Borge v. CIR 2.06 n.49; 15.06
    n.32; 16.21 ns. 77, 78, 124;
        16.27 n.255

Bosch, Est. of, CIR v. 2.01 n.5

Bothin Real Estate Co.
    v. CIR 3.14 n.147

Boulez, Pierre S.17.02 n.17

Bowers v. CIR S.4.09 n.105

Bowersock Mills & Power Co.
    v. CIR 4.03 n.18

Boyer, Robert A. 15.06 n.57

Boyle v. CIR 9.52 n.170

Braddock Land Co. S.11.03
        n.10.1

Bradford, J.C. S.5.04 n.34

Bradford-Robinson Printing Co.
    v. US 8.03 n.52

Bradshaw v. US S.3.04 n.43;
    S.3.15 ns. 153.1, 158, 161, 162;
    S.4.04 n.37; S.6.03 ns. 31, 32

Bramlette Bldg. Corp., Inc.
    v. CIR 6.03 n.38

Brams v. CIR S.2.08 n.88.1

Branch v. US 6.03 n.34

Brans, Stanley H. S.9.32 n.135;
        S.9.33 n.138.1

Braun, W., Co. v. CIR 15.06
        n.32

Braunstein v. CIR 12.01 n.3;
    12.04 ns. 16, 30, 32; 12.07 n.55

Breech, US v. ... 11.05 n.38; 14.54
        ns. 451, 455

Bremerton Sun
    Publishing Co. 8.02
        ns. 19, 27, 34; 8.03
    ns. 45, 52; 8.06 n.81; 8.08 n.93

Brick Milling Co. 16.21
        ns. 89, 99

Briggs, Thomas W. ... 3.17 & n.74

Brigham v. US 17.34 n.154

British Motor Car Distribs.,
    Ltd., CIR v. .. 16.21 & ns. 84, 85

Brittingham, Robert M. 15.06
    ns. 36, 61; S.15.06 n.36;
        17.04 n.59

Broadview Lumber Co.
    v. US (1977) 9.31 n.130;
        S.9.31 n.130

Broadview Lumber Co.
    v. US (1975) 9.31 n.130;
        11.44 ns. 100, 104, 112

Brost Motors, Inc. 15.08 n.109

Brountas, Paul S.3.07 n.75

Brown, Alex, Inc. 8.08 n.96

Brown v. CIR 3.17 n.173;
    S.3.17 n.173; 5.04 n.40;
        14.56 ns. 498, 504

Brown, CIR v. 9.23 n.45;
    11.65 n.192; 11.71 & ns. 256,
        257, 258

Brown v. US 9.24 n.77

Brown, US v. 5.04 n.30

Brown, Clay, CIR v. ..... 11.71 &
        ns. 256, 257, 258

Brown Dynalube Co.
    v. CIR 16.21 n.73

[References are to paragraphs (¶); references to the Supplement are preceded by "S."]

[References are to paragraphs (¶); references to the Supplement are preceded by "S."]

Farha v. CIR 9.25 n.86;
          S.9.25 n.86
Farmer's Loan & Trust Co.,
     Pollack v. .... 1.01 & n.1
Farmers Union Corp.
     v. CIR 5.07 n.94
Farr, Rena 13.09 n.117
Fatland, John L. S.1.05
          ns. 20, 24, 32
Faucher, B.A. 4.09 n.106
Fawn Fashions, Inc. .... 16.22 ns.
          154, 160, 166
F.C. Publication Liquidating
     Corp. v. CIR 16.21 n.78
Fearon, Charles, Est. of 11.62
          n.135
FEC Liquidating Corp.
     v. US 11.67 n.232; 14.32
          n.274; 14.53 n.406
Federal Bulk Carriers, Inc.
     v. US 4.10 n.114
Federal Cement Tile Co.
     v. CIR 16.26 n.217
Federal Grain Corp. 3.08 n.87
Federated Dep't Stores, Inc.,
     CIR v. ...... 3.14 ns. 142, 146
Fed. Mart Corp. v. US .. 4.06 n.59
Fegan, Thos. B. S.15.06 n.57
Fehrs v. US ... 9.23 n.50; 9.31 ns.
          126, 127
Fehrs Fin. Co. v. CIR .. 7.40 n.175;
     9.21 n.22; 9.23 n.50; 9.24 ns.
     68, 71; 9.31 & n.124; 9.32 n.136;
          S.9.33 ns. 138.4, 138.14
Feifer v. US S.14.56 n.511
Feingold, Max 6.03 n.38
Feldman, Joseph W. 6.02 n.22
Fellinger v. US 4.03 n.20
Fender Sales, Inc., CIR v. 3.13
     n.129; 3.17 n.173; 7.05 n.62; 7.61
          n.198; 15.08 & ns. 95, 112
Fenix & Scisson, Inc., US v. .. 16.22
          n.155
Ferguson v. Fidelity Union
     Trust Co. 5.03 n.7
Fergusson, Joseph B. 7.04 n.55
Ferris v. US 9.02 n.4
Fibel, Harriet 11.64 n.177
Fidelity Union Trust Co.,
     Ferguson v. 5.03 n.7

Field v. CIR 5.05 n.49
58th St. Plaza Theatre, Inc.
     v. CIR ... 7.05 n.92; 15.08 n.93
Fine Realty, Inc. v. US .. 8.06 n.81
Fin Hay Realty Co. v. US ... 4.02
          n.16; 4.04 n.28
Fireoved v. US 10.05 n.34
Firestone Tire & Rubber Co. ... 4.11
     n.122; 14.13 n.72; 14.33 ns. 291,
          292
First Fed. Sav. & Loan
     Ass'n v. US 14.11 n.26
First Nat'l Bank of Altoona,
     CIR v. .... 14.14 & ns. 104, 114
First Nat'l Bank
     Little Rock S.15.23 n.153
First Nat'l State Bank
     of N.J. ... 11.44 n.111; 11.45
          n.113
First Sec. Bank of Utah,
     N.A. v. CIR 15.06 n.29;
          S.15.06 n.29; 15.07 n.79;
          15.08 n.106
First State Bank of Stratford,
     CIR v. ..... 7.21 & ns. 134, 136
Fischbein, Dave, Mfg. Co. .. 17.32
          n.139
Fisher, J. Robert 7.61 n.200;
          14.13 n.78
Fischer v. US 5.04 n.16
Fishing Tackle Prods. Co. 2.10
          n.79
Fitzgerald Motor Co.
     v. CIR 15.06 n.55
Fitzpatrick, Philip W. .. 4.09 n.104
Five Star Mfg. Co. v. CIR .. 5.04
          n.32; S.5.04 n.32
525 Co., US v. 6.03 n.36; 8.22
          n.128
Flaccus, William, Oak Leather
     Co., Helvering v. ... 11.65 n.194
Flanagan v. Helvering 9.02 n.6
Fletcher v. US S.8.20 n.106
Flint v. Stone Tracy Co. .. 1.01 &
     ns. 3, 4, 5; 2.01 & n.2
Florida Iron & Metal Co. 8.02
          n.17
Florida Mach. & Foundry Co.
     v. Fahs ...... 3.03 n.27; 3.10 &
     n.107; 3.11 n.115; 3.12 n.119

Floyd v. Schofield 11.62 n.140

Fly, Forrest Hotel Corp. v. .. 14.13 n.72

Focht, Donald D. 3.07 n.76; S.3.07 n.76

Foglesong, Frederick H., Co. ... 1.05 n.24; S.1.05 ns. 20, 24, 32; S.2.06 n.49; 8.22 n.135; S.15.06 ns. 30, 31, 35; S.15.07 ns. 79, 81

Foglesong, Frederick H., Co. v. CIR S.1.05 n.24; S.8.22 n.137; S.15.06 n.30; S.15.07 n.79

Ford v. US 11.03 n.27; 11.04 n.33

Ford Motor Co., Dodge v. .. 8.02 n.11

Foreman v. US 2.06 n.42

Foremost Dairies, Inc. v. Tomlinson 16.26 n.229

Foresun, Inc. v. CIR .. 3.15 n.161; 4.04 n.30

Forman, B., Co. .. 15.06 ns. 38, 55

Forman, B., Co., CIR v. ... 15.06 n.38; 15.08 n.105

Forrest Hotel Corp. v. Fly .. 14.13 n.72

Fors Farms, Inc. v. US 4.10 n.117

Foster, Richard H. ... S.3.17 n.177; S.7.05 n.86; S.7.21 n.140; S.15.06 ns. 23, 24, 31, 32, 32.1, 47

Fostoria Glass Co. v. Yoke .. 5.06 n.57

Fountain, C.D. 6.08 n.74

Fowler Hosiery Co. v. CIR .. 5.06 n.57; 9.52 & ns. 168, 171, 174; S.9.54 n.182.10; 17.11 n.78

Fox, Fontaine 8.20

Fox, Robert L. 7.07 n.108

Fox, CIR v. 7.04 n.60

Fox v. Harrison 9.25 n.96

Fox, Sanders v. 7.05 n.84

Frank v. CIR 3.03 n.25; 4.07 n.81

Frank v. International Canadian Corp. 15.06 n.45

Frankel, E.J. 6.07 n.67

Frantz, Leroy S.3.14

Frazell, US v. .... 3.03 & n.32

Frederick Steel Co. 11.44 n.98

Frederick Steel Co. v. CIR .. 16.26 n.243

Freedom Newspapers, Inc. .. 8.02 n.33; 8.06 n.72; 14.56 n.535

Freeman v. CIR 11.65 n.191

Freitas, George 12.04 n.32

Frelbro Corp. v. CIR .. 8.22 n.119

French, R.T., Co. .... 15.06 n.58; 15.08 ns. 64, 107

French v. US 4.09 n.107

Frentz, J.W. 2.08 n.62

Frentz v. CIR 6.02 n.7

Fribourg Nav. Co. v. CIR .. 11.62 & ns. 148, 149

Friedlander Corp. 15.06 n.36

Friend v. US 9.25 n.84

Friends Wine Cellars, Inc. 6.02 n.10

Frings, Kurt, Agency, Inc. 8.22 n.137

Fruehauf Corp. v. IRS .. 14.01 n.7

F.T.S. Assocs., Inc. .. 12.04 ns. 21, 31

Fulman v. US 8.09 n.100; S.8.09 n.100

Funk, Wilfred J. 4.09 n.105

G

Gabriel, W.E. Fabrication Co 13.05 n.70

Gada v. US .. 13.04 n.55; 13.06 ns. 84, 87, 90; 13.09 n.116

Gage, Robert, Coal Co. .. 5.06 n.57

Galewitz v. CIR ... 5.04 ns. 26, 30

Gallagher, Joseph C. .... 11.05 ns. 38, 41; 14.54

Gallo, E&J Winery v. CIR .. 16.02 n.14

Galt, Arthur T. ... 5.04 n.42; 5.07 n.82

Galt v. US 2.06 n.42

Gamman, W.C. 6.02 n.17

Garfinkel, Julius, & Co. v. CIR ...... 16.26 ns. 219, 235

Garlock, Inc. v. CIR .. 17.31 n.136

Garrett v. Campbell 3.03 n.33

[*References are to paragraphs* (¶); *references to the Supplement are preceded by* "S."]

Garris Inv. Corp. S.2.09 n.63; S.2.10 n.80

Garrow, Ralph R. 11.45 n.124

Garrow v. CIR ... 11.22 ns. 56, 58

Garvey, Inc. v. US .... S.15.23 ns. 148.1, 161

Gawler, John P. 4.09 n.95

Gazette Publishing Co. v. Self 8.07 n.84

Gazette Tel. v. CIR 8.05 n.66

Gelfand v. US 12.03 n.9

General Bancshares Corp. v. CIR 5.04 n.41

General Bancshares Corp., US v. ... 5.07 ns. 78, 92; 11.68 ns. 243, 245

General Elec. Co. v. US .... S.7.21 n.144; S.11.44 n.96.1; S.11.61 n.133; S.11.62 & n.149.2; S.11.62 n.140; S.15.06 ns. 24, 42

General Foods 17.11 n.81

General Geophysical Co. 9.64 n.198

General Guar. Mortgage Co. v. Tomlinson 7.21 n.139

General Housewares, Inc. v. US ... 11.67 n.232; S.11.67 n.232; 14.32 n.274; S.14.32 n.274

General Indus. Corp. .. 15.06 n.27; 15.08 n.109

General Ins. Agency, Inc. ... 11.03 n.23

General Management Corp. v. CIR 8.22 n.136

General Motors Corp. v. US 5.03 n.7

General Utils. & Operating Co. v. Helvering .... 7.21 & ns. 125, 132; S.7.21; S.9.64; S.9.64A

Generes, US v. ..... 4.09 & n.107; 4.10 n.113; S.4.10 n.113

Geneshaft, Arthur 7.05 n.84

Geoli Inv. Co. 16.21 n.75

George, William H. ... 14.14 n.101

Georgia-Pacific Corp. .. 4.04 n.31; 15.23 n.165

Georgia-Pacific Corp. v. US .. 14.33 n.293; 14.53 n.382

Georgia R.R. & Banking Co., US v. ... 5.06 n.58; 7.07 n.106

Gerard v. Helvering 4.08 n.88

Gerli & Co., Inc. S.5.07 n.98; S.11.68 n.246; S.17.40 n.163; S.17.43 n.201

Gerli & Co. v. CIR .. S.17.40 n.163; S.17.41 n.180; S.17.42 n.194; S.17.43 n.195

Giant Auto Parts, Ltd. .. 2.04 n.30

Gibson v. CIR 7.05 n.90; 7.63 n.243

Gidwitz, Victor E., Family Trust .. 7.07 n.115; 14.56 n.532

Gilbert, Gilbert L. S.7.05 n.74

Gilbert v. CIR .. 4.04 & ns. 29, 43; 7.05 n.75

Gilmore, Merrill C. 9.25 n.85

Gilmore, Est. of, CIR v. 14.53 n.388

Given v. CIR 2.10 n.76

Glacier State Elec. Supply Co. S.9.22 n.38; S.9.24 n.77; S.9.25 n.96; S.14.52 n.351

Gladstone Co. 17.04 n.59

Glen Raven Mills, Inc. .. 16.21 ns. 110, 115; 16.22 n.150

Glensder Textile Co. 2.02 n.13; 2.04 n.25

Glickman v. CIR ... 12.04 ns. 17, 19, 31; 12.06 n.49

Gloucester Ice & Cold Storage Co. v. CIR .... 4.04 ns. 25, 37

Glover Packing Co. v. US .. 16.22 ns. 155, 160, 166

Godall Est. v. CIR 8.03 n.53; 8.09 n.98

Godart v. CIR 4.11 n.123

Godley's Est., CIR v. ...... 7.22 & n.156

Golconda Mining Corp. 8.02 n.13; 8.08 n.96

Golden Nugget, Inc. ...... S.14.11 n.45; S.14.17 n.195; S.14.17 ns. 209, 216; S.14.34 n.300

Goldstein v. CIR ...... 7.05 n.95; 15.07 ns. 85, 87

Goldstein's Est., CIR v. 11.04 n.33

Goldwyn, CIR v. 7.04 n.58

Gooch, C.M. Lumber & Sales Co. .... 4.04 ns. 30, 32

[References are to paragraphs (¶); references to the Supplement are preceded by "S."]

Grudberg, H.B. 11.03 n.22
Grunebaum v. CIR 17.02 n.20
Gsell, R., & Co. v. CIR .. 8.02 ns. 17, 33; 8.03 n.44
Gulf Inland Corp. v. US 8.09 n.100
Gulf M. & No. R.R. 5.04 n.42
Gulf M. & No. R.R. v. US .. 14.17 n.196
Gulf Mobile & Ohio R.R. v. US S.4.06 n.59.1
Gunderson Bros. Eng's Corp. 8.22 n.121
Gunlock Corp. S.15.03 n.17; S.15.08 n.123
Gunn v. CIR 3.12 n.123
Gutierrez, Silvio 17.22 n.115
Gyro Eng'r & Supply Co. v. US 3.15 n.161

H

Haft, Robin, Trust v. CIR ... 9.23 n.50; S.9.23 n.50; 9.24 n.73; S.9.24 n.73
Hair Indus. Ltd. v. US .. 1.05 n.15
Hale v. Helvering 11.03 n.19
Hall v. CIR 15.06 n.36
Hallowell, James 3.17 n.186; S.3.17 n.182
Hall Paving Co. v. US .... 15.21 n.130; 15.24 ns. 176, 183; 16.21 n.77
Hamburgers York Road, Inc. .... 15.06 & ns. 26, 31
Hammes, Romy, Inc. 14.18 n.231; 14.53 n.401; 16.12 n.41
Hamrick, James C. .... 3.04 n.51; 7.61 n.198; 14.16 n.152; 14.31 & ns. 246, 247; 14.56 & n.500
H. & G. Indus., Inc. v. CIR .. 5.04 n.32
Hansen v. US 13.04 n.31
Hardee v. US S.7.05 n.94; S.15.08 n.90
Harder Servs., Inc. 5.04 n.32; S.5.04 n.32; 7.21 n.129
Hardin v. US 7.05 n.99; 8.03 n.47; 8.04 n.61
Harlan v. US 4.03 n.19

Harris, B.T., Corp. 5.04 n.25
Harrison, M. Lucille 7.05 n.85
Harrison, Fox v. 9.25 n.96
Harrison, Nat'l Assocs. ...... 3.17 n.178; 15.06 ns. 26, 46, 56
Harrison Property Management Co. v. US 2.10 n.79
Hart, David E. S.17.34 n.153.1
Hartland Assocs. 3.14 n.144
Hartley, Enola C. .. 2.08 n.62; 3.15 n.158
Hartman, Sanford H. .... 15.07 ns. 78, 81
Hart Metal Prods. Corp. v. US 8.20 n.109
Hartzel, Elmer W. .. 14.17 & n.214
Haserot, Henry McK. (1966) .. 3.16 n.167; 9.32 n.135; S.9.33 & n.138.1
Haserot, Henry McK. (1964) .... 9.32 & n.133; S.9.33 & n.138.1
Haserot v. CIR .... 9.32 n.134; S.9.33 & n.138.1
Haskel Eng'r & Supply Co., US v. 4.04 n.29
Hassett, Sears v. 2.03 n.18
Hatfried, Inc. v. CIR ..... 8.22 & n.131
Hauptman v. Director of Internal Revenue .. 6.02 & n.25
Hawaiian Trust Co. v. US .. 15.21 n.131; 15.24 n.180; 16.21 ns. 78, 105, 109, 115
Hawes, J.E., Corp. ... 11.65 n.202
Hawkinson v. CIR 14.34 n.312
Hay v. CIR 17.02 n.13; 17.30 n.130; 17.40 n.162
Hayden, W.O. 4.11 n.123
Hays Corp. v. CIR 14.30 n.237
Haywood Lumber & Mining Co. v. CIR 8.20 n.109
Healy, Alderson v. .. 2.01 n.6; 7.03 n.20
Heber Scowcraft Inv. Co. 9.52 n.161
Hedberg-Freidheim Contracting Co. v. CIR .. 8.02 ns. 10, 14; 8.07 n.84

[References are to paragraphs (¶); references to the Supplement are preceded by "S."]

International Artists, Ltd. ... 7.05 n.92

International Canadian Corp.,
Frank v. 15.06 n.45

International Freighting Corp.
v. CIR 3.13 n.133

International Inv. Corp.
v. CIR ...... 11.41 & ns. 72, 88

International Standard Elec.
Corp. v. CIR 17.02 n.20

International State Bank 11.44 n.112

International Trading Co.
v. CIR 5.03 n.8; 7.05 n.93

Interstate Transit Lines
v. CIR .. 2.10 n.79; 15.08 n.105

Investors Diversified Serv., Inc.
v. CIR 15.07 n.86

Investors Ins. Agency, Inc.
v. CIR S.8.22 n.121

Iowa So. Utils. Co. v. CIR ... 5.04 n.26

Ireland v. US S.7.05 n.93

Isaacson, Rosenbaum,
Spiegleman & Friedman,
P.G. v. US S.2.06 n.51.1

ISC Indus., Inc. 3.07 n.73

ITT & Cos. .. S.3.13 n.130; S.4.06
ns. 79, 126; S.14.11 n.54;
S.14.17 n.186; S.14.33 n.292;
S.14.51 n.350; S.14.53 n.424.1

Ivey, US v. 12.04 n.16

Ix, Frank, & Sons Va. Corp.
v. CIR ..... 16.26 ns. 219, 230, 235, 243

J

Jackson v. CIR 2.10 n.74;
S.3.07 n.75

Jackson Oldsmobile, Inc.,
US v. ... 16.03 ns. 18, 20; 16.22
n.160; 16.26 ns. 226, 235;
16.27 n.258

Jacobs v. CIR ... 12.02 n.7; 12.04
ns. 23, 24

Jacobs v. US .... 11.03 ns. 13, 14

Jacobson v. CIR .. 12.04 ns. 31, 32

Jacqueline, Inc. .... 16.26 ns. 224,
245; 16.27 ns. 257, 258

Jaffe, Ben 9.25 n.84

Jaglom v. CIR 8.22 n.120

James, William S. 3.03 n.25

James v. US .... 7.05 & n.102

James Realty Co. v. US .. 15.02 ns.
5, 11; 16.03 n.22; 16.21 ns. 84,
95, 103

Jamison v. US 4.07 n.86; 4.08 n.88

Jane Holding Corp., Helvering
v. 3.14 n.144

Janeway v. CIR 4.03 n.19

Jarvis, Helvering v. .... 9.65 & ns.
211-213, 216; S.9.65 & n.212

Jeanese, Inc. v. US .. 11.64 n.176;
11.65 n.183

Jeffers v. US 14.31 n.248

Jewell v. US ..... 3.07 ns. 69, 72;
7.05 n.81; 9.25 n.105

Jewell Ridge Coal Corp.
v. CIR 4.03 n.19; 4.04 n.31

JJJ Corp. v. US 8.08 n.96

Johansson v. US .. 1.05 n.24; 2.10 n.72

Johnson, Charles ... S.1.05 ns. 24,
30; S.8.20 n.104; S.15.07 n.79

Johnson, Howard S.7.05 n.84

Johnson, James H. .. S.14.17 n.175;
S.14.34 n.312; S.14.51 n.350

Johnson, Richard L. .. S.6.05 n.54.1

Johnson v. US 3.07 n.74; 7.02
ns. 11, 12; 9.01 n.1; 11.03 n.12

Johnson Bronze Co. ... 15.06 n.56

Johnson's Est. v. CIR ... 3.06 n.62

Johnson Invest. &
Rental Co. ... 8.22 ns. 122, 126;
S.8.22 n.126

Johnson, Rodgers P., Trust .. S.9.23 n.55

Johnston, Mary S.9.24 n.77

Johnston, Steadwell 6.03 n.36;
7.07 n.117

John Town, Inc. 11.64 n.176;
11.69 n.251

Joliet & C.R.R., US v. .. 7.05 n.64;
11.62 & ns. 134, 144

Jones, Edwin L. 9.52 n.161

Jones, Elvin V. 1.05 n.24;
2.06 n.49; 15.06 ns. 30, 56

[References are to paragraphs (¶); references to the Supplement are preceded by "S."]

[References are to paragraphs (¶); references to the Supplement are preceded by "S."]

n.84; 16.22 & n.148; 16.25 &
ns. 204, 206; 16.26 & ns. 213, 214,
216-221, 224, 226, 227, 229, 230,
233, 235, 243, 249, 250; S.16.26
n. 232; 16.27 n.257; 17.11 n.91
Lichtenberg, Herbert .. 4.11 n.125
Liddon v. CIR 14.54 n.434
Liflans Corp. v. US 4.04
ns. 28, 30, 36
Lilly, Eli, Co. v. US 15.06
ns. 46, 60
Linesman, Ken S.17.02 n.16
Lion Clothing Co. 8.06 n.72
Liquidating Co. 5.07 n.75;
14.32 n.268
Liquid Paper Corp.
v. US S.11.72 n.275
Lisle, Claude J. ... 9.23 ns. 45, 46
Liston Zander Credit Co.
v. US 5.06 n.58
Litton Bus Sys., Inc. 4.04 n.31
Livingston, Jefferson 3.01 n.5
Lloyd-Smith v. CIR 3.04 n.37
Local Fin. Corp. v. CIR 15.08
ns. 89, 106
Locke v. CIR ..... 5.04 ns. 18, 38
Locke Mfg. Cos. v. US .. 5.04 n.21
Lockhart, L.M. 9.52 n.161
Lockwood's Est. v. CIR ... 13.04 &
ns. 32, 34, 37, 44, 46, 63;
13.05 & ns. 72, 73, 75
Loewen v. CIR S.3.06 n.58
Loftin & Woodward, Inc.
v. US S.7.05 n.93
Logan, Burnet v. 3.15 n.161;
7.40 n.175; 9.31 & n.128;
11.03 & ns. 16, 18, 23, 26;
S.11.03 & n.26.1; 11.45 n.123;
11.62 & n.145; 14.56 ns. 498, 504
Lombard Trustees, Ltd.
v. CIR 2.07 n.57
Long v. US S.11.61 n.133
Long Island Water Corp. ... 14.12
n.67; 14.13 n.95; 14.33 n.293;
14.53 n.382
Longo, Frank J. 11.03 n.15;
11.44 n.109; 11.68 n.238
Longview Hilton Hotel Co. .. 11.68
n.239; 11.69 n.253
Lorch, Jos. S.4.09 n.107

Lorch v. CIR S.4.09 n.101;
S.4.10 n.114; S.4.17 n.186
Lots, Inc. 4.04 n.37
Louisville Store of Liberty, Ky.,
Inc. v. US 15.02 n.15
Lovett, W.R., Est. of
v. US .... S.17.22 n. 116
Lowery, CIR v. 12.04 n.32
Lowndes v. US 1.05 n.20;
S.2.06 n.64; 2.09 n.64; 3.01 n.1;
11.02 n.8; 11.03 n.30; 11.41 n.89;
11.44 n.107; 11.64 n.179
Lubin v. CIR 4.06 n.69;
8.22 n.120
Lubowitz & Sons, Joseph
v. CIR 7.05 n.74
Lucas, Fred W., Est. of S.8.02
n.29; S.8.09 n.100
Lucas v. Earl ... 1.05 & ns. 21, 22;
S.1.05 n.24; 3.17 & n.171; S.3.17
n.173; 8.20 n.104; 12.02 n.4
Luckman, Sid 7.04 n.54;
16.13 n.46
Luckman v. CIR 4.06 n.72;
7.03 n.52
Ludwig, D.K. 17.32 n.147
Luff Co. 11.65 n.183
Lufkin Foundry & Mach. Co.
v. CIR 15.06 n.73
Luke v. CIR 16.21 n.73
Lukens' Est. 9.20 n.18
Lundgren v. CIR 4.09 n.104
Lupowitz & Sons, Joseph,
v. CIR 7.05 n.74;
8.22 n.121; 15.08 n.101
Lutkins v. US 14.13 n.75
LX Cattle Co. v. US .. S.8.25 n.142
Lynch v. Hornby 7.02 n.8;
7.03 & n.21
Lynch, US v. .... 7.21 & n.141;
9.64 n.201; 11.65 n.192

M

Mackinac Island Carriage Tours,
Inc. v. CIR 15.08 n.108
Macomber, Eisner v. 1.02 n.9;
7.60 & ns. 180, 184, 188;
8.01 & n.3; 9.02 & n.3
Made Rite Inv. Co. v. CIR .. 15.02
n.5; 16.21 n.95

[References are to paragraphs (¶); references to the Supplement are preceded by "S."]

[References are to paragraphs (¶); references to the Supplement are preceded by "S."]

Mulligan, John A. 2.10 n.74
Munter, Est. of 11.65
      ns. 205, 206
Munter, CIR v. 16.02 n.12
Murphy Logging Corp.
   v. US . . . . 3.15 n. 161;
      4.10 & n.116
Murphy, Simon J., Co.
   v. CIR 1.05 n.32;
      11.68 & n.235
Mutual Loan & Sav. Co.
   v. CIR 14.01 n.2
Myerson, Manuel 4.06 n.79
Myron's Ballroom v. US 8.02
      n.20; 8.04 n.63; 8.05 n.66

N

Nadeau v. US 14.05 n.11
Napsky v. CIR 15.02
      ns. 5, 11, 14; 16.21 n.95
Nash v. US 11.65 n.203
Nash, US v. 11.62 n.147
Nassau Lens Co. 3.06 n.63
Nassau Lens, Inc. v. CIR 3.06
      n.63
National Alfalfa Dehydrating &
   Milling Co., CIR v. . . 4.06 n.59;
      4.22 n.144; 14.17 ns. 196, 197
National Bank of Commerce of
   Norfolk v. US 14.14 n.114
National Bellas Hess, Inc.,
   CIR v. 3.10 n.110
National Can Corp. v. US . . S.3.13
      ns. 126, 130; S.4.06 ns. 63, 79;
      S.14.17 n.186; S.14.33 n.292;
      S.14.53 n.424.1
National Carbide Corp.
   v. CIR . . . . 2.10 & n.77;
      S.2.10 n.80
National Farmers Union Serv.
   Corp. v. US . . . . . 4.04 ns. 28, 31
National Grocery Co., Helvering
   v. . . . . 8.01 & n.4; 8.02 n.16;
      17.20 n.112
National Inv. Corp. v. Hoey . . 1.05
      n.18
National Lead Co. v. CIR . . 1.05 &
      n.25; 15.07 n.87
National Metropolitan Bank
   v. US 2.09 n.64

National Secs. Corp.
   v. CIR 15.06 n.43
National Tea Co. . . . S.14.18 n.234;
      S.16.26 ns. 243, 246, 247.1;
      S.16.12 n.41
Natural Gasoline Corp.
   v. CIR 7.21 n.132
Natwick, J. 9.02 n.4
Naylor v. CIR 5.04 n.30
Neditch, Jean 5.04 n.20
Nelson v. CIR 4.10 n.111
Nelson, John A., Co.
   v. Helvering . . . . 14.11 &
      ns. 19, 35; 14.14 n.107
Nemours Corp. 8.02 n.25;
      8.05 n.66; 8.20 n.110
Neustadt's Trust, CIR v. . . 14.17 &
      n.189
Neville Coke & Chem. Co.
   v. CIR . . . . 14.11 & n.40;
      14.17 n.186; 14.31 n.252
Newall, A.T., Realty Co. . . . 11.65
      n.197
Newark Ledger Co. v. US . . . 5.04
      n.30
New Colonial Ice Co.
   v. Helvering . . 16.02 & ns. 9, 14;
      16.10; 16.14 & n.64; S.16.22;
      16.25 n.208; 16.26 n.217
New England Foundry
   Corp. . . . . 15.02 ns. 5, 8
New Jersey Mortgage &
   Title Co. . . . . 14.55 ns. 477, 488
Newman, Lillian M. 7.07 n.107
Newman & Co. v. CIR . . 7.23 n.161
Newman & Co. v. US . . 17.03 n.53
Newmarket Mfg. Co.
   v. US . . . . . . 16.02 & ns. 14, 16;
      16.26 n.216
New York Fruit Auction
   Corp. S.11.44 n.112;
      S.11.45 n.128; S.14.53 n.391
Nichols, North, Buse Co. 7.05
      n.92
Niederkrome v. CIR 9.25 n.93
Niedermayer, Bernard E. 9.23
      ns. 46, 48, 50
Nielsen, Reiner C. 13.04 n.36
Nielsen v. US 4.07 n.81

[References are to paragraphs (¶); references to the Supplement are preceded by "S."]

P

Pacella, Bernard .... S.1.05 ns. 20, 24, 32; S.2.06 n.49; S.15.02 n.15; S.15.06 n.30; S.15.07 ns. 78, 79, 81; S.16.21 n.124

Pacific Coast Biscuit Co. ..... 5.04 n.41; 11.68 ns. 239, 240

Pacific Coast Music Jobbers, Inc. v. CIR ... 6.03 n.28; 7.07 n.121

Pacific Transp. Co. ...... 11.45 & n.118; 14.53 n.382; 16.11 n.32

Pacific Transp. Co. v. CIR ... 3.12 n.120

Pacific Vegetable Oil Corp. v. CIR 9.01 n.1

Page v. CIR 11.65 n.216

Palmer, Daniel D. 11.03 n.14

Palmer v. CIR ...... 3.17 & n.176; 7.05 & ns. 63, 87; S.7.05 n.91; S.7.07 n.108; 7.63 ns. 242, 243, 244; S.7.63 n.244

Palmer, Ex'r v. US ... 9.51 n.150; 11.03 n.22

Paramount Land Co. v. US S.6.06 n.59.1

Paramount-Richards Theaters, Inc. v. CIR ..... 7.05 ns. 66, 84

Park, Latham S.15.06 n.57

Parker, Herbert C. 9.24 n.73

Parker, US v. 3.06 n.57

Parker Oil Co. 6.02 n.16

Parkland Place Co. v. US 3.01 n.11; 3.05 n.53

Parkside, Inc. v. CIR ... 8.22 n.127

Parshelsky's Est. v. CIR ... 13.02 n.9; 13.04 n.55; 13.09 n.116; 14.51 & ns. 341, 342; 15.02 n.11

Parsons, John G. 3.07 n.76

Pastene, R.W. 11.64 n.171; 11.65 n.184

Patten Fine Papers, Inc. v. CIR .. 16.02 n.14; 16.11 n.30; 16.26 n.217

Patterson, Ingalls Iron Works v. 5.04 n.25

Patterson, Mill Ridge Coal Co. v. .... 16.21 ns. 84, 103; 16.26 ns. 220, 221

Patterson, Pizitz v. 7.60 n.195

Patterson Trust v. US .. S.9.21 n.29; S.9.24 ns. 71, 73, 79

Paulsen v. CIR ...... S.4.03 n.21; S.14.31 ns. 242, 244

Paulsen, Herold T. ... S.14.11 n.26

Paymer v. CIR 2.10 n.73

Payne v. CIR .... 12.04 ns. 30, 31, 38, 40; 12.06 n.49

Peabody Hotel Co. ... 14.55 n.477

Peacock v. CIR 7.05 n.93

Pebble Springs Distilling Co. v. CIR 14.51 n.349

Peerless Inv. Co. 11.40 n.68

Pelton v. CIR 2.06 n.42

Pelton Steel Casting Co. v. CIR 8.02 n.15; 8.07 n.84

Penfield v. Davis 9.62 n.193

Penfield, Davis v. ... 14.17 ns. 203, 212

Penn Needle Art Co. ... 8.07 n.84

Pennroad Corp. v. CIR .. 2.03 n.22; 5.04 n.26

Penn-Texas Corp. v. US 3.13 n.128

Penn-Warrington Hosiery Mills, Inc. 13.08 n.103

PEPI, Inc. 16.21 n.114

Perfection Foods, Inc. ... 15.02 n.5

Performance Systems, Inc. v. US .... 14.18 n.232; S.14.18 ns. 234.1, 234.5; 14.53 n.386; 16.12 n.40

Perry, Thos. L. 7.07 n.121

Perry v. CIR 6.07 n.67

Pestcoe, William 6.02 n.22

Peterson, M.Q. 11.03 n.27; S.11.04 n.33

Peterson v. CIR 4.08 n.92

Peterson v. US .... S.11.65 ns. 207, 208, 209, 212

Petroleum Heat & Power Co. v. US 15.23 n.156

Petschek v. US 5.04 n.19

Phellis, US v. .... 7.01 & n.4

Philadelphia & Reading Corp. v. US S.16.14 n.64

Philadelphia Park Amusement Co. v. US 3.13 n.130; 11.04 n.24

Romy Hammes, Inc. .. 14.18 n.231; 14.53 n.401; 16.12 n.41
Ronan State Bank 1.05 n.24; 15.06 n.29
Rooney v. US ...... 3.17 & n.177
Roosevelt Hotel Co. .. 14.14 n.110; 14.55 ns. 477, 481
Rosania, Sam, Sr. 9.61 n.186
Roschuni, Elliott 7.05 n.75
Rose v. US S.14.51 n.349; S.14.54 n.441
Rose, Woolford Realty Co. v. 15.24 n.167; 16.02 n.8
Rosen, David 3.07 n.75
Rosenberg, Est. of 10.01 n.4; 14.35 n.326
Rosenthal, Arthur M. .. 3.15 n.159; 3.16 n.168
Ross v. US 14.34 n.312
Ross Glove Co. .... 1.05 n.20; 15.06 ns. 61, 64
Rosset, B.L., Est. of 7.02 n.11
Rothenberg, US v. 3.06 n.57
Roth, Jake E. S.9.25 n.84
Roubik, Jerome J. .... 1.05 ns. 20, 24; 2.06 & n.48; 15.07 n.75
Routzahn, Mason v. 7.04 n.58
Rowan v. US 4.04 n.37
Royal Oak Apartments, Inc. 11.03 n.28; 11.65 n.214
Royalty Participation Trust ... 2.03 n.19
Royle Co. 15.07 n.78
Rubber Assocs., Inc. v. CIR .. 7.05 n.99
Rubin, Richard 1.05 n.20
Rubin v. CIR ..... 1.05 n.20; 2.06 n.49; 8.20 n.104; 8.22 n.134; 15.06 n.35; 15.07 ns. 79, 81; S.15.07 n.79; 16.27 ns. 254, 255
Ruddick Corp. v. US .. S.7.05 n.86; S.7.21 ns. 140, 144; S.15.06 ns. 24, 42; S.15.08 n.96
Runnels, W.F., Est. of .. 7.05 n.93; 9.24 n.71
Ruprecht, Otto F. 11.69 n.251
Rushing, Mozelle 4.10 n.112; S.4.22
Rushing, W.B. 7.05 n.74; 11.03 n.13; 15.06 n.63

Rushing v. CIR 11.65 n.191
Russell, Edward H. ... 13.05 n.70; 14.12 n.55
Rutter, James H., Mfg. Co. .. S.8.08 n.93

S

Sachs v. CIR 7.05 n.80; 15.06 n.66
St. Louis County Water Co. v. US 4.06 n.80
Salley, James W., Inc. v. US 8.02 n.19; 8.03 n.47
Saltzman, Jack D. 12.04 n.32
Salyersville Nat'l Bank v. US .... S.15.06 ns. 29, 30
Sammons v. CIR .... 7.05 & n.72; 15.08 n.101
San Antonio Transit Co. 14.05 n.11; 14.11 n.33; 14.13 n.81
San Antonio Transit Co., Scofield v. 14.11 n.33
Sanders v. Fox 7.05 n.84
S. & L. Bldg. Corp., Burnet v. 3.07 n.74
Sandy Est. Co. 8.02 n.26; 8.03 n.44; 8.06 n.73
Sansberry v. US 4.02 n.17
Sansome, CIR v. .. 16.02 & ns. 11, 12; 16.13 n.48
Santa Anita Consol., Inc. .... 4.04 n.28; 4.10 ns. 112, 117
Santulli v. US 9.25 n.87
Saperstein, A.M., Est. of 4.09 n.102
Savarona Ship Corp. 5.03 n.8
Sayer v. US 3.06 n.62
Schaefer v. Welch 11.02 n.9
Schahet, Samuel S. 9.61 n.189
Schapiro, Morris 11.03 n.22
Schautz, W.L., Co. v. US 5.03 n.8
Schering Corp. 15.06 n.71; 17.11 n.72
Schleppy v. CIR S.3.14 n.151
Schlumberger Technical Corp. v. US 4.07 n.85
Schmidt, Ethel M. .... 9.51 n.150; 11.03 ns. 15, 22
Schmidt, James G. 7.05 n.100

[References are to paragraphs (¶); references to the Supplement are preceded by "S."]

Transamerica Corp., US v. . . . 5.07
     n.94; 11.68 n.243
Transport Trading & Terminal
     Corp., CIR v. . . . . 7.21 &
     ns. 143, 146
Trent v. CIR 4.09 n.104
Trianon Hotel Co. 9.30 n.118
Tribune Publishing Co. S.15.03
     n.19
Tri-City Dr. Pepper
     Bottling Co. 6.05 n.55
Trico Prods. Corp. 8.02 n.17
Trico Prods. Corp. v. CIR . . 8.02 &
     ns. 13, 15
Trico Prods. Corp., Mahler
     v. . . . . 8.02 & ns. 11, 13, 15
Trico Prods. Corp. v.
     McGowan . . . . 8.02 & ns. 13, 15
Trico Secs. Corp. 8.02 n.28
Tri-Lakes S.S. Co. v. CIR . . 11.41
     n.69
Trotz, Harry 3.06 n.57
Truck Terminals, Inc.
     v. CIR 3.12 n.119; 14.33
     n.287; 15.02 n.8
Truschel, W.H. . . 14.11 n.46; 14.12
     n.57; 14.31 n.243; 14.55 n.485
TSN Liquidating Corp.
     v. US . . . 5.06 n.54; S.5.06 n.54;
     7.07 n.122; S.7.07 n.122;
     7.23 n.162; 9.25 ns. 85, 86;
     S.9.25 n.85
Tufts, John F. 3.07 n.75;
     S.3.07 n.75
Tulane Hardwood
     Lumber Co. 4.07 n.85
Tulia Feedlot, Inc. v. US 4.10
     n.117; 7.05 n.97; S.7.05 n.97
Turnbow, CIR v. 14.13 n.73;
     14.34 & n.304
Turner v. CIR 3.04 n.46
Turner Advertising of Ky.,
     Inc. . . 14.16 n.152; 14.54 n.455
Turner Constr. Co. v. US . . . 3.04
     n.46; 3.10 n.110; 3.11 n.115;
     14.16 n.125; 14.31 n.256
20th Century-Fox Film Corp.
     v. CIR 12.07 n.70
Tyler v. Tomlinson 4.02 n.15;
     4.04 ns. 28, 37

U

Underhill, Wingate E. 11.03
     n.23; 15.06 n.73
Underwood v. CIR 6.07 n.67
Uneco, Inc. v. US . . 4.04 ns. 31, 44
Ungar, J., Inc. v. CIR . . . . 11.62 &
     ns. 137, 142
Union Pac. R.R. Co. v. US . . 3.14
     n.146; 4.07 n.85; 7.03
     n.20; 7.60 n.195
Union Pac. Ry.,
     Helvering v. 5.07 n.70
United Contractors, Inc.,
     CIR v. 15.23 n.143
United Gas Improvement Co.
     v. CIR 14.17 n.165
United Grocers, Ltd. v. US . . 3.14
     n.142
United Mercantile
     Agencies 11.03 n.22;
     11.62 n.138
United Nat'l Corp. v. CIR . . . 7.03
     n.33
U.S. Gypsum Co. v. US 15.06
     n.45
U.S. Holding Co. 3.06 n.62;
     11.66 ns. 227, 228; 14.34 n.324
U.S. Steel Corp. . . 15.06 ns. 45, 56
U.S. Steel Corp. v. CIR . . . S.15.06
     ns. 45, 56
Universal Leaf Tobacco Co.,
     CIR v. 7.03 n.37
University Country Club,
     Inc. 3.13 n.132
Upham, Samuel A. 9.52 n.161
Uris, Percy, Est. of . . . 9.65 n.210;
     S.9.65 n.210
Utilities & Indus. Corp. 3.14
     n.144

V

Valley Loan Ass'n v. US 6.03
     n.34
Van Dale Corp. 15.06 n.36
Van Heusden's Est. v. CIR . . 12.04
     ns. 25, 36; S.12.04 n.25
Van Hummell, Henry, Inc. . . . 8.02
     n. 27; 8.03 ns. 41, 44; 8.06 n.77

[References are to paragraphs (¶); references to the Supplement are preceded by "S."]

Van Keppel, G.W., US v. 9.23 n.50

Van Keuren, James 5.04 n.41

Van Suetendael v. CIR .. 4.07 n.81

Vaughn v. US (Cl. Ct. 1983) S.2.10 n.80

Vaughn v. US (6th Cir. 1983) ...... S.4.10 ns. 112, 113

VCA Corp. v. US .... 14.55 n.479; 16.13 ns. 51, 57, 58; S.16.13 n.51

Velvet O'Donnell Corp. ... S.15.23 n.153

Verito, Frank W. .... 11.63 n.160; 11.65 ns. 207, 209

Vermont Hydro-Electric Corp. 15.21 n.128

Vern Realty, Inc. .... 11.64 ns. 174, 175

Versitron, Inc. v. US ... 6.03 n.30; 6.04 n.40

Vesper Co. v. CIR ... 14.34 n.306

Vest, Earl 3.02 n.17

Veterans Foundation v. CIR .. 3.14 n.147

Viereck v. US .. S.11.05 ns. 43, 44; S.14.34 ns. 314, 315; S.14.53 ns. 441, 443

Vinal, Harry A., Co., Koch v. 8.05 n.70

Vinnell, Allan S. 7.40 n.175; 9.31 n.130

Virginia Ice & Freezing Corp. .... 11.64 & n.166

Virginia Materials Corp. 9.31 n.130

Virginia Metal Prods., Inc. v. CIR 16.21 n.115; 16.26 n.220

Vogel Fertilizer Co. .. S.15.03 n.17

Von Platen, Karl G. ... 9.51 n.152

Vorbleski v. CIR ... S.14.31 n.248

VSG Corp. ..... 11.03 n.15; 11.45 n.127; 16.21 ns. 101, 106, 109

Vulcan Materials Co. v. US .. 5.07 n.80; 16.21 n.86; 16.26 n.243

Vulcan Steam Forging Co. ... 8.04 n.64

Vuono-Lione, Inc. ... 8.02 ns. 25, 33; 8.03 ns. 44, 52

W

WAGE, Inc. 16.21 n.102

Wagner, William S.5.04 n.19

Wagner Elec. Co. v. US 4.04 n.31

Wakefield, CIR v. 7.22 n.155

Wales, Harold O. 11.23 n.62; 11.64 n.163

Walker v. CIR 7.05 n.93; 7.07 n.121

Walker, Ex'r v. Tomlinson .. 11.21 n.51

Wall v. US .. 9.25 & ns. 88, 89, 92, 93, 99, 103, 110; S.9.25 n.96; 9.31 n.121; 9.52 n.170

Wallace v. US 11.02 n.9

Wallace Corp. ..... 16.22 ns. 153, 167; 16.26 ns. 235, 238

Walling Est. v. CIR ... 3.17 n.178

Walter, Jim, Corp. v. US 4.06 n.54; 5.04 n.32; S.5.04 n.32; 5.07 n.94

Waltham Netoco Theatres, Inc. v. CIR 7.21 n.139

Walts, Inc. 7.05 n.97

Wanamaker, John Rodman, Trustee, CIR v. 9.30 n.117

Ward v. US S.6.02 n.19.3

Waring v. CIR 11.03 n.22

Warner, James A. 4.11 n.125

Warren v. CIR 11.03 n.22

Warren v. US .. 11.03 & ns. 24, 25

Warrensburg Board & Paper Corp. S.6.06 n.59.1

Washburne, Elihu 3.03 n.33

Washburn, Helvering v. .. 2.03 n.21

Washmont Corp. v. Hendricksen 8.23 n.138

Waterman, Largen & Co. v. US 4.07 n.85

Waterman S.S. Corp. v. CIR .. 7.07 & ns. 121, 122; S.7.07 ns. 121, 122; 9.01 n.1; 9.25 n.85

Waterman S.S. Corp., CIR v. .... 5.06 ns. 58, 62; 9.25 n.105; 11.71 n.258; 17.11 n.79

Watts, Helvering v. ..... 14.11 ns. 20, 38

Waxenberg, Maynard .. 17.11 n.72

CUMULATIVE TABLE OF
I.R.C. SECTIONS

*[**References** are to paragraphs (¶); references to the Supplement are preceded by "S."]*

[References are to paragraphs (¶); references to the Supplement are preceded by "S."]

[References are to paragraphs (¶); references to the Supplement are preceded by "S."]

[References are to paragraphs (¶); references to the Supplement are preceded by "S."]

[References are to paragraphs (¶); references to the Supplement are preceded by "S."]

[References are to paragraphs (¶); references to the Supplement are preceded by "S."]

[References are to paragraphs (¶); references to the Supplement are preceded by "S."]

[References are to paragraphs (¶); references to the Supplement are preceded by "S."]

SECTION

304 ..... S.3.07 ns. 67, 73; 3.16 &
n.167; S.3.16 ns. 167, 168; S.3.19
n.201; 6.09; 9.03; 9.25 n.93;
S.9.25 ns. 103, 105; 9.26; 9.30;
9.31 & ns. 119, 120, 130; 9.32
& ns. 135, 137; S.9.32 ns. 135,
136; S.9.33 & ns. 138.3, 138.7,
138.15, 138.16, 138.17; 9.62
n.195; 9.64 & ns. 205, 206; 11.05;
14.12; 14.53; 14.54 & ns. 456;
15.09
304–351 .... S.9.31; S.9.32 n.135;
S.9.33 n.138.5
304(a) 9.32; 11.05
304(a)(1)–
304(b)(2)(A) ... S.9.33 n.138.4
304(a)(1) .... 9.31 & ns. 120, 123,
129; S.9.31; 9.32 & ns. 137,
138; S.9.32 n.135; S.9.33 & ns.
138.4, 138.14; S.10.03; 11.44
n.100; S.14.33 n.285; 14.54;
17.33 n.151
304(a)(2) .... 9.31 & ns. 129, 132;
9.32; S.9.33; S.14.33 n.292;
S.14.53 n.424.1
304(b)(1) 9.31
304(b)(2) S.10.03; 11.05;
S.14.35 & n.334.2
304(b)(2)(A) 9.31; S.9.31;
9.32; S.9.32 n.136; S.9.33
& n.138.4; S.10.03; S.14.35 n.329
304(b)(2)(B) ..... 9.31 & n.130;
S.9.31; S.9.33
304(b)(3) S.9.31; S.14.13 n.79
304(b)(3)(A) S.3.16 n.167;
S.9.32 n.135; S.9.33 & n.138.16
304(b)(3)(B) .. S.3.07 ns. 67, 73;
S.3.16 ns. 167, 168; S.9.25 n.103;
S.9.32 n.135; S.9.33
304(b)(3)(B)(ii) .. S.9.33 n.138.7
304(b)(3)(C) S.3.16 n.168;
S.9.33
304(b)(3)(D) S.9.33
304(c) ... S.9.33; S.11.67 n.231.2;
S.14.54 n.455.1; S.14.16 n.164.1;
S.14.52 n.358; S.14.54
304(c)(2) 9.31 n.120; S.9.33
304(c)(3) S.9.33

SECTION

304(c)(3)(B) S.9.33
305 .... 5.06; S.7.06; 7.61;
7.62 & n.205; 7.63; 9.22; 9.25;
9.64 n.206; 10.01 n.1; 13.10
n.121; 14.01; 14.13 n.100; 14.17
& n.184; 14.34; 17.33 n.152
305(a) S.6.08 n.82; 7.61
& n.200; 7.62; S.7.62 n.205;
7.63 & n.237; S.7.63 n.244;
10.03 & n.6
305(b) 4.06 n.68; S.7.61
n.198; 7.62 & n.207; S.7.62 &
ns. 205, 209, 220; 7.63;
10.03; 14.17; 14.18 n.215; 14.34
& n.325; 14.56; 17.02
305(b)(1) .... 7.61 & n.203;
S.7.61; 7.62 & n.205; S.7.62
n.205; 14.13 n.78
305(b)(2) 7.61 n.203; S.7.61;
7.62 & ns. 210, 215, 223, 226;
S.9.25; 10.03; 14.17 n.182;
14.34 n.325
305(b)(3) 4.11 n.127; 7.62;
11.03
305(b)(4) ... 7.62 & n.209; S.7.62
ns. 206.1, 207, 210, 227; 10.03
& n.6; 14.17 & ns. 182, 187;
S.14.17 ns. 170, 181, 182;
14.34 n.325
305(b)(5) .... 7.62 & n.213; 10.03
305(c) 4.06 n.69; S.7.61
n.198; 7.62 & n.232; S.7.62 ns.
205, 210, 220; 9.25; S.9.25 n.108;
14.17; S.14.17 n.181; 14.34 n.325
305(d) .... 7.62 & n.224; 7.63
n.237; 9.21 n.29
305(d)(1) S.6.05 n.56.5; 7.62;
7.63;14.31 n.260; 16.24 n.201
305(d)(2) ... S.6.05 n.56.6; S.6.08
n.84.1; 7.62
305(e) S.7.06; S.7.62
305(e)(3) 7.61 n.198
306 ..... 3.11 n.113; S.3.19 n.201;
4.01; 4.03 n.2; 4.06; 4.07; 4.08;
7.07 n.108; 7.23 n.163; 7.62;
9.01 n.1; 9.23 n.61; 9.25 n.82;
9.32; 9.40 n.141; 9.64 n.206;
S.9.65 n.212; 10.02 & n.5; 10.03

[References are to paragraphs (¶); references to the Supplement are preceded by "S."]

[References are to paragraphs (¶); references to the Supplement are preceded by "S."]

[References are to paragraphs (¶); references to the Supplement are preceded by "S."]

[References are to paragraphs (¶); references to the Supplement are preceded by "S."]

[References are to paragraphs (¶); references to the Supplement are preceded by "S."]

[References are to paragraphs (¶); references to the Supplement are preceded by "S."]

[References are to paragraphs (¶); references to the Supplement are preceded by "S."]

[References are to paragraphs (¶); references to the Supplement are preceded by "S."]

[References are to paragraphs (¶); references to the Supplement are preceded by "S."]

SECTION

357 ..... 3.07; 3.12; S.3.16 n.168; S.4.12; S.9.25 n.103; S.9.32 n.135; S.9.33 & ns. 138.2, 138.3; 14.02; 14.13 n.85; 14.30; 14.32; 14.55 & n.492; 16.13 n.60

357(a) .. 3.07 & n.69; S.3.07 n.67; 3.11; S.3.16 n.167; S.9.25 ns. 103, 105; S.9.32 n.135; 14.15 n.145; 14.32; 14.53; 14.55 & n.495; S.14.55 n.488

357(b) .. 3.07 & ns. 66, 69, 72, 74, 82; S.3.07 ns. 67, 82; 3.11; 3.12 n.120; 9.25 & n.105; S.9.33 n.138.8; S.11.42 n.90; 14.14; 14.32; S.14.32 n.275; 14.55 n.489; S.14.55 n.475; 16.01 n.3; 17.40 n.172

357(c) .... 2.06; 3.07 & ns. 66, 74, 75, 76, 78, 82; S.3.07 ns. 75, 82; S.3.10 n.123; 3.11 & n.116; 3.12 n.120; 3.17 n.175; 3.19 & n.202; S.5.07; 7.21 n.148; 10.04 n.20; 14.16 n.163; S.14.18 n.226; 14.32 & n.275; S.14.32 n.275; 14.53; 14.55 ns. 475, 477; S.14.55 n.475

357(c)(1) 3.19

357(c)(3) 3.07; S.3.07 n.76; 3.11 n.116; 14.55 n.477

358 .... 3.01; 3.07; 3.11 n.112; S.3.11 ns. 113, 115; 3.14 n.149; 3.17; 4.11; 5.07; 11.45 n.116; 13.11; S.13.11 n.130.2; 14.02; 14.15; 14.30; 14.32; 14.33 n.290; 14.34 & ns. 319, 324; 14.54; 17.40

358(a) .. 14.33; 14.34; 14.53 n.409

358(a)(1) 3.11

358(a)(1)(B)(i) 3.11 n.113

358(a)(1)(B)(ii) 3.11

358(a)(2) 3.11; 14.34

358(b)(1) 3.11; 14.34

358(b)(2) 13.11 n.128

358(c) 13.11 n.128

358(d) ...... 3.07; 3.11 & n.116; 14.32

358(d)(2) 3.11 n.116

358(e) ...... 14.33 & n.290; 14.53

361 ...... 3.19; 4.06; 4.22 n.144; 7.03; 12.03; 12.08; 13.05; 14.02;

SECTION

14.11; 14.14 n.118; 14.15; S.14.20; 14.30; 14.31; 14.32; S.14.32 n.274; 14.33 n.284; 14.34; 14.36; 14.53 n.419; 14.54; 17.40; 17.41; S.17.41 & n.189.2; S.17.41A; S.17.42

361(a) ... 3.01; 3.04; 13.03; 13.14 n.146; 14.11; 14.31 & n.259; 14.32 & n.265; S.14.32

361(b) 14.32; S.14.32

361(b)(1) 14.32; 14.33

361(b)(1)(A) .. 13.05 n.67; 14.14; 14.32 & n.278; 14.33; 14.53 & n.406

361(b)(1)(B) 14.14; 14.32; 16.13 n.59

361(b)(2) 13.05 n.67; 14.32

362 .... 3.01; 3.12; 3.13; 3.14; 7.03; 14.33

362(a) .. 3.11 n.112; S.3.11 n.113; 3.12; 3.17; 14.53; 14.54

362(a)(1) .. 3.07; 3.12 n.120; 3.14

362(a)(2) .... 3.14 & n.146; 9.31

362(b) .. 5.07; 11.44 n.112; 13.03; 13.11; 14.02; 14.15; 14.30; 14.33 & n.287; 14.53 & ns. 382, 406, 409; 14.54; 17.40

362(c) .... 3.14 & ns. 139, 146, 147; S.4.06 n.80.1

362(c)(1) 3.14; 4.06

362(c)(2) 3.14

367 .... 3.03 n.34; S.3.03 n.34; 3.14 n.145; 3.19; 3.21 & n.207; S.5.07 n.98; 11.46; S.11.68 n.246; 13.15; S.13.15; 14.12 n.55; 14.13 n.79; 14.16 n.158; 14.36; 14.54 n.445; 15.08 n.97; 15.09; 16.01 n.3; 17.01; 17.04; 17.10; 17.12; 17.13 & n.99; 17.40 & ns. 158, 159, 162, 163, 167, 170, 171, 172; S.17.40 & ns. 163, 167, 170, 367; 17.41 & ns. 179, 180, 187; S.17.41A; 17.42 & n.195; S.17.42 ns. 193, 194, 195; 17.43 & ns. 203, 204; S.17.43 ns. 195, 201; 17.44 & ns. 210, 216, 217, 218, 220

[References are to paragraphs (¶); references to the Supplement are preceded by "S."]

[References are to paragraphs (¶); references to the Supplement are preceded by "S."]

[References are to paragraphs (¶); references to the Supplement are preceded by "S."]

[References are to paragraphs (¶); references to the Supplement are preceded by "S."]

SECTION

533(b) 8.01; 8.02; 8.08 n.96
534 .... 8.01; 8.08 & ns. 92, 93, 96
534(c) 8.08; S.8.08 n.93
535 .... 6.05 n.48; 8.01; 8.09
  & n.99; 17.13; S.17.25
535(b) S.8.09 n.98.1, S.15.23
535(c) 8.09
535(c)(1) 8.02 n.33; 8.03
  n.44; 8.06; 8.08
535(c)(2) 15.01; 15.02; 16.01;
  16.21
535(d) S.17.25 n.126.3
536 .... 8.01
537 .... 8.01; 8.03 8.04; 17.13
537(a) 8.07; 9.40 n.140
537(b) S.8.04
537(b)(1) S.8.04
537(b)(2) S.8.04
537(b)(4) S.8.03 n.52; S.8.04
541 .... 1.02; 1.05; 3.07 n.72; 5.01;
  6.05 n.43; 8.09 n.102; 8.20;
  S.8.20 & n.110; S.8.21 n.116;
  8.22 n.125; 8.24 n.141; 8.25;
  S.8.25; 11.64; 15.20 n.117;
  15.23: S.15.23; 16.01 n.3; 17.04;
  17.05; 17.11 & n.85; 17.13 n.100;
  17.22; 17.23 & n.117; 17.24
542 .... 1.07 n.43; 8.20; 8.21
  & n.113
542(a)(1) 8.21; 8.22
542(a)(2) 1.07 n.43; 5.03;
  8.20 n.107; 8.21; 8.23
542(b) 8.21 n.114;
  S.8.21 n.114
542(c)(1) 8.24
542(c)(2) 8.24
542(c)(3) 8.24
542(c)(4) 8.24
542(c)(5) 8.24; 17.21; 17.23
  n.117
542(c)(6) 8.24
542(c)(7) 8.24; 17.02 n.31;
  17.04; 17.21; 17.23
542(c)(8) 8.24
542(c)(9) S.8.24
542(d) 8.24
543 .... 6.03; 8.20; S.8.22
  ns. 119.1, 126; 17.23

SECTION

543(a) .... 6.03; 8.22 & n.134
543(a)(1) ..... 8.22 & n.119; 8.24
543(a)(1)(C) ... S.9.54 ns. 182.9,
  182.17
543(a)(2) .... 8.22 & n.132
543(a)(3) 8.22; 17.23 n.118
543(a)(4) 8.22
543(a)(5) .... 8.22 & n.122
543(a)(5)(B) 8.22
543(a)(6) .... 8.22 & ns. 132, 133
543(a)(6)(B) S.8.22
543(a)(6)(C) S.8.22
543(a)(7) .... 8.22 & ns. 134, 135;
  8.24 n.141; 17.23
543(b) 8.21
543(b)(1) 8.22 n.134
543(b)(1)(C) 17.02 n.31
543(b)(2)(B) 8.22
543(b)(2)(C) 8.20 n.111;
  8.22
543(b)(3) 8.22 n.125
543(b)(4) 8.22
544 .... 5.03; 8.20; 8.23; 9.21
  n.20; 12.06 n.45; S.17.21 n.113
544(a)(1) 1.05
544(a)(2) 9.21
544(c) S.17.21 n.113
545 .... 6.05 n.48; 8.20; 8.25;
  S.15.23; 17.23 n.118
545(a) .... 17.23 & n.118
545(b) 8.25
545(b)(2) S.8.09 n.98.1
545(b)(5) S.8.09 n.98.1
545(b)(6) .... 8.22 & n.130; 8.25
545(b)(7) S.8.09 n.98.1
545(b)(8) S.8.09 n.98.1
545(c) 8.25 n.143
545(d) 17.23 n.118
546 .... 8.20
547 .... 8.20; S.8.20 n.106;
  8.25; 17.23
547(c) 8.20 n.106
547(d)(1) 8.20 n.106
551 .... 6.01 n.2; 8.22; S.8.22
  n.119.1; 17.05; 17.20; 17.22
  & ns. 115, 116; S.17.22 n.116;
  17.23 & n.117; 17.24; 17.32
  n.146; 17.40 n.171

[References are to paragraphs (¶); references to the Supplement are preceded by "S."]

[References are to paragraphs (¶); references to the Supplement are preceded by "S."]

[References are to paragraphs (¶); references to the Supplement are preceded by "S."]

[*References are to paragraphs (¶); references to the Supplement are preceded by "S."*]

[References are to paragraphs (¶); references to the Supplement are preceded by "S."]

[References are to paragraphs (¶); references to the Supplement are preceded by "S."]

[References are to paragraphs (¶); references to the Supplement are preceded by "S."]

[References are to paragraphs (¶); references to the Supplement are preceded by "S."]

[References are to paragraphs (¶); references to the Supplement are preceded by "S."]

[References are to paragraphs (¶) and footnotes (n.); references to the Supplement

[*References are to paragraphs (¶); references to the Supplement are preceded by "S."*]

CUMULATIVE TABLE OF TREASURY REGULATIONS

[References are to paragraphs (¶); references to the Supplement are preceded by "S."]

[References are to paragraphs (¶); references to the Supplement are preceded by "S."]

[References are to paragraphs (¶); references to the Supplement are preceded by "S."]

[References are to paragraphs (¶); references to the Supplement are preceded by "S."]

[*References are to paragraphs (¶); references to the Supplement are preceded by "S."*]

[References are to paragraphs (¶); references to the Supplement are preceded by "S."]

[*References are to paragraphs (¶); references to the Supplement are preceded by "S."*]

[References are to paragraphs (¶); references to the Supplement are preceded by "S."]

PROPOSED REGULATIONS

[References are to paragraphs (¶); references to the Supplement are preceded by "S."]

[References are to paragraphs (¶); references to the Supplement are preceded by "S."]

CUMULATIVE TABLE OF REVENUE RULINGS, REVENUE PROCEDURES, AND OTHER IRS RELEASES

[References are to paragraphs (¶); references to the Supplement are preceded by "S."]

REVENUE RULINGS

REV. RUL.

92 .... 5.03 n.7
95 .... 11.22 n.56
289 .... 13.02 n.13
54-13 .... 14.35 n.326
54-65 .... 14.17 ns. 171, 172
54-96 ...... 14.52 & ns. 375, 376
54-230 .... 7.03 ns. 31, 46
54-284 .... 8.22 n.122
54-396 .... 11.43 & n.95
54-408 ..... 9.02 n.4; 9.23 n.56; 9.61 & n.187
54-458 .... 9.25 n.82
54-482 .... 14.17 ns. 167, 175
54-518 ..... 11.02 & n.7; 11.23 & n.64; 11.41 n.82
55-15 .... 9.30 n.118
55-38 .... 7.07 n.106
55-45 .... 17.40 n.168
55-59 .... 14.13 n.82
55-103 ...... 13.06 & n.82; 14.52 n.378
55-119 .... 4.06 n.79; 11.45 & ns. 117, 121; 14.56 n.505
55-182 .... 17.02 n.33
55-282 .... 17.02 n.27
55-348 .... 1.07 n.44
55-355 .... 14.34 n.321
55-373 .... 9.20 n.18
55-410 ...... 7.05 n.82; 7.21 n.132
55-440 .... 14.13 ns. 71, 81
55-458 .... 15.21 n.123
55-462 .... 9.24 n.72
55-547 .... 9.20 n.18
55-677 .... 17.02 n.10

REV. RUL.

55-713 .... 7.05 n.94
55-745 .... 9.25 n.82
56-50 .... 12.04 & n.42
56-100 .... 11.04 n.34
56-116 .... 10.05 n.33; 14.35 n.330
56-137 .... 12.04 n.19
56-151 .... 5.06 n.61
56-160 .... 12.04 n.16
56-179 .. 14.17 & ns. 172, 210, 213
56-183 .... 9.24 n.72
56-184 .... 14.13 n.81
56-212 .... 11.21 n.49; 11.43 n.93
56-223 .... 10.05 n.33; 14.35 n.330
56-227 .... 13.05 n.73
56-244 .... 12.04 n.26
56-286 .... 11.23 n.65
56-303 .... 3.15 n.155
56-330 .... 14.51 n.349
56-344 .... 13.05 n.73
56-345 .. 14.13 n.80; 14.14 ns. 101, 110; 14.55 n.481
56-372 .... 11.65 n.194
56-373 .... 13.11 n.134; 16.11 ns. 34, 37
56-387 ..... 11.64 & ns. 180, 181, 182
56-448 ...... 6.09 n.90; 11.65 & n.218
56-450 .... 13.08 n.104
56-451 .... 13.04 n.41
56-510 .... 5.06 n.60

[References are to paragraphs (¶); references to the Supplement are preceded by "S."]

REV. RUL.

56-513 ...... 9.61 & ns. 185, 186; 9.63 n.196
56-542 .... 2.10 n.79
56-554 .... 13.04 n.41
56-555 .... 13.04 n.55; 13.11 n.129
56-556 .... 9.23 ns. 56, 61
56-557 ... 13.04 n.41; 13.11 n.129
56-572 .... 7.63 n.240
56-584 .... 9.23 n.61
56-586 ...... 14.17 n.175; 14.35 n.332
56-613 .... S.3.08 n.88.1
56-653 .... 7.62 n.228
56-655 .... 13.04 n.41
56-681 .... 15.22 n.134
57-103 ... 10.05 n.33; 14.35 n.330
57-106 .... 17.11 n.74
57-114 ... 13.14 n.154; 14.13 n.80; 14.52 ns. 361, 368
57-126 .... 13.05 n.73
57-132 .... 10.03 n.9
57-140 .... 11.64 & n.165
57-144 ... 13.05 n.69; S.13.05 n.69
57-190 ... 13.04 n.41; 13.05 n.74
57-212 ... 10.05 n.33; 14.35 n.330
57-243 .... 11.65 n.196
57-276 .... 14.16 n.164; 14.18 & ns. 219, 225; 16.11 n.38
57-278 .... 14.14 n.129; 14.33 & n.283; S.14.33 n.284; 14.53 n.412
57-296 .. 3.04 n.36; 11.44 ns. 100, 103; S.11.44 n.103
57-328 ... 10.04 & n.21; 10.07 n.39
57-332 ...... 7.03 n.50; 7.04 n.56
57-387 .... 9.23 n.61; S.9.23 n.61; 9.61 n.190
57-465 .. 14.12 n.55; 14.14 n.132; 14.16 n.161; 14.53 & n.391
57-490 .... 7.21 n.146
57-491 .... 11.21 n.48; 12.06 n.51
57-492 ... 13.04 n.50; 13.05 n.76
57-518 .... 14.14 & ns. 108, 110, 111, 114
57-535 .... 14.17 n.172
57-575 .... 12.04 n.32
58-1 .... 7.05 n.92; 15.08 n.93

REV. RUL.

58-54 .... 13.04 n.41; S.13.04 n.41
58-55 .... 17.11 n.75
58-68 ... 13.05 n.79; S.13.05 n.79; 13.06 ns. 83, 91; S.13.06 ns. 83, 91; 13.10 n.123; 14.52 & ns. 361, 368, 374, 378; S.14.52 ns. 361, 374, 378
58-79 .... 11.44 n.100
58-92 .... 11.21 n.51
58-93 ... 14.14 n.130; 14.53 n.410
58-164 .... 13.04 n.49
58-166 .... 2.05 n.40
58-234 .... 4.06 n.71; S.7.63 n.246
58-241 .... 11.66 n.224
58-391 .... 11.41 n.83
58-402 ...... 11.03 & ns. 20, 22; S.11.03 n.26.1
58-471 .... 15.22 n.134
58-479 .... 17.03 n.53
58-486 .... 17.13 n.101
58-546 .... 7.03 n.38; 14.17 n.188
58-603 .. 16.03 & n.21; 16.10 n.24; 16.26 & ns. 232, 233
58-614 .... 9.25 n.95; 9.61 n.184
59-84 .... 14.35 n.328
59-97 ...... 9.30 n.118; 9.61 n.189
59-98 ... 14.17 n.187; 14.31 n.255
59-119 .... 9.23 n.56
59-120 .... 11.65 n.201
59-184 .... 7.05 n.84
59-197 .... 13.06 n.86
59-222 .. 14.11 n.41; 14.13 ns. 84, 86; 14.16 n.152; 14.17 n.188; 14.31 n.255
59-233 .... 9.23 n.53; S.9.23 n.55
59-235 .... 6.02 n.11
59-259 .... 3.08 n.87
59-286 .... 9.25 n.101
59-296 .... 11.42 n.90; 14.16 n.152
59-395 .... 16.26 & ns. 215, 216; 17.11 n.91
59-400 .... 13.05 & n.77
59-412 .... 11.45 n.116
60-1 .... 14.35 n.330
60-18 .... 9.21 n.23
60-37 .... 4.06 n.68; 4.22 n.144; 14.17 & ns. 192, 193, 194
60-48 .... 4.10 n.111

[References are to paragraphs (¶); references to the Supplement are preceded by "S."]

REV. RUL.

60-50	11.02 n.8
60-51	11.02 n.8
60-64	3.10 n.103
60-68	12.06 n.53
60-192	17.24 n.122
60-232	9.52 n.168
60-236	11.65 n.214
60-262	11.44 n.112; 11.45 n.128
60-302	3.07 n.78
60-322	9.52 n.167
60-331	3.17 & n.184; 7.07 n.107; 8.20 n.106
60-370	10.07 n.39
61-18	3.13 n.132; 14.31 n.242
61-96	7.40 n.174
61-97	14.34 n.322
61-112	6.03 n.38
61-115	5.04 n.38
61-134	7.05 n.85
61-156	3.10 n.103; 11.05 n.37; 14.54 & ns. 429, 437, 443, 452, 461
61-175	2.03 n.19
61-191	2.09 n.64; 11.02 n.8; 11.62 n.134; 16.27 ns. 257, 258
62-31	17.02 ns. 33, 34
62-42	S.5.06
62-45	11.68 & n.233
62-116	6.03 n.27
62-128	3.17 & n.179
62-131	7.04 & n.57
62-202	6.05 n.45
62-217	3.13 n.133
63-6	17.11 n.80; 17.43 & n.200
63-28	3.15 n.155
63-29	14.51 n.349; S.14.51 ns. 349, 349.1
63-40	16.03 ns. 18, 19; 16.21 & ns. 120, 121; 16.22 n.145; 16.25 n.206; 16.26 & ns. 225, 227, 234
63-51	17.11 n.74
63-63	7.03 n.44
63-107	2.01 n.7; 11.02 n.6
63-113	17.02 n.33
63-114	11.21 n.48; 12.04 n.20; 12.06 n.44
63-125	11.66 n.224; 12.06 n.44
63-225	4.06 n.71

REV. RUL.

63-226	3.08 n.87; 6.02 ns. 15, 16
63-228	2.03 n.20
63-233	11.65 n.214
63-234	14.13 n.70
63-245	11.64 n.176
63-259	5.07 n.78
63-260	13.03 n.17
64-51	17.03 n.53
64-56	3.03 ns. 34, 35; 8.22 ns. 123, 124; 12.04 n.21; 15.06 n.59; 17.02 n.14; 17.42 n.195
64-73	14.14 & ns. 119, 120; 14.53 & n.417; 14.55 n.495
64-93	15.24 n.179
64-94	6.03 n.30
64-100	11.65 n.194
64-102	13.05 n.79; 13.06 n.92
64-125	12.04 n.20
64-146	7.03 n.44
64-147	13.04
64-155	3.07 n.74; 3.14 n.145; 7.23 n.162; 15.08 n.97
64-156	17.40 n.167
64-157	17.40 n.171; 17.43 n.204
64-158	17.40 n.165
64-177	17.40 n.162; 17.41 n.179; 17.43 n.203
64-220	2.03 n.19
64-225	15.08 n.92
64-232	6.03 n.38
64-235	3.03 n.34; 15.06 n.59
64-236	5.04 n.20
64-250	6.03 n.30
64-257	11.21 n.51
64-290	7.04 n.59
64-308	6.05 n.44; 7.07 n.110
64-328	7.05 n.94; 15.08 ns. 90, 93
65-23	7.04 n.59
65-30	11.64 n.171
65-31	4.06 n.71
65-40	6.03 n.38
65-68	8.05 n.70
65-80	9.52 n.174; 11.64 n.171
65-83	6.03 n.38
65-91	6.03 n.38
65-155	3.06 n.55; S.3.06 n.55; S.14.34 n.301

[References are to paragraphs (¶); references to the Supplement are preceded by "S."]

[References are to paragraphs (¶); references to the Supplement are preceded by "S."]

[References are to paragraphs (¶); references to the Supplement are preceded by "S."]

REV. RUL.

69-617 ...... 14.53 ns. 386, 405
69-623 .... 15.24 n.179
69-630 .... 7.05 n.71; 9.32 n.138;
                   15.06 n.63
70-6 .... 7.23 n.162
70-18 .... 13.03 n.17
70-27 .... 16.12 n.38
70-41 .... 14.13 ns. 78, 86
70-45 .... 3.03 n.34
70-50 .... 6.07 n.67
70-65 .... 14.13 ns. 87, 96
70-83 .... 16.13 n.51
70-93 .... 12.06 n.52
70-101 .... 2.01 & n.8; 2.06 ns. 45,
                      46, 47
70-104 .... 9.23 n.56
70-106 ... 11.41 n.81; 11.44 n.102
70-107 .. 14.14 n.122; 14.55 n.495
70-108 .... 14.13 n.72; 14.31 n.264
70-111 .... 9.32 n.138
70-120 ..... 14.31 n.248; 14.56 &
             n.511; 16.23 n.183
70-128 .... 16.13 n.52
70-140 .. 3.02 & ns. 16, 17; S.3.02
  n.16; 3.10 n.99; 3.17 n.186; 3.19;
  11.21 n.55; 12.04 n.24; 14.13
  n.99; 14.52 ns. 357, 374, 375
70-141 .... S.15.23 n.151
70-153 .... 8.22 n.122
70-172 .... 14.13 n.94; 14.52
              ns. 361, 368
70-199 .... 14.35 n.329
70-223 .... 14.53 n.391
70-224 .. 14.14 n.122; 14.55 n.495
70-225 .... 3.10 n.99; 13.06 n.81;
    14.13 n.99; 14.52 & ns. 370,
                  372, 375
70-232 .... 6.03 n.30
70-238 ..... 16.21 & ns. 122, 123
70-239 ... 3.18 & ns. 195, 196, 197;
         S.3.18 ns. 195, 196
70-240 ... 11.05 n.38; 11.67 n.230;
    14.34 n.307; 14.54 ns. 443, 445
70-241 .. 5.07 ns. 72, 79, 89; 16.13
                  n.51
70-263 .... 17.05 n.64
70-269 ... 14.13 n.78; 14.55 n.476
70-271 .... 3.11 n.113; 7.21 n.129;

REV. RUL.

  11.42 n.91; 11.45 n.116; 11.61
  n.130; 11.67 n.232; 11.69 ns. 250,
  251; 13.03 n.16; 13.11 n.133;
  S.13.11 n.133; 14.17 n.188; 14.32
  & ns. 28, 268, 273, 278; 14.34 &
  ns. 296, 318; 14.53 n.413; 14.55
                   n.492
70-290 .... 17.11 n.75
70-291 .... 3.14 n.149
70-296 .... 7.07 n.111
70-298 .... 14.11 n.25; 14.17 n.175
70-300 .. 14.31 n.248; 14.56 n.507
70-301 .... 8.03 n.52
70-303 .... 17.11 n.75
70-304 .... 17.02 n.19
70-305 ... 3.13 n.126; 14.33 n.285
70-353 .... 5.04 n.43
70-357 .... 11.41 n.73
70-359 .... 5.04 n.43
70-360 .... 5.04 n.43
70-368 .... 4.06 n.56
70-377 .... 17.02 n.12
70-378 .... 15.23 n.156
70-379 .... 17.04 n.58
70-397 .... 12.06 n.52
70-433 ..... 3.19 & n.200; 14.13
  n.97; 14.53 n.394; 17.40 n.168;
            17.44 n.208
70-434 .... 13.06 n.91; 14.13 n.99;
  14.52 ns. 368, 370, 371, 377, 378
70-469 .... 15.21 n.123
70-489 .... 11.42 n.90
70-496 .... 9.31 n.120; 9.62 n.195
70-497 .... 8.09 n.99
70-521 ..... 4.06 n.71; 7.05 n.91;
  S.7.05 n.91; 7.60 n.178; 7.62
  n.230; 7.63 n.244; S.7.63 n.244;
         S.13.13 n.144
70-522 .... 3.10 n.99
70-531 .. 7.02 n.16; 9.65 & ns. 212,
  215, 216, 217; S.9.65 & n.212
70-540 .... 17.02 n.11
70-609 .... 7.04 n.55
70-626 .... 3.07 n.74; 10.04 n.20
70-639 .... 9.23 n.45
71-65 ... 7.23 n.161; 17.11 ns. 77,
                  81

[References are to paragraphs (¶); references to the Supplement are preceded by "S."]

[References are to paragraphs (¶); references to the Supplement are preceded by "S."]

[References are to paragraphs (¶); references to the Supplement are preceded by "S."]

[References are to paragraphs (¶); references to the Supplement are preceded by "S."]

[References are to paragraphs (¶); references to the Supplement are preceded by "S."]

[References are to paragraphs (¶); references to the Supplement are preceded by "S."]

[References are to paragraphs (¶); references to the Supplement are preceded by "S."]

REV. RUL.

80-177 .... S.11.03 n.14.1
80-181 .... S.13.04 n.54
80-189 ...... S.9.31 n.130; S.9.33
    n.138.12; S.14.33 ns. 285, 292;
    S.14.53 n.424.1
80-198 ...... S.3.12 n.120; S.3.17
    ns. 174, 175, 177, 178
80-199 .... S.3.07 n.76
80-213 .... S.7.22 n.152
80-221 .... S.3.01 n.16; S.9.64
    ns. 202, 207.1; S.9.64A n.209.6
80-228 ... S.3.04 n.46; S.3.07 n.69
80-231 ..... S.15.06 n.68; S.17.11
    n.82
80-236 .... S.6.07 n.67
80-238 .... S.5.06 n.62
80-239 ...... S.3.16 n.168; S.9.32
    n.136; S.9.33 ns. 138.3, 138.11
80-240 .. S.3.04 n.46; S.3.07 ns. 67,
    69; S.9.25 n.96; S.9.32 n.135;
    S.9.33 & n.138.5; S.14.55 n.489
80-246 .... S.17.42 n.193
80-247 .... S.17.42 n.193
80-283 .... S.7.21 n.148.1
80-284 .... S.3.05 n.54; S.3.19
    & n.203.2; S.9.33 n.138.18;
    S.14.11 n.31
80-285 .... S.3.05 n.54; S.3.19
    & n.203.2; S.9.33 n.138.18;
    S.14.11 n.31
80-293 .... S.17.42 n.193
80-358 .... S.11.44 ns. 100.1, 105
81-3 .... S.9.52 n.172; S.9.54
    n.182.10
81-4 .... S.17.40 n.173; S.17.41A;
    S.17.42 n.194
81-25 .... S.14.51 n.349
81-41 .... S.9.22 n.34
81-81 ...... S.14.34 ns. 314, 316
81-82 .... S.17.42 n.193
81-84 ...... S.15.23 ns. 144, 163
81-89 .... S.17.42 n.193
81-91 .. S.10.03 n.9; S.14.35 n.326
81-92 .... S.14.51
81-186 .... S.14.35 n.329
81-190 .... S.7.62 n.209
81-197 .... S.6.04 n.38

REV. RUL.

81-204 .... S.14.01 n.2
81-233 .... S.9.23 n.56
81-247 .... S.14.14 n.130; S.14.15
    n.140; S.14.51 n.349.2
81-289 ..... S.9.24 ns. 70, 71, 75,
    77, 79
82-11 ..... S.5.06 n.54; S.7.07 ns.
    116, 118, 119
82-20 ... S.15.23 & ns. 145, 151.2
82-34 ..... S.14.17 n.165; S.14.51
    ns. 349, 349.2
82-45 .... S.15.06 n.29
82-72 .... S.9.32 n.141;
    S.9.65 ns. 210.1, 212
82-80 .. S.15.06 ns. 65.1, 71, 71.1;
    S.15.08 n.99.1
82-112 .... S.17.41 n.192
82-118 .... S.14.51 n.328
82-129 .... S.9.23 n.66
82-130 .... S.13.09 n.114
82-131 .... S.13.09 n.114
82-135 .... S.15.06 n.54
82-150 .... S.3.10 n.109
82-152 .... S.15.24 n.173
82-158 .... S.7.61 n.198; S.7.62
    ns. 205, 220
82-187 ..... S.9.52 ns. 168, 169.1;
    S.9.54 n.182.11
82-191 .... S.14.35 n.328
82-201 .... S.6.03 n.30
82-219 .... S.13.04 n.23
83-14 .... S.15.24 n.176.1
83-23 ...... S.13.06 n.86; S.13.09
    n.114; S.17.44 n.220
83-34 ... S.3.10 n.96; S.14.11 n.28;
    S.14.53 n.416
83-38 ...... S.9.64 ns. 202, 207.1;
    S.9.64A n.209.6
83-42 .... S.7.62 n.207
83-61 .... S.11.21 n.55
83-65 .... S.3.06 n.58
83-68 .... S.7.62 n.205
83-73 ...... S.14.56 ns. 516, 535;
    S.16.13 ns. 51, 57, 58
83-98 .... S.4.03 ns. 21, 24
83-114 ..... S.13.05 n.79; S.13.06
   ns. 83, 91; S.13.09 n.114; S.14.51
    n.350; S.14.52 ns. 374, 378

[References are to paragraphs (¶); references to the Supplement are preceded by "S."]

REVENUE PROCEDURES

[References are to paragraphs (¶); references to the Supplement are preceded by "S."]

GENERAL COUNSEL'S MEMORANDA

[References are to paragraphs (¶); references to the Supplement are preceded by "S."]

INCOME TAX UNIT RULINGS

I.T.

2417	7.62 n.228
3543	7.04 n.54
3706	3.14 n.149
3781	17.03 n.53
3896	15.21 ns. 127, 128

I.T.

3930	2.05 & n.40
3948	2.05 n.40
4007	7.07 n.107
4109	11.42 n.91

INTERNAL REVENUE NEWS RELEASES

I.R.

1703	17.11 n.82
82-145	S.2.02 n.13.1; S.2.04 ns. 24, 33

I.R.

83-56	S.4.05

OFFICE DECISIONS

O.D.

735	7.62 n.228

TECHNICAL INFORMATION RELEASES

T.I.R.

113	6.02 ns. 11, 14, 21
457	7.05 n.82
764	15.23 n.143
773	16.21 n.121; 16.26 & ns. 227, 237
838	15.08 n.89
839	15.06 n.63; 15.08 n.100

T.I.R.

978	17.43 n.213
1160	14.33 ns. 292, 294
1193	17.44 n.218
1248	6.02 n.19
1354	17.44 n.213
1361	13.04 ns. 28, 29, 35

TREASURY DECISIONS

T.D.

4603	4.06 n.67
6378	8.02 n.31
6476	7.61 n.201
6813	15.24 n.170
6990	7.61 n.202
6969	9.21 n.22
7004	7.61 n.202
7343	16.23 n.174; 17.11 n.91
7422	14.15 n.140; 14.33 n.292
7467	17.15 n.111
7515	2.06 n.46
7655	S.12.08 n.71
7685	S.15.23 n.157
7745	S.14.51

T.D.

7781	S.4.06 n.62; S.14.31 n.256; S.14.56 n.507
7791	S.5.03 n.15.01
7863	S.17.41 ns. 185, 190
7872	S.6.02; S.6.03 & n.26; S.6.05 ns. 56.4, 56.5
7889	S.2.04 n.27
7918	S.17.11 n.75.1
7920	S.4.01 n.10; S.4.02 n.14; S.4.03; S.4.04 ns. 29, 36, 37, 39.1; S.6.02 n.19; S.7.05 n.74; S.9.22 n.40; S.9.23 n.46; S.15.06 ns. 54, 63; S.15.08 ns. 100, 101
7942	S.11.47 ns. 129.7, 129.10

CUMULATIVE INDEX
TO CITED ARTICLES

[References are to paragraphs (¶) and footnotes (n.); references to the Supplement are preceded by "S."]

CHAPTER 1: INTRODUCTORY

ARTICLES

Allen, "REIT Provisions Substantially Changed by TRA," 46 J. Tax. 114 (1977) 1.06, n.35

Andrews, "Guide to the Administration of Regulated Investment Companies," 35 Taxes 662 (1957) 1.06, n.34

Asbill, "Cooperatives: Tax Treatment of Patronage Refunds," 42 Va. L. Rev. 1087 (1956) 1.06, n.39

Barr, "A Threat to the Lifeless Corporate Skeleton: Disregarding the Corporate Entity," 51 Taxes 555 (1973) 1.06, n.33

Bittker & Rahdert, "The Exemption of Nonprofit Organizations From Federal Income Taxation," 85 Yale L.J. 299 (1976) . 1.07, n.40

Blum, "Motive, Intent, and Purpose in Federal Income Taxation," 34 U. Chi. L. Rev. 485 (1967) 1.05, n.27

Casazza, "Federal Income Taxation of Farmers and Farmers' Cooperatives, 1913-1976," 2 Del. J. Corp. L. 309 (1977) 1.06, n.39

Chirelstein, "Learned Hand's Contribution to the Law of Tax Avoidance," 77 Yale L.J. 440 (1968) 1.05, n.25

Clark, "The Federal Income Taxation of Financial Intermediaries," 84 Yale L.J. 1603 (1975) 1.06, n.38

Clark, "The Morphogenesis of Subchapter C: An Essay in Statutory Evolution and Reform," 87 Yale L.J. 90 (1977) 1.08, n.46

Cleary, "The Corporate Entity in Tax Cases," 1 Tax L. Rev. 3 (1945) 1.06, n.33

Cohen, "Taxing the State of Mind," 12 Tax Exec. 200 (1960) 1.06, n.33

Couper, "The Farmer, the Cooperative and the Commissioner," 7 Hastings L.J. 143 (1956) 1.06, n.39

Cragg, Harberger & Mieszkowski, "Empirical Evidence on the Incidence of the Corporation Income Tax," 75 J. Pol. Econ. 811 (1967) 1.03, n.13

Eliasberg, "New Controls on 501(c) (3) Entities: What They Mean to Practitioners," 32 J. Tax. 236 (1970) 1.07, n.41

Eliasberg, "New Law Threatens Private Foundations: An Analysis of the New Restrictions," 32 J. Tax. 156 (1970) 1.07, n.41

Eustice, "Contract Rights, Capital Gain, and Assignment of Income —The *Ferrer* Case," 20 Tax L. Rev. 1, 51 (1964) .. 1.05, n.24

Feldstein & Frisch, "Corporate Tax Integration: The Estimated Effects on Capital Accumulation and Tax Distribution of Two Integration Proposals," 30 Nat'l Tax. J. 37 (1977) 1.08, n.46

[References are to paragraphs (¶) and footnotes (n.); references to the Supplement are preceded by "S."]

Feuer, "Section 482, Assignment of Income Principles and Personal Service Corporations," 59 Taxes 564 (1981) S.1.05, n.24

Gombinski & Kaplan, "Demise of the Tax Motivated Personal Service Corporation," 1 J. Copyright, Entertainment & Sports L. 73 (1982) S.1.05, n.24

Gourevitch, "Corporate Tax Integration: The European Experience," 31 Tax L. Rev. 65 (1977) .....
1.08, n.46

Halpern, "Real Estate Investment Trusts and the Tax Reform Act of 1976," 31 Tax Law. 329 (1978) S.1.06, n.35

Harberger, "The Incidence of the Corporation Income Tax," 70 J. Pol. Econ. 215 (1962) ....
1.03, n.13

Hobbet, "The Corporate Entity: When Will It Be Recognized for Federal Tax Purposes?" 30 J. Tax. 74 (1969) 1.06, n.33

Isenberg, "Musings on Form and Substance in Taxation," 49 U. Chi. L. Rev. 859 (1982) ......
S.1.05, n.25

Joint Committee on Taxation, "Tax Policy and Capital Formation" (Comm. Print 1977) ....
1.08, n.46

Klein, "The Incidence of the Corporation Income Tax: A Lawyer's View of a Problem in Economics," 1965 Wis. L. Rev. 576 ....
1.03, n.13

Lamont, "Farmers' Cooperatives: Obtaining and Maintaining the Tax Exempt Status of Section 521," 53 N.D. L. Rev. 519 (1977) 1.06, n.39

Lyon & Eustice, "Assignment of Income: Fruit and Tree as Irrigated by the *P.G. Lake* Case," 17 Tax L. Rev. 293, 396 (1962) ....
1.05, n.24

Lyon & Eustice, "Federal Income Taxation," 36 N.Y.U. L. Rev. 642 (1961) 1.05, n.25

Maxfield, "Capital Gains and Losses," 25 Tax L. Rev. 565 (1970) 1.01, n.7

McFadden, "Section 482 and The Professional Corporation: The *Foglesong* Case," 8 J. Corp. Tax. 35 (1981) S.1.05, n.24

McLure, "General Equilibrium Incidence Analysis: The Harberger Model After Ten Years," 4 J. Pub. Econ. 125 (1975) ... 1.03, n.13

McLure & Thirsk, "A Simplified Exposition of the Harberger Model, I: Tax Incidence," 28 Nat'l Tax J. 1, 195 (1975) 1.03, n.13

McLure, "Integration of the Income Taxes: Why and How," 2 J. Corp. Tax. 429 (1976) 1.08, n.46

McLure, "Integration of the Personal and Corporate Income Taxes: The Missing Element in Recent Tax Reform Proposals," 88 Harv. L. Rev. 532 (1975) 1.08, n.46

Michaelson, " 'Business Purpose' and Tax-Free Reorganization," 61 Yale L.J. 14 (1952) .. 1.05, n.27

Moore, "Current Problems of Exempt Organizations," 24 Tax L. Rev. 469 (1969) ... 1.07, n.40

Murphey, "Income Taxation of Exempt Farmers' Cooperatives," 17 Ohio St. L.J. 58 (1956) ....
1.06, n.39

New York State Bar Ass'n Tax Section, "Report on Foreign Entity Characterization For Federal Income Tax Purposes," 35 Tax L. Rev. 167 (1980) S.2.01, n.5

O'Connor, "Selection of the Form of the Business or Professional Organization," 56 Taxes 880 (1978) 1.03, n.12

Phillips & Cowen, "Tax Reform Implications for Real Estate Invest-

[References are to paragraphs (¶) and footnotes (n.); references to the Supplement are preceded by "S."]

[References are to paragraphs (¶) and footnotes (n.); references to the Supplement are preceded by "S."]

CHAPTER 3: ORGANIZATION OF A CORPORATION— SECTION 351 AND RELATED PROBLEMS

ARTICLES

Adess, "The Role of Section 482 in Nonrecognition Transactions — The Outer Edges," 57 Taxes 946 (1979) S.3.17, n.178

Andrews, "On Beyond Tufts," 61 Taxes 949 (1983) .. S.3.07, n.75

Arent, "Reallocation of Income and Expenses in Connection With Formation and Liquidation of Corporations," 40 Taxes 995 (1962) 3.17, n.170

Baldwin, "Section 351 of the Internal Revenue Code and 'Mid-Stream' Incorporations," 38 U. Cin. L. Rev. 96 (1969) 3.17, n.170

Banoff, "How IRS' New Zero-Basis Approach Will Affect Corporate Tax Planning," 42 J. Tax. 96 (1975) 3.03, n.24

Banoff, "Incorporation of Partnerships With Negative Capital Accounts: Can Gain Be Avoided?" 60 Taxes 411 (1982) S.3.07, n.76; S.3.18, n.196

Barnett, "Problems in Incorporating the Going Business," 59 A.B.A.J. 1090 (1973) 3.07, n.76

Berger, Gilman & Stapleton, "Section 482 and the Nonrecognition Rules: An Analysis of the Boundary Lines," 26 Tax Law. 523 (1973) 3.17, n.178

Bernstein, "Avoiding Zero Basis Problems in Capital Contributions of Debt Obligations," 50 J. Tax. 302 (1979) S.3.07, n.75

Blanchard, "The Service's Recent Attack: Taxation of Section 351 Exchanges Between Shareholders and Newly Organized Holding Companies," 35 Tax L. Rev. 163 (1981) S.3.16, n.168

Bogdanski, "Closely Held Corporation," 10 J. Corp. Tax. 357 (1984) S.3.08, n.75

Bogdanski, "Closely Held Corporation," 11 J. Corp. Tax. 268 (1984) S.3.06, n.55

Bolding, "Non-Pro Rata Stock Surrenders: Capital Contribution, Capital Loss or Ordinary Loss," 32 Tax Law. 275 (1979) S.3.14, n.151

Bowen, "The Reach of Section 351," 59 Taxes 926 (1981) S.3.19, n.203.2

Branda, "Imputed Interest and Fictitious Sales Prices: The Unexpected Effects of Section 483," 21 J. Tax. 194 (1964) .. 3.04, n.43

Burford, "Basis of Property After Erroneous Treatment of a Prior Transaction," 12 Tax L. Rev. 365, 370 (1957) ... 3.11, n.115

Burke & Chisholm, "Section 357: A Hidden Trap in Tax-Free Incorporations," 25 Tax L. Rev. 211 (1970) 3.07, n.66

Chirelstein, "Tax Pooling and Tax Postponement—The Capital Exchange Funds," 75 Yale L.J. 183 1965) 3.02, n.13

Chirelstein & Lopata, "Recent Developments in the Step-Transaction Doctrine," 60 Taxes 970 (1982) S.3.13, n.126

Cooper, "Negative Basis," 75 Harv. L. Rev. 1352 (1962) . 3.07, n.74

Corry, "Preferred Stock Issued in Tax-Free Exchanges: Does Section 306 Apply?" 35 Tax L. Rev. 113 (1979) S.3.19, n.201

Darrell, "Corporate Organizations and Reorganizations Under the Internal Revenue Code of 1954," 32 Taxes 1007, 1009-1010 (1954) 3.10, n.96

Del Cotto, "Section 357(c): Some

[References are to paragraphs (¶) and footnotes (n.); references to the Supplement are preceded by "S."]

Observations on Tax Effects to the Cash Basis Transferor," 24 Buffalo L. Rev. 1 (1974) 3.07, n.76

Dentino & Walker, "Impact of the Installment Sales Revision Act of 1980 on Evidences of Indebtedness in a Section 351 Transaction," 9 J. Corp. Tax 330 (1983) S.3.06, n.55

Eliasberg, "Does the *Knollwood* Decision Augur an End to Cemetery Bootstrap Deals?" 27 J. Tax. 224 (1967) 3.15, n.161

Ellis, "Tax Problems in Sales to Controlled Corporations," 21 Vand. L. Rev. 196 (1968) . . . 3.15, n.154

Eustice, "Cancellation of Indebtedness and the Federal Income Tax: A Problem of Creeping Confusion," 14 Tax L. Rev. 225, 238 (1959) 3.13, n.129

Eustice, "Contract Rights, Capital Gain, and Assignment of Income —The Ferrer Case," 20 Tax L. Rev. 1 (1964) 3.03, n.34

Eustice, "Tax Problems Arising From Transactions Between Affiliated or Controlled Corporations," 23 Tax L. Rev. 451 (1968) 3.17, n.178

Fisher, "Does Rev. Rul. 77-449 Signal a Change in IRS Application of the Step-Transaction Doctrine?" 51 J. Tax. 96 (1979) . . . S.3.10, n.96

Freeman, "Holding Companies: Section 351 as a Lever to Avoid Restrictions Inherent in Section 368, Section 306, and Sections 304 and 302," 6 J. Corp. Tax. 332 (1980) S.3.19, n.203.1

Friedrich, "Recent Developments," 11 J. Corp. Tax. 290 (1984) . . . S.3.19, n.203.2

Gebhardt, "When Are Loss Deductions Available on the Voluntary

Surrender of Stock?," 43 J. Tax. 22 (1975) 3.15, n.151

Goldstein, "Corporate Indebtedness to Shareholders: 'Thin Capitalization' and Related Problems," 16 Tax L. Rev. 1 (1960) 3.04, n.46

Goldstein, "Tax-Free Incorporation: Are Courts Taking Too Restrictive View of Section 351," 39 J. Tax. 165 (1973) . . . 3.17, n.170

Greenberg, "The Use of Holding Companies to Obtain Tax Advantages," 57 Taxes 847, 855 (1979) S.3.19, n.203.1

Greiner, Behling & Moffett, "Assumption of Liabilities and the Improper Purpose—A Re-examination of Section 357(b)," 32 Tax Law. 111 (1978) . . . S.3.07, n.72

Griswold, " 'Securities' and 'Continuity of Interest,' " 58 Harv. L. Rev. 705 (1945) 3.04, n.42

Harley, "Dealings Between Closely Held Corporations and Their Stockholders," 2 Tax L. Rev. 403 (1970) 3.15, n.154

Heng & Parker, "Tax-Free Debt Repurchase Using Stock-for-Debt Exchanges," 60 Taxes 527 (1982) S.3.13, n.126

Herwitz, "Allocation of Stock Between Services and Capital in the Organization of a Close Corporation," 75 Harv. L. Rev. 1098 (1962) 3.03, n.31

Hoffman, "The Substantial Proportionment Requirement of [1939 Code] Section 112(b)(5)," 5 Tax L. Rev. 235 (1950) . . 3.09, n.90

Kahn & Oesterle, "A Definition of 'Liabilities' in Internal Revenue Code Sections 357 and 358(d)," 73 Mich. L. Rev. 461 (1975) . . . 3.07, n.76

Koff, "Judicial Treatment of Covenants Not to Compete: The Third Circuit Takes a Giant Step," 24

[References are to paragraphs (¶) and footnotes (n.); references to the Supplement are preceded by "S."]

Tax L. Rev. 251 (1982) ....
S.3.10, n.103

Truskowski, "Section 358(d) and the Cash Basis Taxpayer," 56 Taxes 555 (1978) ....
S.3.07, n.76; S.3.11, n.116

Walter, "Tax Aspects of Recent Innovative Financings—Strategies for Existing Discount Debt and for New Securities," 60 Taxes 995 (1982) S.3.13, n.126

Walter, "Addendum," 61 Taxes 184 (1983) S.3.13, n.126

Wellen, "New Solutions to the Section 357(c) Problem," 52 Taxes 361 (1974) 3.07, n.76

Winston, "The IRS' No-Ruling Policy on Exchange Offers," 61 Taxes 375 (1983) S.3.02, n.14

Wray, "Transfer of Property by Shareholders to Corporate Employees Under Section 83," 52 J. Tax. 152 (1980) .. S.3.14, n.151

BOOKS

Eustice, The Tax Reform Act of 1984 (   ) ....
S.3.13 n.126; S.3.14 n.132.1

McKee, Nelson & Whitmire, Federal Taxation of Partnerships and Partners ¶ 4.09 (Warren, Gorham & Lamont 1977) 3.02, n.13

NOTES AND COMMENTS

Note, "Accounts Payable Are Not Liabilities for the Purpose of Tax-Free Incorporation — *Bongiovanni*," 40 Brooklyn L. Rev. 1395 (1974) 3.07, n.76

Note, "Contributions to the Capital of a Corporation: A Reexamination," 44 U. Cin. L. Rev. 549 (1975) 3.14, n.138

Note, *"Donald D. Focht*—Section 357 Liabilities Do Not Include Deductible Liabilities of Cash Method Taxpayers," 31 Tax Law. 243 (1977) 3.07, n.76

Note, "Section 351 Transfers to Controlled Corporations: The Forgotten Term—'Securities,' " 114 U. Pa. L. Rev. 314 (1965) ....
3.04, n.46

Note, "Section 482 and the Nonrecognition Provisions: Resolving the Conflict," 77 Nw. U.L. Rev. 670 (1982) S.3.17, n.178

Note, "Taxation of Non-Shareholder Contributions to Corporate Capital," 82 Harv. L. Rev. 619 (1969) 3.14, n.138

SEMINARS AND INSTITUTE PROCEEDINGS

Benjamin, "Problems in Transition From Sole Proprietorship or Partnership to Corporation," 26 N.Y.U. Inst. on Fed. Tax. 791 (1968) 3.17, n.170

Ellicott, "Tax and Related Problems of Going Public," 31 N.Y.U. Inst. on Fed. Tax. 365 (1973) ......
3.10, n.103

Mintz & Plumb, "Step Transactions in Corporate Reorganizations," 2 N.Y.U. Inst. on Fed. Tax. 247 (1954) 3.10, n.110

Schmidt, "Utilizing the Reorganization and Section 351 Provisions to Prepare a Corporation for Public Sale of Its Stock or Securities," 21 N.Y.U. Inst. on Fed. Tax. 1375 (1963) 3.10, n.103

Stone, "Compensation Payments by Shareholders of Employer," 30 N.Y.U. Inst. on Fed. Tax. 349 (1972) 3.14, n.149

[References are to paragraphs (¶) and footnotes (n.); references to the Supplement are preceded by "S."]

CHAPTER 4: THE CORPORATION'S CAPITAL STRUCTURE

[References are to paragraphs (¶) and footnotes (n.); references to the Supplement are preceded by "S."]

[References are to paragraphs (¶) and footnotes (n.); references to the Supplement are preceded by "S."]

CHAPTER 5: THE CORPORATION INCOME TAX

ARTICLES

Bostick & Davis, "Structuring Safe-Harbor Leasing Transactions Under the New Temporary Regulations," 56 J. Tax. 130 (1982) S.5.03

Carroad & Handman, "The Nondeductibility of Certain Losses, Expenses and Interest Items," 33 Taxes 142 (1955) .. 5.05, n.48

Cohen, "The Deductibility of Stock Redemption Expenses," 24 Case W. Res. L. Rev. 431 (1973) ... 5.04, n.18

Fleischer, "The Tax Treatment of Expenses Incurred in Investigation for a Business or Capital Investment," 14 Tax L. Rev. 567, ns. 42, 43, 111 (1959) .. 5.04, n.16

Graetz, "The 1982 Minimum Tax Amendments as a First Step in the Transition to a 'Flat-Rate' Tax," 56 So. Calif. L. Rev. 527 (1983) S.5.01, n.2.2

Grossman, "Tax Treatment of Professional Fees Related to Asset Acquisitions and Changes in Business Entities," 45 Taxes 880 (1967) 5.04, n.17, n.63

Hobbet, "Minimum Tax on Preference Items: An Analysis of a Complex New Concept," 32 J. Tax. 194 (1970) 5.01, n.2

Kaplan, "Effective Corporate Tax Rates," 2 J. Corp. Tax. 187 (1975) 5.01, n.1

Landis, "Liabilities and Purchase Price," 27 Tax L. 67 (1973) ... S.5.07, n.99

Mansfield, Galvin & Craig, "Minimum Tax and Tax Burden Adjustments," 23 Tax Law. 591 (1970) 5.01, n.2

Molloy, "The Ambiguous Tax Nature of the Various Costs of Borrowing Capital," 11 Tax L. Rev. 373 (1956) 5.07, n.70

Mooney, "The Indemnification Dilemma—Tax Problems in Protecting the Corporate Officer and Director From Liability," 51 Taxes 498 (1973) 5.04, n.29

Moore & Tilton, "Golden Parachute Restrictions Require Planning on Existing, Proposed Arrangements," 61 J. Tax. 324 (1984) S.5.05 n.50.1

Paul, "Some Problems Under the New Section 24(c)," 32 Taxes 191 (1954) 5.05, n.48

Schaffer, "The Income Tax on Intercorporate Dividends," 33 Tax Law. 161 (1979) S.5.06, n.51

Schenk, "Arrowsmith and Its Progeny: Tax Characterization by Reference to Past Events, 33 Rutgers L. Rev. 317 (1981) S.5.04, n.19

Schenk, "Minimum Tax for Tax Preferences," 48 Taxes 201 (1970) 5.10, n.2

Sturges, "The Legal Status of the Red Cross," 56 Mich. L. Rev. 1, 20-21 (1957) 5.02, n.5

Taggart, "Fines, Penalties, Bribes, and Damage Payments and Recoveries," 25 Tax L. Rev. 611 (1970) 5.04, n.35

Treasury Department, "Effective Tax Rates Paid by United States Corporations in 1972" (1978) .. 5.01, n.1

Weiss, "Income Tax Deductions on Corporate Termination," 9 Tax L. Rev. 490 (1954) ... 5.07, n.63

Weissman, "Allowable Deductions on the Formation, Reorganization, and Liquidation of a Corporation," 3 Nw. U.L. Rev. 681 (1959) 5.07, n.63

Wilberding, "An Individual's Business Investigation Expenses: An Argument Supporting Deductibility," 26 Tax Law, 219 (1973) 5.04, n.16

[References are to paragraphs (¶) and footnotes (n.); references to the Supplement are preceded by "S."]

COMMITTEE AND STAFF REPORTS

NYS Bar Ass'n, Tax Section, "Report on the Ancillary Tax Effects of Different Forms of Reorganizations," 34 Tax L. Rev. 477 (1979) S.5.07, n.63

NOTES AND COMMENTS

Note, "CA-5 in Allowing Proxy Fight Costs Eases Nonbusiness Expense Definition," 20 J. Tax. 104 (1964) 5.04, n.20

Note, "The Deductibility of Attorneys' Fees," 74 Harv. L. Rev. 1409 (1961) 5.04, n.34

Note, "The Deductibility of Organization Expenses Upon Merger," 21 Tax L. Rev. 447 (1966) 5.07, n.63

Note, "Proxy Fight Expenses: Problems of Tax Deduction," 43 Va. L. Rev. 891 (1957) 5.04, n.20

Note, "Tax Treatment of Section 16(b) Payments," 27 Stan. L. Rev. 143 (1974) 5.04, n.40

SEMINARS AND INSTITUTE PROCEEDINGS

Carruthers, "How to Treat Expenses of Organization, Reorganization and Liquidation," 24 N.Y.U. Inst. on Fed. Tax. 1055 (1966) 5.07, n.63

Graichen, "The Net Operating Loss," 16 N.Y.U. Inst. on Fed. Tax. 865, 867 (1958) 5.06, n.61

Hellerstein, "Intercorporate Dividends and the Interplay Between the Dividends Received Credit and Other Provisions," 7 N.Y.U. Inst. on Fed. Tax. 547 (1949) ... 5.06, n.61

Maier, "Deduction of Expenses Incurred in Corporate Reorganizations and Liquidations," 1968 So. Calif. Fed. Tax Inst. 253 ...... 5.07, n.63

Melnick, "Equipment Leasing Under ERTA," TMM 81-21, Oct. 19, 1981 .... S.5.03, n.15.1

BOOK

Eustice, The Tax Reform Act of 1984 .... S.5.05, n.50.1

CHAPTER 6: CORPORATE ELECTIONS UNDER SUBCHAPTER S

ARTICLES

Braverman, "Special Subchapter S Situations—Regulations Run Rampant," 114 U. Pa. L. Rev. 680 (1966) 6.01, n.1

Briskin, "Use Of Subchapter S Corporations To Shift Income Among Family Members," 59 Taxes 557 (1981) S.6.05, n.44

Caplin, "Subchapter S v Partnership: A Proposed Legislative Program," 46 Va. L. Rev. 6 (1960) 6.01, n.1

Carter, "Selective Election of Subchapter S Status for Net Operating Loss Pass-Through," 27 Tax Law. 465 (1974) 6.07, n.65

Chang, "Recommendations for Restructure of Tax Rules Relating to Subchapter S: A Comparative Summary," 34 Tax L. 403 (1981) S.6.11, n.94

Coven & Hess, "The Subchapter S Revision Act of 1982: An Analysis and Appraisal," 50 Tenn. L. Rev. 569 (1983) ... S.6.11, n.96

Ellett & Tull, "Previously Taxed Income and the New S Corporation," 61 Taxes 569 (1983) S.6.08, n.84.3

Heller, "Shifting Family Income Through Subchapter S Corporations: Problems and Planning," 5 J. Corp. Tax. 157 (1978) 6.05, n.44

[References are to paragraphs (¶) and footnotes (n.); references to the Supplement are preceded by "S."]

[References are to paragraphs (¶) and footnotes (n.); references to the Supplement are preceded by "S."]

(b): Nonremedy for a Nonproblem," 45 So. Calif. L. Rev. 788 (1972) 6.08, n.74

Note, "Shareholder Agreements and Subchapter S Corporations," 19 Tax L. Rev. 391 (1964) ......
6.02, n.15

Note, "Tax Planning With Subchapter S in 1967: Problems and Prospects," 53 Va. L. Rev. 1161 (1967) 6.01, n.1

SEMINARS AND INSTITUTE
PROCEEDINGS

Beck, "Use of the Family Partnership as an Operating Device—The New Regulations," 12 N.Y.U. Inst. on Fed. Tax. 603 (1954) ..
6.05, n.54

Chase & Massen, "What Is Happening To Subchapter S Corporations," 39 N.Y.U. Inst. on Fed. Tax., Ch. 2 (1981) .. S.6.11, n.94

CHAPTER 7: DIVIDENDS AND OTHER NONLIQUIDATING DISTRIBUTIONS

ARTICLES

Adess, "The Role of Section 482 in Nonrecognition Transactions—The Outer Edges," 57 Taxes 946 (1979) S.7.21, n.140

Albrecht, " 'Dividends' and 'Earnings or Profits,' " 7 Tax L. Rev. 157 (1952) 7.03, n.18

Alexander, "Some Earnings and Profits Aspects of the Internal Revenue Code of 1954," 7 Hastings L.J. 285, 297-300 (1956) ..
7.03, n.53

Alvord & Biegel, "Basis Provisions for Stock Dividends Under the 1939 Revenue Act," 49 Yale L.J. 841 (1940) 7.60, n.188

Andrew & Wilson, "Stock Dividend Taxation Under the Tax Reform Act of 1969: Expansion of an Ominous Past," 13 Ariz. L. Rev. 751 (1971) 7.62, n.204

Andrews, " 'Out of Its Earnings and Profits': Some Reflections on the Taxation of Dividends," 69 Harv. L. Rev. 1403 (1956) .. 7.01, n.6

Anthony, "The Involuntary Dividend: A Constant Hazard to the Tax Planner," 16 J. Tax. 194 (1962) 7.05, n.67

Bacon, "Share Redemptions by Publicly Held Companies: A New

Look at Dividend Equivalence," 26 Tax L. Rev. 283 (1971) ....
7.62, n.204

Bashian, "Stock Dividends and Section 305: Realization and the Constitution," 1971 Duke L.J. 1105 ..
7.26, n.204

Blum, "The Earnings and Profits Limitation on Dividend Income: A Reappraisal," 53 Taxes 68 (1975) 7.03, n.18

BNA Tax Mgmt. Memo No. 76-20 (Sept. 27, 1976), "Corporate Payments": Effect on Earnings and Profits 7.03, n.51

Boozman, "Note, Income and Gift Tax Treatment of a Waiver of Rights to Future Undeclared Dividends by a Corporate Shareholder," 32 Vand. L. Rev. 889 (1979) S.7.07, n.113

Carlson, "Taxation of 'Taxable Stock Rights': The Strange Persistence of Palmer v. CIR," 23 Tax L. Rev. 129 (1968) ......
7.05, n.88

Cohen, Survey, Tarleau & Warren, "A Technical Revision of the Federal Income Tax Treatment of Corporate Distributions to Shareholders," 52 Colum. L. Rev. 1, 6-9 (1952) 7.01, n.6

CUMULATIVE INDEX TO CITED ARTICLES   T - 167

[References are to paragraphs (¶) and footnotes (n.); references to the Supplement are preceded by "S."]

Corry, "Stapled Stock—Time For A New Look," 36 Tax L. Rev. 167 (1981) S.7.22, n.152

Cutler, "Dividend Arrearages," 37 Taxes 309 (1959) .. 7.07, n.107

Davis & McGill, "Corporate Charitable Contributions and the Constructive Dividend Problem," 8 J. Corp. Tax. 323 (1982) S.7.05, n.79

de Kosmian, "Taxable Stock Dividends," 28 Tax Law. 57 (1974) 7.62, n.204

Del Cotto & Wolf, "The Proportionate Interest Test of Section 305 and the Supreme Court," 27 Tax L. Rev. 49 (1971) .. 7.62, n.204

Ditkoff, "Inter-Corporate Dividends and Legitimate Tax Avoidance," 4 J. Corp. Tax. 5 (1977) 7.07, n.122

Edelstein, "Earnings and Profits—Effect of Distributions and Exchanges," BNA Tax Mgmt. Portfolio No. 189-2d (1976) 7.03, n.18

Edelstein, "Earnings and Profits: General Principles and Treatment of Specific Items," BNA Tax Mgmt. Portfolio No. 175-2d (1975) 7.03, n.18

Edelstein, "Eighth Circuit's Baker Decision: Filing a Statutory Gap by Judicial Pragmaticism," 38 J. Tax. 66 (1973) .. 7.02, n.15

Emmanuel, "Earnings and Profits: An Accounting Concept?" 4 Tax L. Rev. 494 (1949) 7.03, n.18

Emory, "Is IRS Correct in Treating Corporate Charitable Contribution as Dividends?" 30 J. Tax. 8 (1969) 7.05, n.82

Eustice, "Cancellation of Indebtedness and the Federal Income Tax: A Problem of Creeping Confusion," 14 Tax L. Rev. 225 (1959) 7.03, n.35

Eustice, "Contract Rights, Capital Gain and Assignment of Income: The Ferrer Case," 20 Tax L. Rev. 1 (1964) 7.07, n.105

Eustice, "Corporations and Corporate Investors," 25 Tax L. Rev. 509 (1970) 7.62, n.204

Eustice, "Tax Problems Arising From Transactions Between Affiliated or Controlled Corporations," 23 Tax L. Rev. 451 (1968) 7.05, n.68

Gallant, "Planning Opportunity: The Gifting of Closely Held Stock to Charitable Organizations," 51 Taxes 645 (1973) .. 7.07, n.108

Gann, "Taxation of Stock Rights and Other Options: Another Look at the Persistence of *Palmer v. Commissioner*," 1979 Duke L.J. 911 .. S.7.05, n.88

Gardner, "The Tax Consequences of Shareholder Diversions in Close Corporations," 21 Tax L. Rev. 223 (1966) 7.05, n.100

Goldstein, "Tax Aspects of Corporate Business Use of Life Insurance," 18 Tax L. Rev. 133 (1963) 7.05, n.83

Grayck, "Taxing Income That Is Applied Against the Purchase Price," 12 Tax L. Rev. 381 (1957) 7.07, n.120

Griswold, "New Light on "A Reasonable Allowance for Salaries," 59 Harv. L. Rev. 286 (1945) .. 7.05, n.97

Harley, "Dealings Between Closely Held Corporations and Their Stockholders," 25 Tax L. Rev. 403 (1970) 7.05, n.66

"IRS Attempts to Stop 2-Classes-of-Common Tax-Saving Plan; Legality Questioned," 5 J. Tax. 178 (1956) 7.61, n.201

Jassy, "Dividend Treatment of Distributions of Options to Acquire Assets of the Distributing Cor-

NOTES AND COMMENTS

Note, "Aggregation of Bases Under Sections 301(c)(2) and (3)," 33 Tax. Law. 937 (1980) . . . .
S.7.02, n.11

Note, "Application of Eisner v. Macomber to Pro Rata Stock Distributions in Payment of Salaries: An Opportunity for Tax Manipulation," 64 Yale L.J. 929 (1955)
. . . . 7.61, n.198

Note, "Charitable Donations of Stock—Grove v. CIR," 40 Brooklyn L. Rev. 1410 (1974) . . . . . .
7.07, n.108

Note, "Discounted Preferred Stock Under the New Section 305 Treasury Regulations: On Confusing Debt and Equity," 84 Yale L.J. 324 (1974) 7.62, n.204;
7.62, n.208

Note, "Section 482 and the Nonrecognition Provisions: Resolving the Conflict," 77 Nw. U.L. Rev. 670 (1982) S.7.21, n.140

Comment, "Disguised Dividends: A Comprehensive Survey," 3 U.C. L.A. L. Rev. 207 (1956) . . . . . .
7.05, n.67

Comment, "Taxation of Pre-Sale, Intercorporate Dividends: Waterman S.S. Corp.," 118 U. of Pa. L. Rev. 622 (1969) . . 7.07, n.120

Comment, "Taxation of Stock Rights," 51 Calif. L. Rev. 146 (1963) 7.63, n.243

SEMINARS AND INSTITUTE PROCEEDINGS

Bittker, "Stock Dividends, Distributions in Kind, Redemptions and Liquidations Under the 1954 Code," 1955 So. Calif. Tax Inst. 349, 366-367 . . . . . 7.22, n.158

Brodsky, "What Constitutes Reasonable Compensation: Contingent Compensation Plans; Factors in Proving Reasonableness of Compensation," 19 N.Y.U. Inst. on Fed. Tax. 169 (1961) . . . .
7.05, n.97

Caldwell, "Nonqualified Stock Options and the Effect on Restrictions Imposed," 1970 So. Calif. Tax Inst. 227 . . . . . . 7.05, n.88

Loening, "Section 482 Allocations Resulting in the Creation of Income or in Constructive Dividends to Shareholders," 30 N.Y.U. Inst. on Fed. Tax. 1247 (1972) . . . .
7.05, n.68

McDaniel, "Earnings and Profits, More Than a Cold Accounting Concept: Additions to and Subtractions From," 32 N.Y.U. Inst. on Fed. Tax. 445 (1974) . . . . . .
7.03, n.18

Ray, "Stock Dividends: Section 305(b) and the Conglomerates," 21 So. Calif. Tax Inst. 341 (1969)
. . . . 7.61, n.202

Saltzman, "The New Section 305 Regulations: Planning Problems and Pitfalls," 27 So. Calif. Tax Inst. 41 (1975) . . . 7.62, n.204

Soboloff, "Payment of Compensation in the Form of Restricted Property: Problems of Employer and Employee — The Rules of New Code Section 83," 28 N.Y.U. Inst. on Fed. Tax. 1041 (1970) . . . . .
7.05, n.88

CHAPTER 8: ACCUMULATED EARNINGS AND UNDISTRIBUTED INCOME

ARTICLES

Alexander, "Foreign Personal Holding Companies and Foreign Corporations That Are Personal Holding Companies," 67 Yale L.J. 1173 (1958) 8.24, n.141

[References are to paragraphs (¶) and footnotes (n.); references to the Supplement are preceded by "S."]

[References are to paragraphs (¶) and footnotes (n.); references to the Supplement are preceded by "S."]

An Update," 4 J. Corp. Tax. 101 (1977) 8.07, n.84

Schreiber, "Accumulated Earnings Tax—The Prohibited Purpose," BNA Tax Management Memo. No. 1969-09 (May 5, 1969) 8.02, n.22

Sitrick, "The Computation of Earnings and Profits for Purposes of the Accumulated Earnings Tax," 20 Tax L. Rev. 733 (1965) 8.09, n.99

Tierney & Torkko, "Tax Court's Golconda Mining Decision: What Are Its Implications in the §531 Area?" 37 J. Tax. 290 (1972) ... 8.02, n.13

Ziegler, "The 'New' Accumulated Earnings Tax: A Survey of Recent Developments," 22 Tax L. Rev. 77 (1966) 8.01, n.5

NOTES AND COMMENTS

Comment, "Accumulated Earnings Tax: Burdens of Proof of Reasonableness and Purpose," 54 Calif. L. Rev. 1050 (1966) 8.08, n.94

Comment, "The Accumulated Earnings Tax and the Problems of Diversification," 64 Mich. L. Rev. 1135 (1966) 8.01, n.5

Note, "Derivative Actions Arising From Payment of Penalty Taxes Under Section 102," 49 Colum. L. Rev. 394 (1949) 8.02, n.11

Note, "The Use of Life Insurance to Fund Agreements Providing for Disposition of a Business Interest at Death," 71 Harv. L. Rev. 687 (1958) 8.07, n.85

SEMINARS AND INSTITUTE PROCEEDINGS

Altman, Crampton, Liles, Gannet, Winokur et al., "Improper Accumulation of Earned Surplus and Personal Holding Companies," 24 N.Y.U. Inst. on Fed. Tax. 805-993 (1966) 8.01, n.5

Cohen, "Personal Holding Companies — Entertainment Industry," 1962 So. Calif. Tax Inst. 651 .... 8.22, n.129

Feder, "Relieving the Impact of the Revenue Act of 1964 on 'New' Personal Holding Companies," 23 N.Y.U. Inst. on Fed. Tax. 723 (1965) 8.25, n.145

Ginsburg, "Real Estate Transactions Between Related Taxpayers," 26 N.Y.U. Inst. on Fed. Tax. 311 (1968) 8.22, n.133

Harris et al., "Improper Accumulation of Surplus and Personal Holding Companies: A Functional Presentation," N.Y.U. Inst. on Fed. Tax. 927, 950-958 (1966) 8.06, n.81

Libin, "Accumulations After Bardahl: Developments Affecting the Accumulated Earnings Tax," 30 N.Y.U. Inst. on Fed. Tax. 1143 (1972) 8.03, n.46

McClennen, "Relief Provisions for Personal Holding Companies in the Act of 1964, 1965 So. Calif. Tax Inst. 213 ...... 8.25, n.145

Shapiro, "Personal Holding Companies Under the 1964 Revenue Act," 1965 So. Calif. Tax. Inst. 187 .... 8.20, n.112

CHAPTER 9: STOCK REDEMPTIONS AND PARTIAL LIQUIDATIONS

ARTICLES

ABA Tax Section Report, "Overall Impact of the Tax Reform Act of 1976 on §303," 32 Tax Law. 243 (1979) S.9.40, n.139

Albrecht, " 'Dividends' and 'Earnings or Profits,' " 7 Tax L. Rev. 157, 200-207 (1952); and "Shop Talk," 21 J. Tax. 191 (1964) ... 9.65, n.211

[References are to paragraphs (¶) and footnotes (n.); references to the Supplement are preceded by "S."]

[References are to paragraphs (¶) and footnotes (n.); references to the Supplement are preceded by "S."]

[References are to paragraphs (¶) and footnotes (n.); references to the Supplement are preceded by "S."]

Kadish, "Section 303—Redemptions to Pay Death Taxes and Administrative Expenses: A Relief Provision Liberally Construed," 18 W. Res. L. Rev. 895 (1967) 9.40, n.139

Kahn, "Closely Held Stocks—Deferral and Financing of Estate Tax Costs Through Sections 303 and 6166," 35 Tax Law. 639 (1982) . . . . S.9.40, ns. 139, 143

Kahn, "Mandatory Buy-Out Agreements for Stock of Closely Held Corporations," 68 Mich. L. Rev. 1 (1969) 9.25, n.106

Katcher, "The Case of the Forgotten Basis: An Admonition to Victims of Internal Revenue Code Section 115(g)," 48 Mich. L. Rev. 465 (1950) 9.62, n.193

Kempf, "Section 304 of the Internal Revenue Code: Unmasking Disguised Dividends in Related Corporation Transactions," 33 U. Chi. L. Rev. 60, 66-75 (1965) 9.32, n.134

Kingson, "The Deep Structure of Taxation: Dividend Distributions," 85 Yale L.J. 861 (1976) 9.25, n.85

Kuntz, "Stock Redemptions Following Stock Transfers, An Expanding Safe Harbor," 58 Taxes 29 (1980) S.9.23, n.61

Lange, "Bootstrap Financing: The Redemption Technique," 18 Tax L. Rev. 323 (1963) . . 9.25, n.106

LeMaster, "The Effect of a Stock Repurchase Upon Earnings and Profits of a Public Corporation," 2 J. Corp. Tax. 476 (1976) 9.65, n.212

Marans, "Section 304: The Shadowy World of Redemptions Through Related Corporations," 22 Tax L. Rev. 161 (1967) . . . 9.31, n.119

McCoy, "Revenue Ruling 70-531: Another View," 26 Tax L. Rev. 864 (1971) 9.65, n.212

Moore, "Dividend Equivalency — Taxation of Distributions in Redemption of Stock," 19 Tax L. Rev. 249 (1964) 9.03, n.10

Murphy, "Dividend Equivalency — The End of the Beginning?" 10 Tax L. Rev. 213 (1955) 9.03, n.10

Murphy, "Partial Liquidations and the New Look," 5 Tax L. Rev. 73 (1949) 9.02, n.8

Nazum, "Waiver of the Family Ownership Rules Under Section 302 (c)(2)(A): Retention or Reacquisition of a Prohibited Interest," 11 J. Corp. Tax 19 (1984) S.9.23, n.48

Nolan, "The Uncertain Tax Treatment of Stock Redemptions: A Legislative Proposal," 65 Harv. L. Rev. 255 (1951) 9.02, n.8

Owen, "Waiver of Family Attribution by Entities May Still Present Problems Despite TEFRA," 58 J. Tax 202 (1983) . . S.9.23, n.55.2

Pedrick, "Some Latter Day Developments in the Taxation of Liquidating Distributions," 50 Mich. L. Rev. 529 (1952) 9.02, n.8

Pike, "Proposed Debt-Equity Regulations: Potent New Standards For Characterizing Purported Debt," 7 J. Corp. Tax. 195, 208 (1980) S.9.22, n.40, S.9.23, n.46

Polsky, "Planning for the Disposition of a Substantial Interest in a Closely Held Business," 46 Iowa L. Rev. 516 (1961) . . 9.25, n.106

Porter, "Redemptions of Stock with Appreciated Property: Section 311(d)," 24 Tax Law. 63 (1970) 9.64, n.205

Postlewaite & Finneran, "Section 302(b)(1): The Expanding Minnow," 64 Va. L. Rev. 561 (1978) S.9.24, n.75

Reilly, "An Approach to the Simplification and Standardization of

[References are to paragraphs (¶) and footnotes (n.); references to the Supplement are preceded by "S."]

[References are to paragraphs (¶) and footnotes (n.); references to the Supplement are preceded by "S."]

CHAPTER 10: PREFERRED STOCK BAIL-OUTS

CHAPTER 11: COMPLETE LIQUIDATIONS AND RELATED PROBLEMS

and Shareholders," 27 Tax L. Rev. 215 (1972) 11.65, n.205

Ordower, "Separating Statutory Frameworks: Incompatibility of the Complete Liquidation and Reorganization Provisions of the Internal Revenue Code," 25 St. Louis U.L.J. 9 (1981) S.11.67, n.232; S.14.32, n.274

Peckman, "Simultaneous Liquidation of Parent and Subsidiary Corporations Under Section 337," 63 A.B.A.J. 874 (1977) 11.66, n.228

Pugh, "Combining Acquired and Acquiring Corporations and their Subsidiaries: Some Anomalies of Form and Substance," 35 Tax L. Rev. 359 (1980) S.11.47, n.129.32

Pugh, "The F Reorganization: Reveille for a Sleeping Giant?" 24 Tax L. Rev. 437 (1969) 11.05, n.42

Pustilnik, "Liquidation of Closely Held Corporations Under § 337," 16 Tax L. Rev. 225 (1961) 11.64, n.170

Rock, "Corporate Liquidations Under Section 337," BNA Tax Mgmt. Portfolio No. 18-5th (1975) 11.64, n.160

Rogers, "Purchase Price Allocations in Taxable Acquisitions: New Frontiers—New Hazards," 62 Taxes 812 (1984) ..... S.11.72 ns. 261, 263, 274

Shapiro, "Recapture of Depreciation and Section 1245 of the Internal Revenue Code," 72 Yale L.J. 1483 (1963) 11.61, n.133

Sheppard, "Depreciation Recapture: Some Practical Problems in Working With Section 1245," 24 J. Tax. 194, 196 (1966) 11.44, n.99

Silverman, "Leave It to *Smith* (or 'Refinements' on Section 334(b) (2))," 33 Tax. L. Rev. 545 (1978) 11.44, n.111; S.11.47, n.129.11

Silverman & Serling, "An Analysis of the TEFRA Changes Affecting Corporate Distributions and Acquisitions," 59 J. Tax. 274 (1983) S.11.47, n.129.1

Solari, "Solving Asset Basis Problems Created by 334(b)(2) Liquidations," 29 J. Tax. 150 (1968) 11.44, n.111

Spurgeon, "Avoiding the Waves From Fairfield Steamship," 56 A.B.A.J. 1005 (1970) 11.41, n.73

Stuetzer, "Upstream Debts in Section 112(b)(6) Liquidations," 5 Tax L. Rev. 199, 209 (1950) ... 11.42, n.90

Ward, "The TEFRA Amendments to Subchapter C: Corporate Distributions and Acquisitions," 2 J. Corp. L. (1983) S.11.47, n.129.1

Webster, "The Claim of Right Doctrine: 1954 Version," 10 Tax L. Rev. 381, 399 (1955) 11.63, n.152

Weiss, "Corporate Contingent Income: A Case of Tax Planning," 12 Tax L. Rev. 73 (1956) 11.62, n.136

Yancy, "Section 338: The Result of the Legal Evolution of the Tax Treatment of Two-Step Asset Acquisitions," 61 Tex. L. Rev. 1109 (1983) S.11.47, n.129.1

Yorio, "The Revocability of Federal Tax Elections," 44 Fordham L. Rev. 463, 480-484 .. 11.23, n.62

Yost, "Delayed Section 344(b)(2) Liquidation: The *Smith* Case—A Pyrrhic Victory for the IRS," 5 J. Corp. Tax. 263 (1978) S.11.44, n.111; S.11.47, n.129.11

COMMITTEE AND STAFF REPORTS

Subchapter C Advisory Group, "Re-

CHAPTER 12: COLLAPSIBLE CORPORATIONS

ment," 21 J. Tax. 258 (1964) ... 12.06, n.46

Clark, "The Morphogenesis of Subchapter C: An Essay in Federal Statutory Evolution and Reform," 87 Yale L.J. 90 (1970) 12.08, n.77

Dauber, "Use of Reorganization Techniques to Avoid Collapsible Treatment," 49 A.B.A.J. 1214 (1963) 12.03, n.12

Del Cotto, "The Holding Company as a Collapsible Corporation Under 341 of the Internal Revenue Code," 15 Buffalo L. Rev. 524 (1966) 12.04, n.41

Faber, "Collapsible Corporation Net Expands But Proposed Regs on 341(f) Offer an Escape," 48 J. Tax. 84 (1978) 12.08, n.71

Farer, "Corporate Liquidations: Transmuting Ordinary Income Into Capital Gains," 75 Harv. L. Rev. 527 (1962) 12.01, n.1

Ginsburg, "Collapsible Corporations —Revisiting an Old Misfortune," 33 Tax L. Rev. 307 (1978) 12.03, n.12

Goldstein, "Section 341(d) and (e) —A Journey Into Never-Never Land," 10 Vill. L. Rev. 215 (1965) 12.06, n.46

Hall, "The Consenting Collapsible Corporation—§ 341(f) of the Internal Revenue Code of 1954," 12 U.C.L.A. L. Rev. 1365 (1956) .. 12.08, n.71

Hambrick, "Collapsible Corporations in Oil and Gas: Does the 1958 Act Afford Any Relief?" 28 Geo. Wash. L. Rev. 815 (1960) 12.07, n.55

Mirsky & Willens, "New Developments Auger a Changed View in Applying the Collapsible Corporation Rules," 57 J. Tax. 2 (1982) S.12.04, n.19

Nicholson, "Collapsible Corporations Section 341(f)," BNA Tax Mgmt. Portfolio No. 49-2d (1971) 12.08, n.71

Nordberg, " 'Collapsible Corporations' and the 'View', " 40 Taxes 372 (1962) 12.04, n.30

Odell, "Collapsible Corporations— some 'Softspots' in Section 341," 18 Miami L. Rev. 645 (1964) .. 12.03, n.12

Pelletier, "Shareholder Intent and Congressional Purpose in the Collapsible Corporation Morass," 20 Tax L. Rev. 699 (1965) 12.03, n.12

Sinrich, "New Collapsible Relief Measure Is More Useful Than Most Tax Men Believe," 22 J. Tax. 148 (1965) ... 12.08, n.71

BOOKS

Paul, Federal Estate and Gift Taxation 92 (1946 Supp., Little, Brown & Co.) 12.05, n.43

CHAPTER 13: CORPORATE DIVISIONS

ARTICLES

Alexander, "Some Earnings and Profits Aspects of the Internal Revenue Code of 1954," 7 Hastings L.J. 285, 302 .. 13.11, n.132

Allen & Orechkoff, "Toward a More Systematic Drafting and Interpreting of the Internal Revenue Code: Expenses, Losses and Bad Debts," 25 U. Chi. L. Rev. 1, 42-61 (1957) 13.04, n.22

Caplin, "Corporate Division Under the 1954 Code: A New Approach to the Five-Year 'Active Business' Rule," 43 Va. L. Rev. 397 (1957) 13.05, n.75

[References are to paragraphs (¶) and footnotes (n.); references to the Supplement are preceded by "S."]

Cohen, "Corporate Separations—Active Business Requirements," BNA Tax Mgmt. Portfolio No. 224-2d (1975) 13.04, n.22

Cohen, "Corporate Separations—General Requirements," BNA Tax Mgmt. Portfolio No. 223-2d (1974) 13.03, n.20

Cordes, "The Device of Divisive Reorganizations," 10 Kan. L. Rev. 21 (1961) 13.03, n.20

Emory, "Tax Court Further Narrows Tax-Free Corporate Separations," 47 Taxes 219 (1969) ... 13.04, n.36

Helfand & Lafving, "Filling the Serbonian Bog With Quicksand—Proposed Section 355 Regulations Further Obscure Corporate Separations," Part III, 5 J. Corp. Tax. 133 (1979) S.13.04, n.26

Jacobs, "The Anatomy of a Spin-off," 1967 Duke L.J. 1 .... 13.03, n.20

Jacobs, "Spin-Offs: The Pre-Distribution Two Business Rule—Edmund P. Coady and Beyond," 19 Tax L. Rev. 155 (1964) 13.03, n.20

Lee, " 'Active Conduct' Distinguished From 'Conduct' of a Rental Real Estate Business," 25 Tax Law. 317 (1972) ... 13.04, n.56

Lee, "Functional Divisions and Other Corporate Separations Under Section 355 After Rafferty," 27 Tax L. Rev. 453 (1972) 13.04, n.35

Lee, "Proposed Regulations Under 355 Overhaul Device Test and Single-Business Divisions," 46 J. Tax. 194 (1977) ... 13.04, n.26

Lyons, "Realignment of Stockholders' Interests in Reorganizations Under Section 112(g)(1)(D)," 9 Tax L. Rev. 237 (1954) 13.08, n.103

Massey, "Disposal of Unwanted Assets in Connection With a Reorganization," 22 Tax L. Rev. 439 (1967) 13.06, n.91

Mette, "Spin-Off Reorganizations and the Revenue Act of 1951," 8 Tax L. Rev. 337 (1953) 13.02, n.9

Mintz, "Divisive Corporate Reorganizations: Split-Ups and Split-Offs," 6 Tax L. Rev. 365 (1951) 13.02, n.9

Nesson, "Earnings and Profits Discontinuities Under the 1954 Code," 77 Harv. L. Rev. 450, 474 (1964) 13.03, n.20; 13.11, n.132

O'Dell & Boyd, "Using Stock Rights In A Corporate Spin Off: The *Redding* Case," 8 J. Corp. Tax. 140 (1981) S.13.03, n.15

Redding v. Commissioner: "Step Transaction Doctrine Applied to Distribution of Stock Warrants in a Section 355 Spin-Off," 35 Tax L. Rev. 257 (1981) .. S.13.03, n.15

Whitman, "Draining the Serbonian Bog: A New Approach to Corporate Separations Under the 1954 Code," 81 Harv. L. Rev. 1194 (1968) 13.03, n.20

Wolff, "Divisive Reorganizations as Affected by the Revenue Act of 1951," 31 Taxes 716 (1953) ... 13.02, n.9

Books

McKee, Nelson & Whitmire, Federal Taxation of Partnerships and Partners ¶ 9.05 (1977) 13.04, n.51

Paul, Studies in Federal Taxation 3 (Harvard University Press 1940, 3d series) 13.02, n.9

CHAPTER 14: CORPORATE REORGANIZATIONS

[References are to paragraphs (¶) and footnotes (n.); references to the Supplement are preceded by "S."]

[References are to paragraphs (¶) and footnotes (n.); references to the Supplement are preceded by "S."]

Post-Reorganization Net Operating Loss Carrybacks," 66 Mich. L. Rev. 498 (1968) .. 14.18, n.218

Comment, "Report on Reverse Triangular Mergers and Basis—Nonrecognition Rules in Triangular Reorganizations," New York State Bar Association, Tax Section, 36 Tax L. Rev. 395 (1981) ......
S.14.15, n. 141;
S.14.33, n.284; S.14.33

Comment, "Section 368(a)(1)(F) Loss Carrybacks in Corporate Reorganizations" 117 U. Pa. L. Rev. 764 (1969) 14.18, n.218

Note, "State of Mind Analysis in Corporate Taxation," 69 Colum. L. Rev. 1224 (1969) ....
14.51, n.338

Comment, "The Zero Basis Dilemma," 41 Chi. L. Rev. 93 (1973) 14.33, n.292

Comment, "The Zero Basis Dilemma in Nonqualifying Triangular Acquisitions," 41 U. Chi. L. Rev. 92 (1973) 14.53, n.423

SEMINARS AND INSTITUTE PROCEEDINGS

Asofsky, "Reorganizing Insolvent Corporations," 45 N.Y.U. Ins. Fed. Tax. Ch. 5 (1983) ....
S.14.20, n.236.2; S.14.58, n.543

Baker, "Continuity of Interest Requirement in Reorganizations Reexamined—The Hickok Case," 18 N.Y.U. Inst. on Fed. Tax. 761 (1960) 14.11, n.49

Barker, "Planning Business Transactions in View of Uncertainties in Tax Law," 16 So. Cal. Tax Inst. 79 (1964) 14.56, n.496

Bartolini, "Avoiding or Adjusting to a Change in Status of Acquisition: Taxable to Non-Taxable, or Vice Versa; Obtaining a Ruling; When Not to Apply," 29 N.Y.U.

Inst. on Fed. Tax. 433 ....
14.56, n.496

Bittker, "What Is 'Business Purpose' in Reorganizations?," 8 N.Y.U. Inst. on Fed. Tax. 134 (1950) ..
14.51, n.338

Cohen, "Tax-Free Acquisition of Part of a Corporation's Assets by Combining a Spin-Off With a Unifying Reorganization," 26 N.Y.U. Inst. on Fed. Tax. 849 (1968) ......
14.52, n.369

Cohn, "Downstairs Mergers," 7 N.Y.U. Inst. on Fed. Tax. 1202 (1949) 14.53, n.388

Davis, "Tax Problems of Modification of Previously Entered-Into Tax-Free Reorganizations on Account of Breach of Warranty," 32 N.Y.U. Inst. on Fed. Tax. 593 (1974) 14.56, n.496

Deming, "How 'Solely' Is 'Solely for Voting Stock': Current Problems in 'B' and 'C' Reorganizations," 29 N.Y.U. Inst. on Fed. Tax. 397 (1971) 14.13, n.73

Englert, Podolin, and Oatway, on Tax Accounting in Mergers and Acquisition, 29 N.Y.U. Inst. on Fed. Tax. 491-532 (1971) .....
14.05, n.10

Ferguson & Ginsburg, "Triangular Reorganizations," 1972 So. Calif. Tax Inst. 1 (1972) ....
14.15, n.137

Freling, "Current Problems in Subsidiary Mergers and Other Triangular Reorganizations," 29 N.Y.U. Inst. on Fed. Tax. 347 (1971) ..
14.15, n.137

Friedman & Silbert, "Recapitalizations—Exchanges of Stock, Securities and Property of the Same Corporation Under the Internal Revenue Code of 1954," 13 N.Y.U. Inst. on Fed. Tax. 533 (1955) 14.17, n.215

[References are to paragraphs (¶) and footnotes (n.); references to the Supplement are preceded by "S."]

CHAPTER 15: AFFILIATED CORPORATIONS

Skinner, "What to Do When the Taxpayer Initiates a Change in Accounting Method," 27 N.Y.U. Inst. on Fed. Tax. 583 (1969) .. 15.06, n.49

Watts, "Tax Problems of Regard for the Corporate Entity," 20 N.Y.U.

Inst. on Fed. Tax. 867 (1962) 15.07, n.75

Wiese, "What Is a Method of Accounting: Who Initiates Changes?" 27 N.Y.U. Inst. on Fed. Tax. 565 (1969) 15.06, n.49

CHAPTER 16: CORPORATE TAX ATTRIBUTES: SURVIVAL AND TRANSFER

ARTICLES

Aidnoff, "Utilization of Acquired Net Operating Loss Carryovers and the Tax Reform Act of 1976 —A Face-Lift for Section 382," 55 Taxes 874 (1977) 16.24, n.190

Asimow, "Detriment and Benefit of Net Operating Losses: A Unifying Theory," 24 Tax L. Rev. 1 (1968) 16.10, n.23

Bacon, "Using Acquired Corporation's NOLs Restricted by 1976 Tax Reform Act," 46 J. Tax. 78 (1977) 16.24, n.190

Bacon & Tomasulo, "Net Operating Losses and Credit Carryovers: The Search for Corporate Identity," Tax Notes, Vol. XX, No. 11, p. 385, Sept 12, 1983 ... S.16.28, n.259

Blum, "Motive, Intent and Purpose in Federal Income Taxation," 34 U. Chi. L. Rev. 485 (1967) 16.21, n.101

Bowen & Sheffield, "Section 269 Revisited," 61 Taxes 881 (1983) ... S.16.21, n.87

Brode, "Planning to Use NOL Carryovers: Trafficking in Profit Corporations After 1977," 47 J. Tax. 258 (1977) 16.24, n.190

Campisano & Romano, "On the Benefits of Loss Recoupment: A Response," Tax Notes, Vol. XXI, No. 3, p. 209, Oct. 17, 1983 .... S.16.28, n.259

Cohen, "Taxing the State of Mind," 12 Tax Exec. 200 (1960) 16.01, n.3

Cowan, "*Libson Shops*: A Question of Survival," 34 U. Cin. L. Rev. 462 (1965) 16.26, n.246

Emory, " 'Control' Under Section 269 Is a Labyrinth of Complexity," 53 J. Tax. 181 (1980) S.16.21, n.89

Eustice, "The Tax Reform Act of 1976: Loss Carryovers and Other Corporate Changes," 32 Tax L. Rev. 113 (1977) .. 16.24, n.190

Forer, "Despite PHC Limitations of 1964 Act, Arutunoff Technique May Still Be Effective," 22 J. Tax. 5 (1965) 16.21, n.75

Friedrich, "The Sad Case of Section 382(b)(5): Indirect Stock Ownership May Not Be Taken Into Account for Purposes of Net Operating Loss Carryovers," 2 J. Corp. Tax. 465 (1976) 16.23, n.184

Glancy, "Carrying Losses Through Chapter X and Chapter XI Reorganizations," 28 Tax Law. 27 (1974) 16.10, n.28

Goldstein, "Federal Income Taxation," 1965 Ann. Survey of Am. L. 209, 246 ...... 16.26, n.218

Halperin, "Carryovers of Earnings and Profits," 18 Tax L. Rev. 289 (1963) 16.02, n.12

Hardy, "The Changing Rules on

[References are to paragraphs (¶) and footnotes (n.); references to the Supplement are preceded by "S."]

So. Calif. Tax Inst. 111 (1977) .. 16.24, n.190

Barr, "The Availability of Net Operating Loss Carryovers Following Taxable Changes of Ownership: Section 382(a) of The Internal Revenue Code," 38 NYU Inst. on Fed. Tax. Ch. 5 (1980) S.16.24 n.190

Blake, "Carryovers and Limitations on Carryovers of Net Operating Losses in Corporate Acquisitions," 21 N.Y.U. Inst. on Fed. Tax. 1247 (1963) 16.22, n.147

Eames, "Accounting Method Considerations in Corporate Reorganizations With Special Attention to Section 381 Transactions," 23 N.Y.U. Inst. on Fed. Tax. 853 (1965) 16.13, n.52

Faber, "Net Operating Losses In Corporate Reorganizations Revisited in 1979," 38 NYU Inst. on Fed. Tax. Ch. 4 (1980) S.16.24, n.190

Feder, "The Application of Section 269 to Corporations Having Net Operating Loss Carryovers and Potential Losses," 21 N.Y.U. Inst. on Fed. Tax. 1277 (1963) 16.21, n.87

Harris, *"Libson Shops* and Related Cases," 21 N.Y.U. Inst. on Fed. Tax. 1307 (1963) 16.26, n.246

Kaufman, "Application of a Loss Carryover of One Business Against Profits From Another Business; *Libson Shops,* and Sections 381, 382 and 269," 24 N.Y.U. Inst. on Fed. Tax. 1199 (1966) 16.10, n.23

CHAPTER 17: FOREIGN CORPORATIONS AND FOREIGN SOURCE INCOME

ARTICLES

ABA Tax Section Report, "The Credibility of Foreign Income Taxes: A Critical Analysis of Revenue Rulings 78-61, 78-62 and 78-63," 32 Tax Law. 33 (1978) S.17.11, n.72

Alexander, "Controlled Foreign Corporations and Constructive Ownership," 18 Tax L. Rev. 531 (1963) 17.31, n.135

Alexander, "Foreign Personal Holding Companies and Foreign Corporations That Are Personal Holding Companies," 67 Yale L.J. 1173 (1958) 17.20, n.112

Alpert & Feingold, "Tax Reform Act Toughens Foreign Transfer Provisions of 1491 and Liberalizes 367," 46 J. Tax. 2 (1977) 17.40, n.161; 17.41, n.178

Baker, "Flags of Refuge for the Shipping Industry — Federal Income Tax Considerations," 13 Tax L. Rev. 137 (1958) 17.05, n.64

Bischel "Optimizing Benefits From R&D Expenses Under Allocation and Apportionment Regs," 48 J. Tax. 332 (1978) .. 17.02, n.22

Bischel, "Tax Allocations Concerning Inter-Company Pricing Transactions in Foreign Operations: A Reappraisal," 13 Va. J. Int'l L. 490 (1973) 17.30, n.130

Boffa, "International Finance Subsidiaries," BNA Tax Mgmt. Portfolio No. 215-2d (1972) 17.05, n.67

Clark, "New Temporary Section 367 Regulations," 56 Taxes 405 (1978) 17.41, n.183

Cliff, "Pairing: A Technique For Avoiding Controlled Foreign Corporation Status And Other Burdens Of U.S. Taxation," 57 Taxes 530 (1979) S.17.31, n.135

Cole, "Highlights of the Proposed Regulations on Allocation and Apportionment of Deductions," 39 J. Tax. 272 (1973) .. 17.02, n.22

Corry, "Stapled Stock—Time For A New Look," 36 Tax L. Rev. 167 (1981) S.17.31, n.135

Dailey, "The Concept of the Source of Income," 15 Tax L. Rev. 415 (1960) 17.01, n.3

Dale, "End of Interest Equalization Tax; Analysis of Implications for U.S. Taxpayers," 40 J. Tax. 230 (1974) 17.05, n.68

Dale, "The Reformed Foreign Tax Credit: A Path Through the Maze," 33 Tax L. Rev. 175 (1978) 17.11, n.71

Dolan & Horowitz, "Reorganizations of Foreign Corporations Under § 367(b): Issues and Recommendations," 38 Tax L. Rev. 321 (1983) S.17.41, n.178

Duncan, "Allocation and Apportionment of Deductions Under the Final 1.861-8," 30 Tax Executive 1 (1977) 17.02, n.22

Eustice, "Affiliated Corporations Revisited: Recent Developments Under Section 482 and 367," 24 Tax L. Rev. 101 (1968) 17.40, n.166

Eustice, "Contract Rights, Capital Gain, and Assignment of Income —The Ferrer Case." 20 Tax L. Rev. 1 (1964) 17.02, n.16

Feder & Parker, "The Foreign Investment In Real Property Tax Act of 1980," 34 Tax L. 545 (1981) .. S.17.02, ns. 32.1, 44, S.17.04, n.60

Feingold & Alpert, "Observations on the Foreign Investment in Real Property Tax Act of 1980," 1 Va. Tax Rev. 105 (1981) .... S.17.02, n. 32.1

Feingold & Cappsceio, "U.S. Taxation of OID Income to Foreign Persons After The 1984 Tax Reform Act," 24 Tax Notes 1077 (1984) S.17.03, n.56

Fox & Jackson, "Proposed Regulations Under §861(b)," 4 J. Corp. Tax 47 (1977) 17.02, n.22

Fuller & Granwell, "The Allocation and Apportionment of Deductions," 31 Tax Law. 125 (1977) 17.02, n.22

Garelik, "What Constitutes Doing Business Within the United States by a Non-resident Alien Individual or a Foreign Corporation," 18 Tax L. Rev. 423 (1963) 17.01, n.4; 17.02, n.24

Gifford, "Controlled Corporations— Section 1248," BNA Tax Mgmt. Portfolio No. 240-2d (1975) ... 17.34, n.153

Gifford, "Controlled Foreign Corporations—Section 963," BNA Tax Mgmt. Portfolio No. 105-3d (1975) 17.33, n.151

Gosain, "Foreign Corporations: Recognition of Gain Under § 367—Half a Century of Metamorphosis," 9 J. Corp. Tax. 203 (1982) S.17.40 n.161

Gourevitch, "DISC's Ability to Defer Tax on Income Restricted by TRA of 1976," 46 J. Tax. 9 (1977) 17.14, n.105

Granwell, "Repeal of the 30 Percent Withholding Tax on Interest Paid to Foreigners," 13 Tax Mgmt. Intern. 306 (1984) S.17.03 n.52.2

Griggs, "Operating in Puerto Rico in the Section 936 Era," 32 Tax L. Rev. 239 (1977) 17.13, n.98

Hannes & Levey, "How Regulatory and Judicial Analysis of the Foreign Tax Credit Differ: Regs. v. *Inland Steel*," 57 J. Tax. 162 (1982) S.17.11

[References are to paragraphs (¶) and footnotes (n.); references to the Supplement are preceded by "S."]

[References are to paragraphs (¶) and footnotes (n.); references to the Supplement are preceded by "S."]

eign Persons (Federal Tax Press, Inc. 1968) 17.01, n.1

Owens, The Foreign Tax Credit (Harvard University 1961) 17.02, n.20; 17.11, n.71

Owens & Ball, The Indirect Credit (Harvard University 1975) 17.11, n.71

COMMITTEE AND STAFF REPORTS

Ad Hoc Committee On Foreign Tax Credit, Section of Taxation, "Comments Regarding Proposed Foreign Tax Credit Regulations," 33 Tax Law. 35 (1979) S.17.11, n.72

Committee on Deductions From Foreign Source Income, N.Y.S. Bar Ass'n, Tax Section, "Proposals for Improvement of Rules for Allocation of Deductions Between Foreign and US Source Income," 29 Tax L. Rev. 597 (1974) 17.02, n.22

New York State Bar Ass'n Tax Section, "Report on the Examples Under Section 367(b)," 35 Tax L. Rev. 317 (1980) S.17.41, n.190

New York State Bar Ass'n Tax Section, "Report on the Proposed Regulations Under Section 367" (Aug. 30, 1978), reprinted in 34 Tax L. Rev. 79 (1978) 17.41, n.183

Ross, "United States Jurisdiction to Tax Foreign Income," XLIXb Studies on International Fiscal Law (Int'l Fiscal Ass'n Hamburg 1964) 17.31, n.134

Staff of the Joint Committee on Taxation, 94th Cong., 2d Sess., "General Explanation of the Tax Reform Act of 1976," at 258 (CIR Print 1976), reprinted at 1976-3 Vol. 2 CB 1, 270 .. 17.40, n.176

Treasury Department News Release,

"Study of Administration of §482 to International Business Transactions Between US Corporations and Their Foreign Subsidiaries" (Jan. 8, 1973), reported in 1973 P-H Fed. Taxes ¶54,956 ...... 17.30, n.130

NOTES AND COMMENTS

Comment, "The Off-Shore Hedge Fund," 7 Colum. J. Transnat'l L. 79 (1969) 17.05, n.65

Comments on Guidelines for Ruling Under Section 367 (Report of Special Committee on Section 367 Policies of the Tax Section of the N.Y.S. Bar Ass'n), 23 Tax L. Rev. 151 (1969) .. 17.40, n.168

Note, "Multinational Corporations and Income Allocation Under Section 482 of the Internal Revenue Code," 89 Harv. L. Rev. 12002 (1976) 17.30, n.130

Note, "State of Mind Analysis in Corporate Taxation," 69 Colum. L. Rev. 1224 (1969) 17.40, n.168

Note, "United States Taxation and Regulation of Offshore Mutual Funds," 83 Harv. L. Rev. 404 (1969) 17.05, n.65

SEMINARS AND INSTITUTE PROCEEDINGS

Beimfohr, "Tax-Free Exchanges With a Foreign Corporation: Section 367; The Guidelines Analyzed," 28 N.Y.U. Inst. on Fed. Tax. 455 (1970) .. 17.40, n.166

Brudno, "Export Trade Corporations," 5 Inst. on Private Investments Abroad 59 (Southwestern Legal Foundation 1963) 17.33, n.152

Dale, "Operating a Business in Puerto Rico Under the Industrial Incentive Act of 1963," 28

CUMULATIVE INDEX

[References are to paragraphs (¶); references to the Supplement are preceded by "S."]

[References are to paragraphs (¶); references to the Supplement are preceded by "S."]

[References are to paragraphs (¶); references to the Supplement are preceded by "S."]

[References are to paragraphs (¶); references to the Supplement are preceded by "S."]

[References are to paragraphs (¶); references to the Supplement are preceded by "S."]

[References are to paragraphs (¶); references to the Supplement are preceded by "S."]

[References are to paragraphs (¶); references to the Supplement are preceded by "S."]

[References are to paragraphs (¶); references to the Supplement are preceded by "S."]

[References are to paragraphs (¶); references to the Supplement are preceded by "S."]

[*References are to paragraphs (¶); references to the Supplement are preceded by "S."*]

[References are to paragraphs (¶); references to the Supplement are preceded by "S."]

[References are to paragraphs (¶); references to the Supplement are preceded by "S."]

[References are to paragraphs (¶); references to the Supplement are preceded by "S."]

[References are to paragraphs (¶); references to the Supplement are preceded by "S."]

Liquidating distributions (*cont'd*)
basis of property in, 11.04,
S.11.04
by collapsible corporation, 12.03,
S.12.03,12.07
consolidated returns, 15.23
controlled foreign corporation,
17.30, 17.34
generally, 11.01-11.71, S.11.67A
of installment obligations, 11.65,
S.11.65
Section 482, S.11.62
shareholder gain or loss from,
11.03, S.11.03
Liquidating dividends
See also: Dividends; Liquidations
generally, 11.01, 11.02
Liquidation-reincorporation, 3.20,
9.32, 11.05, S.11.05, 11.67,
S.11.67, S.11.67A, 14.54,
S.14.54
Liquidations
See also: Liquidating
distributions;
Reincorporations;
Reorganizations
carryover rules, S.11.45, S.11.47,
16.02, 16.11, 16.13, S.16.13,
16.14
collapsible corporations, 11.66,
12.01-12.19
complete liquidations, S.9.50,
S.9.51, S.9.52, 11.01-11.71,
S.11.05, S.11.62
continuity of business enterprise,
14.51, S.14.51
controlled foreign corporations,
11.06, 16.11, 17.34
corporate gain or loss on, 9.64,
S.11.47, 11.60-11.71,
S.11.61A, S.11.65, S.11.68,
S.11.69, S.11.71
defined
complete, 11.02
de facto, 16.27
partial, 9.50-9.53
distributions in, 11.01-11.71
divisions, corporate, 13.01,
13.14, S.13.14

expenses of, 5.04, 5.07, S.5.07,
11.68
foreign corporations, S.11.62,
17.34, 17.40-17.44, S.17.40-
S.17.42
foreign subsidiaries, 11.46, 17.43
generally, 2.01, 2.09, 11.01-11.71,
S.11.67A
losses on, characterization as
ordinary or capital, 4.09
nonqualified, §337 aspects,
S.11.61A, 11.66, S.11.67A
nonrecognition of shareholder
gain, 11.20-11.24, S.11.21,
S.11.23
one-month liquidation, 11.20-
11.24, S.11.21, S.11.23,
11.66, 11.70
partial liquidation, 9.50-9.53,
S.9.50, S.9.51, S.9.52, S.9.53,
S.9.54, S.9.64A, S.11.05,
11.68, 13.01, 13.14, 17.34
partnership compared, 1.07,
S.11.61
personal holding company, 8.20,
11.24
personal-service corporation,
S.2.06, S.11.25
plan of, 9.52, 11.23, 11.41, 11.64
reorganization, relation to, 11.67,
S.11.67, 14.32, S.14.32
reincorporation, 11.05, S.11.05,
11.67, S.11.67, S.11.67A,
14.54, S.14.54
Secton 306 stock redeemed in,
10.05
shareholder treatment basis, 11.04,
S.11.04, S.11.65
gain or loss computation, 11.03,
S.11.03
nonrecognition, one-month
liquidation, 11.20-11.22,
S.11.21
subsidiary, 11.40-11.45,
S.11.41-S.11.45
special problems, S.5.07
split-up as, 13.02, 13.14
stepped-up basis on, 11.04,
S.11.44, 12.01, 12.07

Multiple corporations (*cont'd*)
controlled groups, 15.03, S.15.03, 15.04
creation of, business reasons for, 15.02, 16.21
deduction principles, 15.08
generally, 15.01-15.09, 16.02-16.03
limitations on, 15.02-15.04
parent-subsidiary controlled group, 15.03, 15.04, S.15.04
tax avoidance, 15.01, 15.03
tax planning, 15.01, 15.05
transactions between, 7.05, S.7.05, 15.06-15.08

N

Net operating loss
See also: Carryover; Loss; Loss carryover
consolidated return, computation in, 15.23
generally, 4.11, 5.03
Subchapter S pass-through, 6.01, 6.07, S.6.07
Net operating loss carryover
See also: Carryover; Loss carryover; Tax attributes
bootstrap acquisitions, 11.71
change of ownership as affecting, 16.22, S.16.22, 16.24
consolidated return limitations on, 15.24
disallowance of, 16.20, 16.22-16.24, S.16.22
entity theory, 16.02, 16.10-16.14
generally, 2.11, 4.11, 16.10-16.14
Libson Shops doctrine, 16.27
tax benefits, corporate, traffic in, 16.01
transfer or survival of, 16.01
Type E reorganization, effect on, 14.17, S.14.17, 16.22-16.24
Net operating loss deduction
See also: Deductions
accumulated earnings tax, disallowed in computation of, 8.09

earnings and profits, disallowed in computation of, 7.03
generally, 5.03, 16.10
"golden parachute," S.5.05
personal holding company tax, disallowed in computation of, 8.25
survival in reorganization, 16.20-16.27, S.16.22, S.16.23
Nominee corporations, 2.10, S.2.10
Nonrecognition
See also: Gain; Loss; Recognition
boot, 3.06, 14.34
collapsible corporations, 12.07, 12.08
consolidated returns, 15.23
distribution corporation
dividend-in-kind, 7.21
liquidation, 11.61
redemption, 9.64
division, corporate, 13.03, 13.11, 13.14, S.13.14
foreign corporations, 17.40-17.44, S.17.40-S.17.42
generally, 1.04
incorporation transactions, §351, 3.01-3.21, S.3.16
liquidating corporation's gain or loss, generally, 11.61, S.11.61A
liquidation
foreign subsidiary, 17.43
parent corporation's gain, 11.40-11.45, S.11.41, S.11.42, S.11.44, S.11.45
shareholder gain, 11.20-11.24, S.11.21, S.11.23
subsidiary, 11.42, S.11.42
one-month liquidation, 11.20-11.23, S.11.21, S.11.23, 11.66
parent-subsidiary fusion, 14.53
reorganizations
corporate transferee, 14.33
corporate transferor, 14.32, S.14.32
Section 332 liquidations, 11.40
Section 333 elections, 11.23, S.11.23
Section 337 sales, S.11.61A, 11.64, S.11.64

Partnerships (*cont'd*)
switching from to corporate
status, 3.18
Personal holding companies
See also: Foreign personal
holding company
computation of tax, 8.25, S.8.25,
S.15.23
deductions of, 5.05
deficiency dividend procedure,
8.20, 8.25
definition, income tests, 8.21,
S.8.21, 8.22, S.8.22
definition, stock ownership test,
8.23
dividends-paid deduction, 8.25
exemptions, 8.24, S.8.24
foreign corporations as, 17.04,
17.23
foreign personal holding
companies, 17.20-17.23
generally, 8.20-8.25, S.8.21,
S.8.22, S.8.25
income, 8.21, 8.22, S.8.21, S.8.22
incorporated pocketbooks, 8.20
incorporated talents, 8.20, 8.22
liquidation of, 11.01, 11.20, 11.24
minimum tax application, 5.01,
8.20
reorganizations involving, 14.19
tainted income test, 8.21, 8.22
tax preferences of, 5.01
tax-shelter deductions of, 5.03, 5.05
undistributed income, 8.25,
S.8.25, S.15.23
Portfolio shares
distribution of rights to purchase,
7.63
shareholder's option to buy, 7.05
Possessions corporations. *See*:
Foreign corporations
Preferred stock. *See*: Stock
Preferred stock dividends
See also: Dividends
generally, 10.01-10.07
taxability of distribution, 7.60-7.62
Premium
business liability insurance
deduction of, 5.04

deduction, retirement, 4.06, 4.22
Presumptions
accumulated earnings tax, 8.08,
S.8.08
collapsibility, 12.05
tax avoidance under §269, 16.21,
S.16.21
Professional service organizations,
2.06, S.2.06
Property
See also: Assets; Depreciable
property; Distributed
property
acquisitions of, for voting stock,
14.14, S.14.14
appreciated
distribution of, S.6.05, S.6.11,
7.21-7.24, S.7.20, S.7.21,
S.7.24, 9.64, S.9.64A,
S.9.65, 11.61
sale to affiliates, 9.32, 15.07,
15.09
basis of distributed, 7.22, S.7.22,
7.23, 9.63, 11.04, S.11.04,
11.44, S.11.44
collapsible corporation's
production of, 12.04
controlled foreign corporation,
transfer to, 17.42, S.17.42
corporate, use by shareholders,
7.05, 8.22
debt issued for, S.4.23[2]
defined, for §351 exchange, 3.03
depreciable, distribution of, 7.21,
7.24
depreciated, distribution of,
7.20-7.23, S.7.20, S.7.22,
9.64, 11.61
encumbered, distribution of, 7.21,
7.24
expatriating and repatriating,
transfers of under §367,
17.41, S.17.41
export property, DISC provisions,
17.14
foreign corporations
distribution of U.S. real
property by, S.7.21

[References are to paragraphs (¶); references to the Supplement are preceded by "S."]

[References are to paragraphs (¶); references to the Supplement are preceded by "S."]

Reasonable needs of the business test (*cont'd*)
methods of financing, 8.05
stock redemptions as, 8.07
Reattribution, 9.21
Recapitalizations
See also: Reorganizations
as acquisitions under §382(a), 16.22, 16.24
of foreign corporations, §367, 17.40, S.17.40
generally, 7.62, 10.03, 14.10, 14.17, S.14.17
going private transaction, 9.26
recognition of corporation gain or loss on, 14.17
Recapitalization-reorganization, 14.17, S.14.17, S.14.21, 14.54, S.14.54
Recapture
carryover of potential in reorganization, 16.13
depreciation, 3.06
distribution of depreciable property, 7.21, 7.24, 9.64, 11.61
investment credit
dividend in kind, 7.21
incorporation, 3.06
liquidation, 11.61, 11.65
redemption, 9.64
reorganization, 16.13
Subchapter S corporation, 6.05
liquidation distribution or sale, 11.61, 11.65
Subchapter S corporation, 6.05
transfer to controlled corporation under §351, 3.06, S.3.06, 3.17, S.3.17
Receipts
DISC, 17.14
Subchapter S corporation, 6.03
Receivables
corporate, 3.17, 11.03, 12.08
unrealized, 7.24, 11.03, 11.04, 12.04, 12.05
zero basis, transfer in §351 exchange, 3.07, 3.17

Recognition
See also: Nonrecognition
boot
under §333, 11.21, S.11.21
under §351, 3.06
under §355, 13.10, S.13.10
under §356, 14.34, S.14.34
collapsible corporations, 11.66, 12.04, 12.08
consolidated returns, 15.23
distributing corporation in corporate division, 13.11
distribution in redemption of stock, 9.64
foreign corporations, 17.40-17.44
reorganization, 14.30-14.35, S.14.21, S.14.31-S.14.34
Section 351 transactions, 3.01-3.21
Redemptions
See also: Stock
accumulated earnings tax, 8.07
acquisition by subsidiary, 9.31, S.9.31
affiliated corporations, 9.30-9.32, S.9.31-S.9.32, 14.54, S.14.54
appreciated property distributed, 9.64, S.9.64
bail-outs, 9.24, S.9.33, 10.01, 10.02, 10.07
basis of distributed property, 9.63
boot distributions as, 13.10, S.13.10, 14.34
bootstrap acquisitions, 9.22, 9.25, S.9.25
brother-sister acquisitions, 9.31, S.9.31, 14.53, S.14.53
buy-sell agreement, 8.07, 9.25
collapsible corporations, 12.03, 12.07-12.08
consolidated returns, 15.23
constructive stock ownership, 9.21
control-shifting disproportionate, 16.22

[References are to paragraphs (¶); references to the Supplement are preceded by "S."]

[References are to paragraphs (¶); references to the Supplement are preceded by "S."]

[References are to paragraphs (¶); references to the Supplement are preceded by "S."]

Stock (*cont'd*)
  constructive ownership, 9.20, 9.21, 9.24, 9.40
  convertible preferred, 7.62, 10.03, 14.17
  classification, 4.03-4.05, S.4.05
  common, defined, 10.03
  contingent, receipt of, 14.56, S.14.56
  debt, tax-free conversion of to stock, 4.06, 14.17
  debt vs., 4.01-4.22, S.4.05, S.4.07, S.4.09, S.4.20
  debt-financed purchase of, 4.20
  disposition of §306 stock, 10.04
  distributions of, 7.60-7.62, S.7.61, S.7.62
  dividend reinvestment plans, public utilities, S.7.06, S.7.62
  exchanges of, 1.04, 14.17, 14.34
  foreign corporation, exchanges of, 17.40-17.41
  gain or loss on acquisition of, 3.01
  nonparticipating, 4.05
  nonvoting common, 10.03
  nonvoting preferred, 7.60, 9.32, 10.03
  optional distribution of, stock dividend rules, 7.61, 7.62, S.7.62
  ownership under §1563, 15.03
  participating, 4.05, 16.24
  personal holding company definition, 8.23
  preferred
    bail-out, 10.01-10.07, S.10.03
    distribution of
      controlled corporation, 13.12
      divisive reorganization, 10.03, 13.03, 13.12
      reorganization, 10.03, 14.35
    nonvoting excluded from §1563, 15.03
    redemption, 9.01, 10.04
    reorganization, 14.11, 14.35
  public utility, dividends on, 5.03, 5.06

  purchase treated as asset purchase, S.11.44, S.11.47, S.11.64, S.15.24, S.16.22
  recapitalization, exchanges of, 14.17, S.14.17
  redemption of, 9.01-9.40, S.9.22-S.9.25
  reorganization, generally, 14.11, S.14.11
  reorganization, nonrecognition provisions, 14.31, 14.34
  rights, 7.63, S.7.63
  sale of
    foreign corporation, 17.34
    liquidating dividend as, 11.01
  Section 306, 9.32, 10.03, S.10.03, 10.05, 10.06, 13.03, 13.10, 13.12, S.14.31, 14.35
  Section 338, S.11.47, S.11.61A
  Section 351 transaction, 3.01-3.21, S.3.01-S.3.07, S.3.09-S.3.12, S.3.14-S.3.17
  Section 1244, 14.11, S.14.11
  services, issued in exchange for, 3.03, 3.13
  splits of, 7.60, 7.62
  Subchapter S eligibility, 6.02, S.6.02, S.6.11
  subsidiary
    basis, 11.44, S.11.44, S.14.33
    control, 11.41, 15.03, 15.21
    liquidation gain or loss on, 11.41, S.11.41
  transferred basis, §306 stock, 10.03, S.10.03
  Treasury definition of, 4.05
  Treasury stock, 3.13, 14.33
  Type A reorganization, S.14.33
  Type C reorganization, 14.14, S.14.14, S.14.33
  Type D reorganization, S.14.16
  Type E reorganization, 14.17, S.14.17
  voting
    acquisition of property for, 14.14, S.14.14
    acquisition of stock for, 14.13, S.14.13

Subsidiaries (*cont'd*)
  carryover rules, 16.10, 16.11,
    16.13, S.16.13, 16.14
  contingent liability in
    liquidation of, 11.45
  controlled foreign corporation,
    17.30, 17.31
  corporate divisions, 13.01-13.15,
    S.13.15
  distribution of all stock and
    securities in, 13.07, S.13.07
  divisive reorganization, 13.03,
    14.16, S.14.16
  foreign, deemed paid foreign tax
    credit, 17.11
  indebtedness to parents, 11.42,
    S.11.42
  international finance
    subsidiary, 17.05
  liquidations of
    carryover rules, 16.10, 16.11,
      16.13, S.16.13
    cash equivalent assets, 11.45
    foreign subsidiary, 11.46, 17.43
    generally, 11.40-11.45,
      S.11.41-S.11.42, S.11.44-
      S.11.45
    U.S. into foreign parent, 17.43
  merger into parent, 14.12, 14.53
  merger of parent into, 14.53
  merger with controlled, 14.15
  parent-subsidiary fission, 14.53
  parent-subsidiary fusion, 14.53
  redemption by affiliated
    corporation, 9.30-9.32,
    S.9.31, S.9.32
  reorganization of, 17.44
  Section 351 transfers to, 17.41
  spin-off of, 13.01-13.03
  triangular acquisitions, 14.53
Substance vs. form
  affiliated corporations, 15.01
  corporate tax attributes, 16.01
  corporation as entity, 1.05
  exchanges, indirect, 3.02, S.3.02
  redemptions, bootstrap, 9.25,
    S.9.25
  reorganizations, 14.03, 14.51
Substituted basis. *See:* Basis

Successor corporations
  See also: Tax attributes
  generally, 2.11
Surplus. *See:* Corporate surplus
Surtax exemption
  Multiple corporations, 15.01-15.04,
    15.20, 15.23, 16.02, 16.21
Swap-fund exchanges, 3.02, 14.19
Syndicates, 2.05

T

Taxable income
  See also: Foreign source income;
    Gross income; Income
  accumulated, adjustments to, 8.09
  computation of, 1.01, 5.01-5.07,
    S.5.01
  corporate, 5.01, S.5.01
  earnings and profits
    distinguished, 7.03
  noncorporate taxpayer, S.5.01
  personal holding company, 8.25,
    S.8.25
  Subchapter S, 6.05, S.6.05, 6.08,
    S.6.08
  substantial realization of, 12.04
  undistributed, 6.05, 6.08, 8.09,
    8.25, S.8.25
Tax accounting principles. *See:*
  Accounting methods and
  principles
Tax attributes
  carryover rules
    computation mechanics, 16.13
    consolidated returns, 15.24
    generally, 16.01, S.16.01
    items, 16.13
    Libson Shops doctrine, 16.26,
      S.16.26
    limitations on, 16.20-16.27,
      S.16.27
    special operating rules, 16.12
    transactions giving rise to, 16.11
  change of ownership, 16.22,
    S.16.22
  computation mechanics, 16.13
  consolidated returns, 15.24
  foreign corporation, 17.40

[References are to paragraphs (¶); references to the Supplement are preceded by "S."]

[References are to paragraphs (¶); references to the Supplement are preceded by "S."]

Tax Equity and Fiscal Responsibility Act of 1982 (*cont'd*)
stock purchase treated as asset purchase, S.11.44, S.11.47, S.11.64, S.15.24, S.16.22, S.16.25
Type F reorganizations, S.14.18
Tax-exempt corporations
accumulated earnings tax exemption, 8.02
excluded from dividends-received deductions, 5.06
generally, 1.06
Tax-exempt foundations
Section 306 stock donation to, 10.04, 10.05, 10.07
Tax-exempt organizations
personal holding company exemptions, 8.24
transfers to, by foreign corporations, 17.41
Tax haven
U.S. used as by foreign corporations, 17.02
Tax liability, corporate
accumulated earnings tax, 8.09, S.8.09
computation of, 5.01, S.5.01
consolidated returns, 15.20
credits against, 3.01, 8.09, 15.01
deductions, 5.03, S.5.03
dividends-received deduction, 5.06
generally, 1.01-1.03
history, 1.01
income, 5.02
minimum tax, 5.01
penalty taxes, 8.01-8.25
personal holding company tax, 8.25
rates, 5.01, S.5.01
Subchapter S corporations, 6.01
vs. individual, 1.01-1.03
vs. partnership, 1.07
Tax preferences
items of, 5.01, S.5.01, 6.01, 6.05, 6.06
Tax rates
corporate, 5.01, S.5.01
noncorporate taxpayers, S.5.01

Tax Reform Act of 1983, S.12.03, S.12.04, S.12.06, S.17.22
Tax Reform Act of 1984
accrued market discount, S.4.08[9]
bifurcation rule reversion, S.9.33
controlled stock, S.13.12
debt cancellation, S.5.02, S.14.17
debt discharge gain, S.3.13
distributions of appreciated property, S.9.64A
dividend-received-deduction, S.5.06
economic earnings, S.7.01
foreign corporations, S.17.41A
liquidation, S.14.14, S.14.52
nondivisive D reorganization, S.11.05
nonrecognition treatment, S.4.06
"market discount" rules, S.3.05, S.13.11
multicorporation, S.15.04
"portfolio interest" by foreign corporations, S.17.03
"quasi-subsidiary" techniques, S.15.01
related party rules, S.15.06
"stapled stock," S.15.04
transition rules, S.4.23
Tax shelters
foreign corporations, allowed to, 17.03
generally, 5.03, 5.05, 6.05, 6.06, 6.07, 8.20
Tax treaties
force-of-attraction principle, 17.02
Technical Corrections Act of 1982, S.4.06
Tender offer
use of debt securities in, 4.20, 9.26
deductibility of resistance expenses, 5.04
shares, for repurchase of, 9.26
Termination
business expense of, 11.68
shareholder's interest, 9.23, S.9.23